THE CAMBRIDGE COMPANION TO
HUME
Second Edition

Each Cambridge Companion to a philosophical figure is made up of specially commissioned essays by an international team of scholars, providing students and nonspecialists with an introduction to a major philosopher. The series aims to dispel the intimidation that readers may feel when faced with the work of a challenging thinker.

David Hume is now considered one of the most important philosophers of the Western world. Although best known for his contributions to the theory of knowledge, metaphysics, and philosophy of religion, Hume also influenced developments in the philosophy of mind, psychology, ethics, political and economic theory, political and social history, and aesthetic theory. The fifteen essays in this volume address all aspects of Hume's thought. The picture of him that emerges is that of a thinker who, though often critical to the point of skepticism, was nonetheless able to build on that skepticism a constructive, viable, and profoundly important view of the world. Also included in this volume are Hume's two brief autobiographies and a bibliography suited to those beginning their study of Hume.

This second edition of one of our most popular Companions includes six new essays and a new introduction; the remaining essays have all been revised and updated.

David Fate Norton is Professor of Moral Philosophy Emeritus at McGill University and Adjunct Professor of Philosophy at the University of Victoria. He has published widely on Hume and eighteenth-century British philosophy and recently coedited the first critical edition of Hume's *Treatise of Human Nature*.

Jacqueline Taylor is Associate Professor of Philosophy at the University of San Francisco. She has published on Hume's philosophy in *Hume Studies*, *Topoi*, the *Journal of Ethics*, *The Blackwell Guide to Hume's* Treatise, and *Feminist Interpretations of David Hume*.

Continued after the Index

The Cambridge Companion to

HUME

Second Edition

Edited by

David Fate Norton
McGill University and *University of Victoria*

Jacqueline Taylor
University of San Francisco

CAMBRIDGE
UNIVERSITY PRESS

CAMBRIDGE UNIVERSITY PRESS
Cambridge, New York, Melbourne, Madrid, Cape Town,
Singapore, São Paulo, Delhi, Tokyo, Mexico City

Cambridge University Press
32 Avenue of the Americas, New York, NY 10013-2473, USA

www.cambridge.org
Information on this title: www.cambridge.org/9780521677349

First published 1993
Second edition published 2009
Reprinted 2009, 2011

A catalog record for this publication is available from the British Library.

Library of Congress Cataloging in Publication Data

The Cambridge companion to Hume / [edited by] David Fate Norton, Jacqueline
Taylor. – 2nd ed.
    p. cm.
Includes bibliographical references and index.
ISBN 978-0-521-85986-8 (hardback) – ISBN 978-0-521-67734-9 (pbk.)
1. Hume, David, 1711–1776. I. Norton, David Fate. II. Taylor, Jacqueline.
B1498.C26 2008
192–dc22   2007044296

ISBN 978-0-521-85986-8 Hardback
ISBN 978-0-521-67734-9 Paperback

CONTENTS

CONTRIBUTORS

DONALD L. M. BAXTER is Professor of Philosophy, University of Connecticut. He is the author of *Hume's Difficulty: Time and Identity in the* Treatise (New York: Routledge, 2008), as well as various papers in early modern Western philosophy and in systematic metaphysics.

MARTIN BELL is Professor of History of Philosophy, Manchester Metropolitan University. His publications on Hume's philosophy appear as journal articles and as chapters in edited collections, including *Reading Hume on Human Understanding* (2002), *Impressions of Hume* (2005), *New Essays on David Hume* (2007), and *A Companion to Hume* (2008). He also edited Hume's *Dialogues concerning Natural Religion* for Penguin Classics (1990).

JOHN BIRO is coeditor of *Spinoza: New Perspectives* (1978); *Mind, Brain and Function* (1982); *Frege: Sense and Reference a Hundred Years Later* (1995); and *Spinoza: Metaphysical Themes* (2002). He is also the author of papers on a variety of topics in epistemology, the philosophy of mind, and the philosophy of language.

ROBERT J. FOGELIN is Sherman Fairchild Professor in the Humanities and Professor of Philosophy Emeritus, Dartmouth College. He is author of *Hume's Skepticism in the* Treatise of Human Nature (1985), *Wittgenstein* (2nd ed., 1987), *Pyrrhonian Reflections on Knowledge and Justification* (1994), *Berkeley and the Principles of Human Knowledge* (2001), *A Defense of Hume on Miracles* (2003), *Walking the Tightrope of Reason* (2003), and many articles on a wide range of philosophical topics.

J. C. A. GASKIN is a Fellow of Trinity College Dublin, where he also held a personal chair in philosophy. His publications include *Hume's*

Philosophy of Religion (2nd ed., 1988) and *Varieties of Unbelief* (1989). He is the author of numerous articles on Hume and on the philosophy of religion and the editor of the World's Classics edition of Hume's works on religion and Hobbes's *Leviathan*. He is also the author of two volumes of ghost stories, *The Dark Companion* (2001) and *The Long Retreating Day* (2006).

KNUD HAAKONSSEN is Professor of Intellectual History and Director of the Sussex Centre for Intellectual History, University of Sussex. His books include *The Science of a Legislator* (1981); (ed.) *A Culture of Rights* (1991); *Natural Law and Moral Philosophy* (1996); (ed.) *Enlightenment and Religion* (1996); (ed.) *The Cambridge History of Eighteenth-Century Philosophy* (2006); (ed.) *The Cambridge Companion to Adam Smith* (2006); and editions of works by Francis Hutcheson, Hume, Smith, and Thomas Reid.

PETER JONES is Professor Emeritus of Philosophy, University of Edinburgh, where he was also Director of the Institute for Advanced Studies in the Humanities. He has published extensively on philosophical and cultural topics including eighteenth-century aesthetics, the Russian novel, Italian opera, and architecture. Among his books are *Philosophy and the Novel* (1975); *Hume's Sentiments: Their Ciceronian and French Context* (1982); (ed.) *The Reception of David Hume in Europe* (2005); and *Ove Arup: Masterbuilder of the Twentieth Century* (2006).

JANE L. MCINTYRE is Professor Emerita of Philosophy, Cleveland State University, and a past president of the Hume Society. Her numerous publications argue for the centrality of Hume's account of the passions to his overall philosophical position. Notable articles include "Personal Identity and the Passions" (1989) and "Character: A Humean Account" (*History of Philosophy Quarterly* 1990).

DAVID FATE NORTON is Professor of Philosophy Emeritus, McGill University, and Adjunct Professor of Philosophy, University of Victoria. He is the author of *David Hume: Common-Sense Moralist, Sceptical Metaphysician* (rev. ed. 1984) and many articles on Hume and eighteenth-century Scottish philosophy; coauthor of *The David Hume Library* (1996); and coeditor of *David Hume: Philosophical Historian* (1965), *McGill Hume Studies* (1978), and the Oxford

Philosophical Texts and Clarendon editions of Hume's *A Treatise of Human Nature* (2000, 2007).

DAVID OWEN received his B. Phil. and D. Phil. from Oxford University. He has taught in Scotland, England, and Canada and currently teaches philosophy at the University of Arizona. He is the author of *Hume's Reason* (1999) and editor of *Hume: General Philosophy* (2000), and he has published many articles in the history of early modern philosophy, especially on Locke and Hume.

TERENCE PENELHUM is Professor Emeritus of Religious Studies, University of Calgary, where he was formerly Professor of Philosophy and Director of the Calgary Institute for the Humanities. His books include *Hume* (1975), *God and Skepticism* (1983), *Butler* (1985), *David Hume: An Introduction to His Philosophical System* (1992), and *Themes in Hume* (2000).

ANDREW S. SKINNER is Daniel Jack Professor of Political Economy Emeritus, University of Glasgow. In addition to many papers on the history of economic thought, he is the author of *A System of Social Science: Papers Relating to Adam Smith* (1979) and coeditor of *Essays on Adam Smith* (1975) and of Smith's *An Inquiry into the Nature and Causes of the Wealth of Nations* (1976).

JACQUELINE TAYLOR is Associate Professor of Philosophy, University of San Francisco. She has served on the Executive Committee of the Hume Society and currently serves as an editor for *Hume Studies*. Her articles on Hume's philosophy and Humean ethics have appeared in journals and in various anthologies on Hume, including *Feminist Interpretations of David Hume* (2000), *The Practice of Virtue* (2005), *The Blackwell Guide to Hume's* Treatise (2006), and *The Cambridge Companion to Hume's* Treatise (forthcoming).

DAVID WOOTTON is Anniversary Professor of History, University of York. He is the author of *Paolo Sarpi: Between Renaissance and Enlightenment* (2003) and *Bad Medicine: Doctors Doing Harm since Hippocrates* (2006). He has published widely on Renaissance and Enlightenment political theory and is currently writing a biography of Galileo.

This second edition of *The Cambridge Companion to Hume* includes five entirely new essays. These are, in their order of appearance, "Hume and the Mechanics of Mind: Impressions, Ideas, and Association," by David Owen; "Hume's Theory of Space and Time in Its Skeptical Context," by Donald L. M. Baxter; "Hume on Causation," by Martin Bell; "Hume and the Problem of Personal Identity," by Jane L. McIntyre; and "Hume's Later Moral Philosophy," by Jacqueline Taylor. In addition, "The Foundations of Morality in Hume's *Treatise*," by David Fate Norton, bears only a family resemblance to the essay "Hume, Human Nature and the Foundations of Morality" found in the first edition. One essay included in the first edition of this *Companion*, Alexander Rosenberg's comprehensive "Hume and the Philosophy of Science," has been omitted here in favor of the more detailed essays by Owen, Baxter, and Bell.

In addition, the essays by John Biro ("Hume's New Science of the Mind") and Peter Jones ("Hume on the Arts and 'The Standard of Taste': Texts and Contexts") are in this edition substantially revised, while the papers by Terence Penelhum, Knud Haakonssen, Andrew Skinner, and J. C. A. Gaskin have been revised and updated. Moreover, most essays in this volume conclude with a new set of suggestions for further reading related to the topic of the essay, while the Selected Bibliography lists Hume's principal publications and recommends a manageable set of books, both anthologies and monographs, that offer diverse and important interpretations of Hume's thought.

The editors gratefully acknowledge Becca Chase, Miriam Mc-Cormick, Norman Taylor, and especially Mary J. Norton, for their assistance in preparing these essays for publication. At Cambridge University Press we have been graciously and professionally assisted by the late Terry Moore, and also by Beatrice Rehl, Helen Wheeler, and David Anderson.

METHOD OF CITATION

References to Hume's texts are normally given parenthetically, but on some occasions these references may be placed in a note. Parenthetical references follow the form of these examples: *A Treatise of Human Nature:* T followed by Book, Part, Section, and paragraph numbers[1] of the Oxford University Press editions (see T in the list of abbreviations) from which all quotations of this work are taken, to produce, for example, the form (T 3.1.1.26).

An Enquiry concerning Human Understanding: EHU followed by the Section and paragraph numbers of the Oxford University Press editions (see EHU in the list of abbreviations) from which all quotations of this work are taken, to produce, for example, the form (EHU 12.12).

An Enquiry concerning the Principles of Morals: EPM followed by the Section and paragraph numbers in the Oxford University Press editions (see EPM in the list of abbreviations) from which all quotations of this work are taken, to produce, for example, the form (EPM 3.12).

Essays: E-, followed first by an abbreviation of the title of the particular essay cited (for these abbreviations see E in the list of abbreviations), then by the numbers of the paragraphs cited, and last by the relevant page number(s) of the edition of Hume's *Essays Moral,*

---

[1] The use of paragraph numbers in this way allows the cited materials to be found in nearly all of the many editions of Hume's works.

Political, and Literary described at E, to produce, for example, the form (E-ST 3, 228).

The History of England: HE followed first by chapter and paragraph numbers, and then by the volume and page numbers of the edition described at HE, to produce, for example, the form (HE 66.43, 6:307–8).

LIST OF ABBREVIATIONS

A   *An Abstract of a Book lately Published; Entituled* A Treatise of Human Nature, &c. *Wherein the Chief Argument of that Book is farther Illustrated and Explained*
(first published 1740). Cited from the Clarendon Edition of *A Treatise of Human Nature* (Oxford: Clarendon
Press, 2007), or from the 9th and subsequent impressions of the Oxford Philosophical Texts (OPT) Edition
(Oxford: Oxford University Press, 2005) of this same
work; see T later in this list.

D   *A Dialogue* (first published 1751), cited from the Oxford
Philosophical Texts Edition (Oxford: Oxford University
Press, 1998) or the Clarendon Edition of *An Enquiry
concerning the Principles of Morals* (Oxford: Clarendon Press, 1998), both ed. T. L. Beauchamp. Although
these two editions incorporate notably different editorial materials, their texts of D are identical.

DNR   *Dialogues concerning Natural Religion* (first published
1779), ed. N. K. Smith (Oxford: Clarendon Press, 1935;
2nd ed. London: Thomas Nelson & Sons, 1947; 3rd ed.,
New York: Library of Liberal Arts [1964?]). The three
editions are uniformly paginated.

DP   *Dissertation on the Passions* (first published 1757), cited
from *A Dissertation on the Passions* and *The Natural History of Religion*, ed. T. L. Beauchamp (Oxford:
Clarendon Press, 2007).

E   *Essays Moral, Political, and Literary*, ed. E. F. Miller (Indianapolis: Liberty *Classics*, rev. ed., 1987). Abbreviations

of the individual essays cited in this volume, with date of first publication, follow this entry.

E-BG   Whether the British Government inclines more to Absolute Monarchy, or to a Republic (1741)

E-BT   Of the Balance of Trade (1752)

E-CL   Of Civil Liberty (1741)

E-Co   Of Commerce (1752)

E-CP   Of the Coalition of Parties (1760)

E-CR   A Character of Sir Robert Walpole (1742; withdrawn after 1768)

E-DM   Of the Dignity or Meanness of Human Nature (1741)

E-DT   Of the Delicacy of Taste and Passion (1741)

E-Ep   The Epicurean (1742)

E-FP   Of the First Principles of Government (1741)

E-IM   Of Impudence and Modesty (1741; withdrawn after 1760)

E-In   Of Interest (1752)

E-IP   Of the Independency of Parliament (1741)

E-IPC   Idea of a Perfect Commonwealth (1752)

E-IS   Of the Immortality of the Soul (1777, after having been withdrawn in 1757)

E-JT   Of the Jealousy of Trade (1760)

E-LP   Of the Liberty of the Press (1741)

E-Mo   Of Money (1752)

E-NC   Of National Characters (1748)

E-OC   Of the Original Contract (1748)

E-OG   Of the Origin of Government (1777)

E-PA   Of the Populousness of Ancient Nations (1752)

E-PC   Of Public Credit (1752)

E-PG   Of Parties in General (1741)

E-PGB   Of the Parties of Great Britain (1741)

E-PR   That Politics may be reduced to a Science (1741)

E-PS   Of the Protestant Succession (1752)

E-RA   Of Refinement in the Arts (1752)

E-RP   Of the Rise and Progress of the Arts and Sciences (1742)

E-Sc   The Sceptic (1742)

E-SE   Of Superstition and Enthusiasm (1741)

E-SH   Of the Study of History (1741; withdrawn after 1760)

E-SR   Of Simplicity and Refinement in Writing (1742)

E-ST   Of the Standard of Taste (1757)

E-Su   Of Suicide (1777, after having been withdrawn in 1757)

E-Ta   Of Taxes (1752)

E-Tr   Of Tragedy (1757)

EHU   *An Enquiry concerning Human Understanding* (first published, 1748, as *Philosophical Essays concerning Human Understanding*). All quotations and references are to the Oxford Philosophical Texts Edition (Oxford: Oxford University Press, 1999) or to the Clarendon Edition (Oxford: Clarendon Press, 2000), both ed. T. L. Beauchamp. Although these two editions provide significantly different editorial materials, their texts of EHU are identical.

EPM   *An Enquiry concerning the Principles of Morals* (first published 1751). All quotations and references are to the Oxford Philosophical Texts Edition (Oxford: Oxford University Press, 1998) or to the Clarendon Edition (Oxford: Clarendon Press, 1998), both ed. T. L. Beauchamp. Although these two editions provide significantly different editorial materials, their texts of EPM are identical.

HE   *The History of England* (first published 1754–62), 6 vols. (Indianapolis: Liberty *Classics*, 1983).

HL   *The Letters of David Hume*, ed. J. Y. T. Greig, 2 vols. (Oxford: Clarendon Press, 1932).

KHL   *A Kind of History of My Life*, cited from the appendix of this volume.

L   *A Letter from a Gentleman to His Friend in Edinburgh: containing Observations on . . .* the Principles . . . *said to be maintain'd in . . .* A Treatise of Human Nature (first published 1745), cited from *A Treatise of Human Nature*, ed. D. F. Norton and M. J. Norton (Oxford: Clarendon Press, 2007).

MOL   My Own Life (first published 1777), cited from the appendix of this volume.

NHL   *New Letters of David Hume*, ed. R. Klibansky and E. C. Mossner (Oxford: Clarendon Press, 1954).

NHR   *The Natural History of Religion* (first published 1757), cited
         from *A Dissertation on the Passions* and *The Natu-*
         ral History of Religion, ed. T. L. Beauchamp (Oxford:
         Clarendon Press, 2007).

T   *A Treatise of Human Nature* (first published 1739–40). All
         quotations of this work are from the Clarendon Edition
         (Oxford: Clarendon Press, 2007) or the 11th and sub-
         sequent impressions of the Oxford Philosophical Texts
         (OPT) Edition (Oxford: Oxford University Press, 2006).
         Although these two editions provide significantly dif-
         ferent editorial materials, their texts of the *Treatise* are
         identical.[1]

W   *David Hume: The Philosophical Works*, ed. T. H. Green
         and T. H. Grose (London: Longman, 1882–6; reprinted
         Darmstadt: Scientia Verlag Aalen, 1964).

---

[1] A complete set of the corrections and revisions made to the Oxford Philosophical Texts (OPT) Edition of Hume's *Treatise* and *Abstract* may be seen at http://
digital.library.mcgill.ca/hume/Corrections.pdf.

1 An Introduction to Hume's Thought

Much of what David Hume said about a wide range of subjects remains of great importance today. In the first volume of his first work, *A Treatise of Human Nature*, a work in which he articulated a new "science of human nature," Hume focused on an interrelated set of issues in theory of knowledge, metaphysics, and philosophical psychology. More particularly, he explained how it is that we form such important conceptions as space and time, cause and effect, external objects, and personal identity. At the same time, he offered an equally important account of how or why we believe in the objects of these conceptions – an account of why we believe that causes are necessarily connected to effects, that there are enduring external objects, and that there are enduring selves – even though the human mind is unable to provide a satisfactory proof that these phenomena exist. In the second volume of the *Treatise* Hume expanded his account of human psychology, focusing on the origin and role of the passions and the nature of human freedom. In the third and final volume of this work he explored the origins and nature of morality. In later works he returned to many of these philosophical issues, but he also made substantial contributions to our understanding of political theory, aesthetics, economics, and philosophy of religion. In addition, he wrote an influential, six-volume *History of England*, a work published in over 175 editions in the eighteenth and nineteenth centuries, and still in print.

I. LIFE AND WRITINGS

Hume was born in Edinburgh, Scotland's capital, on 26 April 1711. The years of his youth were divided between that city and Ninewells,

1

his family's small landholding at Chirnside, a village near the border with England. Little is known about Hume's childhood. His father died when David was two; his mother thereafter devoted herself to her three children. It is likely that Hume began studies at the College of Edinburgh in 1721 (when about two years younger than the typical entering student) and continued there through the spring of 1725, when he would have turned fourteen.[1] After leaving university he apparently made a desultory effort at learning law, but soon

[1] We lack a detailed account of Hume's early reading and education, but the outlines of his four years at the College of Edinburgh are known. Hume would have studied Latin during his first year, and followed this with a year studying Greek. He would have followed in his third year a course in logic and metaphysics, and in his fourth and final year a course in natural philosophy organized around the writings of Robert Boyle. The plans originally drawn up for this course in 1708 included provision for some instruction in ethics, but there is no firm evidence that ethics were included in the 1724–5 session Hume would have attended. In addition, in December 1724 Hume joined a private library (the Physiological Library) that gave him access to a wide range of books on the sciences then studied. Hume was later to report that in the three years ending about March 1734 he had read "most of the celebrated Books in Latin, French & English," and also learned Italian (KHL 6). Any list of those having a significant (although not necessarily positive) impact on his early thought would likely include not only those writers often mentioned (John Locke, George Berkeley, Isaac Newton, and Francis Hutcheson, for example), but also a great many others, including such relatively well-known figures as Virgil, Cicero, Plutarch, and Seneca from among the ancients, and Michel Montaigne, Francis Bacon, Hugo Grotius, René Descartes, Pierre Gassendi, Blaise Pascal, Samuel Pufendorf, Robert Hooke, Nicolas Malebranche, Pierre Bayle, Anthony Collins, the third Earl of Shaftesbury, Samuel Clarke, Bernard Mandeville, Joseph Butler, Baron Montesquieu, and Lord Bolingbroke, as well as many other individuals now less well known, from the early modern period. Consequently, despite his obvious preference for what he called the "EXPERIMENTAL METHOD OF REASONING," no single writer or philosophical tradition can be relied on to provide a comprehensive key to Hume's thought.

To learn more about Hume's early education, see M. A. Stewart, "Hume's Intellectual Development, 1711–52," in *Impressions of Hume*, ed. M. Frasca-Spada and P. J. E. Kail (Oxford: Clarendon Press, 2005), 11–58, esp. 11–25; and Michael Barfoot, "Hume and the Culture of Science in the Early Eighteenth Century," in *Oxford Studies in the History of Philosophy*, ed. M. A. Stewart, 3 vols. (Oxford: Clarendon Press, 1990–2000) [hereafter *Oxford Studies*], 1:151–90, esp. 151–6. The latter also provides much detail about the Physiological Library. For a more general account of the curriculum at the University of Edinburgh, and of the views of those who taught it, see R. L. Emerson, "Science and Philosophy in the Scottish Enlightenment," also in *Oxford Studies* 1:11–36. Emerson argues that by as early as 1710 the experimentalism of Bacon, Boyle, and Newton was well known in Edinburgh. For extensive suggestions regarding those of his predecessors Hume may have read, see "Editors' Annotations," in *A Treatise of Human Nature*, ed. D. F. Norton and M. J. Norton, 2 vols. (Oxford: Clarendon Press, 2007) [hereafter Norton and Norton], 2:685–978.

enough was devoting his principal efforts to philosophy, and especially to the issues that became central to his philosophical classic, *A Treatise of Human Nature*. In 1734, discouraged by his inability to present his views in satisfactory form, he tried the more active life of a merchant's assistant. Within months he abandoned this experiment and traveled to France, where he remained for three years and at last finished a draft of his long work. In September 1737 he settled in London and continued to revise the *Treatise*. In January 1739 the first two volumes of the work were published and Hume returned to Scotland, where he revised the manuscript of the third and final volume of the *Treatise*. This volume was published in late October 1740. Two volumes of his essays (*Essays, Moral and Political*) appeared in 1741–2.

To help support himself during the next fifteen years Hume took positions first as companion to a mentally unbalanced nobleman, then as aide-de-camp and later secretary to a British general, and finally as Keeper of the Advocates Library in Edinburgh. Although the many works Hume published from 1748 to 1762 made him financially independent, he accepted two further public service appointments: from 1763–5 he was at first Secretary, then chargé d'affaires to the British Embassy in Paris, and in 1767–8 he was Undersecretary of State (Northern Affairs) in the British government. He then retired to Edinburgh where he lived until his death in 1776. In his will Hume left instructions for the publication of his *Dialogues concerning Natural Religion*.

II. EXPERIENCE AND ITS LIMITS

Hume's most often cited works include the three volumes of the *Treatise of Human Nature* mentioned above; an *Abstract* of volumes 1 and 2 of the *Treatise* (1740); a collection of approximately 50 essays, *Essays Moral, Political, and Literary* and *Political Discourses* (most of which were first published from 1741 to 1752); *An Enquiry concerning Human Understanding* (1748);[2] *An Enquiry*

---

[2] This work was first published as *Philosophical Essays concerning Human Understanding*; it was retitled by Hume in 1758. From that date and on through the nineteenth century, Hume's essays and *An Enquiry concerning Human Understanding, Of the Passions* (retitled as *A Dissertation on the Passions*), *An Enquiry concerning the Principles of Morals*, and *The Natural History of Religion* were published together as *Essays and Treatises on Several Subjects*. For a history of

concerning the Principles of Morals (1751); Of the Passions and The Natural History of Religion (1757); his six-volume History of England from Roman times to 1688 (1754–62); a brief autobiography, My Own Life (1777); and Dialogues concerning Natural Religion (1778).[3] These works span an exceptionally wide range of topics and thus are in some ways significantly different from one another. They are nonetheless unified by at least one fundamental characteristic: their author's commitment to the experimental method, or to a form of philosophy that recognizes both the advantages and necessity of relying on experience and observation to provide the answers to intellectual questions of all kinds.[4]

The subtitle of Hume's Treatise describes it as "AN ATTEMPT TO INTRODUCE THE EXPERIMENTAL METHOD OF REASONING INTO MORAL SUBJECTS."[5] In the Introduction to this work Hume traces the beginning of the use of the experimental method in natural philosophy to Francis Bacon (1561–1626).[6] Moral philosophy, Hume argues, and especially the foundational science of human nature that he proposes to develop, must also make use of this method: "And as the science of man is the only solid foundation for the other sciences, so the only solid foundation we can give to this science itself must be laid on experience and observation."[7] A page later he insists that, while we must try "to render all our principles as universal as possible, by tracing up our experiments to the utmost, and explaining all effects from the simplest and fewest causes, 'tis still certain we cannot go beyond experience; and any hypothesis, that pretends to discover

the collected editions of Hume's works published from 1753 to 1777, see Tom L. Beauchamp, "Introduction," in An Enquiry concerning Human Understanding, 2nd impression, corrected (Oxford: Clarendon Press, 2006), xxv–xxxv.

[3] For a chronological list of Hume's writings, see Part I of the Selected Bibliography.

[4] For further reading showing the widely different ways in which Hume has been interpreted, see Parts III and IV of the Selected Bibliography.

[5] The discussion that follows in Parts II–VI of this essay focuses on Hume's first and most comprehensive work, the Treatise of Human Nature.

[6] In Hume's time philosophy had two distinctive branches. One, natural philosophy, included those subjects we now think of as the physical and natural sciences. The other, moral philosophy, focused on humans or human activity and included those subjects we would think of as the core of philosophy (theory of knowledge, metaphysics, ethics, and the philosophy of religion), as well as such subjects as psychology, political science, sociology, economics, and aesthetics (to use our terms).

[7] For more on this topic, see in this volume the essay "Hume's New Science of the Mind."

the ultimate original qualities of human nature, ought at first to be rejected as presumptuous and chimerical" (T Intro. 7–8). Finding that moral philosophy could not, as natural philosophy can, make its experiments "purposely, with premeditation, and after such a manner as to satisfy itself concerning every particular difficulty which may arise," he tells us that

We must therefore glean up our experiments in this science from a cautious observation of human life, and take them as they appear in the common course of the world, by men's behaviour in company, in affairs, and in their pleasures. Where experiments of this kind are judiciously collected and compar'd, we may hope to establish on them a science, which will not be inferior in certainty, and will be much superior in utility to any other of human comprehension. (T Intro. 10)

In his *Abstract* of the *Treatise* Hume describes himself as having promised "to draw no conclusions but where he is authorized by experience" (A 2). He concludes *An Enquiry concerning Human Understanding* with the now notorious injunction to commit to the flames any book of divinity or school metaphysics, for instance, that contains neither "*any abstract reasoning concerning quantity or number*" nor "*any experimental reasoning concerning matter of fact and existence*" (EHU 12.34), but not before he has subjected experimental reasoning itself to a severe, experimental scrutiny (see EHU 4.14–23). In "Of the Original Contract," an essay in political theory first published in 1748, Hume tells us that "A small degree of experience and observation suffices to teach us, that society cannot possibly be maintained without the authority of magistrates," and that, moreover, the "observation of these general and obvious interests [peace and public order] is the source of all allegiance, and of that moral obligation, which we attribute to it" (E-OC 25, 480). *An Enquiry concerning the Principles of Morals* undertakes to discover "the foundation of ethics." As this, Hume says, "is a question of fact, not of abstract science, we can only expect success, by following the experimental method, and deducing general maxims from a comparison of particular instances" (EPM 1.10). In "Of the Standard of Taste," first published in 1756, he tells us that it is obvious that the "rules of composition" are nothing more than "general observations, concerning what has been universally found to please in all countries and in all ages," and that in this regard their "foundation is the same with that of all the practical sciences, experience" (E-ST 9, 231).[8]

To appreciate fully the force of these remarks, we must keep in mind that they carry with them an unspoken but deep distrust of the a priori reasoning characteristic of much earlier philosophy, especially that of the Cartesians. At other times, however, Hume is explicit about the limitations of our faculty of reason and the shortcomings of those philosophical systems that give it priority. He pointedly notes that, although we all believe that every event or object has a cause, there are no valid *arguments* establishing this conclusion (T 1.3.3). And, although we all believe in enduring, external objects, reason cannot establish that such objects exist, and even if it could, it would be of no use to that vast population of people and animals who, without the use of a single argument, believe that such objects exist. Although reason may help us determine how to achieve some desired goal, it has by itself absolutely no motivating force. Although we all make moral distinctions – we take some acts or persons to be virtuous or good, others to be vicious or morally wrong – it is a special kind of feeling, not reason, that makes this possible. It is this distrust of reasoning, coupled with his commitment to

---

[8] Hume was less explicit about his commitment to experience and observation in his primarily historical works, the *Natural History of Religion* and the *History of England*. But the former work attempts to discover "the origin of religion in human nature" by extrapolating from present facts (religion and human nature as they are presently found to be) and the historical record of the beginnings and development of religion. This exercise is a *natural* history because the explanation is constrained within the limits of observable, natural phenomena; no supernatural beings or principles are appealed to or presupposed. For more on this work and Hume's approach to religion, see in this volume the essay "Hume on Religion."

Analogous comment can be made regarding *The History of England*. Motivated to a considerable degree by the exaggerated claims of the two leading political groups in Britain, the Whigs and the Tories, each of whom insisted that the political institutions of eighteenth-century Britain reflected, or should reflect, a perfect model found either in the mists of their Anglo-Saxon beginnings (a Whig tendency) or in a timeless, sacred beginning (a Tory tendency), Hume attempted to write an impartial history of England, a history that recorded the *development* of political institutions over time, one that treated these institutions as the hard-won and still developing products of centuries of experience and observation, and not as something derived from a priori principles ingrained in the human mind. For more on these issues, see in this volume the essays "The Structure of Hume's Political Theory" and "David Hume: 'The Historian.'"

experience and observation, that makes it not entirely inappropriate to think of Hume as an early empiricist.[9] What is often missed, however, is the fact that Hume's commitment to experience and observation is qualified in at least five substantial ways.

1. As we have seen, Hume supposed that moral philosophy cannot make its experiments "purposely, [and] with premeditation" in the way that natural philosophy can because such artificial or laboratory-like experiments would disturb and distort the phenomena being examined. But we also saw that he was not discouraged by this limitation because moral philosophy can collect its experimental data from a careful examination of human life, and having done so, can hope to construct a useful science of human nature.

2. Experience has intrinsic limitations. In our quest to understand human nature, for example, we may follow experience as far as it will take us, but we will still remain ignorant of the most fundamental or ultimate features of our nature. As Hume puts it at the beginning of the *Treatise*, we may try to make our conclusions as general or as universal as possible by "explaining all effects from the simplest and fewest causes," but because we know that experience has limitations, we must remember that any theory that claims to have discovered "the ultimate original qualities of human nature, ought at first to be rejected as presumptuous and chimerical" (T Intro. 8).

3. Hume, as much as any of the Cartesians, insists that all sensory experience is indirect. We do not experience objects themselves. We experience only, in the language of Descartes and Locke, *ideas* or what some suppose to be mental representations of objects. Hume

---

[9] Hume continued his discussion at EPM 1.10 (quoted in the previous paragraph) by contrasting his experimental approach to moral philosophy with what he called the "other scientific method," that in which "a general abstract principle is first established, and is afterwards branched out into a variety of inferences and conclusions." Forms of this latter method came in time to be called *rationalism*, while forms of the "experimental method" to which Hume adhered came (but not during Hume's lifetime) to be called *empiricism*. Retrospectively, then, and while recognizing that there are significantly different kinds of empiricism, it is not a mistake to call Hume an *empiricist*. For a brief discussion of kinds of empiricism, see Nicholas P. Wolterstorff, "Empiricism," in *The Cambridge Dictionary of Philosophy*, ed. R. Audi, 2nd ed. (Cambridge: Cambridge University Press, 1999).

uses different terminology, but is firmly committed to the view that our direct experience is limited to mental phenomena. Early in the *Treatise*, while discussing "*the idea of existence, and of external existence,*" he reports that it is "universally allow'd by philosophers, and is besides pretty obvious of itself, that nothing is ever really present with the mind but its perceptions or impressions and ideas, and that external objects become known to us only by those perceptions they occasion" (T 1.2.6.7). Hume repeats this claim in each book of the *Treatise*, in the *Abstract*, and in the *Enquiry concerning Human Understanding*.[10]

4. Given the fact that we experience only "perceptions," and further facts about the nature of our perceptions, Hume concludes that our deep and virtually ineradicable belief in the existence of external objects is not due to sense experience alone. The senses may play an essential role in the process that brings about this fundamental belief, but the senses operating alone would be unable to produce it. Moreover, the senses operating alone would be unable to account for our belief in causal connections or personal identity.

5. Experience is not the source of certain of our fundamental passions. Locke had argued that there are no innate ideas, and had made this conclusion one of the defining features of his form of empiricism. Locke, according to Hume, was both confused and mistaken. Locke used the term *idea* too broadly and thus failed to distinguish, as he ought to have done, between two kinds of perceptions, impressions (especially impressions of sensation) and the ideas that derive from them. If we make this needed distinction we see that, while it may be true to say that there are no innate *ideas*, it is false to say that there are no innate *impressions*. As Hume puts it, it is clear that some of "our stronger perceptions or impressions are innate, and that natural affection, love of virtue, resentment, and all the other passions, arise immediately from nature" (A 6; see also T 1.1.1.12, EHU 2.9 n.1).

As we will see, these perceived limitations of experience profoundly influenced Hume's conclusions.

---

[10] See also T 1.4.2.21 and 47, 2.2.2.22, 3.1.1.2; A 5; EHU 12.9. For more on Hume's skeptical challenge to experimental reasoning, see in this volume Part II of the essay "Hume's Skepticism."

III. THE ELEMENTS OF HUME'S PHILOSOPHY

For most of the nearly 270 years since the publication of his *Treatise,* Hume was routinely interpreted as the philosopher who advanced his form of philosophy (which has come to be called *empiricism*) to its logical and skeptical conclusion. I suggest that Hume is better understood as a *postskeptical* philosopher. By this I mean to suggest that Hume supposed (a) that earlier philosophers, and especially Nicolas Malebranche, Pierre Bayle, John Locke, and George Berkeley, had already taken traditional metaphysics and epistemology to its skeptical conclusions; (b) that these skeptical conclusions had been soundly and validly established; and (c) that the most important remaining task of philosophy, given these well-established and obvious conclusions, was to show how we manage to get on with our lives, particularly our intellectual lives, without the knowledge of ultimate causes and principles sought by his predecessors. To put this another way, I note that, prior to Hume, one or another philosopher had, perhaps unintentionally, thoroughly discredited the claim of humans to have rationally or experientially derived knowledge of the existence and true nature of space, causal relations, external objects, and mind. But as Hume put it, even the "rabble" outside the philosophical hall – even those who are not philosophers – could see that the philosophical enterprise was not going well. "The most trivial question escapes not our controversy, and in the most momentous we are not able to give any certain decision" (T Intro. 2). It is time, surely, to start anew, to provide moral philosophy with a new foundation, the science of human nature, on which all the other sciences will be founded.

But notice where Hume begins: The "elements of this philosophy" are, in the most literal sense, the immediate objects of thought as well as the relations between or among these "objects" of the "mental world." The elements themselves are called *perceptions,* and are divided into two kinds, *impressions* and *ideas.* Of these, impressions are the more forceful or lively, while ideas are complementary in that they are said to be "the faint images" of impressions. In addition, Hume classifies as impressions "all our sensations, passions and emotions, as they make their first appearance in the soul" or mind, and then divides this class into two subclasses, *impressions of sensation* and *impressions of reflection.* The latter sort, impressions of reflection, are "deriv'd in a great measure from our ideas." On the other hand, impressions of sensation, he says, arise *"in the soul originally, from unknown causes"* (emphasis added). He then adds that the "examination of our sensations [our impressions of sensation] belongs more to anatomists and natural philosophers than to moral; and therefore shall not at present be enter'd upon" (T 1.1.4.3,6–7; 1.1.1.1.; 1.1.2.1). As we work through the *Treatise* we come to realize that the phrase "not at present" in fact means "not in this work," for at no time does Hume take up the task that he has assigned to anatomists and natural philosophers.[11] Indeed, he begins Book 2 of the *Treatise* with much the same disclaimer:

'Tis certain, that the mind, in its perceptions, must begin somewhere; and that since the impressions precede their correspondent ideas, there must be some impressions, which without any introduction make their appearance in the soul. As these depend upon natural and physical causes, the examination of them wou'd lead me too far from my present subject, into the sciences of anatomy and natural philosophy. (T 2.1.1.2)

Between these two remarks Hume tells us clearly why he has left to others the task of explaining impressions of sensation: such an explanation is irrelevant to the philosophical enterprise in which he is engaged. As he puts it:

As to those *impressions*, which arise from the *senses*, their ultimate cause is, in my opinion, perfectly inexplicable by human reason, and 'twill always be impossible to decide with certainty, whether they arise immediately from the object, or are produc'd by the creative power of the mind, or are deriv'd from the author of our being. Nor is such a question any way material to our present purpose. We may draw inferences from the coherence of our perceptions, whether they be true or false; whether they represent nature justly, or be mere illusions of the senses. (T 1.3.5.2)[12]

---

[11] Although Hume wanted nothing to do with a physical anatomy attempting to explain sensation, he does repeatedly describe himself as engaged in *an anatomy of human nature*. See T 1.4.6.23, 3.3.6.6, A 2; HL 1:32–3.

[12] This comment is made in the midst of Hume's attempt to explain how we come to have the idea of, and to believe in, necessary connection. But the suggestion that the explanations of Book 1 are confined to an examination of the "coherence" of "elements" within the "mental world" is repeated in other forms in other places. See, for example, 1.4.2 (*Of scepticism with regard to the senses*), where the discussion is focused on the way in which impressions and ideas cohere to give us, not *knowledge* of, but only *belief* in, external objects; and the Appendix (published

But notice, I say again, where Hume begins: The "elements of this philosophy" are, in the most literal sense, the immediate objects of thought as well as the relations between or among these "objects" in the "mental world." And his concern is not to advance from this base in order to deny dogmatically that there are causes, objects, or minds. His concern is not to make the case for skepticism about these entities. The case for skepticism about these momentous questions was well known to Hume. He knew those sections of Bayle and Locke that reveal the inadequacy of Descartes's attempts to prove by reason that there is an external world. He appreciated the skeptical force of the objections brought by Bayle, then significantly amplified by Berkeley, against the primary-secondary quality distinction championed by Locke.[13] He saw that philosophers of all kinds were, in the matter of explaining the interaction of mind and body, skeptics in spite of themselves. He saw that the leading Cartesian of the day, Malebranche, had concluded that there are no natural causes of any kind, and that there is no human or natural knowledge of the existence of causes or objects. What we do know of these things is, according to Malebranche, the result of an act of divine grace.[14]

in 1740 as a part of Volume 3), where Hume contrasts theories of the material world with his "theory of the intellectual world" (App. 10). For a fuller discussion of Hume's account of impressions and ideas, see in this volume the essay "Hume and the Mechanics of Mind."

[13] Locke had argued that certain ideas (those of extension and shape, for example) caused by what he called the "primary qualities" of objects resemble these qualities in such a way that they provide us with accurate, reliable information about the qualities that cause them. Other ideas (those of color and taste, for example) caused by what he called the "secondary qualities" of objects fail to resemble the qualities causing them, and in fact lead us to attribute to objects characteristics (color, taste) which they do not possess. Bayle suggested, and Berkeley argued (successfully, it is generally believed), that this distinction is untenable. See Pierre Bayle, *Historical and Critical Dictionary: Selections*, ed. and trans. R. H. Popkin (Indianapolis: Library of Liberal Arts, 1965), "Pyrrho," note B; George Berkeley, *A Treatise concerning the Principles of Human Knowledge*, 1.9–15. For a helpful account of Berkeley's impact on Hume, see David Raynor, "Hume and Berkeley's Three Dialogues," *Oxford Studies* 1:231–50.

[14] Hume says, for example: "But so little does any *power* discover itself to the senses in the operations of matter, that the *Cartesians* have made no scruple to assert, that matter is utterly deprived of energy, and that all its operations are performed merely by the energy of the supreme Being" (A 26). For more on Hume's views on causation, see in this volume the essay "Hume on Causation." For others who argued that no causal conection is ever sensed, see Norton and Norton, "Editors' Annotations," 2:735, annotation 55.18.

In short, Hume was satisfied that the battle to establish reliable links between thought and reality had been fought *and lost,* and hence made his contributions to philosophy from a postskeptical perspective that incorporates and builds on the skeptical results of his predecessors.[15]

IV. A SKEPTIC'S IDEAS AND BELIEFS

The once-standard reading of Hume credited him with seeing the skeptical implications of the representative theory of perception, and with seizing on these implications in the cause of a destructive skepticism.[16] It seems likely that Hume was fully aware of the skeptical implications of this theory, but, given his expressed disinterest in the connections between impressions of sensation and their possible causes, we must conclude either that he did not adopt the theory, or that he adopted only one part of it. Hume agrees that the immediate objects of mind are always perceptions, but he does not take these to be, in one cardinal sense, representative of objects. He never claims that impressions or ideas *resemble* objects.[17]

---

[15] It does not follow that Hume made no contributions to the arsenal of skepticism. For a discussion of some of these contributions, see in this volume the essays "Hume's Skepticism" and "Hume on Religion."

[16] This theory maintains that the immediate objects of the mind are *ideas* (in Hume's vocabulary, *perceptions,* or *impressions* and *ideas*), some of which are supposed to represent accurately various kinds of entities outside the mind; see note 13. The problem was to determine which ideas do represent the external existences, and, given that ideas and only ideas are the immediate objects of the mind, to find independent evidence that any given idea represents accurately or even *resembles* the object(s) supposed to be its cause and that it is supposed to represent. That Hume exposed the skeptical implications of this theory was suggested as early as 1751 by his kinsman Henry Home, Lord Kames, and then repeated by such other eighteenth-century philosophers as Thomas Reid. For the relevant works by these early critics of Hume, see the Selected Bibliography, Part IVA.

[17] Hume repeatedly insists that *ideas* are derived from and represent only impressions. Impressions themselves are of two types: impressions of sensation and of reflection. Our senses, he says, cannot represent their impressions as distinct from us, and hence fail to represent a crucial feature of external objects. Nor, he says, can any of our sense impressions, not even our impressions of touch, "represent solidity, nor any real object," because there is not the "least resemblance" between these impressions and solidity (T 1.4.2.8–10, 1.4.4.13). A passion, Hume says, "contains not any representative quality, which renders it a copy of any other existence or modification" (T 2.3.3.5).

In fact, Hume gave the "way of ideas" a kind of phenomenological turn. That is, his primary concern in Book 1 of the *Treatise* is with our perceptions, *qua* perceptions, with perceptions as, simply, the *elements* or *objects of the mind*, and not as *representations* of external existences. Having focused on perceptions as the only objects of the mind, Hume goes on in Book 1 to show how some of these perceptions are interrelated or associated to produce still further perceptions that are then projected onto a world putatively outside the mind.[18] *Somehow* the mind is furnished with impressions of sensation. On examination we find that not one of these *impressions* can of itself be taken as an accurate representation of space or time, causal connection, an external object, or even our own mind. We simply do not have sensory *impressions* of these entities. But, notwithstanding this fact, and the further fact that all our ideas are derived from impressions, we nonetheless do have *ideas* of space, causal connection, and external existences, etc., and we are nonetheless irredeemably committed to believing that there are real entities that correspond to these ideas.[19] The mystery to be explained, given the success of skepticism, is how we come to have these important ideas and, moreover, how we come to believe that they represent, not merely impressions, but independent, external existences or realities. To put this differently, Hume's greater goal can be taken to be showing how, despite the successes of skepticism, we are rescued from skepticism.

The first book of the *Treatise* is an effort to show how our perceptions "cohere" to form ideas of those fundamental items (space, causal connection, external existence) in which, skeptical doubts

[18] Husserl, himself the founder of phenomenology, recognized this feature of Hume's thought. See R. A. Mall, *Experience and Reason: The Phenomenology of Husserl and Its Relation to Hume's Philosophy* (The Hague: Nijhoff, 1973), 19–28.

[19] We remain irredeemably committed to these beliefs in the sense that, while philosophical analysis may on occasion bring us to doubt them (see, e.g., 1.4.2.56–7), this doubt cannot be sustained. Even a skeptic must, with rare exception, believe in causes and objects. The skeptic may very well, however, modify the manner or intensity of these unavoidable beliefs. On this latter point, see my "How a Sceptic May Live Scepticism," in *Faith, Scepticism, & Personal Identity*, ed. J. J. MacIntosh and H. A. Meynell (Calgary: University of Calgary Press, 1993), 119–39, or the shorter version of this paper, "Of the Academical or Sceptical Philosophy," in *Reading Hume on Human Understanding: Essays on the First Enquiry*, ed. P. Millican (Oxford: Clarendon Press, 2002), 371–92.

notwithstanding, we repose belief and on which, as Hume puts it in the *Abstract*, "life and action entirely depend." In Book 1, Part 2, Hume argues that we have no direct impressions of space and time, and yet we have the ideas of both.[20] He accounts for our idea of space by appealing to a "manner of appearance," in the following way. By means of two senses, sight and touch, we have impressions that array themselves as so many points related to one another. These particular impressions are by the *imagination* transformed into a "compound impression, which represents extension" or the abstract idea of space itself. Our idea of time is, *mutatis mutandis*, accounted for in the same way: "As 'tis from the disposition of visible and tangible objects we receive the idea of space, so from the succession of ideas and impressions we form the idea of time."[21] The abstract idea of time, like all other abstract ideas, is represented in the imagination by a "particular individual idea of a determinate quantity and quality" joined to a term, "time," that has general reference (A 4, T 1.2.3.5–7, 15). In short, the imagination, a faculty not typically assigned so significant a role, achieves what neither the senses nor reason can achieve.

Hume's account of our derivation of and belief in the idea of causal connection (of "necessary connexion," in his terms) follows this same pattern. He is often said to have denied that there is physical necessity and that we have any idea of necessary connection. This interpretation is significantly mistaken. Hume had been convinced by the Cartesians, and especially by Malebranche, that neither the senses nor reason can establish that one object (a cause) is connected together with another object (an effect) in such a way that the presence of the the first *necessarily* entails the existence of the second.

[20] It should be understood that Hume is concerned with the source of our most abstract or general ideas of space and time – of space, for example, as something like continuous, unbounded, or unlimited *extension* in every direction, regarded as void of matter, or without reference to matter (*Oxford English Dictionary*). Of such a space we neither have, nor could have, a direct sensory impression, but from the fact that we can intelligibly discuss the subject, it follows, Hume argues, that we have an idea of space to which the word "space" refers: "Now 'tis certain we have an idea of extension [or space]; for otherwise why do we talk and reason concerning it?" (T 1.2.2.9).

[21] For a discussion of Hume's theory of space and time, see in this volume the essay "Hume's Theory of Space and Time."

Hume's own analysis of what we take to be experiences of cause and effect shows that objects that we suppose to be causally related are contiguous in time and space, that the cause is prior to the effect, and that similar objects have been constantly associated in this way, but nothing more. These are the only perceptible features of such putative causal connections. And yet there seems to be more to the matter. "There is," he says, "a NECESSARY CONNEXION to be taken into consideration," and our belief in that relation must be explained (T 1.3.2.11). Despite our demonstrated inability to see or prove that there are necessary causal connections, we continue to think and act as if we had knowledge of such connections. We act, for example, as though the future will necessarily resemble the past, and "wou'd appear ridiculous" if we were to say "that 'tis only probable the sun will rise to-morrow, or that all men must dye" (T 1.3.11.2). To explain this phenomenon Hume asks us to imagine what life would have been like for Adam, suddenly brought to life in the midst of the world and in "the full vigour of understanding." Adam would have been unable to make even the simplest predictions about the future behavior of objects. He would not have been able to predict that one moving billiard ball, striking a second, would cause this second ball to move (A 11). And yet we, endowed with the same faculties, can not only make, but are unable to resist making, this and countless other such predictions. What is the difference between ourselves and this putative Adam? Experience. We have experienced the constant conjunction (an invariant succession of certain paired objects or events) of particular causes and effects, and, although our experience never includes even a glimpse of a causal connection per se, it does arouse in us an expectation that a particular event (a "cause") will be followed by another event (an "effect") previously and constantly associated with it. Regularities of experience give rise to these feelings, and thus determine the mind to transfer its attention from a present impression to the idea of an absent but associated object. *The idea of necessary connection is copied from these feelings* (T 1.3.14.14–23). The idea has its foundation in the mind and is projected onto the world, but there is nonetheless such an idea. That there is an objective physical necessity to which this idea corresponds is an untestable hypothesis, nor would demonstrating that such necessary connections had held in the past guarantee that they will hold in the future. From these considerations we see that Hume does not explicitly and dogmatically deny that there are real causal connections. We have no experience of such necessary connections and hence can be, at best, skeptical or agnostical about their existence. There is, however, an *idea* of necessary connection, but, although we ordinarily and naturally believe that reality corresponds to this idea, the correct philosophical analysis reveals that the idea is derived from a feeling, or an impression of reflection, and it is this that the idea represents. In other words, Hume's analysis leaves the philosopher room to suppose that our belief in causal or necessary connections, however natural, may be mistaken.

Hume's account of our *belief* in future effects or absent causes – of the process of mind that enables us to *plan effectively* – is a part of this same explanation. Such belief involves an idea or conception of the entity believed in, but is clearly different from mere conception without belief. This difference cannot be explained by supposing that some further idea, an idea of belief itself, is present when we believe, but absent when we merely conceive. There is no such idea. Moreover, given our ability to join together any two consistent ideas we choose to so join, if an idea of belief were available we could, contrary to experience, by an act of will combine the idea of belief with any other idea, and by so doing cause ourselves to believe anything. Consequently, Hume concludes that belief can only be a "different MANNER of conceiving an object." It is a livelier, firmer, more vivid and intense conception. Belief in certain "matters of fact" – the belief that because some event or object is now being experienced, some other event or object not yet available to experience *will in the future* be experienced – is brought about by previous experience of the constant conjunction of two impressions. These two impressions have been associated together in such a way that the experience of one of them automatically gives rise to an idea of the other, and has the effect of transferring the force or liveliness of the impression to the associated idea, thereby causing this idea to be believed, or to take on, in effect, the lively character of an impression (T 1.3.7, A 21).

Our beliefs in continuing and independently existing objects and in our own continuing selves are, on Hume's *Treatise* account of these matters, beliefs in entities entirely beyond all experience. We have impressions that we naturally but mistakenly suppose to be themselves continuing, external objects, but careful analysis of our experience reveals that these impressions are by their very nature fleeting and observer-dependent. Moreover, none of our impressions provides us with a distinctive mark or evidence of an external origin (T 1.4.2.1–13; see also EHU 12.5–14). Similarly, when we focus on our own minds, we experience only a sequence of impressions and ideas, and never encounter the mind or self in which these perceptions are supposed to inhere. To ourselves we appear to be merely "a bundle or collection of different perceptions, which succeed each other with an inconceivable rapidity, and are in a perpetual flux and movement" (T 1.4.6.4).[22]

How do we, then, come to believe in external objects or our own selves and self-identity? Neither reason nor the senses, working with impressions and ideas, provide anything like compelling proof of the existence of continuing, external objects, or of a continuing, unified self. Indeed, these two faculties cannot so much as account for our *belief* in objects or selves. If we had only reason and the senses, the faculties championed by previous philosophers, we would be mired in a debilitating and destructive uncertainty. So unfortunate an outcome is avoided only by the operation of a generally unreliable third faculty, the *imagination*. By means of what appear to be a series of outright mistakes and trivial suggestions this faculty leads us to believe in independently existing objects and in our own selves. The skepticism of the philosophers is in this way both confirmed (we can provide no arguments, for example, proving the existence of the external world) and shown to be of little practical import. As Hume summed up his point:

Almost all reasoning is there [in the *Treatise*] reduced to experience; and the belief, which attends experience, is explained to be nothing but a peculiar sentiment, or lively conception produced by habit. Nor is this all. When we believe any thing of *external* existence, or suppose an object to exist a moment after it is no longer perceived, this belief is nothing but a sentiment of the same kind. Our author insists upon several other sceptical topics; and upon the whole concludes, that we assent to our faculties, and employ our reason only because we cannot help it. Philosophy would render us entirely *Pyrrhonian*, were not nature too strong for it. (A 27)

[22] For a discussion of Hume on personal identity, see in this volume the essay "Hume and the Problem of Personal Identity."

V. PASSIONS

At the outset of Book 2 of the *Treatise* Hume turns his attention to another of the elements of his mental world, to the impressions of reflection, or to those impressions he characterizes as "*secondary and reflective.*" He does not in this or the following Book devote significant space to the profound metaphysical or epistemological questions (the existence of causes, objects, or minds, for example) that are the central concerns of Book 1. Having once explained how we form ideas of these core entities, and then how we come to believe in them, Hume takes our belief in them for granted and pushes on to discuss our impressions of reflection.[23] These turn out to be our passions, the principal subject of Book 2, and the moral sentiments, a pair of distinctive passions that, along with the virtues and vices, are dealt with in Book 3.

In general terms, Book 2 of the *Treatise* can be said to have helped rescue the passions from the negative assessments and ad hoc explanations found in many his predecessors. From the time of Plato and the Stoics and well into the eighteenth century the passions were routinely characterized as not just irrational, but as also unnatural and morally dangerous mental elements that, if given their head, would undermine and enslave reason, the nobly defining, essential characteristic of humans. In contrast to this oft-repeated denigration of the passions, Hume supposed the passions to be natural phenomena and undertook to explain them by means of the same experimental or observational method used in Book 1. In short, Book 2 extends Hume's science of human nature to the passions.[24]

---

[23] See, e.g., T 2.1.2.2, 2.1.11.4–8, 2.2.1.2, 2.3.7.1, where Hume's account of the passions touches on our ideas or impressions of the self, and the brief but helpful summary of his account of causation and the source of the idea of necessary connection included near the beginning of his discussion of liberty and necessity (see T 2.3.1.4).

[24] Near the beginning of Book 2 Hume notes that some explanations of the passions resemble "astronomy before the time of *Copernicus.*" They do so because they make use of "a monstrous heap of principles" to explain what is almost certainly "simple and natural." What is needed is an explanation of the passions that respects the maxim "*that nature does nothing in vain*" (T 2.1.3.6–7). When nearly twenty years later he published a much shorter account of the passions, Hume concluded that work by saying: "I pretend not to have here exhausted this subject. It is sufficient for my purpose, if I have made it appear, that, in the production and

Hume begins this task by reminding his readers that perceptions are either impressions or ideas. Noting that impressions are of two kinds, *original* and *secondary*, as we saw above, he again refuses to speculate about the source of original impressions, the "impressions of sensation." His interest is in the *secondary* or *reflective* impressions, those that derive from some original impression either directly or through an idea of that impression, and that make up "the passions, and other emotions resembling them."

These reflective impressions or passions may be, Hume suggests, divided into two kinds, the *calm* and the *violent*. The former includes the "the sense of beauty and deformity" of actions, human creations, and of natural objects, while the latter includes such passions as "love and hatred, grief and joy, pride and humility." But this commonly made distinction is, we are told, "far from being exact." The pleasures of poetry and music may rise to the heights of rapture, while some of the so-called violent passions – love and hatred, grief and joy, for example – may be so gentle as to become virtually imperceptible. A much more useful approach to the passions divides them between the *direct* and the *indirect*. Among the former are "desire, aversion, grief, joy, hope, fear, despair and security," while the latter include "pride, humility, ambition, vanity, love, hatred, envy, pity, malice, generosity" (T 2.1.1.1, 3–4).

The direct passions, to which Hume turns only near the end of Book 2, are of two kinds. There are certain "*original* instinct[s]" of the mind that cause us to respond directly to painful or pleasurable stimuli or to the expectation of such stimuli. If I perceive something good, something that I believe will give me pleasure, that experience alone is enough to arouse the direct passion of desire. If I am certain to obtain this particular good, or if I do in fact obtain it, I experience joy. If it is only probable that I will obtain the good thing, I will feel hope. The perception of things (evils) that I believe will cause pain functions in a like natural way to produce aversion, grief, or fear. Hume observes that these passions continue to be felt only as long as their stimulus or cause continues to have effect (T 2.3.9.1–7, 9–11).

conduct of the passions, there is a certain regular mechanism, which is susceptible of as accurate a disquisition, as the laws of motion, optics, hydrostatics, or any part of natural philosophy" (DP 6.19).

In the midst of his discussion of this first kind of direct passion Hume notes that there is another form of these passions. There are also several "natural" impulses or instincts: "the desire of punishment to our enemies, and of happiness to our friends; hunger, lust, and a few other bodily appetites." These passions, he points out, are unlike the other direct passions in one important respect. These passions are not caused by good or evil or the prospect thereof. On the contrary, they "produce" good or evil. My desire for the happiness of my friends leads me to do good things for them. My hunger leads me to substances which I eat in order to assuage that hunger; these edible things I designate as "good" if they accomplish my desired goal.[25]

Hume gives much more detailed attention to the *indirect* passions, to, that is, pride and humility, love and hatred (and their related compound passions, compassion and malice, for example).[26] He argues that passions of this kind arise as the result of a complex double relation of impressions and ideas that depends in great measure on the association of ideas and impressions. These passions have as their *causes* the qualities or possessions (their virtues or their fine houses, for example) of individuals. On the other hand, these passions have as their *objects* (that is, they are directed toward) the very persons who have the qualities or possessions that cause the passion. As it happens, the object of pride or humility is always the very person feeling pride or humility, while the object of love or hatred is always some other person. If I perceive that I am virtuous, the pleasure this perception resembles, and then gives rise to, is the pleasure of pride, while at the same time the fact that I am the person thought to be virtuous gives rise to the idea of myself. As a result, the impression or passion of pride is directed toward the idea of myself in such a way that I take pride in my own character or possessions. Love or esteem of a friend or relative is explained analogously, so that I love or esteem a virtuous friend. But the important point in the present context has not to do with the details of Hume's account,

[25] T 2.3.9.1–11. At the end of Book 2 Hume identifies what appears to be another passion of this sort, namely, curiosity or "that love of truth" that "was the first source of all our enquiries" (T 2.3.10.1).

[26] Far from considering pride a vice, Hume insists that justified and properly dissimulated pride is a normal and even beneficial concomitant of virtue, as well as of beauty, position, or wealth. See in particular T 2.1.7.8.

but with the fact that in providing these details he demonstrates his commitment to treating the passions as nothing more or less than an integral part of the natural mental world. The passions, like the ideas discussed in Book 1 of the *Treatise*, are further products of the observable natural processes Hume undertook to analyze and explain.

Hume's analysis of the indirect passion of pride leads him to see that a form of sympathy, *sympathy as a principle of communication*, plays a fundamental role in our moral lives.[27] Having asked why it is that the esteem of others increases our pride, Hume replies by drawing attention to a deep-seated human propensity to share, unthinkingly, the sentiments and opinions of others. If, for example, I encounter someone who is grieving, the external signs of that grief (facial expressions, tears, words, etc.) arouse in me the idea of grief. This idea is then by a standard process transformed into an impression of grief, so that I experience the very passion being experienced by the person I am encountering. To put this more generally, in the simplest situations, the observation of another person feeling a given passion will cause the same passion to be felt by the observer (T 3.3.1.7). In other situations, the effect on the observer may be different: Hume also finds that if the misery of another is strongly felt by an observer, that observer feels pity. But if that other's misery is only weakly felt, then the observer may feel contempt (T 2.2.9.16).

Hume's analysis of the passions also leads him to examine the human will. He finds that the will is not a faculty but only "*the internal impression we feel and are conscious of, when we knowingly give rise to any new motion of our body, or new perception of our mind.*" He also finds that the common distinction between *natural* and *moral* evidence – between causal relations as they relate to physical objects and as they relate to human activity – is unfounded. These two kinds of evidence, he concludes, "cement together, and form only one chain of argument betwixt them," a finding he illustrates by pointing out that a "prisoner, who has neither money nor

---

[27] On sympathy as a principle of communication, see, e.g., T 2.1.11.2, 2.2.5.15–16, 2.2.9.13–14, 2.3.6.8. For further discussion of sympathy see in this volume "Hume and the Mechanics of Mind," Part II, and "Hume's Later Moral Philosophy," Part III. For still more on sympathy and the passions, see Jennifer Herdt, *Religion and Faction in Hume's Moral Philosophy* (Cambridge: Cambridge University Press, 1997).

interest, discovers the impossibility of his escape, as well from the obstinacy of the goaler [jailer], as from the walls and bars with which he is surrounded; and in all attempts for his freedom chooses rather to work upon the stone and iron of the one, than upon the inflexible nature of the other" (2.3.1.2–17). He also finds that it is the passions, and only the passions, that influence the will, and thus that the age-old fear that the reason may become enslaved to the passions and consequently fail to be able to direct the will and our actions, makes no practical sense. Reason is inert and entirely unable to direct the will, or, as Hume puts it in what is perhaps the best-known remark from the whole of the *Treatise*, "Reason is, and ought only to be the slave of the passions, and can never pretend to any other office than to serve and obey them" (T 2.3.3.4).[28]

VI. MORALS

In the third and final book of the *Treatise, Of Morals,* Hume looks closely at morality, a subject that "interests us above all others." Once again he pursues his subject by means of the experimental method, this time by focusing on our moral practices or experience (by focusing on morality as we find it in the world) with the intention of discovering those features of our nature and circumstances that give to our moral experience its distinctive features or characteristics.

Having begun Book 3 by reminding his readers of the meaning of his key terms, *impressions* and *ideas,* Hume first shows that our ability to make moral distinctions, our ability to distinguish *virtue* from *vice* or moral good from moral evil, does not derive from reason and the manipulations of *ideas* of which that faculty is capable. Morality is not a speculative matter, but a practical one. That reason lacks the necessary practical force that morality demands had been established in *Treatise* 2.3.3. Now, in 3.1.1 (*Moral distinctions not deriv'd from reason*) Hume adduces several arguments intended to show that reason alone cannot have been the source of the distinction between virtue and vice. In the following section (*Moral*

---

[28] In Book 3 we find that it is because of the activity of sympathy that we come to treat the artificial virtues as genuinely moral virtues (T 3.2.2.24, 3.3.1.9–10). On sympathy and the artificial virtues, see in this volume the essays "The Foundation of Morality in Hume's *Treatise,*" Part IIIC, and "The Structure of Hume's Political Theory," Part III.

distinctions deriv'd from a moral sense) Hume goes on to argue that moral distinctions derive from a natural moral sense that provides human observers with a set of unique impressions or feelings when the motives (the intentions or characters) underlying the actions of human agents are impartially observed. Some of these motives give rise to unique impressions of *approval* or *approbation,* and as a consequence are denominated *virtuous.* Other actions and motives give rise to unique impressions of *disapproval* or *disapprobation,* and as a consequence are denominated *vicious.*

There is, however, much more to be learned. Hume's observations also convince him that there are two kinds of virtue. There are *natural* virtues (benevolence and humanity are examples), and *artificial* virtues (justice and allegiance are examples). These two kinds of virtue differ inasmuch as the natural virtues are inherent features of human nature. They are inherent natural passions that have always motivated specific kinds of human behavior. In addition, Hume says that the natural virtues produce moral good on each occasion of their operation, and that they also give rise to approving moral sentiments whenever they are seen to motivate action.[29]

In contrast, the artificial virtues are not inherent features of human nature, but moralized conventions that have developed over the course of time in response to human needs. Hume concludes from the available evidence that humans in an "uncultivated state" (T 3.2.2.4) would have had no need for the artificial virtues because their natural virtues or dispositions would have been adequate to maintain peace and order in the small, kinship-based units into which they were gathered.[30] But as human groups became larger and more complex, as they became not families, but societies, circumstances would have changed, and these changes would have led to conflicts within or between the existing social units, conflicts with which the natural virtues were unable to deal adequately. As a consequence, a further inherent feature of human nature, self-interest, required the development of conventions (property rights and rules, or the rules of justice) to regulate possessions and still

---

[29] Hume makes other claims that suggest that performing a naturally virtuous act may not, on some occasions, produce good. For a brief discussion of this point, see in this volume the essay "The Foundation of Morals in Hume's *Treatise,*" note 40.

[30] Hume supposed his view to be verified by "the *American* tribes, where men live in concord and amity among themselves without any establish'd government," except in time of war with their neighbors (T 3.2.8.2).

other conventions (the principles of governance) to regulate political behavior.

Given that these conventions or virtues were unknown to humans living in their first or "uncultivated state," it is obvious that they cannot always have motivated or directed human behavior. Moreover, although the uniform practice of an artificial virtue such as justice may be absolutely necessary for the good of society as a whole, the practice of this virtue may on any given occasion be contrary to the good of both individuals and the public generally (T 3.2.2.22, 3.3.1.12). Finally, Hume points out that the artificial virtues have a double foundation. Justice, he says, has "two different foundations." The distinction between justice and injustice begins with "*self-interest,* when men observe, that 'tis impossible to live in society without restraining themselves by certain rules." But this same distinction also comes to be founded in "*morality.*" That happens when this interest is also "observ'd to be common to all mankind, and men receive a pleasure from the view of such actions as tend to the peace of society, and an uneasiness from such as are contrary to it" (T 3.2.6.11).

VII. RECASTINGS AND CONTINUATIONS

1. Within a matter of only a few years after its appearance, Hume came to regret the publication of the *Treatise.* In *My Own Life,* while reviewing the years immediately following publication of the work, he wrote: "Never literary attempt was more unfortunate than my Treatise of Human Nature. It fell *dead-born from the press,* without reaching such distinction, as even to excite a murmur among the zealots." Hume's reasons for this remark are not obvious. From 1739 to 1741, the *Treatise* was reviewed both in Britain and on the continent, and some of these reviews must fairly be described as exciting murmurs among the religious, while the work's skeptical and allegedly atheistical tendencies would by the mid-1740s be a leading cause of Hume's failure to be named Professor of Moral Philosophy at the University of Edinburgh.[31] But despite this

---

[31] The historical material sketched here is discussed in much greater detail in my "Historical Account of *A Treatise of Human Nature* from Its Beginnings to the Time of Hume's Death" (hereafter "Historical Account"), in *A Treatise of Human Nature,* 2 vols. (Oxford: Clarendon Press, 2007), 2:451–526.

notoriety and despite Hume's two published attempts to clarify the work (the *Abstract* of the *Treatise*[32] and the Appendix to Book 3), the work sold so poorly that there was never an opportunity for the second edition Hume looked forward to even before volume 3 was published in late 1740.[33] Thus in describing the *Treatise* as *"dead-born from the press"* Hume may have had this lack of commercial success in mind.[34] It seems more likely, however, that his greatest regret about the *Treatise* had to do with his assessment of his own performance in the work. He came to believe that he had bungled his attempt to introduce a comprehensive new system of philosophy. He was later to say of that performance: "I was carry'd away by the Heat of Youth & Invention to publish too precipitately. So vast an Undertaking, plan'd before I was one and twenty, & compos'd before twenty five, must necessarily be very defective. I have repented my Haste a hundred, & a hundred times" (HL 1:158).[35]

In 1748 Hume published *Philosophical Essays concerning Human Understanding* (later to be titled *An Enquiry concerning Human Understanding*), a recasting of a modest portion of the materials found in Books 1 and 2 of the *Treatise*, along with two essays on religious topics ("Of Miracles" and "Of a Particular Providence and of a Future State") and two systematic discussions: "Of the Different Species of Philosophy" and "Of the Academical or Sceptical

---

[32] The *Abstract of the Treatise*, a short work that attempts *"to render a larger work more intelligible to ordinary capacities, by abridging it,"* or, as the subtitle of the work puts it, to illustrate and explain the "CHIEF ARGUMENT" of that work (A Preface, title page). The *Abstract* was published in March 1740. For a comprehensive effort to establish beyond all reasonable doubt that Hume wrote the *Abstract*, see my "Historical Account," 2:459–71. As it is now settled that Hume wrote the *Abstract*, this short work can be enthusiastically recommended to those who wish to consider Hume's own account of what he took to be the chief argument of the first two volumes of the *Treatise*, namely, his argument about the origin of, and belief in, the idea of causal connection.

[33] In March 1740 Hume wrote to Francis Hutcheson: "I wait with some Impatience for a second Edition principally on Account of Alterations I intend to make in my Performance" (HL 1:38–9).

[34] Hume's contract with the bookseller (John Noon) who published vols. 1 and 2 of the *Treatise* prevented Hume from publishing a second edition of the *Treatise* until all copies of the first edition were sold. But the work sold very poorly, so poorly that, following John Noon's death in 1763, 290 of the 1,000 copies printed in 1739 were sold to the book trade for 7 pence each, about 6 percent of the established retail price of 10 shillings. Four years earlier, it appears that 200 copies of vol. 3 were sold at a similar auction. For further details, see my "Historical Account," 2:583–4.

[35] For a systematic review of Hume's assessments of the *Treatise*, see my "Historical Account," 2:576–88.

Philosophy."[36] Of this work he said that he thought it contained "every thing of Consequence relating to the Understanding, which you woud meet with in the Treatise; & I give you my Advice against reading the latter. By shortening & simplifying the Questions, I really render them much more complete. *Addo dum minuo* [I add while I decrease]. The philosophical Principles are the same in both" (HL 1:158).[37]

The substantially rewritten version of Book 3 of the *Treatise, An Enquiry concerning the Principles of Morals*, the work that Hume took to be, "of all my writings, historical, philosophical, or literary, incomparably the best" (MOL 10), was published in 1751. *A Dissertation on the Passions*, clearly a recasting of Book 2 into what Hume described as one of several "small pieces," was published in 1757. Very late in his life Hume grew impatient with his critics for focusing their attention on the *Treatise* rather than his shorter restatements of his views, and so he composed a brief "Advertisement" that he asked to have included in the appropriate volume of all existing and future copies of his *Essays and Treatises on Several Subjects*.[38] This notice asks that the *Treatise* be ignored:

Most of the principles, and reasonings, contained in this volume, were published in a work in three volumes, called *A Treatise of Human Nature*: A work which the Author had projected before he left College, and which he wrote and published not long after. But not finding it successful, he was sensible of his error in going to the press too early, and he cast the whole anew in the following pieces, where some negligences in his former reasoning and

---

[36] The philosophical position that Hume calls the "Academical" philosophy is that which is now likely to be referred to as *academic skepticism*. Its name derives from the fact that it was first articulated, in the third century B.C., at the Academy founded by Plato.

[37] In *My Own Life* (MOL 8) Hume wrote: "I had always entertained a notion, that my want of success in publishing the Treatise of Human Nature, had proceeded more from the manner than the matter, and that I had been guilty of a very usual indiscretion, in going to the press too early. I, therefore, cast the first part of that work anew in the Enquiry concerning Human Understanding."

[38] On Hume's *Essays and Treatises on Several Subjects*, see note 2 above. After 1758 this collection was for the rest of Hume's life published in either two- or four-volume editions. The "Advertisement" was intended to serve as a Preface to the volume(s) of this work containing *An Enquiry concerning Human Understanding*, the *Dissertation on the Passions*, and *An Enquiry concerning the Principles of Morals*, as it is these "Pieces" that Hume took to represent the *Treatise* "cast . . . anew."

more in the expression, are, he hopes, corrected. Yet several writers, who have honoured the Author's Philosophy with answers, have taken care to direct all their batteries against that juvenile work,[39] which the Author never acknowledged, and have affected to triumph in any advantages, which, they imagined, they had obtained over it: A practice very contrary to all rules of candour and fair-dealing, and a strong instance of those polemical artifices, which a bigotted zeal thinks itself authorized to employ. Henceforth, the Author desires, that the following Pieces may alone be regarded as containing his philosophical sentiments and principles.[40]

Reasonable though his desire to distance himself from the *Treatise* may have seemed to him, few serious readers of Hume have been able to concur with it.[41] For Hume's critics, the *Treatise* is an irresistible target; for those who believe him to have been a profound and constructive student of human nature, the work is too rich to ignore.

2. About the works that are said to represent the *Treatise* "cast... anew," two things are obvious. First, as we saw above, Hume's commitment to the experimental method continued unabated in these later works. Second, Hume does not merely, as he suggests, improve by shortening and simplifying. His *Enquiry concerning Human Understanding* (the "first *Enquiry*") includes some important additions, most notably two attention-getting discussions of religious issues. In an effort to make his views religiously innocuous so that they might be considered calmly and on their philosophical merits, he had carefully excised from the *Treatise* anything that could be taken as antireligious. Nevertheless, the views of the *Treatise* and *Essays, Moral and Political* were too thoroughly secular to

---

[39] For a survey of responses to the *Treatise* from 1739 to 1777, see my "Historical Account," 2:494–576. Of the principal responses written after the publication of the two enquiries (EHU in 1748, EPM in 1751), only that of Thomas Reid, in *An Inquiry into the Human Mind on the Principles of Common Sense* (1764), limits its discussion and criticism of Hume to the views expressed in the *Treatise*.

[40] The "Advertisement" is quoted from *An Enquiry concerning Human Understanding*, ed. T. L. Beauchamp, [1]. The same text is also found in the Oxford Philosophical Texts edition of this work, ed. T. L. Beauchamp (Oxford: Oxford University Press, 1999), [83].

[41] A notable recent exception is the collection of essays edited by Peter Millican cited in note 19 and in the Selected Bibliography. See also Antony Flew, *Hume's Philosophy of Belief: A Study of his First Inquiry* (London: Routledge & Kegan Paul, 1961), and in this volume the essay "Hume's Later Moral Philosophy."

pass unremarked in a religious age, and, as noted, by the mid-1740s Hume had been branded a religious skeptic with atheistic tendencies. He seems in consequence to have decided to challenge openly the rationality of religious belief. In any event, the first *Enquiry*, the first of his recastings, included two of Hume's most provocative forays into the philosophy of religion, "Of Miracles" and "Of a Particular Providence and of a Future State," while *The Natural History of Religion* was denounced as atheistic even before it was published.[42]

These two essays established beyond all doubt Hume's character as a religious skeptic. Taken together, they challenge the foundations of much religious belief and attempt to curb its excesses by undertaking to show that this form of belief has its beginnings in sources or causes about which we must be deeply suspicious. In "Of Miracles," for example, Hume argues that belief in miracles, a kind of putative fact used to justify a commitment to certain creeds, can never provide the secure foundation such creeds require. He sees that these commitments are typically maintained with a mind-numbing tenacity and a disruptive intolerance toward contrary views. To counter these objectionable commitments, he notes that the widely held view that miracles are events that violate established laws of nature means that the evidence for even the most well-attested miracle will always be counterbalanced by the uniform experience (the "proof") that establishes the law of nature that the miracle allegedly violates. Moreover, he argues that the evidence supporting any given miracle is necessarily suspect. His argument leaves open the possibility that unusual events may have occurred, but it shows that the grounds for a *belief* in any given miracle or set of miracles are much weaker than the religious suppose. There are and will be those who believe that miracles have occurred, but Hume's analysis shows that such beliefs

---

[42] Hume at one point thought of including "Of Miracles" in the *Treatise*, but decided not to do so as part of his program to eliminate religiously offensive material from that work. For more on this subject, see in this volume the essay "David Hume: 'The Historian.'" Hume's reputation as a religious skeptic, and even an atheist, was instrumental in his failure, in 1745, to be appointed to the Chair of Moral Philosophy at the University of Edinburgh. See *A Letter from a Gentleman to his Friend in Edinburgh* (Edinburgh, 1745). On the controversy surrounding the publication of *The Natural History of Religion*, see Ernest Campbell Mossner, *The Life of David Hume* (Edinburgh, 1954), 319–35.

will always lack the force of evidence needed to justify the arrogance and intolerance that characterizes so many of the religious.

"Of a Particular Providence and of a Future State," Section 11 of the same *Enquiry*, and the posthumously published *Dialogues concerning Natural Religion* have a similar effect. Philosophers and theologians of the eighteenth century often argued (the *argument from design*, as it is known) that the well-ordered universe in which we find ourselves can only be the effect of a supremely intelligent cause, that each aspect of this divine creation is well designed to fulfill some beneficial end, and that these effects show us that the Deity is caring and benevolent. Hume shows that these conclusions go well beyond the available evidence. The pleasant and well-designed features of the world are balanced by a good measure of the unpleasant and the plainly botched. Our knowledge of causal connections depends on the experience of constant conjunctions; these cause the vivacity of a present impression to be transferred to the idea associated with it, and leave us believing in that idea. But in this case the effect to be explained, the universe, is unique, and its cause unknown. We see, then, that we cannot possibly have experiential grounds for any kind of inference about this cause. On experiential grounds the most we can say is that there is a massive, mixed effect, and, as we have through experience come to believe that effects have causes commensurate to them, this effect probably does have a commensurately large and mixed cause. Furthermore, as the effect is remotely like the products of human manufacture, we can say "*that the cause or causes of order in the universe probably bear some remote analogy to human intelligence*" (DNR 12.33, 227). There is indeed an inference to be drawn from the unique effect in question (the universe) to the cause of that effect, but it is not the "argument" of the theologians, and it provides no foundation for any form of sectarian pretension or even the mildest forms of intolerance.

The *Natural History of Religion* focuses on the question of "the origin of religion in human nature." Hume asks, that is, what features of human nature account for the widespread but not universal belief in invisible and intelligent power(s). He delivers a thoroughly deflationary and naturalistic answer: religious belief "springs not from an original instinct or primary impression of nature," not from any universal and fundamental principle of our natures, but from features of human nature that are derivative and whose operation "may easily be perverted by various accidents and causes [or] . . . altogether prevented" (NHR Intro. 1). Moreover, it is the darker, less salubrious features of our nature that take the principal parts in this story. Primitive peoples did not find nature to be an orderly whole produced by a beneficent designer, but fragmented, arbitrary, and fearsome. As a consequence, motivated by their own ignorance and fear, they came to think of the activities of nature as the effect of a multitude of petty powers – the effects of deities who could, through propitiating worship, be influenced to ameliorate the lives of those who engaged in this worship. Subsequently the same fears and perceptions transformed polytheism into monotheism, the view that a single, omnipotent being created and still controls the world and all that transpires in it. From this conclusion Hume goes on to argue that monotheism, seemingly the more sophisticated position, is in fact *morally* retrograde, for, once having established itself, monotheism tends naturally toward zeal and intolerance, encourages debasing, "monkish virtues," and is itself a danger to society because it proves to be a cause of violent and immoral acts directed against those who fail to act in accord with its tenets. In contrast, polytheism is tolerant of diversity and encourages those genuine virtues that improve the circumstances of humankind, and thus from a moral point of view is superior to monotheism (NHR 9–10). The important point, however, is the suggestion that all religious belief derives initially from fear and ignorance, and, moreover, that it encourages the continued development of these undesirable characteristics.

3. In a number of respects, Hume's *Essays* and his *History of England* constitute *continuations* of his earliest work. They are, of course, further manifestations of his attempt to extend the experimental method into moral subjects. They are also further manifestations of his attempt to gain understanding by means of an examination of origins or beginnings. Their titles alone indicate, often enough, these interests: "That Politics may be reduced to a Science," "Of the First Principles of Government," "Of the Origin of Government," "Of the Rise and Progress of the Arts and Sciences." Others, with less telltale titles, are nonetheless a part of the same project. "Of the Liberty of the Press" traces the unparalleled liberty of the press British subjects enjoyed in the eighteenth century to the "mixed form of government" found in Britain, and thus lends

experiential support to mixed forms of governance (E-LP 2, 10). In "Of the Independency of Parliament" Hume draws attention to the fact that the House of Commons could easily wrest all power from the King and Lords, but does not do so. He explains this unusual situation by looking for an explanation that is "consistent with our experience of human nature," and concludes that a fundamental feature of this nature, the self-interest of the individual members of the Commons, acts as a brake on the expansion of the power of Parliament (E-IP 6, 44–5). "Of Parties in General" looks for the sources, again in human nature, of parties, or those detestable factions that "subvert government, render laws impotent, and beget the fiercest animosities among men of the same nation, who ought to give mutual assistance and protection to each other" (E-PG 2, 55). "Of Superstition and Enthusiasm" outlines the pernicious effects on government and society of the two types of false religion alluded to in the title of the essay.[43] And so on.

There is at least one additional sense in which the *Essays* and *The History of England* represent a continuation of the project that began with *A Treatise of Human Nature:* The work for which Hume is remembered is all fundamentally historical. That is, all this work attempts to explain something that we presently believe, feel, say, think or do, to explain some present state of affairs, whether that state be in the mental, moral, or political world, by tracing these perceptions, actions, or states – by tracing certain noteworthy *effects* – to the prior conditions that appear to have been their *causes*. As we saw above, our experiments in the science of human nature must be gleaned "from a cautious observation of human life," from the "common course of the world, by men's behaviour in company, in affairs, and in their pleasures." Observations of what humans have done, how their minds work, how their institutions have formed: these are all *historical* observations of several different kinds.

Hume reveals something more of his view of explanation in one of the essays just mentioned, "Of the Rise and Progress of the Arts and Sciences." Enquiries into human affairs, he says there, require us to distinguish between "what is owing to *chance*, and what proceeds from *causes*." If we say that an event is owing to chance, we are

---

[43] For a discussion of these issues as they bear on Hume's political theory, see in this volume the essay "The Structure of Hume's Political Theory."

in effect confessing our ignorance, and putting an end to attempts at explanation. But if we suppose some event or state of affairs is the result of causes, we leave ourselves the opportunity of "assigning these causes" and displaying our "profound knowledge." As a general rule, he says, "*What depends upon a few persons is, in a great measure, to be ascribed to chance, or secret and unknown causes: What arises from a great number, may often be accounted for by determinate and known causes*" (E-RP 1–2, 111–12). Consequently, explanations of, say, the course of domestic politics or the rise of commerce will be easier to come by than explanations of artistic development. And yet a careful enquirer may perhaps detect regularities between certain conditions and the flourishing of the arts and sciences. In this particular essay, Hume turns his hand to giving just such an explanation. But, more importantly, the *Essays* taken together, and *The History of England*, are the result of Hume's attempts to push back the frontiers of ignorance or misunderstanding by assigning causes to phenomena previously attributed to the workings of chance, or to that which in Hume's view is equally devoid of content, the workings of providence.

VIII. THE REFORMER

In August 1776, a few days before his death, Hume was visited by Adam Smith, one of his closest friends. On observing that Hume, who had been seriously ill for some months, was cheerful and apparently full of the spirit of life, Smith "could not help entertaining some faint hopes" of his friend's recovery. "Your hopes are groundless," Hume replied, and eventually turned the conversation onto Lucian's *Dialogues of the Dead*, and the excuses offered to Charon the boatman for not entering his boat to be ferried to Hades. None of the classical excuses fitted him, Hume noted. He had no house to finish, no children to provide for, no enemies to destroy. "He then diverted himself," Smith continues,

with inventing several jocular excuses, which he supposed he might make to Charon, and with imagining the very surly answers which it might suit the character of Charon to return to them. "Upon further consideration," said [Hume], "I thought I might say to him, 'Good Charon, I have been correcting my works for a new edition. Allow me a little time, that I may see how the Public receives the alterations.' But Charon would answer, 'When you have seen the effect of these, you will be for making other alterations. There will be no end of such excuses; so, honest friend, please step into the boat.' But I might still urge, 'Have a little patience, good Charon, I have been endeavouring to open the eyes of the Public. If I live a few years longer, I may have the satisfaction of seeing the downfal[l] of some of the prevailing systems of superstition.' But Charon would then lose all temper and decency. 'You loitering rogue, that will not happen these many hundred years. Do you fancy I will grant you a lease for so long a term? Get into the boat this instant, you lazy, loitering rogue.'"[44]

Of the many anecdotes about Hume that have survived, none, I suggest, better reveals his character. There is, first, the fact that a man, correctly convinced of his imminent death, and equally satisfied that death is simply annihilation, would treat the matter lightly.[45] Serious topics treated at times with nonchalance: this has been enough to lead some of his critics to suppose, mistakenly, that Hume lacked seriousness of purpose, to suppose that rhetorical *effect* was to him more important than *truth*. Hume did at times treat serious topics lightly, and he did have reservations about claims to have found ultimate principles or The Truth, but these facts are entirely consistent with his most fundamental and unmistakably serious aim.[46]

In the conversation with Smith, for example, Hume's humor is focused on two topics of genuine concern to him. He was, surely, as he candidly tells us in *My Own Life,* concerned with his literary reputation, and he just as surely took great pleasure in being recognized as one of Europe's leading intellectual figures. But it was not merely *fame* that Hume sought; it was also *reputation*. Before he had published anything he said that he "wou'd rather live & dye in Obscurity" than publish his views in a "maim'd & imperfect" form (KHL 6). With the *Treatise* finally published, he discouraged a friend

---

[44] Letter from Adam Smith, LL.D. to William Strahan, Esq. (DNR 244–5).

[45] A few weeks before his death Hume was able to satisfy James Boswell that he sincerely believed it "a most unreasonable fancy" that there might be life after death (DNR 76–7). Hume's essay on the topic "Of the Immortality of the Soul," intended for publication in 1755, was published in a French translation in 1770, and in English in 1777, a year after Hume's death (see E-IS 590–8).

[46] For further discussion of this point, see in this volume the essay "Hume's Moral Psychology."

from pursuing a scheme to increase sales. His first concern, he said, was not with commercial success, but with earning the approbation of those capable of judging his writings (NHL 4). And, as his first excuse to Charon indicates, he constantly revised and altered his *Essays and Treatises,* and *History of England* – indeed, he did so, apparently, on his death bed – at a time, in other words, when he had no other reason for revising his work than his own interest in improving it. We can agree that Hume wrote for effect, but we need not conclude from his occasional lightness of tone that he lacked serious purpose.[47]

Hume's second excuse to Charon reveals much about that purpose. He has, he says, "been endeavouring to open the eyes of the Public" and would like to remain alive long enough to have "the satisfaction of seeing the downfal[l] of some of the prevailing systems of superstition." Hume the *reformer* is only seldom noticed.[48] And yet from early days *reform* was the effect at which he aimed. In the beginning it was reformation through the science of man at which he aimed, a reformation that would, if successful, have the effect of reforming all the other sciences, for all of these – even *"Mathematics, Natural Philosophy,* and *Natural Religion"* – are dependent on the science of human nature (T Intro. 4). In the Preface to the *Abstract* he describes himself as, by his *Treatise,* suggesting that *"were his philosophy received, we must alter from the foundation the greatest part of the sciences."* Habit, his skeptic says, is a "powerful means of reforming the mind, and implanting in it good dispositions and inclinations," while the great value of philosophy derives from the fact that, properly undertaken, "It insensibly refines the temper, and it points out to us those dispositions which we should endeavour to attain, by a constant *bent* of mind, and by repeated *habit"* (E-Sc 30, 170–1). "MORAL philosophy," he says at the very beginning of *An Enquiry concerning Human Understanding,*

---

[47] In the letter cited in note 44, Smith went on to add: "And that gaiety of temper, so agreeable in society, but which is so often accompanied with frivolous and superficial qualities, was in him certainly attended with the most severe application, the most extensive learning, the greatest depth of thought, and a capacity in every respect the most comprehensive" (DNR, 247).

[48] An important exception is John B. Stewart, *Opinion and Reform in Hume's Political Philosophy* (Princeton: Princeton University Press, 1992); see especially 194–317.

"may contribute to the entertainment, instruction, and reformation of mankind" (EHU 1.1).

Hume had no thought of reforming the fundamental dispositions of human nature itself. These he took to be settled, and utopian schemes dependent on a changed constitution of humanity he dismissed without qualification: "All plans of government, which suppose great reformation in the manners of mankind, are plainly imaginary" (E-IP 4, 514). Reformation, if it is to take place, will affect individuals, and will be in the form of that refinement of character that results from new *habits of mind*, and, most particularly, from new *habits of belief*. It will be the effect of individuals melding, as Hume melded, the "EXPERIMENTAL METHOD OF REASONING" into an updated version "Of the Academical or Sceptical Philosophy." This latter species of philosophy has, he says, a clear advantage over all other kinds: by its very nature it protects those who adopt it from the excesses characteristic of other forms of philosophy. The academic skeptic, noting the dangers of hasty and dogmatic judgment, emphasizes continually the advantages of "doubt and suspence of judgment... of confining to very narrow bounds the enquiries of the understanding, and of renouncing all speculations which lie not within the limits of common life and practice" (EHU 5.1). Hume's postskeptical philosophy does not counsel us to suspend all judgment, belief, and affirmation. Instead, accepting the basic lessons of skepticism, it attempts to show us how to moderate our beliefs and attitudes. Those who practiced his principles would, Hume thought, learn how to avoid that combination of arrogance, pretension, and credulity that he found so distasteful and stifling, so *dangerous* in its typical manifestations, religious dogmatism and political faction. Hume did not suppose that he would effect changes in human nature itself, but he did hope that he could moderate individual belief and opinion, and, as a result, moderate the opinions, institutions, and behavior of the public at large. A simple but profound goal: "to open the eyes of the Public," with the aim of undercutting the "prevailing systems of superstition."[49]

---

[49] Paul Russell argues that Hume supposed the reformation of character to be difficult and even unlikely. See his *Freedom and Moral Sentiment: Hume's Way of Naturalizing Responsibility* (New York: Oxford University Press, 1995), 102–5, 128–30. For a discussion of Hume's less pessimistic views about the reformation of belief, see the papers cited in note 19 above.

IX. FOURTEEN ESSAYS ON HUME'S THOUGHT

Although perhaps now best known for his contributions to the theory of knowledge, metaphysics, and philosophy of religion, Hume also made substantial and influential contributions to moral theory and moral psychology, political and economic theory, political and social history, and, to a lesser extent, aesthetic and literary theory. The essays in this volume approach Hume in this topical way. They introduce readers to his wide-ranging thought by focusing on fourteen overlapping areas of interest. The essays themselves are arranged in a pattern that reflects, first, the structural order of *A Treatise of Human Nature*, Hume's most systematic philosophical publication, and then the pattern of his later publications. Some essays show how Hume's thought may be linked to that of his predecessors and contemporaries. Others are more concerned with links to the twentieth century. Each provides an accessible account of some central aspects of Hume's thought.

The first essay outlines Hume's plans for a new science of human nature, a science that is to serve as the foundation of all the other sciences, moral as well as natural. This science, John Biro argues, has significant affinities with modern cognitive science and offers insights that will be of use to those engaged in this contemporary enterprise.

David Owen points out the innovations Hume made to the theory of ideas accepted by his predecessors, and then shows how his views about impressions and ideas and the principles of association enable him to provide explanations of causal reasoning, belief, several key passions (pride, humility, love, and hatred), and the principle of sympathy, and thus form the core of his science of human nature.

Donald Baxter explains Hume's perplexing account of space and time, and of our ideas of them, in the context of his skeptical reliance on appearances. The explanation shows the surprising force of Hume's arguments against infinite divisibility, the exactness of geometry, vacuums, and time without change, while illuminating his relational account of space and time as manners in which colored or tangible points exist.

Martin Bell's essay takes up Hume's widely discussed account of causation or necessary connection. The essay focuses on Hume's efforts to answer two questions of great importance: How do we acquire the idea of cause and effect? And how are we able to infer effects from causes and vice versa? Contrary to what we might have expected, we are shown that Hume's answer to the first question depends on his answer to the second. The essay also examines Hume's two definitions of cause and some recent interpretations of Hume's views on causation.

Jane McIntyre situates Hume's discussion of personal identity in its broader historical context, including the important debate between Anthony Collins and Samuel Clarke. She also lays out the textual evidence supporting the view that in his later writings Hume continued to hold, and even expand on, his *Treatise* account of the self.

Noting that Hume describes the philosophy of the *Treatise* as "very sceptical," Robert Fogelin attempts to see what this skepticism amounts to, and how it is related to other aspects of his philosophical program. He concludes that while Hume clearly did not recommend a wholesale suspension of belief (he thought this impossible), he is, insofar as he presents us with a thoroughgoing critique of our intellectual faculties, a radical, unreserved, unmitigated skeptic, and that to think otherwise is to miss much of Hume's genius.

Of the four essays that take Hume's moral theory as a point of departure, that by Terence Penelhum considers those elements – the self, the passions, and the will, for example – of Hume's view of human nature that are most intimately related to his objectives as a moral philosopher, but not before he has considered Hume's character and the important questions that some have raised about his psychological qualifications for doing philosophy.

David Fate Norton situates the moral theory of the *Treatise* within a centrally important debate about the foundations of morality. According to Hume, we are by nature motivated by both altruistic and self-interested dispositions. We are also by nature sensitive to the motivations – the desires, intentions, or character – of those we encounter, and as a consequence we come to denominate some of these motivations, and those who have them, virtuous, and others vicious. He also reviews Hume's suggestions about the origin of the ideas of blame and obligation.

Jacqueline Taylor examines Hume's post-*Treatise* writings on morals, drawing attention to the emphasis these place on the language of morality and its role in moral conversation and debate. She also discusses the importance of Hume's sentiment-based ethics when he considers apparent cultural differences of moral outlook.

Knud Haakonssen argues that Hume undertook to show that most early modern views of society and politics, founded as they were on two forms of false religion, *superstition* or *enthusiasm*, were philosophically misconceived, empirically untenable, and, often enough, politically dangerous. In contrast, Hume provided a humanistic account of political morality – an account that sees our political institutions as human constructs that depend on human nature and human experience.

With the publication of his *Political Discourses* in 1752, Hume established himself as an important political economist. Andrew Skinner sketches the background of economic theory in which Hume's work appeared, outlines Hume's insightful alternative views, and concludes by noting Hume's influence on the economic writings of, among others, his good friend Adam Smith.

In 1757, with the publication of "Of the Standard of Taste" and "Of Tragedy," Hume provided his readers with what may be some of the surviving pieces of what may once have been intended to be a systematic work on "criticism" – a combination of aesthetics, literary theory, and moral psychology. Peter Jones's essay brings together Hume's somewhat scattered remarks on these topics, thus enabling us to see and understand his general perspective on the arts, and how it relates to his other views about humanity and society.

Because of the popularity of his six-volume *History of England*, Hume has often been identified as "David Hume the Historian." David Wootton examines the motivations – personal, moral, and political – that led to Hume's monumental narrative of social and political circumstance, and suggests that it is, to a large extent, Hume's story of the development of the uncommon liberty enjoyed by the English.

The last of Hume's major publications, his *Dialogues concerning Natural Religion*, was published only in 1779, three years after his death. In the final essay in this volume, J. C. A. Gaskin reviews the whole of Hume's critique of religion – a critique that is at least implicit in all of his works, and that, we are shown, is "subtle, profound and damaging to religion in ways which have no philosophical antecedents and few successors."

An Appendix supplies the reader with two brief autobiographies. Hume wrote the first of these in 1734, some years after he had begun work on, but still five years before he published, the *Treatise*. The second he wrote forty-two years later, only a few months before his death in 1776.

A Selected Bibliography supplements the suggestions for further reading found at the end of each of the fourteen essays just described.[50] A comprehensive Index completes the volume.

---

[50] Readers are again reminded that, as the works listed in the Selected Bibliography show, Hume has been interpreted in widely different ways.

2 Hume's New Science of the Mind

"Human Nature is the only science of man."

T 1.4.7.14

For Hume, understanding the workings of the mind is the key to understanding everything else. There is a sense, therefore, in which to write about Hume's philosophy of mind is to write about all of his philosophy. With that said, I shall nonetheless focus here on those specific doctrines that belong to what we today call the philosophy of mind, given our somewhat narrower conception of that subject. It should also be remembered that Hume describes his inquiry into the nature and workings of the mind as a *science*. This is an important clue to understanding both the goals and the results of that inquiry, as well as the methods Hume uses in pursuing it. As we will see, there is a thread running from Hume's project of founding a science of the mind to that of the so-called cognitive sciences of the late twentieth century. For both, the study of the mind is in important respects just like the study of any other natural phenomenon. While it would be an overstatement to say that Hume's entire interest lies in the construction of a science in this sense – he has other, more traditionally "philosophical," concerns – recognizing the centrality of this scientific aim is essential for understanding him.[1]

---

[1] For a discussion of the relations among Hume's different concerns, see John Biro, "Cognitive Science and David Hume's Science of the Mind," in *Truth, Rationality, Cognition, and Music*, ed. K. Korta and J. Larazabal (Dordrecht: Kluwer Academic Publishers, 2004), 1–20.

I. A NEW SCIENCE OF HUMAN NATURE

In one of the best-known passages in all his writings, in the Introduction to *A Treatise of Human Nature*, Hume declares his aim of founding what he calls a new science of human nature. He argues that the development of such a science, based on "THE EXPERIMENTAL METHOD OF REASONING," must precede all other inquiry, since only it can serve to ground the rest of our knowledge:

There is no question of importance, whose decision is not compriz'd in the science of man; and there is none, which can be decided with any certainty, before we become acquainted with that science. In pretending therefore to explain the principles of human nature, we in effect propose a compleat system of the sciences, built on a foundation almost entirely new, and the only one upon which they can stand with any security. (T Intro. 6)

Although the principles of human nature to be explained may "lie very deep and abstruse," the new method, modeled after that used with such spectacular success by Galileo, Boyle, and Newton in what may be called the new science of matter, holds out the hope of similarly far-reaching results here.[2] The method calls for "careful and exact experiments," to enable us to "render all our principles as universal as possible." This, in turn, requires "tracing up our experiments to the utmost, and explaining all effects from the simplest and fewest causes" (T Intro. 8).

Hume's expectations for his project are at once great and modest. He sees his new science as the key to all others, indeed, to all knowledge: "Human Nature is the only science of man." Yet his modest aim is only to bring it "a little more into fashion," as, in spite of its importance, it "has been hitherto the most neglected." Even more than the other sciences, it is still in its infancy: "Two thousand years with such long interruptions, and under such mighty discouragements are a small space of time to give any tolerable perfection

---

[2] There is controversy among scholars about the precise extent and nature of Newton's influence on Hume. For a sampling, see Nicholas Capaldi, *David Hume: The Newtonian Philosopher* (Boston: Twayne, 1975), 29–70; James Noxon, *Hume's Philosophical Development* (Oxford: Clarendon Press, 1973), 27–123; and Michael Barfoot, "Hume and the Culture of Science in Early Eighteenth-Century Britain," in *Oxford Studies in the History of Philosophy*, ed. M. A. Stewart (Oxford: Oxford University Press, 1990), 151–90.

to the sciences; and perhaps we are still in too early an age of the
world to discover any principles, which will bear the examination of
the latest posterity" (T 1.4.7.14). Still, Hume's hope is that the new
science may "discover, at least in some degree, the secret springs and
principles, by which the human mind is actuated in its operations"
(EHU 1.15).

Thus we should substitute this new science for the "many
chimerical systems" spawned by the "warm imagination" of meta-
physicians. "Were these [metaphysical] hypotheses once remov'd,
we might hope to establish a system or set of opinions, which if not
true (for that, perhaps, is too much to be hop'd for) might at least
be satisfactory to the human mind, and might stand the test of the
most critical examination" (T 1.4.7.14). "The only solid foundation
we can give to this science... must be laid on experience and observation." This is, of course, true of all human knowledge; for Hume,
there is no other source of knowledge besides experience, and no
claim to knowledge based on anything else is legitimate. Where the
application of the experimental method to "moral subjects" must
differ from its more established use in "natural philosophy" is in
the impossibility of making experiments "purposely, with premeditation." Here Hume is speaking of controlled experiments (typical of
the modern laboratory sciences) contrasting them with "glean[ing]
up our experiments... from a cautious observation of human life,
and tak[ing] them as they appear in the common course of the world,
by men's behaviour in company, in affairs, and in their pleasures."
In spite of this limitation, the science of man need "not be inferior
in certainty, and will be much superior in utility to any other of
human comprehension" (T Intro. 7–8, 10). As we have seen, Hume
holds that all other sciences depend on this one for whatever certainty they may have: it is in this science alone that we "can expect
assurance and conviction" (T 1.4.7.14).

Such assurance and conviction cannot extend to any claim about
why the principles governing human nature are the way they are:
"we can give no reason for our most general and most refin'd principles, beside our experience of their reality" (T Intro. 9). Hume is
adamant on this point. When he introduces his principles of association, resemblance, contiguity, and cause and effect (the three "universal principles" that guide the operations of the imagination in
uniting our ideas; see below, Section III), he says that their reality

requires no special proof beyond recognizing their "effects which are every where conspicuous."[3] By contrast, why they cause these effects is "mostly unknown, and must be resolv'd into *original* qualities of human nature, which I pretend not to explain" (T 1.1.4.1, 6). It would be a mistake, however, to complain about this "impossibility of explaining ultimate principles" in the science of man, as it is "a defect common to it with all the sciences, and all the arts, in which we can employ ourselves" (T Intro. 10). With respect to "natural phænomena," all we can do is "to resolve the many particular effects into a few general causes, by means of reasonings from analogy, experience, and observation. But as to the causes of these general causes, we should in vain attempt their discovery.... These ultimate springs and principles are totally shut up from human curiosity and enquiry" (EHU 4.12). Such skepticism about the possibility of ultimate metaphysical explanations need not, however, make us skeptical about the possibility of a science of the mind that contents itself with a careful description, based on observation, of the operation of these principles.

Hume is, as we have seen, fully explicit about the nature and status of the project he wants to undertake. Yet his declarations have had remarkably little effect on the interpretation of that project by champions and critics alike, from his day to ours. It is only recently that he has begun to be seen as engaged in an inquiry at least continuous with what we think of as the scientific study of the mind. Philosophers of mind today often see themselves as being so engaged, as participating in an interdisciplinary inquiry they are happy to label "cognitive science." But it is an irony that would not be lost on Hume that some have explicitly contrasted that inquiry with his science of man, rather than recognizing it as the latter's descendant.[4]

---

[3] Hume regarded his explanation of "all the operations of the mind" by means of the three principles of association (resemblance, contiguity, and causation) as his most noteworthy discovery, and famously described these principles as being *"to us* the cement of the universe" (A 35).

[4] Jerry A. Fodor, "Mental Representation: An Introduction," in *Scientific Inquiry in Philosophical Perspective,* ed. N. Rescher (Lanham, MD: University Press of America, 1987). More recently Fodor has had a change of heart: "Hume's account of the mind . . . seems, in a number of respects, to anticipate the one that informs current work in cognitive science"; see his *Hume Variations* (Oxford: Clarendon Press, 2003), 2.

This is not to say, of course, that there are no differences between the two projects, separated as they are by two and a half centuries during which both science and philosophy have changed in important respects. The passages I have cited from Hume's announcement of his new science should alert us to some features of it that contrast sharply with those of its twentieth-century offspring. While Hume anticipated many of the difficulties and problems recently "discovered," the solutions he offers – or, at least, hints at – are often different and, I shall suggest, compare favorably with those currently on offer. One reason for this is that the method he so clearly outlines in the Introduction to the *Treatise* is more suited to the subject matter of the new science than is one modeled on that of the so-called hard sciences and favored by many of his modern successors. (See below, Sections III and VI.)

II. SKEPTIC OR SCIENTIST?

For two centuries after its appearance, Hume's philosophy was commonly seen as essentially, perhaps entirely, negative. His inquiries were thought to have been undertaken in a spirit of skepticism and as aiming to show how far that outlook can – and must – be carried if some seemingly compelling empiricist principles were followed out to their inevitable consequences. The barrage of skeptical arguments in the first book of the *Treatise* were seen not as directed against various philosophical accounts of our knowledge of the world and of ourselves (as they are, increasingly, today), but against the very possibility of such knowledge. That such skepticism is on the face of it incompatible with the project Hume announced in the Introduction to the work was either not noticed or dismissed as unproblematic by the simple expedient of not taking him at his word.

There was, to be sure, some reason for such a response. After Descartes, epistemological questions moved to center stage in philosophy, and epistemology came to be seen as primarily consisting in coming to terms with, in one way or another, the kind of skeptical threat posed in the opening pages of the *Meditations*. It was natural for Hume's contemporaries and for later philosophers until fairly recently to see him as struggling with the same problems that preoccupied them and as responding to his predecessors' treatment of them. His extensive and devastating criticisms of attempts to deal with the skeptical threat by relying either on reason to discover truths about the world a priori or on experience to convey those truths to us through perception seemed to these contemporaries, and to many since, evidence that he shared their preoccupation with that threat. Yet Hume repeatedly disclaims such an interest and tells us clearly, in a variety of contexts and ways, that the main aim of his enquiries is something quite different. An example is his admonition, in the opening paragraph of the section in the *Treatise* entitled *Of scepticism with regard to the senses*, not to be concerned with the usual skeptical question about the existence of the external world: "We may well ask, *What causes induce us to believe in the existence of body?* but 'tis in vain to ask, *Whether there be body or not?* That is a point, which we must take for granted in all our reasonings." That such an injunction should appear in this very section, nominally concerned with skepticism, is surely not an accident and should clinch the case that, whatever Hume is doing, it is neither pressing nor looking for (and failing to find) an answer to the usual skeptical challenges. He tells us explicitly what he *is* doing: "The subject, then, of our present enquiry is concerning the *causes* which induce us to believe in the existence of body" (T 1.4.2.2). As noted earlier, Hume is skeptical about various philosophical attempts at justifying our beliefs, especially when it comes to the most basic of these, such as the belief in bodies, in the identity of our person, and in causal connections, beliefs that even a skeptic cannot seriously reject or live without. It is, he often insists, just as well that nature has made sure that, in spite of all philosophy, we take these for granted, as without them "human nature must immediately perish and go to ruin" (T 1.4.4.1). But this recognition of our unreflective, instinctive, and unavoidable acceptance of certain basic beliefs must not be confused with claiming to have a philosophical justification of those beliefs. Hume's skeptical arguments target attempts to provide such justifications, based on either reason or experience: " 'Tis impossible upon any system to defend either our understanding or senses." The recognition of this fact is skepticism of a sort – "a malady, which can never be radically cur'd" – but it is different from the usual kind of skepticism in a crucial respect: our inability to justify a belief of this fundamental sort is not seen as a reason for withholding assent to it. There cannot be a reason to do something we cannot do. As for the malady, "Carelessness and in-attention alone can afford us any remedy" (T 1.4.2.57).

In the crucial case of personal identity (to be discussed at greater length below),[5] Hume makes it equally clear that his interest lies in examining how one comes to form one's belief in one's identity and in what accounts for one's confidence in that belief, rather than in a philosophical justification of the belief. After dismissing the claim of philosophers that we are "every moment intimately conscious of what we call our SELF," he asks: "What then gives us so great a propension to ascribe an identity to these successive perceptions, and to suppose ourselves possest of an invariable and uninterrupted existence thro' the whole course of our lives?" (T 1.4.6.1, 5). It should be clear that his powerful negative arguments are given not in the service of a purely skeptical conclusion, but as a necessary preliminary to refocusing our attention on giving an answer to these other questions in the manner of a descriptive and explanatory science.[6]

Thus while there is a sense in which Hume can be said to be a skeptic, his skepticism is better understood as one about pretended supra-scientific metaphysical knowledge, rather than about scientific knowledge itself. It is this that separates him from those who conceive of philosophy as going beyond mere scientific knowledge to give us a deeper and more certain knowledge of reality. Hume, by contrast, thinks of explanation in a thoroughly scientific spirit. The total alteration or revolution he claims his new science brings to the intellectual scene consists in becoming what he calls an *anatomist* of human nature. As we saw earlier, Hume believes that if we "anatomize human nature in a regular manner," we *can* discover the laws governing the mind (A 2). These may be hidden or secret until the right method is brought to bear, but, unlike the supposedly deeper truths of the metaphysician, they are not occult, destined forever to elude discovery.

---

[5] See also in this volume the essay "Hume and the Problem of Personal Identity."

[6] On the relation between description and explanation, see João Paulo Monteiro, "Hume's Conception of Science," *Journal of the History of Philosophy* 19 (1981): 327–42, and John Biro, "Description and Explanation in Hume's Science of Man," *Transactions of the Fifth International Congress on the Enlightenment* (Oxford: Voltaire Foundation, 1979), 449–57.

This shift of focus from a vain attempt to give a philosophical jus-tification of our fundamental beliefs to a scientific account of their origin in the operations of our minds, is what Hume, with deliber-ate paradox, calls a "Sceptical Solution" to the skeptical challenge (EHU 5). The questions such a scientific account must answer are How do we form our beliefs? How do we move from one belief to another? and What mechanisms and principles underlie and gov-ern such processes? These are the questions to which Hume always turns as soon as he has discredited the claims of those who think that they know what entitles us (by some nonimmanent, external standard) to hold the beliefs we in fact, and inevitably, do hold.

III. AN ANATOMY OF THE MIND

The raw materials from which all mental life is constructed are *impressions* and their copies, *ideas,* both species of the genus, *per-ception:* "All the perceptions of the human mind resolve themselves into two distinct kinds, which I shall call IMPRESSIONS and IDEAS." What Hume calls his "first principle" (sometimes also labeled *the copy principle*) states *"that all our simple ideas in their first appear-ance are deriv'd from simple impressions, which are correspondent to them, and which they exactly represent"* (T 1.1.1.1, 7, 12).[7] Many of the most skeptical-sounding passages of the *Treatise* and the *Enquiry concerning Human Understanding* are devoted to showing that our stock of these materials is more limited than philosophers have supposed. Hume shows us again and again that the impressions from which some putative idea posited by the metaphysician would have to derive are just not to be found in experience. But he does not deny the obvious, and remarkable, fact that from the rather lim-ited stock of impressions that come my way, I am able to construct an edifice of beliefs that go far beyond those impressions and the ideas traceable to them. First, my complex ideas are not confined to the complex impressions I have had: I can combine both simple and complex impressions in novel ways, thus forming new complex ideas. These, often called by Hume "fictions," may or may not give rise to belief, and often they do not, as with fictional ideas in the

---

[7] For more on impressions and ideas and related topics, see also in this volume the essay "Hume and the Mechanics of Mind."

usual sense (such as those of Eldorado or Santa Claus). Second, the course of my experience, the various regularities among the perceptions that make it up, is exploited by the mind in forming beliefs. The idea of a rock flying toward a window will give rise to the idea of the window's shattering, given the "constant conjunction" of these events in one's experience. An *impression* of the rock flying toward the window will give rise to the *belief* that the window will break, which, of course, involves the idea of the window's breaking, but also something more. That something more comes from the relation of the idea to a present impression; being so related is what makes an idea into a belief (T 1.3.7.5). In both these ways, the mind must be conceived as essentially active. It is what it does with what it gets that matters, and it is this activity that Hume's science aims to describe.

Hume's answer to questions about how we come to have the beliefs we have is that they are, one and all, the product of a nonrational faculty. This faculty, which he usually labels "the imagination" (and sometimes describes as an instinct), produces a "habit" or "custom," which consists in a tendency to move from an idea one has to another idea linked to the first idea by one of the principles of association (resemblance, contiguity, or cause and effect). He contrasts this faculty with reason or the understanding, the faculty whose standards and operations some philosophers think can serve to provide an answer to the skeptic's challenge. This distinction between reason (understood in one way, though, as we will see, not in another) and the imagination is fundamental to Hume's anatomy of the mind. In one sense, *reason* is the reflective faculty we employ when we make a comparison between two ideas concerning their similarity or difference in some respect and when we engage in chains of demonstrative reasoning concerning these similarities and differences. These relations and thus this kind of reasoning depend exclusively on the ideas compared: change the idea and you change the relation. The idea of a thing may bring to mind other things thought of as similar, adjacent, or causally connected to it. However, relations in this sense are merely "philosophical." We *can* ask of any two objects, what is the distance or, more generally, the difference, between them, and in so doing, be said to be asking how they are related. But if they are very far, or wholly different, from each other, the natural thing to say is that they are *not* related. Hume contrasts such "relations" with relations in a more common sense, which he calls "natural" relations. These we think of as connecting two ideas in such a way that "the one naturally introduces the other" (T 1.1.5.1). The principles of association involve such natural relations. (The shade of blue I now see does not make me think of all the others I have experienced, but it does bring to mind things exactly, or very similarly, colored.) The *imagination* is the *non*reflective faculty that takes us from an idea or an impression to another idea connected to it by one of these "natural" relations. To quote again from his discussion of our belief in external objects: "our reason neither does, nor is it possible it ever shou'd, upon any supposition, give us an assurance of the continu'd and distinct existence of body. That opinion must be entirely owing to the IMAGINATION; which must now be the subject of our enquiry" (T 1.4.2.14). Nor is this particular kind of belief unique in this respect. In general, *"belief is more properly an act of the sensitive, than of the cogitative part of our natures"* (T 1.4.1.8). Our most general and most fundamental beliefs (such as those in our own identity, in the existence of an external world, and in causal relations) are impervious to the influence of reason, which can neither ground nor destroy them. Here *cogitative part,* and thus *reason,* refer to our faculty of theoretical reasoning, at work when we construct demonstrations and philosophical arguments. There is, however, another sense of *reasoning,* applicable to some of the natural and instinctive transitions we make from one perception to another, from perception to belief, and thus from one belief to another. We are engaged, for example, in reasoning when we make a causal inference; indeed, that is what we primarily mean by *reasoning* in ordinary, nontheoretical, contexts: "this inference is not only a true species of reasoning, but the strongest of all others" (T 1.3.7 n.20). Hume calls this kind of reasoning "experimental" or "probable" reasoning and insists that we share it with infants, "nay even brute beasts" – who presumably do not engage in theoretical reasoning. It is this kind of reasoning "on which the whole conduct of life depends, [and it] is nothing but a species of instinct or mechanical power, that acts in us unknown to ourselves; and in its chief operations, is not directed by any such relations or comparisons of ideas, as are the proper objects of our intellectual faculties" (EHU 4.23, 9.6).[8]

---

[8] In the concluding paragraph of *Treatise* 1.3.16, "Of the reason of animals," Hume makes a similar claim: "To consider the matter aright, reason is nothing but a wonderful and unintelligible instinct in our souls, which carries us along a certain

Reasoning of this latter sort is the business of the imagination, the ever-active, sometimes overactive, nonrational faculty whose workings Hume's new science sets out to describe. According to that science, the mind moves from one idea to another by way of the three principles of association just mentioned. Responsible for these transitions are custom or habit and, most importantly, the mind's tendency to continue any motion or process once it has begun it. This is a fundamental property of the imagination that plays a role in Hume's explanations of some of the most remarkable facts about the mind. These include the fact that in the absence of corresponding impressions from which the ideas could have been copied, one nonetheless comes to believe that there are bodies and that one is the same person at one time as at another, and even that one can "extend [one's] identity beyond [one's] memory" (T 1.4.6.20).

In the pivotal section *Of scepticism with regard to the senses,* where he undertakes his enquiry "concerning the *causes* which induce us to believe in the existence of body" (the legitimately scientific inquiry he distinguishes from the vain attempt to answer the skeptic), Hume reminds us of his earlier explanation of the – he argues, mistaken – belief in the infinite divisibility of space and time in terms of this natural tendency, which can appear to take us beyond what is given in experience: "I have already observ'd, in examining the foundation of mathematics, that the imagination, when set into any train of thinking, is apt to continue, even when its object fails it, and like a galley put in motion by the oars, carries on its course without any new impulse" (T 1.4.2.2, 22). This tendency, automatic and nonreflective, is everywhere: nothing, says Hume, is "more usual, than for the mind to proceed after this manner with any action, even after the reason has ceas'd, which first determin'd it to begin." In the sections on our ideas of space and time, this tendency was also appealed to in explaining how we generate an "imaginary standard of equality," of "correction[s] beyond what we have instruments and art to make," and of notions of "perfection beyond what [our]

train of ideas, and endows them with particular qualities, according to their particular situations and relations. This instinct, 'tis true, arises from past observation and experience; but can any one give the ultimate reason, why past experience and observation produces such an effect, any more than why nature alone shou'd produce it?"

faculties can judge of." This, in turn, enabled Hume to account for the fictions, "useless" and "incomprehensible," of the mathematicians who claim to give exact definitions and demonstrations (T 1.2.4.24, 29).

Hume's purpose in that earlier discussion was to expose these fictions as "absurd" (T 1.2.4.29–30, 32). His recommendation there was to resist this tendency of the mind and thus avoid the absurdity. In the discussion of our belief in body, the same tendency is invoked in the interest of a different goal: that of explaining how naturally, even unavoidably, we form our "opinion of the continu'd existence of body." He writes: "Objects have a certain coherence even as they appear to our senses; but this coherence is much greater and more uniform, if we suppose the objects to have a continu'd existence; and as the mind is once in the train of observing an uniformity among objects, it naturally continues, till it renders the uniformity as compleat as possible" (T 1.4.2.22).[9]

Hume distinguishes between "principles which are permanent, irresistible, and universal" and those "which are changeable, weak, and irregular" (T 1.4.4.1). This distinction is essential to the double use made by Hume of this tendency of the mind. When the tendency is guided by principles of the first sort, as it is in the formation of our fundamental common-sense beliefs, we have a skeptical solution to the skeptic's doubts, whether that doubt be about the external world or about personal identity. While Hume sometimes uses the term *fiction* to denote a fundamental natural belief produced by this property of the mind, we must be careful not to be misled by this into thinking of such a belief as somehow fanciful and arbitrary. Fictions of this sort are not optional: they are forced on us by our nature. Distinguishing such fictions from those resulting from philosophical speculation floating free of common sense is a large, arguably, the central, part of the overall aim of Hume's philosophy.

In these cases of what we may call *natural fictions*, the mind's inertial tendency operates "in such an insensible manner as never

---

[9] For a classic discussion of how we form our belief in the existence of bodies, see H. H. Price, *Hume's Theory of the External World* (Oxford: Clarendon Press, 1940). For a briefer account, see David Fate Norton, "Editor's Introduction," in Hume's *Treatise of Human Nature*, Oxford Philosophical Texts Edition (Oxford: Oxford University Press, 2000), 138–42.

to be taken notice of," and "the imagination can draw inferences from past experience, without reflecting on it; much more without forming any principle concerning it, or reasoning upon that principle." Hume adds that this tendency "may even in some measure be unknown to us." It is important to see that by this he means only that we have no direct, introspective, access to the processes in question. In making causal inferences, for example, we obviously do not consciously recall the previous instances of constant conjunctions on which the inference is based: "The custom operates before we have time for reflection," and "I never am conscious of any such operation," so that in deciding to "give the preference to one set of arguments above another, I do nothing but decide from my *feeling* concerning the superiority of their influence" (emphasis added). Thus it is that "all probable reasoning is nothing but a species of sensation" (T 1.3.8.13, 10, 12).

Of the three relations Hume calls "natural" relations, cause and effect is the only one by which we "can go beyond what is immediately present to the senses," since it is "the only one, that can be trac'd beyond our senses, and informs us of existences and objects, which we do not see or feel" (T 1.3.2.3). The causal inferences that thus take us beyond our present impressions are, for Hume, indeed a form of reasoning, even though they are, as we have seen, automatic and nonreflective. This sort of reasoning is "stronger" than that which involves "the separating or uniting of different ideas by the interposition of others, which show the relation they bear to each other" (T 1.3.7). The latter, while constituting demonstrations, as the former do not, do so only with respect to philosophical relations.

It is appeals to reasoning of the demonstrative sort to establish facts about the world that Hume's skeptical arguments are intended to show to be futile. Causal reasoning, by contrast, has the power to yield belief. The difference between mere idea and belief is easy to know but difficult to explain. While it is Hume's official and oft-expressed view that a belief is nothing but a lively idea (T 1.3.5, for example), the matter is rather more complicated. When he reflects, in the Appendix to Book 3 of the *Treatise*, on his earlier doctrine that perceptions can differ only in their respective degrees of force and vivacity, he realizes that "there are other differences among ideas, which cannot properly be comprehended under these terms. Had I said, that two ideas of the same object can only be different by their different *feeling*, I shou'd have been nearer the truth" (T App. 22).[10]

Yet, as we have just seen, the special feeling that marks out belief – "that certain *je-ne-sais-quoi*, of which 'tis impossible to give any definition or description, but which every one sufficiently understands" (T 1.3.8.16) – is not altogether involuntary and beyond rational control. The "great difference," Hume says, between "a poetical enthusiasm, and a serious conviction... proceeds in some measure from reflection and *general rules*.... A like reflection on *general rules* keeps us from augmenting our belief upon every encrease of the force and vivacity of our ideas.... 'Tis thus the understanding corrects the appearances of the senses" (T 1.3.10.11–12). Thus not all transitions between ideas grounded in natural relations deserve the title *reasoning* in the more honorific sense. We must remember the distinction between the two sorts of principle that guide the imagination, those "permanent, irresistible, and universal" and those "changeable, weak, and irregular." Only the former, and they only when tempered by the proper use of "general rules," are to be relied on in forming beliefs (T 1.3.13.7–19, 1.3.15.2–10). This "second influence of general rules" is the work of our judgment and understanding, and it must be distinguished from the first, which involves their rash use by the uncontrolled imagination or fancy, as when we generalize hastily or from too small a sample. This "first influence" of general rules is what is at work in the kind of inertial extrapolation to an imaginary standard in mathematical reasoning that we saw Hume criticize. It is also what happens when we declare that "an *Irishman* cannot have wit, and a *Frenchman* cannot have solidity" on the basis of a few examples we have encountered; and in this use they are "the source of what we properly call PREJUDICE" (T 1.3.13.12, 7). The "second influence" of general rules consists in applying second-order principles to observed first-order regularities, such as the principle "Do not judge on the basis of small samples." Such principles are, of course, themselves based on experience: in

---

[10] The *Treatise* was first published in three separate volumes, the first two in 1739, the third in 1740.

this case, on the experience of mistaken judgments resulting from neglecting to pay attention to them.[11]

This, in brief, is Hume's account of how we come by our beliefs, an account intended to replace futile attempts to give philosophical justifications of them. Providing such an account is what Hume means when he says he has given a skeptical solution to the skeptic's challenge (EHU Sect. 5). It is to give up being a "metaphysician" and to become a scientist – an "anatomist" – of the mind, of human nature. This recommendation bears a striking resemblance to the "naturalizing" programs common in recent philosophy of mind and epistemology. Here, too, the leading idea is to abandon an a priori method perceived as bankrupt in favor of an empirical one that holds out the promise of genuine progress. Many epistemologists have, in recent years, come to feel that the time-honored method of armchair conceptual analysis is unlikely to tell us much about the nature of knowledge.[12] Philosophers of mind, too, interested in understanding reasoning, perception, memory, language, and a host of other mental phenomena, increasingly look to the new discipline (or constellation of disciplines), cognitive science, rather than to traditional methods of philosophical analysis and argument.[13]

One of the most striking findings of modern cognitive science has been that the mechanisms and processes involved, whether in perception, in linguistic processing, or in reasoning generally, are what

---

[11] For helpful discussions of general rules, see Thomas K. Hearn, "'General Rules' in Hume's *Treatise*," *Journal of the History of Philosophy* 8 (1970): 405–22; and "General Rules and the Moral Sentiments in Hume's *Treatise*," *Review of Metaphysics* 30 (1976): 57–72.

[12] The uninspiring history of the so-called Gettier problem, involving increasingly arcane and artificial counterexamples to ever more byzantine definitions of knowledge, is often taken to be proof of this. For details of this history, see Robert K. Shope, *The Analysis of Knowing: A Decade of Research* (Princeton, NJ: Princeton University Press, 1983).

[13] The fountainhead of so-called naturalizing programs in epistemology and the philosophy of mind is W. O. Quine. See *Word and Object* (Cambridge, MA: Technology Press of the Massachusetts Institute of Technology, 1960); and "Epistemology Naturalized," in *Ontological Relativity, and Other Essays* (New York: Columbia University Press, 1969), 69–90. For recent examples, see Alvin Goldman, *Epistemology and Cognition* (Cambridge, MA: Harvard University Press, 1986), and Stephen Stich, *The Fragmentation of Reason: Preface to a Pragmatic Theory of Cognitive Evaluation* (Cambridge, MA: MIT Press, 1990). For a useful volume of papers on the subject, see *Naturalizing Epistemology*, ed. H. Kornblith (Cambridge, MA: MIT Press, 1985).

it calls *subdoxastic, modular,* and *automatic.* They are subdoxastic because they usually take place below the threshold of consciousness, hence, "below" the level of belief. They are modular, because they are, in the overwhelming majority of cases, task-specific; they do their work largely in isolation from each other, as well as from the cognitive states we would attribute to the person as a whole. The processes underlying one particular kind of cognitive capacity or performance do not interact with those involved in others, and their respective outputs are similarly independent. (Think of the common case of different senses delivering different verdicts on the properties of one and the same object or event – as on the stick, half-immersed in water seen to be bent, yet felt to be straight.) They are also insensitive to the thinker's beliefs, even if these are reflective and conscious, rather than merely tacit, and even if he makes an effort to bring them to bear. (Think of the robustness of perceptual illusions known to be such – parallel railroad tracks that seem to converge as they recede.) Finally, they are automatic because they are not under the thinker's control. They are not really operations and processes of the thinker's mind, but of some component subsystem we construe as their "agent." As a result of these features, the thinker is not a reliable source of information about these processes. Hence the preference for laboratory experiments over armchair introspection. (Compare Hume's preference, noted earlier, for observation "of the common course of the world" over "experiments [made] with premeditation.")

I have already remarked on Hume's recognition of our tendency to overgeneralize. The same sort of inductive overgeneralization, sometimes benign, sometimes not, has been found to be ubiquitous by recent empirical studies of our cognitive processes. We see it in language learning, and in various kinds of processing, phonological, morphological, even syntactic – as, for example, with "garden-path" sentences, where we leap ahead to complete a sentence in the wrong way.[14] We see it in perception, for example, in the detection of the edges and boundaries of objects and in the perception of the movement of rigid bodies. We see it in problem solving and reasoning generally, as in our lamentable tendency to make clearly fallacious

---

[14] Such sentences as "The horse raced past the barn fell," or "The florist sent the flowers was very pleased."

probabilistic inferences. What all these instances of the tendency have in common is that the meanings we assign, the beliefs we form, and the inferences we draw, while often far outrunning the evidence available to us and, in many cases, recognized as doing so, are nonetheless all but irresistible. Hence the common characterization of many of the processes posited to explain our cognitive capacities and performance as "cognitively impenetrable" or "informationally encapsulated."[15]

This recognition, common to Hume and to modern cognitive scientists, of these features of our cognitive make-up raises some deep methodological issues. What these are, and how Hume's distinctive response to them differs from those of the latter, will help us see the full complexity of his approach to the task he has set himself, as well as the source of some of the tensions we may detect in it. But before turning to these matters, we must look in some detail at the topic on which discussion of Hume's philosophy of mind has traditionally centered, that of personal identity. Here, too, the continuity with some central concerns of modern cognitive science will be striking. After highlighting these, we will be in a better position to reflect on some differences between Hume's approach and that of recent cognitive science.

IV. PERSONAL IDENTITY

One of the central philosophical questions about the mind has always been an ontological one: What is it? But Hume's eschewal of speculative metaphysics leads him to substitute for this question others to which he thinks there are clearer answers. First, what *kind of thing* is my belief that I am an identical thing over time, *a self*, about? Second, how do I acquire my *idea* of such a thing? Third, how do I come to *believe* that I am such a thing? It is important that these questions be approached from the first-person point of view, rendering irrelevant the easy answer that to believe in one's identity is to

---

[15] Details about these matters may be found in Shimon Ullman, *The Interpretation of Visual Motion* (Cambridge, MA: MIT Press, 1979); *Judgment under Uncertainty: Heuristics and Biases*, ed. D. Kahneman, P. Slovic, and A. Tversky (Cambridge, MA: Cambridge University Press, 1982); and Zenon W. Pylyshyn, *Computation and Cognition: Toward a Foundation for Cognitive Science* (Cambridge, MA: MIT Press, 1984).

believe that one is, or is at least associated with, a body that is the same over time. Hume *is* interested in the concept of identity in general and in how we come to attribute identity to bodies. His account of what is involved in such attributions, however, cannot be used to explain how we come to attribute identity to ourselves, since that account appeals to activities such as remembering and associating and in so doing presupposes the identity of a mind whose activities they are. For talk of a mind *doing* things to make sense, there must be a temporally extended thing of some sort denoted by the term *mind* (or the pronoun *I*), one to which the predicate "same at time$_2$ as at time$_1$" can apply.[16] How does one come to believe, though, that one is such a thing? As Hume recognizes, the fundamental belief standing in need of an analysis and a genetic account is the belief one has in one's own identity (T 1.4.2.5–6).

Consequently, Hume gives an account of what one believes when one has that belief and of how one could come by a belief of that sort. The fact that in this account he must make use of the more general concepts that themselves presuppose having such a belief can obscure this all-important point, as can, on occasion, Hume's language. But when he asks whether "in pronouncing concerning the identity of a person, we observe some real bond among his perceptions," he must be taken to be talking about a person's pronouncing on his own identity on the basis of observing his own perceptions (T 1.4.6.16). There *is* no observing another's perceptions, as there is another's body. So, for an answer to the question that must be most basic – How do I come to think of myself as a self? – I must turn inward. I must look to see what there is in my experience that leads me to think of myself as the same person or mind over

---

[16] Hume's general account of identity involves thinking of the mind as surveying objects and "trac[ing] the succession of time" – something that seems to presuppose *its* identity over time (T 1.4.2.29). So, it may seem, does talking of *one's* believing and reidentifying, as I just have. This may seem to beg the question against the very skeptic Hume is often taken to be, namely, one who doubts that there *is* a self. But does such talk not already imply, by virtue of its grammar alone, that there is one? One may be tempted to say that if the skeptic were right, "he" could not state "his" view. However this may be, Hume's discussion is better seen, as I suggested above, as being about what kind of thing the self is, rather than one about whether there is one. For further discussion, see John Biro, "Hume on Self-Identity and Memory," *Review of Metaphysics* 30 (1976): 19–38, and "Hume's Difficulties with the Self," *Hume Studies* 5 (1979): 45–54.

time. *That* I do think of myself is a datum, a fact, one that Hume is seeking to explain within the new scientific framework he has adopted.[17]

Hume's treatment of the idea of the self has two parts. The negative one consists in the argument he gives against the widely held (among philosophers, at least) belief that one has an idea of oneself as a simple substance, one that endures essentially unchanged through accidental changes, especially through one's changing perceptions. The argument depends on the copy principle: "from what impression cou'd this idea be deriv'd?" Having found no such impression ("when I enter most intimately into what I call *myself*, I always stumble on some particular perception or other"), Hume concludes that we have no idea of such an entity (T 1.4.6.3). This means that we cannot believe ourselves to be such a thing, belief (at least, with respect to matters of fact) being nothing but a lively idea related to a present impression.[18]

The positive part of Hume's account is his famous "bundle" theory, according to which a mind (a self or person) is a collection of perceptions related to each other in certain ways, constituting a complex entity to which identity of one sort, though not of another, may be intelligibly and truly ascribed. The sort of identity the self has is what Hume calls "imperfect identity," distinguishing this kind of identity from "perfect" (or "strict") identity, a feature that only those entities that undergo no change whatever have, or, as he puts it, a feature of only those entities that are wholly "invariable and uninterrupted." The conclusion of his negative argument is not that we have no idea of the self. It is only that we have no "idea of *self*, after the manner it is here explain'd" – that is, no idea of the self as a simple, unchanging substance (T 1.4.6.9, 6, 5, 1–2). It does not follow that the same experience that fails to deliver such an idea

---

[17] The relation between the first-person and the second-person elements in Hume's method is discussed in Section VI and in the paper cited in note 1.

[18] In the second book of the *Treatise*, concerned with the passions (with what we would today call moral psychology), Hume insists that "the idea of ourselves is always intimately present to us" (T 2.2.4.7). The appearance of inconsistency here evaporates once we remind ourselves that the kind of self-awareness Hume requires in his account of the passions does not entail anything about the nature of the object we are aware of. What our idea of the self is, and the role it plays in our emotional life, are different questions, largely independent of one another.

of the self cannot serve to explain how one comes to *believe* that one is *a self*, understood as a thing having *imperfect* identity. We do have the required impressions for forming the idea of the self as a thing of that sort: a complex thing that is nothing but a bundle of perceptions united by certain relations. The belief I have in my own identity over time is a belief about such a thing even if I do not realize this and need Hume's help to do so.[19] And it is a belief implicated in all our other beliefs, a belief without which, arguably, even the skeptic's position could not be understood.

What, above all, unites the perceptions that collectively constitute a mind or self is *memory*, and the natural relation of causation with which memory is inextricably bound up. Memory is in one way the more fundamental here, since without it the natural relation of cause and effect itself could not obtain. Hume's account of causation requires that I remember the constant conjunction of pairs of events of two different types if experience of such conjunctions is to lead me to think of events of these two types as cause and effect. The mere occurrence of such constant conjunctions in my experience would not suffice. Suppose that my experience did include such repetitions of pairs of type A and of type B events, but that it did not also include perceptions that are rememberings of previous co-occurrences of these pairs. Perhaps such experience could give rise, on a fresh observation of an event of type A, to an expectation that an event of type B will follow. (There are reasons to doubt

---

[19] We could say that the idea is an idea *of* an imperfectly identical self (an idea *de re*, or of a thing), even if it does not have that as its content (*de dicto*, or of what is said). What, then, is its content? One answer is, as Hume sometimes appears to say, *nothing*. Another, better one, is to say that it is the self as a simple substance. I do have an idea of identity (one of the seven "philosophical" relations Hume thinks exhaust the ways in which any two arbitrarily chosen ideas may be compared), "as apply'd in its strictest sense to constant and unchangeable objects" (T 1.1.5.4). To apply that idea to "variable or interrupted objects" is to "attribute identity [to them], in an improper sense," requiring a "fiction, either of something invariable and uninterrupted, or of something mysterious and inexplicable" (T 1.4.6.7). Believing of a self that it is strictly identical is simply a mistake, consisting of misapplying the idea of perfect identity. But it is a mistake of which I can be freed by careful attention to experience. "When I enter most intimately into what I call *myself*," what I do not find is an impression of an object to which *that* idea could be *properly* applied (T 1.4.6.3). If I draw the right lesson, I shall cease applying this idea improperly and will come to see that there is another idea I have of myself, as an imperfectly identical thing, whose simple components can be traced to impressions in my experience.

this: What would be the mechanism? What, in the absence of memory, would distinguish the present, nth experience of A from the first experience of it?) Still, even that expectation would not be enough to explain the *felt* "determination of the mind" to move from the new A-type event to a yet-to-be-observed B-type event. Such determinations of the mind, according to Hume, result from an exposure to the constant conjunctions in question, and they serve in place of the not-to-be-experienced impression of necessary connection. It is from these determinations of mind that the idea of necessary connection derives.[20] My expectation of an event of type B, while brought about by the constant conjunction between events of this type and events of type A in my experience, would, in the absence of a memory of that constant conjunction, fail to be an expectation of an *effect*. Being caused to expect something is not the same thing as expecting something for a reason. When I expect something as the effect of some cause, I reason (however unreflectively) from the remembered constant conjunction to the event I expect. This reasoning is, of course, matter-of-fact or causal reasoning, not demonstrative reasoning, and hence it lacks the kind of certainty that characterizes demonstrative reasoning. But, as we have already seen, Hume insists that causal reasoning is not only a true form of reasoning, but is, indeed, "the strongest of all," the form of reasoning "on which the whole conduct of life depends" (Section III above). Thus it is that Hume can say, "Had we no memory, we never shou'd have any notion of causation, nor consequently of that chain of causes and effects, which constitute our self or person" (T 1.4.6.20). It is the presence of memories among my perceptions that is the ultimate source of my belief that I am a temporally extended being.[21]

---

[20] For further discussion of these issues see in this volume the essay "Hume on Causation."

[21] These memories need not be veridical: what matters is that they are of events I *believe* to have occurred earlier. Memory, no less than belief itself, is a "manner of conceiving," of a special *feel* – familiar but indefinable – that ideas merely entertained (imagined) lack (T 1.3.8.7; see also EHU 5.12). In the full story, forward-looking perceptions – anticipations – also play a role, as does the inertial tendency we have already seen at work elsewhere: "But having once acquir'd this notion of causation from the memory, we can extend the same chain of causes, and consequently the identity of our persons beyond our memory, and can comprehend times, and circumstances, and actions, which we have entirely forgot, but suppose in general to have existed" (T 1.4.6.20).

One thing that emerges from this discussion of personal identity, with implications that go far beyond that topic, is that an entity of the sort Hume takes the mind to be (complex, dynamic, ever-changing) must and *can* be thought of as an active agent in the formation of its beliefs about everything (including, even, as we have seen, the formation of the belief in its own identity). A generalization of this insight underlies virtually all of Hume's analyses of the concepts we employ in thinking about the world and our relation to it. Most importantly, it drives all Hume's hypotheses about how we come to believe what we believe, whatever the content and object of the belief in question. From the earliest parts of the *Treatise*, with its picture of complex ideas being constructed from simple ones, through the account of the nature of belief, to his principles of moral psychology, and to the principles of his practical philosophy (his ethics, politics, and aesthetics), it is the constant activity of this mind that dominates the story and ties it together into a unified and coherent whole.[22] It is no wonder that Kant, while never tiring of pointing out the limitations of empiricism, nonetheless owns that it was Hume who woke him from his "dogmatic slumbers."[23]

V. HUME'S SELF AND SOME RECENT THEORIES OF THE MIND

With this sketch of Hume's account of the self in place, we are now in a position to explore some parallels between it and influential recent theories. Doing so will both illustrate the continuing relevance of his thought and help guard against some common misunderstandings of it. While the morals I shall draw apply to other parts of these theories, I have singled out the topic of personal identity as my chief illustration, for three reasons. First, this is the topic that has received, historically, and continues to receive, today, the most attention from those interested in Hume's philosophy of mind. Second, while this emphasis on the subject of personal identity may

---

[22] The account also includes an account of belief formation, of belief transition by way of the principles of association, and of causal beliefs as expectations produced by experience and habit.

[23] See Kant's Letter to Christian Garve in his selected *Philosophical Correspondence, 1759–99*, ed. and trans. A. Zweig (Chicago: University of Chicago Press, 1986), 252.

have stood in the way, at least until recently, of achieving a satisfactory overall interpretation of Hume's account of the mind, it is
nonetheless true that any interpretation of that account must offer,
or presuppose, answers to the questions Hume asks concerning the
idea of the self, namely, what this idea is an idea of, and how is it
acquired. For Hume, given his unique account of the workings of
the mind and his self-imposed empiricist constraints, finding a satisfactory answer to these questions is especially pressing. Third, it
is necessary that we understand the answers Hume gives to these
questions if we are to understand the rest of his science of man,
particularly those aspects of that science that center on the constant
activity of the mind, aspects that I have suggested are fundamental.

A much-favored strategy in recent philosophy of mind has been
to look for decompositions, along functional lines, of the various
kinds of behavior we think of as intelligent – of, that is, behavior
involving rational, and not merely causal, properties and processes.
My arm's rising may be completely explained as the effect of your
lifting it (as at the end of the boxing match), but *your* lifting of it,
or my *raising* it when I want to claim the floor, cannot be explained
in these terms. The first is an event requiring merely a causal explanation. The latter are *actions,* and, as such, require explanation in
terms of reasons, beliefs, desires, and the like. Similarly with blink-
ing on emerging into bright sunlight, in contrast to putting on sunglasses. The first involves no inference or thought on my part, but
the second *requires* it. However many difficulties there may be in
explaining the first response, giving one of the second kind involves
more.

The aim of these functional decompositions is to identify simple processes, which, in combination, would explain, even, perhaps,
literally constitute, the complex rational behavior in question. We
assume that the agent whose behavior we are trying to explain is in
various mental states (sensing the bright light, desiring to avoid it,
believing that he can do so by putting on sunglasses...) related in
various regular ways. We think of our subject as going through various transitions from mental state to mental state (from the painful
sensation to the intention to act to the carrying out of the act to end
the painful sensation) by way of specifiable steps falling into specifiable patterns. Within this framework, it is the business of normal
empirical science – of the burgeoning field of "cognitive science"
that includes cognitive psychology, linguistics, neurophysiology,

and more – to generate hypotheses about what states and processes would best explain the subject's observable behavior.

The simple processes we hope to identify as underlying, or even in some sense constituting, complex intelligent behavior are supposed themselves to be "dumb," that is, merely mechanical. The chief reason for this is a metaphysical concern: it is felt that only then will the mental have been explained in respectably physicalistic terms, showing it to be subject to the same laws as the rest of the natural world. In our day this physicalistic assumption is not considered to be in need of defence: the historical alternative of accepting, with Descartes, a radical division of nature into separate material and mental realms, and the concomitant bifurcation of our knowledge, is deemed a nonstarter, incompatible with the scientific outlook.

This so-called top-down approach, which sees intelligent behavior as the tip of an iceberg of unintelligent, mechanical, processes subserving it, has indeed proven to be fruitful in the cognitive sciences, though it has not gone unchallenged.[24] Of course, functional decomposition can be illuminating and useful even when couched in thoroughly mentalistic language, as it often is in empirical psychology and the other social sciences. (Identifying the perceptual processes and mental states and events that are involved in a complex act, that, say, of driving a car, is a nontrivial task, and success in the task yields understanding of a nontrivial sort.) The demand that there be a point at which such mentalism *pro tem* is redeemed in physicalistic coin is rooted in the metaphysical assumption just mentioned, one we need not make, and one that would be regarded by Hume as one of the metaphysical hypotheses he denounces (T Intro. 8). Nonetheless, we can ask how various theories, Hume's included, fare in meeting this demand, supposing it to be legitimate and pressing.

One thing that seems to stand in the way of discharging the debt to physicalism is the fact that the mental states posited in such decompositions are typically what philosophers, following Franz Brentano, have called *intentional* or, what is much the same thing, *representational*. Simply put, this means that mental states are *about* things other than themselves (not necessarily physical things – a belief

---

[24] The chief challenge has come from connectionism; for a useful introduction, see William Bechtel and Adele Abrahamsen, *Connectionism and the Mind: An Introduction to Parallel Processing in Networks* (Cambridge, MA: Blackwell, 1991).

can also be about, say, another belief).[25] It is precisely this feature
that makes them useful in rationalizing explanations: I explain your
reaching for the glass by attributing to you the belief that it contains a thirst-quenching liquid and your desire to have your thirst
quenched. That belief and that desire explain that piece of behavior
because of what they are about – the liquid and the thirst, respectively. (As we have already noted, only if it can be explained in this
way does the bit of behavior in question count as an *action*.) But
since a representation represents only *to* or *for* someone, a state that
is said to represent must be thought of as having an interpreter. The
natural thing to think in this case, of course, is that this interpreter
is the agent. But if we say that, we have not even made a start toward
explaining our intelligence in the way the decompositional strategy
is committed to doing. The alternative is to posit a subpersonal interpreter, that is, think of some component of the person as doing the
interpretation. (Such a subpersonal interpreter is often referred to as
a *homunculus*.) Unless, however, we are ultimately able to get rid
of this homunculus by explaining how *its* functions, including the
interpretive one, can be carried out by dumb, mechanical, components of the system, we are left with an "exempt agent," one whose
own intelligence is unexplained. If so, we will not have discharged
our debt and, from a philosophical point of view (though not, perhaps,
from a scientific one), we may as well not have started. Daniel Dennett, one of the pioneers of the approach we are discussing, explicitly dubs this "Hume's problem." He concedes that "Hume wisely
shunned the notion of an inner self that would intelligently manipulate the ideas and impressions." But, Dennett says, this left him
"with the necessity of getting the ideas to 'think for themselves.'"
Even though "this associationistic coupling of ideas and impressions, [the] pseudo-chemical bonding of each idea to its predecessor
and successor, is a notorious non-solution to the problem," Dennett
thinks that Hume had no alternative but to take it seriously.[26]

[25] This is not, perhaps, true of all mental states: sensations, such as pains, moods,
emotions, and the like are perhaps not – at least not straightforwardly – about anything. But the kind of states most centrally involved in understanding intelligent
behavior – beliefs and desires – do seem to be intentional in this sense (a sense
different from, though related to, the usual one of "intentional" as it modifies
actions, a sense close to that of "deliberate").

[26] See Daniel C. Dennett, *Brainstorms: Philosophical Essays on Mind and Psychology*
(Montgomery, VT: Bradford Books, 1978).

Is Hume really forced into the position Dennett attributes to him? Only if there are no options but a homunculus-self, the very thing Hume claims not to find in experience, or no self at all. To think that these are the only possibilities is, however, a mistake, and a surprising one, given the fact that Hume's bundle theory may plausibly be seen as designed precisely to find a middle way between these two unacceptable extremes. While Hume does not deny that there is a self, something that thinks, has beliefs, desires, and other cognitive states and dispositions, he does spend considerable time telling us what it is not, namely, the unchanging substance philosophers have typically taken it to be.[27] In doing this, he can appear to be saying that the self is not anything. But this appearance is misleading, as is that which prompts Dennett's reading. The mistake is, one must concede, an easy one to make. Hume does, indeed, often make perceptions, as opposed to bundles of them, the subject of certain verbs that look intentional: they are said to "produce" and "attract" each other. This can encourage the attribution to Hume of the so-called Newtonian picture. (So called because, in an effort to describe the bonds among perceptions, it makes obvious reliance on metaphors drawn from Newton's account of the gravitational attraction among bodies.) Taken at face value, such language suggests that it is these subpersonal components of a person that are the fundamental bearers of intentional properties, with attributions at the personal level being derivative. The problem with this line of thought is that we now have to make sense of perceptions doing other, much more puzzling, things, such as understanding each other and themselves. As Dennett points out, this parallels the modern cognitivist's problem of having to make sense of representation either without an exempt agent, or by accepting an unending regress of components, and thus ending up with an uninformative theory.[28]

---

[27] If one did take Hume to be really denying that there is a self, what would one take him to be talking about in Book 2 and Book 3 of the *Treatise*, which unmistakably take it for granted?

[28] For discussion of the "Newtonian" picture of the self, in which it is ideas that are the subject of intentional verbs, see Jane L. McIntyre, "Is Hume's Self Consistent?" in *McGill Hume Studies*, ed. D. F. Norton, N. Capaldi, and W. L. Robison (San Diego: Austin Hill Press, 1979), 79–88, and Biro, "Hume's Difficulties with the Self." For further discussion of personal identity, see in this volume the essay "Hume and the Problem of Personal Identity."

Is Hume really forced into the position Dennett describes? In fact, there is evidence that he is more successful than some modern cognitivists in avoiding the trap. In brief, the evidence is that he never makes anything other than a person the subject of a seriously intentional – as opposed to what we may call a quasi-intentional – predication. While he talks of perceptions "attracting," "producing," "destroying," and "influencing" each other, he never talks of them as thinking, understanding, willing, or desiring. Expressions of the former sort should be taken for the metaphors they are. We also say things like "Clouds produce rain" and "Magnets attract nails," without taking ourselves to be attributing genuine intentional states to clouds and magnets. The literal meaning of such sentences is that clouds or magnets are the causes of certain effects. We have already seen that Hume is happy to say that an idea (better: the occurrence of an idea) can cause (the occurrence of) another idea – that is what an idea's "introducing" another idea comes to, and the various ways in which this happens is what the principles of association describe.

There may indeed be a mystery about how a mind constituted of perceptions, as Hume's account has it, can do the things we say it does in our ordinary, nonphilosophical, discourse. But there is no mystery about how the *perceptions* that constitute a mind can do these same things, for the simple reason that they are not said by Hume to do them, and, *contra* Dennett, nothing in Hume's theory commits him to saying that they do. On the contrary, Hume's point is that only selves constituted in the way he describes can be intelligibly said to do the things people (or any other intelligent beings) are said to do.

VI. SCIENTIST OR PHILOSOPHER?

As I remarked earlier, one of the surprising consequences of the picture both Hume and modern cognitive science present of the cognitive agent is that he is not always the best source of information and insight about his own cognitive life. If we want to find out what processes are involved in the performance of some cognitive task and how they work, asking the cognizer is often unhelpful and sometimes even misleading. One of the most robust general findings in recent cognitive science has been that we often get more interesting, more detailed, and more reliable information about these processes from experiments that measure response times, uncover error patterns, test comprehension, and so on.

The modern cognitive scientist can accept this lesson with equanimity, even with relish. But can Hume, in spite of his scientific ambitions? I have suggested that his own general picture of the science of the mind, and some of his specific insights about how the mind works, anticipate some of these results. And he certainly emphasizes the need for experiments, although, as we have noted, what he has in mind is rather different from the kind of laboratory experiment on which modern science in general thrives and that is, as I have just noted, common in cognitive science. But Hume still has a deep commitment, inherited from the "way of ideas" followed by both the Cartesians and his British empiricist predecessors, to introspection as a way of finding epistemological bedrock. So, for him, the need to find the right balance between the subjective, phenomenological, approach so central to the introspective tradition, and the objective, third-person, experimental methods standard in scientific theory, is indeed a pressing one.

Hume's commitment to the introspective method should not be seen as merely the result of his inability to free himself from a pervasive pattern of thought, one that contributes nothing to the substance of his account of the mind. Hume's aims are, as we saw earlier, ambitious, and require him to look for a certain kind of grounding of the concepts and beliefs that a nonphilosophical scientist can take for granted. Unlike the latter, he cannot be a naive realist about external objects, causation, or the self in the way a working scientist can and, indeed, must be. He needs to give an account of fundamental concepts and beliefs that are, from a purely scientific point of view, unproblematic. It is not that cognitive science has nothing to say about such concepts and beliefs and about their role in our mental life. Indeed, it does. But it does so without raising philosophical questions about their legitimacy, without, in particular, taking the possibility of skepticism seriously. Hume, of course, does take this possibility seriously. As I noted earlier, one of the features common to Hume's science of the mind and the so-called naturalization programs in recent epistemology and philosophy of mind is a shift from the justification of beliefs in the traditional sense, to an explanation of their provenance through an examination of our cognitive endowments and history. In both cases the shift leads to doubt about the value, even the coherence, of traditional epistemological projects. But only in Hume's case does it also lead to rethinking the very notion of justification.[29]

Thus the similarity between Hume's project and modern cognitive science should not be overemphasized. There are significant differences, as well. Among these are Hume's continued adherence to the introspective method he inherited from his predecessors, as well as his refusal to abandon those elements of the traditional framework that derive from common sense and our everyday practices, rather than from the rarified and esoteric activities of philosophers *or* scientists. That is why, to return once again to the clear and explicit explanation of his method set out at the start of his project, the experiments in his science must consist of a "*cautious* observation of human life" and must be taken "as they appear *in the common course of the world*" (emphasis added).

Hume, then, has a much more complex task than the modern cognitive scientist, or even the modern naturalizing philosopher. He must try to fit together into a coherent whole a number of elements that do not easily go together: innocent scientific theorizing, the introspective method he inherits from his predecessors, philosophical analysis, and an ultimate allegiance to common sense as the touchstone for the deliverances of each of the former. Hume does not, one must grant, fully succeed in weaving together the different strands in his thought responsive to these different demands. It is no wonder that the debates that have dogged the interpretation of his work since his own day, debates about whether he is a philosopher or "just" a psychologist, a naturalist or a skeptic, continue unabated. Take, for example, the thesis that our natural beliefs are

---

[29] Fodor, while now conceding, indeed, emphasizing, that Hume anticipates some of the central insights of modern cognitive science, still argues that Hume's empiricism, in particular, his commitment to the copy principle, stands in the way of his recognizing that an account of what beliefs are, what they are about, and how they interact (the proper concerns of a scientific theory of the mind) must be distinct from, and independent of, a theory of how the beliefs we actually have may be proven to be true, as well as of one of how we come to have them, the twin concerns of boring old epistemology. See *Hume Variations*, especially Chap. 2. Perhaps Hume's point is precisely to fashion a new notion of justification, one in which a belief is justified *because* of how we come to have it. Perhaps he supposes that a belief is justified if it is unavoidable given our cognitive make-up and our experience.

irresistible. We have seen that a recognition of, indeed, insistence
on this is a cornerstone of Hume's account of the mind. Yet even
if no amount of philosophical reflection can halt the processes that
yield these beliefs, that does not mean that such reflection cannot
lead us to question their epistemological status. When unchecked by
common sense, such philosophical reflection can lead to the "deepest darkness" of total skepticism. Fortunately, when common sense
reasserts itself, as it inevitably does, the skeptic's speculations are
seen as "cold, and strain'd, and ridiculous" (T 1.4.7.8–9). Yet they,
too, are in a sense, natural and, at least for some minds, irresistible.
If one is a philosopher, the deepest challenge is to find a way of living
with these irreconcilable demands of one's nature.

SUGGESTIONS FOR FURTHER READING

In addition to the works cited in the notes to this essay, for further reading
the following are recommended.

Baxter, Donald L. M. *Hume's Difficulty: Time and Identity in the* Treatise.
New York: Routledge, 2008.

Biro, John. "David Hume." In *The Encyclopedia of Cognitive Science*, L.
Nadel, ed. (New York: Macmillan, 2002).

Bower, Kennett. "Imagery: From Hume to Cognitive Science." *Canadian
Journal of Philosophy* 14 (1984): 217–34.

Bricke, John. *Hume's Philosophy of Mind*. Princeton, NJ: Princeton University Press, 1980. 74–123.

Broughton, Janet. "What Does the Scientist of Man Observe?" *Hume Studies*
18 (1992): 155–68.

Garrett, Don. *Cognition and Commitment in Hume's Philosophy*. New
York: Oxford University Press, 1997.

Owen, David. *Hume's Reason*. Oxford: Clarendon Press, 1999.

Stroud, Barry. *Hume*. London: Routledge and Kegan Paul, 1977.

Waxman, Wayne. *Hume's Theory of Consciousness*. Cambridge: Cambridge
University Press, 1994.

Winkler, Kenneth. "The New Hume." *Philosophical Review* 100 (1991):
541–79.

3   Hume and the Mechanics
     of Mind

Impressions, Ideas, and Association

By the time Hume started to work on his *Treatise*, the notion of
an idea as the primary, most general sort of mental item dominated
European philosophy. Although Descartes noted that, strictly speaking, only those "thoughts that are as it were images of things" were
appropriately described as ideas, in practice he used "the word 'idea'
to refer to whatever is immediately perceived by the mind."[1] Not
only do we have ideas of trees and the sun, but we also have ideas
of our own activities of thinking and willing. Locke characterizes
"idea" as "being that Term, which, I think, serves best to stand for
whatsoever is the Object of the Understanding when a Man thinks."
Locke also thinks that we not only have ideas that derive from things
or objects in the world (ideas of sensation), but also of the activities
and operations of our own minds (ideas of reflection). Ideas of sensation are acquired through the operation of external objects on our
sense organs, while ideas of reflection come from introspection, from
thinking about what happens within our own minds. He also thinks
that these ideas of reflection are of two basic sorts of mental activity,
perception and willing, that correspond to two faculties of mind: the
understanding (or the power of thinking) and the will (or the power
of volition).[2]

Hume introduced important innovations concerning the theory of
ideas. The two most important are the distinction between impressions and ideas, and the use he made of the principles of association

---

[1] Rene Descartes, *Meditations on First Philosophy*, in *The Philosophical Writings of
Descartes*, trans. J. Cottingham, R. Stoothoff, and D. Murdoch, 3 vols. (Cambridge:
Cambridge University Press, 1984), 2:25, 127.

[2] John Locke, *An Essay concerning Human Understanding*, ed. Peter Nidditch
(Oxford: Clarendon Press, 1975), 1.1.8, 2.6.2.

in explaining mental phenomena. Hume divided the perceptions of the mind into two classes. The members of one class, impressions, he held to have a greater degree of force and vivacity than the members of the other class, ideas. He also argued that ideas are causally dependent copies of impressions. And, unlike Locke and others, Hume makes positive use of the principle of association, both of the association of ideas, and, in a more limited way, of the association of impressions. Such associations are central to his explanations of causal reasoning, belief, the indirect passions (pride and humility, love and hatred), and sympathy. These views about impressions and ideas and the principles of association form the core of Hume's science of human nature. Relying on them, he attempts a rigorously empirical investigation of human nature. The resulting system is a remarkable but complex achievement.

I. IMPRESSIONS AND IDEAS

Hume begins Book 1 of the *Treatise, Of the Understanding,* by saying: "All the perceptions of the human mind resolve themselves into two distinct kinds, which I shall call IMPRESSIONS and IDEAS" (T 1.1.1.1). In his *Enquiry concerning Human Understanding* (hereafter *Enquiry*) he says much the same thing, but adds an example: "Every one will readily allow, that there is a considerable difference between the perceptions of the mind, when a man feels the pain of excessive heat, or the pleasure of moderate warmth, and when he afterwards recalls to his memory the sensation, or anticipates it by his imagination" (EHU 2.1). In neither work does he make an attempt to explain what he means by the phrase *perceptions of the mind,* but it would have been obvious to any eighteenth-century reader that he is using that expression much as Descartes and Locke had used the term "idea": for anything that mind is aware of or experiences. As he had put it in the *Treatise:* "To hate, to love, to think, to feel, to see; all this is nothing but to perceive" (T 1.2.6.7).

Hume's initial step in the *Treatise* is to show that perceptions of the mind may divided into "two distinct kinds," impressions and ideas. These two kinds commonly differ, he says, "in the degrees of force and liveliness, with which they strike upon the mind." Among our impressions, those perceptions with the most "force and vivacity" are sensations (including those of pain and pleasure) and the passions and emotions. Ideas are described as "the faint images" of impressions that are found "in thinking and reasoning." The distinction between ideas and impressions is further characterized as "the difference betwixt feeling and thinking." Perceptions also differ in being either simple or complex. Simple perceptions, he says, "are such as admit of no distinction nor separation," a single color or taste, for example. Complex perceptions, in contrast, are those that "may be distinguish'd into parts," for example, the several qualities (color, taste, smell, etc.) "united together" in the perception of an apple (T 1.1.1.1–3; cf. EHU 2.3).

Impressions and Ideas of Sensation

Hume says that there are two kinds of impressions, "those of SENSATION and those of REFLECTION." Although he has much to say about the causal origin of impressions of reflection, he says that impressions of sensation arise "in the soul originally, from unknown causes."[3] He says almost nothing about the causes of sense impressions and has, strictly speaking, no theory of perception. How we come to have impressions of sensation is a problem that he leaves to "anatomists and natural philosophers" (T 1.1.2.1; cf. T 2.1.1.2). His concern in Book 1 of the *Treatise* and the first *Enquiry* is limited principally to the ideas that are derived from such impressions.

While Hume initially divides impressions into sensations, passions and emotions, ideas are characterized only as the images of impressions, and as the materials of thinking and reasoning. It is important to remember that Hume's initial discussions in *Treatise* 1.1.1.1 and in *Enquiry* 2.1 are provisional, intended, by the use of examples, to introduce the reader to the distinction he has in mind. Once roughed out, this distinction is made "with the more accuracy" as Hume proceeds with "a more accurate survey." Thus, while the official distinction between impressions and ideas is made in terms of force and liveliness or vivacity, we get an initial grip on it only as Hume gives us examples of impressions (of sensations, passions, and emotions), and then tells us more about ideas, the faint images of impressions. One might think that the characterization of ideas as faint images of impressions prejudges Hume's important copy

---

[3] Discussion of this important point is deferred until Section III.

principle. Hume took great pains to argue for this principle – that all simple ideas are derived from simple impressions – on empirical grounds. He then says that this is "the first principle I establish in the science of human nature" (T 1.1.1.3–4, 12). His efforts to establish it are meant to be a paradigm of empirical rigor. But if both the truth of this principle and Hume's method of establishing it are suspect because of an apparent prejudgment of the issue, then his new science is off to a shaky start.[4] The copy principle is not merely the first and one of the most important results of Hume's science and its method. In addition, because impressions effectively constitute or delineate our experience, the claim that all simple ideas derive from simple impressions gives substantial content to Hume's methodological determination to stay within the bounds of experience.

As long as one remembers that Hume's initial discussion is deliberately loose and inexact, this issue can be resolved in Hume's favor. It is true that the term *image* suggests a relationship of dependence: an image is dependent on that of which it is an image. But all Hume needs is the weaker concept, resemblance, of which he makes explicit use in the next few pages. The official distinction between impressions and ideas is in terms of force and vivacity. The reference to "sensations, passions and emotions," on the one hand, and "faint images of these," on the other, is not part of the official theory, *at this stage*. These examples are introduced early on in order to help us grasp the distinction that Hume goes on to make officially, as it were, in other terms. If, in the course of giving these examples to help us to understand the content he intends to give the terms *impressions* and *ideas*, he uses a stronger term than he should, no harm is done. No harm, that is, so long as, in the course of establishing the precedence of impressions over ideas, the real work is done by the notion of resemblance, not by that of image.

Thus when Hume goes on to consider "with the more accuracy" how it is that impressions and ideas interact among themselves and with each other, he shifts from talk of images to that of resemblance: "The first circumstance, that strikes my eye, is the great

---

[4] Perhaps the most important aspect of Hume's science of human nature is his determination not to go beyond experience, both with respect to the content of our mental states and with respect to the explanation of mental phenomena. As he says: "'tis still certain we cannot go beyond experience" (T Intro. 8).

resemblance betwixt our impressions and ideas in every other particular, except their degree of force and vivacity." He then mentions
that one kind of perception seems to be a reflection of the other,
but he does not say which kind is the original and which the reflection. He first establishes the correspondence between simple ideas
and impressions: "every simple idea has a simple impression, which
resembles it; and every simple impression a correspondent idea."
Hume "affirms" this rule on the basis of observation, and further
supports it by issuing a challenge to anyone who doubts the rule:
find a counterexample. He then turns to a central task in his science of human nature, that of tracing the connections, especially
the causal connections, between impressions and ideas. "The *full*
examination of this question," he says, "is the subject of the present
treatise" (T 1.1.1.3, 5, 7).[5]

At this early stage Hume limits himself to a precise enuncia-
tion of the copy principle: "we shall here content ourselves with
establishing one general proposition, *that all our simple ideas in
their first appearance are deriv'd from simple impressions, which
are correspondent to them, and which they exactly represent.*" He
establishes this principle in two stages. He first reassures himself
"by a new review . . . that every simple impression is attended with
a correspondent idea, and every simple idea with a correspondent
impression." In a foreshadowing of his analysis of our idea of causation, he describes this relationship as a "constant conjunction."
And he argues that this constant conjunction is evidence of a causal
connection between impressions and ideas: "Such a constant conjunction, in such an infinite number of instances, can never arise
from chance; but clearly proves a dependence of the impressions on
the ideas, or of the ideas on the impressions" (T 1.1.1.7–8).

The question of dependence, Hume argues, can be decided
by determining which of a pair of resembling impressions and
ideas appears first. He finds "by constant experience" that simple

---

[5] In the *Enquiry*, Hume skips the step of establishing the correspondence rule and
goes straight to proving that "all our ideas or more feeble perceptions are copies of
our impressions or more lively ones" (EHU 2.5). The lack of the correspondence
rule in the *Enquiry* leaves open a plausible option apparently ruled out by the
presence of the rule in the *Treatise:* one might have a simple impression without a
correspondent simple idea, though one cannot have a simple idea without a simple
impression.

impressions are always experienced before their corresponding ideas. He also finds that our practice confirms this: when we want to introduce a person to the idea of orange, we convey to her the impression "but proceed not so absurdly, as to endeavour to produce the impressions by exciting the ideas." He summarizes his argument by saying that the "constant conjunction of our resembling perceptions, is a convincing proof, that the one are the causes of the other; and this priority of the impressions is an equal proof, that our impressions are the causes of our ideas, not our ideas of our impressions." He also provides a second causal argument, pointing out that whenever

by any accident the faculties, which give rise to any impressions, are obstructed in their operations, as when one is born blind or deaf; not only the impressions are lost, but also their correspondent ideas; so that there never appear in the mind the least traces of either of them. Nor is this only true, where the organs of sensation are entirely destroy'd, but likewise where they have never been put in action to produce a particular impression. We cannot form to ourselves a just idea of the taste of a pine-apple, without having actually tasted it. (T 1.1.1.8–9)[6]

This first principle of the science of human nature is important for many reasons. Perhaps most important is Hume's determination to use the principle as a way of testing the content of ideas and thus limiting metaphysical speculation. If ideas of sensation are copies of impressions, then the content of such an idea cannot outstrip the content of the impression from which it is derived. In the *Enquiry* this test is explicitly put forward as a check on the meaning of philosophical terms: "When we entertain, therefore, any suspicion, that a philosophical term is employed without any meaning or idea (as is but too frequent), we need but enquire, *from what impression is that supposed idea derived?* And if it be impossible to assign any, this will serve to confirm our suspicion" (EHU 2.9; cf. A 7).[7] In the *Treatise*, Hume first uses this check to test the notion of substance in 1.1.6, but the most famous deployment occurs in his discussion of the idea of necessary connection.

---

[6] See also EHU 2.7.

[7] Since the claims about impressions and ideas are empirical, it is, of course, possible to conceive that, in a particular case, the order might be reversed. The missing shade of blue example (see T 1.1.1.10) might well be Hume's way of emphasizing the empirical nature of his claims.

Ideas and Impressions of Reflection

In *Treatise* 1.1.2, Hume distinguishes between impressions of sensation and impressions of reflection. Impressions of reflection are "deriv'd in a great measure from our ideas." On this account, we first experience impressions of sensation, including "heat or cold, thirst or hunger, pleasure or pain." Copies of these impressions are retained as ideas, and when we recall such an idea of pleasure or pain it "produces the new impressions of desire and aversion, hope and fear." These Hume calls "impressions of reflection" because they are derived from a reflection on previous experience. Among impressions of reflection he initially includes the "passions, desires, and emotions," but this classification is apparently provisional. In Book 2 he speaks of secondary impressions, which can be caused by either impressions or ideas. Only the latter are properly called impressions of reflection.[8] Moreover, Hume often uses *emotion* to refer, not to an impression of reflection, but to the feeling such an impression has.[9] He also sometimes uses *sensation* in the same way, as when he says of calm passions that they "produce little emotion in the mind, and are more known by their effects than by [any] immediate feeling or sensation" (T 1.1.2.1, 2.3.3.8).

At *Treatise* 2.1.1, Hume replaces the distinction between impressions of sensation and reflection with a more accurate distinction between original and secondary impressions. As a term of classification, *impressions of sensation* is either too narrow or too broad. If *sensation* means "comes from the senses," then it is not clear that "impressions of sensation" include pleasures and pains. But if *sensation* just means *feeling*, then there is no clear difference between impressions of sensation and those of reflection. Furthermore, the category "impressions of reflection" is misleading. Not all passions, emotions, and desires are caused by reflection, by, that is, the consideration of our ideas. Some are caused immediately by other impressions. Original impressions, he says, "are such as without any antecedent perception arise in the soul." They include "all

---

[8] T 2.1.2.4; see also T 2.3.9.2. Hume does not seem to have a name for those secondary impressions that are not impressions of reflection.

[9] See the discussion at T 2.2.8.4, and "emotion" in the Glossary of the Oxford Philosophical Texts (OPT) edition of *A Treatise of Human Nature*, ed. D. Fate Norton and M. J. Norton (Oxford: Oxford University Press, 2000), 575.

the impressions of the senses, and all bodily pains and pleasures."[10] When Hume says that these original impressions make their appearance in the soul "without any introduction," he does not mean "without cause," but rather "without any preceding thought or perception."[11] Every impression has a causal history, but the causal history of original impressions does not, typically, involve other perceptions of the mind. Moreover, Hume here reiterates the policy established at the beginning of Book 1. He will not look for the "natural and physical causes" of original impressions. To do so, he says again, would lead him away from his "subject, into the sciences of anatomy and natural philosophy" (T 2.1.1.1–2).

For the remainder of the *Treatise*, Hume treats the passions as secondary impressions. Secondary impressions are caused by original impressions or by an idea derived from an original impression. The original impressions are usually pleasures or pains.[12] Consider, for example, the bodily pain associated with an attack of gout. This "produces a long train of passions, as grief, hope, fear." These passions may also be produced, not by any present pain from this condition, but by remembering the pain it caused in the past or anticipating its future pain. As Hume says, "Bodily pains and pleasures are the source of many passions, both when felt and [when] consider'd by the mind" (T 2.1.1.2).

Hume also distinguishes between direct and indirect passions. Among the former he lists desire, aversion, grief, joy, hope, fear, despair, security, and, interestingly, volition (T 2.1.2.4). These direct passions arise immediately from an impression or idea of pain or pleasure, or what Hume often calls "good or evil" (see T 1.3.10.2,

---

[10] Hume lists as possible causes of these original impressions "the constitution of the body," "the animal spirits," and "the application of objects to the external organs" (T 2.1.1.1). Note that any of these causes might as well be causes of bodily pains and pleasures as causes of impressions that come from the senses. The significance of our ignorance of the causes of original impressions is discussed in Section III.

[11] In the same paragraph he says that original impressions "arise originally in the soul, or in the body, which-ever you please to call it." I take the extremely casual nature of this controversial remark to be further evidence that Hume refuses to be drawn about the causal background of original impressions, including impressions of sensation.

[12] "'Tis easy to observe, that the passions, both direct and indirect, are founded on pain and pleasure, and that in order to produce an affection of any kind, 'tis only requisite to present some good or evil" (T 2.3.9.1).

for example). Furthermore, the "mind by an *original* instinct tends to unite itself with the good, and to avoid the evil, tho' they be conceiv'd merely in idea, and be consider'd as to exist in any future period of time." By "*original* instinct," Hume means a basic feature of human nature, a feature that explains behavior, but that cannot itself be explained. These fundamental connections between pleasure and desire or pain and aversion help explain human motivation. As Hume puts it, "the WILL exerts itself, when either the good or the absence of the evil may be attain'd by any action of the mind or body" (T 2.3.9.1–2, 7).[13]

In addition to those direct passions that arise from the perception of pleasure and pain, there are also those that "arise from a natural impulse or instinct, which is perfectly unaccountable." These instinctively based passions include "the desire of punishment to our enemies, and of happiness to our friends; hunger, lust, and a few other bodily appetites." Unlike the other direct passions, these passions are not caused by pleasure or pain or the prospect thereof. On the contrary, these passions "produce" pleasure or pain, as, for example, when hunger leads us to eat, an act that gives pleasure. Given the central role that these two kinds of direct passion play in human motivation, one would expect Hume to have a lot to say about them. But, apart from the extensive discussion of hope and fear in *Treatise* 2.3.9, he tells us that none "of the direct affections seem to merit our particular attention" (T 2.3.9.8–9). He is much

---

[13] Hume has a rather deflationary account of the will. Although in T 2.3.9.2 he counts "volition" as a direct passion, in T 2.3.1.2 he says that the will, "properly speaking" is "not comprehended among the passions." He goes on to define the will as "*the internal impression we feel and are conscious of, when we knowingly give rise to any new motion of our body, or new perception of our mind.*" I think the situation is this. The term, *the will*, is a term for a faculty; other faculties that Hume talks about include memory, the senses, the imagination, judgment, and reason. Faculties produce impressions or ideas. Hume does not seem to have a term for the faculty that produces passions. Looked at in this way, of course, the will, as a faculty, is not a passion. But what the will produces, volitions, are passions. I describe this as a deflationary account of the will because Hume does not think that appeals to such a faculty are explanatory. What is important is not the postulation of faculties, but the tracing of causes and effects among impressions and ideas. An action is not explained by saying that it was caused by a volition, which was produced by the faculty of the will. It is explained by saying it was caused by a volition, which was caused by a desire or aversion, which was in turn caused by the perception of pleasure or pain. For additional discussion of the will, see in this volume the essay "Hume's Moral Psychology."

more interested in what he calls the indirect passions, discussion of which occupies roughly two-thirds of Book 2 of the *Treatise*.

Hume has an extraordinarily rich and interesting story to tell about the indirect passions, their nature and their causal origins. In some ways his account of these is the most technically sophisticated part of his science of human nature. The basic indirect passions are pride and humility, love and hatred. Others that derive from these four are ambition, vanity, envy, pity, malice, generosity, and "their dependants" (T 2.1.1.4).

Several features of the indirect passions stand out.

1. The indirect passions, like all passions, are "simple and uniform impressions." As a result, "'tis impossible we can ever, by a multitude of words, give a just definition of them, or indeed of any of the passions" (T 2.1.2.1).
2. The feeling of the passions of love and pride is pleasant, while hatred and humility feel painful. The causes of love and pride produce a pleasure distinct from those passions themselves, while the causes of hatred and humility produce a pain distinct from those passions themselves.
3. The indirect passions have both causes and objects, which must be distinguished. The object of pride and humility is always the self. "Here the view always fixes when we are actuated by either of these passions." The object of love and hatred is always another person. "Our love and hatred are always directed to some sensible being external to us" (T 2.1.2.2, 2.2.1.2).
4. The indirect passions, like all passions, do not purport to represent anything. I return to this issue in Part III.

Because this account of the indirect passions relies heavily on a double relation of impressions and ideas, further discussion of it will be deferred until we have considered Hume's theory of relations.

II. RELATIONS

In both the *Treatise* and the *Enquiry* Hume introduces three principles of association: resemblance, contiguity, and cause and effect. These are "universal principles, which render [the imagination], in some measure, uniform with itself in all times and places" (T 1.1.4.1). In the *Enquiry*, he somewhat more cautiously says that it "is evident, that there is a principle of connexion between the different thoughts or ideas of the mind, and that, in their appearance to the memory or imagination, they introduce each other with a certain degree of method and regularity" (EHU 3.1). In the *Treatise*, these three principles of association are called *natural* relations, and are given this name because in each such relation one idea involuntarily or "naturally introduces" another. Natural relations contrast with a second set of relations, the *philosophical* relations, or those in which one idea is voluntarily compared with another. As Hume sums up his view: "The word *relation* is commonly us'd in two senses considerably different from each other. Either for that quality, by which two ideas are connected together in the imagination, and the one naturally introduces the other ... or for that particular circumstance, in which, even upon the arbitrary union of two ideas in the fancy, we may think proper to compare them" (T 1.1.5.1). These two kinds of relation require our attention.

Philosophical Relations

Hume draws attention to philosophical relations in *Treatise* 1.1.5 and again in 1.3.1. The earlier discussion is essentially a list, with a brief description of each of the seven philosophical relations. In the later discussion, he divides these relations into two classes. The first class includes *resemblance, contrariety, degrees in quality*, and *proportions in quantity or number*. Hume says of these four relations that "they depend entirely on the ideas, which we compare together" and illustrates his view by saying: "'Tis from the idea of a triangle, that we discover the relation of equality, which its three angles bear to two right ones; and this relation is invariable, as long as our idea remains the same" (T 1.3.1.1). He is saying, in other words, that as long as we take the idea of a triangle to be that of an enclosed plane figure made up of three straight lines, we will find that the sum of the internal angles of this figure will be exactly equivalent to the sum of two right angles. This is a demonstrative judgment, the conclusion, that is, of a piece of demonstrative reasoning the contrary of which cannot be conceived, and that results in *knowledge*.

It is tempting to think of this first class of relations as being broadly logical in character or instantiating metaphysical necessity. But this cannot be right. Such relations include *degrees in quality*, of which Hume gives this example: "And tho' it be impossible to judge exactly of the degrees of any quality, such as colour, taste, heat, cold, when the difference betwixt them is very small; yet 'tis easy to decide, that any of them is superior or inferior to another, when their difference is considerable" (T 1.3.1.2). If I have an idea of something being pretty hot, and another idea of something being pretty cold, then *as long as those ideas remain the same*, the relation between the two ideas will always be the same. Note that this recognition that one thing is noticeably hotter than another thing is an example of a relation known, in Hume's terms, with "knowledge and certainty."

Relations of the second class, those involving *time and place, identity,* and *causation,* are different. These relations "may be chang'd without any change in the ideas." Hume says, for example, that "the relations of *contiguity* and *distance* betwixt two objects may be chang'd merely by an alteration of their place, without any change on the objects themselves or on their ideas; and the place depends on a hundred different accidents, which cannot be foreseen by the mind" (T 1.3.1.1). Consider this example of two objects subject to such changes. Suppose I have two cars, a Jaguar and a BMW. These could be side-by-side in my driveway. The same cars could equally well be separated by a continent, the Jaguar in New York and the BMW in LA. Whatever their location, my ideas of these cars remain exactly the same, but the spatial relationship between them may have changed. Or, suppose I think that the golf ball I just hit down the fairway is the same one that I used when I made a hole-in-one last week. But then I remember that I put the hole-in-one ball away as a souvenir, and so it and the one just struck cannot be identical. The *ideas* of these golf balls are indistinguishable – the ideas are effectively the same –but the relationship between them is not one of identity. Judgments regarding this second set of relations are not, according to Hume, demonstrative and certain, but only probable.[14]

Hume's distinction between these two classes of philosophical relations is replaced in the *Enquiry* with the more famous distinction between *relations of ideas* and *matters of fact.* The former

---

[14] For further discussion of this difficult distinction between the two classes of philosophical relations, see David Fate Norton, "Editor's Introduction" to the *Treatise,* 124–7, and the Annotations to *Treatise* 1.3, 446–7, both in the OPT edition of the *Treatise.*

includes "every affirmation, which is either intuitively or demonstratively certain" and which is "discoverable by the mere operation of thought, without dependence on what is any where existent in the universe." Any proposition that is intuitively or demonstratively true is such that its denial "would imply a contradiction, and could never be distinctly conceived by the mind" (EHU 4.1–2). This gives Hume a criterion: any proposition the falsehood of which we can conceive without contradiction is neither intuitively nor demonstratively certain. It must therefore fall into the other class, matter of fact.[15]

In both the *Treatise* and the *Enquiry* Hume also distinguishes between *intuition* and *demonstration*, between those relations that we can perceive immediately, and those relations that we perceive as the result of a reasoning process. Three relations, *resemblance*, *contrariety*, and *degrees in quality*, are, Hume says, "discoverable at first sight, and fall more properly under the province of intuition than demonstration." We intuit a relation when we can just see, without the aid of any other ideas, that two ideas stand in a certain relationship with each other. Think of the ideas of a hot coal and an ice cube. We understand, without further thought, that the qualities of temperature represented by those ideas are significantly different. Now consider a relation involving *proportions in quantity or number*. Hume illustrates his position by means of a geometrical example, the relationship of the internal angles of a triangle and two right angles. This is a relationship of equality, but most of us cannot intuit or see that this is true. We have to demonstrate this truth to ourselves, or proceed, as Hume puts it, "in a more *artificial* manner" (T 1.3.1.2–3). This process of demonstration is a matter of constructing a chain of ideas, the first of which is the idea of the internal angles of a triangle, and the last of which is the idea of two right angles. Each of the intermediate ideas must be seen to be intuitively

[15] Hume's distinction in EHU between relations of ideas and matters of fact *seems* closer to our distinction between necessary and contingent than does the distinction found in the *Treatise*. It is extremely unclear how and to what extent Hume's thinking has changed and developed here. It is worth noting that Hume often uses the phrase "matter of fact" to mean "matters of fact that are not observed by the sense or memory," i.e., matters of fact that are the conclusions of causal inference. See the quotation from the *Enquiry* in note 17 below. For further discussion and references, see Norton, "Editor's Introduction" to the *Treatise*, 133 and note 38.

connected to the ideas with which it is adjacent in the chain. We in effect see that two things equal to a third thing are equal to one another. In this case the way to proceed is to discover an angle that we can just see is equal to both the internal angles of a triangle and to two right angles.[16]

Hume also distinguishes between the immediate and the inferential in "matters of fact." The relations of identity and of time and place are grasped, he says, as the result of "a mere passive admission of the impressions thro' the organs of sensation." Consequently, "we ought not to receive as reasoning any of the observations we may make" concerning them (T 1.3.2.2). In other words, we immediately sense that one impression or idea is or is not identical with another, or was or was not prior to another. It is only the relation of cause and effect that enables, and even forces us, to move from the experience of something presently observed to the idea of something not presently observed.[17] But it is the natural relation of causation that has this all-important feature: "Thus tho' causation be a *philosophical* relation, as implying contiguity, succession, and constant conjunction, yet 'tis only so far as it is a *natural* relation, and produces an union among our ideas, that we are able to reason upon it, or draw any inference from it" (T 1.3.6.16).

Natural Relations, or Association

All ideas are derived from impressions, and ideas can stand in philosophical relations to each other. But more importantly for Hume, ideas and impressions can stand in natural relations to each other. The central role played by association is one of the most distinctive

---

[16] In spite of the fact that this geometrical example is Hume's own, a few pages later, Hume limits demonstrative reasoning to algebra and arithmetic. This is because in those subjects we have a "precise standard, by which we can judge of the equality and proportion of numbers." This standard is the "unite," so that we can always tell, no matter how long our demonstrative chain of ideas, when one number "has always a unite answering to every unite of the other" (T 1.3.1.5). Hume appears to have dropped this limitation in the *Enquiry.*

[17] The point is well made in the *Enquiry:* "It may, therefore, be a subject worthy of curiosity, to enquire what is the nature of that evidence, which assures us of any real existence and matter of fact, beyond the present testimony of our senses, or the records of our memory.... All reasonings concerning matter of fact seem to be founded on the relation of *Cause* and *Effect*" (EHU 4.3–4).

aspects of Hume's science of human nature, an aspect of which he was proud, as the *Abstract* shows:

Thro' this whole book, there are great pretensions to new discoveries in philosophy; but if any thing can entitle the author to so glorious a name as that of an *inventor*, 'tis the use he makes of the principle of the association of ideas, which enters into most of his philosophy... there is a secret tie or union among particular ideas, which causes the mind to conjoin them more frequently together, and makes the one, upon its appearance, introduce the other.... 'Twill be easy to conceive of what vast consequence these principles must be in the science of human nature, if we consider, that so far as regards the mind, these are the only links that bind the parts of the universe together... they are really *to us* the cement of the universe, and all the operations of the mind must, in a great measure, depend on them. (A 35)

We noted Hume's careful empirical establishment of the copy principle (all simple ideas are derived from simple impressions), and saw that this is an aspect of his determination not to go beyond experience and what can be derived from experience. His account of the association of ideas is similarly empirical but proceeds in a different fashion. Hume's proof of the copy principle depended on a survey that led to a generalization. In contrast, the principles of association are postulated to explain uniformities in phenomena. A complete defence of these principles cannot be given when they are first enunciated in *Treatise* 1.1.4. In fact, the adequacy of Hume's account of the principles of association can be judged only by the success or failure of the *Treatise* as a whole. Hume observes that it is common that "the same simple ideas... fall regularly into complex ones." Such patterns would be impossible were "ideas entirely loose and unconnected." Thus there must be "some universal principles, which render [the imagination], in some measure, uniform with itself in all times and places." Consistently with having found that the imagination is free to join any two simple ideas it chooses, the principles of association link ideas with "a gentle force, which commonly prevails," rather than by "an inseparable connexion" (T 1.1.4.1).

Hume lists three "qualities, from which this association arises, and by which the mind is after this manner convey'd from one idea to another" (T 1.1.4.1). These are resemblance, contiguity in time and place, and cause and effect. He makes no attempt at this stage to show that there are no other principles of association. He simply claims that it is "plain" and "evident" that "these qualities produce an association among ideas, and upon the appearance of one idea naturally introduce another" (T 1.1.4.1–2). In the first *Enquiry*, he does claim that "this enumeration is compleat" while admitting the difficulty of proving his claim: "All we can do, in such cases, is to run over several instances, and examine carefully the principle, which binds the different thoughts to each other, never stopping till we render the principle as general as possible" (EHU 3.3). This is a typical feature of Hume's science of human nature. Regularities at one level are to be explained by overarching principles, but we cannot expect that those principles themselves can always be explained.[18]

The Uses of Association

Although Hume says in the *Abstract* that it is the use he makes of the principles of association of ideas that is innovative, two of his most important uses of association involve impressions. Hume specifically speaks of the association of impressions, noting "this remarkable difference, that ideas are associated by resemblance, contiguity, and causation; and impressions only by resemblance" (T 2.1.4.3). This second sort of association is central in explaining the indirect passions. The other use of association involving impressions is perhaps the most important use of association in the *Treatise*. The central argument of *Treatise* 1.3 concerns probable or causal reasoning, and the production of beliefs in what is presently unobserved or unobservable on the basis of what is presently observed, of, that is, a present impression.[19]

---

[18] Although Hume wants his most basic principles to be "as universal as possible," he recognizes the "impossibility of explaining ultimate principles" (T Intro. 8; T Intro. 10).

[19] Hume's first example of the association of ideas in the *Enquiry* is an instance of the association between an impression and an idea: "A picture naturally leads our thoughts to the original" (EHU 3.3). An impression of a picture leads us, by means of the relation of resemblance, to think of what the picture is a picture of.

Belief and Causal Reasoning

The act of believing, for Hume, is the act of assenting or judging. But Hume's central case of belief is not the assent we might attach to any proposition, whether known or merely believed, but rather the belief we have in unobserved existents. Belief in these is contrasted with knowledge, knowledge of mathematical propositions, for example. The central issue of *Treatise* 1.3 is how, on the basis of past experience, we come to believe in the existence of objects or events that we are not currently experiencing. His negative account is that in coming to have such beliefs, we are not determined by reason.[20] His positive account involves both his theory of association and his account of belief. Past experience shows us that one sort of object or event, B, has always followed another contiguous object or event, A. This sets up an association, so that whenever we have an impression of A, we are led to have an idea of B and, furthermore, to believe that B will again occur. But what is it to believe that B will occur, as opposed to merely thinking or conceiving B? Hume's answer is that we believe that B will occur – in the coming existence of B – when the force or vivacity of our idea of B approximates that which an impression of B would have. A belief in such a matter of fact is simply a more forceful or lively idea. What distinguishes beliefs from mere conceptions is the same thing that distinguishes ideas from impressions: force and vivacity, or liveliness.[21]

---

[20] This has come to be known as "the problem of induction." There is, of course, a huge literature on the subject. See Don Garrett, *Cognition and Commitment in Hume's Philosophy* (New York: Oxford University Press, 1997), Chap. 4; Peter Millican, "Hume's Sceptical Doubts concerning Induction," in *Reading Hume on Human Understanding,* ed. Peter Millican (Oxford: Clarendon Press, 2002); and Kenneth Winkler, "Hume's Inductive Scepticism," in *The Empiricists: Critical Essays on Locke, Berkeley, and Hume,* ed. Margaret Atherton (Lanham, MD: Rowman and Littlefield, 1999), 183–212.

[21] It is important to realize that on Hume's view, as that of Descartes, we can make judgments or form beliefs with only one idea. Locke held the more traditional view, which Hume describes as "the separating or uniting of different ideas." Hume thinks this is a mistake because "'tis far from being true, that in every judgment, which we form, we unite two ideas; since in that proposition, *God is,* or indeed any other, which regards existence, the idea of existence is no distinct idea, which we unite with that of the object" (T 1.3.7, n.20). See Descartes's discussion of the idea of God and the existence of God in Meditation 3, and Locke's account of belief, opinion or assent in *Essay* 4.14–16.

Association works in two ways in causal reasoning and the production of belief. The first explains why it is that on the appearance of one sort of impression the mind comes to have another sort of idea. Hume here appeals explicitly to the principles of association:

When the mind, therefore, passes from the idea or impression of one object to the idea or belief of another, it is not determin'd by reason, but by certain principles, which associate together the ideas of these objects, and unite them in the imagination. Had ideas no more union in the fancy than objects seem to have to the understanding, we cou'd never draw any inference from causes to effects, nor repose belief in any matter of fact. The inference, therefore, depends solely on the union of ideas. (T 1.3.6.12)

This explains why the mind makes the transition from a first impression or idea to another idea, but it does not explain why that idea is believed, and not merely conceived. For example, if I see a patch of scorched earth, I might then believe that this patch was recently burned, for fire and scorched earth have in my past experience been associated as, respectively, cause and effect. But so far, Hume has only accounted for the occurrence of the idea *fire* and not for my belief that there has been a fire. For an idea to be a belief, it must have a greater degree of force and vivacity; it must in this respect approximate to an impression.[22] But what is the source of extra force and vivacity that constitute my belief that a fire has scorched the earth? This force and vivacity come from the impression with which the idea is associated. Again, Hume is explicit: "I wou'd willingly establish it as a general maxim in the science of human nature, *that when any impression becomes present to us, it not only transports the mind to such ideas as are related to it, but likewise communicates to them a share of its force and vivacity*" (T 1.3.8.2). The three principles of association are features of human nature, and so is the fact that force and vivacity is transmitted from one associated perception of the mind to another. Both are crucial to Hume's account of causal reasoning and the production of belief.[23]

---

[22] Hume does not distinguish the belief from what is believed or what we might call the content of the belief.

[23] It is extremely difficult not to read this account into Hume's discussion of the same topic in the *Enquiry*. But in fact he never mentions either of these two uses of association in EHU 5, "Sceptical Solution of these Doubts." Nor, for that matter, does he describe what turns an idea into a belief as the very same thing as

Hume's account of those beliefs reached by causal or probable reasoning does not explain the assent we give to knowledge. Concerning propositions known by intuition or demonstration, Hume says that "the person, who assents, not only conceives the ideas according to the proposition, but is necessarily determin'd to conceive them in that particular manner." If one understands that A is equal to B, and that B is equal to C, one has no choice but to suppose that A is also equal to C. In other words, the assent that attaches to *knowledge* comes from our inability to conceive an item of knowledge to be false. In contrast, so far as probable or causal *belief* is concerned, "the imagination is free to conceive both sides of the question," and belief, as we have seen, depends on the force and vivacity of the idea associated with some present impression (T 1.3.7.3).

Double Relation

Hume's account of the indirect passions is summarized in *Treatise* 2.1. The basic indirect passions are pride and humility, love and hatred. Although the cause of each occurrence of any of these passions varies (I can be proud of my new car, of my daughter's grades, and even of the quality of a local restaurant), Hume thought it absurd to think that there is a distinct or fundamental feature of human nature that explains each such instance of pride. It is more in keeping with a science of human nature to think that each of these items can produce pride "by partaking of some general quality, that naturally operates on the mind" (T 2.1.3.5). The relevant qualities, it turns out, are those that produce a pleasure resembling but distinct from love and pride, or a pain resembling but distinct from hatred and humility. And these qualities "naturally operate" on the mind through association. Consider my pride in my new car. When I survey this car I see an expensive and colorful object capable of safely transporting me and my family. This survey causes me to feel pleasure. But the feeling of pride is also pleasant, and, by resemblance (the only principle of association that links impressions), the feeling of pleasure

---

what distinguishes an idea from an impression, viz., force and vivacity. There is no scholarly consensus as to whether Hume has changed his mind, or whether he has just suppressed technical details for ease of presentation.

arising in such circumstances is associated to a distinct feeling, the passion of pride. Furthermore, as the car is mine, the survey of it, by the association of ideas, brings to mind the idea of my self, the idea of the person who is the natural object of my pride. In a second way, then, association facilitates the production of pride. Using Hume's text to sum up:

That cause [some quality of my new car], which excites the passion [pride], is related to the object [of pride, my self], which nature has attributed to the passion; the sensation [pleasure], which the cause separately produces, is related to the sensation [another pleasure] of the passion: From this double relation of ideas and impressions, the passion is deriv'd. (T 2.1.5.5)

This double relation of impressions and ideas is another example of the importance of association in Hume's philosophy. As he says: "Any thing, that gives a pleasant sensation, and is related to self, excites the passion of pride, which is also agreeable, and has self for its object." It is the association of a pleasant sensation with pride, and the further association of the idea of what produces that pleasant sensation with the idea of self, that explain the occurrence of pride. We have seen that association is crucial in explaining the formation of causal beliefs. Hume draws attention to the similarities between that account and his account of the indirect passions. He even uses the same expression "a kind of attraction" that he used when he first discussed association at *Treatise* 1.1.4. In the formation of causal beliefs, he says,

the present impression gives a vivacity to the fancy, and the relation [of association] conveys this vivacity, by an easy transition, to the related idea. . . . There is evidently a great analogy betwixt that hypothesis, and our present one of an impression and idea, that transfuse themselves into another impression and idea by means of their double relation: Which analogy must be allow'd to be no despicable proof of both hypotheses. (T 2.1.5.8, 10–11)

Sympathy

Another important concept introduced in Book 2 is that of sympathy. It too is handled with technical facility, and explained in terms of Hume's account of impressions, ideas, and association. In the

Treatise, at least, *sympathy* has a special meaning for Hume. We sympathize with others when we "receive by communication their inclinations and sentiments, however different from, or even contrary to our own." Hume explains this process in two stages. We are first made aware of the sentiment or opinion of another "only by its effects, and by those external signs in the countenance and conversation, which convey an idea of it." But there is more to sympathy than having an idea of another's feeling. By sympathy, the relevant idea is "converted into an impression, and acquires such a degree of force and vivacity, as to become the very passion itself, and produce an equal emotion, as any original affection." Hume has to explain both the source of our idea of another's feeling and how this idea comes to have the extra force and vivacity that transforms it from an idea of a feeling into the very feeling it represents. His explanation is simple: a lively idea, indeed an impression, of our self is always present to us,[24] and thus: "Whatever object... is related to ourselves must be conceiv'd with a like vivacity of conception, according to the foregoing principles," namely, the principles of association. The greater the resemblance or contiguity to us of the person feeling the original sentiment, the more likely our idea of that feeling is to be converted into the feeling itself: "The stronger the relation is betwixt ourselves and any object, the more easily does the imagination make the transition, and convey to the related idea the vivacity of conception, with which we always form the idea of our own person" (T 2.1.11.2–5).

Resemblance functions here in two ways. There is "the general resemblance of our natures," so that we have some tendency to sympathize with any other human being. Furthermore, where "there is any peculiar similarity in our manners, or character, or country, or language, it facilitates the sympathy." The greater the resemblance between ourselves and others, the more likely we are to sympathize with them. Contiguity and causation also play a role: "The sentiments of others have little influence, when far remov'd from us, and require the relation of contiguity, to make them

---

[24] This claim creates difficulties for Hume. See Jane McIntyre, "Personal Identity and the Passions," *Journal of the History of Philosophy* 27 (1989): 545–57, and Donald Ainslie, "Scepticism about Persons in Book II of Hume's *Treatise*," *Journal of the History of Philosophy* 37 (1999): 333–61.

communicate themselves entirely. The relations of blood, being a species of causation, may sometimes contribute to the same effect" (T 2.1.11.5–6).[25]

As in his account of belief, this explanation of how an idea can be turned into an impression works only because of Hume's doctrine of impressions and ideas. If an idea differs from its correspondent impression only in terms of force and vivacity, then we can explain the operation of sympathy simply by accounting for the source of the additional force and vivacity that accounts for the conversion of a relevant idea into a resembling impression or passion. In general terms, Hume's account of sympathy runs parallel to his account of belief. As he says: "Let us compare all these circumstances, and we shall find, that sympathy is exactly correspondent to the operations of our understanding; and even contains something more surprizing and extraordinary" (T 2.1.11.8). The association of ideas plays a crucial role in each, and in each case an idea is enlivened by the addition of extra force and vivacity. In the case of belief, the source of the extra force and vivacity is an associated impression. In the case of sympathy the source is an ever-present impression of the self, and because of the strength of this idea, sympathy is even more extraordinary than belief, for, while belief enlivens an idea so that it approximates to an impression, sympathy actually turns an idea into an impression.[26] Sympathy can enliven an idea so that it becomes an

---

[25] In *Treatise* 3.3.1, *Of the origin of the natural virtues and vices*, Hume argues "that sympathy is the source of the esteem, which we pay to all the artificial virtues" (T 3.3.1.9). Because sympathy is facilitated by resemblance, contiguity, and causation, the esteem we feel will have a tendency to favor those who are closest to us, most resemble us, or are linked to us by ties of blood. Sometimes this is appropriate. It is proper to favor one's own family, to some extent. But in general, we do not want our judgments of character to depend on these factors. So we must correct our moral sentiments, in just the way we correct our sense impressions and the influence of the passions and our beliefs. See Part III of this essay, and J. L. Mackie, *Hume's Moral Theory* (London: Routledge and Kegan Paul, 1980), Chap. 5, as well as Rachel Cohon, "The Common Point of View in Hume's Ethics," *Philosophy and Phenomenological Research* 57 (1997): 827–50. See also in this volume the essay "Hume's Later Moral Philosophy."

[26] This difference is important. If a sensory idea actually turned into a sense impression, it would presumably be a hallucination. Part of the point of belief is to enable us to deal with objects or events that we are not currently experiencing, so beliefs could not perform their role if they were impressions. But they must imitate impressions in the sense that both involve judgments about existence.

actual passion. But sympathy can also enliven other kinds of ideas. It can, for example, enliven beliefs so that they too are transferred from individual to individual. Because of sympathy, Hume says, "men of the greatest judgment and understanding... find it very difficult to follow their own reason or inclination, in opposition to that of their friends and daily companions" (T 2.1.11.2).[27]

III. REPRESENTATION, INTENTIONALITY, AND CORRECTION

Sensation and Representation

Hume's first principle in the science of human nature is that all simple ideas are derived from simple impressions, "*which are correspondent to them, and which they exactly represent*" (T 1.1.1.7). Ideas represent impressions, and they do so in virtue of resembling them, and being caused by them.[28] Because ideas are causally dependent on impressions and differ from them only in the degree of their force and vivacity, they can in another important respect resemble impressions: the content of the two kinds of perception can be exactly identical. But this leads us to a question of the greatest importance. If ideas represent impressions because of causal dependence and resemblance, how and what do impressions represent? We want our idea of the telephone in the next room, for example, to be an idea of an actual, physical object in the next room, and not merely the idea of an impression, which after all is just another perception of the mind. But it looks as if this can be so only if the impression we had of a telephone when we were in the next room represented an actual, physical telephone.

The question What do impressions represent? turns out to be extremely difficult to answer. In order to address it, we must first remember to distinguish between impressions of sensation and impressions of reflection or secondary impressions. The question

---

[27] Note the suggestion that this tendency should be resisted. Here again we have a case where correction may be necessary. See the discussion in *Treatise* 2.1.11.9, and later in the next section of this essay.

[28] Hume is explicit about this: "Our ideas are copy'd from our impressions, and represent them in all their parts;" "All ideas are deriv'd from, and represent impressions" (T 1.3.7.5, 1.3.14.11).

about what and how impressions represent does not arise for impressions of reflection. Hume is clear about this: a passion, the paradigm impression of reflection, is, he says, "an original existence, or, if you will, modification of existence, and contains not any representative quality, which renders it a copy of any other existence or modification" (T 2.3.3.5).[29] So the issue concerning the representative nature of impressions is limited to impressions of sensation.[30] But as we saw above in Part I, Hume supposes that the sources or causes of impressions of sensation are beyond our reach. Such impressions, he says, arise "in the soul originally, from unknown causes." This is enough to rule out any investigation of the causes of such impressions, and is in addition consistent with his limitation of enquiry to experience. If experience itself is constituted by impressions, then it is clear that the cause of impressions cannot itself be a subject of empirical inquiry.[31] We cannot, for example, sensibly ask whether our impression of a tree is caused by and represents a tree. We can inquire into the causes of our *beliefs* about trees, as Hume does with great subtlety in 1.4.2 (*Of scepticism with regard to the senses*), but that is a different matter. We can also examine the character of our sensations and how they are interrelated to each other and to other perceptions of the mind, but beyond that we cannot go. "We may," he says, "draw inferences from the coherence of our perceptions," but as to "those *impressions*, which arise from the *senses*, their ultimate cause is, in my opinion, perfectly inexplicable by human reason, and 'twill always be impossible to decide with certainty, whether they arise immediately from the object, or are produc'd by the creative power of the mind, or are deriv'd from the author of our being" (T 1.3.5.2).[32]

---

[29] This is not to say that no questions of intentionality arise with respect to the passions. When we love, our love is directed toward another person, and hunger is often directed toward a certain item of food. We will return to this issue below.

[30] We should note that the question of representation does not arise for all impressions of sensation. Hume classifies the "pains and pleasures, that arise from the application of objects to our bodies" as impressions of sensation (T 1.4.2.12).

[31] This ignorance is limited to impressions of sensation; we do, of course, know something of the causal origins of impressions of reflection. The difference seems to be that the causes of impressions of reflection are themselves perceptions of the mind.

[32] See also T 1.2.6.7–9; EHU 12.11–14.

Consequently one answer to the question What do impressions of sensation represent? is: As far as we know, nothing! Impressions of sensation may no more represent than do impressions of reflection.[33] Ideas represent impressions, because they are caused by and resemble impressions. But Hume says more than once that we cannot know the causes of impressions of sensation. This may be why he calls them "original impressions."[34]

And if we cannot know the causes of our sense impressions, we can never be in a position to know whether these impressions resemble their causes. On the other hand, we certainly talk as if our sense impressions represent objects in the world and distinct from our minds, and Hume owes us an account of this. This he provides in 1.4.2. Hume is well aware that what he calls "the philosophical system" does "suppose external objects to resemble internal perceptions." But he claims to have already shown, in arguments made earlier in the section, "that the relation of cause and effect can never afford us any just conclusion from the existence or qualities of our perceptions to the existence of external continu'd objects." He goes on to add "that even tho' they cou'd afford such a conclusion, we shou'd never have any reason to infer, that our objects resemble our perceptions" (T 1.4.2.54).[35]

---

[33] This is a controversial claim. For a further defense, see Rachel Cohon and David Owen, "Representation, Reason and Motivation," *Manuscrito* 20 (1997): 47–76. For a contrary view, see Don Garrett, "Hume's Naturalistic Theory of Representation," *Synthese* 152 (2006): 301–19.

[34] As we saw earlier, Hume sometimes uses "original" to describe something about human nature for which we have no explanation. For further discussion, see Miriam McCormick, "Hume on Natural Belief and Original Principles," *Hume Studies* 19 (1993): 103–16.

[35] Hume thinks that his distinction between impressions and ideas, and his claim that we cannot know the causes of sensation, brings clarity to the debate about innate ideas. On a natural reading of innateness, the fact that all ideas are derived from impressions shows that no ideas are innate. But what about impressions? In the *Enquiry* the fact that impressions are not copies of other mental items is enough to show that all impressions are innate (EHU 2, n.1). In the body of the *Treatise*, Hume is more cautious, apparently not committing himself (T 1.1.1.12). The *Abstract* is ambiguous: "it is evident our stronger perceptions or impressions are innate, and that natural affection, love of virtue, resentment, and all the other passions, arise immediately from nature" (A 6). Hume could be saying here either that all impressions are innate (a reading in accord with the *Enquiry*), or just that impressions of reflection are.

The fact that Hume does not discuss in detail what and whether impressions of sensation represent until late in Book 1 explains another fact. It is pretty clear that Hume takes sense impressions to be not just content but also judgments, judgments about the existence of things. The nature of those judgments is not clarified until *Of scepticism with regard to the senses*, but even in the early stages of the *Treatise* Hume seems committed to something like the following view: when we have an impression of an apple, we do not simply have an apple-like experience; we also judge an apple to exist. Of course, Hume is reluctant at this stage to say much about this, because of the problematic nature of our beliefs in the world we experience. Nonetheless, he does talk about "the *belief* or *assent*, which always attends the memory and senses" and goes on to say that this belief is "nothing but the vivacity of those perceptions they present.... To believe is in this case to feel an immediate impression of the senses, or a repetition of that impression in the memory. 'Tis merely the force and liveliness of the perception, which constitutes the first act of the judgment" (T 1.3.5.7). Sense impressions are not mere sense data. To have an impression is to make a judgment. If it were not so, Hume could not explain the nature of beliefs reached by causal reasoning by showing that these approximate to impressions.

Intentionality and the Passions

Hume's discussion of the origins of the indirect passions as the result of a double relation of ideas and impressions shows great technical sophistication, and further illustrates his commitment to the formation of a science of human nature.[36] Attention to this aspect of Hume's account can help soften, perhaps disarm, some fairly obvious criticisms of his account of the passions, especially with respect to intentionality.[37] We noted that Hume thinks of all the passions as "simple and uniform impressions, [so that] 'tis impossible we can ever, by a multitude of words, give a just definition of them"

---

[36] See, e.g., *Treatise* 2.2.2, *Experiments to confirm this system.*

[37] Intentionality is that characteristic of a mental state in virtue of which it is "of" or "about" something. So, typically, we think that our visual representation of a tree is of or about the tree. But a state can be intentional without being representational. When I am angry with you, my anger does not represent you, but it is directed at you.

(T 2.1.2.1). When taken out of context, this may seem implausible. How could something as rich and complex as love be a simple impression of reflection? Simple impressions may have no logical relations, but the love Desdemona bears for Othello necessarily involves Othello. Hume captures this feature when he says that the object of love is another person. It is true that, on Hume's account, the relation between Desdemona's love (an impression) and the idea of Othello is causal and not logical.[38] But the indirect passions are determined to have their objects, "not only by a natural but also by an original property" of the human soul. "Now these qualitites, which we must consider as original, are such as are most inseparable from the soul, and can be resolv'd into no other: And such is the quality, which determines the object of [the indirect passions]" (T 2.1.3.2– 3).[39] Love, as a basic fact of human nature, just does take another person as its object. And Desdemona's love for Othello would not be the love it is if it took some other person, for example, Cassio, as its object. Although strictly speaking a passion is a simple impression, incapable of definition, each passion is bound in a relational nexus of a double relation of impressions and ideas, and cannot be understood independently of that context.[40]

Hume not only says that passions are simple impressions, he also says that they do not purport to represent anything. As we have seen, he insists that a passion contains no "representative quality, which renders it a copy of any other existence or modification" (T 2.3.3.5). This may look like an implausible denial of the intentionality of passions and desires.[41] We should first note what Hume

---

[38] "Here then is a passion plac'd betwixt two ideas, of which the one produces it, and the other is produc'd by it. The first idea, therefore, represents the *cause*, the second the *object* of the passion" (T 2.1.2.4).

[39] Hume is actually talking about pride and humility here, but it is clear he intends the same to be true of the objects of love and hatred. Note again the use of "original" to describe something as a basic, unexplained part of human nature.

[40] "That we may understand the full force of this double relation, we must consider, that 'tis not the present sensation alone or momentary pain or pleasure, which determines the character of any passion, but the whole bent or tendency of it from the beginning to the end" (T 2.2.9.2).

[41] It seems so implausible that Annette Baier regards this claim of Hume's as an isolated mistake that should be ignored. See Annette C. Baier, *A Progress of Sentiments: Reflections on Hume's Sentiments* (Cambridge, MA.: Harvard University Press, 1991), Chap. 6. For further discussion of this issue, see in this volume the essay "Hume's Moral Psychology."

is concerned to deny in this passage. As we have seen, impressions of sensation are as much judgments as they are pure sensations. We normally think of this as meaning that an impression represents an external object, and that, if the representation is accurate, our judgment is true.[42] What Hume is claiming about the passions is that they are differently structured. Having a passion is not akin to making a judgment. Passions or secondary impressions do not carry with them this representational character. As they do not purport to copy or represent anything, they cannot be true or false, reasonable or unreasonable.[43]

To deny that passions are judgments is not to answer all questions about their intentionality. They may not express truths or falsehoods, but they are nonetheless directed. If Desdemona loves Othello, then there is an alternative sense in which Othello is represented by the passion. Othello is the object of Desdemona's love. The passion of love is a simple impression, so the idea of Othello cannot be part of that impression. But the idea of Othello is the object of that passion, and is brought to mind by it. When the passions are considered in their relational context, their alternative form of intentionality becomes apparent.

The direct passions are also intentional in this limited sense. Anger is typically directed toward an individual, as is lust. But these are direct, not indirect passions, and we thus cannot appeal to the double relation of ideas and impressions to account for their intentionality. Nonetheless, direct passions often bring to mind ideas, just as the passion of pride, for example, brings to mind the idea of self. Hume says, "The sensations of lust and hunger always produce in us the idea of those peculiar objects, which are suitable to each appetite" (T 2.1.5.6). And he explicitly compares this with the production of the idea of self by pride. Similarly, desire and aversion arise in response to an impression or idea of pleasure and pain, and produce in turn ideas of various things that can produce the

---

[42] Hume is usually perfectly happy to speak this way, in spite of his qualms about impressions of sensation representing something external to the mind.

[43] Although Hume claims that it is in general "impossible, that reason and passion can ever oppose each other," he is careful to add that there are two ways in which a passion may "be call'd unreasonable... when founded on a false supposition, or when it chooses means insufficient for the design'd end" (T 2.3.3.7).

envisaged pleasure or help to avoid pain.[44] So Hume explains the intentionality of all passions, not just the indirect ones, in terms of the complex nexus of relations passions bear to various impressions and ideas. And, of course, passions must stand in such relations, or they would be unable to interact with beliefs in the determination of the will and the production of behavior. Beliefs about sources of pleasure and pain produce desires, which in turn produce ideas of what will satisfy those desires.

Correction

Hume notes that the passions have commonly been divided into the calm and violent. An example of the former is "the sense of beauty and deformity in action, composition, and external objects." The latter seem to include such passions as "love and hatred, grief and joy, pride and humility." But Hume thinks that this division is "far from being exact"; indeed it is "vulgar and specious." The "raptures of poetry and music frequently rise to the greatest height; while those other impressions, properly call'd *passions*, may decay into so soft an emotion, as to become, in a manner, imperceptible" (T 2.1.1.3). The distinction between calm and violent occurs again later, not as a means of classifying impressions of reflection, but as a manner of describing the different ways that passions can be experienced. This is important for at least two reasons. First, reason "exerts itself without producing any sensible emotion." There are also "certain calm desires and tendencies, which, tho' they be real passions, produce little emotion in the mind, and are more known by their effects than by the immediate feeling or sensation." Since it is natural, but mistaken, "to imagine, that those actions of the mind are entirely the same, which produce not a different sensation," it is common to mistake the influence of the calm passions on our behavior for the influence of reason. Second, although both the calm and violent passions influence the will, and hence our behavior, it is natural to think that the more violent the passion, the more effect it will have on us. But this is not so. Hume says that what "we call

---

[44] "The mind by an *original* instinct tends to unite itself with the good, and to avoid the evil, tho' they be conceiv'd merely in idea, and be consider'd as to exist in any future period of time" (T 2.3.9.2).

strength of mind, implies the prevalence of the calm passions above the violent" (T 2.3.3.8, 10).[45]

At first glance, it looks as if there is a disanalogy between, on the one hand, the assent we attach to our beliefs (that is to the force and vivacity or liveliness of ideas) and the subsequent effect of beliefs on our behavior, and, on the other hand, a passion's violence and the subsequent effect of that passion on our behavior. A belief influences the will because it approximates to an impression: the effect of belief is to "raise up a simple idea to an equality with our impressions, and bestow on it a like influence on the passions. This effect it can only have by making an idea approach an impression in force and vivacity. For as the different degrees of force make all the original difference betwixt an impression and an idea, they must of consequence be the source of all the differences in the effects" (T 1.3.10.3). So the assent we attach to beliefs, and its effect on behavior, just is equivalent to an idea's force and vivacity, and Hume is happy to speak of this force and vivacity as "a feeling or sentiment."[46] If the effect of a passion on the will was exactly parallel to that of a belief, then the stronger in feeling the passion, the more it would influence behavior. But this is just to say that a passion's influence is directly proportional to its violence. But we have seen that Hume denies this conclusion.

This apparent disanalogy is easy to overstate. In both cases there is an initial correlation between the strength in feeling of the perception and its effect on the will. But, as we have seen, toward the end of his important discussion, *Of the influencing motives of the will,* Hume allows that this correlation can be corrected, at least with respect to the passions. It is not always the case that the more violent a passion is, the more it affects behavior. There is a virtue, strength of mind, that comes with maturity and reflection. Although we are inclined to act on our most violent impulses, we learn not to. Hume frequently speaks of correcting our feelings or sentiments, and even of correcting our sense impressions. "'Tis thus the understanding corrects the appearances of the senses, and makes us imagine, that

---

[45] Hume admits, quite rightly, that "there is no man so constantly possess'd of this virtue, as never on any occasion to yield to the sollicitations of passion and desire." Nonetheless, calm passions can and do counteract more violent passions. Hume says that it is "not therefore the present uneasiness alone, which determines" us (T 2.3.3.10).

[46] See, e.g., App. 2–3.

an object at twenty foot distance seems even to the eye as large as one of the same dimensions at ten" (T 1.3.10.12).[47] He also speaks of correcting the moral sentiments, and then says: "Such corrections are common with regard to all the senses; and indeed 'twere impossible we cou'd ever make use of language, or communicate our sentiments to one another, did we not correct the momentary appearances of things, and overlook our present situation" (T 3.3.1.16).[48]

If we can correct our moral sentiments, and even our sense impressions, then surely we can correct our beliefs. This Hume suggests we can do on at least two occasions. First, he points out that whenever we make a causal judgment, there are both essential and superfluous circumstances. Where there is a great similarity of superfluous circumstances, but few of essential ones, we are tempted to make false causal judgments. Hume says that we "may correct this propensity by a reflection on the nature of those circumstances." The second case occurs in the very same paragraph in which Hume talks about correcting "the appearances of the senses." There he says: "A like reflection on *general rules* keeps us from augmenting our belief upon every encrease of the force and vivacity of our ideas. Where an opinion admits of no doubt, or opposite probability, we attribute to it a full conviction; tho'... its force [be] inferior to that of other opinions" (T 1.3.13.9, 1.3.10.12). Here Hume explicitly differentiates between the degree of belief or assent, and the amount of force and vivacity, and thus it looks as if beliefs can be corrected in the same way that sense impressions, passions, and moral sentiments can be corrected.[49]

---

[47] See also T 3.3.3.2.

[48] See note 25 above.

[49] Hume's distinguishing here between degree of assent and amount of force and vivacity is problematic for his theory of belief. According to the official theory, the degree of force and vivacity just is the degree of belief, so no such distinction is possible. It is not hard to think of ways to make the overall account consistent. He could distinguish first- and second-order beliefs: a first-order belief may be initially strong, but we might have a second-order belief that beliefs of the first sort tend to be misleading. This second-order belief might actually cause the force and vivacity, that is, degree of assent, of the first-order belief to decline. I am not suggesting Hume actually thought this, though it is a not implausible way of reading "We may correct this propensity by a reflection on the nature of those circumstances." The whole issue of the correction of belief, especially in the context of general rules, including the rules by which to judge of causes and effects, is extremely interesting and deserves further study.

IV. CONCLUSION: IMPRESSIONS, IDEAS, AND THE SCIENCE OF HUMAN NATURE

Hume's science of human nature was modeled on the physical sciences, which achieved such stunning successes in the seventeenth and eighteenth centuries. The analogy between his intended methodology for his science of human nature and the physical sciences is revealed in the full title of the *Treatise: A Treatise of Human Nature: Being an Attempt to Introduce the Experimental Method of Reasoning into Moral Subjects*. Hume thinks that humans have a nature and that it can be empirically investigated. Although practioners of the science of human nature cannot hope to perform the "careful and exact experiments" of the physical sciences, they can "glean up our experiments in this science from a cautious observation of human life, and take them as they appear in the common course of the world, by men's behaviour in company, in affairs, and in their pleasures" (T Intro. 8, 10). Such "cautious observation" is not simply a matter of paying attention to what is going on around one; it also involves the study of history and literature, ancient and modern:

> Would you know the sentiments, inclinations, and course of life of the GREEKS and ROMANS? Study well the temper and actions of the FRENCH and ENGLISH: You cannot be much mistaken in transferring to the former *most* of the observations, which you have made with regard to the latter. Mankind are so much the same, in all times and places, that history informs us of nothing new or strange in this particular. Its chief use is only to discover the constant and universal principles of human nature. (EHU 8.7)

The reliance on careful observation is the central feature of Hume's methodology, and it has two consequences. One is his determination not to go beyond experience, and the other is the limitation of explanation. Hume's theory of ideas and impressions, especially the copy principle, plays a crucial role in both of these. If all ideas are ultimately derived from impressions, from, that is, what we experience, the very content of our thought is limited by what we have experienced: "we can give no reason for our most general and most refin'd principles, beside our experience of their reality" (T Intro. 9). It is impossible to explain the ultimate principles of human nature;

we just observe them. Hume's three principles of association are like this, as is the general desire of the good or the pleasant and the general aversion to the bad or the painful. His theory of impressions and ideas is the central part of, and partially instantiates, the empirical methodology of his science of human nature. Described at this level of generality, Hume's methodology and the role played by the theory of impressions and ideas is common both to the *Treatise* and the *Enquiry*.

This essay is a study of how Hume's theory of impressions and ideas and his principles of association feature in the empirical methodology he uses to establish some of his most important positions, first, in Books 1 and 2 of the *Treatise*, and then later in the *Enquiry*. Simple ideas are derived from and exactly resemble simple impressions, and this fact is crucial to Hume's empirical establishment of "the first principle . . . in the science of human nature." Hume has little to say about sense impressions and their causes, though it is clear that they are judgments, and not simply sense data. Beliefs and their production in probable reasoning are explained, not by appeal to a traditional faculty of reason, but by the principles of association and the transfer of vivacity from impressions to ideas. A belief just is a forceful, vivacious idea. So one of the most important stories Hume has to tell in Book 1 of the *Treatise* relies crucially in all its aspects on the theory of impressions and ideas and the principles of association.

In a like manner, two of the most important accounts in Book 2 center round both association and the theory of impressions and ideas. First, these components are used extensively in Hume's theory of the indirect passions, which Hume explicitly compares to his account of causal beliefs. Second, the mechanism of sympathy turns ideas into impressions. If ideas did not resemble and represent the impressions from which they were derived, this account would not work. Furthermore, association is used to explain just how through the operation of sympathy an idea can turn into an impression. Hume also compares the operations of sympathy with the operations of the understanding.

In the process of establishing the copy principle, the first principle in the science of human nature, Hume says that the subject of the *Treatise* is the full examination of ideas and impressions and of how these stand with respect to each other, especially causally.[50] This is a remarkable claim, but the way Hume develops his arguments and positions bears it out. All the issues we have explored in Books 1 and 2 come down to tracing the relations ideas bear to impressions and to one another. This has the effect of lessening the importance of faculties in Hume's account of the understanding and the will. As we have seen, Hume argues that a volition is simply an impression we feel when we move our body or give rise to a new perception of the mind.[51] The will is the faculty that produces volitions, but appeal to such a faculty does no work for Hume. The work is done by tracing connections among such impressions and ideas as desires, aversions, and perceptions of pleasure and pain. Hume's account of reason, especially causal reason, is similarly deflationary. Reason is the faculty that gives rise to beliefs, but it is not an appeal to reason that explains why we have the beliefs we have or their nature. That work is done by appeal to the association of ideas set up by past experience, and by the enlivening of certain ideas related to present impressions. Although Hume is happy to talk about the senses, memory, and reason, just as he is happy to talk about the will, all the real work of the mind is done by the connections, especially the associative and causal connections, among ideas and impressions.

SUGGESTIONS FOR FUTHER READING

In addition to the works cited in the notes to this essay, for further reading the following are recommended.

On the Science of Human Nature

Biro, John. "Hume's New Science of Human Nature." This volume.

On Ideas, Impressions, and the Copy Principle

Everson, Stephen. "The Difference between Feeling and Thinking." *Mind* 97 (1988): 401–13.
Stroud, Barry. *Hume.* London: Routledge & Kegan Paul, 1977. Chap. 2.

---

[50] "Let us consider how they stand with regard to their existence, and which of the impressions and ideas are causes, and which effects. The *full* examination of this question is the subject of the present treatise" (T 1.1.1.7).
[51] See note 13 above.

On the Indirect and Direct Passions

Árdal, Páll S. *Passion and Value in Hume's* Treatise, 2nd ed. Edinburgh: Edinburgh University Press, 1989. Chap. 1.

McIntyre, Jane L. "Hume's 'New and Extraordinary' Account of the Passions." In *The Blackwell Guide to Hume's Treatise*, edited by Saul Traiger. Malden, MA: Blackwell Publishing, 2006. 199–215.

On Belief

Bell, Martin. "Belief and Instinct in Hume's First *Enquiry.*" In *Reading Hume on Human Understanding: Essays on the First Enquiry*, edited by P. Millican. Oxford: Clarendon Press, 2002. 175–85.

Norton, David Fate. "Of the Academical or Sceptical Philosophy." In *Reading Hume on Human Understanding: Essays on the First Enquiry*, edited by P. Millican. Oxford: Clarendon Press, 2002. 371–92.

Owen, David. "Locke and Hume on Belief, Judgment and Assent." *Topoi* 22 (2003): 15–28.

On Representation and the Intentionality of the Passions

Alanen, Lilli. "Reflection and Ideas in Hume's Account of the Passions." In *Persons and Passions: Essays in Honor of Annette Baier*, edited by J. Jenkins, J. Whiting, and C. Williams. Notre Dame: University of Notre Dame Press, 2005. 117–42.

4   Hume's Theory of Space and Time in Its Skeptical Context

In *Treatise* 1.2, *Of the ideas of space and time,* Hume examines our ideas of spatial extension and temporal duration, our ideas of geometric equality, straightness, flatness, and mathematical point, and our ideas of a vacuum and of time without change. Hume does not, however, restrict his attention to these ideas; he also draws conclusions about space and time themselves. He argues that space and time are not infinitely divisible, that their smallest parts must be occupied, and that as a consequence there is no vacuum or interval of time without change. His treatments of matters beyond the scope of the section's title have received harsh criticism.[1] His conclusions have seemed contrary to mathematics and physics. His method of arguing – applying features of our mere ideas of space and time to space and time themselves – has seemed philosophically inept. The apparent success of these criticisms has led to widespread neglect of this part of Hume's work.

The neglect is unfortunate. In *Of the ideas of space and time* Hume gives important characterizations of the skeptical approach that will be developed in the rest of the *Treatise*. When that approach is better understood, the force of Hume's arguments concerning

---

[1] See Norman Kemp Smith, *The Philosophy of David Hume* (London: Macmillan, 1941), 287; C. D. Broad, "Hume's Doctrine of Space," *Proceedings of the British Academy* 47 (1961): 161–76; Antony Flew, "Infinite Divisibility in Hume's *Treatise*," in *Hume: A Re-evaluation*, ed. D. W. Livingston and J. T. King (New York: Fordham University Press, 1976), 257–69; and Robert Fogelin, "Hume and Berkeley on the Proofs of Infinite Divisibility," *Philosophical Review* 97 (1988): 47–69, and *Hume's Skepticism in the* Treatise of Human Nature (London: Routledge and Kegan Paul, 1985), 25–37.

space and time can be appreciated, and the influential criticisms of them can be seen to miss the mark.

Hume's "system concerning space and time consists of two parts, which are intimately connected together." First, he concludes that finite portions of space and time are not infinitely divisible, but are composed of a finite number of "simple and indivisible" parts. Second, he concludes that these indivisible parts are inconceivable unless occupied by something "real and existent," and so space and time must each simply be "the manner or order, in which objects exist." In consequence it is impossible both to conceive of empty space and to conceive of time without anything changing (T 1.2.4.1–2).

The arguments composing the first part of Hume's system are the ones most derided. Not many readers bother with the second part of his system, since it is, by Hume's own characterization, a consequence of the first and thus dependent on its success. A new evaluation of Hume on space and time should begin, then, with a new interpretation and defense of his main arguments against infinite divisibility.

I. THE FIRST PART OF HUME'S SYSTEM

Against Infinite Divisibility

Hume means to show that not every part of space has parts.[2] The argument relies on a claim established in Section 1: "that the *idea*, which we form of any finite quality, is not infinitely divisible." Ideas for Hume are like images.[3] Just as the image of a chessboard in a mirror can be seen to have parts, so any idea of anything that takes up space will have parts. No idea will have an infinite number of parts, however. This conclusion follows from two premises. The first is "that the capacity of the mind is limited, and can never attain a full and adequate conception of infinity." Hume means simply that the mind cannot have an infinite number of ideas. The second premise

---

[2] He does not state this explicitly in the *Treatise*, but see EHU 12.18.

[3] Here, following Hume, I use *image* in a sense that extends beyond visual images. Cf. Thomas Hobbes, *Human Nature*, in *The English Works of Thomas Hobbes*, ed. W. Molesworth, 11 vols. (London, 1839–45), 4:3–9 (Chap. 2).

is "that whatever is capable of being divided *in infinitum*, must consist of an infinite number of parts." From these two premises it immediately follows that no idea is infinitely divisible. After all, an infinitely divisible idea would have an infinite number of parts, and so the mind would have an infinite number of ideas (T 1.2.1.2).

The second premise contradicts a long tradition going back to Aristotle, who concluded that something divisible need not have parts that exist actually, but need only have parts that exist potentially.[4] However, a rejoinder can be made to the Aristotelians on Hume's behalf. Some – but not all – of a whole would become its left half, were the whole divided in half. The rest would become the right half. The former is actually on the left, and the latter is actually on the right. They actually differ. Since something can't differ from itself, they are actually numerically distinct. Since these lesser amounts of the whole are actually distinct from each other, then they are actually parts of the whole. So anything divisible actually has the parts it is divisible into.[5]

From the conclusion that no idea is infinitely divisible, Hume concludes that we have some minimal ideas – ideas that cannot be divided. As he says, "'Tis therefore certain, that the imagination reaches a *minimum*, and may raise up to itself an idea, of which it cannot conceive any sub-division, and which cannot be diminish'd without a total annihilation." Likewise there are minimal impressions, where impressions are the vivid images we get in sensory or introspective experiences. Hume describes an experiment to allow one to see a minimal visual impression: "Put a spot of ink upon paper, fix your eye upon that spot, and retire to such a distance, that at last you lose sight of it; 'tis plain, that the moment before it vanish'd the image or impression was perfectly indivisible" (T 1.2.1.3–4). Note that Hume is not saying that the spot of ink is

---

[4] Aristotle, *Physics* Book III, Chap. 6, and Book VIII, Chap. 8; and *On Generation and Corruption* Book I, Chap. 2. *The Basic Works of Aristotle,* ed. R. McKeon (New York: Random House, 1941).

[5] Bayle gives a similar argument against "Epicurean atoms": Pierre Bayle, *Historical and Critical Dictionary: Selections,* trans. R. H. Popkin (Indianapolis: Hackett Publishing, 1991), s.v. "Zeno of Elea," note G, p. 360. There was widespread support for Hume's position on this issue. See Thomas Holden, "Infinite Divisibility and Actual Parts in Hume's *Treatise*," *Hume Studies* 28 (2002): pp. 3–25, and *The Architecture of Matter: Galileo to Kant* (Oxford: Clarendon Press, 2004).

indivisible. With a small telescope one could certainly discern its parts. Rather, Hume is talking about the vivid image caused in the mind by the spot of ink. When the spot of ink is close, the image of it in the mind has many parts. As the spot moves further away it causes a smaller image with fewer parts. Just before the spot is too far away to cause any image at all, it causes an image that cannot be further diminished – one with no parts. This last image is indivisible; it is a minimal impression. Minimal ideas are simply less vivid copies of such minimal impressions.

Armed with minimal ideas Hume proceeds in *Treatise* 1.2 to argue confidently that space, or (as he also calls it) "extension," is not infinitely divisible. More precisely, he argues that no "finite extension," no portion of space with finite length, is infinitely divisible. The basis for his argument is his claim that minimal ideas are "adequate representations of the most minute parts of extension." For, he says, "Wherever ideas are adequate representations of objects, the relations, contradictions and agreements of the ideas are all applicable to the objects" (T 1.2.2.1). He is about to argue that because there are smallest, indivisible ideas of the parts of space, there are smallest, indivisible parts of space. The adequacy of the ideas is supposed to justify this inference.[6] What makes them adequate is that "nothing can be more minute" than they are, "since these are ideas and images perfectly simple and indivisible" (T 1.2.1.5). Being too small to be divided, they are perfect representations of anything too small to be divided.

The argument begins with the assumption used previously, "Every thing capable of being infinitely divided contains an infinite number of parts" (T 1.2.2.2). So any portion of space, if it is infinitely divisible, has an infinite number of parts. So even a portion of space with finite length, if it is infinitely divisible, has an infinite number of parts. However, Hume thinks he can show that any portion of space with an infinite number of parts must have infinite length. It would follow that it is contradictory to talk of an infinitely divisible

---

[6] Hume likely borrows this notion of the adequacy of an idea from Locke, who says, "Those [ideas] I call *Adequate*, which perfectly represent those Archetypes which the Mind supposes them taken from." *An Essay concerning Human Understanding*, ed. P. H. Nidditch (Oxford: Clarendon Press, 1975), 2.31.1.

portion of space with finite length. So there can be no such thing. He uses the minimal ideas from Section 1 to explain the contradiction. He forms a minimal idea in his imagination. "I then repeat this idea once" – that is, he imagines a second minimal idea right next to the first. Now he has an idea of the smallest possible extension, the smallest possible length. Note that, because extension has parts, a single minimal idea is not an idea of extension at all (see T 1.4.4.8). One must resist the temptation to think that two minimal ideas are twice as long as one. One minimal idea has no length at all; it is simply a single point, whereas something with length must have two distinct endpoints. The two form a length simply because they are at their closest approach while still being distinguishable from each other, which is a fact about the mind, not about any bulk the minimal ideas have. So, again, with the first repetition Hume forms the idea of the smallest possible length. Now "I then repeat this idea . . . twice" – that is, he imagines a third minimal idea right next to the second. With the addition of a third minimal idea, the original length doubles. In other words, to the original length composed of the first and second minimal ideas is added an equal length composed of the second and third minimal ideas. On the third repetition of the original idea, that is, the addition of a fourth minimal idea, the original length triples. And so on. Or as Hume put it, "I then repeat this idea once, twice, thrice, &c. and find the compound idea of extension, arising from its repetition, always to augment, and become double, triple, quadruple, &c. till at last it swells up to a considerable bulk, greater or smaller, in proportion as I repeat more or less the same idea" (T 1.2.2.2).

From here Hume moves swiftly to his conclusion. He sees that only an idea composed of a finite number of minimal ideas will have finite length. Since the length is proportional to the number of parts, an idea composed of an infinite number of minimal ideas would be infinitely long. Since the minimal ideas are adequate, what is true of them is true of the smallest parts of extension itself. He concludes "that no finite extension is capable of containing an infinite number of parts; and consequently that no finite extension is infinitely divisible" (T 1.2.2.2).

This conclusion seems to overlook the obvious mathematical possibility that the parts that are added could be proportionately smaller each time. Take the addition of proportionately smaller fractions, for instance, $1/2 + 1/4 + 1/8 + 1/16 + 1/32 + \cdots$, and so on. With each addition the sum approaches 1. No matter how close to 1 you might choose to be, the sum of the whole infinite series is even closer. For this reason the sum of the series has been defined as 1. However, 1 is a finite number, nowhere near an infinite number. Similarly, to a part of length $1/2$ could be added a nonoverlapping part of length $1/4$ and then one of length $1/8$ and then..., and so on, to arrive at a whole of length 1, a decidedly finite length.

Hume considered this objection, but refused to acknowledge its force. In a footnote he says,

> It has been objected to me, that infinite divisibility supposes only an infinite number of *proportional* not of *aliquot* parts, and that an infinite number of proportional parts does not form an infinite extension. But this distinction is entirely frivolous. Whether these parts be call'd *aliquot* or *proportional*, they cannot be inferior to those minute parts we conceive; and therefore cannot form a less extension by their conjunction. (T 1.2.2.2 n.6)

Aliquot parts are of uniform size, whereas proportional parts are of successively smaller size.[7] Hume is saying that no parts of extension, proportional or aliquot, will, when added together, yield a length smaller than the length yielded by the addition of the same number of minimal ideas. Why? Because our minimal ideas are "adequate representations of the most minute parts of extension" (T 1.2.2.1). Perhaps everything in space is bigger than these minimal parts, perhaps some things are the same size, but at least nothing can be smaller than they are. One might worry that Hume is assuming that there are most minute parts of extension in order to prove that there are. But he is not. He is only assuming that his minimal ideas are at least as small as any part of extension.

Hume's proof that finite extension is not infinitely divisible depends crucially, even excruciatingly, on the assumption that our minimal ideas are adequate. On this assumption depends the inference from features of minimal ideas, and features of compounds of

[7] Bayle distinguishes the two kinds of parts, then defines *aliquot parts* as "parts of a certain magnitude and of the same type." Bayle, *Historical and Critical Dictionary,* 362, 367. For more on the distinction see Marina Frasca-Spada, *Space and the Self in Hume's* Treatise (Cambridge: Cambridge University Press, 1998), 33–8.

them, to features of space or extension itself. It is this assumption, however, that seems the least defensible.[8]

Ideas are simply images in the mind that may or may not accurately reflect reality. How can Hume assume with so little argument that in the case of minimal ideas the reflection is accurate? His assumption is especially troubling since the reflection seems so clearly inaccurate, as appears easy to show.

First, distinguish (as Hume does not) between imagining and conceiving. Descartes illustrates the distinction by pointing out that although it is impossible accurately to imagine a chiliagon – a thousand-sided closed plane figure – it is easy to conceive of one. A geometer can even prove some of the properties of such a figure, for instance, that the sum of the interior angles is 179,640 degrees.[9] Second, grant that we cannot imagine something as having an infinity of parts. However, surely we can conceive it. We can, for instance, conceive of a line as a set of dimensionless points as Georg Cantor did.[10] Third, grant that we can only imagine the smallest parts of a line being ordered sequentially, one next to another. However, we can conceive of different ways points can be ordered. They might be ordered densely – between any two points is another – as are the rational numbers.[11] Or points might even be ordered the way a continuum is, such as the real numbers, where there are even more of them than there are rational numbers.[12] Fourth, note that often our best natural science uses mathematics such as geometry or calculus for successful explanation and prediction. This successful use of mathematics presupposes that space is not as we imagine it, but is a continuum the way we conceive it to be. Thus, our best science tells us that space is not the way our imaginations represent it.

---

[8] Besides Fogelin, "Hume and Berkeley," 54, see James Franklin, "Achievements and Fallacies in Hume's Account of Infinite Divisibility," *Hume Studies* 20 (1994): 85–101.

[9] Or as Hume puts it "1996 right angles" (T 1.3.1.6). The sum of the interior angles of a polygon is equal to the number of sides minus 2, multiplied by 180 degrees.

[10] See Adolf Grünbaum, "Modern Science and Refutation of the Paradoxes of Zeno," in W. C. Salmon, ed., *Zeno's Paradoxes* (Indianapolis: Bobbs-Merrill, 1970), 165–70.

[11] The rational numbers are those that can be expressed as a ratio of two whole integers, e.g., 2/3.

[12] The real numbers are the rational numbers along with the algebraic irrational numbers such as the square root of 2 and the transcendental irrational numbers such as pi (π).

Therefore there is no reason to accept Hume's assumption that our minimal ideas are adequate. They are not perfect representations of the dimensionless points ordered as a continuum, the way scientists presuppose space to be.[13]

The trouble with this criticism of Hume's adequacy assumption is that it overlooks the skeptical context of Hume's treatment of space and time. In that context this criticism, powerful as it is, remains beside the point.

Hume's Skepticism

From a modern, narrowly epistemological standpoint, Hume is a Pyrrhonian skeptic who emulates a late Academic skeptic.[14] Whether by accident or design, he is a Pyrrhonian more in the way described by Sextus Empiricus than in the way Hume describes Pyrrhonism. Perhaps Hume's interpretation of Pyrrhonism was somewhat distorted by the commentators he was familiar with, or perhaps he found it useful just to appeal to a widely extant interpretation.[15] In any event, to understand the complexities of Hume's skepticism, it helps to disregard his own characterizations and to apply the nuanced descriptions of ancient skepticism given by the ancient sources themselves and some exacting commentators of our own

---

[13] For strands of this line of thought see Flew and Fogelin cited in note 1 above.

[14] Here I supplement the account of Hume's skepticism given by Fogelin in the essay "Hume's Skepticism" in this volume. He gives the details of Hume's specific skeptical arguments, while I give a more general characterization. Our treatments are consistent, I think, except that whereas Fogelin says that Hume's theory of belief explains his Pyrrhonism, I am inclined to say that Hume's Pyrrhonism explains his theory of belief. This disagreement may well be merely apparent, however, since Fogelin seems to use *Pyrrhonism* in Hume's own sense. An expanded version of this section appears in Chap. 1 of my *Hume's Difficulty: Time and Identity in the Treatise* (New York: Routledge, 2008).

[15] See Frede's extended argument that the Pyrrhonians and earlier Academics were subsequently interpreted to be more dogmatic than they really were. Michael Frede, "The Skeptic's Two Kinds of Assent and the Question of the Possibility of Knowledge," in *Essays in Ancient Philosophy* (Minneapolis: University of Minnesota Press, 1987), 201–22. Popkin thinks Hume's characterization of Pyrrhonism fits this description. Richard H. Popkin, "David Hume: His Pyrrhonism and His Critique of Pyrrhonism," in *Hume: A Collection of Critical Essays*, ed. V. C. Chappell (Garden City, NY: Anchor Books, 1966), 55–6. Commentators on which Hume relied were, e.g., Cicero, Diogenes Laertius, Montaigne, and Bayle.

day.[16] Such descriptions give us some key features to look for in a skeptic's position that we might otherwise overlook.

The Pyrrhonians distinguished two kinds of assent – (1) active endorsement of a view as true based on an appropriate reason, and (2) passive acquiescence in a view forced on one by appearances. In seeking after truth they found that any reasons for endorsing a view as true could be counterbalanced by reasons for not so endorsing it. They found themselves suspended, unable to endorse any view or the opposite of any view. This suspension of judgment was not, contrary to the contentions of Hume and many of his predecessors, supposed to be a suspension of all assent whatsoever. The Pyrrhonians, while continuing to seek the truth about reality, allowed themselves to acquiesce in whatever view happened to be forced on them by the appearances of things. If they appeared to be at the edge of a cliff in danger of falling, they would try not to fall. They would do so, however, without endorsing as true the views that were motivating them.

The late Academics were a bit more dogmatic than the Pyrrhonians. They found that they retained certain beliefs after weighing the conflicting arguments, and regarded this fact as evidence that some beliefs were more likely true – more probable – than others. Thus they found it plausible that truth could at least be approached.[17]

---

[16] I am relying for my remarks mainly on Sextus, Frede, and Popkin. See Sextus Empiricus, *Outlines of Scepticism*, ed. J. Annas and J. Barnes (Cambridge: Cambridge University Press, 2000). See also David Fate Norton, *David Hume: Common-Sense Moralist, Sceptical Metaphysician* (Princeton: Princeton University Press, 1982), 255–79. Annas hints at an account like the one I will give, but does not develop it and ends up reading Hume as a dogmatist. Julia Annas, "Hume and Ancient Scepticism," *Acta Philosophica Fennica* 66 (2000): 271–85, especially 276 and 279. My characterization of Pyrrhonism is selective in accordance with modern epistemological concerns, so that I ignore, e.g., tranquillity as its aim.

[17] Hume would have been familiar with the modern revival of such a view in Mersenne and Gassendi, its development by Anglican theologians and the Royal Society, and its expression in Boyle, Newton, and Locke. See Richard H. Popkin, "Constructive or Mitigated Scepticism," in *The History of Scepticism from Savonarola to Bayle* (Oxford: Oxford University Press, 2003), 112–27; and Henry van Leeuwen, *The Problem of Certainty in English Thought: 1630–1690* (The Hague: Martinus Nijhoff, 1963). For a wide-ranging history of reasoning without certainty see James Franklin, *The Science of Conjecture: Evidence and Probability before Pascal* (Baltimore: Johns Hopkins University Press, 2001).

The Pyrrhonians undercut philosophy, science, and mathematics. The late Academics, with their reliance on probable beliefs, provided for these endeavors. Hume admired the modern flowering of such an approach in Newton.[18] However, the Academics in their degree of dogmatism were still vulnerable to a Pyrrhonian-type challenge. Hume gives it in *Of scepticism with regard to reason,* where he critiques an Academic reliance on the probable. He argues in effect that the Academics cannot justify any degree of belief in any conclusion (T 1.4.1). However, Hume invents a Pyrrhonian facsimile of Academic probability, as follows.[19]

Like the Pyrrhonians, Hume finds no final reason actively to endorse any views as true, or even as probable. He is content passively to acquiesce in whatever views are forced on him by appearances. He says, "After the most accurate and exact of my reasonings, I can give no reason why I shou'd assent to it; and feel nothing but a *strong* propensity to consider objects *strongly* in that view, under which they appear to me" (T 1.4.7.3). His main innovation is to make distinctions between the relative strength or weakness of the forcing. It is by feeling that the mind distinguishes the degree to which an idea is forced on it: "An idea assented to *feels* different from a fictitious idea, that the fancy alone presents to us: And this different feeling I endeavour to explain by calling it a superior *force,* or *vivacity,* or *solidity,* or *firmness,* or *steadiness*" (T 1.3.7.7). Because they concern feeling, the distinctions Hume makes are like aesthetic distinctions: "'Tis not solely in poetry and music, we must follow our taste and sentiment, but likewise in philosophy. When I am convinc'd of any principle, 'tis only an idea, which strikes more strongly upon me. When I give the preference to one set of arguments above another, I do nothing but decide from my feeling concerning the superiority of their influence" (T 1.3.8.12).[20] Sometimes ideas are imposed on us by principles of reasoning that are

---

[18] David Hume, *The History of England, from the Invasion of Julius Caesar to the Revolution in 1688,* Vol. 6 (Indianapolis: Liberty *Classics,* 1983), Chap. 70.

[19] It may be that Hume was following in the footsteps of the early Academic Carneades, if Carneades is read as a "classical skeptic" in Frede's sense; see "The Skeptic's Two Kinds of Assent," 201.

[20] Hume's restriction in this passage to belief as a result of "probable reasoning" is no real restriction since he thinks "all knowledge resolves itself into probability" (T 1.4.1.4).

"changeable, weak, and irregular." Their influence can be undercut by a due contrast with ideas imposed on us by principles that are "permanent, irresistible, and universal" (T 1.4.4.1). In this way "we might hope to establish a system or set of opinions, which if not true (for that, perhaps, is too much to be hop'd for) might at least be satisfactory to the human mind, and might stand the test of the most critical examination" (T 1.4.7.14). Thus Hume is able to distinguish between, on the one hand, views that would remain stable through time and from place to place, and, on the other hand, views that would vary by time or place. The latter would include superstitions, myths, the fictions of the ancient philosophers. Some of our stable views will be fundamental common sense beliefs, such as those in the unitary self and the external world, but there is also room for views in philosophy, science, and mathematics. And so Hume makes room for "refin'd reasoning" and "the most elaborate philosophical researches" in his skeptical approach.[21] Like a critic in the arts who tries to distinguish classic works from passing fancies, Hume tries to distinguish the most stable of the views forced on us by appearances. He extends the Pyrrhonian approach beyond active daily life into theoretical matters. Thus Hume is a Pyrrhonian skeptic whose discrimination concerning the force and stability of passive acquiescence in views gives him a procedure for doing philosophy, science, and mathematics with results akin to those of the later Academic skeptics and their modern heirs. The difference is that Hume makes no connection between the degree to which a view is forced on him and the degree to which it is likely to be true.

Much success in arriving at stability is to be hoped for when our views concern sensory appearances of objects. There are views provoked by other sorts of appearances, but few as stable: "As long as we confine our speculations to the *appearances* of objects to our senses, without entering into disquisitions concerning their real nature and operations, we are safe from all difficulties, and can never be embarrass'd by any question" (T 1.2.5.26 n.12). Note the appeal to objects as they appear to the senses. Hume's skepticism explains his empiricism. That is, his assent only to views forced on him by appearances explains his reliance on experience. He says that "we can never

---

[21] The phrase "refin'd reasoning" is from T 1.4.7.7 and "elaborate philosophical researches" from T 1.4.7.15.

pretend to know body otherwise than by those external properties, which discover themselves to the senses." Extension and duration will turn out to be two such properties. When discussing them he contents himself "with knowing perfectly the manner in which objects affect my senses, and their connexions with each other, as far as experience informs me of them" (T 1.2.5.26). This approach is the one he promises in introducing his "science of man." Thus he says that "the only solid foundation" for his theory of human nature "must be laid on experience and observation" (T Intro. 7). This empiricism, which he learned from Boyle, perhaps Newton, and others, Hume takes simply to be an aspect of his Pyrrhonism:

And tho' we must endeavour to render all our principles as universal as possible, by tracing up our experiments to the utmost, and explaining all effects from the simplest and fewest causes, 'tis still certain we cannot go beyond experience; and any hypothesis, that pretends to discover the ultimate original qualities of human nature, ought at first to be rejected as presumptuous and chimerical. (T Intro. 8)

As with the study of human nature, so with all sciences. "None of them can go beyond experience, or establish any principles which are not founded on that authority" (T Intro. 10). Hume's Pyrrhonian Empiricism is thus concerned only with objects as they appear to us in experience.[22]

Some incautious uses of the words *real* and *really* might be thought to belie this claim.[23] When characterizing his skepticism Hume contrasts the appearances of objects with their unknowable real natures, as one would expect. However, once he takes it to be understood that he is confining his attention to these appearances, he sometimes feels free to reapply the contrast between appearance and reality. In effect he is then distinguishing how an object really appears from how it apparently appears – a contrast allowed by his distinction between more stable and less stable views of things. At other times he contrasts being real with being a nonentity, or, in

---

[22] Cf. Berkeley's distinction between, for instance, "sound as it is perceived by us, and as it is in itself," and his exclusive concern with the former. George Berkeley, *Three Dialogues between Hylas and Philonous*, in *The Works of George Berkeley, Bishop of Cloyne*, ed. A. A. Luce and T. E. Jessop, 9 vols. (London: Thomas Nelson and Sons, 1948–57), 2:174–5, 180–2.
[23] I will note these in the course of the essay.

other words, with being something that appears as opposed to being nothing. Sometimes he uses "in reality" to distinguish a view forced on the mind from the view being criticized. Sometimes he contrasts being real with being only in the mind, though again this contrast is within the world as it appears. Such uses of "real" "imply no dogmatical spirit" any more than phrases such as "'tis evident, 'tis certain, 'tis undeniable." The propensity to use such expressions is, as Hume says, "so natural" that they were "extorted from me by the present view of the object" (T 1.4.7.15). But despite such expressions, he is still confining his attention to objects as they appear to us in experience.

One of Hume's innovations was to find out about objects as they appear to us by examination of the ideas we use to represent them. For instance, he comes to the conclusion that a mathematical point must have color or solidity in order to be an entity that can "by its conjunction with others form a real existence" (T 1.2.4.3).[24] In the course of this investigation he asks, "What is our idea of a simple and indivisible point?" and comments, "No wonder if my answer appear somewhat new, since the question itself has scarce ever yet been thought of. We are wont to dispute concerning the nature of mathematical points, but seldom concerning the nature of their ideas" (T 1.2.3.14). Examining our ideas can help in finding out how objects appear to us. When our ideas are obscure, we can settle controversies about them by examining the impressions from which the parts of the ideas are copied (T 1.2.3.1). Hume's famous copy principle – that all simple ideas are copied from impressions – is part of his skeptical view that the ultimate source of all our views is appearances (see T 1.1.1.7).

As Pyrrhonian, Hume does not even actively endorse the philosophical framework he uses to characterize his skeptical approach. That there are external physical objects (what Hume calls in general "body") is not something Hume finds any justification to believe. It is a belief forced on us. As he says, "'tis in vain to ask, Whether there be body or not? That is a point, which we must take for granted in all our reasonings" (T 1.4.2.1). Further, that there is an internal world of perceptions caused by the external world of objects is a belief philosophers find themselves with when they reflect on experience.

---

24 Here Hume contrasts being real with being a nonentity.

This belief lacks justification as well, yet it is durable. One might focus on passages in which Hume is questioning this philosophical framework, or is thinking along the lines of ordinary nonphilosophical people, to conclude that by talk about the external world he means to be talking about our impressions of it. But when doing philosophy one cannot shake the framework for long (T 1.4.2.41–57).[25] When Hume is operating within it, he means really to be talking about the external world as it is experienced via our impressions and as it is represented by our most stable ideas. This framework may seem for a moment to be less justified than the conclusion that there are only perceptions, but the framework is actually more stable.

We might be misled by Hume's claim that his philosophy "pretends only to explain the nature and causes of our perceptions, or impressions and ideas" (T 1.2.5.26). We are more easily misled if we confuse objects as they appear with the impressions they occasion. Certainly Hume devotes attention and care to characterizing our perceptions. But the context of the above remark is a paragraph in which Hume is contrasting what he is *not* trying to do – "penetrate into the nature of bodies" – with what he *is* trying to do – to "know body ... by those external properties, which discover themselves to the senses." Part of the task in examining perceptions is to discover the properties of the objects of those perceptions, that is, objects as they appear to us. In other words, as Pyrrhonian, he is concerned to characterize the external world by those appearances that force views on us.

The Skeptical Context of Hume's Argument

Hume's assumption that our minimal spatial ideas are adequate representations of the least part of extension falls out of this skeptical approach. Our ideas of the external world are images of the world as it appears to us. Being copied from sense impressions, their characteristics are determined by the way external objects "discover themselves to the senses" (T 1.2.5.26). Not all complex ideas are faithful

---

[25] The considerations against a framework of both an external world of objects and an internal world of perceptions "*admit of no answer and produce no conviction,*" as Hume famously says of Berkeley's philosophy. See EHU 12.15 n.32.

to the world as it appears because of *"the liberty of the imagination to transpose and change its ideas"* (T 1.1.3.4). By rearrangement of their parts we can invent new complex ideas differing from any complex impressions we have had. But simple ideas are completely forced on us. They give us the elements of the world as it appears. They are adequate representations of these elements. And so our minimal spatial ideas are adequate representations of the least part of extension as it appears. If they can only be ordered sequentially, one next to the other, then the same holds of extension as it appears. If no extended idea of finite length can contain an infinite number of adequate minimal ideas, then no extension as it appears can contain an infinite number of parts.

Talk by Hume's critics of infinitely divisible space as a set of points ordered as a continuum would for him amount merely to empty words. Given the copy principle, since there could be no impression of such a set with its elements ordered in such a way, there could be no idea of it. Beyond that, this conceit of a mathematical continuum is not forced on us by appearances, and there is no way to know if it is true of reality.[26] If we try to apply it to the world as it appears, we end up in contradiction. Not only is assent to the conceit not forced, dissent from it *is* forced: "For 'tis evident, that as no idea of quantity is infinitely divisible, there cannot be imagin'd a more glaring absurdity, than to endeavour to prove, that quantity itself *[as it appears to the senses]* admits of such a division; and to prove this by means of ideas, which are directly opposite in that particular" (T 1.2.4.32). I have added the phrase *as it appears to the senses* as a reminder of the skeptical context of all such inferences from idea to object. The phrase helps bring out the force of Hume's remark just quoted: one cannot use ideas that are adequate representations of quantity as it appears, in order to prove that quantity as it appears is different than it appears. Hume's incautious use of the phrases *"really* impossible and contradictory" and *"real quality of extension"* in the argument at 1.2.2.1–2 must not mislead us about Hume's skepticism. He is merely expressing the views forced on

---

[26] Even if taking space to be a continuum yields the best explanation for the successful use of geometry and the calculus, there is no conclusive reason why the best explanation must be true.

him by appearances, whatever incautious expressions happen to be extorted from him.[27]

If one is still dubious about Hume's appeal to ideas to prove his point, then one should return to impressions. Look at grains of sand from the furthest distance at which they are still visible, perhaps arm's length.[28] Move them around with a needle. Ones too close together cannot be distinguished from a single one. Pairs that can be distinguished from a single grain form a tiny extension. The apparent length of the extension grows with the number discernibly added, just as Hume says. The length is proportional to the number discernibly added, just as Hume says. It is of no use to look more closely to see how the grains are really arranged and if there is really any space between them or if they really touch. The grains are not the concern; of concern are only the impressions caused by them at the maximum distance at which the grains are visible. From these impressions the conclusion is forced on one that an extension of merely finite length cannot be built up from an infinite number of such parts.[29] It seems obvious that space as it appears is not infinitely divisible.

As with space, so with time, Hume thinks. He adds one argument peculiar to time that, again, is best understood as an argument concerning time as it appears. In our experience, all moments occur successively, one immediately after the other. So they exist one at a time in the present. So only the present moment exists. Thus if the present moment were divisible into further moments its parts would each be present. So they would coexist. But since all moments are successive, no moments coexist. So if all moments were divisible

[27] When Hume says, "That whatever *appears* impossible and contradictory upon the comparison of these [adequate] ideas, must be *really* impossible and contradictory, without any further excuse or evasion," he is talking about what is really true of what the ideas are adequate of, in other words, what is really true of the world as it appears. When he speaks of "a real quality of extension" he is speaking of extension as it really appears (T 1.2.2.1–2). For further support of the claim that Hume is concerned with "space and time as apprehended by us," see Michael Ayers, "Berkeley and Hume: A Question of Influence," in *Philosophy in History: Essays on the Historiography of Philosophy*, ed. R. Rorty, J. B. Schneewind, and Q. Skinner (Cambridge: Cambridge University Press, 1984), 313–14.

[28] For me it was arm's length. The distance will depend on grain size and color, amount of light, background color, one's visual acuity, etc.

[29] A carefully designed experiment would be needed to conclusively establish these conclusions. I write only from my own crude experiment.

into further moments, the present moment would be as well, so its parts would be coexisting moments that do not coexist – an "arrant contradiction" (T 1.2.2.4).

Hume's Pyrrhonian Empiricism is presupposed by his main arguments concerning space and time. All his conclusions about space and time should be read as claims about space and time *as they appear*. If one is going to disagree with Hume on infinite divisibility, then one is going to have to take issue with his Pyrrhonian Empiricism by showing, for example, that knowledge is possible, or that there is another way to be a skeptic than by acquiescing to views forced on one by appearances, or by showing that the appearances of the external world are not always so closely tied to what is conveyed by the senses. One cannot, however, simply accuse Hume of ineptly reasoning from idea to reality or of making mathematical blunders. Such accusations overlook his sceptical approach to issues concerning space and time, and are irrelevant to judging its success.

The General Argument against Geometric Proofs of Infinite Divisibility

Hume gives various other arguments that space has indivisible parts, that is, parts without parts.[30] He supports these with a crucial general argument against any supposed geometric proof of the infinite divisibility of space. Hume argues that no such proof can succeed (T 1.2.4.17–31). He does so "by denying geometry to be a science exact enough to admit of conclusions so subtile [subtle] as those which regard infinite divisibility" (A 29). The importance he gives to this argument is evidenced by its mention in the Abstract – a piece written to promote the *Treatise*. Besides the long summary of his views on causation and causal inference, the only other highlights of Book 1 of the *Treatise* mentioned there are his bundle theory of the self and his general argument against geometric proofs of infinite divisibility.

All such proofs pretend to be demonstrations based on precise definitions and exceptionless geometric axioms. Hume argues to the contrary that "they are not properly demonstrations, being built on ideas, which are not exact, and maxims, which are not precisely true." The principles of geometry do not apply beyond a certain

---

[30] At T 1.2.2.3, 1.2.2.5, 1.2.2.9, 1.2.4.14.

level of precision and certainly not to "such minute objects" as are envisioned by the defenders of infinite divisibility (T 1.2.4.17).

Hume takes for granted that what is at issue is the status of geometry as it applies to the space which we explore by means of our senses. Given the copy principle, a pure geometrical space would not be something of which we could have ideas. But beyond that, as before, the conceit of pure geometrical space is not forced on us by appearances and there is no way to know if it is true of reality beyond appearances.

Geometry is inexact, Hume says, because the ultimate standard of equality for geometric figures, of straightness for lines, and of flatness for planes is merely appearance to the senses or the imagination. Thus our ideas of these geometric properties are merely ideas of appearing equal, appearing straight, and appearing flat. Thinking that there is a more exact, yet still useful, standard than mere appearance is a natural fiction, but a fiction nonetheless. For what could that standard be? Hume shows that nothing besides appearance will do. Consider equality. Hume's own theory affords a precise standard of equality. Two figures are equal "when the numbers of points in each are equal." However, this proposed standard is useless because we cannot discern the indivisible parts of things outside the mind. They are too small, or as Hume says, "so minute and so confounded with each other, that 'tis utterly impossible for the mind to compute their number." Further this proposed standard is not available to those Hume is arguing against, viz., those who contend that every part has parts, "since, according to their hypothesis, the least as well as greatest figures contain an infinite number of parts" (T 1.2.4.19–20). The only other alternative is that the standard of equality for two figures is simply their appearing equal. Actually, first appearances can sometimes be misleading. We have learned to correct them by determining whether the figures continue to appear equal even after they have been juxtaposed or compared in size to some movable third figure (the "common measure"). The result, as Hume puts it, is that "the very idea of equality is that of such a particular appearance corrected by juxta-position or a common measure" (T 1.2.4.24). Thus the notion of equality in geometry is based on this standard determined by appearance.

We are well aware that the standard is not exact. Addition or removal of a single minute part would make no difference to equality according to this standard, since it would be "not discernible either in the appearance or measuring." Yet we imagine that such action renders equals unequal, so we "suppose some imaginary standard of equality, by which the appearances and measuring are exactly corrected." The relatively crude process of correction we are capable of impels the mind to continue, by a kind of inertia, to imagine that there is the possibility of correction beyond that of which we are capable. We imagine there to be facts about how things would appear – things too small to make any difference to any possible appearance – if only the right conditions enabled us to discern them. But this standard of equality is "a mere fiction of the mind, and useless as well as incomprehensible," Hume says. There is no reason to believe that what cannot appear would appear a certain way in certain conditions. Since our notion of equality is derived only from appearance, there is no applying it beyond possible appearance. Thus appearance (or at least appearance corrected by juxtaposition or use of a common measure) is our best, though inexact, standard of equality (T 1.2.4.24).[31]

---

[31] This imprecision of geometric equality enables Hume to answer some standard objections to his discrete geometry. The first objection is that for any unit of extension, no matter how minimal, there is a line segment not composed of a whole number of these units. Simply let there be a right triangle with sides of n units. The hypotenuse will be $\sqrt{n^2}$ units. Hume's answer is that there will always be a line segment, for figures large enough to yield an appearance, that is *equal* in his sense to $\sqrt{n^2}$ units. The other objection is that on Hume's discrete geometry some line segments have no midpoint, viz., those composed of an even number of minima, so cannot be bisected by another line. Hume's answer is that for line segments large enough to yield an appearance, the *halves* will be *equal*. These answers require two amendments to Hume's geometry of minuscule imprecision. First, he would have to expand his idea of a *common measure* to include not only figures the same size or smaller than the ones being tested, but also ones larger. The danger is that some figures equal on Hume's definition, repeated the same number of times, would compose unequal figures. This problem would occur if there were an indiscernible difference between the original figures that, after sufficient repetition of them, summed to a discernible difference between the resulting composite figures. Hume would have to say that in such a case the original figures failed the test for equality. Additionally, he would have to say that there is a maximum size beyond which geometry does not apply, just as there is a minimum size. Otherwise even a difference of a single minimum would count against equality, for a huge number of repetitions could make that difference discernible. Both these amendments would be in the spirit of Hume's empirical approach. The first gives a way of making the nonapparent apparent; the second rules out figures too large to yield an appearance. For the objections see, for instance, Don Garrett, *Cognition and Commitment in Hume's Philosophy* (Oxford: Oxford University Press, 1997), 74–5. For additional discussion, see Dale Jacquette, *David Hume's Critique of Infinity* (Leiden: Brill, 2001).

We have only the same sort of standard for straightness. "Nothing is more apparent to the senses, than the distinction betwixt a curve and a right [straight] line." However, we cannot define either in terms of how their tiniest parts are arranged, because "this order is perfectly unknown, and nothing is observ'd but the united appearance." Geometers may try to define a straight line as the "*shortest way betwixt two points*," but this overlooks the fact that the connection between straightness and shortness is a discovery, not something true by definition (T 1.2.4.25–6).[32]

The situation is the same for flatness. "The idea of a *plane surface* is as little susceptible of a precise standard as that of a right line; nor have we any other means of distinguishing such a surface, than its general appearance." Geometers may try to define a plane as what is "produc'd by the flowing of a right line," but that would work only if the line flowed along a plane, so the definition in order to be true would have to be circular (T 1.2.4.28).

Analogous to the case of the equality of geometric figures, we realize that there could be curvings of an apparently straight line or warpings of an apparently flat plane that are not noticed at first but that can be detected by juxtaposition or use of a common measure. And analogously our practices of correcting initial appearances leads us to "form the loose idea of a perfect standard to these figures, without being able to explain or comprehend it" (T 1.2.4.25).

Hume concludes that for cases in which it is "in any degree doubtful" whether figures are equal or not, whether a line is straight or not, and whether a plane is flat or not, there is no standard that determines which of the options is in fact true. The ideas "most essential to geometry" are not "exact and determinate." That is, again, because the only standard for the application of these ideas is "the weak and fallible judgment, which we make from the appearance of the objects, and correct by a compass or common measure" (T 1.2.4.29).

Hume continues: "Now since these ideas are so loose and uncertain, I wou'd fain ask any mathematician what infallible assurance

---

[32] The worry that mimima cannot be arranged in a triangle having sides incommensurable with its hypotenuse without leaving a subminimal gap, is assuaged by realizing that the worry presupposes a precise standard of straightness. See Garrett, *Cognition and Commitment*, 75.

he has, not only of the more intricate and obscure propositions of his science, but of the most vulgar and obvious principles?" For example suppose two lines have a line segment in common. If they form an obvious angle with each other, it is clear that at least one of the lines is not straight. At least one of them must bend or curve in order for the lines to overlap for a bit. But what if the angle is very, very small? What if the lines "approach at the rate of an inch in twenty leagues?" Even if they "become one" at some point, they will give every appearance of being straight. There is no further "rule or standard" that makes it true of either line that it is not straight. Thus the seemingly obvious assumption of Euclid's geometry that distinct straight lines cannot share a common segment fails in such a case, because there is no more to being straight than giving every appearance of being straight: "The original standard of a right line is in reality nothing but a certain general appearance; and 'tis evident right lines may be made to concur with each other, and yet correspond to this standard, tho' corrected by all the means either practicable or imaginable" (T 1.2.4.30).[33]

Thus geometrical axioms are liable to fail in cases in which their success would require differences too subtle to make a difference to appearance. Reliable application of our geometric principles is restricted to clear appearances.[34] This restriction entails that it is illegitimate to apply these principles to figures too small to yield any possible appearance. Yet such illegitimate application is what the geometers do in their proofs of infinite divisibility:

if they employ, as is usual, the inaccurate standard, deriv'd from a comparison of objects, upon their general appearance, corrected by measuring and juxta-position; their first principles, tho' certain and infallible, are too coarse to afford any such subtle inferences as they commonly draw from them. The first principles are founded on the imagination and senses: The conclusion, therefore, can never go beyond, much less contradict these faculties. (T 1.2.4.31)

---

[33] Here with the phrase *in reality* Hume indicates the view forced on the mind as opposed to the view being criticized.

[34] Hume allows that because the fundamental principles of geometry "depend on the easiest and least deceitful appearances," they enable us to draw some conclusions more exact than the eye or touch could determine by themselves. Geometry allows a high degree of "exactness." It just "falls short of that perfect precision and certainty, which are peculiar to arithmetic and algebra" (T 1.3.1.6).

The general proof against arguments for infinite divisibility explains the caution against applying geometrical principles beyond
clear appearance. The caution against contradicting appearance
harks back to Hume's initial argument that our idea of extension
consists of indivisible parts. Thus mathematicians who argue that
every part of extension has parts not only illegitimately go beyond
appearance, they actually contradict it. However, it is absurd to try
to use ideas that copy appearance in order to prove that appearance
differs from these ideas (T 1.2.4.32).

Hume gives an example of the failure of trying to use ideas derived
from experience to go beyond and contradict experience. He considers the class of arguments that every part of extension has parts
"deriv'd from the *point of contact*" (T 1.2.4.33). Hume gives more
detail about such arguments in the first *Enquiry*. For example, consider a circle and a straight line tangent to it. For any angle formed
by two straight lines, no matter how small, the "angle of contact"
between a circle and its tangent is less (EHU 12.18). Think of the
angle formed by the tangent and some chord from the point of tangency. No matter how small the angle, the space between the two
lines is divided by the arc of the circle. Thus, Hume's opponents
argue, for every portion of space there is a smaller portion.

Far from helping his opponents, however, the circle and tangent
example brings up a dilemma they cannot escape. So Hume argues.
Consider the point of tangency. If it is an indivisible part, then
Hume's opponents are wrong that every part has parts. If the point
of tangency is a part with parts, then a straight line and a curved
line coincide for a distance, which establishes that at a certain level
of minuteness there is no standard for distinguishing a straight line
from a curved one. "Which-ever side he chooses, he runs himself
into equal difficulties" (T 1.2.4.33). Proponents of infinite divisibility must either accept indivisible points or must accept his general
argument against their supposed geometric proofs of their position.[35]

The general argument supports Hume's conclusion that there are
indivisible parts of extension. In addition, showing the ideas "most

[35] Disciples of modern geometry who take a line to be an infinite set of dimensionless
points will be untroubled by Hume's dilemma. However, they would still owe a
Pyrrhonian Empiricist an account of the source of their basic concepts, and an
explanation why someone should believe in the pure space their geometry purports
to describe.

essential to geometry" to be derived simply from appearance is part of Hume's skeptical view that in doing geometry we are simply acquiescing in views forced on us by appearances.

II. THE SECOND PART OF HUME'S SYSTEM

Colored or Tangible Points

The first portion of Hume's system concerning space and time concludes that they are not infinitely divisible, but consist of indivisible parts. In the second portion he concludes that these parts are inconceivable unless occupied by something real, and so space and time must simply be manners in which real things are arranged.[36] In consequence it is impossible to conceive both of empty space and of time without anything changing (T 1.2.4.1–2).

Here Hume might seem to be opposing the view endorsed by Newton that space and time are absolute in the sense of existing independently of the things that occupy them.[37] However, Hume's approach is subtler than mere opposition. Newton contended that space as it really is, is absolute; space as it appears is relative to perceived objects:[38]

I do not define time, space, place, and motion, as being well known to all. Only I must observe, that the common people conceive those quantities under no other notions but from the relation they bear to sensible objects.

. . .

II. Absolute space, in its own nature, without relation to anything external, remains always similar and immovable. Relative space is some movable dimension or measure of the absolute spaces; which our senses determine by its position to bodies.[39]

[36] Here being real contrasts with not existing.
[37] Hume might further be seen as opposing Newton's view that space and time are absolute in the sense of providing nonrelative frames of reference for inertial motion and the passage of time.
[38] The apparent tension between Newton's skeptical empirical method and his pronouncements about absolute space and time was noticed early on. See Mary Shaw Kuypers, *Studies in the Eighteenth Century Background of Hume's Empiricism* (Minneapolis: University of Minnesota Press, 1930), 19–20.
[39] Isaac Newton, "Scholium" to the "Definitions," in *Mathematical Principles of Natural Philosophy*, Vol. 1, trans. A. Motte and F. Cajori (Berkeley: University of California Press, 1962), 6.

Hume follows this lead. As skeptic he suspends endorsement of Newton's first contention that space as it really is, is absolute, while acquiescing in the second that space as it appears is relative to perceived objects.

The thinker whose views Hume had most prominently in mind, however, was Bayle. Hume's system as a whole was most likely written as a response to the general problem Bayle posed for the divisibility of space and time: "Extension cannot be made up of either mathematical points, atoms, or particles that are divisible to infinity; therefore its existence is impossible."[40] In other words, there are only three candidates for the parts of space – unextended indivisible parts (what Bayle and Hume both call "mathematical points" and sometimes Hume calls "atoms"), extended, indivisible parts (what Bayle calls "atoms" and what Hume calls "physical points"), and extended, divisible parts (thus infinitely divisible parts since every part, being divisible, would itself have parts).[41] Bayle gives arguments against each alternative. He intends to show that reason cannot make sense of the composition of extension. As a fideist, his overall goal is to humble reason so it will not presume to challenge religious faith.

Bayle gives several arguments against infinitely divisible parts. However, he thinks the absurdity of the view is "as clear and evident as the sun" to the unprejudiced: "An infinite number of parts of extension, each of which is extended and distinct from all the others, both with regard to its being and to the place that it occupies, cannot be contained in a space one hundred million times smaller than the hundredth thousandth part of a grain of barley."[42] Hume agrees, of course, and has his own arguments in support of the absurdity of infinite divisibility. Bayle's argument against physical points is as follows: Anything extended has distinct parts, for instance, a left half

---

[40] Bayle, *Historical and Critical Dictionary*, 359. A source for Bayle's trilemma is likely Aristotle, *On Generation and Corruption*, Book I, Chap. 2, 316a17–317a13. It is likely that Berkeley, who was also influenced by Bayle, was another influence on Hume here. See David Raynor, "'Minima Sensibilia' in Berkeley and Hume," *Dialogue* 19 (1980): 196–200; and Ayers, "Berkeley and Hume," 306–14.

[41] Bayle lets it go without saying that what might seem to be a fourth option, namely, unextended, divisible parts, makes no sense. Presumably the explanation is that something that takes up no space cannot have spatial parts.

[42] Bayle, *Historical and Critical Dictionary*, 362.

and a right half. Having distinct parts entails being divisible in the relevant sense of divisible. So there cannot be extended, indivisible points. Hume agrees with this argument as well, noting that the "system of *physical* points ... is too absurd to need a refutation" (T 1.2.4.3).

Bayle's argument against mathematical points derives from Zeno's paradox of extension. Mathematical points are unextended. Thus they have zero length. Adding parts of zero length together yields a whole of zero length no matter how many parts are involved. So no finite interval can be composed of mathematical points. As Hume puts Bayle's argument, "a mathematical point is a non-entity, and consequently can never by its conjunction with others form a real existence" (T 1.2.4.3).[43]

Here Hume disagrees. We do have, after all, an idea of extension as consisting of a conjunction of unextended, indivisible points – the very idea appealed to in Hume's first argument against infinite divisibility. Since we have the idea, extension composed that way must be possible. As Hume says, "'Tis an establish'd maxim in metaphysics ... *that nothing we imagine is absolutely impossible*" (T 1.2.2.8). The extent to which a skeptic is entitled to use established maxims in metaphysics might be debatable, but in this case Hume's reliance on appearance leaves little room for debate. As my sand experiment shows, the idea Hume appeals to can be directly copied from an impression of extension. So we can be sure that extension as it appears can conform to the idea.

Bayle goes wrong by assuming that there is no way to conjoin parts of no length to form a whole of some length.[44] To find a way, Hume thinks, we merely have to use our imaginations. Alternatively we could use the sand experiment. The key is that we do not try to conceive how things are in some pure conceptual space. We stick with appearance. That amounts to "bestowing a colour or solidity on these points," in other words, it amounts to imagining or

---

[43] This contrast with being "a nonentity" is what Hume has in mind when he says the smallest parts of space are filled with something "real and existent" and form "a real existence" (T 1.2.4.2–3).

[44] Bayle's assumption has been questioned also by supporters of Georg Cantor's conception of a line as a set of unextended points. See Adolf Grünbaum, *Modern Science and Zeno's Paradoxes* (Middletown, CT: Wesleyan University Press, 1967), Chap. 3.

sensing them to be occupied by things detectable by sight or touch (T 1.2.4.3). Bayle was right concerning *un*occupied mathematical points that they are no better than nonentities and cannot be conjoined to form an entity. Such points are "inconceivable when not fill'd with something real and existent" (T 1.2.4.2). But filled ones avoid Bayle's conclusion:

'Tis not only requisite, that these atoms shou'd be colour'd or tangible, in order to discover themselves to our senses; 'tis also necessary we shou'd preserve the idea of their colour or tangibility in order to comprehend them by our imagination. There is nothing but the idea of their colour or tangibility, which can render them conceivable by the mind. Upon the removal of the ideas of these sensible qualities, they are utterly annihilated to the thought or imagination. (T 1.2.3.15)

One might object that color and tangibility do not help. The indivisible points must have edges that either touch or not, and they must have shape. If they have edges or shape, then they must have differentiable parts and so can be further subdivided, after all. Further, if they touch, they must totally penetrate each other, since they would have no parts that do not touch (T 1.2.4.4). Alternatively, if they do not touch then there is more to space than Hume's points. Such objections seem forceful, but misunderstand Hume's concern with appearance. The impression received from a barely visible grain of sand accurately reflects a colored or tangible mathematical point. That impression has no edges, no shape. It can "touch" another impression, but only in the sense of there being no indivisible impression between them – a sense that neither entails penetration nor there being something else between them.[45] To understand Hume, we must not make the mistake of thinking that such impressions have geometric characteristics at a level below our ability to discern them.[46]

---

[45] Cf. Richard Sorabji, "Atoms and Time Atoms," in N. Kretzman, ed., *Infinity and Continuity in Ancient and Medieval Thought* (Ithaca, NY: Cornell University Press, 1982), 67. In light of the discussion of vacuums to follow, the definition of *touch* could be emended to read "there being no visible or tangible nor invisible and intangible distance between."

[46] An additional objection to an atomistic theory of space is given by H. Weyl. "If a square is built up of miniature tiles, then there are as many tiles along the diagonal as there are along the side; thus the diagonal should be equal in length to the side." Again this objection assumes that Humean points have precise shapes and

It is not just the points that must be conceived as colored or tangible. As Hume says, "Now such as the parts are, such is the whole." We can only conceive of extension by conceiving of its parts and we can only conceive of them by conceiving of them as colored or tangible. "We have therefore no idea of space or extension, but when we regard it as an object either of our sight or feeling" (T 1.2.3.16).

Manners in Which Objects Exist

The idea of space is the idea of a whole composed of indivisible parts. It is an "*abstract* or *general*" idea, however, not a "*particular*" idea (T 1.1.7.1, 1.2.3.5). In other words, the idea of space is not an idea of a particular vast container or dimension, as one might commonly suppose. Rather, in accordance with Hume's theory of abstract or general ideas, the idea of space is an idea of some arbitrary extended whole, such as a tabletop or a wall, with an eye to the way it resembles other extended wholes. The way extended wholes resemble is specifically the manner in which their indivisible parts are arranged. Thus "space" is synonymous with "extension" for Hume, in the sense of "extendedness."

Hume's view belongs to a family of views about space termed "relational" or "relationist." Contrasting views are termed "absolute" (in the sense given above) or "substantival." In a famous correspondence, Leibniz defended a relational view against the absolute view of the Newtonian, Samuel Clarke.[47] The basis of Hume's relational view of space is his reliance on the copy principle, the principle "*that all our simple ideas in their first appearance are deriv'd from simple impressions, which are correspondent to them, and which they exactly represent*" (T 1.1.1.7). Note that Hume's skepticism, his exclusive concern with appearances, helps motivate the copy principle. An idea of space concerns space as it appears to our senses, or

arrangements below our ability to detect them – an assumption Hume does not grant. He need only say that we find there to be more points along the diagonal of a square than along a side. The arrangement that allows this to happen is beyond us to discover. This situation would be analogous to the way we would find more grains of sand along the diagonal of a square shadow on the beach, when looking down from a boardwalk perhaps. Hermann Weyl, *Philosophy of Mathematics and Natural Science* (Princeton: Princeton University Press, 1949), 43.

[47] H. G. Alexander, ed., *The Leibniz-Clarke Correspondence* (Manchester: Manchester University Press, 1956).

132 DONALD L. M. BAXTER

in other words, as it appears in our sense impressions. Not only does the copy principle help codify his reliance on how things appear in our experience, it gives him a method of making ideas clear. "No discovery cou'd have been made more happily for deciding all controversies concerning ideas, than that above-mention'd," viz., the copy principle. Our ideas are often "obscure" but our impressions "are all so clear and evident, that they admit of no controversy" (T 1.2.3.1).

The idea of space must be derived in some way from some of our impressions. It cannot be derived from "internal impressions" – "our passions, emotions, desires and aversions" (T 1.2.3.3). Such feelings are not spatial. They cannot be conjoined to form something that takes up space (T 1.4.5.9). So the idea must come from impressions conveyed by the senses. The relevant impressions are sensory impressions of things in space, such as a tabletop. "But my senses convey to me only the impressions of colour'd points, dispos'd in a certain manner." It follows "that the idea of extension is nothing but a copy of these colour'd points, and of the manner of their appearance" (T 1.2.3.4).[48]

Without the preparation afforded by the ink spot experiment and without a consideration and rejection of infinite divisibility (especially in the light of the answer to Bayle's challenge), we readers of Hume might easily have overlooked the colored points in our experience. After all, because each is so small and is right next to its nearest neighbor, we too easily run together such points in perception (T 1.2.4.19). However, given that preparation, Hume's characterization is a natural one. When we perceive a table we perceive an expanse with parts we can distinguish even if they are seamlessly connected. Such parts have discernible parts, which themselves have discernible parts, and so on, down to the level of indivisible, partless parts. These last are hard to distinguish precisely, but with the suitable preparation we cannot help but believe they are there.[49]

---

[48] Kemp Smith's suggestion that appeal to ideas of manners is inconsistent with Hume's empiricism is decisively refuted in Lorne Falkenstein, "Hume on Manners of Disposition and the Ideas of Space and Time," *Archiv für Geschichte der Philosophie* 79 (1997): 179–201.

[49] Broad's criticism of Hume here seems to confuse *continuous* in the sense of not having discernible gaps between parts, with *continuous* in the mathematical sense ("Hume's Doctrine of Space," 166–7).

Thus seeing a tabletop gives us an impression, and so an idea, of colored points, perhaps "of a purple colour," arranged in a certain manner. Seeing expanses of other colors, "violet, green, red, white, black, and of all the different compositions of these," gives us the idea of different colored points with similar arrangement. Merely feeling expanses such as marble floors, pillows, oven doors, and so on, that are hard or soft, hot or cold, gives us further ideas of points, tangible ones without color yet with a similar arrangement. It is by noticing the similar manner of being arranged that we get the idea of space (T 1.2.3.5).

Here Hume appeals to his account of abstract ideas, better thought of as *general* ideas. An abstract idea is an idea of some characteristic, some respect in which particular things resemble. For instance, the abstract idea of color would be an idea of the respect of resemblance between colored things; that of green would be an idea of the respect of resemblance between green things. We cannot have an idea of a respect of resemblance without thinking of the things that resemble, according to Hume. We cannot think separately of redness, say; we can only think generally of red things. So we come to have abstract ideas as follows: An idea of a particular thing naturally brings to mind ideas of particulars that resemble it in a certain way. For example, an idea of a tulip may remind one of a similarly colored rose. Which respect of resemblance is in play at a given time is at first arbitrary and inexplicable. But after a while some such associations become habitual and we, by another inexplicable process, begin to associate a word with the particular ideas joined by a given habit. For instance, the word *salty* may bring to mind the idea of the taste of olives and engage the habit of bringing to mind the ideas of other salty tastes such as that of pickles (T 1.1.7). As Hume says, "All abstract ideas are really nothing but particular ones, consider'd in a certain light; but being annex'd to general terms, they are able to represent a vast variety, and to comprehend objects, which, as they are alike in some particulars, are in others vastly wide of each other" (T 1.2.3.5).[50] Thus an abstract idea is the idea of some particular thing insofar as it resembles in a certain way various other particular things. The particular idea is used as a general

---

[50] Here *really* indicates the view forced on the mind as opposed to the view being criticized.

representative or proxy for the various ideas of the various particulars that share the characteristic.[51]

The idea of extension is an abstract or general idea in just the way described. The ideas of a whole composed of purple points, a whole composed of cold points, and so on, all resemble in a certain respect, namely, in the manner in which their indivisible parts are arranged. The abstract idea of extension is an idea of some particular extended whole, insofar as it resembles other extended wholes. In other words, the abstract idea is an idea of an extended whole in general. Now it is clearer why Hume uses the terms *space* and *extension* interchangeably. For us the first word suggests a container of extended things while the second suggests a characteristic of them. For Hume, however, both terms are terms for extended things in general.[52]

Hume does not say much of the manner of arrangement except that the parts coexist. "For that quality of the co-existence of parts belongs to extension, and is what distinguishes it from duration" (T 1.2.3.8). There is more to the arrangement than coexistence, however, because tastes and smells – qualities that Hume thinks cannot have spatial location – can coexist (T 1.4.5.10–12). From his discussion of infinite divisibility it follows that each indivisible part of extension is right next to its nearest neighbors; there is no distance between them. However, this arrangement could be true of simultaneous, barely distinguishable sounds. The best Hume can do to characterize the relevant arrangement of parts is to refer to the arrangement in the context of talking about something extended. This is fine. He is not defining the arrangement; he is only calling our attention to it.

Hume has been charged with circularity in his account of acquiring the idea of space, for it seems as if we must already have the idea of the manner of being arranged in order to notice it.[53] However,

---

[51] For the medieval background of such an account see Julius R. Weinberg, "The Nominalism of Berkeley and Hume," in *Abstraction, Relation, and Induction* (Madison: University of Wisconsin Press, 1965).

[52] The Cartesians also used the terms interchangeably. See Descartes, *Principles of Philosophy*, in *The Philosophical Writings of Descartes*, trans. J. Cottingham, R. Stoothoff, and D. Murdoch, 2 vols. (Cambridge: Cambridge University Press, 1984), 1:227 (Pt. II, Sect. 10).

[53] For instance, in paragraph 259 of T. H. Green's General Introduction to Hume's *A Treatise of Human Nature* (London: Longmans, 1878). The charge may be inspired by Kant's claim that we must have the concept of space – the ability to represent

the charge results from misunderstanding. The manner in which the points are arranged merely serves to bring to mind other points arrayed in a similar manner by the inexplicable process mentioned above. Such association of particular ideas is a quasi-mechanical causal process. Any noticing of a resemblance is no more than the coming to mind of an associated particular idea. It is certainly not the application of a general idea. The general idea of space is not had before the habit of associating the particular ideas with each other is established.

The account of the idea of time is very similar to that of the idea of space:

The idea of time, being deriv'd from the succession of our perceptions of every kind, ideas as well as impressions, and impressions of reflection as well as of sensation, will afford us an instance of an abstract idea, which comprehends a still greater variety than that of space, and yet is represented in the fancy by some particular individual idea of a determinate quantity and quality. (T 1.2.3.6)

The idea of time is an idea of a particular succession of objects, insofar as it resembles other successions of objects. Thus the idea of time is the idea of successiveness, or better, of a succession in general. Cases of succession for Hume are any cases of replacement, or alteration, or movement. He gives the example of five successive notes played on a flute (T 1.2.3.10). This account explains why Hume uses *time* and *duration* interchangeably. For us, the first word suggests some sort of container for objects with duration, while the second suggests a characteristic of them. For Hume, however, they are both terms for enduring things – that is, things with duration – in general.

Hume concludes, "The ideas of space and time are therefore no separate or distinct ideas, but merely those of the manner or order, in which objects exist" (T 1.2.4.2). The idea of a manner or order is not separable from ideas of the things ordered. An idea of a manner

---

things in spatial arrays – logically prior to experiencing space. This claim, however, is not something Hume would disagree with. His ideas are not like Kant's formal concepts. Immanuel Kant, *Critique of Pure Reason*, trans. N. K. Smith (New York: St. Martin's Press, 1965), "Transcendental Aesthetic," Sect. 2; see also Sect. 4 about the concept of time.

or order is a general idea of objects insofar as they are ordered in that manner.

As in the case of indivisible points, Hume investigates the nature of space and time by investigating their ideas. And again this method of investigation is justified by the fact that his concern is with space and time as they appear.

Against the Idea of a Vacuum

Hume's view is that we can only conceive of space and time by means of abstract, that is, general, ideas. In other words we can only conceive them by means of particular ideas – ideas of particular things – used generally to represent resembling particular things. A consequence of this view is that we cannot conceive of a vacuum, or empty space. Nor can we conceive of time passing with nothing changing. Hume's view seems open to the objection that of course we can conceive of both a vacuum and a period of time without change. The possibility of such ideas is provided for by Newton's authoritative conceptions of absolute space and absolute time. Hume responds, however, that we do not actually have these ideas. We only imagine (in some sense) that we do.

These ideas of a vacuum and changeless time would be possible only if the ideas of time and space were literally separable from the ideas of things that occupy them – separable as in Locke's account of abstraction.[54] However, Hume has taken care to show that they are not separable. He details his point for time:

In order to know whether any objects, which are join'd in impression, be separable in idea, we need only consider, if they be different from each other; in which case, 'tis plain they may be conceiv'd apart. Every thing, that is different, is distinguishable; and every thing, that is distinguishable, may be separated, according to the maxims above-explain'd.[55] If on the contrary they be not different, they are not distinguishable; and if they be not distinguishable, they cannot be separated. But this is precisely the case with respect to time, compar'd with our successive perceptions. The idea of time is not deriv'd from a particular impression mix'd up with others, and plainly distinguishable from them; but arises altogether from the manner, in

---

[54] See Locke 2.11.9, 2.12.1, 3.3.6–9, 3.6.32.
[55] These maxims are first mentioned at T 1.1.3.4, 1.1.7.3.

which impressions appear to the mind, without making one of the number. (T 1.2.3.10)

Nor is the idea of space derived from a particular, separable impression mixed up with the impressions of colored and tangible points. As Hume puts the inference for space: "If the second part of my system be true, *that the idea of space or extension is nothing but the idea of visible or tangible points distributed in a certain order;* it follows, that we can form no idea of a vacuum, or space, where there is nothing visible or tangible" (T 1.2.5.1).

Hume restricts his attention here to the impossibility of the *idea* of a vacuum, and does not explicitly say that a vacuum is impossible. There is no need to. He has already said that space consists of indivisible parts that would be nonexistent unless they were colored or tangible. The "absurdity" of alternative views demonstrates the "truth and reality" of his own. Thus space not only must be conceived to be "fill'd with something real and existent," it also must really be so (1.2.4.1–3).[56] Section 1.2.4 is an extended defense of the claim that space consists of colored or solid points. Later he calls extension, a "composition of visible and tangible objects" (1.2.5.14). In the case of time Hume explicitly switches from talk of there being no *idea* of changeless duration to talk of there being no changeless duration. Since what is at issue, given Hume's Pyrrhonian Empiricism, is time and space as they appear, it follows that neither empty space nor changeless time can exist. Neither time nor space can appear to us except as indivisible, partless things arranged in the appropriate manner.

Having shown that space is filled with colored or tangible things, Hume is concerned to show that we do not even have an idea of a vacuum, despite seemingly strong arguments to the contrary. Hume puts his point in a potentially confusing way: Even though we "falsly imagine we can form such an idea" of a vacuum, we cannot really have such an idea (T 1.2.5.14).

How could we literally imagine that we have an idea without having an idea of the imagined idea? On Hume's account, ideas are like pictures. A picture of a picture of a centaur can be used as a picture of a centaur. Likewise an idea of an idea of a vacuum could

---

[56] Here again Hume is talking about what is really true of the world as it appears.

be used as an idea of a vacuum. So it does not make sense to say that we literally imagine we have ideas that we cannot really have.

Hume must be using the phrase "falsly imagine we can form such an idea" in another legitimate but not absolutely literal sense. He must mean that we falsely talk as if we have such an idea. We use the phrases "empty space" or "vacuum" as if there were a coherent idea corresponding to these terms. There is not really one, he argues. Instead of a coherent idea we have a confounding of distinct ideas (see also T 1.2.5.21). In explaining Hume's thinking I will limit myself to considering vision, though he gives analogous details for the sense of touch.

One might think we could get the idea of empty space from an experience of darkness. But, Hume argues, darkness fails to give us any visual impression from which an idea could be copied. Being in a lightless cave, for instance, gives one no visual experience, rather than a visual experience of black. When one sees something black, one can discern parts of it, Hume thinks. However when, as a result of darkness, one lacks visual experience, there are no parts to discern. One gets "no perception different from what a blind man receives from his eyes" (T 1.2.5.11). Thus there are no visual ideas of the lack of something visible. There is only the lack of visual ideas.

This conclusion holds true even if distant visible things appear in the darkness, such as stars in a night sky. The stars give the viewer visual impressions and so ideas, but the darkness does not. In such a case the stars are experienced as distant from each other yet not as spatially separated. They are not experienced as spatially separated because between the impressions of the stars there is no extended impression that could give rise to an idea of space. There is no impression at all, much less one with parts. So, he says of "the very distance, which is interpos'd betwixt them," it is "nothing but darkness, or the negation of light; without parts, without composition, invariable and indivisible" (T 1.2.5.11). Such a distance cannot give rise to the abstract idea of space, so the idea cannot properly be applied to it (see T 1.2.3.11). Nonetheless the stars are perceived as distant from each other in some sense, because they affect different parts of the eye so that the impressions of them are not directly adjacent. Hume uses the word "distance" of this separation, but calls it an "invisible and intangible distance" to contrast with extension that is visible or tangible distance.[57] Thus he distinguishes "two kinds of distance" (1.2.5.16–17).

Such a distinction might well seem strange, but it is appropriate if we confine our attention to the world as it appears. We can distinguish distant things between which other things appear, from distant things between which no other things appear. The former distance is "mark'd out by compounded and sensible objects," whereas the latter is "known only by the manner, in which the distant objects affect the senses" (T 1.2.5.17). The differing ways in which things are experienced can render important differences in the world as it appears. In this case what makes the difference is whether or not the stars are experienced by means of impressions that have impressions in between. In the world as it appears, the stars are either separated by visible or tangible distance or by invisible and intangible distance, depending, for example, on whether or not the sky is dark.

In a case of stars in the darkness, although we perceive no intervening locations, no parts of space, we assume there are such. Why? Because the idea of invisible and intangible distance is closely related to the idea of visible or tangible distance, and so we confuse them.

First, the angle at which light rays from the distant things strike the eye can be the same whether the distance is invisible and intangible or is visible or tangible: "two visible objects appearing in the midst of utter darkness, affect the senses in the same manner, and form the same angle by the rays, which flow from them, and meet in the eye, as if the distance betwixt them were fill'd with visible objects, that give us a true idea of extension" (T 1.2.5.15). Hume later retracts his claim that we know the angle, perhaps under further consideration of Berkeley's New Theory of Vision (A 22).[58] But the fact is that the sensations of moving the eye from direct contemplation of one thing to direct contemplation of another are the same whether the distance is invisible and intangible or is visible or tangible (T 1.2.5.15).

---

[57] Broad gives an attractive but less textually bound account of the contrast between the two sorts of distance ("Hume's Doctrine of Space," 173). Hume also calls invisible and intangible distance "imaginary" when arrived at purely by kinesthetic sensations (T 1.2.5.13) and "fictitious" when confused with extension (T 1.2.5.23).

[58] George Berkeley, An Essay towards a New Theory of Vision, in The Works of George Berkeley, 1: 171–4 (Sects. 4–15).

Second, invisible and intangible distance can be "converted" into visible or tangible distance merely by putting something between the things. For instance, as dawn approaches and the sky gains some color, the distance between two stars can shift to a visible distance. Given Hume's concern solely with the world as it appears, it is irrelevant that beyond our atmosphere the real space between the stars remains uncolored. He is concerned only with the way the distance is experienced. In fact, as far as Hume is concerned one could convert the invisible and intangible distance between the stars into visible or tangible distance merely by holding a strip of white paper so that the distant stars appear adjacent to each end of the strip. His distinction between visible or tangible distance and invisible and intangible distance is purely a matter of how things appear to the senses. The impressions of points of the paper are between the impressions of the stars, he thinks, even if the paper is not literally between the stars. Hume assumes, as does for instance Locke,[59] that our visual field is like a flat plane: "'Tis commonly allow'd by philosophers, that all bodies, which discover themselves to the eye, appear as if painted on a plane surface, and that their different degrees of remoteness from ourselves are discover'd more by reason than by the senses" (T 1.2.5.8; see also T 1.2.5.16). In any event invisible and intangible distance has the capability of being converted into visible or tangible distance.

Third, both kinds of distance diminish the force of other qualities of a distant object: "For as all qualities, such as heat, cold, light, attraction, &c. diminish in proportion to the distance; there is but little difference observ'd, whether this distance be mark'd out by compounded and sensible objects, or be known only by the manner, in which distant objects affect the senses" (T 1.2.5.17). The further your friend's flashlight is from an object, the dimmer it shines on that object. This is so whether you see the flashlight and the object at the shore, against the backdrop of a lightless sky, or in the woods, against the backdrop of mist and trees.

The first and third of these close relations are instances of resemblance. The second, Hume says, is an instance of cause and effect. Presumably he is assuming that capability, like power, is understood in terms of cause and effect (T 2.1.10). So the capability of being

---

[59] Locke, *Essay concerning Human Understanding*, 2.9.8.

converted into visible or tangible distance is understood in terms of cause and effect. These close relations make it easy for the mind to use one idea in the place of the other. When we talk about a case in which the distance is properly speaking invisible and intangible, an idea of visible or tangible distance is likely to come to mind instead. (The mental slip does not seem to go in the other direction, perhaps because the perception of visible or tangible distance is so much more common.) Thus when we think of two distant stars in the night sky we have two ideas without any ideas between them. Immediately and unawares we add between them an array of spatially minimal ideas endowed, say, with the color black – an array of ideas that can serve as the general idea of space. At first, there is nothing between the star ideas, so we characterize the distance as *empty*. Then immediately there are ideas in between, so we go on to characterize the distance as *space*. We do not notice, however, that we have shifted from an idea of an invisible and intangible distance to an idea of a visible or tangible distance. Thus we talk of *empty space* although we have no coherent idea of such a thing. An idea that would literally be an idea of empty space would have to be an idea with both nothing and something between the ideas of the stars. It would be an idea of invisible and intangible distance that is visible or tangible. Oblivious to the incoherence we come, as time goes on, to use other expressions, such as *vacuum*, interchangeably with *empty space*.

Hume uses this account to answer the three seemingly strong arguments for the claim that we have an idea of a vacuum. The first is that we must have an idea of vacuums since we argue about them. Hume's response is just that we "imagine," in the way just explained, that we have the idea. The second argument is that we can conceive the matter within a cube to be annihilated without motion of the sides of the cube, and in so doing we are having an idea of a vacuum. Not so, Hume replies, we are rather having an idea of what he has called invisible and intangible distance. The third argument is that we must conceive there to be vacuums in the world in order to conceive there to be room for things to move. If the world were a plenum there would always be something in the way to prevent motion. Invisible and intangible distance can do the same work, says Hume. It is easily converted into visible or tangible distance by things moving in between the bodies that border the invisible and intangible distance. Invisible and intangible distance, not a vacuum, is what we have an idea of (T 1.2.5.22–4).

One might object that Hume's claim to have no idea of empty space is just an artifact of his decision to use the word *space* to refer to one kind of distance. Why not use it to refer to distance in general? Then invisible and intangible distance could be called *empty space* without contradiction. Hume's reply would be that geometry gives the properties of space. There can be no geometry, however, of invisible and intangible distance. There would be no points to compose lines and planes. A spatial point with neither color nor solidity is a "non-entity" (T 1.2.4.3). Since there can be no geometry of invisible and intangible distance, it is not space. In sum, space as dealt with in geometry has parts; invisible and intangible distance lacks parts.

One might further object that Hume is simply discussing appearances of things but not their real natures: "'Twill probably be said, that my reasoning makes nothing to the matter in hand, and that I explain only the manner in which objects affect the senses, without endeavouring to account for their real nature and operations." Thus the charge is that he is merely finessing arguments that there must really be vacuums in the world. Hume blithely responds, "I answer this objection, by pleading guilty, and by confessing that my intention never was to penetrate into the nature of bodies, or explain the secret causes of their operations." The world as it appears is the only legitimate concern of the Pyrrhonian Empiricist (T 1.2.5.25–6).

Against the Idea of Time without Change

Just as one cannot conceive of space except by conceiving of objects coexisting, so one cannot conceive of time except by conceiving of objects in succession. Hume's "doctrine" is "that time is nothing but the manner, in which some real objects exist" (T 1.2.5.28).[60] From this doctrine he concludes that we cannot conceive of a "stedfast and unchangeable" object enduring through time. We only imagine that we can conceive it. Hume promises to consider, "By what fiction we apply the idea of time, even to what is unchangeable, and suppose, as is common, that duration is a measure of rest as well as of motion" (T 1.2.3.11).

---

[60] Here again being real contrasts with not existing; see notes 24, 36.

The connection between the doctrine and the conclusions is Hume's denial that a steadfast object endures through time. Here Hume is roughly concerned with the general issue raised by Aristotle, whether there can be time without change.[61] His concern is not whether there can be time in a steadfast, changeless universe, or in an empty universe. Clearly, for time as it appears he would think not; if there is no succession, then there is no manner in which successive objects exist. As for Newton's claim that "absolute true, and mathematical time, of itself, and from its own nature, flows equably without relation to anything external," he would suspend judgment.[62] In any event, his concern is rather with the more immediate cases of particular steadfast objects, such as stones and houses. His claim that these do not endure might seem implausible, and so he has to explain himself:

I know there are some who pretend, that the idea of duration is applicable in a proper sense to objects, which are perfectly unchangeable; and this I take to be the common opinion of philosophers as well as of the vulgar. But to be convinc'd of its falshood we need but reflect on the foregoing conclusion, that the idea of duration is always deriv'd from a succession of changeable objects, and can never be convey'd to the mind by anything stedfast and unchangeable. (T 1.2.3.11)

Because the idea of time or duration is a general idea of successions, nonsuccessions cannot convey it to the mind. Changeable objects are ones that alter, move, or are replaced by others. Steadfast and unchangeable objects are ones that neither alter nor move, and that are not replaced for a while. The flames in a fireplace are examples of changeable objects, whereas the mantle above the fireplace is an example of a steadfast one. The examples do not have to be external objects, however. When a person is "strongly occupy'd with one thought," that thought is a steadfast object. Hume specifically contrasts steadfast objects with successions. Steadfast objects are not successions, so cannot convey the idea of duration: "an unchangeable object, since it produces none but co-existent impressions, produces none that can give us the idea of time; and consequently that idea must be deriv'd from a succession of changeable objects, and time in its first appearance can never be sever'd from such a

---

[61] *Physics* IV, 11.
[62] Newton, *Principia*, 1:6.

succession" (T 1.2.3.7–8). Hume goes on to conclude that steadfast objects do not endure, that is, do not have duration:

For it inevitably follows from thence, that since the idea of duration cannot be deriv'd from such an object, it can never in any propriety or exactness be apply'd to it, nor can any thing unchangeable be ever said to have duration. Ideas always represent the objects or impressions, from which they are deriv'd, and can never without a fiction represent or be apply'd to any other. (T 1.2.3.11)

Note that Hume has not argued that steadfast objects are not in time. They are in time, insofar as they are members of larger successions. It is just that they do not have duration because they are not successions themselves.

Once it is clear that steadfast objects are not successions, it becomes obvious why Hume says we can have no idea of a steadfast object with duration. Duration is successiveness. No impression could give rise to the idea in question unless it were an impression of a succession without successiveness. "But if you cannot point out *any such impression*, you may be certain you are mistaken, when you imagine you have *any such idea*" (T 1.2.5.28).

Despite not being successions and so lacking duration, individual steadfast objects can coexist with successions. For example, the single thought with which the person is strongly occupied can coexist with a "real succession in the objects."[63] That person would be "insensible of time" though it would be passing, because there would not be a succession of impressions reflecting the successions in the world (T 1.2.3.7).

If a steadfast object were a whole made up of a succession of parts, then it would endure. It would be the succession of its parts. Since it does not endure, it has no parts. Yet it coexists with some successions. So bigger, temporally partless things can coexist with smaller temporally partless things.

It is because all steadfast objects coexist with successions that we tend, falsely, to imagine in a confused way that they have duration as well: "But tho' it be impossible to show the impression, from which

---

[63] Here by *real* Hume means that the succession of objects is outside the mind in the world as it appears, instead of merely being a succession of perceptions in the mind. (Of course, there is more to the world as it appears than just what appears to the person "strongly occupy'd with one thought.")

the idea of time without a changeable existence is deriv'd; yet we can easily point out those appearances, which make us fancy we have that idea" (T 1.2.5.29; see also T 1.2.3.11, 1.2.5.28, 1.4.2.29). Just as there are two kinds of spatial distance so there are two kinds of temporal separation. Objects in time can be separated by an intervening steadfast object (temporal separation by something unchanging, that is, by something without duration), as well as by an intervening succession (temporal separation by something changing, that is, by something with duration). Because of the close relations between these two separations, we tend inadvertently to substitute the second when thinking about the first. Just as we imagine that we have an idea of a vacuum, we imagine we have the idea of an enduring steadfast object.

The relations between the two kinds of temporal separation parallel those between the two kinds of distance, and so Hume only briefly explains the process of arriving at the falsely imagined idea of changeless duration. The reader is clearly meant to fill in the details based on the previous discussion. First, we can "consider a stedfast object at five-a-clock, and regard the same at six," just as we can consider the chiming of the clock at 5:00 and then at 6:00. Between these noticings the action of the mind about its other business can be the same. "The first and second appearances of the object, being compar'd with the succession of our perceptions, seem equally remov'd as if the object had really chang'd."[64] This is analogous to the motion of the eye being the same whether attending to things at invisible and intangible distance or at visible or tangible distance. Second, "the object was susceptible of such a number of changes betwixt these appearances." It might have changed even if it did not. It might have been moved or painted or whatever. So the potential for change in a case of changeless temporal separation puts one in mind of change in a duration. This is analogous to the way the capacity of invisible and intangible distance to be converted into visible or tangible distance relates those two in the mind. Third, qualities of objects separated by a perceived changeless temporal separation undergo the same changes as those separated by a perceived duration: "the unchangeable or rather fictitious duration has the same effect

---

[64] Here *really* indicates how appearance really is as opposed to how it is falsely supposed to be.

upon every quality, by encreasing or diminishing it, as that succession, which is obvious to the senses." When one returns one's gaze to the fire after contemplating the unchanging view out the window for a while, the fire is perceived to have burned down as much as if one had been continuously watching it dance. Analogously, invisible and intangible distance has the same effect on the qualities of distant objects as visible or tangible distance (T 1.2.5.29).

These close relations make us "fancy we have that idea" of duration in which nothing changes. The idea of the steadfast object accompanying the phrase *nothing changes* is replaced by an idea appropriate to the word *duration*. Perhaps the replacement idea is of a close succession of objects each resembling the steadfast object. Thus one talks as if the phrase *duration in which nothing changes* stands for a coherent idea. We then come to use other phrases as equivalent, such as *time without a changeable existence* (T 1.2.5.29).

CONCLUSION

Hume's system concerning space and time cannot be understood without seeing it as a consequence of his Pyrrhonian Empiricism. His exclusive concern with views forced on him by appearances leads him to claim that space and time consist of indivisible points and cannot be conceived without them. Very likely he expected that agreement from his readers would come rather easily. After all he was arguing, as he saw it, on the side of common sense concerning the core issue of infinite divisibility, an issue over which "philosophy and common sense . . . have waged most cruel wars with each other" (A 29). Ironically, his discussion of space and time has met with determined resistance. The resistance has been misdirected, however. If one wants to engage Hume concerning his views on space and time, one must at the same time grapple with the skepticism on which they depend.

5   Hume on Causation

Hume's theory of causation is one of the most famous and influential parts of his philosophy. When compared with the accounts provided by earlier philosophers whom Hume studied, such as René Descartes (1596–1650), John Locke (1632–1704), and Nicolas Malebranche (1638–1715), his theory is revolutionary. It is also controversial, and has been interpreted in a number of different ways. This is not surprising, because Hume's ideas about causation are not only challenging in themselves, but also lie at the heart of much of the rest of his thought. As a result, interpretations of Hume on causation influence, and are influenced by, interpretations of his general philosophical aims, methods, and purposes.

Hume's account of causation is part of his theory of human nature or "science of man." The theory is a partly epistemological, partly psychological investigation of how human beings acquire beliefs and knowledge, make moral, political, and aesthetic judgments, and act in and react to the natural and social world. Hume's approach to these questions is genetic. He sets out to identify the origins of thoughts, feelings, judgments, and patterns of behavior and response. His theory of causation, therefore, is not primarily a metaphysical account of what causality consists in, although it has implications for that. Rather, it is an investigation of two main questions. First, how do human beings come to have the idea of causation? Second, how do human beings come to be able to infer effects from causes and causes from effects? Hume's answer to the first question is that the idea of causal connections between objects and events depends genetically on the capacity to infer causes from effects and vice versa. His answer to the second question is that the capacity to make causal inferences does not originate in reason or a priori knowledge but in

147

the way in which experience of repeated regular sequences of events affects the imagination. Thus in Hume's theory the answer to the first question depends on the answer to the second, and not, as one might expect, the other way round.

While Hume's answers to these questions are the core of his account of causation, there are other ways in which causation is central to his philosophy. The theory of human nature, or science of man, as a genetic investigation of the origins of human cognitive and emotional life, is itself a causal theory. It is, he says, "AN ATTEMPT TO INTRODUCE THE EXPERIMENTAL METHOD OF REASONING INTO MORAL SUBJECTS."[1] By the use of the experimental method Hume means the attempt to discover causal laws on the basis of observation and experience rather than on the basis of supposed rational insight into the essence or nature of things.[2] The distinction between the experimental method on the one hand and supposed rational insight into the nature of things on the other, and Hume's adoption of the one and rejection of the other, is itself supported by his central arguments about the idea of causation and the nature of causal inference. The arguments have consequences for the methodology of both natural and moral philosophy.[3] The application of the experimental method to human nature is predicated on the assumption that there can be no knowledge of the "essence" of the mind, or of "the ultimate original qualities of human nature." Knowledge of the principles of human nature, like knowledge of the principles of nature in general, is built up gradually from observation of particular events, the formation of beliefs about their causes, the bringing of particular causal connections under more general causal laws, and the "endeavour to render all our principles as universal as possible, by tracing up our experiments to the utmost, and explaining all effects from the simplest and fewest causes" (T Intro. 8). Causation, it is clear, is central to Hume's methodology.

---

[1] From the subtitle of the *Treatise*.

[2] See T Intro. 7.

[3] In Hume's time *natural philosophy* meant roughly what is meant today by *natural science*, although what sciences these terms cover and how they are differentiated has changed. *Moral philosophy* meant the study of what today we regard as history, economic and political theory, logic, epistemology and metaphysics, aesthetics, and ethics.

Hume also uses his theory of causation in critical discussions of philosophical questions in moral philosophy and natural theology. In both the *Treatise* (T 2.3.1–2) and the first *Enquiry* (Sect. 8) he examines the question "of liberty and necessity," that is, the question whether human actions are causally determined and whether, if so, this should lead us to revise or abandon the ways in which we ascribe and accept moral responsibility for them. Exactly what Hume argues in these sections is not something that can be considered in this essay.[4] But certainly part of Hume's arguments in both books is that his revolutionary theory of causation enables him to throw new light on a perennial problem and, he thinks, to resolve it. Another equally famous application of his theory comes in his critical attacks, in the first *Enquiry* (Sect. 11) and the *Dialogues concerning Natural Religion*, on the design argument for the existence of God. In these attacks Hume argues that any inference from what we can observe of the nature of the world considered as an effect, to an omnipotent and wholly benevolent Deity considered as its cause, violates a range of principles that follow from his theory of causal inference.[5]

In short, Hume's theory of causation is a revolutionary and influential discussion that plays a central role in his overall philosophical project and is used both constructively and critically in examining other philosophical issues. The sections that follow examine the theory in detail and consider some of the interpretative problems that it poses.

---

[4] For discussion of these sections see in this volume the essay "Hume's Moral Psychology." Other discussions include Paul Russell, *Freedom and Moral Sentiment* (New York: Oxford University Press, 1995); Don Garrett, *Cognition and Commitment in Hume's Philosophy* (New York: Oxford University Press, 1997), 118–36; George Botterill, "Hume on Liberty and Necessity," in *Reading Hume on Human Understanding: Essays on the First Enquiry*, ed. P. Millican (Oxford: Clarendon Press, 2002), 277–300; James Harris, *Of Liberty and Necessity: The Free Will Debate in Eighteenth-Century British Philosophy* (Oxford: Clarendon Press, 2005), 64–87.

[5] See, for example, J. C. A. Gaskin, *Hume's Philosophy of Religion*, 2nd ed. (London: Macmillan, 1988); David O'Connor, *Routledge Philosophy Guidebook to Hume on Religion* (London: Routledge, 2001). It should be noted that in both the *Enquiry* and the *Dialogues* criticisms of the design argument are put forward by fictional characters rather than by the author of the work in his own voice.

I. CAUSAL INFERENCE

One task for the theory of human nature is to explain how belief and knowledge arise. Empirical beliefs about matters of fact may result from sense perception and memory alone, but a great many beliefs of this kind concern matters of fact that lie beyond the evidence provided by perception and memory. Where such beliefs are products of reasoning they are conclusions inferred from other factual beliefs, and ultimately from beliefs produced by perception and memory. To take one factual belief as evidence for another, to infer one from the other, Hume claims, is to assume that there is a causal connection between the states of affairs that are believed to obtain. For example, to take puddles on the pavement as evidence that it has been raining is to assume that rain caused the puddles. Someone whose assumption about the cause of the puddles was different, for example, someone who supposed that they were caused by a water sprinkler, would draw a different conclusion from observing the puddles. In the kind of reasoning in which human beings draw conclusions about the existence of something they do not observe from the existence of something they do observe, they "trace the relation of cause and effect" (T 1.3.5.7). Hume's theory is that reasoning from factual evidence is reasoning from causes to effects, or from effects to causes.

Hume's account of causal reasoning is, as part of his theory of human nature, an investigation into how human beings acquire the capacity to infer causes from effects and vice versa. He argues that in no case can such inferences be made a priori. This is an important part of Hume's theory, and his reason for it plays a major role not only in the explanation of causal inference, but also in the account of the origin of the idea of causation. He means that when we observe an object or event, we cannot infer, merely from the idea we acquire from this impression, any other object or event as the cause or the effect of what we observe:

'Tis easy to observe, that in tracing [the relation of cause and effect], the inference we draw from cause to effect, is not deriv'd merely from a survey of these particular objects, and from such a penetration into their essences as may discover the dependance of the one upon the other. There is no object, which implies the existence of any other if we consider these objects in themselves, and never look beyond the ideas which we form of them. Such an inference wou'd amount to knowledge, and wou'd imply the absolute contradiction and impossibility of conceiving any thing different. But as all distinct ideas are separable, 'tis evident there can be no impossibility of that kind. When we pass from a present impression to the idea of any object, we might possibly have separated the idea from the impression, and have substituted any other idea in its room [or place]. (T 1.3.6.1)

In the first *Enquiry*, Hume argues that even if two objects or events are causally connected, they are, nevertheless, distinct and different from each other. Their ideas in the imagination are separable, and so, if we are proceeding a priori and not on the basis of previous experience, when we think of one object we could always think of any other object we like as a possible cause or effect. Any choice is as arbitrary as any other. The imagination is free to put together any two different and separable ideas. Nothing about the idea of a particular object or event fixes, or, to use Hume's terminology, *determines* the imagination to put them together:[6]

In a word, then, every effect is a distinct event from its cause. It could not, therefore, be discovered in the cause, and the first invention or conception of it, *a priori*, must be entirely arbitrary. And even after it is suggested, the conjunction of it with the cause must appear equally arbitrary; since there are always many other effects, which, to reason, must seem fully as consistent and natural. In vain, therefore, should we pretend to determine any single event, or infer any cause or effect, without the assistance of observation and experience. (EHU 4.11)

Causal inference, Hume concludes, is impossible a priori and is dependent on observation and experience. The feature of experience that he identifies as crucial is repetition. A person who experiences for the first time the occurrence of an event of kind A succeeded by the occurrence of an event of kind B will not think of A-type events as causes of B-type events, nor, if and when an event of either type is next experienced, will the person normally infer that an event of the

---

[6] For Hume's notion of *determination* and its importance in his thought, see Annette C. Baier, *A Progress of Sentiments: Reflections on Hume's* Treatise (Cambridge, MA: Harvard University Press, 1991), 78–100. For Hume's notion of a priori inference, and the contrast between "arbitrary" and "determined," see Peter Millican, "Hume's Sceptical Doubts concerning Induction" in *Reading Hume on Human Understanding*, 107–69.

other type has occurred or will occur.[7] However, Hume claims, if AB sequences occur repeatedly in a person's experience the person will come to infer that a B-type event will occur when he or she experiences an A-type event, and to infer that an A-type event has occurred when a B-type event is experienced. At the same time the person will come to believe that A-type events cause B-type events. In brief, on this theory human beings require experience before they can make causal inferences, and this experience takes the form of repetition of regular sequences of events.

Experiencing repeated regular sequences of events is a causally necessary condition for acquiring the capacity to make causal inferences. After such experience the conjunction of the cause and the effect no longer appears to the mind as arbitrary. Rather, after repeated experience of a regular sequence of events of types A and B, when a token (an example) of the one type is next experienced the mind is "determined" to infer the occurrence of a token of the other type. We make causal inferences, then, "in conformity to our past experience" (T 1.3.6.2). Hume now asks what else, besides experience of what he calls the "constant conjunction" of events, is needed in order to make causal inferences. How does the experience of regularity result in the determination of the mind to expect the regularity to continue? Why do we expect that further instances of the same types of event will occur "in conformity to our past experience"?

Causal inferences are always made in a way that manifests the assumption that causal connections are uniform in all times and places. In one of his most famous arguments, Hume claims to prove that this assumption of the uniformity of causal connections cannot be established as the conclusion of any form of reasoned argument. There are, he says, no *"demonstrative arguments"* to prove the principle *"that instances, of which we have had no experience, must resemble those, of which we have had experience, and that the course of nature continues always uniformly the same"* (T 1.3.6.4–5). By a *demonstrative argument* Hume means the kind of proof of a proposition that shows that it could not possibly be false, that it is necessarily true in what he calls the "absolute" sense that

---

[7] However, Hume does grant that once the habit of causal inference has been established, a single, carefully designed experiment may be enough to produce inference. See, for example, T 1.3.8.14, 1.3.15.6.

characterizes mathematical truths such as "$2 + 2 = 4$."[8] Where
something can be demonstrated, Hume thinks, the mind is determined to conceive the proposition by reason alone: "When a demonstration convinces me of any proposition, it not only makes me conceive the proposition, but also makes me sensible, that 'tis impossible to conceive any thing contrary. What is demonstratively false
implies a contradiction; and what implies a contradiction cannot be
conceived" (A 18). But we can conceive that the constant conjunctions of events that we have experienced so far will not continue in
the future; we can conceive a change in the course of nature.

If the principle of the uniformity of nature is not provable a priori, by a demonstrative argument, can it be inferred on the basis of
evidence? Hume argues that it cannot. Any proof of it by inference
from what we have so far experienced would be circular, because
inference from past experience would already assume the point in
question. Therefore, it is not possible to explain how experience
enables human beings to make causal inferences and acquire causal
beliefs by appealing to their capacity for reason.

This famous argument, commonly referred to as Hume's skepticism about induction, is central to his account of the origin of
the ability to make causal inferences. Because memory and reason
alone cannot be the basis on which we make causal inferences and
draw on our previous experience to form our expectations of what
will happen in new cases, Hume concludes that there is another
principle of human nature whose effect on the mind accounts for
our causal inferences. This is the principle of "custom" or "habit"
(T 1.3.8.12, 1.3.12.9). When there is repeated experience of the conjunction of types of events, the ideas of these types of events become
associated in the imagination by custom. What this means is that
the imagination comes to be structured in such a way that within it
the ideas of types of events that have been repeatedly experienced as
conjoined are connected together. The imagination becomes habit-
uated to move from one idea to another without any intermediate
step.[9] Repeated experience of the conjunction of A-type events with

---

[8] T 1.3.7.3.
[9] Although Hume sometimes uses the terms *custom* and *habit* as if they designated
the same phenomenon, it seems better to think of *custom* as denoting the way
in which repetitions of experience lead to ideas being associated in the imagination, and *habit* as denoting a resulting tendency for the imagination to transfer its

B-type events produces a belief in the occurrence of a token event of the one type when a token event of the other type is experienced. Hume, then, gives a causal explanation of the ability to make causal inferences, an explanation that presents this ability as the effect of a fundamental principle of human nature, custom, or habit. After experiencing events of types A and B constantly conjoined, when another instance of an A-type event is observed it is not reason that determines the mind to infer that a B-type event will occur. What determines the mind is custom and habit.[10]

II. THE IDEA OF NECESSARY CONNECTION

In arguing for his theory of how we come to be able to make causal inferences Hume claims (1) that no such inference can be made a priori, (2) that experience of the constant conjunction of types of events is necessary before we can infer one from the other, and (3) that even after we have such experience it is not reason but custom that determines the mind to make the inference. One might be inclined to object that the move from (2) to (3) rests on too thin a notion of what experience of regular sequences of events reveals. As we have seen, Hume speaks of the experience of "constant conjunctions." He means by this experience of events of two types, A and B, always occurring in "a regular order of contiguity and succession": that is, A-type and B-type events always occur without any spatial or temporal interval between them, and A-type events always precede B-type events (T 1.3.6.2).[11] However, as Hume himself points out, the idea that A causes B is not just the idea that A-type events and B-type events are constantly related by priority and contiguity. The idea that A causes B includes as a most important element the idea that B *must* occur if A occurs. This idea, that a B-type event

---

attention and the vivacity of its conception from one idea to another customarily associated with it. Hume refers to the habitual movement of the mind from one idea to another as a "transition," and he says that the transition of the mind is essential to relations (see, e.g., T 1.3.5.1, 1.4.2.34).

[10] For Hume's own summary account of the process by which we come to make causal inferences and believe in causal connections, see A 8–26.

[11] In the *Treatise* Hume argues that there cannot be an event that is the direct effect of a cause that is spatially distant from it; cause and effect must be contiguous. In the first *Enquiry* he no longer treats the contiguity of cause and effect as essential to direct causation. In both works he says, however, that causes must be temporally prior to their effects.

necessarily occurs whenever an A-type event occurs is what Hume calls the idea of *necessary connexion* (T 1.3.2.11). But if experience shows that A-type events are necessarily connected to B-type events, would that not imply, once there has been sufficient experience to reveal this connection, that the inference from the observation of an A-type event to a B-type event is, after all, determined by reason?

For Hume, this line of thought is misconceived. He seeks to show that the idea that causes and effects are necessarily connected is one that could not arise simply from the experience of the constant conjunctions of events. In fact, once there has been experience of such a conjunction, it is only because the mind is determined by custom to infer future events in conformity to past experience that the idea of a necessary connection between causes and effects arises. The experience of mere constant conjunctions alone, without the effect of custom and habit on the imagination, would not produce this idea. That is why in both the *Treatise* and the first *Enquiry* the sections entitled *Of the idea of necessary connexion* (T 1.3.14, EHU 7) come after Hume has argued that inferences from causes and effects depend not on reason but on custom and habit. These sections provide an answer to the question *"What is our idea of necessity, when we say that two objects are necessarily connected together!"* (T 1.3.14.1). The answer appeals to the customary associations between ideas of objects that have been repeatedly experienced as occurring together in succession, and the resulting habitual transitions of the mind from the one to the other.

In the *Treatise* the section on the idea of necessary connection briefly outlines Hume's theory of the origin of this idea right at the start, in the first paragraph. Following his principle that ideas are derived from impressions, Hume considers what relevant impressions we have of any two objects that we take to be related as cause and effect. Examining a single case, he says, reveals only that impressions of the cause are temporally prior to the effect, and that the two impressions are spatially and temporally contiguous. There is no impression of a third relation that could give rise to the idea of a necessary connection.[12] If we proceed to consider multiple instances of the same kind of cause and effect, these same relations of priority

---

[12] See T 1.3.2.12 and the Editors' Annotation to this text in *A Treatise of Human Nature*, ed. D. F. Norton and M. J. Norton, 2 vols. (Oxford: Clarendon Press, 2007), 2:735.

and contiguity are repeated. At first sight it appears that repetition does not produce any new impression. Hume says, however, that repetition does in fact produce a new impression, for it changes the way the mind responds to an experience of one of the constantly conjoined objects: "For after a frequent repetition, I find, that upon the appearance of one of the objects, the mind is *determin'd* by custom to consider its usual attendant, and to consider it in a stronger light upon account of its relation to the first object. 'Tis this impression, then, or *determination*, which affords me the idea of necessity" (T 1.3.14.1).

After this brief statement of his positive theory, Hume proceeds by drawing attention to its significance. Following his empiricist principle that tracing the origin of an idea to its source in impressions serves to clarify the idea and make more precise the meaning of terms that are used to express it, he claims to "have just now examin'd one of the most sublime questions in philosophy, viz. *that concerning the power and efficacy of causes*" (T 1.3.14.2). The relevance of discovering the origin of the idea of necessary connection to metaphysical accounts of causality is also emphasized at the start of the corresponding section of the first *Enquiry:*

There are no ideas, which occur in metaphysics, more obscure and uncertain, than those of *power, force, energy,* or *necessary connexion,* of which it is every moment necessary for us to treat in all our disquisitions. We shall, therefore, endeavour, in this section, to fix, if possible, the precise meaning of these terms, and thereby remove some part of that obscurity, which is so much complained of in this species of philosophy. (EHU 7.3)

It can be seen from these quotations that Hume supposes that the idea of a necessary connection between a cause and effect is pretty well the same as the idea that the cause has a power or force or energy that produces the effect. Indeed, he says, "the terms of *efficacy, agency, power, force, energy, necessity, connexion,* and *productive quality,* are all nearly synonimous" (T 1.3.14.4). To understand his discussions of the idea of necessary connection one must keep this assumption in mind throughout. Philosophical accounts of causation have been given according to which the sense in which a cause is necessarily connected to its effect is to be explained by saying, very roughly, that the occurrence of the effect is logically deducible from the occurrence of the cause, assuming that a set of initial conditions and a nonnecessary law of nature obtain.[13] A theory of causal necessity of this kind need not employ concepts such as power and efficacy at all. Hume's account of the origin of the idea of necessary connection is, however, given in a philosophical and historical context in which the ideas of causal necessity are bound up with ideas about causal powers and forces. He describes a causal power as a "quality, which binds the effect to the cause, and renders the one an infallible consequence of the other" (EHU 7.6). Similarly, he describes "the efficacy of causes" as "that quality which makes them be follow'd by their effects" (T 1.3.14.3). Thus Hume assumes that to think that a cause is necessarily connected to its effect is to think that the cause has a power or efficacy whose operation in producing the effect is "infallible" or unfailing.

Given this way of understanding causal necessity, it is natural to assume that the idea of a necessary connection must arise from experience of causal powers. Indeed, Hume thinks that before we start to think philosophically about the matter we usually take it that we do directly perceive causal powers operating:

The generality of mankind never find any difficulty in accounting for the more common and familiar operations of nature; such as the descent of heavy bodies, the growth of plants, the generation of animals, or the nourishment of bodies by food: But suppose, that, in all these cases, they perceive the very force or energy of the cause, by which it is connected with its effect, and is for ever infallible in its operation. (EHU 7.21)

---

[13] It is interesting (but mistaken) that theories of this kind, so called nomological accounts of causation, are often claimed to have their origin in Hume's work. For example, Ernest Sosa, arguing that nomological accounts cannot capture all kinds of causation, says: "It is an essential feature of 'nomological' accounts of causation that according to them an event or state of affairs P (partially) causes (or is 'a cause' or 'causal factor' of) another [state of affairs] Q only if there are actual ('initial') conditions I and a law of nature L such that, by necessity, if P and I and L all obtain then Q must obtain, where L is essential in that P and I alone do *not* necessitate Q. It is further commonly assumed, especially by Humeans (regularists), (i) that laws make no essential reference to any particulars: that laws are purely general, and (ii) that laws are not necessary truths" ("Varieties of Causation" in *Causation*, ed. E. Sosa and M. Tooley [Oxford: Oxford University Press, 1993], 234–42).

This illustrates the widespread assumption that Hume, in denying that we have an idea of causal power as a property of objects, denied that causes necessitate their effects in any sense other than that expressed by such nomological theories. For example, A. H. Basson claims that Hume "says that causality is nothing more than uniformity of sequence," *David Hume* (London: Pelican, 1958), 75.

It is Hume's view, however, that this common supposition is mistaken. We never do, and in fact we never can, observe any quality or property of causes that constitutes causal power. In observing a single instance of a causal relation, he argues, none of the perceivable qualities of the objects involved constitutes power or necessary connection because none of them is a "quality, which binds the effect to the cause, and renders the one an infallible consequence of the other." Perceivable or "sensible" qualities are always "compleat in themselves, and never point out any other event which may result from them." But for a perceivable quality to count as a causal power it would need to be such as to "point out" the effect it produces. Indeed, if causal powers were sensible qualities, then knowledge of the effects of an object would become possible a priori: "But were the power or energy of any cause discoverable by the mind, we could foresee the effect, even without experience; and might, at first, pronounce with certainty concerning it, by the mere dint of thought and reasoning" (EHU 7.6–8).

Hume argues for the same conclusion in considering the causal relation between volition and bodily movement or mental actions. He discusses this briefly in the *Treatise* (T 1.3.14.12) and at greater length in the first *Enquiry*. We know from experience that volition can result in bodily motion, as, for example, the voluntary movement of an arm. But there is no impression of the power of the will. Hume gives three arguments in support of this conclusion. The first is that it is a mystery how the soul and the body are united: "But if by consciousness we perceived any power or energy in the will, we must know this power; we must know its connexion with the effect; we must know the secret union of soul and body." The second is that we can voluntarily move some parts of the body but not others, and we discover this only by experience; whereas, were we conscious of the power of the will in the one case and its impotence in the other, "we should then perceive, independent of experience, why the authority of will over the organs of the body is circumscribed within such particular limits" (EHU 7.11–12). The third is that if we had an impression of the power of the will, we would then know the effect of the will; but in fact we do not know the effects of the will when we move an arm, for example, because

the immediate object of power in voluntary motion, is not the member itself which is moved, but certain muscles, and nerves, and animal spirits, and, perhaps, something still more minute and more unknown, through which the motion is successively propagated, ere it reach the member itself whose motion is the immediate object of volition. Can there be a more certain proof, that the power, by which this whole operation is performed, so far from being directly and fully known by an inward sentiment or consciousness, is, to the last degree, mysterious and unintelligible? (EHU 7.14)

Hume gives three similar arguments to show that there is no impression of power or necessary connection when we voluntarily perform mental actions. As before, the arguments turn on the claim that if there were such an impression, there would be knowledge of a kind that we do not actually possess. We know that we can direct our thoughts, exercising some control over our ideas. But we have no knowledge of how the mind produces ideas: "the manner, in which this operation is performed; the power, by which it is produced; is entirely beyond our comprehension." Again, as in the case of volition and bodily motion, there are limits to the control of the will over ideas and passions that can be discovered only from experience. They are not known by "acquaintance with the nature of cause and effect," or by, that is, acquaintance with the nature of the power of the will over thoughts and passions. Finally, the fact that the mind's command of thoughts and feelings varies in different circumstances, such as in sickness and in health, suggests that there is "some secret mechanism or structure of parts, upon which the effect depends, and which, being entirely unknown to us, renders the power or energy of the will equally unknown and incomprehensible" (EHU 7.17–19).

In considering whether the idea of necessary connection arises from observation of the behavior of material bodies, from experience of the interaction of human minds and bodies, or from introspection into the workings of our minds, Hume's arguments are close to those given by Malebranche.[14] Hume rejects Malebranche's conclusions about causation, but seeing the extent of the agreement between the two philosophers, and the points of difference, helps to highlight what is revolutionary about Hume's theory. Like Hume, Malebranche sees a close relation between necessary connection and causal power. For him, a true cause is something that has an active

---

[14] At T 1.3.14.7, n.29, Hume refers to Malebranche's *Search after Truth* 6.2.3 and to *Elucidation* 15 of this work. See Nicolas Malebranche, *The Search after Truth and Elucidations of the Search after Truth*, trans. T. M. Lennon and P. J. Olscamp (Columbus: Ohio State University Press, 1980).

power to bring about the effect, and true causes necessitate their effects.[15] It is impossible that the power of a cause acts, but that the relevant effect does not follow from that act. Consequently he holds that if the mind has an idea of a true cause, there will be a conceptual connection between the idea of the cause and that of the effect. The mind will perceive or see a necessary connection between the cause and the effect, meaning by that that it will be inconceivable that the cause should operate without the effect resulting. With this understanding of necessary connection and causal power in place, Malebranche seeks to show that there is only one causal power, God's will, and only one case in which we can perceive necessary connection: between the will of God and everything that happens. According to this doctrine, when a moving billiard ball collides with a stationary one, it is not the first ball that causes the second to move. The impact is no more than the "occasion" on which God wills that the second ball should move, while it is just this act of willing that causes it to move.[16]

In Malebranche's occasionalist theory, the regularities we observe in natural events like the collisions of moving bodies are the result of the fact that God's acts of will are themselves regular and uniform. On any occasion where a particular type of event occurs, God always wills, miracles aside, that a particular type of event should follow. Thus we come to experience constant conjunctions of events. Given experience of the constant conjunction of events of types A and B, he says, we assume that A causes B, and form the habit of expecting B when we observe A. Unfortunately, in his view, we are also prone to assume that A has a power or nature to produce B. But this is "a prejudice from which it is almost impossible to deliver oneself without the aid that can be drawn from the principles of a philosophy that has not always been sufficiently known."[17] The prejudice that B is an effect of A's power blinds us to the realization that B is in

---

[15] Malebranche distinguishes between a power to act, which is a true cause, and a passive capacity to undergo change. See Nicolas Malebranche, *Dialogues on Metaphysics*, trans. W. Doney (New York: Arbaris Books, 1980), 147, 151.

[16] For this reason Malebranche's theory is referred to as "occasionalism." The motion of the first ball is also said to be a "secondary" cause of the motion of the second ball, because the true, or "primary" cause is the divine will. Hume uses the terminology of secondary causes at T 1.3.14.11.

[17] Malebranche, *Search after Truth*, Elucidation 15, 657–8.

fact the effect of divine power, and that A is not the true cause of B, but only the occasion for God to produce B in accordance with his general will. Thus, for Malebranche, belief in natural force, efficacy, or power is contrary to sound philosophy and true religion.

When Malebranche argues that secondary causes are not true causes, for there is no necessary connection between them and any other natural event, he sounds very like Hume. According to occasionalist theory, when the white billiard ball strikes the red one, there is no necessary connection between this impact and the ensuing movement of the red ball, for it is conceivable that the red ball will react in some way different from usual. It may shatter, or disappear, or do anything imaginable. There is never a necessary connection between the motion of one body and the motion of another. And when I will my arm to move, it is conceivable that my arm does not move. There is never a necessary connection between volition and bodily movement. When I will to think of some object, there is never a necessary connection between my volition and the occurrence of the idea of that object in my mind. Furthermore, no one really has any idea of what he or she means by talking of causal powers in bodies or in finite minds:

There are many reasons preventing me from attributing to *secondary* or natural causes a force, a power, an efficacy to produce anything. But the principal one is that this opinion does not even seem conceivable to me. Whatever effort I make in order to understand it, I cannot find in me any idea representing to me what might be the force or the power they attribute to creatures. And I do not even think it a temerarious judgment to assert that those who maintain that creatures have force and power in themselves advance what they do not clearly conceive. For in short, if philosophers clearly conceived that secondary causes have a true force to act and produce things like them, then being a man as much as they and participating like them in sovereign Reason, I should clearly be able to discover the idea that represents this force to them. But whatever effort of mind I make, I can find force, efficacy, or power only in the will of the infinitely perfect Being.[18]

Despite the similarities between some of the arguments used by the two philosophers, Hume's conclusion is significantly different

---

[18] Malebranche, *Search after Truth, Elucidation* 15, 658.

from that of Malebranche. First, Hume denies that it follows from the fact that there is no conceptual connection between ideas of natural causes and effects that natural causes are not true causes and have no powers to produce their effects. Second, he rejects Malebranche's claim to "find force, efficacy, or power" in "the will of the infinitely perfect Being." Third, he denies that we can think that there is a necessary connection between a cause and its effect only if we cannot conceive of the cause occurring without the effect (T 1.4.5.31, 1.3.14.10, 33).

At the heart of Hume's critique of Malebranche is his empiricist account of the nature of ideas. For Hume, all ideas are ultimately derived from impressions of sense or reflection. And impressions are what ideas represent. "Ideas always represent their objects or impressions; and *vice versa*, there are some objects necessary to give rise to every idea" (T 1.3.14.6).[19] Ideas do not, therefore, represent the essences of things, where this means a level of reality underlying the appearances of these things; on the contrary, ideas represent the appearances of things and nothing more.[20] For Malebranche, however, there are clear ideas that are not derived from impressions of sense or feeling, and these, he claims, do represent the essences of things. This notion is used by Malebranche in stating a principle of certainty and evidence, namely, that, in asserting of a thing whatever is included in the clear idea that represents it, one can be certain.[21] As Andrew Pyle explains, Malebranche regards this principle as licensing inference from "the clear idea of X does not contain F" to "X is non-F."[22] Hence Malebranche supposes that the

---

[19] For discussion of Hume's theory of ideas and impressions see in this volume the essay "Hume and the Mechanics of Mind." In the quoted sentence Hume is using *object* to mean *object of the mind*. Thus *object* and *impression* are interchangeable in this context. See Marjorie Grene, "The Objects of Hume's *Treatise*," *Hume Studies* 20, no. 2 (1994): 163–77.

[20] "My intention never was to penetrate into the nature of bodies, or explain the secret causes of their operations. For besides that this belongs not to my present purpose, I am afraid, that such an enterprize is beyond the reach of human understanding, and that we can never pretend to know body otherwise than by those external properties, which discover themselves to the senses" (T 1.2.5.26).

[21] For textual references and discussion of this principle, see Jean-Christophe Bardout, "Metaphysics and Philosophy," in *The Cambridge Companion to Malebranche,* ed. S. Nadler (Cambridge: Cambridge University Press, 2000), Chap. 6.

[22] Andrew Pyle, *Malebranche* (London: Routledge, 2003), 102.

fact that ideas of secondary causes never contain anything representing causal powers justifies the conclusion that secondary causes are
causally impotent. In contrast, Hume does not infer from "there are
no ideas of causal powers in objects" that "there are no causal powers in objects." Certainly, there are no appearances of causal powers
in objects or the mind. But if causal powers belong to the essences
or natures of things, then the proper thing for an empiricist to say
is that they, like anything else to do with the essence or nature of
things, are "unknown" (or are, as he often says, "inconceivable,"
"unintelligible," "hidden," "secret," and so on).

Hume uses his empiricist theory of ideas to refute Malebranche's
view that God is the one true cause. The demolition is swift. Malebranche has asserted that secondary causes are not true causes
because our ideas of them do not contain representations of causal
powers. But then, Hume objects, because all ideas are derived from
impressions and there are no impressions of power, neither can the
idea of God, which itself must derive from impressions, contain a
representation of power. It follows, then, that one can no more perceive a necessary connection between the divine will and natural
events than one can perceive a necessary connection between the
events themselves:

For if every idea be deriv'd from an impression, the idea of a deity proceeds
from the same origin; and if no impression, either of sensation or reflection,
implies any force or efficacy, 'tis equally impossible to discover or even
imagine any such active principle in the deity. Since these philosophers [the
occasionalists], therefore, have concluded, that matter cannot be endow'd
with any efficacious principle, because 'tis impossible to discover in it such
a principle; the same course of reasoning shou'd determine them to exclude
it from the supreme being. (T 1.3.14.10)[23]

---

[23] Malebranche also argues that God is the only true cause because He is infinitely
powerful and thus that whatever he wills must result. God's will is necessarily
connected to every event. There is, he says, a contradiction in the thought that
God wills that X occurs and yet X does not occur. Hume reveals the muddle that
Malebranche is in. "We have no idea of a being endow'd with any power, much less
of one endow'd with infinite power," and so we are unable to use the conceivability
test for necessary connection. On the other hand, if we simply define the infinite
power of God's will in terms of the impossibility that anything happens contrary
to this will, the claim that the divine will is the true cause of everything becomes
tautological, for then "we really do no more than assert, that a being, whose volition
is connected with every effect, is connected with every effect" (T 1.4.5.31).

Malebranche insists that nothing is a true cause unless its power is knowable in such a way that the necessary connection between cause and effect is perceivable by the mind. Hume shows that there is no case in which this requirement is satisfied. All causes and effects are objects or events distinct and different from each other. They never have discoverable, knowable properties or qualities that relate them together so that conceptual connections of the kind that Malebranche requires can be seen. This appeal of Malebranche to the idea of God is, on empiricist principles, a failure. Consequently, Hume concludes, if true causation requires knowable necessary connections, if it requires ideas that represent impressions of causal powers in objects, then there is no true causation at all.[24] The way out Hume offers the occasionalists is the central feature of his own positive theory.[25] Because there is no idea of power or necessary connection as a property or quality of objects, all that the experience of causes and effects provides us is those regularities of contiguity and succession that Hume calls "constant conjunctions" and that Malebranche identifies as characteristic of the behavior of what he supposes are secondary causes and effects. What Hume's positive theory does is make experience of constant conjunction, together with the principle of custom and habit, sufficient in the circumstances of human nature to give rise to the idea of causality as a necessary relation. It is precisely because the idea of necessary connection that Hume identifies is *not* a representation of any property or quality of objects that secondary causes and effects can be thought of as necessarily connected. What is revolutionary in his theory is that he solves the problem by turning from the observation of objects to the effect of that observation in the mind, and presents the idea of cause and effect as a complex phenomenon that includes an idea that does not represent anything in the objects:

The several instances of resembling conjunctions lead us into the notion of power and necessity. These instances are in themselves totally distinct from each other, and have no union but in the mind, which observes them, and collects their ideas. Necessity, then, is the effect of this observation, and is nothing but an internal impression of the mind, or a determination to carry our thoughts from one object to another. Without considering it in

---

[24] See T 1.4.5.31.
[25] T 1.3.14.10.

this view, we can never arrive at the most distant notion of it, or be able to attribute it either to external or internal objects, to spirit or body, to causes or effects. (T 1.3.14.20)

When we say, therefore, that one object is connected with another, we mean only, that they have acquired a connexion in our thought, and give rise to this inference, by which they become proofs of each other's existence (EHU 7.28).

There are two aspects to the way in which, on this empiricist theory, experience produces the idea of cause and effect. On the one hand, there is experience of the constant and invariable conjunctions of types of objects or events. On the other hand, there is the resulting habitual association of the ideas of these things and the feeling of the customary transition of thought from one to the other. From these two perspectives Hume forms two definitions of cause. On the one hand a cause is "*an object, followed by another, and where all the objects, similar to the first, are followed by objects similar to the second.*" On the other hand a cause is "*an object followed by another, and whose appearance always conveys the thought to that other*" (EHU 7.29).[26] There are two points to note about these definitions. First, they are definitions in Hume's sense, namely, identifications of the impressions from which a particular idea arises. The relations between objects mentioned in the definitions, namely, succession, resemblance, and habitual association, are all observable in the sense that they can be perceived or felt. Second, they are, as Hume later points out, as much his proposed definitions (in, again, his sense of identifying the origin of an idea in impressions) of necessity as they are definitions of cause.[27] The concluding section of this essay discusses these definitions and some of the problems of interpretation that arise in seeking to understand Hume's theory of causation.

III. THE DEFINITIONS OF *CAUSE* AND THEIR IMPLICATIONS

The first definition of cause (call this C1) refers to constant conjunctions of objects and events. A cause is "*an object, followed by another, and where all the objects, similar to the first, are followed*

---

[26] Similar definitions are given in the *Treatise* at 1.3.14.31.
[27] EHU 8.5.

by objects similar to the second." The second definition (call this C2) refers to the effect on the imagination of observing constant conjunctions. A cause is *"an object followed by another, and whose appearance always conveys the thought to that other"* (EHU 7.29). It has been objected that the two definitions are neither logically nor extensionally equivalent.[28] If the reference in C1 to "all the objects, similar to the first" is read as meaning all the similar objects that have existed, do exist and will exist, then there could be many causes (by C1) that are not causes (by C2) because no one has observed any or enough resembling cases for ideas of these objects to become associated in the imagination. Conversely, there could be causes (by C2) that are not causes (by C1). Someone may have experienced sufficient resembling instances of the conjunction of two types of objects or events for the ideas of these objects to become associated in the imagination, although the cases that have been observed do not constitute a representative sample of these types of objects or events.

These considerations might suggest that the two definitions should be read as defining different senses of *cause.* C1 might be read as an objective sense, expressing what it is for an object or event to be a cause of an effect in reality, independently of the experience and resulting inferential tendencies of observers. C2 might then be read as a subjective sense, expressing what it is for an observer to assume or believe that an object or event is a cause of another. If the definitions are so understood, there seems to be a further implication about the idea of necessity. Although neither definition explicitly mentions a necessary connection between causes and effects, Hume traces the origin of that idea to the feeling of the determination of the imagination in habitual causal inferences. That seems to mean that necessity is properly speaking a feature of causes only in the sense of C2, and that objectively speaking, in the sense of C1, causes do not necessitate their effects. This way of reading Hume, as holding what is called a "regularity theory" of causation in the objective sense, is widespread. For example, it has been claimed that "about causation as it really is in the objects Hume usually says that it is regular

---

[28] For example, J. A. Robinson, "Hume's Two Definitions of 'Cause,'" *Philosophical Quarterly* 12 (1962): 162–71, reprinted in *Hume: A Collection of Critical Essays,* ed. V. C. Chappell (Garden City, NY: Doubleday, 1966), 129–47.

succession and nothing more."[29] In this tradition, C1 is "supposed to be the complete definition of causation, as it exists objectively in nature."[30] Furthermore, because Hume's account of the origin of the idea of necessity ties it to the mental habits referred to only in the definition of the subjective sense of *cause*, it would seem that he must rule out as meaningless talk of causes as objectively and necessarily connected to their effects, or of objects as really possessing causal powers.

There are passages in the *Treatise* that seem to support the view that Hume regards talk of objective causal necessity or causal power as meaningless or confused.[31] In these passages he describes his thesis that the idea of causal necessity arises from our awareness of the determination of the mind in causal inferences as a "paradox." But he does not mean that the doctrine involves some kind of contradiction.[32] He means, rather, that readers will be prone to think that his view does involve a contradiction, and will likely reject it as "a gross absurdity." The reason why this reaction is to be expected is, he says, that "the mind has a great propensity to spread itself on external objects, and to conjoin with them any internal impressions, which they occasion" (T 1.3.14.25–6). He returns to this notion, the notion that the mind "conjoins" the "internal impression," that is, the feeling of determination in the imagination, with the impressions of external objects, in the conclusion of Book 1. The view that his theory is "a gross absurdity" is the expected reaction of those who fail to realize "that in the most usual conjunctions of cause and effect we are as ignorant of the ultimate principle, which binds them together, as in the most unusual and extraordinary." The propensity of the mind about which he is speaking is, consequently, that which leads people to imagine that the internal impression is in fact a sense impression, an impression of a property or quality of an object. Because the internal impression is the origin of the idea of a necessary connection between objects, those who manifest the propensity mistakenly think that they perceive, and so are acquainted with,

---

[29] J. L. Mackie, *The Cement of the Universe: A Study of Causation* (Oxford: Clarendon Press, 1974), 20.

[30] Georges Dicker, *Hume's Epistemology and Metaphysics* (London: Routledge, 1998), 115.

[31] For example, T 1.3.14.14, 22–8.

[32] By "paradox" Hume means a strange or unusual opinion.

"that energy in the cause, by which it operates on its effect; that tie, which connects them together; and that efficacious quality, on which the tie depends." It is the belief that experience acquaints us with causal powers in objects that is "an illusion of the imagination." The correct conclusion to draw, Hume thinks, is that we are ignorant of causal powers or necessary connections in objects. There is a "deficiency in our ideas," an absence or a gap, which, because of the propensity of the mind to conjoin internal with external impressions, we commonly fail to perceive (T 1.4.7.5–6).

The theme of the deficiency or inadequacy of our ideas of causal powers and necessary connections occurs also in what Hume says about the two definitions of cause. In the *Treatise* he talks about the possibility that the definitions may be judged to be "defective, because drawn from objects foreign to the cause" (T 1.3.14.31). It is not immediately clear what is meant by "objects foreign to the cause," nor why reference to them makes the definitions defective. In the corresponding passage in the first *Enquiry*, however, Hume makes it clearer why someone might make these objections. Hume there speaks of the idea of cause and necessity that we actually have, the idea that the two definitions refer to, as "imperfect." The idea we actually have is not, as we have seen at length, an idea that represents "that circumstance in the cause, which gives it a connexion with its effect. We have no idea of this connexion; nor even any distinct notion what it is we desire to know, when we endeavour at a conception of it" (EHU 7.29). Hume does not agree that his definitions are defective. In his view they capture the idea we actually have of cause and effect and so define the term *cause* correctly by indicating the idea it expresses. They do not, of course, indicate an idea we do not have, an idea of power or necessary connection as a quality of, or relation between objects. Compared to that which perhaps we would wish to mean, the idea we actually have is "imperfect," while the definitions of cause can be regarded as "drawn from objects foreign to the cause" because they invoke ideas of entities that are causally connected, but not an idea of something that does the connecting.

In these discussions of the meaning of causal language, Hume points to a tension between what he argues we actually mean, the ideas we actually have and express, and what we have a strong tendency to think we mean. We think we have ideas that in reality we do not have, and we think that our words express them. In short, our everyday thinking about causation is confused. This confusion seems to be a prime candidate for illustrating the method of clarifying ideas by tracing them to their origin in impressions. But Hume seems conscious that the tensions and confusions he has identified continue to operate even as we try to understand his theory. At the end of his account in the first *Enquiry*, he writes:

I know not, whether the reader will readily apprehend this reasoning. I am afraid, that, should I multiply words about it, or throw it into a greater variety of lights, it would only become more obscure and intricate. In all abstract reasonings, there is one point of view, which, if we can happily hit, we shall go farther towards illustrating the subject, than by all the eloquence and copious expression in the world. This point of view we should endeavour to reach, and reserve the flowers of rhetoric for subjects which are more adapted to them. (EHU 7.30)

It is difficult to be sure that one has succeeded in reaching Hume's point of view. His theory of causation is still the subject of competing interpretations. John Wright, for example, has argued that Hume himself regarded his definitions as "imperfect."[33] According to Wright, Hume held that causation in reality involves "real physical force," and that such forces do necessitate their effects. Hume's purpose, he argues, is to show that we have no idea of such things, no idea of the causal powers that constitute the "ultimate" reasons why things happen the way they do. He points out that, as we have already seen, Hume claims that if we had ideas of ultimate causes we would be able to infer effects from causes a priori. That we cannot make such inferences is because our ideas of causes and effects are always distinct from each other and separable. As a result, Wright says, Hume regards our ideas as "inadequate." Hume's purpose, he says, was not to deny that there are such ultimate causes on which depend the regularities of nature, but only to show that we have no knowledge of them: "Hume's whole argument assumes the existence of force or necessary connection in the material universe."[34] Consequently, "it must be stressed that Hume's definitions of causality

---

[33] John P. Wright, "Hume's Causal Realism: Recovering a Traditional Interpretation" in *The New Hume Debate*, ed. R. Read and K. A. Richman (London: Routledge, 2000), 88–99. See, by the same author, *The Sceptical Realism of David Hume* (Manchester: Manchester University Press, 1983), 123–86.

[34] Wright, *Sceptical Realism*, 147, 144.

are clearly presented as definitions which are wholly inadequate to what they purport to define."[35] Wright's reading differs, therefore, from that given above, according to which *inadequate* or *imperfect* applies to the ideas we have, not to the definitions. The ideas we have, I have argued, are inadequate or imperfect compared to the idea we do not have, that of qualities of or relations between objects that constitute the "ultimate principle" that binds a cause to its effect (T 1.4.7.6). Hume can refer to the idea we do not have, the idea of an ultimate principle, consistently with saying that all ideas originate in impressions, because he explains the idea of an ultimate cause in terms of human cognitive powers (in terms of what we could infer if we had such an idea), as indeed Wright has granted.[36] Thus Hume can give content to the thought of what an idea of causal power or force or necessary connection in the objects would be, although we lack it, and in these terms can speak of the idea we do have as "inadequate." Wright, however, says that the definitions "purport to define" ultimate causes and that Hume recognizes that they do not do so. This is part of Wright's evidence for his interpretation of Hume as a "sceptical realist." He reads Hume as holding that to believe that A causes B, properly speaking, is to believe that there exists some feature of A such that if we were aware of it we would be able to infer B from A a priori. The belief that such features exist is Hume's realism about causes, while his denial that we ever have any idea of such features is his skepticism. This entails that, for Hume, our experience of causes and effects as distinct and different from each other does not represent the world as it really is. As Wright says, the consequence of the position he ascribes to Hume is that, in reality, causes and effects are not distinct and different events: "[Custom] leads us to ascribe an absolute necessity relating those objects which we call cause and effect. And it leads us to suppose that there is no absolute existential distinction between them."[37]

---

[35] Wright, "Hume's Causal Realism," 91.

[36] Hume usually speaks of an ultimate cause as something such that, were we acquainted with it, we could infer the effect a priori. He does not treat this epistemologically defined notion as an idea of necessary connection between objects. For discussion of this point see Ken Levy, "Hume, the New Hume, and Causal Connections," *Hume Studies* 26 (2000): 41–75; Peter Kail, "Projection and Necessity in Hume," *European Journal of Philosophy* 9 (2001): 24–54.

[37] Wright, *Sceptical Realism*, 161.

Wright's skeptical realist reading is one of those that have been described, by Ken Winkler, as "New Hume" readings.[38] These are readings according to which Hume's theory of causation includes the thesis that there exist causal powers that necessitate their effects even though we can have no knowledge of them. However, these revisionist readings differ among themselves. Galen Strawson, for example, argues that Hume's frequent references to secret powers and principles are evidence that he "takes the existence of something like natural necessity or causal power for granted not only in common life but also as a philosopher." But Strawson does not think that this belief is a belief in causal connections of the kind Wright ascribes to Hume. Rather, Hume's belief in causal power is described, essentially, as a denial of the regularity theory of objective causation. It is the belief that "there must be and is something about reality given which it is ordered and regular in the way that it is."[39] To believe that "there must be" an underlying ground of nature's regularity, implies, however, some kind of evidence or argument to this effect, but no such argument ever appears in Hume's texts.[40]

The denial that Hume held the regularity theory of causation does not entail ascribing to him causal realism in either Wright's or Strawson's sense. For example, both Annette Baier and Don Garrett attack the ascription to Hume of the regularity theory, and both argue that definition C1 is misinterpreted when it is read as supporting this ascription.[41] Garrett argues that C1 and C2 do not define different senses of *cause*, but are two different ways of indicating the same idea. There are good reasons for this interpretation. At EHU 8.5, Hume refers in the singular to "our idea... of necessity and causation," not to "ideas." This idea "arises entirely from the uniformity, observable in the operations of nature." It is this observation of uniformity that has two aspects, the "two circumstances" that taken together "form the whole of that necessity, which we ascribe to

---

[38] Ken Winkler, "The New Hume," *Philosophical Review* 50 (1991): 541–79, reprinted with a new postscript in *The New Hume Debate*, 52–87.

[39] Galen Strawson, *The Secret Connexion: Causation, Realism and David Hume* (Oxford: Clarendon Press, 1989), 1–2; see also, by the same author, "David Hume: Objects and Powers," in *The New Hume Debate*, 31–51.

[40] Levy, "Hume, the New Hume, and Causal Connections," 42.

[41] Baier, *A Progress of Sentiments*, 92: Garrett, *Cognition and Commitment*, 111.

matter."[42] For Hume, definitions of terms are given by invoking the ideas that the terms express, and in this case the idea is of a relation between objects or events. In the *Treatise* he says that he can give two definitions, not because there are two different ideas (as it were, objective and subjective), but because the relation of cause and effect is both a "philosophical" relation and a "natural" relation (T 1.3.14.31). The two definitions present the idea of the relation either as "a comparison of two ideas" (a philosophical relation), or as "an association betwixt them" (a natural relation). To understand why Hume gives two definitions that seem not to be equivalent it is necessary to understand how the definition of the philosophical relation, C1, and the definition of the natural relation, C2, provide different perspectives on the same object.

As Garrett says, Hume's initial definition of the relation of cause and effect is in terms of the three component relations of priority, contiguity, and necessary connection.[43] It is only because the idea of the relation of necessary connection is obscure that this is not yet a satisfactory definition. Garrett explains that, for Hume, an abstract idea, such as that of cause and effect, is a particular idea (in this case a particular idea of some pair of objects or events) associated to a term (*cause*) whose use is connected to a custom of calling to mind other particular ideas (in this case of pairs of objects) that resemble each other in a certain respect. When Hume first discusses ideas of philosophical relations in the *Treatise*, he says that they arise from comparison, and that comparison requires some respect in which the things compared resemble each other. Speaking of the relation of cause and effect, he states that this is at once both a philosophical and a natural relation, and then comments that "the resemblance imply'd in this relation, shall be explain'd afterwards" (T 1.1.5.9). What Hume's theory eventually shows is what it is that all the pairs of objects or events that are brought under the abstract idea of the causal relation have in common: they resemble each other in that in each pair the first element is related to the second element by priority

---

[42] In fact, Hume argues in this section of the first *Enquiry* that we find that the same "two circumstances take place in the voluntary actions of men, and in the operations of the mind," and thus we can ascribe causal necessity to human action in the same sense that we can ascribe it to matter.

[43] Garrett, *Cognition and Commitment*, 99.

and contiguity, while all objects that resemble the first element stand in the same relations of priority and contiguity to objects that resemble the second element. Therefore, Garrett explains, the pairs of objects whose ideas are included in the set of ideas associated with the term *cause and effect* are pairs of objects that are perceived as resembling each other in this rather complex way. But in that case on Hume's theory the ideas of these objects will also be related by the *natural* relation of causation, for they will be habitually associated in the imagination, and there will be a settled disposition to infer one from the other. The connection between cause and effect as a philosophical relation based on comparison and as a natural relation based on custom also works the other way round. All the ideas of pairs of objects or events that fall under the *natural* relation by being ideas between which the imagination is disposed to make habitual transitions will also be ideas of pairs of objects or events that fall under the *philosophical* relation. The connection between the two definitions that justifies Hume's claim that they simply present different views of the same object is, of course, that one kind of experience (that referred to in C1) causes another kind of experience (that referred to in C2). As Annette Baier has shown, Hume's definitions are "arrived at by a causal investigation into our concept of cause."[44] The habitual association of ideas that gives rise to the feeling of being determined to infer one from the other is the effect of the experience of the constant conjunction of objects that causes the mind to think of these objects as related by the philosophical relation of cause and effect. Either definition is, as Hume claims, a definition of cause and necessity.

The way in which Garrett interprets the two definitions and their relation enables him to offer an interesting solution to the problem that C1 seems to be an objective definition while C2 seems to be a subjective one. He compares the two definitions of cause to the two definitions of virtue Hume gives in the second *Enquiry*. In the case of causation, we have constant conjunctions of objects, and a feeling of determination. In the case of virtue, we have qualities of mind that are useful or agreeable to the possessor or to others, and a feeling of approbation. Garrett argues that, in the case of the

---

[44] Baier, *A Progress of Sentiments*, 91.

definitions of virtue, it makes sense to distinguish between a subjective reading, in which the feeling of approbation is one that arises in some particular empirical observer, and an objective reading in which the feeling arises in an ideal spectator who has a properly developed moral sense and is free from bias, prejudice, or other distorting influences. Similarly, Garrett suggests, we could read both definitions of cause as having a subjective sense, one in which the *constant conjunctions* are just those that happen to have occurred in the experience of some particular empirical observer, while the *ideas* that are associated are, similarly, just those associated in that person's mind. Alternatively, we could read both definitions as having an objective sense, one in which the constant conjunctions are such as to hold at all times and in all places, while the habitual transitions of the mind are those that would occur in an ideal observer who has a properly developed capacity for making causal inferences freed from prejudice, bias, or other distorting influences. In this context it is also important to recognize, as Baier stresses, that in the *Treatise,* after giving the definitions of cause, Hume formulates a set of rules for judging what really causes what. That Hume derives normative rules from the theory that led to the definitions provides some support for Garrett's interpretation.[45]

The proposal that Hume's account of causation is best interpreted by considering its similarity with his account of the ideas of vice and virtue is a major part of the so-called quasi-realist reading given by Simon Blackburn. Blackburn agrees that Hume did not hold the regularity theory. He did not intend to reduce causation to regularity. But, Blackburn says, it is wrong to think that the only alternative is realism of the kinds ascribed to Hume by Wright and Strawson. It is possible that Hume was a realist about causal powers insofar as he was convinced that reference to them could not be eliminated from everyday ways of thinking and speaking about causation. But at the same time, Hume could have been an antirealist about causal powers insofar as he held that a theoretical account of what we are doing in thinking and speaking as we do does not mean that we

---

[45] As Garrett puts it, "these rules become, in part, rules for making oneself more like an idealized mind" (*Cognition and Commitment,* 112).

are responding to the presence of causal powers as entities in the world.[46]

The final section of this essay has shown that, in the attempt to understand Hume's theory of causation and arrive at that point of view that, he himself confessed, might continue to elude his readers, the rival interpretations of contemporary scholars testify to the continuing interest and significance of Hume's ideas on causation. It also demonstrates that interpretations of Hume on causation must also be interpretations of Hume's philosophical work as a whole.

SUGGESTIONS FOR FURTHER READING

In addition to the works cited in the notes to this essay, for further reading the following are recommended.

On the Will and Bodily and Mental Acts

Harris, James. "Hume's Reconciling Project and 'The Common Distinction betwixt *Moral* and *Physical* Necessity.'" *British Journal for the History of Philosophy* 11 (2003): 451–71.

Pitson, Tony. "Liberty, Necessity, and the Will." In *The Blackwell Guide to Hume's* Treatise, edited by S. Traiger. Oxford: Blackwell Publishing, 2006. 216–31.

Norton, David Fate. "Editor's Introduction." In David Hume, *A Treatise of Human Nature*, edited by D. F. Norton and M. J. Norton. Oxford: Oxford University Press, 2000. 165–72.

On Relations, Conceivability and Possibility, and Demonstration

Costa, Michael. "Hume on the Very Idea of a Relation." *Hume Studies* 24 (1998): 71–94.

Falkenstein, Lorne. "Space and Time." In *The Blackwell Guide to Hume's* Treatise, edited by S. Traiger. Oxford: Blackwell Publishing, 2006. 67–9.

Lightner, D. Tycerium. "Hume on Conceivability and Inconceivability." *Hume Studies* 23, no. 1 (1997): 113–32.

Norton, David Fate. "Editor's Introduction." In David Hume, *A Treatise of Human Nature*, 124–6.

---

[46] Simon Blackburn, "Hume and Thick Connexions," *Philosophy and Phenomenological Research* 50 (supplement) (1990), 237–50, reprinted with a postscript in *The New Hume Debate*, 100–12.

Owen, David. *Hume's Reason.* Oxford: Oxford University Press, 1999. 83–112.

On Projectivist and Realist Interpretations of Hume on Causality

Beebee, Helen. *Hume on Causation.* London: Routledge, 2006. 142–225.
Kail, Peter. *Projection and Realism in Hume's Philosophy.* Oxford: Clarendon Press, 2007. 75–124.
Millican, Peter. "Humes Old and New: Four Fashionable Falsehoods, and One Unfashionable Truth." *Proceedings of the Aristotelian Society* supplementary volume 81 (2007): 163–99.

6   Hume and the Problem of Personal Identity

I. BACKGROUND

The problem of personal identity, as philosophers understand it today, emerged from the discussion of identity that Locke added to the second edition of *The Essay concerning Human Understanding*, published in 1694. In the forty-five years between the publication of that work and the publication of the *Treatise*, the literature on the problem of personal identity mushroomed, prompting Hume to observe wryly: "We now proceed to explain the nature of *personal identity*, which has become so great a question in philosophy, especially of late years in *England*, where all the abstruser sciences are study'd with a peculiar ardour and application" (T 1.4.6.15). Hume's own explanation of the nature of personal identity drew on the resources of his accounts of the imagination and the passions, and was therefore unique in many respects. Nevertheless, the debates of the preceding decades had covered considerable ground, and the distinctive features of Hume's own view emerge more clearly when seen in the context of what had come before.

Locke added the chapter *Of Identity and Diversity* to the second edition of his *Essay* to address issues about personal identity that arose from his arguments against the Cartesian view that the soul always thinks.[1] Locke's basic assumption was that questions about identity had to be understood in relation to the kind of object under consideration: one and the same object could instantiate different kinds, each of which would have different conditions of identity.

---

[1] John Locke, *An Essay concerning Human Understanding*, ed. P. H. Nidditch (Oxford: Clarendon Press, 1975). References to this work will cite the book, chapter, and section numbers in this edition.

He argued that a tree, considered as an organized living body, could be distinguished from a given mass of particles. It may be correct to say, Locke held, that the tree remains the same tree through time even though all of its particles may have gradually changed: it may be the same *tree,* but it is not the same *mass of matter.* For Locke, therefore, the crucial question about *personal* identity was the question of what kind of thing persons are: his answer outraged some of his contemporaries. Locke argued that the term *person* does not stand for the same concept as *immaterial substance,* or *soul,* or *spirit.* Locke also distinguished the concept of a person from that of a man, which he usually understood to mean "nothing else but ... an Animal of such a certain Form."[2] According to Locke, a person is "a thinking intelligent Being, that has reason and reflection, and can consider it self as it self, the same thinking thing in different times and places; which it does only by that consciousness, which is inseparable from thinking, and as it seems to me essential to it: It being impossible for any one to perceive, without perceiving, that he does perceive."[3] And, for Locke, the identity of persons depends only on consciousness. He argued:

For it is by the consciousness it has of its present Thoughts and Actions, that it is *self* to it *self* now, and so will be the same *self* as far as the same consciousness can extend to Actions past or to come; and would be by a distance of Time, or change of Substance, no more two *Persons* than a Man be two Men, by wearing other Cloaths to Day than he did Yesterday, with a long or short sleep between: The same consciousness uniting those distant Actions into the same *Person,* whatever Substances contributed to their Production.[4]

Locke explicitly argued that personal identity could persist through a change of substance and that the sameness of an underlying substance did not guarantee that personal identity was preserved.[5] Substantial identity, therefore, was neither necessary nor sufficient for personal identity. For Locke, consciousness alone constitutes personal identity. Locke's theory of personal identity thus broke not only with the Cartesian view that the self is an immaterial

<hr>

[2] Locke, *Essay* 2.27.4, 8.
[3] Locke, *Essay,* 2.27.9.
[4] Locke, *Essay,* 2.27.10.
[5] Locke, *Essay,* 2.27.13–14.

substance, but also with any view that took personal identity to be, or be dependent on, the identity of the human body.

Locke described the concept of a person as a "Forensick" term, that is, as one tied to ascriptions of moral and legal responsibility. Consciousness alone, Locke argued, makes us concerned and accountable for our past actions: "For supposing a Man punish'd now, for what he had done in another Life, whereof he could be made to have no consciousness at all, what difference is there between that Punishment, and being created miserable?" Although Locke himself allowed that "the more probable Opinion is, that this consciousness is annexed to, and the Affection of one individual immaterial Substance," he did not hold that there was anything about thought or consciousness itself that required this. Locke argued that it is "not much more remote from our Comprehension to conceive, that GOD can, if he pleases, superadd to Matter a Faculty of thinking, than that he should superadd to it another Substance, with a Faculty of Thinking."[6]

Locke was not unaware of the implications that might be drawn from his view, and added that

All the great Ends of Morality and Religion, are well enough secured, without philosophical Proofs of the Soul's Immateriality; since it is evident, that he who made us at first begin to subsist here, sensible intelligent Beings, and for several years continued us in such a state, can and will restore us to the like state of Sensibility in another World, and make us capable there to receive the Retribution he has designed to Men, according to their doings in this Life.[7]

We can see, then, that Locke's position on personal identity involved three controversial claims: first, that personal identity is constituted by consciousness; second, that the identity of an underlying substance (whether material or immaterial) is neither necessary nor sufficient for the existence of the same consciousness; and third, that as a consequence the self is not necessarily an immaterial substance.

In the first half of the eighteenth century, philosophical debate about these claims was intense, and Locke's novel account of

---

[6] Locke, *Essay*, 2.27.25–6, 4.3.6.
[7] Locke, *Essay*, 4.3.6.

personal identity won few followers. As early as 1702 Henry Lee attacked Locke's central thesis that consciousness constitutes personal identity. Lee argued that a person could be "decay'd in his Memory and Intellectuals" without losing his identity. He appealed primarily to what he took to be our common notion of a person, which he thought Locke failed to adhere to, but he also held that Locke's position could not give an adequate account of commonly accepted moral judgments. According to Lee, when a person's memory and intellect fails, we nonetheless have an obligation to treat that individual as the person he or she was before.[8] The nature of the self was also central to Shaftesbury's widely read dialogue *The Moralists*, published in 1709 and regularly reprinted in his popular *Characteristics*, a three-volume work first published in 1711. Shaftesbury maintained that the identity of the self persists "when neither one atom of body, one passion, nor one thought remains the same."[9]

Perhaps the most influential critic of the Lockean account of personal identity, however, was the Newtonian philosopher and theologian Samuel Clarke. Clarke had defended the view that the soul is necessarily immaterial and immortal in his Boyle lectures of 1704 and 1705. A lively published exchange with Anthony Collins, a proponent of Locke's position, extended over the next several years and explored in detail the problems associated with a Lockean account of personal identity.[10]

Clarke attacked the view that consciousness could exist in anything but a simple immaterial substance. His arguments focused on what he took to be the essential features of matter and

---

[8] Henry Lee, *Anti-scepticism* (London, 1702; fac. ed., New York: Garland Publishing, 1984), 124–30.

[9] Anthony Ashley Cooper, Third Earl of Shaftesbury, *Characteristics of Men, Manners, Opinions, Times*, ed. Lawrence E. Klein (Cambridge: Cambridge University Press, 1999), 301. Hume purchased a copy of this work in 1726 and refers to *The Moralists* in the discussion of personal identity in a footnote to T 1.4.6.6. For details concerning Hume's purchase, see David Fate Norton and Mary J. Norton, *The David Hume Library* (Edinburgh: Edinburgh Bibliographical Society, 1996), 16.

[10] The published exchange of letters between Clarke and Collins is reprinted in its entirety in Samuel Clarke, *The Works of Samuel Clarke*, 4 vols. (London, 1739; fac. ed., New York: Garland Publishing, 1978). Citations to both Clarke and Collins will be to Clarke's *Works*.

consciousness – that matter is divisible, or made up of parts, and that consciousness itself has a unity that is incompatible with being made up of parts. If hundreds of particles of matter set miles from each other could never constitute one "individual Conscious Being," Clarke argued, then bringing these particles together into a single system, however organized, could never make them into one. For, if the parts themselves were conscious, the system they created would be no more than a collection of distinct conscious beings. And if the parts were *not* essentially conscious, Clarke held, it would be impossible that consciousness could result from joining them together.[11]

Collins replied that Clarke had begged the question: systems of matter could, and did, have individual powers that their parts did not possess separately. Consciousness could therefore be a quality of a compound material substance such as the brain.[12] In response, Clarke raised a further problem: "The Spirits and Particles of the Brain," he argued, "being loose and in perpetual Flux" could not be the seat of consciousness of past actions "by which a Man not only remembers things done many Years since: but also is Conscious that He himself, the same Individual Conscious Being, was the doer of them."[13] According to Clarke, the experience of being conscious that one did something in the past depends on the existence of a simple, unchanging substance. Collins countered that in fact "we are not conscious, that we continue a Moment the same individual numerical Being." Rather, the "continual intermediate repeating" of ideas before they are lost preserves memories of the past in the ever-changing brain.[14] Not surprisingly, Clarke maintained that continuity of consciousness of this kind would be "mere Deceit and Delusion," destructive of moral agency. Persons would have no real connection to the past, and therefore no grounds for taking responsibility for past actions: nor would they have a basis for thinking about the consequences of their actions in the future, since they themselves will not exist to suffer them. Similarly, Clarke argued that on the Locke-Collins view the justice of reward and punishment is undermined, since the person rewarded or punished would

---

[11] Clarke, *Works*, III:730.
[12] Collins, in Clarke, *Works*, III:751–2.
[13] Clarke, *Works*, III,:798.
[14] Collins, in Clarke, *Works*, III:819–20, 870.

not be the same as the one who committed the action.[15] Collins, like Locke, argued that continuity of consciousness alone makes us accountable for past actions, but he added that the distinct beings that are united by consciousness into a single self are also bound to each other by "Sympathy and Concern."[16]

Contemporary cognitive scientists may find Collins's arguments to be suggestive, but in the philosophical discussion of personal identity prior to the *Treatise* it was Clarke's view, not those of Locke or Collins, that took on the status of the received opinion. Nevertheless, the debate between Clarke and Collins had provided their readers with a comprehensive review of questions faced by any account of the nature of the self, or personal identity. Joseph Butler's "Dissertation on Personal Identity" (1736), one of the best-known critiques of Locke's account, cited Clarke and deployed many of the same arguments. A few years later, many of the positions Collins had defended found a congenial home in Hume's *Treatise*.

II. *TREATISE* 1.4.5 AND HUME'S ACCOUNT OF THE SELF

Hume's extended account of the nature of the self begins in *Treatise* 1.4.5, "Of the immateriality of the soul." As the title indicates, this section analyzes one of the central questions debated by Clarke and Collins. Of course, even before they reached 1.4.5, readers of the *Treatise* could not be in much doubt about the broad outline of Hume's position. *Treatise* 1.4.2, *Of scepticism with regard to the senses*, had provided a clear précis of what was to follow: "what we call a *mind*, is nothing but a heap or collection of different perceptions, united together by certain relations, and suppos'd, tho' falsly, to be endow'd with a perfect simplicity and identity" (T 1.4.2.39).

Hume's opening argument in *Treatise* 1.4.5 continues the critique of the concept of substance initiated in earlier sections of *Treatise* 1.4. Every simple idea must be derived from a precedent simple impression (T 1.1.1.7). However, the "curious reasoners" who debate whether our perceptions inhere in a material or immaterial substance cannot point to an impression that produces the idea of substance – a prima facie proof that the term *substance* lacks

[15] Clarke, *Works*, III:845, 851.
[16] Collins, in Clarke, *Works*, III:877.

significance. Appeals to the traditional definition of substance as *"something which may exist by itself"* provide no help, since every perception is distinguishable and separable from every other, and therefore satisfies this definition. Hume concludes that the question *"Whether perceptions inhere in a material or immaterial substance"* is devoid of meaning (T 1.4.5.2, 5–6).

Somewhat surprisingly, Hume is nonetheless interested in providing a more detailed analysis of one of the arguments presented by the defenders of the immateriality of the soul: the argument championed by Clarke that thought, or perceptions, cannot exist in a being made up of parts. Hume's strategy here requires some comment. As Hume understood it, because the metaphysical concept of substance is meaningless, there could be no serious philosophical debate over the question of whether the substance of the soul is material or immaterial. Why then should he continue to participate in a dispute he believed to be meaningless? Part of the answer may be that Hume could not resist the temptation to offer a clever argument against a formidable opponent, even though it was somewhat superfluous. Hume's audacious claim that defenders of the immateriality of the soul hold a theory indistinguishable from that of Spinoza (see T 1.4.5.17–25), whom they reviled, certainly suggests this; but other, philosophically deeper, reasons for pursuing this strategy will emerge in the discussion below.

Hume begins his new analysis of the issue with a review of the argument that thought and extension are "qualities wholly incompatible, and never can incorporate together into one subject" (T 1.4.5.7). In the light of his previous conclusion about the meaninglessness of the concepts of substance and inhesion, Hume maintains that the question at issue is more accurately whether thought and matter are susceptible of local conjunction (of, that is, conjunction in space – do thoughts or sensations have locations?), rather than about the underlying substance of the soul. Hume argues that such perceptions as passions, desires, moral reflections, smells, sounds, and tastes can exist *"and yet be no where"* (T 1.4.5.10). These perceptions have no size or figure, and thus cannot be located in space. Nor are they like mathematical points that can be manipulated to create a figure with spatial dimensions. Perceptions of this kind cannot have any spatial relation to matter. They cannot be part of matter, and in that sense cannot literally inhere in matter: "in this view of things,"

Hume observed, "we cannot refuse to condemn the materialists, who conjoin all thought with extension." But, he continued "a little reflection will show us equal reason for blaming their antagonists, who conjoin all thought with a simple and indivisible substance." There are some perceptions, namely, those derived from sight and touch, that are extended. The perception of a table, for example, has parts that are arranged to form a figure having all the features of extension. "To cut short all disputes, the very idea of extension is copy'd from nothing but an impression, and consequently must perfectly agree to it. To say the idea of extension agrees to any thing, is to say it is extended" (T 1.4.5.15). Since there are extended as well as unextended perceptions, those who argue that perceptions inhere in an immaterial substance face the same problem as the materialists. Just as the materialist cannot explain how perceptions that lack extension can exist in an extended substance, so the immaterialist cannot explain how extended perceptions exist in immaterial substance. Neither view, according to Hume, can be correct. Defenders of materialism and defenders of the immateriality of the soul both run afoul of the diverse nature of perceptions. This sheds further light on why, having concluded that the debate over the substance of the soul was meaningless, Hume did not just let the argument drop and move on. His analysis is intended to show that even if the concept of substance were not meaningless, accounts of the mind that attempt to ground perceptions in an underlying substance would fail.

The fact of the irreducible diversity of our perceptions is the starting point of Hume's own account of the self. The mind, according to Hume, is inherently complex and composite. Hume therefore goes beyond Locke's controversial conclusion that the mind is not necessarily an immaterial substance, to the stronger proposition that it could not be an immaterial substance. And, while Hume is critical of both materialism and immaterialism, on this central point his own account of the mind is similar to that of Collins, and fundamentally at odds with theologians like Clarke.

Of the immateriality of the soul concludes with a discussion of another issue debated by Clarke and Collins, whether matter and motion could be the cause of thought. This question, Hume argues, can be resolved by appeal to his own account of the nature of causality in *Treatise* 1.3. Although there is no apparent connection between motion and thought, the same is true for all causal relations.

It is only through the experience of their constant conjunction that we conclude that two objects are related as cause and effect: "we find by comparing their ideas, that thought and motion are different from each other, and by experience, that they are constantly united; which being all the circumstances, that enter into the idea of cause and effect, when apply'd to the operations of matter, we may certainly conclude, that motion may be, and actually is, the cause of thought and perception" (T 1.4.5.29–30). Hume acknowledged that this argument "gives the advantage to the materialists above their antagonists." But, while he does not seem reluctant to acknowledge this association, his previous grounds for rejecting materialism still stand: he reiterates that "all our perceptions are not susceptible of a local union, either with what is extended or unextended; there being some of them of the one kind, and some of the other" (T 1.4.5.32–3). As Hume has just argued, however, the diverse nature of perceptions is no obstacle to their standing in causal relations to each other. Thus *Treatise* 1.4.5 ends having established three central elements of Hume's account of the mind: there is no substance in which perceptions inhere; the self is comprised of perceptions of different types; and, in spite of their diverse natures, these perceptions may be linked together by the relation of cause and effect. These metaphysical conclusions provide the foundation for the discussion of personal identity that immediately follows.

III. *TREATISE* 1.4.6: PERSONAL IDENTITY AS IT REGARDS THE IMAGINATION

Of the immateriality of the soul addressed those philosophers who claim "that we have an idea of the substance of our minds" (T 1.4.5.4), without direct discussion of their views concerning the existence of the mind over time. The opening sentence of *Treatise* 1.4.6 signals an expanded focus. There are, Hume grants, "some philosophers who imagine we are every moment intimately conscious of what we call our SELF; that we feel its existence and its continuance in existence; and are certain, beyond the evidence of a demonstration, both of its perfect identity and simplicity." But, Hume argues, we have no idea of the self "after the manner it is here explain'd," that is, as something simple and identical through time. As we have seen, every simple idea must be derived from a simple impression.

If any impression were to give rise to the idea of the self as a being that exists over time, "that impression must continue invariably the same, thro' the whole course of our lives; since self is suppos'd to exist after that manner." But Hume finds no such impression in himself, and doubts that anyone, after "serious and unprejudic'd reflection," will be able to do so either.[17] "Pain and pleasure, grief and joy, passions and sensations succeed each other, and never all exist at the same time. It cannot, therefore, be from any of these impressions, or from any other, that the idea of self is deriv'd; and consequently there is no such idea."[18] The mind is "nothing but a bundle or collection of different perceptions, which succeed each other with an inconceivable rapidity, and are in a perpetual flux and movement. . . . There is properly no *simplicity* in it at one time, nor *identity* in different; whatever natural propension we may have to imagine that simplicity and identity" (T 1.4.6.1–4).[19] This last sentence indicates how Hume will bring the principles he has developed throughout Book 1 of the *Treatise* to bear on the problem of personal identity. Hume is not uninterested in the metaphysical question of the nature of the self: he had already argued for the complexity of the mind, and would develop his account to explain the relations that connect the self over time. But in *Of personal identity* Hume's focus is on explaining our tendency to believe in the perfect identity of the self over time, given that we have no impression or idea on which to ground that belief.

The distinction Hume introduces at this juncture, between personal identity "as it regards our thought or imagination" and personal identity "as it regards our passions or the concern we take in ourselves," reflects the way in which he had reconceptualized the problem of personal identity. A theory of personal identity as it

[17] Earlier comments in the *Treatise* reflect this view as well. Hume argued that the vulgar "have nothing like what we can call a belief of the eternal duration of their souls." Hume also argued that "in common life 'tis evident these ideas of self and person are never very fix'd nor determinate" (T 1.3.9.13, 1.4.2.6).

[18] As the passage quoted indicates, Hume here is denying that we have an idea of a simple self. We can, and do, have a complex idea of the self, of the self as a *collection* of perceptions.

[19] When introducing the philosophical relation of identity Hume said: "This relation I here consider as apply'd in its strictest sense to constant and unchangeable objects; without examining the nature and foundation of personal identity, which shall find its place afterwards" (T 1.1.5.4). Of course, Hume also said that the mind is falsely supposed "to be endow'd with a perfect simplicity and identity" (T 1.4.2.39).

regards the imagination should explain our tendency to suppose – incorrectly, according to Hume – that we are "possest of an invariable and uninterrupted existence thro' the whole course of our lives" (T 1.4.6.5). Hume thus recasts the underlying philosophical problem of personal identity as one about the causes of a particular and mistaken belief. Given the structure of the *Treatise*, Hume limits himself in Book 1 to the discussion of this aspect of personal identity. A theory of personal identity as it regards our passions focuses not on our belief, but on our concern for ourselves. As we saw earlier, Clarke (and others) had raised a troubling objection to Locke's account of personal identity, one that would apply to any theory on which the self is a compound entity. How, Clarke asked, could a self that was not strictly identical through time be a responsible moral agent? What basis could there be for concern with past acts, or consequences for the future? Hume acknowledged that this is a part of the problem of personal identity, but he does not in 1.4.6 address the problem at any length.

Hume's approach to the problem of personal identity can therefore be summed up in the following way: the arguments of *Treatise* 1.4.5 show that the mind is a collection of perceptions without an underlying substance. When we consider the existence of this kind of entity over time, there is no single perception that continues unchanged throughout a person's life. Nevertheless, we tend to think of ourselves as the same person, and to feel concerned with distant portions of our lives. The problem of personal identity, as Hume understood it, is to account for these beliefs and feelings about ourselves. There is, first, personal identity "as it regards our thought or imagination." Discussion of the details of this part of Hume's theory of personal identity continues below. And then there is personal identity "as it regards the passions," the subject of the next section of the present discussion.

Hume begins with his first task – with, that is, a general account of the idea of identity as that of an object that remains "invariable and uninterrupted" over time. When we think carefully and accurately, we recognize that any succession of objects exhibiting variation, even when they are closely related, is not an example of identity. However, the experience the mind has when it considers an unchanging object is very similar to the experience it has when it considers a closely connected series of objects. Resemblance is one of the principles by which perceptions are associated, and thus these two experiences become associated with each other. The idea of identity consequently becomes linked in the imagination with the experience of a succession of related objects, and we tend to attribute identity to the related sequences. This is a mistake, but one we can understand in light of the principles of association. We fall into this error so easily and readily, that "to justify to ourselves this absurdity, we often feign some new and unintelligible principle, that connects the objects together," or we are "apt to imagine something unknown and mysterious, connecting the parts, beside their relation" (T 1.4.6.6).

Hume analyzes the situations in which we attribute identity to physical objects, plants, and animals to support this general account. A physical body – a mass of matter with contiguous and connected parts – remains strictly the same over time only if all its parts remain unchanged. But when small changes are made gradually, we scarcely notice them, and the mind "feels an easy passage" as it surveys the object from one moment to the next. We continue to ascribe identity to the object because of this smooth transition of thought. But strictly speaking, a small change destroys the identity of the object just as much as a large change would. The only difference is that a large change does not usually go unnoticed. Even a considerable degree of variation can be compatible with accepting the continued identity of an object, if there is something, a common end or a functional organization, that facilitates the transition of the imagination when it considers the object at different times. In animals and plants, the parts are also causally related to each other, making it more likely that the object will act on the imagination as if it were strictly identical through time. To the imagination, a ship remains the same ship after major repairs, an oak is the same as it grows from a small plant to a mature tree, and an "infant becomes a man, and is sometimes fat, sometimes lean, without any change in his identity" (T 1.4.6.8–12).

Personal identity "as it regards our thought or imagination" is no different: "The identity, which we ascribe to the mind of man, is only a fictitious one, and of a like kind with that which we ascribe to vegetables and animal bodies. It cannot, therefore, have a different origin, but must proceed from a like operation of the imagination upon like objects." The mind at any one time is a collection of perceptions: over time, it is a series of such collections, interconnected but not identical. The interconnections make possible an "uninterrupted progress" of thought as a present self reflects on the successive experiences that have preceded it and led up to it. This feeling of easy transition creates "our notions of personal identity" (T 1.4.6.15–17).

Of the three relations that associate ideas, only two, resemblance and causation, have a role in creating the fiction of the self's identity over time. Memory is involved in both of these associations. Within the flux and variation of continuing experience, most people retain memories of past thoughts and experiences. Since memories resemble the perceptions that caused them, the existence of memories creates numerous links of resemblance within the succession of perceptions that constitutes a mind over time. In this respect, Hume argues, memory produces personal identity "by producing the relation of resemblance among the perceptions" (T 1.4.6.18).

Memory, however, is only one of many causal relations that connect the perceptions of the mind: impressions give rise to ideas, which may in turn produce impressions of reflection; beliefs influence the passions, and passions figure among the sources of other beliefs (T 1.1.2.1, 1.3.10.3–4). The centerpiece of Book 2 of the *Treatise*, the account of the indirect passions, is built on a double association of impressions and ideas that involves both causation and resemblance (T 2.1.5). For Hume, "the true idea of the human mind, is to consider it as a system of different perceptions or different existences, which are link'd together by the relation of cause and effect, and mutually produce, destroy, influence, and modify each other." Memory is necessary if one is to experience the idea of causation. Similarly, one cannot have the idea of the self, a series of causally related perceptions, without memory. However, once we have this idea, we extend the idea of our identity to our entire causal history, whether remembered or not. "In this view, therefore, memory does not so much *produce* as *discover* personal identity, by showing us the relation of cause and effect among our different perceptions" (T 1.4.6.19–20).

Hume's discussion of the role of memory in personal identity is motivated by his desire to avoid one of the problems associated with Locke's earlier account. Locke had argued that personal identity depends only on continuity of consciousness. On his view, consciousness of past thoughts and actions makes a present self identical with the person who had those thoughts and performed those actions. This account was criticized on the grounds that, in many ordinary judgments, including situations where we assign moral responsibility or evaluate moral obligations, personal identity is assumed to be more extensive than this account suggests. Indeed, in the eyes of the critics, personal identity *must* be something maintained from the start of life through the Last Judgment. Hume's theory is like Locke's in giving memory a role in actually producing personal identity, and not merely giving evidence of the existence of something else, such as a soul or immaterial substance that is independent of memory. However, on Hume's account, the true idea of the mind is that of a system of causally related perceptions. This enables his theory to extend personal identity beyond memory without appealing to the persistence of substance. The thoughts and emotions of the person "decay'd in his Memory and Intellectuals," as Henry Lee put it, are still causally dependent on earlier impressions and ideas, and the habits and associations built up over time. As a consequence, there is no need for Hume to deny that the later self is the same person as the earlier one when memory fails. Nonetheless, it is unlikely that Hume's appeal to causality would have satisfied many (or any) of the critics of Locke's view. Hume acknowledged without reluctance that relations like resemblance and causality occur in degrees. Memory, and the cognitive capacities that rely on memory, often fade or fail: there is no "just standard," according to Hume, to determine precisely when identity ceases. Questions of this kind about identity, and even about personal identity, are examples of what Hume calls "verbal" disputes. Complex relations of resemblance and causation connect perceptions over time: these explain the tendency to speak of a self, and attribute identity to it, even though there is nothing invariable and uninterrupted. The one issue about personal identity that is not verbal, and that can be definitively resolved, concerns the substance that is purported to connect our perceptions through time: no such substance exists (T 1.4.6.21).

IV. PERSONAL IDENTITY AS IT REGARDS OUR PASSIONS

We return now to the distinction Hume made between personal identity as it regards the imagination and personal identity as it regards our passions. As the previous two sections have shown, Hume argued that the self – either at a given time or over time – is nothing more than a complex collection of perceptions: there is no underlying substance in which the perceptions inhere, and no perception that remains through the whole course of a person's life. Personal identity is thus a fiction. And as Hume conceived it the twofold problem of personal identity is, first, to explain why we tend to *believe* in the identity of the self, and, second, to explain why a present self who is not, in fact, identical with a self who existed in the past or will exist in the future is nonetheless *concerned* with a set of "past or future pains or pleasures" (T 1.4.6.19). Hume limited the discussion in *Treatise* 1.4.6 to the former question, which is directly connected to his theory of the imagination. Thus by Hume's own characterization, the treatment of the problem of personal identity in Book 1 of the *Treatise* is incomplete.

The history of the discussion of personal identity after Locke makes it clear why Hume would have seen the latter problem, the explanation of self-concern, as an important issue. For both Clarke and Butler had argued that without a substantial self that remains identical through time a person would have no reason to feel responsible for past actions, nor any reason to be concerned about the future consequences of present actions. Both philosophers took this to be a reductio ad absurdem of Locke's view. The same argument could, of course, be urged against Hume. It might be thought that a Humean account of the mind has no avenue of response to this criticism. Since Hume denies that any substance identical to me, now, existed in the past, or will exist in the future, there might appear to be nothing for my present self to be concerned about: no past actions *I* am responsible for, no future consequences that will affect *me*. This argument begs the question, however. As we have seen, Hume supposes that the self is extended through time, but it is not so extended by means of the persistence of substance. On Hume's view, my past encompasses those perceptions, thoughts, and actions related to a present self by resemblance and causation. What Hume's account of the passions needs to explain is how those past perceptions, thoughts, and actions affect my present feelings, and therefore why they are of interest and importance to me. And, similarly, his account must explain why I sometimes act out of concern for a future self – a future collection of perceptions – that will bear to me, now, the relation I bear to my past. Hume's theory of the passions does, in fact, accomplish both of these tasks. It is by providing an account of self-concern that Book 2 of the *Treatise* completes Hume's account of personal identity.

Let us first consider what Hume's account of the passions has to say about the relationship of a present self to its past. A theme that is common to Hume's explanation of the passions and his moral theory is that certain actions and characters naturally evoke pleasure or pain in those who observe or contemplate them. (See, for example, T 2.1.5.2, 2.1.7.3–5, 3.1.2.3.) As sources of pleasure and pain, actions and characters have a role to play in the genesis of what Hume calls the *indirect passions*. Hume's innovative theory of the indirect passions has many subtleties, but the central concept can be briefly summarized. Although some passions, desires, or aversions arise *directly* from the observation or contemplation of something pleasurable or painful, other feelings have a different origin. These latter feelings or passions occur only when the source of pleasure or pain is related either to oneself, or to another person. Pride and humility, love and hatred, are in this sense indirect passions.

Hume's explanation of a person's concern with her past is rooted specifically in his account of the indirect passions of pride and humility. When something relevantly related to me is also a source of pleasure or pain, the result is a feeling of pride or humility, respectively. These passions have the self for their object, that is, they reintroduce the idea of the self (understood as a connected succession of perceptions) into the mind. Hume describes the underlying mechanism as a double relation (or sometimes as an "association") of impressions and ideas (T 2.1.2.3, 2.1.5.5, 10). The pleasure caused by something closely related to me (my virtue or my house, for example) is associated with the pleasurable feeling of pride; this is the association of two impressions. The idea of the cause is associated with the idea of the self. These two associations reinforce each other, simultaneously turning my attention to myself and generating the feeling of pride.[20]

---

[20] As an illustration: a well planned garden is a source of pleasure no matter who planned it, or who owns it. If the garden is mine, or designed by me, however, I will feel not merely pleasure, but pride. Due to the association of ideas, looking at the garden causes me to think to myself ("I made that" or "I own that"). This enhances another association, between the pleasure of looking at the garden and the pleasurable glow of pride. The cause of pride is the fact that something pleasurable is related to me. This is not the result of a process of reasoning, but of mutually reinforcing associations.

Analogously, when something related to me is a source of pain, the resulting feeling is humility.

Hume's analysis of pride and humility provides an explanation of a concern with the past that is a natural extension of the account of personal identity in *Treatise* 1.4.6. In light of this account Hume can explain why, for example, my past actions continue to concern me, even though they are not the actions of a single substance, and even though the self is not strictly identical through time. My present self stands in relations of resemblance and causation to various past perceptions, thoughts, and actions: this is what makes them mine. This same fact of relatedness to my present self gives a past occurrence a role to play in the generation of my passions. Insofar as it is independently a source of pleasure or pain, a past action will affect me with pride or humility. My shame in a past failure is the result of two circumstances: the past act is relevantly related to me, and it is of a kind that evokes feelings of pain or displeasure. Concern with the past therefore depends on the relations that hold among perceptions – specifically the appropriate double association of ideas and impressions – and not on identity of substance.

The present self extends its concern to the future as well as the past. Even the most ordinary plans can require that our present actions are governed by a future interest that we see as our own. We think of ourselves in the future, and are motivated (at least sometimes) by the prospect of future pain or pleasure, punishment or reward (T 2.3.2.5, 2.3.3.3, 3.3.12). But, on Hume's view, what is involved in thinking of oneself in the future? How do such thoughts affect our passions and serve to motivate our present actions? Book 2 of the *Treatise*, like Book 1, takes causation to be the primary connection between the perceptions that constitute the self through time. But Book 2 introduces another causal relation into the account of the self: the relation between intention and action. Hume argued that although some might refuse to apply the terms *cause* or *necessity* to that relation, the constant conjunction between intention and action, and the inference from the one to the other, is "universally, tho' tacitly" allowed (T 2.3.2.4). Even in common life, therefore, my future is believed to be causally related to my present and my past. In thinking of myself in the future, I am thinking of the actions that follow from my motives, intentions, and character, rather than of some substance in which these actions inhere.

To understand why the passions are affected by our ideas of the future requires at least a brief examination of the relationship between the imagination and the passions, and the influence on them of spatial and temporal relations. The imagination tends to focus on the vivid ideas of what is present and near: it "passes easily from obscure to lively ideas, but with difficulty from lively to obscure." Ideas of things that are distant in either space or time tend to be relatively faint, and as such might be expected to have little influence on the passions. But the passions have a dynamic of their own that counteracts this: they tend to spread themselves out. The feeling of love or hatred I have for another person transfers readily to their relations (to, that is, members of their family) and other acquaintances (T 2.2.2.15, 19). Further experience may change or correct these transferred feelings, but the passions are naturally expansive. One of the most fundamental traits of human nature, the mind's ability to turn, as it does in sympathy, from the idea of myself to the idea of another person presupposes this expansive tendency. And the operation of sympathy explains the influence of our ideas of the future on our present actions.

Hume initially presents sympathy as the propensity to "receive by communication" the sentiments of others. We first form an idea of another person's feeling by perceiving its effects on "countenance and conversation." The resemblance between other persons and ourselves enlivens that idea, transferring to it the vivacity of our own passions. As a result of this process, we are not merely convinced, by a piece of causal reasoning, of the reality of the other person's feeling, but the idea of that feeling is actually converted into an *impression* that copies the feeling of that person. In other words, the operation of sympathy allows us to share (and thus to know) the feelings of others (T 2.1.11.2–8). The basic functioning of sympathy is interpersonal, but it can also be extended beyond the present to pains and pleasures that are only anticipated. Hume wrote:

Sympathy being nothing but a lively idea converted into an impression, 'tis evident, that, in considering the future possible or probable condition of any person, we may enter into it with so vivid a conception as to make it our own concern; and by that means be sensible of pains and pleasures, which neither belong to ourselves, nor at the present instant have any real existence. (T 2.2.9.13)

The identification of my interest with the interests of a future person – the identification of myself with that person – is the result of the extended operation of sympathy. When I think of myself in the future I think of the actions that follow from my present intention, motives, and character: I think of the consequences of those actions, and the circumstances in which they will take place. This causal connection between something central to my present self (to, that is, my intentions, motives, and character) and the actions and circumstances of a future person facilitates the operation of sympathy. The "possible or probable condition" of that future person becomes my own present concern.

This account explains why, even though there is no strict identity of the self through time, we identify a future interest as our own. A mere fiction of the imagination would have no influence on the passions, according to Hume, but sympathy with a future self can serve as the motivation for action. This does not entail, however, that we always act on the basis of that future interest. To think of myself at a point of time in the future requires that I trace a causal chain between myself and that future time (T 2.3.6.10, 2.3.7.2). The more remote the time, the harder it is to trace the connection, thus lessening the effect of sympathy.[21]

V. THE DISCUSSION OF PERSONAL IDENTITY IN THE APPENDIX TO THE *TREATISE*

The argument of the previous sections reveals a remarkable consistency in Hume's account of the self throughout Books 1 and 2 of the *Treatise*. The mind, or self, is a compound entity – a collection of perceptions of different types connected to each other by causation and resemblance. As a consequence of this view, the problem of personal identity has two dimensions. First, to explain why we tend to *believe* in the identity of the self, and, second, to explain why a present self who is not, in fact, identical with a self in the past or the future is nonetheless *concerned* with a past and a future it identifies as its own. Hume addressed the first part of the problem of

---

[21] On this account, self-concern and concern for others differ in degree, rather than in kind. To adopt the disinterested perspective Hume took to be necessary for moral evaluation is to recognize the essential similarity of these relations.

personal identity in *Treatise* 1.4.6, and the second part through the
account of the indirect passions and sympathy in Book 2. Taken as a
whole, then, the *Treatise* presents a complete analysis of the nature
of the self and its identity – an account that was crafted to be responsive to the issues about personal identity raised in the fifty years
following Locke's discussion in his *Essay*. Nevertheless, in twelve
paragraphs of the Appendix to the *Treatise* (T App. 10–21) Hume
famously expressed dissatisfaction with the central arguments he
had given in *Of personal identity*. These paragraphs confess a mistake, but the argument behind them is cryptic, and scholars have
not been able to agree on the nature of the mistake to which Hume
refers.[22] This section aims to clarify the issue raised by the Appendix.

The opening sentences of Hume's discussion of personal identity
in the Appendix set the stage for the discussion that follows:

I had entertain'd some hopes, that however deficient our theory of the intellectual world might be, it wou'd be free from those contradictions, and
absurdities, which seem to attend every explication, that human reason can
give of the material world. But upon a more strict review of the section concerning *personal identity*, I find myself involv'd in such a labyrinth, that, I
must confess, I neither know how to correct my former opinions, nor how
to render them consistent. (T App. 10)

Hume goes on to say that he will review the arguments "on both
sides" of the issue, beginning with those that lead him to deny the
simplicity and identity of the self. He proceeds to repeat, briefly,
that we have no idea of a simple and individual self or substance
because we have no impression of such a substance; that all perceptions may be *conceived* as existing separately, and thus may in fact
exist separately; that there is no contradiction involved in holding
that perceptions do not inhere in a simple substance; that reflection
on the mind reveals nothing but perceptions, so that "'Tis the composition of these, therefore, which forms the self" (T App. 15). Hume
notes that these conclusions are similar to those that philosophers

---

[22] For reviews of various proposals concerning Hume's argument in the Appendix, see
Don Garrett, *Cognition and Commitment* (New York: Oxford University Press,
1997), 167–80; and Corliss Swain, "Personal Identity and the Skeptical System of
Philosophy," in *The Blackwell Guide to Hume's* Treatise, ed. S. Traiger (Malden,
MA: Blackwell Publishing, 2006), 133–50.

have already drawn with respect to external substances (T App. 11–15, 19).

At this juncture Hume remarks: "So far I seem to be attended with sufficient evidence" (T App. 20). What then prompts him to have reservations about the account of personal identity presented in *Treatise* 1.4.6? When we turn to the remainder of Hume's discussion – to the critique of his own view – the source of his dissatisfaction is difficult to make out. Hume's focus in Appendix 20 and 21 is on the principles that bind the distinct perceptions together and make "us attribute to them a real simplicity and identity." The analysis of causality in *Treatise* 1.3 led to the conclusion that the connections between distinct existences are only the "determination of the thought, to pass from one object to another." Applying that conclusion to the self, it follows that "thought alone finds personal identity, when reflecting on the train of past perceptions, that compose a mind." That is, thought finds that the ideas of past perceptions are felt to be connected together, and naturally introduce each other. Hume draws a parallel between this view and the position that personal identity arises from consciousness, which he surprisingly says "most philosophers" are inclined to accept.[23] However, he takes this to be a further "promising aspect" of his own account, not a negative one. So, although philosophers such as Clarke and Butler would have viewed this as a devastating criticism of Hume's account of the self, Hume endorses it as a consequence of his account of causal relations. In spite of this, paragraph 20 concludes with Hume's assertion that he cannot discover any theory that provides a satisfactory explanation of the principles that "unite our successive perceptions in our thought or consciousness."

Paragraph 21 of the Appendix is even more perplexing, for there Hume says that there are two principles that he can neither render consistent nor renounce, namely, "*that all our distinct perceptions are distinct existences*, and *that the mind never perceives any real connexion among distinct existences*." Virtually every commentator has acknowledged that these principles are not inconsistent, and that they are essential not merely to Hume's account of the self, but to many of the central arguments of Book 1 of the *Treatise*. What

---

[23] As we have seen in Section I of this essay, this Lockean view was notoriously controversial from the moment of its publication.

then is Hume's specific disappointment with his account of personal identity?

An answer to this question can be found by reexamining Appendix 10, the paragraph quoted above in which Hume said that he had hoped that his theory of the intellectual world would be "free from those contradictions, and absurdities, which seem to attend every explication, that human reason can give of the material world."[24] This sentence refers to the first paragraph of *Treatise* 1.4.5, *Of the immateriality of the soul,* where Hume had claimed that the account of the intellectual world "is not perplex'd with any such contradictions, as those we have discovered in the natural" world. Through that comment, it also refers indirectly to the arguments of 1.4.2, *Of scepticism with regard to the senses,* and 1.4.4, *Of the modern philosophy,* and to the summaries and comments on those arguments at T 1.4.4.15 and 1.4.7.3–5. Each of these passages discusses a contradiction within the imagination. In them, Hume argues that two operations of the imagination lead to contradictory results. The associations of ideas described in *Treatise* 1.4.2 lead to belief in the continued and independent existence of objects. On the other hand, reasoning from causes and effects, another association of ideas, leads to the conclusion that there are no objects with continued and independent existence. The account of the intellectual world in *Treatise* 1.4.5, *Of the immateriality of the soul,* was *by itself* able (as it claimed to) to avoid this inconsistency. It did so because it did not consider belief in the *continued* existence of any substance. It argued that the mind is nothing but perceptions, without an underlying substance. There is no need, then, in 1.4.5 to posit a feigned "double existence" resulting from adherence to two contrary principles. In fact, 1.4.5 presents a clever argument showing why there *could not be* a double existence of perceptions and an underlying substance. It argued that some perceptions are extended, and some unextended, and as a result it is clear that they cannot all inhere in either a material or an immaterial substratum.

The argument of *Treatise* 1.4.6, *Of personal identity,* however, reopens the problem of inconsistency. In this section, as in 1.4.2,

---

[24] This general approach is also taken by A. E. Pitson in Hume's *Philosophy of the Self* (London: Routledge, 2002), Chap. 4; and by Corliss Swain, "Personal Identity and the Skeptical System of Philosophy." Pitson and Swain develop their analyses in ways different from that followed here.

the association of ideas is appealed to as the source of the *belief* that something continues to exist (in this case soul or mental substance) in spite of all the variation in our perceptions over time. The structure of the argument in T 1.4.6.6 is the same as that of the argument in T 1.4.2.31–43. Consequently, the account of the intellectual world, like the account of the material world, reveals inconsistent tendencies or principles in the imagination. Both accounts face the same problem: the imagination produces belief in the continued existence of something other than perceptions (a substratum), while at the same time revealing that nothing of that kind exists.

Of personal identity presents a view that Hume explicitly called "the true idea of the human mind," the view of the mind as a system of different perceptions or existences linked together by the relation of cause and effect. We arrive at this idea in the following way: (1) Memory acquaints us with the continuance and extent of a succession of perceptions. (2) From memory we also get the idea of causation. And (3) once we have the idea of causation, we extend the chain of perceptions beyond memory (T 1.4.6.19–20). This progression is the natural development of the position arrived at in 1.4.5, namely, that there could not be a substance in which perceptions inhere, and hence that the mind can be nothing but perceptions and their causal relations. In 1.4.5 and 1.4.6 Hume never expresses any reservations about this view of the mind, which is grounded in his own account of causality. This is a point of contrast with his discussion of the belief in the existence of body, where no view is singled out as the "true" view.

Hume held that the *belief* that the self is identical over time is the result of another operation of the imagination – the tendency of the imagination to associate by resemblance, and to confuse the experience of closely related succession with the experience of an unchanging thing. The belief in the identity of the self is false, but it is produced by operations of the imagination that are as entrenched as causal reasoning. The imagination therefore leads both to the *true* view of the mind as a causal system of perceptions, and the *false* view that the self is a substance that is identical through time. In this way Hume's argument about the self recapitulates the dilemma he articulated concerning belief in the existence of body. As a consequence, the theory of the intellectual world is not free from the contradictions that bedeviled the theory of the material world.

We can now see why Hume said in the Appendix that he did not know how to correct his former opinions, or to make them consistent. He had formerly held that his account of the intellectual world was free from the contradictions that faced his account of the material world. He now sees that both accounts face the same problem, namely, that certain fundamental tendencies of the imagination lead to inconsistent conclusions. Furthermore, there is no way (or no way acceptable to Hume) to give an account of why we *believe* in the identity of the self over time that avoids this problem. Belief is the result of the enlivening of ideas, an enlivening that is a product of association. On Hume's account, the only connections that exist among perceptions are *felt* connections that are the product of the association of ideas. The feeling produced by these connections is the source of the belief in the continued existence of both mind and body.

We can see why Hume might not have recognized this problem earlier. First, Hume's basic theory of the intellectual world is internally consistent, however unsatisfactory it was to theologians on other grounds. He holds that

1. The mind is nothing but perceptions
2. There is no substance (material or immaterial) underlying those perceptions
3. The existence of the self through time can be explained, without contradiction, as a succession of causally related perceptions
4. Nothing more than this is necessary to explain the operation of the passions, particularly the concern we have for our future selves.

Furthermore, Hume did not reject the belief in a continually existing self so long as that was not taken to include the false belief in continually existing substance or soul. Although Hume was ambivalent about the strength of the general tendency to endorse this false belief, he clearly found it possible to correct it in himself. Elsewhere in the *Treatise* Hume argued that education and indoctrination artificially promote the belief in a future state of the soul after death (T 1.3.9.13). Initially, therefore, there did not appear to be a problem with the account embedded in 1.4.5 and 1.4.6.

Unfortunately, if Hume's later reflections are correct, the view before the Appendix underestimates the tendency of the imagination to arrive at the *false* belief in a continually existing mental substance or self. If we look back to the account of the belief in the existence of body, and the contradictions that occur in the theory of the material world, we can see some of the difficulties emerging in his account of the self. Hume's theory of the material world depicts such a strong tendency to take resembling perceptions to be identical over time that it is impossible really to eradicate it. We also cannot give up the opinion that resembling impressions are interrupted and different from each other (T 1.4.2.51–2). This leads to the unsatisfactory philosophical theory of the double existence of perceptions and objects.

The operation of the imagination should be the same when considering the perceptions that constitute the mind. This would lead to two opposing beliefs: an ineradicable (though still false) belief in the identity of self or substance over time; and the opinion, well established by reflection, that all our perceptions are distinct existences. The analogous unsatisfactory philosophical position would be that there is a substance, different from perceptions, that continues identically the same, in which the variable perceptions inhere. As an account of a dilemma in early modern philosophy of mind, this is not implausible. In fact, it seems to reflect the view of personal identity held by nearly all of Locke's critics. But there is no longer a complete theory of "the intellectual world" that is free of contradictions. The internal world is beset by the same contradiction discovered in the theory of the material world. A greater cause for despair, however, is that it does not leave much hope that the "true idea of the human mind" will be one that we can believe.

VI. "MATURE REFLECTION": HUME'S VIEW OF THE SELF AFTER THE *TREATISE*

Of personal identity presented the tendency to believe in a self that was strictly identical through time (and therefore was not a bundle of perceptions) as one that could be explained through the operation of the imagination and potentially corrected through reflection. Hume's later claim in the Appendix that the theories of the intellectual and material worlds are subject to the same inherent

contradictions indicated that he had lost his confidence that philosophical arguments like those in *Treatise* 1.4.5–6 could counterbal-
ance the false belief in a substantial self. The Appendix, however,
does not retract the positive account of the self argued for in the
Treatise. And, although Hume did not directly address the problem
of personal identity again, both his published and his unpublished
work after the *Treatise* reveal a view of the self strikingly similar to
the earlier account.

After the *Treatise*, Hume's expression of his views on the self was
more guarded in his published works than in those he left unpublished. Nevertheless, the *Enquiry concerning Human Understanding* provides examples of the persistence of many of the main tenets
Hume sought to establish in T 1.4.5–6, even in passages not trans-
planted from the *Treatise*. *Enquiry 7*, in which Hume discusses the
idea of necessary connection, provides an important example of this.
The *Treatise* contained only a brief mention, added as a note in the
Appendix, of the impossibility of deriving the idea of power from the
feeling of volition (T 1.3.14.12). By contrast, the argument against
this origin of the idea of power is more extensive in the *Enquiry*,
incorporating discussions of both the influence of mind on body,
and the relation of the mind to its own ideas and passions. In both
works Hume denied that we have any idea of a connection other than
observed conjunction. Even within the mind there is no stronger tie
to be discovered among our perceptions. Both T 1.3.14.12 and the
Enquiry agree with the view expressed in *Of the immateriality of
the soul*, the view that "tho' there appear no manner of connexion betwixt motion or thought, the case is the same with all other
causes and effects." This was a central part of the argument Hume
gave in support of his view of the compound nature of the self. Further, *Enquiry 7* continues to reject the concept of immaterial substance, referring to the mysterious union of the soul and the body
"by which a supposed spiritual substance" acquires influence over
a material one (EHU 7.11). Thus the argument of this section of
the *Enquiry* supports many of the conclusions Hume argued for in
T 1.4.5–6. Everything we know about the connection between mind
and body, or the relationship of a mind to its ideas, comes through
experience. Experience reveals that there are such relations, but not
how they operate. Hume concludes by saying: "So that, upon the
whole, there appears not, throughout all nature, any one instance

of connexion, which is conceivable by us. All events seem entirely loose and separate. One event follows another; but we never can observe any tye between them" (EHU 7.26). The nature of the mind provides no exception to this principle.

Unlike the *Treatise,* the *Enquiry* includes extended discussions of theological issues. This change of emphasis is also reflected in Hume's treatment of questions about the self. While *Enquiry* 7 shows that Hume continued to reject the view that there are necessary connections among the components of the mind, in Section 11, "Of a Particular Providence and of a Future State," Hume endorses the radical theological consequences of his view of the self.

As was noted in Part I of this essay, Butler's "Dissertation on Personal Identity" was one of the best-known critiques of the Lockean account. Butler opened with the following statement:

Whether we are to live in a future State, as it is the most important Question which can possibly be asked, so it is the most intelligible one which can be expressed in Language. Yet strange Perplexities have been raised about the Meaning of That Identity or Sameness of Person, which is implied in the Notion of our living Now and Hereafter, or in any two successive Moments.[25]

Like Clarke, Butler argued that the soul's existence in a future state, or its reward and punishment in that state, required a substantial self, strictly identical through time. We can only speculate whether Hume had read Butler's account of personal identity before writing his own, but it would be very surprising if he had not read it by the time he composed the *Enquiry.* Although the account of personal identity presented in the *Treatise* clearly did not satisfy the conditions held by theologians to be necessary for a future existence, the *Treatise* contains only a brief criticism of the belief in the soul's state after death (T 1.3.9.13). Section 11 of the *Enquiry,* however, presents a direct attack on a major argument for this belief. Written in the form of a dialogue, it develops a critique of the argument from design. In this context Hume considers and rejects the claim that distributive justice requires the existence of a future state in which souls are rewarded or punished. Our experience of justice in the world provides no ground for expecting a future state of the

[25] Joseph Butler, Dissertation I in *The Analogy of Religion* (London, 1736), 301.

soul in which justice will be more perfectly satisfied (EHU 11.22). Rather than retreating from the analysis of the self in the *Treatise*, the *Enquiry* embraces one of its most controversial implications.

Of Hume's unpublished works, "Of the Immortality of the Soul" sheds the most light on his view of the self after the *Treatise*. This essay was one of two intended for publication in 1755, but suppressed by Hume before it was distributed.[26] It includes some of the arguments from *Of the immateriality of the soul* and Section 11 of the *Enquiry*, but its scope is considerably broader. "Of the Immortality of the Soul" touches on the full range of problems about the self found in the *Treatise*, including the concern of the self with the past and the future, and the relationship of self-concern to facts about our bodily existence.

The organization of this essay indicates some of its overlap with Hume's related published work. Hume considers, in turn, metaphysical, moral, and physical arguments as they bear on the question of the immortality of the soul. The metaphysical argument, he contends, is that the soul is immaterial, and therefore immortal. Hume repeats the arguments explicitly presented in the *Treatise* (and only slightly less explicitly in the *Enquiry*) that the essence of matter and spirit are equally unknown; we cannot rule out, a priori, that matter might be the cause of thought (E-IS 4, 591).

At this point, however, Hume introduces an argument not found in his previous works. Even if immaterial substance does exist, this would not prove the immortality of individual personal souls: "As the same material substance may successively compose the body of all animals, the same spiritual substance may compose their minds: Their consciousness, or that system of thought, which they formed during life, may be continually dissolved by death; and nothing interest them in the new modification" (E-IS 5, 591–2). Two aspects of this passage are significant. First, contrary to Hume's claim in Appendix 21, the inherence of ideas in a substance would not, according to this argument, adequately account for personal identity. Second, Hume argues that we would not be *interested* in the underlying substance once our own conscious system of thought

---

[26] E. C. Mossner, *The Life of David Hume*, 2nd ed. (Oxford: Clarendon Press, 1980), Chap. 24; J. C. A. Gaskin, *Hume's Philosophy of Religion*, 2nd ed. (New Jersey: Humanities Press, 1988), Chap. 9.

is dissolved. Our concern is with the organized conscious system, not with a substance supporting it. In this respect, Hume reiterates the view of *Treatise* 1 and developed in his account of the passions, the view that the causal connections among the components of the self make "our distant perceptions influence each other," and give us a present concern for our "past or future pains or pleasures" (T 1.4.6.19). Underscoring this, Hume wrote: "what is incorruptible must also be ingenerable. The soul, therefore, if immortal, existed before our birth: And if the former state of existence no wise concerned us, neither will the latter" (E-IS 6, 592). The metaphysical argument fails, according to Hume, precisely because it fails to prove the existence of an object whose fate we would be interested in, or about which we would be concerned.

The issue of self-concern plays an important part as well in Hume's reformulation of his critique of the moral arguments for the immortality of the soul. These maintain that the soul must be immortal so that there will be an arena in which virtue will unfailingly be rewarded and vice punished. Although Hume repeats the argument concerning distributive justice given in Section 11 of the *Enquiry,* his emphasis here is on arguing that a person's concerns are all "limited to the present life." Hume asked: "With how weak a concern, from the original, inherent structure of the mind and passions, does he ever look farther? What comparison, either for steddiness or efficacy, between so floating an idea, and the most doubtful persuasion of any matter of fact, that occurs in common life." Rather than assuring justice, the immortality of the soul would in fact conflict with it. Moral ideas are derived from the reflection on the interests of human society and relate to the present life. Eternal rewards and punishments serve no purpose, "after the whole scene [of the present life] is closed," and are out of proportion to the limited interests they supposedly guard (E-IS 11, 19–22, 28, 592, 594–5).

The arguments in the final section of the essay, which Hume describes as "*physical* arguments from the analogy of nature," have an important tie to Hume's references to mind and body in Book 2 of the *Treatise* (E-IS 30, 596). In the *Treatise* the passions of pride and humility are among the primary expressions of the concern we take in ourselves. Hume identified qualities of both mind and body as parts of the self, and as causes of pride and humility (T 2.1.9.1). From the point of view of the passions, mind and body are on a par. In the final section of "Of the Immortality of the Soul" this perspective on the passions, in which the body is fully integrated into the concept of the self, becomes the dominant view. In the present life, which Hume argues is our only concern, "Every thing is in common between soul and body. The organs of the one are all of them the organs of the other. The existence therefore of the one must be dependent on that of the other" (E-IS 36, 596).

Hume's conclusion that the soul is dependent on the body, however, goes beyond even the enhanced view of the self in Book 2 of the *Treatise*. The body is no longer depicted as a part of what we consider as ourselves. On the contrary, our mental qualities depend for their existence on the existence of our bodies. Both the *Treatise* and the *Enquiry* accepted the existence of causal connection between mind and body because of the experienced constant conjunctions between them. In "Of the Immortality of the Soul" Hume appeals to analogical arguments to support the stronger conclusion that changes in the body are always accompanied by changes in the mind. From infancy to old age, the powers of the body and the mind are "exactly proportioned." Hume continued: "The step farther seems unavoidable; their common dissolution in death" (E-IS 33, 596).

VII. CONCLUSION

"Of the Immortality of the Soul" provides an account of the belief in the future existence of the soul that draws more on the passions than the imagination. Although our concerns all relate to this life, and we cannot help but recognize that the dissolution of the body results in the annihilation of the soul, that thought terrifies us. The horror that we feel has the utility of helping to preserve the human species, but this in itself makes the belief in immortality problematic, for "All doctrines are to be suspected, which are favoured by our passions" (E-IS 43, 598).

"Of the Immortality of the Soul" and the related essay "Of Suicide" also revive and extend the argument Hume presents only briefly in the *Treatise*, the argument that education and indoctrination contribute to the strength and entrenchment of the belief in the existence of the soul, and a continued life after the death of the body. In these essays, belief in the soul is not the outcome of the workings of the imagination, but the result of artificially fostered superstition that exploits our natural horror of annihilation. As Hume says in "Of the Immortality of the Soul": "There arise, indeed, in some minds, some unaccountable terrors with regard to futurity: But these would quickly vanish, were they not artificially fostered by precept and education. And those, who foster them; what is their motive? Only to gain a livelihood, and to acquire power and riches in this world" (E-IS 12, 593). "Of Suicide" reiterates this account of the influence of superstition and appeals to "true philosophy" to counter the false opinion that suicide is criminal (E-Su 1, 579). And, in a similar vein, in Part XII of the *Dialogues concerning Natural Religion*, Philo classifies belief in a future state as a vulgar superstition. Religious motives, such as the concern for eternal punishments and rewards, "operate only by starts and bounds" and "must be roused by continual efforts" (DNR 12.13, 17, 221, 222).

In Hume's later works, therefore, it is not the imagination alone that is the source of an ineradicable belief in a simple self that remains strictly the same through time. The passions, assisted by education and indoctrination, also play a part in enlivening this belief. In this respect, we find some resolution to the problem that worried Hume in the Appendix, for the imagination alone is no longer implicated in a labyrinth of contradiction in its account of the intellectual world.

The final evidence that Hume maintains his view of the self in his later philosophy is revealed in the *Dialogues concerning Natural Religion*. There we find both Demea and Cleanthes explicitly endorsing the analysis Hume put forth in the *Treatise*. At the end of Part III Demea eloquently proclaims: "Our thought is fluctuating, uncertain, fleeting, successive, and compounded; and were we to remove these circumstances, we absolutely annihilate its essence" (DNR 3.13, 156–7). He continues at the beginning of Part IV:

What is the soul of man? A composition of various faculties, passions, sentiments, ideas; united, indeed, into one self or person, but still distinct from each other. When it reasons, the ideas, which are the parts of its discourse, arrange themselves in a certain form or order; which is not preserved entire for a moment, but immediately gives place to another arrangement. New opinions, new passions, new affections, new feelings arise, which continually diversify the mental scene, and produce in it the greatest variety and most rapid succession imaginable. How is this compatible with that perfect immutability and simplicity, which all true theists ascribe to the Deity? (DNR 4.2, 159)

Cleanthes asserts slightly later: "A mind, whose acts and sentiments and ideas are not distinct and successive; one, that is wholly simple, and totally immutable; is a mind which has no thought, no reason, no will, no sentiment, no love, no hatred; or in a word, is no mind at all" (DNR 4.3, 159). Philo takes no exception to these descriptions of the mind, and enjoys pointing out to Cleanthes that, on his view, all the "orthodox divines" are atheists – an argument strongly reminiscent of Hume's in *Of the immateriality of the soul* in the *Treatise*. Hume was obviously having fun here, for neither Clarke nor Butler, the supposed models for Demea and Cleanthes, would have embraced those Humean sentiments. Yet by having all three participants in the *Dialogues* agree on this view of the human mind Hume left little possibility for doubt about his final view of the self. After thirty-seven years of mature reflection, the account of the self in the *Treatise* emerged again, unscathed.

SUGGESTIONS FOR FUTHER READING

In addition to the works cited in the notes to this essay, for further reading the following are recommended.

Baier, Annette. "Hume on Heaps and Bundles." *American Philosophical Quarterly* 16 (1979): 285–95.

    A Progress of Sentiments: Reflections on Hume's Treatise. Cambridge, MA: Harvard University Press, 1991. Chap. 6.

Garrett, Don. "Hume's Self-Doubts about Personal Identity." *Philosophical Review* 90 (1981): 337–58.

Penelhum, Terence. *Themes in Hume: The Self, The Will, Religion.* Oxford: Clarendon Press, 2000.

7   Hume's Skepticism

> By all that has been said the reader will easily perceive, that the
> philosophy contained in this book is very sceptical, and tends to
> give us a notion of the imperfections and narrow limits of human
> understanding. Almost all reasoning is there reduced to experience;
> and the belief, which attends experience, is explained to be nothing
> but a peculiar sentiment, or lively conception produced by habit.
> Nor is this all. When we believe any thing of *external* existence, or
> suppose an object to exist a moment after it is no longer perceived,
> this belief is nothing but a sentiment of the same kind. Our author
> insists upon several other sceptical topics; and upon the whole
> concludes, that we assent to our faculties, and employ our reason
> only because we cannot help it. Philosophy would render us entirely
> *Pyrrhonian*, were not nature too strong for it.
>
> A 27

The above passage comes from a pamphlet written by David Hume to
secure a readership for his largely unappreciated *Treatise of Human
Nature.* Although not successful in this regard, the *Abstract* remains
a valuable guide to Hume's *Treatise,* through offering his own assessment of the significance of that work. Here, at least, Hume is
unequivocal in describing his philosophy as "very sceptical." But
even if Hume describes his philosophy in this way, and even if, at
the time, his philosophy was almost universally taken in this light, it
remains unclear, first, what this skepticism amounts to and, second,
how this skepticism is related to other aspects of his philosophical
program. The goal of this essay is to answer both of these questions.
I begin by giving a broad sketch of the role of skepticism in Hume's

philosophy and then, in succeeding sections, offer a detailed analysis of the central skeptical arguments.

I. SKEPTICISM AND BELIEF

One clue to the nature of Hume's skepticism is given in the sentence that immediately follows his claim that the philosophy found in the *Treatise* "is very sceptical, and tends to give us a notion of the imperfections and narrow limits of human understanding": "Almost all reasoning is there reduced to experience; and the belief, which attends experience, is explained to be nothing but a peculiar sentiment, or lively conception produced by habit" (A 27). Now, the reduction of all reasoning to experience (*empiricism*) does not, by itself, yield skeptical consequences, at least of the strong (Pyrrhonian) kind referred to at the end of the passage. Empiricism can lead to a mild version of skepticism if we insist (perhaps incorrectly) that knowledge must involve certainty, and then further insist (perhaps incorrectly) that empirical claims that go beyond reports of immediate experience always fall short of certainty. Skepticism of this kind might better be called *fallibilism*, not skepticism. In fact, a thorough-going empiricist typically abandons claims to certainty over a wide range of cases where most people think they possess certainty, but traditional empiricists did not think that their position forced a wholesale suspension of belief. With an important exception to be noted later,[1] it is not Hume's empiricism but primarily his theory of belief that pushes his philosophy in the direction of extreme (or Pyrrhonian) skepticism.

The story, broadly sketched, is this: a central part of Hume's project of introducing the experimental method of reasoning into moral subjects involved giving a naturalistic account of how human beings come to believe certain things about the world that (they suppose) surrounds them. A single example will serve our purposes. As human beings we naturally suppose that we are directly aware of a world that is independent of us and continues to exist when we are not aware of it. What is the source of this belief? It cannot be the result of sound argument, for, first, the great bulk of mankind

---

[1] This occurs in his skepticism concerning the senses, discussed in Part IV of this essay.

is wholly unacquainted with any arguments on these matters. They believe, but do so in a total absence of justifying arguments.[2] Furthermore, those arguments intended to prove the existence of an enduring external world are easily shown to be irreparably no good. Thus, for Hume, the common belief in an external world is not based on any sort of reasoning to begin with, and cannot be supported by sound reasoning after the fact. This is one side of Hume's skepticism.

A second side of Hume's skepticism emerges when he lays bare what he takes to be the mechanisms that do, in fact, govern the formation of beliefs on these matters. The wording in the passage from the *Abstract* is revelatory: "the belief, which attends experience, is explained to be nothing but a peculiar sentiment, or lively conception produced by habit. Nor is this all. When we believe any thing of *external* existence, or suppose an object to exist a moment after it is no longer perceived, this belief is nothing but a sentiment of the same kind" (A 27). Now, in describing a belief as *nothing but* a peculiar sentiment produced by habit, Hume is obviously contrasting his position with that of others who hold that there must be more to belief formation than this. That view, crudely put, is that belief is the result of reasoning, and sound beliefs are the result of sound reasoning. Over against this rationalist or Cartesian conception of belief formation, Hume holds that reasoning, by itself, is generally incapable of fixing belief and, in this particular case, incapable of establishing a belief in the existence of an external world.

These skeptical motifs are further developed by the details of Hume's explanation of how this fundamental belief is formed. Presented with Hume's causal account of the actual mechanisms that lead us to believe that we are aware of an independent external world, we are simply appalled that our beliefs should be formed on such an arbitrary basis. Furthermore, when this arbitrary basis for our fundamental beliefs is revealed to us, then, for a time at least, belief

---

[2] Hume makes this point explicitly: "And indeed, whatever convincing arguments philosophers may fancy they can produce to establish the belief of objects independent of the mind, 'tis obvious these arguments are known but to very few, and that 'tis not by them, that children, peasants, and the greatest part of mankind are induc'd to attribute objects to some impressions, and deny them to others" (T 1.4.2.14).

itself evaporates. In the *Enquiry concerning Human Understanding*, Hume describes skepticism generated in this way as follows:

There is another species of scepticism, *consequent* to science and enquiry,
when men are supposed to have discovered, either the absolute fallacious-
ness of their mental faculties, or their unfitness to reach any fixed determination in all those curious subjects of speculation, about which they are
commonly employed. Even our very senses are brought into dispute, by a
certain species of philosophers; and the maxims of common life are subjected to the same doubt as the most profound principles or conclusions of
metaphysics and theology. (EHU 12.5)[3]

From all this it appears that Hume's writings contain two skeptical strategies. The first we might call the *argumentative* strategy;
the second the *genetic* strategy. When using the argumentative strategy, Hume adopts the common skeptical ploy of presenting arguments intended to show that some class of beliefs is not capable
of rational justification. In this class we find many of the enduring features of Hume's philosophy,[4] most importantly, his skepticism concerning induction, his skepticism concerning the external
world (T 1.4.2; EHU 12, Part 2), and, more exotically, his skepticism
with regard to reason (T 1.4.1). His criticism of the argument from
design found in the *Dialogues concerning Natural Religion* and his
examination of arguments involving miracles found in Section 10
of the *Enquiry* can also be placed in this category of argumentative
skepticism.

What I have called Hume's *genetic* strategy reflects his idea of a
skepticism that is consequent on science and enquiry. A system of
beliefs can be discredited by revealing its disreputable provenance.
Thus, in his discussion of *Scepticism with regard to the senses*,
Hume offers a detailed account of the manner in which fictions are

---

[3] Hume's *Enquiry concerning the Principles of Morals* is not discussed in this essay,
although its opening two sections do discuss skeptical motifs. I discuss Hume's ethical skepticism in *Hume's Skepticism in the* Treatise of Human Nature (London:
Routledge & Kegan Paul, 1985). There are excellent discussions of Hume's ethical
skepticism in J. L. Mackie, *Ethics: Inventing Right and Wrong* (Harmondsworth:
Penguin, 1977); *Hume's Moral Theory* (London: Routledge & Kegan Paul 1980); and
David Fate Norton, *David Hume: Common-sense Moralist, Sceptical Metaphysician* (Princeton: Princeton University Press, 1982).

[4] This is at least foreshadowed in *Treatise* 1.3, then stated explicitly in the *Abstract*,
and in Section 4 of the *Enquiry*.

piled on fictions in a way that leads us to adopt what he calls "so extraordinary an opinion" that the objects of our awareness (which, for Hume, are perceptions) can enjoy a continued and distinct existence (T 1.4.2.20). Here, then, is a double movement in the development of Hume's skeptical position. First, *reasoning* shows us that our belief in an external world is not based on sound argument, for no such sound argument on this matter exists, and, second, when *empirical investigation* lays bare the actual mechanisms that lead us to embrace this belief, we are immediately struck by their inadequacy.

This contrast between argument-based and genetic-based skepticism has another side. If, as is not true, our most general beliefs about the world rested on arguments, then sound skeptical arguments, once encountered, would deprive us of these beliefs. But this does not happen. Skeptical arguments may confound us for the moment, but lack lasting effects. Hume makes this point nicely in commenting on the nature and force of some of Berkeley's arguments: "But that all his arguments, though otherwise intended, are, in reality, merely sceptical, appears from this, *that they admit of no answer and produce no conviction.* Their only effect is to cause that momentary amazement and irresolution and confusion, which is the result of scepticism" (EHU 12.15, n.32).

I think that we can now understand why, on Hume's terms, skeptical arguments "*produce no conviction.*" An examination of the actual mechanisms of belief formation shows that beliefs are rarely based on ratiocination. For this reason, a skeptical argument, even if correct, removes nothing that previously supported beliefs. It is more deeply disturbing to come face to face with the actual mechanisms that do generate beliefs, for then we cannot help but being struck by their inadequacy. With these mechanisms explicitly displayed before us, we do, in fact, *find* ourselves in a state of radical doubt. But as our thoughts return to the common concerns of life, the authority of these normal mechanisms is restored, and we *find* ourselves believing largely as we had before we began our inquiries. This is our sole defense against radical skepticism, for philosophy, as Hume tells us in the *Abstract*, "would render us entirely *Pyrrhonian*, were not nature too strong for it" (A 27). The irony is that the ways of nature, when revealed, hardly fill us with confidence or with a sense of human dignity.

II. HUME'S INDUCTIVE SKEPTICISM

1. From his lifetime down to the present, no aspect of Hume's philosophy has attracted more attention than the things that he says
about the related notions of causality, necessity, and induction. The
limitations of the present essay preclude a close examination of his
important ideas on necessity and causality,[5] but, very broadly, for
Hume, causality and inductive reasoning are related in the following
way. In both the *Treatise* and the *Enquiry* Hume argues that causal
connections cannot be established by any form of a priori reasoning. Nor can a causal relationship be ascertained through immediate
experience, for inspection of the cause reveals no connecting link
between it and its effect. Simplifying, it is only our experience of a
constant conjunction between two sorts of events that leads us to
suppose that one is the cause of the other. We reach the problem
of induction by raising the following question: How does the experience of events being consistently conjoined in the past license an
inference to the claim that they will continue to be so conjoined in
the future? That, as it turns out, raises a question that proves very
difficult to answer. In Hume's words: "But if we still carry on our
sifting humour, and ask, *What is the foundation of all conclusions
from experience?* this implies a new question, which may be of more
difficult solution and explication" (EHU 4.14).

Hume poses his difficult question three times – first in the *Treatise,* then in the *Abstract,* and finally in the *Enquiry* – and though
there are important differences in detail, the basic move is the same
in each. Our reliance on past experience rests, he tells us, on the
principle *"that those instances, of which we have had no experience, resemble those, of which we have had experience,"* and, with
respect to the future, this amounts to the assumption there will not
be "a change in the course of nature." On what basis, Hume asks,
can we justify this assumption? His claim – and this is his core

---

[5] My *Hume's Skepticism,* Chap. 4, provides a detailed discussion of Hume's treatment of the interrelated notions of causality, necessity, and induction. Detailed
examinations of Hume's definition of causality can be found in Tom L. Beauchamp
and Alexander Rosenberg, *Hume and the Problem of Causation* (New York: Oxford
University Press, 1981), and in J. L. Mackie, "Causes and Conditions," *American
Philosophical Quarterly* 2 (1965): 245–64, and *The Cement of the Universe* (Oxford:
Clarendon Press, 1974).

thesis – is that no argument can justify this assumption. There can be no demonstrative argument to prove it for it is at least conceivable that the course of nature might change: what is conceivable is possible; what is possible cannot be demonstrated to be false; therefore, it cannot be demonstrated that the course of nature will not change (T 1.3.6.5).

For Hume, the only alternative to demonstrative reasoning is reasoning involving probability. In the *Treatise* Hume dismisses this alternative quickly, and somewhat obscurely:

probability is founded on the presumption of a resemblance betwixt those objects, of which we have had experience, and those, of which we have had none; and therefore 'tis impossible this presumption can arise from probability. The same principle cannot be both the cause and effect of another; and this is, perhaps, the only proposition concerning that relation, which is either intuitively or demonstratively certain. (T 1.3.6.7)

By *probability* (as opposed to *demonstration*), Hume seems to mean any form of inductive reasoning based on past experience. His basic point, which he puts rather quaintly, is that such reasoning itself presupposes that the course of nature will not change, and thus cannot be used, without circularity, to prove it. Hume makes this point more cleanly in the *Abstract*, where he tells us that it is not possible to "prove by any *probable* arguments, that the future must be conformable to the past. All probable arguments are built on the supposition, that there is this conformity betwixt the future and the past, and therefore can never prove it" (A 14). Given that neither demonstrative nor probable arguments can prove that the future must be conformable to the past, it seems that nothing could prove this.[6]

---

[6] Janet Broughton has argued that the *Treatise* does not contain a skeptical argument concerning induction, but that Hume is simply arguing that it is past experience plus the imagination, rather than past experience plus reason, that cause us to project past regularities into the future. See "Hume's Skepticism about Casual Inferences," *Pacific Philosophical Quarterly* 64 (1983): 3–18. I think that Broughton is right in identifying this contest between the faculties of imagination and reason as the major theme of *Treatise* 1.3. I think she is also right to say that the examination of the causes of our causal reasoning is the central theme of *Treatise* 1.3.6. All the same, it seems to me that part of Hume's attack against the claims of reason is that reason cannot account for our tendency to project past regularities into the future simply because no argument derived from reason can justify such projections. Hume's skepticism concerning induction is present in the *Treatise*, but

Hume's basic argument for inductive skepticism gets its most elaborate statement in the *Enquiry*. In the *Abstract* he brought the core argument into sharp focus; in the *Enquiry* he made it a centerpiece of his philosophy. The argument in the *Enquiry* has the same underlying structure as those in the *Treatise* and the *Abstract*, but it employs an essentially new argumentative device: the distinction between *relations of ideas* and *matters of fact* for argumentative purposes.[7] Presented with any claim on any subject, we can always ask: can this claim be established as a relation of ideas? If not, can it be established as a matter of fact? If its truth can be established in neither way, then its truth cannot be established at all. Antony Flew calls this argumentative device *Hume's Fork*.[8]

Unfortunately Hume's distinction between relations of ideas and matters of fact raises problems of its own. First, the distinction is hastily, and perhaps incoherently, drawn. Second, by resting his argument on this distinction, Hume opens himself to serious objections concerning the distinction itself, objections that do not bear directly on the problem of induction. I will take up these points one at a time.

Hume introduces his distinction between relations of ideas and matters of fact as follows:

ALL the objects of human reason or enquiry may naturally be divided into two kinds, to wit, *Relations of Ideas* and *Matters of Fact*. Of the first kind are the sciences of Geometry, Algebra, and Arithmetic; and in short, every affirmation, which is either intuitively or demonstratively certain.... Propositions of this kind are discoverable by the mere operation of thought, without dependence on what is any where existent in the universe....

Matters of fact, which are the second objects of human reason, are not ascertained in the same manner; nor is our evidence of their truth, however great, of a like nature with the foregoing. The contrary of every matter of fact is still possible; because it can never imply a contradiction, and is conceived by the mind with the same facility and distinctness, as if ever so conformable to reality. (EHU 4.1–2)

deeply embedded in a larger program. In contrast, in both the *Abstract* and the *Enquiry concerning Human Understanding* this argument is given prominence as a freestanding philosophical move.

[7] The distinction between relations of ideas and matters of fact appears in the *Treatise* as well, but its use as a dialectical weapon emerges clearly only in the *Enquiry*.

[8] Antony Flew, *Hume's Philosophy of Belief* (London: Routledge & Kegan Paul, 1961), 53.

Though it is not spelled out fully, in this passage Hume divides relations of ideas and matters of fact along *two* lines: one logical, the other epistemological. His criterion for a relation of ideas is epistemological, that is, the criterion is drawn in terms of how we come to know such relations: "Propositions of this kind are discoverable by the mere operation of thought." Thus statements expressing relations of ideas can be known to be true a priori.[9] In contrast, Hume's criterion for a matter of fact is both epistemological and logical. First, matters of fact differ epistemically from relations of ideas in that they "are not ascertained in the same manner;" that is, they are not ascertained by the mere operations of thought. Second, they differ logically from relations of ideas, in that the "contrary of every matter of fact is still possible; because it can never imply a contradiction."

Now, given Hume's initial claim that "All the objects of human reason or enquiry may naturally be divided into two kinds," his use of dual criteria for distinguishing relations of ideas from matters of fact has the following consequence: no proposition that is not a relation of ideas can be known to be true a priori. Thus, in the guise of merely classifying the "objects of human reason or enquiry," Hume has embraced a very strong thesis without offering any argument in its behalf.

Furthermore, by basing his argument on the distinction between relations of ideas and matters of fact, Hume has opened himself to criticisms that have nothing to do with the issue at hand, namely, the problem of induction. In particular, propositions exist that seem not to fit into either of Hume's categories, for example, that the west wall of a building cannot be simultaneously both entirely white and entirely green. Of course, if propositions exist that cannot be accommodated within Hume's classification, then that classification is no longer exhaustive, and the argumentative strategy known as Hume's Fork fails. It seems, then, that before we can evaluate the argument in the *Enquiry* in behalf of inductive skepticism, we will have to

---

[9] In passing, we can note that Hume seems to forget that the *falsehood* of certain propositions can also be discoverable by the mere operation of thought. As a result, if we take Hume's statement literally, it seems that he would have to classify a proposition like $2 + 2 = 5$ as a matter of fact. A similar confusion occurs in Kant's classification of judgments in the Introduction to his *Critique of Pure Reason*.

enter into a more general investigation of the kinds of propositions that exist and the methods of justification appropriate to them. This is an excursion from which we might never return.

Perhaps there is a shorter route back to Hume's original concern with inductive skepticism. The drawing of a distinction between relations of ideas and matters of fact can be viewed as the argumentative counterpart of a tactic used in both the *Treatise* and in the *Abstract*, namely, that of holding (or just assuming) that all arguments fall into two distinct categories: demonstrative and probable. Hume, of course, can be challenged on just this point. But we can get back to the center of Hume's argument if we recall that he was interested in the possibility of an argument establishing the truth of quite a specific claim, namely, that *the future must be conformable to the past*. On its face, this seems to be a substantive claim about how the future will unfold and thus not something susceptible to any form of a priori justification.[10] Furthermore, the second part of Hume's argument seems persuasive as well: any attempted inductive justification of this claim will be question-begging.

Elsewhere I have claimed that Hume put forward what I called a *no-argument argument* concerning induction, namely, an argument intended to show that no argument could possibly justify the claim that the future will be conformable to the past.[11] The text, I believe, clearly shows that this was his intention. It now also seems clear to me that Hume's no-argument argument fails. In both the *Treatise/Abstract* version and the *Enquiry* version an important step is missing. In the early version, we need a proof showing that all arguments may be divided into demonstrative arguments and probable arguments in the sense in which Hume describes them. In the later version, we need a proof showing that: "All the objects of human reason or enquiry may naturally be divided into two kinds, to wit, *Relations of Ideas* and *Matters of Fact.*" In fact, Hume seems to face a more difficult problem with the *Enquiry* version of his

---

[10] Barry Stroud emphasizes this point, for, among other things, it helps to clear Hume of the charge of being a deductive chauvinist, that is, of holding or assuming that the only form of proof is a sound deductive argument. See his *Hume* (London: Routledge & Kegan Paul, 1977), 56–67.

[11] See my *Hume's Skepticism*, Chap. 4 and Appendix A.

argument than with the earlier versions, for there seem to be a number of clear examples of propositions that fall into neither of his two categories. But perhaps a related complaint might be made against the *Treatise/Abstract* version of the argument, namely, that there are legitimate modes of argumentation that Hume has not considered. Again, because Hume has not eliminated this possibility, his argument fails as a no-argument argument.

2. In the first part of this essay I indicated that Hume's skepticism had two chief sources, one based on arguments, the other based on accounts of how human beings actually form beliefs. The second theme will play a central role in the discussion of Hume's skepticism with regard to reason and his skepticism with regard to the senses, but his account of how we actually come to project past regularities into the future has skeptical consequences as well. As we shall see, however, these are not as dramatic as those found in his discussion of reason and the senses.

In the *Treatise* Hume's skeptical argument concerning induction is embedded in a psychological account of the component parts of our reasoning concerning causes and effects.[12] In the *Enquiry* the two discussions are neatly partitioned into two successive sections. Section 4 of the *Enquiry* is entitled "Sceptical Doubts concerning the Operations of the Understanding." Its intended results are essentially negative: no argument can justify inference from past to future experience. Section 5 has the curious title "Sceptical Solution of these Doubts." The following passage gives some idea of what Hume has in mind in speaking of a "sceptical" solution: "If the mind be not engaged by argument to make this step, it must be induced by some other principle of equal weight and authority; and that principle will preserve its influence as long as human nature remains the same. What that principle is, may well be worth the pains of enquiry" (EHU 5.2). Presumably a nonskeptical solution to the doubts raised in Section 4 would be some sort of argument that would justify the step in question. In that sense of *solution,* a *skeptical solution* is no solution at all; instead, it is a mere description of the mechanisms

---

[12] This discussion stretches over 1.3.4–14. The skeptical argument appears (or at least is adumbrated) in T 1.3.6.

that lead the mind to operate as it does. The description of these mechanisms will not resolve skeptical doubts, and, to the extent that their operations strike us as arbitrary, our skeptical doubt may be heightened by their discovery.

What principle leads us to make this transition to a belief in a matter of fact beyond the present testimony of the senses given that no argument can vindicate it? "This principle is CUSTOM or HABIT. For wherever the repetition of any particular act or operation produces a propensity to renew the same act or operation, without being impelled by any reasoning or process of the understanding; we always say, that this propensity is the effect of *Custom.*" More specifically, after experiencing "the constant conjunction of two objects, heat and flame, for instance, weight and solidity, we are determined by custom alone to expect the one from the appearance of the other (EHU 5.5).[13]

A recognition that all our inferences beyond present or past experience derive from this source may or may not make us more sceptical concerning them, but this discovery, at the very least, deflates our intellectual pretensions by revealing that some of our most important modes of inference are made in the complete absence of rational insight.

As nature has taught us the use of our limbs, without giving us the knowledge of the muscles and nerves, by which they are actuated; so has she implanted in us an instinct, which carries forward the thought in a correspondent course to that which she has established among external objects; though we are ignorant of those powers and forces, on which this regular course and succession of objects totally depends. (EHU 5.22)

We are so constructed that under certain circumstances our minds irresistibly make transitions from one idea to another. In this regard we do not differ in any essential way from animals who also learn from experience and who also do so without any comprehension of the underlying mechanisms that bring this about – a point that Hume dwells on in both the *Treatise* and the *Enquiry* (T 1.3.14.15–23; EHU 9).

---

[13] Hume seems to have forgotten liquid mercury.

Hume gives the argument a nice turn by commenting on the wonder we feel concerning the complex instinctual endowment possessed by animals:

But our wonder will, perhaps, cease or diminish; when we consider, that the experimental reasoning itself, which we possess in common with beasts, and on which the whole conduct of life depends, is nothing but a species of instinct or mechanical power, that acts in us unknown to ourselves; and in its chief operations, is not directed by any such relations or comparisons of ideas, as are the proper objects of our intellectual faculties. (EHU 9.6)

We can think of skepticism as a set of arguments intended to undercut claims for knowledge or even rational belief. Section 4, with its skeptical doubts concerning the human understanding, illustrates this first strategy. We can also think of the central aim of skepticism as an attempt to destroy the pretensions of reason. Section 5, with its skeptical – as opposed to rational – solution to these doubts, illustrates this second strategy.

III. HUME'S SKEPTICISM WITH REGARD TO REASON

1. The target of Hume's skepticism is not simply the writings of philosophers, but the faculties of the mind that generate these writings. Hume does, of course, discuss the philosophical positions of others, and allusions to other philosophical standpoints occur throughout his writings, but, more often than not, such references are made in the service of developing his science of man. Bad, even nonsensical, philosophical arguments are revelatory of the underlying faculties that generate them.[14]

Although Hume is not careful in his use of terminology, the first book of the *Treatise* is largely concerned with four faculties: understanding, reason, the senses, and the imagination. By the understanding, Hume usually has in mind reasoning from experience, notably causal reasoning. By reason, Hume usually has in mind demonstrative and intuitive reasoning.[15] By the senses, Hume has in mind that

---

[14] This is the central theme of Part V of this essay.

[15] In a number of places Hume does not honor this contrast between reason and understanding, but this, at least, is his general tendency.

faculty that (seemingly) gives us information about a surrounding world. By the imagination, Hume has in mind a faculty that generates new ideas from old by means of principles of association. Hume's general strategy is to argue that the operations of the first three faculties are ultimately grounded in the operations of the fourth: the imagination or, as he sometimes calls it, the fancy. Hume's standard strategy in furthering this project is to produce skeptical arguments intended to show that beliefs generated by the first three faculties cannot be grounded in any form of ratiocination. He then attempts to show how they are generated by the instinctive mechanisms of the imagination.[16] We have already seen this double strategy at work in Hume's treatment of our reasoning from past experience, but its most striking occurrence appears in the section of the *Treatise* entitled *Of scepticism with regard to reason* (T 1.4.1).

Hume's skepticism with regard to reason has not fared well. Most writers on Hume say little or nothing about it. Hume did not repeat it in his later writings. This almost universal neglect probably springs from one of two sources: (1) a belief that the basic skeptical argument is no good, or (2) a revulsion against the total skepticism that it would entail if it were correct. However this may be, it is clear in the *Treatise* that Hume accepted the skeptical argument he put forward and explicitly embraced the radical skeptical consequences it entailed.

Hume's overall argument depends on two subarguments that I will call, respectively, the *regression argument* and the *diminution argument*. This wider argument, presented largely in Hume's own words, has the following form.

The Regression Argument

a. "In every judgment, which we can form concerning probability, as well as concerning knowledge, we ought always to correct the first judgment, deriv'd from the nature of the object, by another judgment, deriv'd from the nature of the understanding."

---

[16] For more details on this, see my *Hume's Skepticism*, Chap. 5. This same theme is developed by Annette C. Baier, *A Progress of the Sentiments: Reflections on Hume's* Treatise (Cambridge, MA: Harvard University Press, 1991), Chaps. 2–3.

b. "As demonstration is subject to the controul of probability, so is probability liable to a new correction by a reflex act of the mind, wherein the nature of our understanding, and our reasoning from the first probability become our objects" (T 1.4.1.5).

The Diminution Argument

a. "Having thus found in every probability, beside the original uncertainty inherent in the subject, a new uncertainty deriv'd from the weakness of that faculty, which judges, and having adjusted these two together, we are oblig'd by our reason to add a new doubt deriv'd from the possibility of error in the estimation we make of the truth and fidelity of our faculties."

b. "No finite object can subsist under a decrease repeated in infinitum; and even the vastest quantity, which can enter into human imagination, must in this manner be reduc'd to nothing."

c. Thus, "all the rules of logic require a continual diminution, and at last a total extinction of belief and evidence" (T 1.4.1.6).

I have called the first step the *regression argument* because it tells us that in our judgments we must not only attend to the object under consideration, but we must also *step back* and ask the prior question whether – or to what extent – those procedures we use in dealing with the object are reliable. For example, that someone has been very careful in casting a horoscope should not lead us to trust his predictions until we satisfy ourselves on the prior question whether horoscopes can be trusted. Similarly, Hume tells us that we should rely on our faculties only to the extent that they have shown themselves to be trustworthy: "We must, therefore, in every reasoning form a new judgment, as a check or controul on our first judgment or belief; and must enlarge our view to comprehend a kind of history of all the instances, wherein our understanding has deceiv'd us, compar'd with those, wherein its testimony was just and true" (T 1.4.1.1). For Hume, all faculties are subject to this restraint, including reason – the source of demonstrative and intuitive knowledge. Even with reason, before trusting it, we must step back and ask how reliable it has proven to be. The upshot of this, Hume tells us, is that "all knowledge degenerates into probability; and this probability is greater or less, according to our experience of the veracity or deceitfulness of our understanding, and according to the simplicity or intricacy of the question" (T 1.4.1.1). Hume is here probably wrong in saying that "knowledge *degenerates* into probability," for the fact that there may be some chance that a demonstrative argument is invalid does not change it into a different kind of argument.[17] But for Hume's purposes, it might be sufficient to claim that every claim for knowledge inevitably *leads us* to a prior claim concerning probability that must be answered before we assess the knowledge claim.

Part (b) of the *regression argument* tells us that just as every knowledge claim must be checked by regressing to a probability claim, so too must every probability claim be checked against a further probability claim. This leads to an infinite regress of probability judgments concerning probability judgments, forming a stack of the following kind:

$$\ldots\ldots$$
$$\ldots\ldots$$

(4) (3) has a probability of n_4.
(3) (2) has a probability of n_3.
(2) (1) has a probability of n_2.
(1) $17 + 39 = 56$ has a probability of 1.

Here probability claims are being nested *inside* one another. What (4) says is this:

That that that $17 + 39 = 56$ has the probability 1 has the probability n_2 has the probability n_3 has the probability n_4.

The human mind buckles under the complexity of such a proposition: a fact that Hume will exploit in offering what might be called his skeptical solution to the problem he here raises.

At this point Hume could have moved directly to a traditional skeptical conclusion by pointing out that as rational creatures we are committed to an unstoppable regress of higher-order probability

---

[17] The expression "invalid demonstrative argument" is not a solecism.

assessments. That, it would seem, would be sufficient for his purposes. Instead, he gives this traditional skeptical argument a turn
of his own by arguing that with each ascent to a higher probability
assessment, the base proposition $(17 + 39 = 56)$ loses some measure
of its probability. Finally, since we must perform infinitely many
such assessments – each diminishing the initial probability at least
to some extent – Hume concludes that "all the rules of logic require
a continual diminution, and at last a total extinction of belief and
evidence" (T 1.4.1.6).

This is not the place to examine the technical details of Hume's
probabilistic arguments, but it is important to note both the breadth
and the depth of Hume's skeptical conclusion.[18] With respect to
breadth, Hume's skepticism seems very nearly all encompassing.
His original target was demonstrative reasoning, but, having reduced
demonstrative reasoning, as he thought, to probabilistic reasoning,
he then applies the same argument to probabilistic reasoning, finally
depriving us of all those things we believe on that basis as well. The
only things we may be left with as objects of belief are immediate
reports of experience, and, perhaps, certain simple intuitive truths.
This is not a mere fallibilism – a cautionary reminder that we lack
certainty in areas where people commonly suppose we possess it. If
Hume's argument is correct, we find ourselves in the deep skepticism
traditionally associated with Pyrrhonism.[19]

When I reflect on the natural fallibility of my judgment, I have less confidence in my opinions, than when I only consider the objects concerning
which I reason; and when I proceed still farther, to turn the scrutiny against
every successive estimation I make of my faculties, all the rules of logic
require a continual diminution, and at last a total extinction of belief and
evidence (T 1.4.1.6).

---

[18] For more on this, including references to others who have discussed this topic, see
my *Hume's Skepticism*, Chap. 2, and Ian Hacking, "Hume's Species of Probability,"
Philosophical Studies 33 (1978): 21–37.

[19] A good introduction to the effects of Pyrrhonism on early modern philosophy is
Richard H. Popkin, *The History of Scepticism from Savonarola to Bayle* (New
York: Oxford University Press, 2003), and *The High Road to Pyrrhonism* (San
Diego: Austin Hill Press, 1980). For a helpful introduction to the character of
ancient Pyrrhonism, see Myles Burnyeat, "Can the Sceptic Live His Scepticism?"
in *Doubt and Dogmatism: Studies in Hellenistic Epistemology*, ed. M. Schofield,
M. Burnyeat, and J. Barnes (Oxford: Clarendon Press, 1980), 20–53.

2. Yet for all of Hume's skeptical arguments, experience shows that this total extinction of belief does not take place. Of course, most people – indeed, most philosophers – have never heard of Hume's skepticism with regard to reason. Others, who have heard of it, hold that it is incorrect and are thus immune to its force. But Hume, who propounded the argument, thinks that it is irrefutable while yet continuing to believe many things on many topics. How, on his own terms, is this possible? In response to this question, Hume offers what again amounts to a "sceptical solution" to his doubts: since rational mechanisms cannot sustain our beliefs, and, indeed, lead to their extinction, there must be nonrational mechanisms that do this for us. Hume describes them as follows:

I answer, that after the first and second decision; as the action of the mind becomes forc'd and unnatural, and the ideas faint and obscure; tho' the principles of judgment, and the ballancing of opposite causes be the same as at the very beginning; yet their influence on the imagination, and the vigour they add to, or diminish from the thought, is by no means equal.... The attention is on the stretch: The posture of the mind is uneasy; and the spirits being diverted from their natural course, are not govern'd in their movements by the same laws, at least not to the same degree, as when they flow in their usual channel. (T 1.4.1.10)

The sole reason that we are not total skeptics is that we lack the mental capacity to pursue our reflections to this, their predetermined end. Toward the end of the concluding section of Book 1, Hume puts the matter this way: "We save ourselves from this total scepticism only by means of that singular and seemingly trivial property of the fancy, by which we enter with difficulty into remote views of things, and are not able to accompany them with so sensible an impression, as we do those, which are more easy and natural" (T 1.4.7.7). Thus it is the weakness of the mind, not its strength, that saves reason from the skeptical destiny implicit in it.

IV. HUME'S SKEPTICISM WITH REGARD TO THE SENSES

1. Hume's examination of the senses begins with a comparison between the skeptical problem concerning reason and the skeptical problems concerning the senses: "Thus the sceptic still continues to reason and believe, even tho' he asserts, that he cannot defend his reason by reason; and by the same rule he must assent to the principle concerning the existence of body, tho' he cannot pretend by any arguments of philosophy to maintain its veracity" (T 1.4.2.1).

Hume holds that there are unanswerable skeptical arguments against the pretensions of both of these faculties, but his mode of exposition is different in the two cases. As we have just seen, in his discussion of skepticism with regard to reason, Hume begins by stating his skeptical argument and then, very briefly, describes those nonrational mechanisms that preserve belief despite the existence of a contrary skeptical argument.[20] In his discussion of the senses, Hume reverses this order. He begins by merely alluding to a skeptical argument concerning the senses and then announces that his main task will be to examine "the *causes* which induce us to believe in the existence of body" (T 1.4.2.2). What follows is a long, complex, and rather perplexing examination of those causal mechanisms that lead human beings to adopt the false belief that our inner perceptions can enjoy an existence distinct from our minds, and can continue to exist even when unperceived. The standard skeptical argument concerning the external world appears only after this causal account of the common belief is completed.

The skeptical argument, when it does appear in the *Treatise*, has two parts. The first is intended to show that "our perceptions [those things, that is, of which we are aware] are not possest of any independent existence." Here Hume uses standard arguments from perceptual variability:

When we press one eye with a finger, we immediately perceive all the objects to become double, and one half of them to be remov'd from their common and natural position. But as we do not attribute a continu'd existence to both these perceptions, and as they are both of the same nature, we clearly perceive, that all our perceptions are dependent on our organs, and the disposition of our nerves and animal spirits. (T 1.4.2.45)

Convinced, perhaps wrongly, that we are only aware of our own private perceptions, the philosopher steps in and suggests that some of these perceptions are images or representations of external objects. This theory, sometimes called representational realism, holds that

---

[20] Later, in the *Enquiry*, Hume adopted this same order of exposition in discussing inductive inference.

we are not directly aware of external objects, but we are aware of perceptions that serve as their representations. Here Hume speaks of "the opinion of a double existence and representation," a view he obviously associates with the philosophy of John Locke (T 1.4.2.31).

The second step in Hume's skeptical argument is aimed at such double existence theories and is intended to show that no argument can establish the existence of external objects resembling our perceptions. In the *Treatise*, Hume states the basic argument in only a few sentences:

> The only conclusion we can draw from the existence of one thing to that of another, is by means of the relation of cause and effect, which shows, that there is a connexion betwixt them, and that the existence of one is dependent on that of the other. The idea of this relation is deriv'd from past experience, by which we find, that two beings are constantly conjoin'd together, and are always present at once to the mind. But as no beings are ever present to the mind but perceptions; it follows that we may observe a conjunction or a relation of cause and effect betwixt different perceptions, but can never observe it betwixt perceptions and objects. 'Tis impossible, therefore, that from the existence or any of the qualities of the former, we can ever form any conclusion concerning the existence of the latter, or ever satisfy our reason in this particular. (T 1.4.2.47)

The counterpart argument in the *Enquiry* is equally succinct:

> It is a question of fact, whether the perceptions of the senses be produced by external objects, resembling them: How shall this question be determined? By experience surely; as all other questions of a like nature. But here experience is, and must be entirely silent. The mind has never any thing present to it but the perceptions, and cannot possibly reach any experience of their connexion with objects. The supposition of such a connexion is, therefore, without any foundation in reasoning. (EHU 12.12)

Hume thought that this skeptical argument was completely unanswerable, telling us that "This is a topic, therefore, in which the profounder and more philosophical sceptics will always triumph, when they endeavour to introduce an universal doubt into all subjects of human knowledge and enquiry" (EHU 12.14). It seems that sound reasoning leads us to abandon our naive belief in a direct awareness of an external world, and then further sound reasoning leads us to a skepticism that casts doubt on the very existence of such a world. For Hume, things get worse the more we reason.

There is another important side of the story that cannot be pursued in detail here. We have seen before that Hume's skepticism is strengthened by his account of the actual mechanisms that fix belief. In the *Treatise*, though not as much in the *Enquiry*, Hume emphasizes the sheer arbitrariness of the mental mechanisms that lead us to believe, quite falsely, that we are directly aware of an external world. The upshot of this move, combined with the skeptical argument that forecloses any help from the philosopher, is one of Hume's deepest expressions of skepticism:

Having thus given an account of all the systems both popular and philosophical, with regard to external existences, I cannot forbear giving vent to a certain sentiment, which arises upon reviewing those systems. I begun this subject with premising, that we ought to have an implicit faith in our senses, and that this wou'd be the conclusion, I shou'd draw from the whole of my reasoning. But to be ingenuous, I feel myself *at present* of a quite contrary sentiment, and am more inclin'd to repose no faith at all in my senses, or rather imagination, than to place in it such an implicit confidence. I cannot conceive how such trivial qualities of the fancy, conducted by such false suppositions, can ever lead to any solid and rational system. (T 1.4.2.56)

2. The literature on the so-called problem of the external world – on the questions Whether the external world exists, and How one would prove that it does – is too large to summarize in any detail. Here there is only room to note that the form of Hume's argument suggests two possible strategies for responding to these questions. First, we can attempt to block the argument intended to show that we are only directly aware of our own perceptions and not directly aware of external objects; second, we can grant this much of the argument and then attempt to find some form of inference that will take us from beliefs concerning our private perceptions to well-founded beliefs concerning objects external to them. The first strategy was championed in Hume's day by Thomas Reid and in the last century most notably by J. L. Austin; the second is the more traditional way of responding to skepticism concerning the external world.[21]

---

[21] See Essay I in Thomas Reid, *Essays on the Intellectual Powers of Man*, ed. D. R. Brookes and K. Haakonssen (University Park: Penn State University Press, 2002), a work first published in 1785; and J. L. Austin, *Sense and Sensibilia* (Oxford: Clarendon Press, 1963). Among Hume's predecessors, Locke and Descartes attempted the second strategy. Since the early twentieth century it has been adopted by

Although tremendous effort has been expended on these matters, no consensus has emerged that either of these approaches is successful in meeting Hume's challenge.

V. THE WORDS OF PHILOSOPHERS

In the previous section we saw that Hume presented a skeptical challenge to those who held what he called a "double existence" theory of perception.[22] Hume cannot be credited with a great deal of originality in presenting this challenge for here he is largely casting into his own vocabulary arguments found in the writing of George Berkeley.[23] But in this same context, Hume makes a move that seems to be entirely original and of great importance for understanding his attitude toward philosophical reflection.

According to Hume – and surely he was right in this – the theory of double existence (or representational realism) was introduced by philosophers as a replacement for the naively realistic view of perception held by the plain man. We have already seen that Hume rejected this replacement since it was subject – or so he thought – to a decisive skeptical refutation. Here Hume follows Berkeley. But Hume goes beyond Berkeley in making the following further criticism of double existence theories: "There are no principles either of the understanding or fancy, which lead us directly to embrace this opinion of the double existence of perceptions and objects, *nor can we arrive at it but by passing thro' the common hypothesis of the identity and continuance of our interrupted perceptions*" (T 1.4.2.46, emphasis added). Hume's remarkable suggestion is that the theory of double existence is not simply the result of rational

---

many philosophers, including Bertrand Russell in *Problems of Philosophy* (London: Oxford University Press, 1912).

[22] Much of what is said in this section is stated in more detail in my *Hume's Skepticism*, Chap. 7.

[23] See, for example, Berkeley's *Principles of Human Knowledge*, Part I, Sects. 9–15, and the first dialogue of *Three Dialogues between Hylas and Philonous*. In *Treatise* 1.4.4, *Of the modern philosophy*, Hume follows Berkeley in deriving skeptical consequences from the distinction between primary and secondary qualities, but he does not say so. On Berkeley and Hume see David Raynor, "Hume and Berkeley's *Three Dialogues*," in *Studies in the Philosophy of the Scottish Enlightenment*, ed. M. A. Stewart (Oxford: Clarendon Press, 1990), 231–50.

reflection, but is the *causal* product of competing forces operating in the mind:

The imagination tells us, that our resembling perceptions have a continu'd and uninterrupted existence, and are not annihilated by their absence. Reflection tells us, that even our resembling perceptions are interrupted in their existence, and different from each other. The contradiction betwixt these opinions we elude by a new fiction, which is conformable to the hypotheses both of reflection and fancy, by ascribing these contrary qualities to different existences; the *interruption* to perceptions, and the *continuance* to objects. (T 1.4.2.52)

Thus the double existence theory is not simply a rational replacement for the naive view; instead, it is a position that naturally presses itself on philosophers because the naive view still exerts a force on them. The doctrine of double existence is not simply a hypothesis that philosophers conjure up; it is something they find themselves constrained to believe. Paradoxically, the source of this belief is the naive position they claim to have overcome:

Nature is obstinate, and will not quit the field, however strongly attack'd by reason; and at the same time reason is so clear in the point, that there is no possibility of disguising her. Not being able to reconcile these two enemies, we endeavour to set ourselves at ease as much as possible, by successively granting to each whatever it demands, and by feigning a double existence, where each may find something, that has all the conditions it desires. (T 1.4.2.52)

Hume tells a similar story concerning the traditional idea of *substance*. Briefly, provided that the changes in an object are gradual, the easy transition from one perception of it to the next will lead us to believe that an object has remained the self same thing even though it has undergone considerable alteration: "The smooth and uninterrupted progress of the thought ... readily deceives the mind, and makes us ascribe an identity to the changeable succession of connected qualities." Yet a shift in perspective can lead us to the reverse opinion:

But when we alter our method of considering the succession, and instead of tracing it gradually thro' the successive points of time, survey at once any two distinct periods of its duration, and compare the different conditions of the successive qualities; in that case the variations, which were insensible when they arose gradually, do now appear of consequence, and seem entirely to destroy the identity. (T 1.4.3.4)

So whether a changing object will seem to preserve its identity or lose it depends on the perspective we take on it. Furthermore, since both perspectives are readily available and seem entirely natural, the mind, following its own principles, seems to be driven toward what Hume calls a contradiction. From one perspective, we are naturally inclined to ascribe identity to an object gradually changing over time; from another perspective we are inclined to withdraw this ascription.[24]

Again, the mind seems to be at odds with itself, and again it tries to extricate itself from this difficulty through the introduction of a fiction. "In order to reconcile which contradictions the imagination is apt to feign something unknown and invisible, which it supposes to continue the same under all these variations; and this unintelligible something it calls a *substance,* or *original and first matter*" (T 1.4.3.4).

I do not think that Hume supposes that this fiction of substance, or original and first matter, is part of the ordinary person's conceptual apparatus. For Hume, ordinary human beings (the *vulgar* in his eighteenth-century vocabulary) live blissfully innocent of the fact that the greater part of their beliefs is either false or unfounded. It is the philosophers who, having lost their innocence, stand in need of the notion of substance, or original and first matter. They need this notion precisely because they cannot fully stifle their natural inclination to suppose that changing objects preserve their identity over time, while yet holding that we are only aware of fleeting internal perceptions. The notion of substance is a surrogate for these lost beliefs of the vulgar.

This philosophical fiction of substance has a feature that ordinary fictions lack: strictly speaking it is unintelligible. Examination reveals that the term *substance,* at least as employed by the philosopher, has no idea, either simple or complex, associated with it. All

---

[24] Hume follows this discussion of the identity of an object over time with a parallel discussion of the simplicity or unity of an object at a given time (T 1.4.3.5–8).

the same, if we press our enquiries far enough, at a certain stage we are naturally led to embrace this doctrine. "The whole system, therefore, is entirely incomprehensible, and yet is deriv'd from principles as natural as any of those above-explain'd" (T 1.4.3.8).

But how can a system that is "entirely incomprehensible" become an object of belief? What would the object of such a belief be? Hume answers these questions in a passage that anticipates developments in twentieth-century linguistic philosophy. Since it has been neglected, it is worth citing in its entirety:

But as nature seems to have observ'd a kind of justice and compensation in every thing, she has not neglected philosophers more than the rest of the creation; but has reserv'd them a consolation amidst all their disappointments and afflictions. This consolation principally consists in their invention of the words *faculty* and *occult quality*. For it being usual, after the frequent use of terms, which are really significant and intelligible, to omit the idea, which we wou'd express by them, and to preserve only the custom, by which we recal the idea at pleasure; so it naturally happens, that after the frequent use of terms, which are wholly insignificant and unintelligible, we fancy them to be on the same footing with the precedent, and to have a secret meaning, which we might discover by reflection. (T 1.4.3.10)

Broadly speaking, this is Hume's assessment of man's intellectual condition: for the most part, the fundamental beliefs of ordinary persons are either false or unfounded. The philosophers' attempts to put something better in their place is "wholly insignificant or unintelligible."

VI. HUME'S SKEPTICISM

To what extent was Hume a skeptic? This question does not admit of a direct answer for two reasons. First, describing a philosopher as a skeptic can mean a variety of things, and, depending on what is meant, our assessment of Hume's skepticism can vary. Second, and more deeply, Hume's own philosophical position precludes any simple attribution of doctrines to him.

Concerning the first point, various things can be meant by describing a philosopher as a skeptic. Skepticism is often associated with doubt or with the suspension of belief. The Pyrrhonists, at least as

Hume understood them, recommended something close to a total suspension of belief.[25] Clearly Hume did not recommend a whole-sale suspension of belief, for he held, first, that it would be disastrous to human life, and, second, that it is not something we are capable of achieving. We are naturally determined – hardwired, as it were – to form certain beliefs in certain circumstances. If skepticism is equated with Pyrrhonism (as Hume understood it), then Hume was not a skeptic – but he at several places says that he is a skeptic.[26]

Skepticism can also be understood as a critique of the capacities of our intellectual faculties. Taken this way, Hume is a radical, unre-served, unmitigated skeptic. The doctrine of the *Treatise* is that our rational faculties, left to themselves, are wholly destructive of belief. To repeat a passage already cited: "sceptical doubt arises naturally from a profound and intense reflection on those subjects, it always encreases, the farther we carry our reflections, whether in opposition or conformity to it" (T 1.4.2.57). As we have seen, Hume supports this claim in two ways: by producing what he takes to be irrefutable skeptical arguments and through displaying the arbitrariness of our actual, nonrational modes of belief formation. His fundamental idea is that we are saved from total skepticism only because the non-rational aspects of our nature overwhelm the doubts that reason attempts to force on us, but we must not lose sight of the fact, as some have, that this is a skeptical conclusion.

The second, deeper, reason it is difficult to decide whether, or to what extent, Hume was a skeptic is that his own account of belief formation precludes simple ascriptions of beliefs. On his own theory, a person's beliefs, including a philosopher's beliefs, will be a func-tion of the level of inquiry at which they are formed. This applies to Hume's expression of his own beliefs, even in his theoretical writing.

---

[25] Hume's understanding of Pyrrhonism was probably historically inaccurate, but this is rather a complex topic, since scholars today disagree on the proper inter-pretation of Pyrrhonism. Discussions revealing the competing views on the nature of Pyrrhonism are to be found in Jonathan Barnes, "The Beliefs of a Pyrrhon-ist," in *Proceedings of the Cambridge Philological Society* NS 28 (1982): 1–29; Myles Burnyeat, "Can the Sceptic Live His Scepticism"; and Michael Frede, "The Skeptic's Beliefs," in *Essays in Ancient Philosophy* (Minneapolis: University of Minnesota Press, 1987), 201–22.

[26] In addition to the several passages already cited, see, for example, the closing paragraph of *Treatise*, Book 1.

In these writings he often expresses himself in a manner that suggests that he accepts a completely naive notion of perception. There are passages that suggest a commitment to a causal theory of perception – what Hume called a "double existence" theory. There are also passages intended to show the inadequacies of both these positions. Finally, there are passages that reflect a near-Pyrrhonian despair of basing any belief on the senses. Which is the real Hume? The most appropriate answer on Hume's own terms is that his writings simply exhibit "that propensity, which inclines us to be positive and certain in *particular points*, according to the light, in which we survey them in any *particular instant*" (T 1.4.7.15). This radical perspectivalism had historical precedents – perhaps in Protagoras, certainly in Sextus Empiricus – but Hume was one of very few philosophers to understand it and trace out its implications.

In the closing section of the *Enquiry*, Hume recommends a moderate or mitigated skepticism as a middle way between naive acceptance and Pyrrhonism. This may suggest that he was a sensible fellow after all. His skepticism might be nothing more than a version of fallibilism, the appropriately cautious attitude of a hard-working social scientist attempting to "INTRODUCE THE EXPERIMENTAL METHOD OF REASONING INTO MORAL SUBJECTS." This reading diminishes Hume's genius. His own account of how one arrives at a moderate or mitigated skepticism is of a piece with his account of how other philosophical positions emerge: they come into existence because of a clash between brute irresistible common beliefs and philosophical reflection that shows these beliefs to be groundless:

[A] species of *mitigated* scepticism, which may be of advantage to mankind, and which may be the natural result of the PYRRHONIAN doubts and scruples, is the limitation of our enquiries to such subjects as are best adapted to the narrow capacity of human understanding. The *imagination* of man is naturally sublime, delighted with whatever is remote and extraordinary.... A correct *Judgment* observes a contrary method, and avoiding all distant and high enquiries, confines itself to common life, and to such subjects as fall under daily practice and experience.... To bring us to so salutary a determination, nothing can be more serviceable, than to be once thoroughly convinced of the force of the PYRRHONIAN doubt, and of the impossibility, that any thing, but the strong power of natural instinct, could free us from it. (EHU 12.25)

Like other philosophical positions, mitigated skepticism is the product of a conflict between philosophical doubts and instinctual beliefs. Here, as in other cases where philosophy and instinct clash, it is instinct, not philosophical reflection, that maintains belief.

SUGGESTIONS FOR FURTHER READING

In addition to the works cited in the notes to this essay, the editors recommend the following.[27]

Bell, Martin, and Marie McGinn. "Naturalism and Scepticism." *Philosophy* 65 (1990): 399–418.

Broughton, Janet. "Hume's Naturalism and Scepticism." In *A Companion to Hume's* Treatise, edited by E. S. Radcliffe. Oxford: Blackwell Publishing, 2008.

Cummins, Phillip D. "Hume's Diffident Skepticism." *Hume Studies* 25 (1999): 43–65.

Falkenstein, Lorne. "Naturalism, Normativity, and Scepticism in Hume's Account of Belief." *Hume Studies* 23 (1997): 29–72.

Fogelin, Robert J. *A Defense of Hume on Miracles*. Princeton: Princeton University Press, 2003.

Garrett, Don. "'A Small Tincture of Pyrrhonism': Skepticism and Naturalism in Hume's Science of Man." In *Pyrrhonian Skepticism*, edited by W. Sinnott-Armstrong. New York: Oxford University Press, 2004. 68–98.

McCormick, Miriam. "A Change in Manner: Hume's Scepticism in the *Treatise* and the First *Enquiry*." *Canadian Journal of Philosophy* 29 (1999): 431–47.

"Hume, Wittgenstein and the Impact of Skepticism." *History of Philosophy Quarterly* 21 (2004): 417–34.

Millican, Peter. "Hume's Sceptical Doubts concerning Induction." In *Reading Hume on Human Understanding*, edited by P. Millican. Oxford: Clarendon Press, 2002. 107–73.

Morris, William Edward. "Hume's Conclusion." *Philosophical Studies* 99 (2000): 89–110.

Norton, David Fate. "How a Skeptic May Live Skepticism." In *Faith, Scepticism, and Personal Identity*, edited by J. J. MacIntosh and H. A. Meynell.

---

[27] For their assistance in compiling this list, the Editors gratefully acknowledge William Edward Morris and David Owen. See also the relevant sections of the books listed in the Selected Bibliography by, among others, Annette Baier, Donald Baxter, Stephen Buckle, Don Garrett, John Laird, Louis Loeb, David Fate Norton, David Owen, Thomas Reid, Norman Kemp Smith, and John Wright.

Calgary: University of Calgary Press, 1994. 119–39. For Terence Penelhum's response to this essay, see in the same volume 267–71.

Owen, David. "Scepticism with Regard to Reason." In *The Cambridge Companion to Hume's* Treatise, edited by D. Ainslie. Cambridge: Cambridge University Press, forthcoming. A pre-publication version of this paper may be seen at http://phil.web.arizona.edu/faculty/extra/dowen/ dowen_swrtr.htm.

"Hume and the Irrelevance of Warrant." In *Ensaios sobre Hume*, edited by Livia Guimarães. Belo Horizonte: Editora Segrac, 2005. 23–58. http:// phil.web.arizona.edu/faculty/extra/dowen/dowen_hiw.htm.

Read, Rupert, and Kenneth A. Richman, eds. *The New Hume Debate*. London: Routledge, 2000.

Roth, Abe. "Causation." In *The Blackwell Guide to Hume's* Treatise, edited by S. Traiger. Oxford: Blackwell Publishing, 2006. 95–113.

Singer, Ira. "Nature Breaks Down: Hume's Problematic Naturalism in Treatise I iv." *Hume Studies* 26 (2000): 225–43.

Stroud, Barry. "Hume's Scepticism: Natural Instincts and Philosophical Reflection." *Philosophical Topics* 19 (1991): 271–91.

Winkler, Kenneth. "Hume's Inductive Skepticism." In *The Empiricists: Critical Essays on Locke, Berkeley, and Hume*, edited by M. Atherton. Lanham, MD: Rowan & Littlefield, 1999. 183–212.

8   Hume's Moral Psychology

In 1927 A. E. Taylor concluded his Leslie Stephen Lecture on "David Hume and the Miraculous" with a judgment of Hume's attitude to his philosophical work that has been held by many other readers of Hume:

What kind of response one makes to life will, no doubt, for better or worse, depend on the sort of man one is for good or bad. . . . But we can all make it our purpose that our philosophy, if we have one, shall be no mere affair of surface opinions, but the genuine expression of a whole personality. Because I can never feel that Hume's own philosophy was that, I have to own to a haunting uncertainty whether Hume was really a great philosopher, or only a "very clever man."

Taylor is here expressing an attitude to Hume that many of us have felt: that his philosophy does not deserve to be taken too much to heart, because for all his intellectual vitality and the disturbing character of much that he says, there is a streak of frivolity in him that leads him to follow arguments to outrageous conclusions without serious consideration of the effect such conclusions may have on those who are driven to them; and that the love of literary reputation that he openly expressed was of far greater personal importance to him than philosophical truth.[1]

This estimate of Hume is a deeply mistaken one, and it involves a misconstruction of elements in his writings and his personality that have a very different explanation.

---

[1] A. E. Taylor, *David Hume and the Miraculous* (Cambridge: Cambridge University Press, 1927), 53–4.

I. HUME AND HIS PHILOSOPHICAL SYSTEM

There is no doubt that Hume writes with a lightness of touch, an ironic humor, and a degree of self-depreciation that are rare among great philosophers. He is not hard enough to read for a judgment of greatness to come readily to our minds, in fact. He is also able to deal with the issue immediately before him without belaboring its connections with those other parts of his system not presently being considered; this, too, to readers in an era when system building is unfashionable makes it harder to suppose he is trying to construct one in the way great philosophers do. And no thinker who is so frequently successful in the art of philosophical criticism can escape seeming to care first and foremost about scoring points. Such features are most easily explained as the result of a temperamental immunity to philosophical anxieties.

But the evidence is clearly against this, and another explanation is called for. The lightness is deliberately assumed for philosophical reasons by someone who is not immune to philosophical anxieties, but knows very well, and says, what it is like to be their victim. There are two well-known places where he tells us about this. One, not originally destined for our eyes, is the letter he wrote to an unnamed physician in 1734, yet did not (it seems) send, but rather preserved (KHL 4). In this he outlines, with remarkable acuity, the symptoms of breakdown that he had suffered as a result of his philosophical exertions in the period prior to the composition of the *Treatise* – symptoms such as "Scurvy Spots on my Fingers," "Watryness in the mouth," and a compulsive appetite, which he interpreted as signs of the "Disease of the Learned." The other is the famous concluding section of Book 1 of the *Treatise* itself, where he tells us of the effects that his researches have upon him. He fancies himself to be "some strange uncouth monster," to be "in the most deplorable condition imaginable, inviron'd with the deepest darkness, and utterly depriv'd of the use of every member and faculty" (T 1.4.7.2, 8). On both occasions he seeks release from these anxieties, which are the dark underside of the intellectual exhilaration that so frequently bursts through in the text of the *Treatise*; and this release is something he thinks to be available to him only if he makes himself balance the excesses of his philosophical reflections with deliberate absorption in business or social activities. These allow the resources of his nature to overcome the debilitating effects of overindulgence in philosophical reasoning.

This clear evidence shows us that Hume was not someone for whom philosophy was an activity of minor consequence, but someone who saw himself as likely to be thrown off balance by his predilection for it. So the affable and corpulent gentlemanly loiterer (to use Taylor's phrase)[2] whom some see as the historical Hume is, at most, a deliberately assumed *persona*, beneath which a much more complex and serious reality is at work. The *persona* is not a mere duplicate of the reality, but a product of experience and theory: experience of what philosophy leads to when practised in a way that does violence to our nature, and a theory that puts philosophy in its proper place.

What sort of theory is it? Any theory that suggests limits be placed on philosophy itself has an appearance of inconsistency if it is itself a philosophical theory; and the fact that Hume belongs somewhere in the skeptical tradition might seem to accentuate this risk. To a large extent Hume's theory of human nature is not, in our terms, philosophical, but psychological, even though one of its key purposes is to determine the proper limits of philosophical thought. He certainly thinks that philosophical activity, properly pursued, sustains personal equilibrium and can keep threats to it in check – as when it protects us from the far more dangerous risks that arise from superstition (T 1.4.7.13). But to know when to pursue philosophy and when not, one has to understand human needs and weaknesses, and make philosophy take account of them. Hume does not *confuse* philosophy and psychology, as some suppose; but he does mix them, in a special blend of his own.

Hume is a Socratic thinker. He believes that in order to avoid being plagued by anxiety we must achieve self-knowledge. The philosopher stands in need of it as much as his or her fellows do. Socrates would have agreed; but he appeared to think that self-knowledge was to come through the pursuit of the dialectical questioning in which the philosopher is expert, and Hume does not think this. Hume thinks that he has available a scientific mode of understanding that illuminates our nature for us, and that the philosopher must turn

[2] Taylor, *David Hume and the Miraculous*, 53.

to this to save himself. Our nature is intelligible; and once we have learned its key features, we can avoid those influences in philosophy (and in religion) that would lead us to do violence to it. The understanding of human nature that Hume urges on us is different indeed from that deriving from Socrates, at least as Plato presents him to us.

II. HUMAN NATURE, THE SELF, AND THE PASSIONS

Hume confidently proclaims the importance of his theory of human nature in the introduction to the *Treatise:*

Here then is the only expedient, from which we can hope for success in our philosophical researches, to leave the tedious lingring method, which we have hitherto followed, and instead of taking now and then a castle or village on the frontier, to march up directly to the capital or center of these sciences, to human nature itself.... There is no question of importance, whose decision is not compriz'd in the science of man; and there is none, which can be decided with any certainty, before we become acquainted with that science. In pretending therefore to explain the principles of human nature, we in effect propose a compleat system of the sciences, built on a foundation almost entirely new, and the only one upon which they can stand with any security. (T Intro. 6)

This is ambitious language, fully comparable to the claims Descartes had made in the previous century to be rebuilding all knowledge afresh. But the bases the two thinkers offer for this rebuilding are very different. The differences help us to understand why Hume has always had the reputation of being a spoiler rather than a builder, in spite of the positive thrust of this programmatic proclamation.

In Descartes's reconstruction of human knowledge, the metaphysical separation of the mental and the physical dictates limits to science: science is accorded the autonomy it deserves (and which the church had denied it in condemning Galileo) because it is confined in its subject matter to the physical world; the soul is exempted from its scrutiny because of its simplicity, its freedom, and its self-consciousness. The essence of Hume's reconstruction is to be found in the insistence that there can indeed be a science of mind, and that it is "experimental," or observational. The scientific ideal Hume has is often described as Newtonian, and the evidence for this is his proclamation of the theory of the association of ideas. This seems to duplicate Newtonian explanation in the physical realm. It does this by identifying, first, the ultimate corpuscular units that our observation of mental life reveals to us; Hume calls these perceptions, and divides them into impressions and ideas. It then provides a principle roughly corresponding to that of gravitation to account for the constant inner movement and change that characterizes the mental life we are able to introspect. This analogue to gravitation is association, which determines one perception to call up, or lead on to, another. In spite of a wise and cautionary statement that "we are only to regard it as a gentle force, which commonly prevails" (T 1.1.4.1), the gravitational analogy is offered with pride, along with a similarly Newtonian reticence about what may lie beneath that gentle force:

Here is a kind of ATTRACTION, which in the mental world will be found to have as extraordinary effects as in the natural, and to show itself in as many and as various forms. Its effects are every where conspicuous; but as to its causes, they are mostly unknown, and must be resolv'd into *original* qualities of human nature, which I pretend not to explain. (T 1.1.4.6)

In the *Abstract*, his own anonymous review of the *Treatise*, in which we can suppose he would draw particular attention to features of the work he thinks central, he says that if anything justifies calling "the author" an inventor, it is the use he makes of the principle of association.

Peter Jones has argued that the influence of Newton on Hume has been overrated, and that Hume's direct acquaintance with Newton's writings was probably limited.[3] Even if this is so, and even though the doctrine of association is less prominent in his later writings than it is in the *Treatise* (and even though the *Treatise* itself, as we shall see, leans heavily on psychological theories that do not combine with it without difficulty), I think that the impact of something like a Newtonian picture of the science of mind lingered in Hume's system long after the details of associationism ceased to interest him. There are two places where this can be seen most clearly. One is in his view of the self. The other is in his famous claim that reason

---

[3] Peter Jones, *Hume's Sentiments: Their Ciceronian and French Context* (Edinburgh: Edinburgh University Press, 1982), 11–19.

is, and ought only to be, the slave of the passions. In both these places we find ourselves at the heart of his moral psychology.

To say there can be a science of the mental, as Hume sees the matter, is to say that what we think, feel, or will can be explained as the effect of a cause and the instance of a natural law. Human minds are not strangers in nature, but inextricably part of it. Hume tries to demonstrate this in detail in the *Treatise* by showing how our beliefs and our emotive and conative commitments arise. The accounts are intended to treat thoughts and feelings and volitions (all perceptions, in his vocabulary) as the units of explanation, and to show how they give rise to one another. This form of explanation, at least nominally, gives the mind *itself* no role to play. If the never-ending changes in the physical world are all to be explained in terms of the attraction of material particles to one another, there is no room for the suggestion that the world itself, which merely *contains* them, exerts a force of its own. It is just the place where the events being described occur. Similarly, if the course of my mental history is determined by the associative attraction of my perceptions, so that they cause one another to arise, there seems no place, perhaps even no clear sense, to the suggestion that *I*, the mind or soul that *has* them, can exert any influence over their course. All it does is *include* them. The self, or ego, as he says, is just "a kind of theatre, where several perceptions successively make their appearance." The denial of an independent real self is not an awkward consequence of Hume's theory of knowledge, which requires us to say that it is not there because we cannot find it when we look for it (although this is true); it is a cornerstone of his system, required by the supposed fact of a science of man conceived in quasi-Newtonian terms. This science is deterministic, since mental events occur as a result of laws that supposedly govern the sequences of such events alone; and if it mentions minds or agents themselves, these are construed to be mere bundles, collections, or sequences of such events. "They are the successive perceptions only, that constitute the mind; nor have we the most distant notion of the place, where these scenes are represented, or of the materials, of which it is compos'd" (T 1.4.6.4).

This understanding of human nature stands in sharp contrast to another, which for convenience I shall call the rationalist model. This derives, historically, from Plato's *Phaedo*, in which Socrates is presented as teaching that the human soul is not part of nature, but is alien to it. It can choose how far it allies itself with the alien forces of its present environment, and how far it asserts its independence from them. These alien forces make inroads on it through the passions and desires, to which the soul can say yes or no. The implication of this is that some of the elements of our inner life, namely, the passions and desires, are not truly parts of ourselves at all; what is to be identified with the true self is the reason which says yes or no to them.

This Platonic view of the soul has taken deep root in our culture in many popular, and sophisticated, doctrines that are not overtly ascribed to him. There is the common contrast between reason and the passions, a contrast that yields the assumption that when one acts from passion one acts *in passivity,* so that what one does is not fully an act at all, and that one is not fully oneself in doing it. There is the correlative assumption, philosophically expressed in modern times in the Cartesian tradition, that the self is to be equated with the rational faculty, and that one is fully oneself when it dictates what one believes and what one chooses. Descartes indeed carried this to the extent of holding that one has full freedom whether to say yes or no, not only to the passions, but to the presentations of sense, so that we can always suspend judgment on these when our grounds are inconclusive.[4] This theory is the epistemological aspect of the general view that the unique dignity of the human soul consists in its possession of a special kind of freedom to assent to, or to reject, the promptings of the senses, the emotions, and the instincts. We can readily wonder whether all the elements in this view of ourselves are necessarily connected, and even whether they are consistent, but they are all powerfully present in both popular culture and rationalist philosophical theory.

Hume's understanding of human nature is at odds with this rationalist picture of it at every important point, and he sees its main contentions as inconsistent with the very possibility of a science of man. So he assaults it in every possible way, and in assaulting it has acquired a destructive reputation among philosophers who feel the dignity of human nature and the dignity of their own profession are both linked to the truth of the rationalist picture. One way Hume assaults that picture is by making statements of high shock value

[4] See his Fourth Meditation.

for those imbued with it. The most famous is his dictum that "Reason is, and ought only to be the slave of the passions, and can never pretend to any other office than to serve and obey them" (T 2.3.3.4). This is fundamentally an insistence that there can be a science of human nature in a way the rationalist picture would (in Hume's opinion) make impossible. It is, of course, more than this: it is also a claim that when we look and see, we shall find that human beings are creatures of instinct and feeling whose rational powers cannot, or at least should not, be used in any way at odds with the dominance of instinct and feeling.

Norman Kemp Smith and others have made clear that Hume's theory of knowledge is itself an application of this claim about human nature.[5] Hume sees our most fundamental beliefs as products of instinct; and he thinks we are lucky that they are. The rational queries of the philosophical skeptic would have the effect, if the rationalist view of the mind were true, of reducing us to a condition of chronic anxiety and indecision through our inability to justify the claims of our senses or the expectation of regularity in nature or the identity of the self. The skeptic is quite right about what we cannot rationally justify, but is also, fortunately, quite wrong about what we are able to disbelieve. Skeptical doubts are intellectually correct, but are *vain* or impotent doubts. Hume is himself a skeptic in his estimate of the soundness of skeptical arguments, but sides with the most truculent of the Common Sense thinkers in denying that these arguments can disturb us for more than brief periods.[6] These brief periods, however, are anxious ones, to be avoided by distraction, social or intellectual. Hume rejects the contention of the Sceptics of antiquity that the recognition of reason's inability to support the commitments of Common Sense leads of itself to inner peace. On the contrary, as he makes clear in the concluding Section 7 of Book 1 of the *Treatise,* such recognition would lead to despair if not overcome by the resources of instinct.

Hume does see our nature as creative: in generating our fundamental beliefs, it invests our perceptions with meaning. But it is instinct and not reason that does this.

---

[5] Norman Kemp Smith, "The Naturalism of Hume," *Mind* 14 (1905): 149–53, 335–47, and *The Philosophy of David Hume* (London: Macmillan, 1941).
[6] See Essay 9 in Terence Penelhum, *Themes in Hume* (Oxford: Clarendon Press, 2000).

Why is it that our instincts manage to invest our perceptions with meanings that are so useful and adaptive? Hume does not profess to know, and contents himself with an ironical suggestion that there must be a preestablished harmony at work (EHU 5.21). He never says the lifeworld our instincts create for us is one we know to be the true one.[7] His view of our beliefs is essentially a Darwinian view.

I turn now to a more detailed account of the way Hume's view of human nature underlies his account of our conduct and our morality, leaving aside his epistemology with the comment that, as Kemp Smith made clear to us, Hume's views on the interrelation between reason and passion run parallel in the two areas.

III. HUMAN CHOICE AND THE PASSIONS

Epistemology has never had much of a place in popular culture. But the rationalist understanding of human nature has a strong hold on the common understanding of our choices. We pride ourselves on the supposed fact that we are able sometimes to choose courses of action that override our passions and desires in the light of a greater good. We pride ourselves on the supposed fact that when we do this, we exercise the power to be free from the influences and temptations that would otherwise condemn us to what Kant called heteronomy. And we particularly pride ourselves on the supposed fact that we are able to pursue the austere demands of duty and so function as pillars of society by putting inclinations aside.

Hume denies none of the experiences on which these popular self-estimates depend. We can, and do, choose the good over the attractive, and resist many of the passions that agitate us. We are indeed entitled to talk of ourselves as acting freely on many such occasions – as well as equally on those when we yield to passions, and choose the attractive rather than the good. And we do, indeed, choose many actions because they are our duty, even though they do not appeal to us, and our society depends for its health on the fact that we do this. But he maintains that none of these familiar experiences is to be interpreted in the way rationalists interpret them. I shall

---

[7] This is what separates him so clearly from the common-sense school. See David Fate Norton, *David Hume: Common-Sense Moralist, Sceptical Metaphysician* (Princeton: Princeton University Press, 1982), Chap. 5.

take each of these three popular views in order, and try to show how Hume offers an alternative account of the relevant phenomena. I begin with those occasions when we pursue our good in the face of inclination.

The rationalist holds that when I do this, reason triumphs over passion. Hume's alternative account of this familiar experience depends on his analysis of the passions, which he develops at length in the largely neglected second book of the *Treatise*.[8]

The two technical classifications that are essential for understanding Hume's analysis of conflict and choice are his distinctions between direct and indirect passions, and between calm and violent passions. Both distinctions are introduced in the first section of Book 2 (T 2.1.1). Every passion, in Hume's view, is a unique, simple secondary impression. What makes it the passion it is, rather than some other, is therefore the felt quality it has. More simply, each passion is a distinct feeling; and questions about how it arises and how it leads to other experiences or to actions are construed by Hume as causal questions to be dealt with within his Newtonian mental science. In calling them secondary impressions, Hume seeks to distinguish them from the sensory impressions, which he calls "original" – a term indicating (here at least) that they do not occur in us in consequence of prior perceptions, as the secondary ones do. Passions, then, always arise in us from mental causes: from sensory impressions, from ideas, or from other passions. When they arise from other passions, they do so by association. There is, therefore, an association of impressions (based on resemblance) as well as an association of ideas.

---

[8] What follows here is not an attempt at the impossible feat of summarizing Book 2 in a few paragraphs, but merely an attempt to indicate the parts of its argument that are of most importance in assessing Hume's alternative to rationalism in moral psychology. I give a more detailed treatment in Chap. 5 of Penelhum, *Hume* (London: Macmillan, 1975), and in an essay "The Indirect Passions, Myself, and Others," in *The Cambridge Companion to Hume's* Treatise of Human Nature, ed. D. Ainslie (New York: Cambridge University Press, forthcoming). Important accounts of Book 2 are to be found in Páll Árdal, *Passion and Value in Hume's* Treatise (Edinburgh: Edinburgh University Press, 1966); Nicholas Capaldi, *Hume's Place in Moral Philosophy* (New York: Peter Lang 1989), Chap. 5; and Annette C. Baier, *A Progress of Sentiments: Reflections on Hume's* Treatise (Cambridge, MA: Harvard University Press, 1991), Chaps. 6 and 7. But the best place for any reader to go first in a serious study of Book 2 is David Norton's Editor's Introduction to the Oxford Philosophical Texts Edition of the *Treatise* (2000), 146–72.

The distinction between direct and indirect passions is a distinction between two ways in which passions arise. Direct passions "arise immediately from good or evil, from pain or pleasure." This seems to mean that they arise when something has given us pleasure or pain, or is believed to offer us the prospect of one or the other. This at least is what he says at the outset of Book 2; but when he discusses the direct passions in more detail in Section 9 of Part 3, he adds that some of them "frequently arise from a natural impulse or instinct, which is perfectly unaccountable" – a remark that comes close to making them original after all.[9] The indirect passions "proceed from the same principles, but by the conjunction of other qualities" (T 2.1.1.4, 2.3.9.8). This "conjunction" is described in much detail in Parts 1 and 2 of Book 2; but the key element in it is the fact that the indirect passions require a distinction between their *causes* and their *objects*:[10] roughly, the qualities that occasion them and the *persons* (that is oneself or another or others) who have these qualities, and to whom the indirect passions are directed. The fundamental indirect passions are those of pride and humility (that is, shame), where the object is oneself, and love and hatred, where the object is another person or persons. In each case the passion arises only when we are conscious both of the quality that causes it and of the fact that this quality is possessed by oneself or by another – that is, by the person who is the "object, to which [the passion] is directed" (T 2.1.3.4).

The direct passions are a mixed group indeed; but the critical fact about them for present purposes is that they not only include such

---

[9] This remark is probably intended to avoid the appearance of psychological hedonism that could be left by the earlier classification. Kemp Smith and Árdal have said that the passions Hume refers to here should be classified separately as "primary" rather than as direct. Norton divides the passions into productive and responsive, the former being desires that may yield pleasures but are not prompted by them, and assumes a distinction in the present passage between the instincts and the passions to which they give rise. These classifications amend Hume's own divisions, which are certainly made more problematic by the remark I quote here and by what Hume says at 2.3.3.8. I cannot explore these matters here beyond noting that Hume's regard for the facts of our emotional life has won out over his architectonic tendencies.

[10] This should not be equated too readily with what analytical philosphers in our time have meant by these terms. I have attempted to spell out the differences in Chapter 5 of *Hume* (1975) and in "The Indirect Passions, Myself, and Others," in *The Cambridge Companion to Hume's* Treatise of Human Nature.

reactive emotions as joy or grief or despair, but also include some of the most fundamental determinants of human conduct, namely, the *desires*. Hume does not only include desires for perceived objects like clothes, or for bodily satisfactions like food or sex, but mentions "the desire of punishment to our enemies, and of happiness to our friends" and even "the general appetite to good, and aversion to evil, consider'd merely as such" (T 2.3.9.8, 2.3.3.8). It does not seem natural to write of desires as passions, unless they are very agitating and overwhelming ones, but Hume's psychology depends on his being able to counter our resistance to his doing this. He attempts to counter it through his very important distinction between calm and violent passions. When introducing it, Hume says that it is common for us to distinguish between gentle and intense emotions, and to use the word "passion" only of the latter, but he calls this a "vulgar and specious division." One and the same passion can be both mild and intense, though on any occasion a given passion will usually be one or the other. It is critically important that when a passion has become "the predominant inclination of the soul, it commonly produces no longer any sensible agitation" (T 2.1.1.3, 2.3.4.1). We must therefore distinguish between the violence of a passion, which is a matter of its felt intensity, and its strength, which is a matter of its degree of influence on our choices and conduct. A passion can be strong but calm; and such a passion may overcome a more violent or agitating one. This is presumably what happens when we choose the good over the alluring – so that the aching longing for the dessert loses out to the wish to stay slim, which agitates not at all. So those occasions when we think our reason has won out over passion are actually cases where a calm passion has shown more strength than a violent one.[11]

The doctrine of calm passions is Hume's main card in the game against rationalist psychology. Its main internal difficulty is the fact that it requires him to say that passions can be "in a manner, imperceptible," while classing them as impressions; when he has earlier distinguished impressions from ideas on the basis of their force and vivacity, even using the very word "violence" in doing so (T 2.1.1.3, 1.1.1.1).

---

[11] We owe the clear understanding of Hume's distinction between calm and violent passions to Árdal's *Passion and Value in Hume's* Treatise, 95ff.

He supports his positive analysis of choice by some famous negative arguments against rationalism. They are to be found in Section
3 of Part 3 of Book 2, entitled *Of the influencing motives of the will.*
These arguments are intended to show that "reason alone can never
be a motive to any action of the will" and that "it can never oppose
passion in the direction of the will" (T 2.3.3.1). Hume argues for the
first contention in two ways: he says that reason has two functions
only, namely, the discovery of relations of ideas, as in mathematics,
and the description of matters of fact, as in the empirical sciences and
common life.[12] Reason in the former function has practical import
only when calculation plays a role in empirical investigation; and
in its empirical function reason can affect practice only by showing
us the causes or effects of objects that we already desire or shun. In
other words, it is our desires that prompt us to pursue or flee from
the objects of our choice. Reason merely shows us what leads to,
or away from, that in which our desires make us take interest. It is
never itself the source of such interest.

If reason is thus shown to be incapable of originating our choices
and inclinations, then on those occasions when we make choices in
opposition to a passion, it cannot be reason that moves us: it cannot
provide the necessary contrary "impulse" itself. At most it can serve
some desire or aversion that is the real counterforce to the passion
that loses the contest.

Hume tries to clinch these arguments by drawing on a fundamental feature of his theory of the passions: that they are secondary
impressions, and not ideas. Only ideas have "reference to any other
object," because they are copies, whereas passions, as impressions,
do not have any such "representative quality." They cannot, therefore, be "contradictory to truth and reason," since such contradiction entails a defect in that very representative quality. This self-
containedness, or lack of reference, that supposedly characterizes
all passions is a feature of them even when they are desires. Hume
gives the example of anger, which on his view is a desire for harm
to another (what we would call hostility). When I am angry, he says,
"I am actually possest with the passion, and in that emotion have
no more a reference to any other object, than when I am thirsty, or
sick, or more than five foot high" (T 2.3.3.5).

---

[12] I am here using the terminology Hume introduced later in EHU 4. It is clear that
the same distinction is intended in T 2.3.3.

As a consequence of this apparent denial of the intentionality of passions and desires, Hume maintains that they cannot properly be called unreasonable.[13] This term, though often applied to them, should, he says, be applied only to the judgments that *accompany* them: "In short, a passion must be accompany'd with some false judgment, in order to its being unreasonable; and even then 'tis not the passion, properly speaking, which is unreasonable, but the judgment" (T 2.3.3.6). Hence there is no unreasonableness in preferring "the destruction of the whole world to the scratching of my finger" or in choosing "my total ruin, to prevent the least uneasiness of an *Indian* or person wholly unknown to me," or to prefer my lesser good to my greater. None of these preferences require any false judgments, and could only be unreasonable if they did.

If we put aside the attention-drawing rhetoric, we can see that Hume does not deny reason an essential role in human conduct. It shows us how to satisfy our desires, and in enabling us to recognize that which we then come to want, it can even prompt them, although he does not concede this explicitly. What reason cannot do is to motivate us of itself. It is the *slave* of the passions. But there are many things that we can do with the help of a slave that we could not do if we did not have him, and for all the air of paradox with which Hume pronounces his theories, he does not deny this.

IV. FREEDOM

Hume believes that if there is to be a science of human nature, our actions and choices must show the same sort of regularity that we find in the physical world. In tracing our choices to the workings of

---

[13] A defender of Hume might say here that in spite of the rhetoric he is merely insisting that passions are not themselves representative of their objects, and that such representation is confined, in his theory, to the ideas that generate the passions or are generated by them. His theory entails that the intentionality of a passion (its being *about* a person or a quality) is a fact about its ideal accompaniments or its effects and is not a feature of the feeling in which the passion itself consists. This is what enables him to argue that the passion itself is immune to appraisals of its rationality. I argue against this later in this essay. For further discussions of these complicated questions, see Chapter 3 of David Norton, *David Hume: Common Sense Moralist, Sceptical Metaphysician;* Chapter 7 of Annette Baier, *A Progress of Sentiments;* and Chapter 1 of John Bricke, *Mind and Morality: An Examination of Hume's Moral Psychology* (Oxford: Clarendon Press, 1996). An older but still rewarding treatment is to be found in Rachel M. Kydd, *Reason and Conduct in Hume's* Treatise (Oxford: Clarendon Press, 1946).

the passions that arise in us through the mechanisms of association, he has tried to show that these regularities do indeed govern them. Such a program seems to imply a denial of the freedom that we think distinguishes us from other beings, and that is associated in rationalist theory with the assertion of the supposed authority of reason. Hume seeks to show that his human science can accommodate our freedom without exempting human choice from the regularity and predictability that he finds in our natures. Hence his philosophical system contains the best-known classical statement of what is now known as Compatibilism.[14]

Compatibilism is the thesis that there is no inconsistency in holding that human actions are caused and yet are free. This is a logical thesis, normally combined with the substantive claim that our actions always *are* caused, and that they are sometimes free as well. I shall use the title to comprise the combination of all three propositions. I shall use the common term Libertarianism to name the view that it is indeed inconsistent to hold that human actions can be free yet always caused; that some of them are indeed free; and that some are therefore, in some manner, exempt from causation.

Hume's position is presented most clearly in Section 8 of the first *Enquiry*, though most of what he says there is anticipated in Sections 1 and 2 of Part 3 of Book 2 of the *Treatise*. The *Treatise* version is more aggressive, and in the *Enquiry* he describes his argument as a "reconciling project." This phrase might suggest that he thinks his position is fully in accord with common sense, but it clearly is not, and Hume does not seriously pretend it is. What he thinks he is reconciling are the needs of a human science and the needs of our ordinary moral discourse, and he argues that common opinion is in error about the latter needs. Popular opinion holds that we need one sort of freedom that we do not have, instead of another that we do have.

In the *Treatise* he uses scholastic terminology to name these two kinds of freedom: he distinguishes between "liberty of *spontaneity*"

---

[14] He was anticipated by Hobbes in Chap. 21 of *Leviathan* (1655), and by Anthony Collins in his *Philosophical Inquiry Concerning Human Liberty* (1717). Collins's work is often overlooked (e.g., by myself), even though its existence was pointed out by T. H. Huxley in his *Hume* (London: Macmillan, 1886). It is conveniently available in *Determinism and Freewill*, ed. J. O'Higgins (The Hague: Martinus Nijhoff, 1976). I have attempted to examine Hume's views on freedom more fully in Chapter 8 of my *Themes in Hume*.

and "liberty of *indifference*" (T 2.3.2.1). Liberty of spontaneity consists in the absence of hindrances to the execution of one's decisions. He describes it in the *Enquiry* thus: "*a power of acting, or not acting, according to the determinations of the will*; that is, if we choose to remain at rest, we may; if we choose to move, we also may." He immediately adds that it is possessed by "everyone who is not a prisoner and in chains" (EHU 8.23). He thinks, correctly, that this last claim is not controversial. He is also correct in thinking that liberty of spontaneity, so defined, is compatible with universal causation; for it is merely the absence of interference with the exercise of one's choices, not the absence of causal determination in the making of those choices.

Where he is controversial is in what he says about the other sort of freedom that we think we have, but in his view do not have. We think that sometimes, when we choose one way, we could equally have chosen another way. In Hume's language we believe that sometimes, when we choose to remain at rest, we might (even though we do not) choose instead to move; and that if we choose to move, we might (even though we do not) choose instead to remain at rest. We believe in the reality of unexercised powers of choice, and see this reality as essential to our freedom as agents. Hume calls this sort of freedom "liberty of *indifference*" and interprets it as a denial of the universality of causation in human affairs, and insists we neither have it nor need it. Indeed, he believes the requirements of our moral thinking and decision making are inconsistent with its existence.

He attacks liberty of indifference in three ways. First, he asserts the universality of causation, and the unreality of chance, and emphasizes that human affairs do not differ in these respects from the natural world. For example: it "is universally allowed, that nothing exists without a cause of its existence, and that *chance*, when strictly examined, is a mere negative word, and means not any real power, which has, any where, a being in nature" (EHU 8.25). To this dogmatic metaphysical argument, he adds that we can infer and predict human actions from the motives and characters of human agents in a way that is fully comparable to our ability to explain and predict natural phenomena; and when people seem to act in bizarre or unpredictable ways, we can postulate and discover hidden causes that account for this – again, as we are able to do for surprising physical events. So we must acknowledge "necessity" in human affairs as well as in physical nature – this term being under-stood, as he stresses, in the same way as he has interpreted it in his earlier analysis of causal inferences. It is important to recall that when he outlines what he calls some "corollaries" of that analysis in the *Treatise* he remarks, with astonishing casualness, that "the distinction, which we often make betwixt *power* and the *exercise* of it, is... without foundation" (T 1.3.14.32, 34). One of the ways in which we "often make" this distinction is, of course, in the popular ascription to agents of the unexercised power of choice.

Hume's second line of attack on liberty of indifference is the more practical one that we need predictability in human affairs in order to make our decisions. He gives the melancholy example of the prisoner condemned to the scaffold, who recognizes he will get no help in escaping from his gaoler or his guards after observing their characters, and decides he would be better employed in trying to weaken the bars of his cell than in trying to change their resolution (T 2.3.1.17). The multitude of examples that human experience offers us of regular connections between character and action would not be open to us if liberty of indifference were a reality.

Hume's third argument against liberty of indifference consists in refutations of the natural, but in his view misguided, suggestion that we can introspect its reality (T 2.3.2.2). What he says here parallels the many important things he says in opposition to the claim that we can detect within ourselves the experience of the power that we ascribe to physical causes (see, for example, EHU 7.9–20). Hume does not deny there are volitions, as some have;[15] he sees them as a readily detectable component in the mechanism of human choice.[16] But he denies that we can ever detect that they are themselves "subject to nothing" (EHU 8.22, n.18).

Liberty of indifference, then, is a myth; but we have never had any need of it, and in fact presuppose its absence in practical reflection. Its reality would be inconsistent with the possibility of a science of man, as conceived by Hume. It is impossible here to explore the question of the relationship between human science and determin-ism that is raised by Hume's stance. Instead, I mention an important implication of his view for his moral psychology.

---

[15] The best-known case is Chapter 3 of Gilbert Ryle, *The Concept of Mind* (London: Hutchinson, 1949).

[16] See Penelhum, *Hume* (1975), 111–17, and Bricke, *Mind and Morality*, 49–59.

If Hume is right, we are often in a position to enact the choices we make, and also to enact the alternative choices that we do not make. But we are never in a position to choose in a way other than the way we do choose. He believes in the reality of unexploited opportunities; but not in the reality of unexercised powers of choice. This entails, however, that moral praise or blame can never be applied on the ground that someone has chosen a course of action that he or she *need not have chosen.* Common opinion follows rationalism in thinking that this is in fact the basis of much praise or blame; and Hume must deny it.

He does in fact deny it, and offers an account of moral virtue that connects it with the very predictability that he insists we can find in human affairs, not with the liberty of indifference that he says does not exist.

V. OBLIGATION AND VIRTUE

We have seen that Hume traces all choices to the passions, and rejects the rationalist understanding of human freedom. But this leads us to what he seems to see as the major problem of his moral philosophy. Rationalists might concede the main features of his account of prudential choice, but still say that when I choose what I think is good for me instead of what I am now inclined to desire, I remain the servant of my desires. I do not cease to serve them when I merely postpone their satisfaction to the future. We do, however, sometimes manage to act in the face of *all* our desires, short term or long term. We do this when we act from duty. When we do this, reason does indeed triumph over passion.

The best-known version of this view from Hume's time is that of Joseph Butler, who insists on the supremacy of conscience in human nature.[17] He accords it supremacy over all other springs of action, including self-love, benevolence, and particular desires. Hume's account of our regard for duty is one that concedes its reality, but still derives it from our emotional natures as his science of man depicts them.

---

[17] Butler avoids commitment on whether conscience is a rational power or a moral sense. See *The Works of Bishop Butler*, ed. J. H. Bernard, 2 vols. (London: Macmillan, 1900), 2:287. But the role he ascribes to it is one to which Hume must find an alternative within his own human science.

His account depends on a principle he enunciates as an "un-doubted maxim," namely, "*that no action can be virtuous, or morally good, unless there be in human nature some motive to produce it, distinct from the sense of its morality*" (T 3.2.1.7). He recognizes that this claim looks to be at odds with the fact that we sometimes act from a sense of duty alone. His attempt to show that his claim can accommodate this fact is at the heart of his account of justice.

We must begin with his account of the role of the passions, or sentiments, of approval and disapproval, since he views the sense of duty as a derivative of these. Hume holds that moral judgments, in which we describe behavior as virtuous or vicious, express these sentiments. Like all other passions, they are unique secondary impressions, and cannot therefore be analyzed; but we can say how they arise and what their effects are. The story is complex, but we can see at the outset that if indeed the sense of duty is a product of the sentiments of approval and disapproval, it is a product of sentiments that arise when we pass judgment on human behavior that must already be produced by something other than the approval and disapproval to which it gives rise. I draw in what follows on Sections 1, 2, and 3 of Part 3 of Book 3 of the *Treatise,* and Sections 5 through 7 of the second *Enquiry.*

Hume maintains that moral approval and disapproval have human characters, rather than individual actions, as their objects. It is significant that he takes the terms "virtuous" and "vicious" as the paradigms of moral language, thus making it easier to persuade us that evaluations are directed toward persons rather than their deeds: "If any *action* be either virtuous or vicious, 'tis only as a sign of some quality or character." He says that actions that do not reflect settled states of character in their agents "are never consider'd in morality." Reason assists in the generation of approval and disapproval by showing us the effects that certain states of character have. If, by a disinterested examination (an examination conducted "without reference to our particular interest"; T 3.3.1.4, 3.1.2.4), we find that a particular character trait is agreeable or useful, or disagreeable or harmful, to the agent who has it, or to others, then the mechanism that generates approval or disapproval can commence.

The mechanism is complex, and involves the workings of *sympathy.* This psychological principle is not to be confused with the sentiment of compassion, which is merely one of its products. The principle is the one that enables us to participate in the emotional life, and the pleasures and pains, of others. Hume introduces it in *Treatise* 2.1.11.[18] According to his account of it there, I become aware of the passion of another by observing its manifestations in his or her behavior; I have, therefore, an *idea* of it. So far, however, I am not moved by the other's passion. For this to happen, my idea has to be enlivened: then it will turn into an impression, and I shall *have* the very passion I have inferred to be present in the other person. Hume says, to the surprise of the readers who encounter this so early in Book 2, with their memories of *Treatise* 1.4.6 in their minds, that what enlivens the idea I have of the other's passion is the "idea, or rather impression" of myself. He cannot here refer to the impression of the pure ego that he was so emphatic in Book 1 that he did not have, but must refer to "that succession of related ideas and impressions, of which we have an intimate memory and consciousness" (T 2.2.11.4, 2.1.2.2). This is so lively and vivid that its liveliness is communicated to the idea of the other's passion, which I then come to have myself. It can then lead on to other passions through the principle of association.

The sympathetic mechanism enables me to share in the pleasures and pains that are the effects, in the agent or others, of those character traits I am disinterestedly surveying. The association of impressions causes me then to experience approval (when these effects are pleasant) or disapproval (when they are painful). I *express* these sentiments in my moral judgments, and I call the character traits I have assessed in this way virtues or vices, respectively. Their virtuousness or viciousness consists in their capacity to arouse these sentiments in observers; but these sentiments have not, of course, caused these character traits to be present in the observed agents in the first place.

Hume describes approval and disapproval as calm forms of the indirect passions of love and hatred (T 3.3.5.1).[19] Love and hatred are

---

[18] Sympathy seems to drop out of sight in the second *Enquiry*, and it has been a matter of controversy whether this shows Hume to have abandoned it or not. For the negative view, see the appendix to J. B. Stewart, *The Moral and Political Philosophy of David Hume* (New York: Columbia University Press, 1963); for the positive, see Capaldi, *Hume's Place in Moral Philosophy*, Chap. 7. Whatever its place in the second *Enquiry*, its role in the *Treatise* is much greater than I have described here. See also in this volume the essay "Hume's Later Moral Philosophy."

[19] This passage is key to Árdal's interpretation of the relation between Hume's theory of the passions and his moral philosophy. In this essay I have followed him, as the passage seems quite explicit. Its importance has been questioned, however,

caused by the qualities or actions of persons, but have the persons themselves as their objects. Approval and disapproval are aroused by the qualities agents display, but are directed toward the agents themselves as the bearers of the characters they manifest.

We have yet to account for the sense of duty, however. The account comes in two parts. The first is Hume's explanation of how it is that we sometimes perform acts from a sense of duty that others perform from (say) benevolence. He says that someone may be conscious of the fact that he lacks a character trait (such as kindness to children) that causes us to approve of those who have it. He may then come to "hate himself upon that account" and may perform the action "from a certain sense of duty, in order to acquire by practice, that virtuous principle" (T 3.2.1.8). On this view, the sense of duty is a conscious substitute for more natural motives, and is a product of self-hatred. To feel it is to feel the disapproval of your own lack of a virtuous inclination.

These phenomena occur, though I think we may doubt whether they are the key to the *origin* of the sense of duty. But even if they are, they do not include a much larger range of cases: those occasions when we seem willing to act from duty even when there is no prior natural motive, either in ourselves or in others. These are the cases when we act from *justice.* There is no natural inclination (such as benevolence) to explain our willingness to pay our taxes, or to return money we have borrowed from our bankers. Yet justice is esteemed as a virtue, and its denial is judged vicious. Hume's understanding of this fact is of primary importance in his psychology of duty. In Hume's system justice is not a natural virtue but an artificial one: that is, it is not a settled state of character that is due to innate causes within us, but a condition we acquire because of the influence on us of social institutions. We do have some socially unifying motives in

---

by Donald Ainslie, in his essay "Scepticism about Persons in Book 2 of Hume's *Treatise," Journal of the History of Philosophy* 27 (1999): 469–92. If Árdal is right, Hume's account of obligation is a direct application of his theory of the passions; if he is not, and we need to distinguish more carefully than this passage seems to between persons and their characters or mental qualities as objects of approval and disapproval, the great emphasis that Hume places on his account of the indirect passions needs further explanation. Ainslie offers such an explanation. I incline to think that the role Ainslie gives to these passions is one they indeed have; but I do not see that this shows Árdal to be mistaken.

our natural benevolence and love of family; but these motives are too restrictive to sustain large social groupings. We are able, however, to see the value of conventions that would safeguard such things as property rights, and we adopt them through an implicit recognition of common interests. Both in the *Treatise* and in the second *Enquiry* Hume uses the analogy of oarsmen who row together without any explicit mutual undertaking to do so. Such conventions often entail inconvenience for us, but we sustain them through self-interest.

Once they are established, it is easy to understand how they acquire the extra status given them through the operation of approval and disapproval. Each of us is able, through sympathy, to be conscious of the unpleasant results of unjust actions for those who suffer from them. We may suffer from them ourselves. We express our displeasure at these effects by saying that just actions are our duty, and avoid inner discomfort by doing our duty ourselves. Hence justice becomes virtuous without first being attractive. Hume's most succinct summary of his account of the genesis of the sense of duty is perhaps this: "All morality depends upon our sentiments; and when any action, or quality of the mind, pleases us *after a certain manner*, we say it is virtuous; and when the neglect, or non-performance of it, displeases us *after a like manner*, we say that we lie under an obligation to perform it" (T 3.2.5.4).

VI. HUME AND COMMON OPINION

For all his willingness to express himself paradoxically, Hume's moral psychology is designed to accommodate the phenomena of our daily moral experience, and only to reject a rationalist interpretation of them. He does not seek to overturn the moral conventions of common sense but, on the contrary, seeks to support them anew on foundations of experiment and observation, free of misleading and disruptive theory.[20] It is therefore important, in assessing his successes and failures, to determine how far his opinions conform to common opinion, and how far not.

I begin with a comment on his theory of obligation. Its very ingenuity presents an immediate difficulty. Is it so obvious that the sense

[20] I am in agreement here with the position in Norton, *David Hume: Common Sense Moralist, Sceptical Metaphysician.*

of duty is derivative? Hume is free of the worldly wise cynicism of psychological egoism. In the second appendix to the second *Enquiry* he argues against it, much in the manner of Joseph Butler, and maintains that those who hold it (like Hobbes) are forcing a theory on the observable facts of conduct. But why not follow Butler further and say that the observable facts also show we have a natural tendency to feel and act on a sense of obligation?[21] The reason is probably to be found not only in the determination to undermine ethical rationalism, but also in the equally strong determination, in Hume, to avoid any theory that might seem to require, or invite, theological underpinnings, and to offer instead a purely secular account of all the phenomena he explains. But in seeking to offer an explanation of conscience at all, instead of taking the fact of it as a datum as he takes benevolence to be, he is forced to interpret it as a product of the institutions of social justice, when the latter are probably regarded by most as deriving some of their hold on us from the power of our sense of obligation, not the other way about. The fact that many other philosophers try to explain them as deriving from self-interest, much as Hume does, puts them at odds with common opinion also.

There is another place where Hume's account of moral virtue puts him at odds with common sense, and where he himself shows signs of greater discomfort at the fact. In his story of the ways we come to feel moral approval, he tells us that it is directed toward established character traits in our natures, and arises when we disinterestedly recognize that these character traits are useful or agreeable to ourselves or others: that they have utility, in the language of the second *Enquiry.* This account prompts a question: there are many human characteristics that have utility in this way that we delight in, but are not objects of moral approval. Similarly, many human traits that are harmful or disagreeable do not elicit moral disapproval. We praise charm, wit, or eloquence, but not *in the manner* of benevolence, industry, or temperance. Why not? Hume addresses this potentially vexing question in *Treatise* 3.3.4–5, and in the fourth appendix to the second *Enquiry.* He tries to dismiss it as not "very material" and in entitling the *Enquiry* appendix "Of Some Verbal Disputes"

[21] For Butler's arguments, see the first, second, and third Sermons in *The Works of Bishop Butler,* Vol. 1, 25–57.

evinces a lamentable and atypical inclination to dismiss a serious conceptual issue as what misguided theorists today sometimes call a "mere" question of semantics.

But it *is* a problem; and he shows a degree of recognition of the sort of problem that it is by trying to fend off one possible explanation of the distinction we do indeed make between virtues on the one hand and talents on the other. This is the suggestion that virtues are voluntarily acquired and talents are not. He says, perhaps correctly, that there is no ground for maintaining this, and suggests instead that the relevant consideration is that virtues (and vices) can be changed by laws and by education, whereas talents cannot. This is interesting, but seems wrong: one thinks of the work of remedial language instructors, long-suffering piano teachers, or physiotherapists, who all seem to be in the thankless but not wholly ineffectual business of modifying our talents by training.

What, then, is the ground of our distinction? We can approach it by noticing that in order to assimilate talents to virtues, Hume has to assume that the talents are used well or wisely. A virtue cannot (necessarily cannot) be used badly by its possessor, but a talent can.[22] A virtue is, in part, the predictable tendency to use some talent well, rather than badly. But using a talent well involves using it at the right times and not using it at the wrong times. We praise someone who can be predicted to do this (by calling him virtuous), because that person *chooses* to use that talent when it is good to, and not to use it when it would be bad to. He or she is praiseworthy because they use it in good ways when they *could* use it in bad ways instead. We praise the predictability of virtuous action precisely because we think it could be done otherwise. On Hume's view of freedom this is what we can never say about anyone's choices.

Hume's science of human nature, then, seems to have the unattractive consequence that we accord moral approval and disapproval to patterns of choice that could not be other than what they are. A good character is just a piece of good fortune. While popular ethical thinking is frequently forced to give ear to this view, it is still seen as paradoxical. Good character is, for the most part, still

---

[22] One recalls here the definition of a virtue in Aquinas: "a good disposition of the mind, by which we live righteously, and of which no one can make bad use." *Summa Theologiae* 1a2ae55,4.

regarded as the regular tendency to make free choices that are good, not merely to perform pleasing acts habitually.

This brings us to the bedrock of Hume's understanding of what a science of human nature has to be like. I have suggested that the common distinction between virtues and talents, which he finds a source of difficulty, exists because the popular ascription of virtue to someone involves ascribing some degree of what Hume calls liberty of indifference to that person. But Hume would respond that this entails the denial of the very predictability of human conduct that our ethical thinking requires, and is inconsistent with the scientific status of the study of mankind. Critics of a libertarian turn of mind would say that Hume's difficulties merely show we must jettison the Newtonian model of the human sciences. We must, they would say, accept that the social sciences are able to predict human behavior (such as voting patterns) as well as they do because, in fact, most people do choose in roughly the same ways in similar situations, even though they could, *if* they chose, not do so. But some people do, now and then, surprise us (when they could have chosen not to!) and we have to be content with statistical predictions in consequence.

So far we have found aspects of Hume's moral psychology that are at odds with common opinion in ways that seem inevitable consequences of his understanding of the science of human nature. There is another well-known claim that he makes that is indeed at odds with common opinion, but in a way he could have avoided. This is his claim that erroneous or bizarre emotions are not contrary to reason.

He recognizes that the understanding can give rise to passion by producing opinions that give rise to such states as grief or joy or resentment, or by prompting desires or volitions when we see that some course of action will lead to what we already want or think good. But he insists that this does not ever entitle us to call the passions or desires unreasonable, or to hold that "reason and passion can ever oppose each other, or dispute for the government of the will and actions" (T 2.3.3.7). What Hume has done here is emphasize the importance of passion and/or desire in the genesis of choice and conduct, while continuing to accept, indeed to stress, the rationalist insistence on the sharp separation of reason and emotion. Hume teaches the *a*-rationality of passion where the rationalist teaches the *ir*-rationality of passion. Both, in fact, misinterpret common moral opinion, which is committed to neither view, but accepts that emotion, as well as opinion, can be both reasonable and unreasonable.

Hume seems to think that the only cases where the moral evaluations of common sense require the ascription of irrationality to the passions are cases where these are deemed to be the result of false judgments. But this is not so. On the contrary: if I pursue an objective that is harmful to me, because I mistakenly think it will be good for me, then my desire for it may be judged to be erroneous, since my judgment is; but it is not thereby judged to be unreasonable. If common sense agrees that the course I am following will lead to the objective I am pursuing, but holds me to be mistaken in thinking it will be good for me; or if it holds me to be right in thinking it would be good for me but wrong in thinking the course I am following will help me attain it, it is still likely to call my choice a *reasonable* one. The falsity of my judgment is the very thing that makes my action reasonable in cases of this sort. If I grieve at the supposed loss of a loved one who is in fact alive and well, my grief is mistaken, but not unreasonable. We apply the term "unreasonable" to an emotion or to a desire where that emotion or desire is thought to be in some way *inappropriate* to the situation that the agent considers himself, or herself, to be in: when it is the wrong way to respond, emotionally or conatively, to a situation of that sort. If the situation is not of that sort, the response is mistaken as well. But it can be quite free of error, and still be either reasonable or unreasonable: by being moderate or excessive, helpful or unhelpful, sane or silly. These are all dimensions of rationality that can be manifested *by the passions themselves.* Hume has perceived the importance of the passions for all our choice and conduct, but has mistakenly felt obliged to deny their rationality in order to accommodate this importance. In this respect he shares an estimate of them with the rationalists whose theories he contests. The estimate is one from which common sense is already free.

VII. MORAL PSYCHOLOGY AND THE SELF

We have seen that Hume's conception of a science of human nature reduces mental life to the interplay of impressions and ideas, and treats the mind itself as the theater where this interplay occurs, not as a participant in it. The scholarly literature contains many criticisms and reappraisals of what Hume says about the self, almost all directed to his treatment of it in Book 1 of the *Treatise*. Two of the criticisms prominent in this literature are of particular importance.

The first criticism is that in spite of the Newtonianism of perceptions that Hume proclaims at the outset of the *Treatise*, and again in the first *Enquiry*, his accounts of the origins of our beliefs lean heavily on the ascription to us of propensities, tendencies, or habits. This leads some to suggest that he is committed to a crypto-Kantian psychology in which the subject of explanations is the mind and its dispositions, rather than the perceptions it contains.[23] The second criticism is that the ascription of a propensity (in this case the propensity to confuse one sort of succession with another) is essential to Hume's account of the genesis of the belief in the unity of the mind itself – thus opening him to the objection that he cannot explain how we come to have the belief he criticizes without first assuming its truth.

It is possible to respond on Hume's behalf to the first criticism by suggesting that talk of the mind's propensities should be construed as popular shorthand for a genuinely Newtonian account that speaks instead of how impressions and ideas give rise to one another *in* the mind. It is possible to respond similarly to the second by saying that the perceptions the mind has can well include perceptions *of* the series that constitute it, without there having also to be any supervenient subject beyond the series' successive members. Such responses seem to save him from charges of formal inconsistency.[24]

But the transition to the passages about the self in Book 2 is still a surprising one for the reader of Book 1. Hume has tried to prepare us for it by telling us to distinguish "betwixt personal identity, as it regards our thought or imagination, and as it regards our passions or the concern we take in ourselves" (T 1.4.6.5). He also tries to ease the transition by clarifying his use of the term "self" in its first

---

[23] The two fundamental and classic essays on this theme are Robert Paul Wolff, "Hume's Theory of Mental Activity," *Philosophical Review* 69, no. 3 (July 1960): 289–310; and Fred Wilson's essay of the same title in *McGill Hume Studies*, ed. D. Norton, N. Capaldi, and W. Robison (San Diego: Austin Hill Press, 1979), 101–20.

[24] See Nelson Pike, "Hume's Bundle Theory of the Self: A Limited Defense," *American Philosophical Quarterly* 4 (1967), and Essay 3 in Penelhum, *Themes in Hume*, 40–60.

introduction in Book 2 as the name of the object of the indirect passion of pride: "This object is self, or that succession of related ideas and impressions, of which we have an intimate memory and consciousness" (T 2.1.2.2). This makes it clear that he is not reverting to the pure owner-self whose existence he rejects so brusquely in Book 1. But this does not prepare us for the claim that "the idea, or rather impression of ourselves is always intimately present with us, and that our consciousness gives us so lively a conception of our own person, that 'tis not possible to imagine, that any thing can in this particular go beyond it" (T 2.1.11.4). More serious, perhaps, is the fact that the account of the aetiology of the indirect passions requires the use of the idea of the self *as distinct from others;* and the account of the origins of our belief in self-identity in Book 1 is confined to our belief in the self's own inner unity over time, and tells us nothing of how we come to be aware of the existence of other minds. This is a serious gap in his system, but perhaps not a manifest inconsistency. Let us turn instead to the role he ascribes to this lively notion of the self in our emotional life.

Whatever this role is, he does not think it undermines his Newtonian mental science. There is no place in his system for the suggestion that choices are the product of anything other than the series of passions and cognitions that lead to them. His denial of liberty of indifference permits no consideration of what has been called agent causation: the theory that in free action it is the agent, rather than the agent's desires or volitions, that is the *locus* of causality.[25] This denial is coupled with great stress on the claim that our understanding and evaluation of human agency depends on our recognition of settled states of character. This raises, in the sphere of action, a perplexity parallel to that raised by his critics in the sphere of epistemology: that his view seems to require a continuing self that *has* the character traits he feels necessary for prediction and evaluation. We can perhaps offer a similar answer: that talk of an agent's character is shorthand for talk of that agent's emotions and desires.

However we respond to these difficulties of interpretation, there is a vital dimension to Hume's theory of the self in Book 2 that

---

[25] For a classic treatment of this notion, see R. M. Chisholm, "Freedom and Action," in *Freedom and Determinism,* ed. Keith Lehrer (New York: Random House, 1966), 11–44.

is only lately recognized as central to his moral psychology.[26] It permeates his whole vision of the human condition. We find its clearest expression in the introduction of the principle of sympathy, in *Treatise* 2.1.11. Scholars have interpreted sympathy as a mechanism to explain my concern for others, which emerges through my having myself the very feelings I discern in them. This is correct, but seriously incomplete. The principle is introduced by Hume as a "secondary" source of the *self*-regarding indirect passions of pride and humility. Pride does not merely come about through my taking pleasure in qualities that I recognize to belong to me; it also comes about through my sympathetically sharing the admiration (that is, in Hume's view, the love) that others have toward me when they, too, discern these pleasing qualities. So my own pride is in part the product of the mentality of others, not only of my own. And since I am loved, or admired, for qualities I have or objects I possess, my emotional life is such that I shall pride myself on those qualities or objects for which others admire me, and be ashamed of those qualities or objects for which they hate (or despise) me. They are the cocreators of my self-image, and to understand the character of my self-concern it is necessary to take the measure of the society of which I am a member.

As Baier points out, many of the features others thus make part of my self-image will be physical ones, so the self of the passions is a physicalized construct, and not the quasi-solipsist monster of Book 1.[27] Once this is recognized, it is also evident that I sometimes come to have pride or humility in some characteristic I ascribe to myself only after others admire or despise it: their evaluation of it and of me may not only augment my own, but actually engender it. And I may, of course, come to simulate, or actually develop, some character trait they would praise in order to prevent their blaming me (and hence my blaming myself) for its absence: this, as we have already seen, is part of Hume's account of the origin of the sense of duty (see again T 3.2.1.8), an account that seeks to turn the rationalist's key ethical endowment into an internalized social product.

---

[26] It is given its due place in Baier's *A Progress of Sentiments;* see especially Chap. 7. See also in this volume the essay "Hume and the Problem of Personal Identity," Sect. IV.

[27] Baier, *A Progress of Sentiments,* 136.

The sort of story this tells us about the self as social construction is one we have heard since from Freud, Marx, and the existentialists, always with ideological accretions wholly foreign to Hume's naturalism. His own summary statement is as follows: "In general we may remark, that the minds of men are mirrors to one another, not only because they reflect each other's emotions, but also because those rays of passions, sentiments and opinions may be often reverberated, and may decay away by insensible degrees" (T 2.2.5.21).

It is easy to see from this insistence – that the self is not discernible within but largely ascribed by transference from without – why Hume has such deep hostility to all systems that view persons as alien to the social world they inhabit. His negativity toward rationalism and its craving for autonomy is the result of its being a theoretical force that can only encourage self-distancing from the sources of emotional nourishment that make us what we are. And his intemperate rejection of the religious austerities of the "monkish virtues" can be seen as having the same theoretical source.[28] Each is life-denying, and in a quite literal sense self-destructive. Human nature does not need to be mastered, nor does it need to be redeemed. It needs social nurture. Both reason and "true" religion are the *slaves* of the passions.

VIII. CONCLUSION

I have argued that Hume is a neo-Hellenistic thinker who follows the Stoics, Epicureans, and Skeptics in maintaining that we should avoid anxiety by following nature. This prescription is notorious among philosophers for combining descriptive and normative elements. Hume is not, in any general way, confused between descriptive and normative claims: there is nothing in principle confused about seeing an understanding of our nature as a guide to one's way of life, or even to the proper practice of philosophy. There is more than one way of getting and using such guidance. Hume thinks a philosopher must, first and foremost, learn to accept his or her nature for what it is. This means recognizing that it is so programmed that our instincts furnish us with beliefs that we cannot survive without, or supply independently, or seriously question. Faced with this

[28] EPM 9.2.

fact, the philosophical enterprises of skeptical doubt and rationalist reconstruction are doomed to failure on psychological grounds alone, and the attempts to pursue them can only generate and exacerbate anxiety.

When we turn to Hume's moral thought, we find the parallel insistence that we must recognize the dominance of the passions in our nature, and not risk misery by attempting to follow eccentric programs of choice that frustrate them in the supposed interests of reason, or the mortifications of religion. Here again, we have to accept our nature, not violate it. Here Hume risks confusion in a fundamental respect: while there is nothing incoherent in describing our nature and then saying we must accept it and not violate it, this *is* incoherent if we are *unable* to violate it. To combine the descriptive with the normative without incoherence, it is necessary to permit freedom of choice in a form for which Hume's own account of liberty allows no space. The price of using the study of human nature as a guide to choice is the price of recognizing that it is part of our nature to be *able* to choose. But if this is admitted, we can then follow him in saying that if we make certain kinds of choices, we may ruin ourselves, and end up anxious, or incapacitated, or otherwise miserable, by frustrating our basic needs. Read this way, his system tells us that the polite society human beings had developed in property-owning Western Europe by his day, with all its protective artifices, meets the needs of human nature better than its alternatives. While this may be judged by some to be complacent or enervating, the experience of more radical programs that are based on ideologies that attend less to the details of human nature should make us hesitate to dismiss his advice too readily.

SUGGESTIONS FOR FURTHER READING

In addition to the works cited in the notes to this essay, for further reading the following are recommended.

Harris, James. *Of Liberty and Necessity: The Free Will Debate in Eighteenth-Century British Philosophy*. Oxford: Clarendon Press, 2005.

Kane, Robert, ed. *The Oxford Handbook of Free Will*. Oxford: Oxford University Press, 2002.

Kenny, Anthony. *Action, Emotion and Will*. London: Routledge and Kegan Paul, 1963.

McIntyre, Jane. "Personal Identity and the Passions." *Journal of the History of Philosophy* 27 (1989): 545–57.

Mercer, Philip. *Sympathy and Ethics*. Oxford: Clarendon Press, 1972.

Russell, Paul. *Freedom and Moral Sentiment: Hume's Way of Naturalizing Responsibility*. New York: Oxford University Press, 1995.

9   The Foundations of Morality in Hume's *Treatise*

I found that the moral Philosophy transmitted to us by Antiquity, labor'd under the same Inconvenience that has been found in their natural Philosophy, [namely,] of being entirely Hypothetical, & depending more upon Invention than Experience. Every one consulted his Fancy in erecting Schemes of Virtue & of Happiness, without regarding human Nature, upon which every moral Conclusion must depend. This therefore I resolved to make my principal Study, & the Source from which I wou'd derive every Truth in . . . Morality.

KHL 6

In Book 2 of the *Treatise of Human Nature* Hume reports that a question concerning the foundation of moral distinctions had "of late years" been of great public interest. The question is whether *"moral distinctions"* (distinctions between *virtue* and *vice*) are *"founded on natural and original principles,"* or arise *"from interest and education."* He then suggests that those who traced the distinction between virtue and vice to "self-interest or the prejudices of education" supposed that morality has "no foundation in nature." In contrast, those who said that moral distinctions are founded on natural and original principles supposed that "morality is something real, essential, and founded on nature" (T 2.1.7.2–3, 5). This debate, as we will see, raised both an ontological question (which features of the world, if any, do our moral judgments reflect?) and an epistemological question (which of our faculties, reason or sense, enables us to grasp moral distinctions?).[1] The first section of this essay focuses

---

[1] These issues are both addressed in *Treatise* 3.1.1–2, but are more explicitly stated in Hume's later *Enquiry concerning the Principles of Morals; see* EPM 1.3. For an

on the views of four of the principal early eighteenth-century participants in this debate in order to understand the controversy, which Hume hoped his own moral theory would resolve. The remainder of the essay outlines some key features of Hume's response, in Book 3 of the *Treatise*, to these and other questions about the foundations of morality.[2]

I. THE FOUNDATIONS DEBATE: SOME PRINCIPAL POSITIONS

Two turn-of-the-century philosophers whose writings carried the debate regarding the foundations of morality into the eighteenth century were Samuel Clarke and Anthony Ashley Cooper, Lord Shaftesbury. Bernard Mandeville and Francis Hutcheson were central figures in the early eighteenth-century debate.[3] The works of all four writers were well known to Hume.

Samuel Clarke (1675–1729)

In the first of two discourses published in 1705–6,[4] Samuel Clarke argued that there has necessarily existed from eternity a unified, unchangeable, and self-existing Being who is not only infinite, omnipotent, and the cause of everything, but also a Being of infinite goodness and justice and all the other moral characteristics appropriate to the Supreme Governor and Judge of the world. In the

---

account of Hume's later views on morals, see in this volume the essay "Hume's Later Moral Philosophy."

[2] Hume's moral theory is interpreted in widely different ways. The books and articles recommended at the end of this essay represent some of these different interpretations.

[3] For the views of additional eighteenth-century writers who engaged in this debate, see David Fate Norton and Manfred Kuehn, "The Foundations of Morality," in *The Cambridge History of Eighteenth-Century Philosophy*, ed. K. Haakonssen, 2 vols. (Cambridge: Cambridge University Press, 2006), 2:939–86. For discussion of seventeenth-century contributions to the controversy, see in this volume the essay by Knud Haakonssen, or, for greater detail, see, by the same author, *Natural Law and Moral Philosophy: From Grotius to the Scottish Enlightenment* (Cambridge: Cambridge University Press, 1996).

[4] These works are *A Demonstration of the Being and Attributes of God* (London, 1705) and *A Discourse concerning the Unchangeable Obligations of Natural Religion* (London, 1706).

second discourse Clarke argued that there are eternal and necessary differences between created things, and that these differences are alone sufficient to make it morally right that creatures should act in certain ways, and morally wrong that they should act in other ways. Prior to any command of the Deity, and prior to any convention or positive law, there are, in the very nature of things themselves, characteristics and relations (and especially differences) that translate immediately into real moral differences. Because there are "*certain necessary and eternal differences* of things," humans can see that moral differences are "founded unchangeably in the nature and reason of things, and unavoidably [arise] from the differences of the things themselves," with the consequence that "some things are in their own nature *Good* and *Reasonable* and *Fit* to be done."[5]

That Clarke means to say that these real and enduring factual differences provide both a necessary and a sufficient ground for morality is confirmed by what he has to say about moral knowing and moral obligation. The differences and relations he is speaking of are, he argues, absolutely fixed and unalterable, and no more open to willful change than are the differences between "*Light* and *Darkness*" or "*Mathematical* or *Arithmetical Truths*."[6] Furthermore, the differences that constitute morality are known, by means of the activities of reason, in just the way these other differences are known, either immediately or by demonstration. For any rational being to deny that there are such differences would be equivalent to denying that twice two is not equal to four, or that a whole is not larger than any of its constituent parts.[7]

Clarke grants that there is one notable difference between our response to nonmoral truths and our response to perceived moral differences. Assuming we understand the terms, seeing the proposition "$2 + 2 = 4$" leaves us with no choice but to *assent*. In contrast, the perception of a moral truth leaves us free to *act* in a manner that is contrary to what we have perceived.[8] But, he argues, acting in this contrary way is not only absurd; it is also immoral. We perceive that there is an infinite Deity and that we are finite creatures

[5] *Discourse, The Works of Samuel Clarke*, ed. B. Hoadly, 4 vols. (London, 1738), 2:611–12.

[6] *Discourse, Works*, 2:626.

[7] *Discourse, Works*, 2:609, 613.

[8] *Discourse, Works*, 2:615.

dependent on Him. Where there is such a difference between beings, we also perceive that we as the inferior creatures *ought* to honor, imitate, and obey the vastly superior being. To fail to act consistently with these perceptions is absurd because it is in effect to deny the very truths we have perceived; it is absurd in the same sense that it is absurd to deny that twice two is four. In addition, failing to act consistently with these perceptions is also blameworthy. Once we have seen the real and eternal differences between these beings, our minds, of their own accord, are "compelled to own and acknowledge" that there really are such obligations unavoidably binding us to a particular course of action.[9] The "*original Obligations of Morality*," as Clarke calls them, follow immediately from our recognition of "the *necessary and eternal*" relations of things themselves. The ground or foundation of morality is nothing more than a set of real and perceivable relations between existing things, relations the mere perception of which is sufficient to inform us of what is right and wrong, and to oblige us to the right or virtuous course of action.[10]

Anthony Ashley Cooper, the third Earl of Shaftesbury (1671–1713)

At the beginning of his *Inquiry concerning Virtue or Merit*, Shaftesbury observes that religion and virtue seem so closely related that they appear inseparable.[11] To know how virtue relates to religion we must know, as he says, what "virtue is, considered by itself." To this end, he draws our attention to what he calls the "frame" of nature, the systematic interconnections of nature. Although there is much we do not know about nature, and particularly about the role some species are intended to play in the larger scheme of things, there is also much that we do know. We know, for example, that each creature is better off in some conditions than in others, and thus that "there is in reality a right and a wrong state of every creature" and "a certain end to which everything in [its] constitution must naturally

[9] *Discourse, Works*, 2:613–14; see also 2:618.
[10] *Discourse, Works*, 2:630.
[11] Shaftesbury's *Inquiry* was first published from an "Imperfect Copy" in 1699. An authorized version was published in 1711 as a part of *Characteristicks of Men, Manners, Opinions, Times*, and is here quoted from the edition of John Robertson, 2 vols. (London, 1900; reprinted, Indianapolis: Bobbs-Merrill, 1964).

refer." We can see, too, that what is good for individuals is good for their species, and thus that what we might call antisocial behavior is against the interest of each individual. We can also see that, as the wing of the fly is suited to the web of the spider, so are many species suited to the existence and well-being of other, very different species. In consequence of many such perceived interdependencies, it is reasonable to conclude not only that all animals form a system, but also that everything found in the universe is part of a general system. And it is also reasonable to conclude that whatever contributes positively to this system is good, and whatever is destructive of it is ill or bad. The terms *good* and *ill*, in other words, can be used to refer to real or objective differences between existing or possible states of affairs.[12]

Shaftesbury goes on to say that we do not consider a creature virtuous merely because it contributes positively to the good of itself, its species, or the universe in general. To be *virtuous*, this creature must also satisfy other requirements. She must first be a sensible, reflective creature who is aware of what she does. That is, she must not act merely from instinct in the manner of a thoughtless and unreasoning automaton. She must also have a notion of the public interest and a sense of right or wrong – she must grasp the moral character of situations and of what she does. And finally, she must act from a self-determined motive to do good or avoid evil. A creature who lacks self-consciousness or the ability to grasp the moral character of situations cannot be virtuous. A person who contributes to the public good merely as a consequence of selfish motives is not counted among the virtuous.[13] The virtuous individual is the individual who, aware of what contributes to or detracts from the public good, undertakes, by conscious intent or from settled character, to add to the store of good or to avoid increasing the supply of evil.

These features of virtue established, Shaftesbury returns to the question of the relation of religion and virtue. It is clear, he argues, that neither virtue nor what comes to the same thing, the practice of virtue, is dependent on religion. It is true that belief in a providential, judging Deity and a future state of reward or punishment may provide an incentive to act in ways that are consistent with virtue. And

[12] *Inquiry, Characteristics*, 1:238, 243–6.
[13] *Inquiry, Characteristics*, 1:247–58.

yet virtuous behavior does not depend on holding religious beliefs, and may even be hindered by such beliefs. Many religions teach that "treachery, ingratitude, or cruelty" have been given a divine sanction, or call on their followers to persecute friends, to offer human sacrifices, or to abuse and torment themselves out of religious zeal. But nothing, Shaftesbury insists, not even religion, can justify brutality or barbarity or make them beneficial. Nothing, neither custom, law, nor religion can ever "alter the eternal measures and immutable independent nature of worth and virtue."[14]

Whether an act is judged to be moral or immoral, according to Shaftesbury, depends on the different motives available to rational agents. That he supposed this distinction of motives an effective, practical foundation of morality is made clear in his attacks on what he took to be the moral skepticism of Thomas Hobbes and John Locke. Shaftesbury knew, of course, that both of these earlier philosophers had proposed moral theories. He nonetheless considered them to be moral skeptics because their theories have the effect of questioning or denying the reality of moral distinctions.[15] Hobbes had attempted to explain every human act by the one principle of self-interest or self-regard,[16] an explanation that has the consequence of making apparent moral distinctions meaningless. If Hobbes is right, then such words as *friendship, love, public interest,* all those words that appear to make reference to altruistic acts or motives, have ultimately the same meaning as their contraries because there are no differences in motivation. If Hobbes is right, then there can be, according to Shaftesbury, "no such thing in reality as virtue." To Shaftesbury, who alludes to himself as a "realist in morality," reducing all motivations to selfish ones is to introduce a "general scepticism" about morality, a skepticism that denies that there is any real virtue or moral good and natural justice.[17] Locke's moral theory, because more subtle than that of Hobbes, is even worse. Locke argued that our moral ideas are mere inventions, constructs based on no real model or archetype in the world, and he credulously repeated stories of cultures that have no idea of virtue. He

---

[14] *Inquiry, Characteristics,* 1:255.
[15] See *Life, Letters, and Philosophical Regimen,* ed. B. Rand (New York, 1900), 37–8.
[16] This view is now called *psychological egoism.* In this essay the term *egoism* always refers to this form of egoism.
[17] *Characteristics,* 1:61–5, 79; 2:53.

then concluded that "virtue ... has no other measure, law, or rule, than fashion and custom; [that] morality, justice, equity, depend only on law and will. . . . And thus neither right nor wrong, virtue nor vice, are anything in themselves; nor is there any trace or idea of them naturally imprinted on human minds."[18]

Such views Shaftesbury took to be dangerous. Because Hobbes and Locke explicitly deny either that moral distinctions are real, observer-independent distinctions, or that they derive from real differences in the nature of things, their views encourage individuals to disregard moral considerations and as a consequence threaten to undermine morality and society itself. To counter this danger, Shaftesbury rejects speculation and a priori reasoning in favor of an observationally based study of human nature, a study that leads him to conclude that humans are inherently moral and inherently capable of recognizing moral distinctions. Just as animals have instincts or dispositions that enable them not only to survive, but also to thrive, so too do humans have the dispositions they need to thrive. Humans cannot survive without society. It is not surprising, then, that humans are motivated not only by the selfishness that Hobbes describes, but also by public spirit or a concern for the general good. Humans also develop the ability to distinguish benevolence from indifference or malice. We find, to sum up, that humans have a kind of moral instinct, a natural "moral sense" that enables them to be just the kind of creature Hobbes says they never are, and that provides for us an archetype, an objective model, of those moral ideas that Locke says are only arbitrary constructs. In addition, to show that morality is not founded on religious decree and that it has a real foundation in nature, Shaftesbury argues that morality rests on the distinctions of motive available to rational human agents. These agents are able to act not only from self-regarding, but also from *other-regarding* or *altruistic*, motives and do often enough *act* from these other-regarding motives. When they do so, they are acting virtuously.

Bernard Mandeville (1670–1733)

The decade following the appearance of Shaftesbury's *Characteristicks* was a relatively quiet one for the foundations debate, but

---

[18] *Life, Letters, and Philosophical Regimen*, 403–5.

the publication in 1723 of an expanded version of Bernard Mandeville's *The Fable of the Bees* changed that. Mandeville took direct aim at Shaftesbury, and particularly at his optimistic view of human nature and his account of the foundation of the moral distinctions we make. But Mandeville's challenge may easily be misunderstood. Shaftesbury had traced morality to distinctions of motive, arguing that virtuous individuals are those and only those who consciously act from other-regarding motives. Mandeville accepted this conclusion and made it a key premise in an argument leading to the conclusion that the distinction between virtue and vice lacks an adequate foundation in morals. Moral distinctions are merely conventions created by a class of inventive humans and foisted onto the rest of us.

Mandeville's analysis takes this form. Shaftesbury's claim about motivation and moral distinctions is accepted as a first premise: the only virtuous acts are those motivated by other-regarding motives. It is, Mandeville says, "impossible to judge of a Man's Performance, unless we are th[o]roughly acquainted with the Principle and Motive from which he acts."[19] Mandeville's second premise is stated in the opening words of his *Enquiry into the Origin of Moral Virtue*: all animals, including humans, he says, "are only solicitous of pleasing themselves, and naturally follow the bent of their own Inclinations, without considering the good or harm that from their being pleased will accrue to others."[20] But if only other regarding acts are (genuinely) virtuous, and if there are no other-regarding acts because all of us are motivated only by self-interest, then it follows that there are no virtuous acts. Mandeville does not deny that we (appear to) make moral distinctions. He grants that we describe some acts or persons as "virtuous" and others as "vicious," but he denies that this fact of our experience establishes that this moral language represents *real* moral differences.

Mandeville brings home his point with a striking analysis of pity, a passion supposed to derive from pure kindness. Pity, says Mandeville, "is the most gentle and the least mischievous of all our Passions," but it is still as much a passion as "Anger, Pride, or Fear." As a consequence, he goes on, whoever acts from pity, no matter

[19] *An Enquiry into the Origin of Moral Virtue, The Fable of the Bees: or, Private Vices, Publick Benefits*, ed. F. B. Kaye, 2 vols. (Oxford: Clarendon Press, 1966), 1:56.
[20] *Enquiry, Fable*, 1:41.

how much good he happens to do, really acts from a self-interested impulse and

has nothing to boast of but that he has indulged a Passion that has happened to be beneficial to the Publick. There is no Merit in saving an innocent Babe ready to drop into the Fire: The Action is neither good nor bad, and what Benefit soever the Infant received, we only obliged our selves; for to have seen it fall, and not strove to hinder it, would have caused a Pain, which Self-preservation compell'd us to prevent.[21]

Suppose Mandeville is correct about these basic facts. Moral distinctions depend on a specific distinction of motives, which are said to be either other-regarding or self-regarding (the view he shares with Shaftesbury). He finds, however, that no such distinction of motives exists, and thus we must conclude that there are no *real* moral distinctions.

How does it happen, then, that we commonly denominate some acts and persons virtuous and other acts and persons vicious? Mandeville's answer to that question takes the form of an *inventors story.* No animal, Mandeville tells us, is so headstrong, selfish, cunning, and difficult to control or govern as human beings are. Indeed, humans are so difficult to govern that, if we are to be governed, it will never be by force alone. From this beginning, he goes on to explain that humans have become governable through the invention of morality. Those who have undertaken to establish society (to establish a well-ordered group of humans) have been engaged in a massive and long-standing deceit. Knowing that humans are all selfish and self-willed, these inventors have nonetheless told us that we will each be better off if each of us effectively subjugates his or her appetites and sacrifices personal interests to the general good of the public.

In Mandeville's view, the claim that our self-interest is best served by sublimating it to the general good is nothing more than an outright lie. In order for this lie to be effective, it had to be attractively packaged. That is, if this lie was to serve the end for which it was

---

[21] *Enquiry, Fable,* 1:56. On the following page Mandeville grants that some may appear to perform good actions "from no other Motive but their Love to Goodness," but he then argues that "the Reward of a Virtuous Action, which is the Satisfaction that ensues upon it, consists in a certain Pleasure [the agent] procures to himself by Contemplating on his own Worth: Which Pleasure, together with the Occasion of it, are ... certain Signs of Pride."

(and is) told, those who curtail their naturally selfish inclinations (their self-interest) because of it had (and have) to be rewarded, while those who fail to curtail these selfish inclinations must be punished. The rewards offered include tangible or material benefits, but they are not limited to benefits of that kind. There are not, for one thing, enough tangible goods to satisfy everyone, and, even if there were enough, there would be problems with their distribution. As it happens, the most important of the nontangible rewards offered has been found to be a particular form of moral praise or "flattery." Having found such praise an effective means to their end, the inventors also convinced the individuals making up one part of humanity that they were a class superior to the remaining part. That is, some humans were made to feel morally superior to those "low-minded" types who, "always hunting after immediate Enjoyment... yielded without Resistance to every gross desire, and made no use of their Rational Faculties but to heighten their Sensual Pleasure." Characteristically, individuals of the "superior Class," supposing themselves to be of a loftier sort altogether, make war on themselves (they fight against their natural but allegedly irrational inclinations) and seek the *general good* through the "Conquest of their own Passion." In short, these individuals were duped by their own pride and the machinations of the inventors, and this induced many of them, especially "the fiercest, most resolute, and best among them, to endure a thousand Inconveniences, and undergo as many Hardships, that they may have the pleasure of counting themselves Men of the [superior] Class." In this way, Mandeville says, "Savage Man was broke," or, in other words, trained in pseudo-morality. Moreover, in the course of time, even the sensual lower class came to believe that their individual interests would best be served by moderating their natural inclinations. Taken generally, the story leads to the conclusion that morality is best described as "the Political Offspring which Flattery begot upon Pride."[22]

Francis Hutcheson (1694–1746)

The *Inquiry into the Original of our Ideas of Beauty and Virtue* of Francis Hutcheson was first published in 1725. The subtitle of the first edition describes the work as a defense of Shaftesbury's

---

[22] *Enquiry, Fable,* 1:43–51.

principles "against the Author of the *Fable of the Bees.*" In his Preface Hutcheson says that his aim is to show that *"Human Nature was not left quite indifferent in the Affair of Virtue,"*[23] and the work continually reverberates with explicit concern with moral foundations. Noting that we humans distinguish between moral good and evil, Hutcheson asks "what general Foundation there is in Nature for this Difference." After examining "the Springs of the Actions which we call virtuous, as far as it is necessary to settle the general Foundation of the Moral Sense," he undertakes to show that neither esteem nor benevolence is or can be "founded on Self-Love, or Views of Interest," and that "the universal Foundation of our Sense of moral Good" is benevolence, while the foundation of our sense of moral evil is "Malice, or even Indolence, and Unconcernedness about... manifest publick Evil."[24]

Given his stated aim of defending Shaftesbury's views, Hutcheson's association of virtue with other-regarding motives comes as no surprise. And given that Mandeville had also accepted the principle that moral differences derive from differences of motive, it is clear that he and Hutcheson reached their crucially different conclusions about the reality of virtue because they affirmed contrary views about certain factual matters. Mandeville's survey of human behavior led him to the view that individuals never act from benevolent or other-regarding motives. Hutcheson counters with a survey showing that Mandeville is mistaken about the relevant facts: at least some human actions are motivated by a regard or concern for others. Consequently, Hutcheson can validly conclude that there are genuinely virtuous individuals and that virtue is something with a real, objective foundation in the nature of things, in, more specifically, minds of human agents.[25]

Hutcheson's conclusion depends heavily on the results of his new and, he argues, more careful survey of our moral approvals or disapprovals, of the circumstances in which we say individuals are virtuous or vicious. Among other things, this survey reveals

---

[23] *An Inquiry into the Original of our Ideas of Beauty and Virtue,* 4th ed. (London, 1738; facsimile reprint, Westmead: Gregg International Publishers, 1969), xiii.

[24] *Inquiry,* 105, 132, 154, 172. Hutcheson's plentiful italics have been eliminated.

[25] For Hutcheson's concern to prove "the *Reality of Virtue,*" and that "no Action of any Person was ever approv'd by us, but upon the Apprehension... of some *really good moral Quality,*" see *Inquiry,* xi, 201.

- That of many long-dead individuals who can no longer contribute to our interest or pleasure, some are morally approved, some are morally disapproved, and about some we are morally indifferent.
- That, although the generous acts of an agent and the products of a plot of land may equally be of benefit to us and thereby gain our approval, it is only the agent who is thought to be *virtuous*, and, although the fraudulent acts of a partner and a falling beam may both injure us, it is only the partner who is thought to be *vicious*.
- That if two individuals contribute in similar ways to our well-being, the one from an intent to benefit us, the other from a purely self-interested motive, we count as *virtuous* only the individual who intended to benefit us; moreover, because our moral assessments of individuals depend upon the *motives* from which individuals act, we find that we may morally disapprove an agent whose behavior causes no actual injury to others, and morally approve agents whose behavior has accidentally caused them harm.
- That although we can be bribed to perform an action that we think to be morally wrong, we cannot be bribed to feel that this same action is morally right or that we were right to undertake it. We can bribe an enemy to betray his country and benefit ours, thereby furthering our own interest, but we nonetheless feel moral disapproval of the enemy who has been bribed, taking him to be a traitor and vicious. More generally, we find that we cannot by any act of our will alter our moral approvals and disapprovals.[26]

Facts of this sort, Hutcheson concludes, establish beyond doubt that Mandeville and other egoists such as Hobbes are mistaken. Facts of this sort show that there are natural or unlearned differences in our responses to actions or events, differences that would not arise if the egoists had correctly described human nature. But they have not done so. The egoists have badly misdescribed our moral experience. When we look carefully at our moral approvals and disapprovals we find that we quite naturally make some important distinctions:

[26] *Inquiry*, 111–15, 123–7.

Without training or indoctrination we distinguish between *natural* and *moral* goods, and we also distinguish between moral *good* or *virtue* and moral *evil* or *vice*.

Moral good, Hutcheson argues, is a characteristic of, or at least attributable to, only rational agents *as* agents, while *natural good* may be a characteristic of many different classes of things. Hutcheson's crucial claim is that we recognize this distinction, and show that we recognize it, because we respond in one way to the honesty, kindness, or generosity of an agent, and in a substantially different way to the beneficial qualities of an inanimate object, or to the wealth, houses, lands, health, sagacity, or strength possessed by human beings. We necessarily hold in high esteem those who possess such qualities as generosity, but we may very well envy or hold in disesteem those who possess wealth or power, and we simply do not take possessions or bodily endowments to be or to have *moral* characteristics. In addition, our idea of *moral good* is the "Idea of some Quality apprehended in Actions," a quality that produces "Approbation, attended with Desire of the Agent's Happiness," while our idea of *moral evil* is of a quality that produces disapprobation, and is attended with a desire for the agent's misery. He goes on to suggest that *approbation* and *disapprobation* probably cannot be further explained because they are simple or primitive ideas, and even these descriptions of moral good and evil are offered provisionally. They are the best we can do until we find out whether we really do have such ideas and what general and natural *foundation* there is for this distinction between the morally good and the morally evil.[27]

We have been reviewing Hutcheson's attempt to show, contrary to Mandeville, that some actions are performed from other-regarding motives, and thus that there is a real, well-founded distinction between virtue and vice. Assuming that Hutcheson's description of our approving experiences is accurate, he is on track to accomplish his goal. If it is true that our responses to different kinds of good and to different kinds of action are themselves significantly different, and if it is true that what constitutes the relevant differences between these actions is recognition that there is a significant difference in the motivations that give rise to them, so that we feel a special kind of approval (*approbation*) only in response to

---

[27] *Inquiry*, 105–6.

other-regarding actions, then it is clear that some actions are the result of such other-regarding motives. Our experience is significantly more complex than Mandeville had supposed. Given these facts, it follows, contrary to Mandeville, that there are genuinely virtuous individuals, and that *virtue* and *vice* are real and founded in the minds of agents. Given these important facts, the question becomes, as Hutcheson typically frames it, what features of human nature are presupposed by the fact that we can and do make these moral distinctions? Elaborating on Shaftesbury's suggestion, Hutcheson devotes a section of his *Inquiry* to showing that we have "implanted in our Nature" a complex moral disposition, a *moral sense*, whose presence and operation provide a foundation for morality.[28] The moral sense provides this foundation by making it possible for us to be moral agents and moral observers. But even before he reaches this part of his account, Hutcheson has argued that the moral sense comprises both an inherent benevolence able "to direct our Actions," and an innate "disinterested ultimate Desire of the Happiness of others."[29] It is this aspect of the moral sense that motivates us to participate in society, to pursue the public good, and to take pleasure in the realization of that good. Had we lacked this disposition we might have developed an abstract or speculative idea of virtue, but our concern for our own interest would have caused us, contrary to fact, to be concerned only with this interest and to approve only those agents and actions that serve this interest.

Hutcheson also finds that the moral sense includes a cognitive function, a power that enables us to respond differently to benevolence and self-interest and the actions they motivate. The human mind is formed in such a way that it can and often does approve or condemn actions or agents without concern for its own pleasure or interest. Thus if two individuals contribute in similar ways to our well-being, but the one acts "from an ultimate Desire of our Happiness, or Good-will toward us; and the other from Views of Self-Interest, or by Constraint," we respond differently.[30] In response to the first we feel gratitude and approbation; to the second we are indifferent. Or, if we know that an individual has benevolent

---

[28] *Inquiry*, title to Part II, Sect. V, 218.
[29] *Inquiry*, 129, 152.
[30] *Inquiry*, 113.

dispositions, but has been prevented from exercising these, we approve of her and count her as morally good even though she has not been able to act, even though she has done nothing to benefit us. The nature and complexity of these responses show that we have a perceptual power, a sense of moral discrimination, for without such a sense we would assess fields and agents, or patriots and traitors, in the same way and only with regard to our own interests and well-being.

Because Hutcheson held that the moral sense discriminates between virtue and vice by means of feelings of approval and disapproval, some of his critics supposed that he had reduced virtue and vice to these feelings or sentiments. Hutcheson explicitly denied such an intent and such a result. The moral sense relies on feelings to distinguish virtue or vice, but moral qualities are themselves independent of the observer who feels approbation or disapprobation of them. The "admired Quality," he says, is a *quality of the agent judged,* and entirely distinct from any approbation or pleasure felt by either the approving observer or the agent himself. The moral perceptions or approbation experienced "plainly represents something quite distinct from this Pleasure."[31] Feelings play both a motivating and a cognitive role, but virtue is constituted by the benevolent disposition that gives rise to approbation, while vice is constituted by the malevolent or indifferent dispositions that give rise to disapprobation. Virtue and vice, although known by means of the feelings they arouse, are real, observer-independent qualities of agents.

II. HUME, HUMAN NATURE, AND THE FOUNDATIONS OF MORALITY

As we have seen, Hume was aware of the controversy about the foundations of morals. And although he voiced substantial disagreement with his predecessors, he did agree that morality has its foundation in human nature and in differences of motivation. In the spring of 1734, he wrote in the autobiographical letter included at the end of this volume that he had found the moral philosophy of the ancients too speculative to be of any value. These philosophers formed moral

---

[31] *Inquiry,* 130–1. Hutcheson added this comment to the third edition (1729) of his *Inquiry* in order to prevent what he took to be misunderstandings of his position.

systems by relying on their inventive imaginations, and without regard for "human Nature," the foundation "upon which every moral Conclusion must depend." Consequently, he resolved to make human nature "my principal Study, & the Source from which I would derive every Truth in . . . Morality" (KHL 6).

When in 1739–40 Hume published the *Treatise of Human Nature*, he described it by its subtitle as "AN ATTEMPT TO INTRODUCE THE EXPERIMENTAL METHOD OF REASONING INTO MORAL SUBJECTS." In the Introduction to this work he said that "all the sciences," but especially the human sciences of "*Logic, Morals, Criticism,* and *Politics,*" are fundamentally dependent "on the knowledge of man." So far as these sciences are concerned there is "no question of importance, whose decision is not compris'd in the science of man; and there is none, which can be decided with any certainty, before we become acquainted with that science" (T Intro. 4–6).

Hume also said that, just "as the science of man is the only solid foundation for the other sciences, so the only solid foundation we can give to this science itself" is "experience and observation." He also supposed that any science of human nature that attempted to carry the explanation of that nature to unobserved principles or causes allegedly more ultimate than this nature itself as it is observed would be a poor science indeed.[32] To say that morality is founded on human nature is to suggest that, with respect to morals, human nature is a *primitive element,* an ultimate fact, beyond which explanation cannot go. He saw, however, that he could not gain a sound knowledge of human nature by undertaking the kind of carefully planned experiments made familiar by natural philosophy. He saw that we must collect our experiments in the science of human nature through "a cautious observation of human life," by, that is, observing human behavior "in the common course of the world." When "experiments of this kind" have been carefully "collected and compar'd," he argues, "we may hope to establish on them a science, which will not be inferior in certainty, and will be much superior in

---

[32] Later in the *Treatise* Hume says that the causes of effects in the "mental world" are "mostly unknown, and must be resolv'd into *original* qualities of human nature, which I pretend not to explain," and also mentions the "particular *original* principles of human nature, which cannot be accounted for" (T 1.1.4.6, 3.3.1.27; see also EPM, n.19).

utility to any other of human comprehension" (T Intro. 7–10). But, isolated as he was in the Scottish countryside or the only marginally wider society offered by Edinburgh, Scotland's small, provincial capital, and the small French town (La Flèche) where he wrote much of the *Treatise,* it was books, books of philosophy, literature, history, and politics that gave Hume a wider window on human nature.[33] Through this window he saw that "It requires but very little knowledge of human affairs to perceive, that a sense of morals is a principle inherent in the soul, and one of the most powerful that enters into the composition," and he set about describing the principal features of this powerful sense (3.3.6.3).

Moral Distinctions Not Derived from Reason

As he had promised in *Treatise* 2.1.7, Hume takes up the dispute regarding the origin of moral distinctions in "Of Morals," the third and final book of the *Treatise.* He begins by reminding his readers that *perceptions* are found in only two forms, *impressions* or *ideas,* and then asking which of these two forms enables us to recognize moral differences and to make moral judgments (T 3.1.1.2).[34] In raising this question, Hume directly confronts the rationalists' account of morality. He notes first that those who, like Clarke, claim that morality rests on a kind of conformity between actions and certain unchanging relations of things in effect claim that moral distinctions can be traced to ideas and their relations, and thus implicitly claim that it is reason alone that enables us to make moral distinctions. Drawing on important facts that characterize morality as it is practiced, Hume challenges this account with a battery of arguments intended to show that moral distinctions are neither the immediate effect of reason, nor known by reason alone, and that as a consequence we must conclude that moral distinctions are not derived from reason (T 3.1.1). Of these arguments, the following are representative.

1. The claims of the rationalists are inconsistent with the fact that the very act of making a moral distinction influences our behavior.

---

[33] On Hume's early education and reading, see my introductory essay, n.1.

[34] For an account of Hume's views on perceptions, impressions, and ideas, see in this volume the essay "Hume and the Mechanics of the Mind."

Moral distinctions directly and by themselves arouse passions and motivate us to action. But Hume had earlier argued that reason is effectively inert and that any influence it has on the will is indirect and merely instrumental.[35] Reason can inform us of the nature of things and how to obtain them, but it can neither arouse nor extinguish desire for them. In short, reason is unable to bring about the effects attributed to it by the rationalists. Consequently, morality cannot be founded on reason alone (T 3.1.1.4–8, 10).

2. The claims of the rationalists are inconsistent with the fact that moral assessments admit of degrees. So far as rationalist theory is concerned, the theft of a piece of fruit and the theft of a kingdom, actions equally inconsistent with the relations said to hold between owners and their property, should be judged equally immoral. In fact, we take the second to be significantly more reprehensible than the first (T 3.1.1.13).

3. The claim that reason alone is capable of making moral distinctions entails that such distinctions are either derived from some distinctive relation of ideas or from some matter of fact discoverable by the understanding. Our moral experience shows that moral distinctions are not derived in either of these ways. First, such distinctive relations of ideas cannot be found. Precisely the same relation that characterizes human ingratitude in the form of parenticide, of all human "crimes . . . the most horrid and unnatural," is taken to be morally innocent when found among other living species. Incest, to take a second example, is taken to be vicious when engaged in by humans, yet the same relations characterize animal instantiations of this practice, and these are found to be morally innocent. In addition, the rationalists insist that morality, like mathematics, is capable of demonstration. That they hold such a view shows they do not take morality to be a factual matter, for it is universally agreed that it is probable arguments, not demonstrations, that establish matters of fact. Moreover, however closely our reason or understanding analyzes an action taken to be virtuous or vicious, we never discover virtue or vice among the features of that action. Using the senses, a principal tool of the understanding to examine a case of willful murder, we never discover virtue or vice among the features associated with this act. We may initially learn about this action by means

---

[35] See T 2.3.3, *Of the influencing motives of the will.*

of *impressions of sensation,* and there may be some ways in which vice and virtue resemble color or heat or certain *ideas of sensation,* but Hume explicitly denies that virtue and vice are known through impressions or ideas of *sensation* (T 3.1.1.17–27).

Moral Distinctions Derived from a Moral Sense

If, as Hume says, perceptions are of only two forms, impressions and ideas, and if analysis or comparisons of ideas are not the source of the distinction we make between virtue and vice, then it must be by means of impressions that we make this distinction. But, from Hume's brief analysis of the morally significant act of wilful murder, we already know that vice and virtue do not produce impressions of sensation. Consequently these distinctive moral qualities must make themselves known by means of impressions of reflection or feelings. "Morality, therefore," Hume says, "is more properly felt than judg'd of" (T 3.1.2.1). *Treatise* 3.1.2, *Moral distinctions deriv'd from a moral sense,* explains how this happens. It explains, in other words, how certain impressions of reflection or feelings enable us to make moral distinctions.

Treatise 3.1.2. begins by drawing our attention to the fact that those things that we call *virtuous* produce in those who observe them an agreeable impression or feeling, a *pleasure,* while those things called *vicious* produce in those who observe them a disagreeable impression or feeling, a *pain.* Hume then points out that it is not the case that every item desired because it gives pleasure is taken to be morally good, or that every item that produces pain is taken to be morally evil. The relevant feelings are "particular" or *distinctive* pleasures and pains. They are those pleasures and pains that Hutcheson and Hume often call *approbation* and *disapprobation,* and they are only aroused in unique circumstances. That this is so means, Hume says, that explaining how we come to feel these unique moral sentiments will be equivalent to understanding moral distinctions themselves. If we call a motive or action virtuous or vicious "because its view causes a pleasure or uneasiness of a particular kind," then by explaining those distinctive pleasures and pains we will also, he says, "sufficiently explain the vice or virtue" that causes them (T 3.1.2.3).

In the course of explaining the moral sentiments, Hume makes three important claims:

1. There are many different kinds of pleasure and pain. The pleasure produced by good music, for example, is different from that produced by good wine. The pleasures and pains (the moral sentiments) produced by the motives or actions of humans are different from those produced by other kinds of thing.

2. It is only the qualities or actions of *persons* that give rise to the "*particular* pains or pleasures" known as the *moral sentiments.* Hume also says that virtue and vice consistently excite one of the four indirect passions (pride, humility, love, or hatred) that have oneself or other persons for their objects. Drawing on his earlier discussion of the passions, he further refines his view, saying that it is only certain "durable principles of the mind" (motives, including character and intentions) that give rise to the moral sentiments, and that actions themselves are neither virtuous nor vicious, but only signs of the virtue or vice (the signs of virtuous or vicious qualities) in those who perform them (T 3.1.2.3, 5; 3.3.1.3–5).[36]

3. These unique moral sentiments are aroused only in very special circumstances. We do not, for example, experience disapprobation every time some individual's "durable principles of mind" cause some form of pain. The unique sentiment of disapprobation is felt only if we abstract from or ignore our own interest: "'Tis only when a character is consider'd in general, without reference to our particular interest, that it causes such a feeling or sentiment, as denominates it morally good or evil." Thus, for example, although the "good qualities of an enemy," his valor or courage, may cause us harm, these qualities "may still command our esteem and respect," and we

---

[36] Hume's clearest statement of the view that actions are *signs* of motives is perhaps that made at T 3.2.1.2: "'Tis evident, that when we praise any actions, we regard only the motives that produc'd them, and consider the actions as signs or indications of certain principles in the mind and temper. The external performance has no merit. We must look within [the agent] to find the moral quality. This we cannot do directly; and therefore fix our attention on actions, as on external signs. But these actions are still consider'd as signs; and the ultimate object of our praise and approbation is the motive, that produc'd them." See also, e.g., T 2.1.2.2; 2.2.1.2; 2.2.3.3–8; 2.3.2.6; 3.2.1.4, 8.

may still judge this enemy to be honorable and virtuous (T 3.1.2.4; see also 3.3.1.3).

Imagine, then, that you observe a specific case of intentional killing. On Hume's view of the matter, as a consequence of experiencing this action, you will first experience certain impressions of sensation that inform you of the physical features of the event. Suppose that these sensations inform you that one person, A, has pointed a pistol at another person, B, demanded B's wallet, and, when B resisted, shot him. Further impressions of sensation inform you that B has fallen lifeless to the ground. None of these impressions of sensation has a moral dimension. None of them even suggests that A's action has moral connotations. But in response to this extended action you can also expect to have, among a number of impressions of reflection (shock, pity, and fear, for example), a particular impression of reflection. You can also expect to experience the distinctive impression of moral disapproval or disapprobation. If that impression does arise it will mean that you have determined that A, the person who carried out the killing action, is vicious or morally evil. Moreover, you will have made this determination simply because you have had this distinctive moral sentiment. You will have no need to make use of reason in order to compare, step-by-step, the action to a rule of behavior, find that the action violates that rule, and then conclude that as a consequence moral evil has been present and observed.[37] Should it be asked why, in contrast, a leopard, seen to have deliberately stalked and killed a gazelle, is not said to be vicious, Hume would say that this second action, because it does not involve a human agent, does not arouse disapprobation, the distinctive moral sentiment. He does not attempt to explain why this should be the case. He simply takes it to be a fact of our nature (a fact illustrated by our moral practice) that our moral sense is aroused by certain features or actions of humans, but is not aroused by the apparently analogous features or actions of animals, plants, or other external objects.[38]

---

[37] We have seen that Hume denies that virtue and vice are known by means of the senses, the tool by which the understanding attempts to discover matters of fact.
[38] See T 3.1.2.4.

III. THE VIRTUES

A. A Comparison of Kinds

We saw above that when Hume first mentioned the debate over the foundations of morality he described it as a debate between those who suppose that moral distinctions are based "*on natural and original principles,*" and those who say that they "*arise from interest and education.*" Although in Book 3 Hume argues that morality has a substantive foundation in human nature, he also argues that there are two kinds of virtue, *natural* and *artificial*, and that while in important senses all moral distinctions derive from natural and original principles of human nature, the artificial virtues (justice, fidelity, allegiance, treaty keeping, and chastity are discussed) are at first the product of self-interest and education. *Treatise* 3.2 focuses on the artificial virtues, while 3.3 focuses on the natural virtues and vices. But before turning to Hume's extended discussions of each of these kinds of virtue, it will be useful to sketch these kinds and the principal differences between them.

The *natural virtues*:

a. Are inherent features of human nature (T 3.3.1.1)
b. Are specific passions that have always motivated specific kinds of human behavior; examples include generosity, humanity, love of children, greatness of mind, compassion, gratitude, friendship, and disinterestedness[39]
c. Are motivating passions that are said to produce good on each occasion that they motivate behavior (T 3.3.1.12)[40]

---

[39] See T 3.2.1.5, 3.2.5.6, 3.3.2, 3.3.3.3. There are also natural vices. These include ingratitude, cruelty, villainy or baseness, and inhumanity; see T 3.1.1.24; 3.1.2.2, 4; 3.3.3.8–9. For another discussion of the two kinds of virtue, see in this volume the essay "The Structure of Hume's Political Theory," Part II.

[40] Given that Hume in 3.3.1.12 goes on to say that one of the most important natural virtues, humanity, may come into conflict with the established scheme of justice, it appears that on his account it could happen that pursuing a natural virtue would undercut the scheme of justice and would thus not, all things considered, produce good. A father's love of his children could also have this effect. This problem is more directly addressed in the second *Enquiry*; App. 3.2–6 ("Some Farther Considerations with Regard to Justice").

d. Produce in observers positive sentiments of moral approval whenever they are seen to motivate the behavior of another person (T 2.1.7.5, 3.1.2.3–5).

In contrast, the *artificial virtues:*

a'. Derive from human nature, and thus are in that attenuated sense *natural,* but these virtues were unknown to humans living in their first "rude and more *natural* condition" (T 3.2.1.9)

b'. Derive from our natural self-interest, as it has been modified by contingent circumstances and necessities, and have developed over the course of time in response to just such circumstances and necessities (T 3.2.2.1–22)

c'. Constitute a system of rules or conventions to which it is necessary that we conform for the public good, but which may yet on any given occasion require actions or behavior contrary to both individual and public good; in such cases, the relevant virtuous acts produce only weak sentiments of approval (T 3.3.1.12)

d'. Are, once established, "*naturally* attended with a strong sentiment of morals" owing to "our sympathy with the interests of society" (T 3.3.1.12).[41]

For humans in their original or "uncultivated state," the artificial virtues and the constraints they introduce were unnecessary. In that original state the natural virtues were adequate to maintain order in the small, kinship-based groups that humans formed. As human society became larger and more complex, circumstances changed (some material goods became scarce, for example), and these changes led to conflicts within or between the existing social units, conflicts that the natural virtues were unable to resolve. As a consequence, conventions regulating first property, then promises, and then government were (gradually) developed.

---

[41] There are also corresponding or parallel artificial vices. These include the contraries of the artificial virtues, e.g., injustice, infidelity, treason, licentiousness, and cowardice, as well as ill-breeding and overweening pride (see T 3.2, *passim*, 3.3.2.10). Hume offers a similar comparison between natural and artificial *duties* in "Of the Original Contract," an essay first published in 1748; see E-OC 33–5, 479–80.

Hume's account of the artificial virtues undertakes to explain three related matters having to do with this development: the origin of these conventions in self-interest; the development of *moral* motives adequate to produce actions conforming to these conventions; and the fact that we now have sentiments of *approbation* in response to actions that conform to these conventions, and *disapprobation* in response to those that fail to conform to them.

B. Motives and Moral Qualities

Hume begins his explanation of the artificial virtues with a discussion of the relationship between the motives of an agent's actions and the moral character of that agent. As we saw above, Hume supposes that the moral sentiments arise in response to the actions and motives of human agents. In 3.2.1 (*Justice, whether a natural or artificial virtue?*) he again argues that, although *actions* may appear to be virtuous or vicious, they are in reality only *signs* of "certain principles in the mind and temper." These "principles," the underlying features of mind of which actions are signs, are the *motives* that cause agents to perform the actions in question. Given that it is these motives that are the objects of moral assessment, it follows that to say of a given individual that he or she is virtuous is to say this individual has motives (passions and desires as well as dispositions, intentions, and character) of a distinctive kind (T 3.2.1.2, quoted in full, note 36).

In making this claim, Hume is agreeing with many other philosophers. We have seen that Shaftesbury, Mandeville, and Hutcheson agree that the motives of agents determine the moral character of the actions performed by those agents.[42] These moralists agreed that an action is morally good only if it has been produced by an other-regarding motive, with the obvious consequence that an action

---

[42] Hume traced this view to Cicero, whom he found to have argued that it is "on the Goodness or Badness of the Motives that the Virtue of the Action depends" (Letter to Francis Hutcheson, 17 Sept. 1739; *Letters* 1:35). For Cicero's discussion, see *De finibus bonorum et malorum* [*About the Ends of Goods and Evils*] 4.16–17.43–8. For some of the many others who took this view, see "Editors' Annotations," in *A Treatise of Human Nature*, ed. D. F. Norton and M. J. Norton, 2 vols. (Oxford: Clarendon Press, 2007), 2:845, 896–7, 949 (annotations 226.1, 307.7, 373.19).

motivated by self-interest is never virtuous. Such an action may benefit someone or the public generally, but benefit alone is not enough to make the agent who performed the action virtuous. Given that Hume maintains that actions in themselves are always morally neutral, and that virtuous actions derive their virtue "only from virtuous motives, and are consider'd merely as signs of those motives," it is clear that he also supposes that actions are morally good only when motivated by a regard for others (T 3.2.1.2, 4).[43] But Hume's position on this issue is substantially different from that of his predecessors. Although he never abandons the view that the moral character of actions is determined by their motives, we will see that he maintains that the artificial virtues are initially motivated by self-interest. It is only over the course of time that these virtues come to be motivated by a regard for others, and thus to meet Hume's standard for a *moral* virtue.

C. Justice

Hume begins his discussion of the artificial virtues with justice, the conventions governing property.[44] Imagine, he begins, that someone has borrowed a sum of money, and said that he will return the equivalent amount by some specified later date. This date has now been reached, but the borrower asks, "*What reason or motive have I to restore the money?*" We, far removed from the time when justice originated, would say that *justice* obliges one to repay a loan when it is due, and a person asking the question now would understand that answer. Hume's example, however, is intended to direct our attention to an earlier time, a time when humanity was in that "rude and more *natural* condition" to which he refers. The reply we would now make, if made to a borrower still in that rude state, would make no sense to that person. That hypothetical person would reply, Hume

---

[43] Hume observes that actions may be thought to have moral character because we have a tendency to focus on them rather than on the motives from which they derive. As a consequence, moral assessments are directed to the actions. As Hume puts it: "Actions are at first only considered as signs of motives: but 'tis usual, in this case, as in all others, to fix our attention on the signs, and neglect, in some measure, the thing signify'd" (T 3.2.1.8).

[44] In Hume's account, the rules of justice have to do only with external goods or property (see T 2.1.10.1, 3.2.2.7).

suggests: What do you mean by *justice?* And what does this *justice,* of which I have never heard, have to do with me? In this way Hume forces us to ask still another question: In such a morally undeveloped environment, what motive could there be to repay the loan? His answer to this last question: None. In those circumstances there could be no motive to repay the loan (T 3.2.1.9).

Hume undertakes to establish this point by arguing that there are exactly three original motives to action: *self-love,* or a concern for one's own private interest; *general benevolence,* or a concern for the well-being of others generally; and *private benevolence,* or a concern to do what benefits some other individual or limited set of individuals. Hume maintains that none of these motives is a natural, universal motive to be just or a foundation of the virtue of justice as we now know it. In support of this conclusion he points out that self-love appears to motivate more unjust actions than just ones,[45] that there is in human nature no general regard for the well-being of others (we are by nature generous, but the scope of this generosity is significantly limited), nor is such a regard essential to acts of justice, and that private benevolence is sometimes best served by violating the rules of justice.

There is, then, no effective answer to the first question posed by the uncultivated individual. In the rude or uncultivated condition envisaged, there is no morally compelling reason or motive to repay the loan. To conclude that a morally uncultivated person would neither understand what justice is, nor have an effective motivation to act justly, is to conclude that justice, given that it is now a virtue, is an *artificial* virtue. It is to conclude that our "sense of justice and injustice" (our sense that acting justly is the right way to act) "is not deriv'd from nature, but arises artificially, tho' necessarily from education, and human conventions" (T 3.2.1.9–17).

---

[45] Hume also argues that, before the conventions of justice were developed, acting in accordance with the impartiality demanded by these conventions would have been seen to be vicious. In our original state, self-interest motivates us to act partially or selfishly. Moreover, the partiality we feel in that original state leads us to expect such partial behavior, and to treat any significant deviation from this expectation as wrong: such partiality, he says, has an influence not only on our "behaviour and conduct in society, but even on our ideas of vice and virtue; so as to make us [when in that state] regard any remarkable transgression of such a degree of partiality . . . as vicious and immoral" (T 3.2.2.8).

Having reached this important conclusion, Hume turns his attention to two related questions. How is it that humans have developed the conventions of justice? And why is it, given what we have learned about the origin of these conventions, that we treat their observance or neglect as a *moral* matter?

In response to his first question Hume emphasizes humanity's natively perilous condition. Of all animals, individual humans appear to have the fewest natural advantages in proportion to their needs and desires. Individually, humans are weak, inept, and in constant danger of losing whatever material goods they may have acquired. It was only by joining forces that humans could remedy these deficiencies. That is, it was only by forming societies that humans could enhance, as they needed to do, their strength, abilities, and security. Hume assumes that our most remote ancestors had no experience of societies, no experience of, that is, *convention-* or *rule-governed* social units. Fortunately, the development and recognition of the advantages of such units depends on an ineradicable feature of human nature, sexual appetite. Rule-governed social groups were not a part of our rude and uncultivated beginnings, but such groups emerged naturally as a consequence of the process of socialization that begins with sexual appetite and leads to families, themselves miniature social units or proto-societies. In the beginning, then, a powerful and entirely natural but amoral motive gave rise to small proto-societies characterized by a significant degree of cooperation.[46]

This initial development then led some of our ancestors to realize that the leading source of conflict between their proto-societies was disputes about external goods. Some also realized that it would be in the interest of each individual and each family to reduce these conflicts, and that this desirable end could be achieved by adopting conventions or rules that stabilized the possession of such goods.

---

[46] Hume suggests that in the rude and natural condition of which he speaks, not even the rudiments of justice were present, needed, or known. He compares the situation to that of close friends and married couples or to circumstances in which there is a great plenty of some item: "'Tis easy to remark, that a cordial affection renders all things common among friends; and that marry'd people in particular mutually lose their property, and are unacquainted with the *mine* and *thine*, which are so necessary, and yet cause such disturbance in human society. The same effect arises from any alteration in the circumstances of mankind; as when there is such a plenty of any thing as satisfies all the desires of men: In which case the distinction of property is entirely lost, and every thing remains in common" (T 3.2.2.17).

On Hume's account, the unreflective self-interest that characterizes humanity's "wild uncultivated state" and that inhibits the development of genuine societies was gradually restrained and redirected. But it was self-interest itself, a partially enlightened self-interest, that brought about this important change and made society possible. The initial conventions of justice were the result of individuals tacitly recognizing that they would each gain by including in their routine behavior certain restraints regarding property, provided only that others would do the same thing (I refrain from taking your goods as long as you refrain from taking mine).[47] In fact, the restraints and expectations that produced the peace and order of society were articulated as explicit rules of property only after they had begun to have effect (T 3.2.2.1–22).

If this account of the origins of justice is correct, what have we learned from it? First, Hume has shown that justice is the product of a historical process that depended on unwitting contrivance. Second, he has shown that the conventions of justice arose because certain contingent conditions made human well-being or survival dependent on them. Had those conditions been different (had not necessary material goods been in relatively short supply, for example), rules of property would not have been necessary for peace and order. Even now, were there to be a bountiful supply of these material goods or were humans all generous without limit, justice would alter or wither away. Hume has also confirmed that justice is not founded on ideas or their allegedly eternal and immutable relations. It was only *after* the practice of mutual restraint had resulted in the relevant conventions that the ideas of justice and injustice, as well as the ideas of property, right, and obligation, were formed. The ideas and the relevant relations do not precede, but follow after, experience.

The portion of his theory just outlined explains, Hume says, our "*natural* obligation to justice, *viz.* interest." Hume is satisfied that he has shown why, as the result of the gradual process he has described, individual humans have gained an effective motive, *enlightened* self-interest, to establish the conventions of justice, a motive that the uncultivated members of our species lacked. He has

---

[47] In direct opposition to Hobbes and Locke, Hume insists that this development was not the result of a promise or social contract; see T 3.2.2.10.

also shown why these same individuals have come to feel that they *ought* to act justly. He has explained how we as a species developed conventions to which we are now motivated to conform, and thus how we came to feel, when we find ourselves in certain circumstances, that (for self-interested or prudential reasons) we *ought* to conform to those conventions, or to feel that we *ought* to act justly where *justly* means in our own enlightened self-interest. We have developed conventions that serve our interests and that also call for each individual to keep up his or her part in what is at least a tacit agreement to respect property rights. But Hume goes on to say that he must still explain why it is that we treat the observance or neglect of the conventions of justice as a *moral* matter. Given his commitment to the view that motives determine moral merit, and that only other-regarding motives secure moral approbation, he still must explain, "*Why we annex the idea of virtue to justice, and of vice to injustice?*" or how it happens that, in matters pertaining to justice we develop a "*moral* obligation, or the sentiment of right and wrong" (T 3.2.2.23).

When Hume equates the "*moral* obligation" to justice with "the sentiment of right and wrong," he reminds us that one of the aims of *Treatise* 3 is to discover the foundations of morality, and that the preceding account of the development of justice omits an essential part of that story. Hume saw the development of the virtue of justice as passing through three stages. He is now about to sketch the third and final stage.

What Hume describes as our original or "wild uncultivated state" would have been the first stage in the development of justice. In that portion of *Treatise* 3.2.2 just outlined, he has explained our movement from an initial stage in which there were no conventions of justice and in which any reference to such conventions would have been unintelligible, to a second stage. As we have seen, this second stage is characterized by the fact that the conventions defining and protecting property have been developed. To say this is to say that when groups of individuals have reached this stage – when genuine *societies* have been developed – individuals composing these societies routinely respect each other's possessions. They also have a working understanding of the concepts of justice, injustice, and property, as well as the sense that they as individuals have an obligation to respect the property rights of others. These newly developed conventions have also gained an action-guiding force. As Hume describes the situation, "After this convention, concerning abstinence from the possessions of others, is enter'd into, and every one has acquir'd a stability in his possessions, there immediately arise the ideas of justice and injustice; as also those of *property*, *right*, and *obligation*" (T 3.2.2.11). Thus, while individuals in the first stage were unable to understand talk about justice or property rights and consequently could not know what it meant to respect such rights, some of their descendants were capable of understanding these key notions. These individuals also understood that being just means that one conforms one's behavior to the conventions of justice, that conforming to these conventions is in one's best interest, and, consequently, that this is the prudent thing to do. In short, individuals who have reached the second stage of this development have acquired important new capabilities. They have developed, and thus they understand, the conventions or rules of justice. They have also discovered a motive (enlightened self-interest) for maintaining these rules. Finally, these individuals experience a form of approval in response to actions that conform to these rules, and a form of disapproval in response to those that do not. Still remaining to be answered, however, is Hume's second question: Why do acts of justice and injustice arouse these sentiments of approval or disapproval, and what circumstances eventually cause these approvals to take the form of the distinctive moral sentiments? The initial motive to justice is self-interest, not that regard for others that was earlier said to be an essential component of our moral approvals. Why, then, do we in the third and final stage of the development of justice give *moral* approval to acts of justice? Or, to press even further, how and why is there a third stage, a stage in which we suppose we have a "*moral obligation*" to be just? (T 3.2.2.23).

Near the end of *Treatise* 3.2.2 Hume says that a complete answer to this question depends on discussions found only in *Treatise* 3.3, but he nonetheless provides an enlightening sketch of how he supposes that we come to attach *moral* significance to what is initially only self-regarding concern that the conventions of justice be maintained. In the normal and slowly changing course of events, the societies made possible by the conventions of justice grew significantly larger and more complex. As a result, it became more difficult for individuals to see how their private interests were being served by adherence to the conventions of justice that had been developed. As a result, some individuals began to disregard these conventions. They began to act unjustly, perhaps without even noticing that they were doing so. Other individuals, however, did notice when these conventions were violated because they were harmed by the actions taking place. Moreover, even when such unjust actions were remote from these observers and consequently did not harm them, these distant observers nonetheless disapproved of these actions. They did so, according to Hume, because they found such unjust behavior "prejudicial to human society, and pernicious to every one that approache[d] the person guilty of it" (T 3.2.2.24). In fact, even those individuals who acted unjustly were made to feel uneasy by their own unjust actions. Somehow, a further stage of development had been reached. What in the second stage had been a self-regarding concern that the conventions of justice be maintained, became in addition *an other-regarding concern* that these conventions be followed.[48]

Hume finds that two features of human nature made this important moral development possible. The first feature is our tendency to form general rules, and to give to these rules an inflexibility that can withstand even the pressures of self-interest.[49] Once we have

---

[48] Later in his discussion of justice Hume says, "Upon the whole, then, we are to consider this distinction betwixt justice and injustice, as having two different foundations, *viz.* that of *self-interest*, when men observe, that 'tis impossible to live in society without restraining themselves by certain rules; and that of *morality*, when this interest is once observ'd to be common to all mankind, and men receive a pleasure from the view of such actions as tend to the peace of society, and an uneasiness from such as are contrary to it. 'Tis the voluntary convention and artifice of men, which makes the first interest take place; and therefore those laws of justice are so far to be consider'd as *artificial*. After that interest is once establish'd and acknowledg'd, the sense of morality in the observance of these rules follows *naturally*, and of itself" (T 3.2.6.11). Note that Hume here and elsewhere grants that the "instructions" of politicians and of parents contribute to the development of justice, but he also says, surely with Mandeville in mind, that this account of the matter "has been carry'd too far by certain writers on morals, who seem to have employ'd their utmost efforts to extirpate all sense of virtue from among mankind," and that this account is "erroneous" (T 3.2.2.25, 3.3.1.11).

[49] Hume's first account of general rules suggests that they are what would now be called *generalizations,* and indicates that they may be well- or ill-founded. But the relevant general rule in the present case is a definition that characterizes property as "a stable possession, deriv'd from the rules of justice, or the conventions of men," or, as Hume had earlier said, an understanding of property as "*such a relation*

established the conventions that are to govern the possession and exchange of property, our sentiments may be influenced by these conventions even when they or their use conflicts with the self-interest that has produced them. Conventions having that kind of continuing force exercise at least a partial check on self-interest.

The second feature is sympathy. Hume recognizes that any particular act of justice may be contrary to both private and public good:

> a single act of justice, consider'd in itself, may often be contrary to the public good; and 'tis only the concurrence of mankind, in a general scheme or system of action, which is advantageous . . . if we examine all the questions, that come before any tribunal of justice, we shall find, that, considering each case apart, it wou'd as often be an instance of humanity to decide contrary to the laws of justice as conformable to them. Judges take from a poor man to give to a rich; they bestow on the dissolute the labour of the industrious; and put into the hands of the vicious the means of harming both themselves and others. The whole scheme, however, of law and justice is advantageous to the society and to every individual. (T 3.3.1.12)

Hume tells us, in other words, that only an unremitting commitment to the system of justice is beneficial to all concerned, and yet few would seem to have sufficient motive to maintain such a commitment. It is an inherent principle of communication, sympathy, that makes this commitment possible. Sympathy enables us to transcend our narrowly selfish interests and to feel approbation in response to actions that maintain the system of justice, and disapprobation in response to those that fail to give such support. It does so by enabling observers to feel the pleasures and pains produced in others affected by just or unjust acts that have no direct bearing on those observers. Hume argues at length that self-interest was "the original motive to the *establishment* of justice," but he then goes on to insist that we feel the moral sentiments in response to just and unjust actions only because of sympathy. If, for example, I observe that Doe is pained by the unjust action of Roe, then the

---

betwixt a person and an object as permits him, but forbids any other, the free use and possession of it, without violating the laws of justice and moral equity" (T 1.3.13.7–13, 3.2.3.7, 2.1.10.1). For more on these general rules, see Thomas K. Hearn, "'General Rules' in Hume's *Treatise*," *Journal of the History of Philosophy* 8 (1970): 405–22; and "General Rules and the Moral Sentiments in Hume's *Treatise*," *Review of Metaphysics* 30 (1976): 57–72.

operation of sympathy causes me to feel not only Doe's pain, but also the disesteem this pain has caused her to feel for Roe. More generally, as Hume later sums up the matter, once the conventions of justice are established, just actions are *"naturally* attended with a strong sentiment of morals; which can proceed from nothing but our sympathy with the interests of society" (T 3.2.2.24, 3.3.1.12).[50] Our disposition to form and follow general rules and our ability to share sentiments with our fellow humans have enabled morality to evolve to the point that at least some of us feel the distinctive moral sentiments in response to just or unjust actions.[51]

D. The Natural Virtues

Hume announces at the beginning of *Treatise* 3.3.1, *Of the origin of the natural virtues and vices,* that he is ready for "the examination of such virtues and vices as are entirely natural, and have no dependance on the artifice and contrivance of men." Later in this section he notes that great men are praised for two kinds of qualities, those that enable them to "perform their part in society," namely, *"generosity* and *humanity,"* and those that make them "serviceable to themselves, and enable them to promote their

---

[50] Hume also said of sympathy that it "produces, in many instances, our sentiments of morals.... No virtue is more esteem'd than justice, and no vice more detested than injustice; nor are there any qualities, which go farther to the fixing the character, either as amiable or odious. Now justice is a moral virtue, merely because it has that tendency to the good of mankind; and, indeed, is nothing but an artificial invention to that purpose. The same may be said of allegiance, of the laws of nations, of modesty, and of good-manners. All these are mere human contrivances for the interest of society. The inventors of them had chiefly in view their own interest. But we carry our approbation of them into the most distant countries and ages, and much beyond our own interest. And since there is a very strong sentiment of morals, which has always attended them, we must allow, that the reflecting on the tendency of characters and mental qualities, is sufficient to give us the sentiments of approbation and blame. Now as the means to an end can only be agreeable, where the end is agreeable; and as the good of society, where our own interest is not concern'd, or that of our friends, pleases only by sympathy: It follows, that sympathy is the source of the esteem, which we pay to all the artificial virtues" (T 3.3.1.9; see also 3.3.6.1–2). For further discussion of sympathy, see in this volume "Hume's Moral Psychology," Part V, and "Hume's Later Moral Philosophy," Part IV.

[51] For further discussion of Hume's account of justice, see in this volume "The Structure of Hume's Political Theory," Part III.

own interest," namely, "*prudence, temperance, frugality, industry, assiduity, enterprize,* [and] *dexterity.*" In 3.3.3, *Of goodness and benevolence,* he describes "*generosity, humanity, compassion, gratitude, friendship, fidelity, zeal, disinterestedness,* [and] *liberality*" as the "qualities, which form the character of good and benevolent," but the inclusion of *fidelity,* elsewhere described as an artificial virtue, requires us to ask if all the qualities listed here are natural virtues. Later, while discussing natural abilities, he notes that "*industry, perseverance, patience, activity, vigilance, application,* [and] *constancy,*" as well as "*temperance, frugality, œconomy,* [and] *resolution,*" are useful "*virtues,*" while "*prodigality, luxury, irresolution* [and] *uncertainty, are vicious.*" If these qualities are all to be classed among the natural virtues, they constitute a wide spectrum of motivating qualities (T 3.3.1.1, 3.3.1.24, 3.3.3.3, 3.3.4.7).

Although the *Treatise* never provides us with a comprehensive and unambiguous list of the natural virtues, we can be sure that *generosity* and *humanity* are two such virtues. Knowing this, knowing that at least these two instinctive desires or motivations are an intrinsic part of human nature, means that we have, as Hume puts it, "a proof, that our approbation has, in [some] cases, an origin different from the prospect of utility and advantage, either to ourselves or others." We have, in other words, proof that the accounts of human nature given by Mandeville or other egoists are mistaken. The descriptions of our "selfishness" that these philosophers give, Hume said, "are as wide of nature as any accounts of monsters, which we meet with in fables and romances." It may be rare, he grants, to encounter anyone "who loves any single person better than himself," but it is just "as rare to meet with one, in whom all the kind affections, taken together, do not over-ballance all the selfish" (T 3.3.3.4, 3.2.2.5).

E. Duty and Obligation

Although Hume follows the development of the artificial virtues to the point of explaining how these conventions become *moral* virtues and that many humans feel a moral obligation to act justly or keep their promises, he does not in the *Treatise* (or elsewhere) provide us with a sustained discussion of how it is we come to feel moral obligation, of how we come to feel that we *ought* to behave humanely or justly. Moreover, in one of the most widely discussed paragraphs in the *Treatise*, Hume reports that in "every system of morality" that he has encountered the author begins "in the ordinary way of reasoning" and in this way presents readers with "propositions" that connect their parts with *is* or *is not* ("There is a God," for example). Soon enough, however, these authors go on to present us with propositions that connect their parts with *ought* or *ought not* ("We ought to obey the commands of God," for example). Hume describes this shift as a subtle or "imperceptible" one, but considers it to be of the greatest consequence: "For as this *ought*, or *ought not*, expresses some new relation or affirmation, 'tis necessary that it shou'd be observ'd and explain'd; and at the same time that a reason shou'd be given, for what seems altogether inconceivable, how this new relation can be a deduction from others, which are entirely different from it" (T 3.1.1.27).

This paragraph has led some to suppose that Hume is arguing that all moral imperatives (all propositions of the form, "*X* ought to do/ought to have done *Y*") are unfounded, and that he is inconsistent when he later suggests that humans do in fact have both natural and moral duties or obligations, and that these obligations derive from relevant facts. Such interpretations fail to notice that, although this paragraph begins with a reference to "every system of morality," it is in effect an addendum to a section of the *Treatise* devoted to showing that moral distinctions are not derived from reason, and that it concludes with the comment that merely noticing that this important shift of language infects many moral systems will be enough to "subvert all the vulgar" or common "systems of morality, and let us see, that the distinction of vice and virtue is not founded merely on the relations of objects, nor is perceiv'd by reason" (T 3.1.1.27).[52]

We can begin to understand the account of the origins of moral obligation or duty found in the *Treatise* by observing that when Hume says that "no action can be laudable or blameable, without

---

[52] From the fifteenth into the nineteenth century, the meanings of the adjective "vulgar" included "In common or general use; common, customary, or ordinary, as a matter of use or practice" (*Oxford English Dictionary*, vulgar, *a*. 2). Circa 1740, when Hume wrote this sentence, the most common "system" of morals was most likely that of Clarke and his many rationalist disciples.

some motives or impelling passions, distinct from the sense of morals," he goes on to say that these distinct and motivating passions not only have "a great influence" on our sense of morals, but also that "we blame or praise" according to the "general force in human nature" these passions have. He also says that we "always consider the *natural* and *usual* force of the passions, when we determine concerning vice and virtue," and that our "sense of duty always follows the common and natural course of our passions." And he later summarizes his view of morality saying: "All morality depends upon our sentiments; and when any action, or quality of the mind, pleases us *after a certain manner*, we say it is virtuous; and when the neglect, or non-performance of it, displeases us *after a like manner*, we say that we lie under an obligation to perform it" (T 3.2.1.18, 3.2.5.4).

These comments suggest that Hume takes the origin of the idea of duty or obligation to resemble the origin of the idea of causal or necessary connection. This latter idea, the idea that certain events of type A necessarily cause certain other events of type B derives, he explains, from an impression of expectation ("a determination of the mind") felt when, after events of type B have been repeatedly experienced to follow closely the experience of events of type A, we again experience a particular event of type A. When this latest experience of an A-type event occurs, we expect a B-type event to follow. If, for example, we are familiar with lightning and the thunder that follows it, then, if we see lightning, we expect thunder to follow.[53]

The remarks quoted in the last paragraph but one suggest that an impression or feeling of expectation plays an analogous role in the formation of both the *sense* of obligation and our *idea* of this phenomenon. They also suggest that another impression of expectation

---

[53] The *Treatise* account of the origin of our idea of the causal relation and necessary connection is set out in detail in Sections 1.3.3–8, 14–15. Hume later summarizes his conclusions by saying, "If objects had not an uniform and regular conjunction with each other, we shou'd never arrive at any idea of cause and effect; and even after all, the necessity, which enters into that idea, is nothing but a determination of the mind to pass from one object to its usual attendant, and infer the existence of one from that of the other" (T 2.3.1.4). At 1.3.15.8 Hume speaks of the "expectation" produced by a uniform experience, and also of the disappointment felt if that expectation is not met.

plays the same kind of role in the production of the impression of blame and of at least some forms of moral approval. That is, from the common course of actions motivated by "the common and natural course of our passions" there arises in us the expectation that, in specifiable circumstances, certain actions will be performed. If these actions are performed, we approve or feel approbation. If they are not performed, we disapprove or feel disapprobation. Feelings or sentiments of disapproval of this particular type (those feelings that have the causes and features characteristic of moral sentiments), become, when copied, the *idea* of blame. They become, that is, the idea that an individual *ought* to have acted in a particular way, but failed to do so. This idea of blame, understood as applying to all those who fail to perform in accordance with the common and natural course of the passions, is itself the *idea* of duty or obligation. In short, the *idea* of obligation is derived from a unique impression of expectation, an impression that is unique insofar as it is a response to specific features of our experience. Duty or obligation cannot be deduced from factual premises. But an impression of obligation – a feeling that something ought to have been done – can be derived from our experience of those actions that have moral relevance insofar as they serve as "signs" of the relevant virtuous or vicious motives (see note 36).

This interpretive hypothesis is supported by Hume's brief comments about the obligations associated with a natural virtue, the affection of parents for children. He says: "We blame a father for neglecting his child. Why? because it shows a want of natural affection, which is the duty of every parent." He then goes on to say that, "were not natural affection a duty, the care of children cou'd not be a duty," thus suggesting that, because affection for one's children is a standard feature of human nature, the care of children is not only *expected* of parents, but as a consequence becomes their duty (T 3.2.1.5). He later returns to this example and lends further support to the suggestion that he supposes that moral obligation arises from a process of the sort just outlined. He says:

No action can be requir'd of us as our duty, unless there be implanted in human nature some actuating passion or motive, capable of producing the action. This motive cannot be the sense of duty. A sense of duty supposes an antecedent obligation: And where an action is not requir'd by any natural passion, it cannot be requir'd by any natural obligation; since it may be omitted without proving any defect or imperfection in the mind and temper, and consequently without any vice.

Then, after a comment regarding our obligation to keep promises, an artificial virtue, he goes on to speak again of the natural virtues, and says that

Tho' there was no obligation to relieve the miserable, our humanity wou'd lead us to it; and when we omit that duty, the immorality of the omission arises from its being a proof, that we want the natural sentiments of humanity. A father knows it to be his duty to take care of his children: But he has also a natural inclination to it. And if no human creature had that inclination, no one cou'd lie under any such obligation. (T 3.2.5.6)

Duty or obligation, Hume says, cannot be deduced from factual premises, but he indicates that a "natural obligation" may be derived from a "natural passion" or "natural sentiments" – from an "inclination" to humanity or to care for one's children. These implanted or innate natural virtues lead humans to behave, ordinarily, in predictable ways that benefit others. When one of our species fails to behave as we expect, we feel blame or moral disapproval, and from this impression we go on to form the idea of moral obligation.[54] Here again Hume traces a central aspect of morality to human nature.

IV. THE FOUNDATION IN HUMAN NATURE

We have seen several ways in which Hume in the *Treatise* makes good on his commitment to make "human Nature" his "principal Study, & the Source from which [he] wou'd derive every Truth in . . . Morality." We have seen that, having directed his attention to human nature, he has found in that nature features ("principles,"

---

[54] Hume allows for unavoidable exceptions to the expected behavior: "Where a person is possess'd of a character, that in its natural tendency is beneficial to society, we esteem him virtuous, and are delighted with the view of his character, even tho' particular accidents prevent its operation, and incapacitate him from being serviceable to his friends and country. Virtue in rags is still virtue; and the love, which it procures, attends a man into a dungeon or desert, where the virtue can no longer be exerted in action, and is lost to all the world" (T 3.3.1.19; see also 2.2.3.3–4).

he often calls them) that explain the origin and basic workings of morality. Central among the features or principles discovered are those that we have briefly reviewed in this essay:

1. Humans are motivated by the passions, not by reason.
2. Humans have a natural moral sensitivity, so that they respond to actions seen to have been motivated by a regard for the welfare of others with a sentiment of approbation, and to those actions motivated by malice or overweening self-concern, they respond with a sentiment of disapprobation.
3. Human nature includes important natural virtues: natural desires or dispositions to act in humane, generous, or compassionate ways, but the scope or strength of these virtues is limited.
4. Human nature also encompasses in each individual the strongest of all human passions, self-interest.
5. The rude self-interest natural to humans can with time and reflection be changed from unprincipled selfishness to an enlightened self-interest that enables groups of us to develop such valuable conventions or "artificial virtues" as justice (an understanding of and respect for property), fidelity (an understanding of and respect for promises or contracts), and allegiance (an understanding of and respect for political society).
6. Human nature also includes "a very powerful principle," sympathy, which is "the chief source of moral distinctions" and which (among other things) serves to transform the fundamentally self-regarding artificial virtues of justice, fidelity, and allegiance into forms of behavior (being just, faithful, and loyal) motivated by a regard or concern for the well-being of others, even of others with whom we have no acquaintance or connection (T 3.3.6.1).
7. Human nature includes a further disposition to respond to customary human behavior in much the way that we respond to the customary behavior of natural objects: by forming expectations, expectations in moral matters that, when they are disappointed, give rise to the impressions and ideas of blame and obligation.

Although Hume's account of morality is significantly different from that of Hutcheson, he could clearly join Hutcheson in saying that *"Human Nature* was not left quite indifferent in the Affair of Virtue."

SUGGESTIONS FOR FURTHER READING

For alternative points of view on the issues raised in this essay, see, in addition to the the books and essays cited therein:

Anthologies

Chappell, V. C., ed. *Hume: A Collection of Critical Essays.* New York: Doubleday, 1966. See esp. the contributions on Hume's theory of obligation by A. C. McIntyre, R. F. Atkinson, W. D. Hudson, and Bernard Wand.

Cohon, Rachel, ed. *Hume: Moral and Political Philosophy.* Aldershot, England: Dartmouth Publishing, 2001. This volume includes relatively recent papers on virtually all the issues taken up in Parts II–IV of this essay.

Monographs and Papers

Árdal, Páll. *Passion and Value in Hume's Treatise,* 2nd ed. Edinburgh: Edinburgh University Press, 1989. 41–79, 109–89.

Baier, Annette C. *A Progress of Sentiments: Reflections on Hume's* Treatise. Cambridge, MA: Harvard University Press, 1991. 127–259.

Darwall, Stephen. "Hume and the Invention of Utilitarianism." In *Hume and Hume's Connexions,* edited by M. A. Stewart and J. P. Wright. Edinburgh: Edinburgh University Press, 1994. 58–82.

Ferreira, M. Jamie. "Hume and Imagination: Sympathy and 'the Other.'" *International Philosophical Quarterly* 34 (1994): 39–57.

Green, T. H. "Introduction." In *David Hume: A Treatise of Human Nature, The Philosophical Works of David Hume,* edited by T. H. Green and T. H. Grose, 4 vols. London, 1875, 1882. 2:1–71.

Herdt, Jennifer A. *Religion and Faction in Hume's Moral Philosophy.* Cambridge: Cambridge University Press, 1997.

Korsgaard, Christine M. *The Sources of Normativity.* Cambridge: Cambridge University Press, 1996. 51–66, 86–9.

Mackie, J. L. *Hume's Moral Theory.* London: Routledge & Kegan Paul, 1980.

Martin, Marie A. "Hutcheson and Hume on Explaining the Nature of Morality: Why It Is Mistaken to Suppose Hume Ever Raised the Is-Ought Question." *History of Philosophy Quarterly* 8 (1991): 277–89.

McGilvary, E. B. "Altruism in Hume's *Treatise." Philosophical Review* 12 (1903): 272–98.

McIntyre, Jane L. "Hume's 'New and Extraordinary' Account of the Passions." In *The Blackwell Guide to Hume's* Treatise, edited by S. Traiger. Oxford: Blackwell Publishing, 2006. 199–215.

Mounce, H. O. *Hume's Naturalism*. London: Routledge, 1999. 62–98.

Norton, David Fate. "Editor's Introduction." In *David Hume: A Treatise of Human Nature*, edited by D. F. Norton and M. J. Norton. Oxford: Oxford University Press, 2000, reprinted with corrections, 2005. I47–97.

Stroud, Barry. "'Gilding or Staining' the World with 'Sentiments' and 'Phantasms.'" *Hume Studies* 19 (1993): 253–72.

Taylor, Jacqueline. "Justice and the Foundations of Social Morality in Hume's *Treatise*." *Hume Studies* 24 (1998): 5–30.

10 Hume's Later Moral Philosophy

Hume writes in his autobiographical essay, "My Own Life," that he regarded his *Enquiry concerning the Principles of Morals* as "of all my writings, historical, philosophical, or literary, incomparably the best."[1] This work, like the *Enquiry concerning Human Understanding*, was a part of his *Treatise on Human Nature* that he had decided to "cast anew" (MOL 9–10).[2] In an advertisement composed late in his life, Hume wrote that the volume of essays that included these two works afforded him an opportunity to correct "some negligences in his former reasoning and more in the expression" of the *Treatise*, and that he wanted the later work, and not the *Treatise*, to be "regarded as containing his philosophical sentiments and principles."[3] The second *Enquiry* is often considered a more eloquent work than the *Treatise*. But Hume's correction of some "negligences" in reasoning, the addition of new arguments, and a restructuring of main themes give the later work a philosophical significance in its own right.

---

[1] In a letter of 1755 to the Abbé le Blanc, Hume wrote that the *Enquiry concerning the Principles of Morals* "is my favorite Performance" (HL I:227).

[2] Hume's earliest reviews were primarily negative. For an extensive discussion and the full text and an English translation of the only review of Book 3 of the *Treatise*, see "The *Bibliothèque raisonnée* Review of Volume 3 of the *Treatise*: Authorship, Text, and Translation," by David Fate Norton and Dario Perinetti, *Hume Studies* 32 (April 2006): 3–52. See also James Fieser, ed., *Early Responses to Hume*, Vols. 3 and 4 (Bristol, England: Thoemmes Press, 2000).

[3] See the Advertisement prefacing the OPT edition of *Hume's Enquiry concerning Human Understanding*, ed. Tom L. Beauchamp. Hume mentions the advertisement in a letter of October 1775 to the printer William Strahan; see HL 2:301. The advertisement was first printed in January 1776 and was to be included in all unsold and future copies of the volume of essays containing the two *Enquiries*.

311

This essay examines Hume's later moral philosophy. I also look at some differences between the *Treatise* and his later works. But the main aim of the essay is to draw attention to what makes the later work philosophically interesting and important in comparison with Hume's earlier work. In particular, I show the importance of the mature Hume's attention, in the second *Enquiry*, "A Dialogue," and some of his essays, to the role of language and reason in morality. He also has important things to say about the issue of the universality and relativity of morals. I begin with a brief overview of the second *Enquiry* to draw attention to Hume's method and the main themes of the work. I then discuss in more detail the relation between sympathy, reason, and discourse or language, on the one hand, and moral sentiment, on the other. In the concluding sections, I reconstruct Hume's account of how we assess moral communities when their values differ from our own, drawing attention once more to the importance of moral discourse.

I. BRIEF SURVEY OF THE METHOD AND THEMES OF THE SECOND *ENQUIRY*

The second *Enquiry* opens with a discussion of moral controversies. Hume first identifies two sorts of philosopher not worth engaging with, the dogmatist and the "disingenuous disputant" who denies the reality of moral distinctions. Both sorts adhere blindly to their own views, and show contempt for whoever opposes them. Thus, "as reasoning is not the source, whence either disputant derives his tenets; it is in vain to expect, that any logic, which speaks not to the affections, will ever engage him to embrace sounder principles." A better controversy to take up concerns the foundation of morality: does it lie in reason or sentiment? Some think that morality is a matter of truth, arrived at through a consideration of the facts and arguments. Others insist that morality must engage our feelings, for otherwise we would be indifferent to it. Hume says he will not begin by examining in depth the seemingly convincing arguments that might be made on either side of this controversy. Instead, he proposes first to collect together all those mental qualities that make up "what, in common life, we call PERSONAL MERIT," by which he means those character traits we find praiseworthy or blameworthy (EPM 1.1–2, 10).

The starting point is thus "common life" and the everyday terminology we use to talk about character and other qualities of human nature. By attending to the names we use for the attributes of the mind we will find that the "very nature of language guides us almost infallibly in forming" our moral judgments, and that "the least acquaintance with the idiom suffices, without any reasoning, to direct us in collecting and arranging the estimable or blameable qualities of men." We can simply ask ourselves which qualities we want to have attributed to us: for example, would we rather have others find us benevolent and honest, or cruel and disloyal? With the virtues and vices appropriately cataloged, the task of reason is to examine the circumstances common to the virtues and those common to the vices. Through this "experimental" approach we can finally reach "the foundation of ethics, and find those universal principles" that explain why we praise some mental qualities and blame others. Determining these principles "is a question of fact." The artful construction of the *Enquiry* allows Hume to set out arguments against a range of opponents, including dogmatic divines and disingenuous selfish theorists, in the course of following "the experimental method" (EPM 1.10).

The careful survey of mental qualities leads, in Section 9, to the definition of virtue as any mental quality that is useful or agreeable to the moral agent herself or to others. Hume implicitly relies on this definition to structure the discussion of the qualities that make up personal merit. Instead of distinguishing, as he did in the *Treatise*, between natural and artificial virtues, he begins with benevolence and justice, treating them together as the two fundamental kinds of social virtue (that is, virtues useful for society). In Section 2, Hume notes that it is almost "a superfluous task" to show that we admire benevolence. The terms that name benevolent qualities, *humane, merciful, generous,* and so on, "universally express the highest merit, which *human nature* is capable of attaining" (EPM 2.1). One important reason we approve of benevolence as a virtue lies in its usefulness both for the possessor and for society. It can guide the development and exercise of such other qualities as courage or ambition, and it promotes the general interest as well as the happiness of those for whom we care most. Hume argues that in recommending something as useful, whether a fertile field, a comfortable house, or a virtuous character, we express our approval of it. Usefulness, or utility, is a source of merit or value. Useful character traits have *moral* merit, and earn our moral admiration.

Justice is a second kind of socially useful virtue. Hume's aim in Section 3 is to show that utility is the sole origin of justice, and hence "the *sole* foundation of its merit," and the admiration we feel for it (EPM 3.1). He makes his case by showing that the human condition is a medium between the extremes of material abundance and absolute scarcity, as well as between extremes of temperament. We are not self-sufficient, and we naturally live in family settings where we form friendships and enjoy conversation. But our benevolence, including our love, compassion, and generosity, is naturally limited, typically to those to whom we are most partial, such as family and friends. Hence, the rules of justice are the most useful means of extending cooperation for mutual advantage. Civil laws are formed in response to the needs and convenience of each community, and the complexity of particular laws shows the influence of reasoning, custom, and education. Section 4 extends the explication of justice, showing that utility is also the source of the merit of those virtues, such as loyalty and honor, associated with good government and citizenship. Indeed, utility explains the merit of other convention-based virtues, including those specific to women (chastity and modesty), and good manners.

Section 5 forms the heart of the second *Enquiry*, and examines more fully the reason why utility, or more precisely, why qualities useful to the agent or to others and said to be virtues are a source of merit or value. Hume's explanation centers on the importance of our capacity to sympathize with the interests, pleasures, and pains of others. Sympathy, not considerations of self-interest, explains why we find useful character traits so valuable. In the second part of Section 5, Hume details the pervasive influence of sympathy in human life. Without sympathy we would be indifferent not only to humanity but to morality. The rest of this section discusses the connection between sympathy and the moral sentiments. Section 6 shows how the same principle of sympathy produces approval of self-regarding qualities, such as industry or prudence, useful primarily for the person who possesses them. Sections 7 and 8 discuss another kind of quality that produces attributions of merit. We approve of some traits of character simply because they are "agreeable" to the person possessing them or to others, even though they may not have any tendency to the good of the individual or society. Cheerfulness, for example, pleases us immediately. So traits of character that are agreeable are virtues and those that we find disagreeable are vices.

Hume, having in Sections 2 through 8 explained the merit of various mental qualities, gives us in Section 9 the definitions of virtue and vice. Virtues are those mental qualities that are useful or agreeable to oneself or to others, while vices are the mental qualities that are harmful or disagreeable to oneself or others. Hume makes it clear that some character traits meet more than one of the criteria for virtue. Benevolence, for example, meets all four criteria: it is useful and agreeable, for the possessor as well as for others. Hume also argues that some virtues, such as pride, benevolence, and justice, are essential for successful cooperative living, while the more immediately agreeable qualities, such as wit or good manners, enhance our quality of life. Linking in this way the aim of virtue with living well provides Hume with good grounds for concluding that the obligation to cultivate virtue coincides with our "true interest." In the second part of Section 9, Hume argues that from the point of view of interest, where this includes a concern for our reputation, the cultivation of virtue recommends itself to us. A "sensible knave" might think that self-interest and morality come apart in the case of justice, but then he lacks a sense of integrity and the pleasing consciousness that, for the rest of us, reflect "the force of many sympathies" and ensure that we keep "a character with ourselves" and not simply for appearances (EPM 9.16, 22, 11).

Hume's strategy for establishing the foundation of morality in the *Enquiry* is significantly different from the one he pursued in the *Treatise*. In the earlier work, Hume invoked the principles of association and sympathy to give a causal story of how the moral sentiments, a particular kind of impression, originate in the mind. In the *Enquiry*, Hume sets the hypothesis regarding association to one side and concentrates on our actual experience of moral evaluation as a social process grounded in language and discourse. The *Enquiry* also offers new arguments that mark substantive additions or changes to the moral philosophy of the *Treatise*. First, Hume explicitly argues that neither our social motives nor the moral sentiments reduce to self-interest. Second, moral evaluation explicitly requires good reasoning, reflection on experience, and conversation with others. Finally, Hume shows a new awareness of historical and cultural change, an awareness that shapes his discussion of the scope of merit and of possible variations in just which qualities we recognize as virtues or vices. The importance of these additions to Hume's philosophy is underscored insofar as each is treated in the main body of the text and in a separate appendix.

II. SELF-INTEREST AND BENEVOLENCE

Hume in the *Treatise* did not discuss the importance of the virtues that make up the benevolent character until the final part of the book. Prior to that, he emphasized only the limited scope of our benevolence in order to make the case that we have no natural motive to act justly, and so justice must be established through conventions. The *Treatise* strategy was not particularly successful, though, since his critics seized on his claims about justice as an artificial virtue and tried to link him with the selfish theorist Thomas Hobbes.[4] In the *Enquiry*, Hume takes a different tack. Benevolence is the first virtue discussed. As noted earlier, Hume presents justice and benevolence as the fundamental social virtues, and he reserves discussion of the differences between benevolence and justice until Appendix 3. In Section 2 and Appendix 2, the focus is on the genuineness of our benevolent dispositions and affections. In fact, the issue of how selfish we are by nature is immaterial to moral practice since in common life we recognize real friendship and gratitude, and distinguish between the person who obviously does us a good turn out of self-interest and one who genuinely desires our well-being. Nevertheless, the question of universal selfishness "is certainly of consequence in the speculative science of human nature." Hume has two targets here: those who think "that all *benevolence* is mere hypocrisy," a fair disguise by means of which we can manipulate others to serve our own interests, as well as those who think that all

---

[4] In the 1741 review in *Bibliothèque raisonnée des ouvrages des savans de l'Europe* (referred to in note 2 above), the reviewer wrote that Hume's account of justice was "Hobbes's system clothed in a new fashion" (see *Hume Studies* 32 [2006]: 36). In his *Letter from a Gentleman*, Hume cites William Wishart's charge that the *Treatise of Human Nature* aimed at "sapping the Foundations of Morality, by denying the natural and essential Difference betwixt Right and Wrong, Good and Evil, Justice and Injustice; making the Difference only artificial, and to arise from human Conventions and Compacts" (L 19).

generous actions are done out of self-love (EPM App. 2.1–5). Bernard de Mandeville's work was regarded as an instance of the first kind of selfish theory, and Hume identifies Epicurus, Hobbes, and Locke as among the second.

Hume argues that the selfish school can maintain its tenets only by distorting the evidence. Language provides key evidence in favor of benevolence as a principle of human nature. When we examine common life we find numerous terms for the "amiable qualities" that show evidence of our altruistic nature. Such terms as "*sociable, good-natured, humane, merciful, grateful, friendly, generous, beneficent*" not only describe other-regarding motives but also "express the highest merit" we can accord to one another (EPM 2.1). In both Section 2 and Appendix 2 Hume advances further arguments to support the contention that benevolence is real. For example, animals show kindness to one another, and it seems specious to attribute hypocrisy or narrow self-interest to them. If we allow disinterested benevolence in the lower animals, then "by what rule of analogy can we refuse it" in mankind (EPM App. 2.8)? Hume cites Juvenal, who credits the more extensive benevolence of the human species to our superiority to the other animals, and notes that this superiority gives us "larger opportunities of spreading our kindly influence" (EPM 2.4).

Hume continues to maintain his *Treatise* stance that benevolence is limited. Our benevolent attitudes and actions are for the most part instances of "particular" benevolence (EPM App. 2, n.60). We direct our love or gratitude, our kindness or generosity, not toward mankind in general, but rather toward particular others, especially those whom we esteem as virtuous, or who have done us a service, or who stand more intimately connected to us through family or friendship than the general run of mankind. The long dependency of our children, for example, is evidence of strong parental affections. As Hume notes, "It is wisely ordained by nature, that private connexions should commonly prevail over universal views and considerations; otherwise our affections and actions would be dissipated and lost, for want of a proper limited object" (EPM 5.42, n.25). Our admiration of benevolence in turn reflects our acceptance of this natural partiality.

Hume presents another argument against reducing all motives to self-interest, versions of which were also advanced by Joseph

Butler and Francis Hutcheson, and which he describes as being "conformable to the analogy of nature" (EPM App. 2.12). Natural appetites such as hunger or thirst alert us to the body's need for certain things, viz., food or liquid, which are the ends of the appetites and precede any enjoyment we may get from them. Of course, we often do enjoy our meals, and pleasure can become a secondary object, so that when hunger strikes us we now desire delicious food. The same can be true of our benevolent desires. When we act from benevolent motives we aim at the good of another person. It often turns out that we enjoy helping others, so that, as in the case of bodily appetites, the pleasure we receive from helping others can become a secondary object of desire.

III. SYMPATHY AND THE MORAL SENTIMENT

After appealing to utility as a source of moral merit, Hume is keen to show that we do not approve of it only when it benefits ourselves. We approve of benevolence and a range of other useful virtues from "a more public affection," that is, one more socially oriented than self-interest (EPM 5.17). Hume sets out his account of our moral sentiments, that is, of what he generally terms our moral "approbation" and "disapprobation," in stages. He first shows the importance of sympathy for our preference for utility, and then shows how sympathy serves as the foundation of the moral sentiments. The discussion in the beginning of Section 5 suggests that Hume thinks moral philosophers tend to associate utility with moral skepticism. A skeptic like Mandeville, for instance, thinks that morality is an invention of politicians. Clever politicians persuade us to attach praise to those actions that promote and maintain social order. Hume notes, however, that in common life most of us appeal to utility and think of morality as something real. He asks us to consider an analogy between the virtuous character and those features of the environment or human inventions that make life more comfortable for us. We praise the fertile field, the well-built house, and the virtuous character for very similar reasons: each possesses qualities that make it useful for an individual or society in general. Like the fertile field, the virtuous person has "a natural beauty" that we find pleasing even if it provides no direct benefit for us. That is, we take a disinterested pleasure in the natural beauty exhibited in the actions of the virtuous character.

It is our capacity for sympathy that explains our disinterested admiration and blame. Hume insists that usefulness is a tendency to an end, and what tends to the end cannot affect our sentiments unless we also care about the end. In the case of character, the useful quality is indeed useful for somebody: for the agent herself in some cases, or for particular others, or for the interests of society. The useful virtues tend to promote well-being, prevent harm, or alleviate distress. Sympathy makes us care about the interests of others and of society generally.

Now we should note that in addition to the term *sympathy*, Hume also uses the terms *humanity* and *general benevolence* to refer to the capacity that explains why we tend to be pleased by others' happiness or pained by their misery.[5] Linking together *general benevolence* and *sympathy* is a departure from the association-ist account of the principle of sympathy that Hume gave in the *Treatise* (EPM App. 2.5, n.60). Some scholars have thought that, in the *Enquiry*, Hume's references to general benevolence signal that he is being more conciliatory toward Hutcheson's moral sense theory, which puts benevolence squarely at the center of morality.[6] There are, however, substantive differences between Hume's view in the *Enquiry* and Hutcheson's position. First, Hume indicates in the *Enquiry* that sympathy functions, as it did in the *Treatise*, as a principle of communication. That is, sympathy is the means by which we communicate our passions and sentiments to one another.

---

[5] Hume also uses the terms "general concern" and "natural philanthropy" (see EPM 5.16, 40).

[6] See L. A. Selby-Bigge, who writes that "in the Enquiry sympathy is another name for social feeling... rather than the name of a process [as it was in the *Treatise*] by which the social feeling has been constructed out of non-social or individual feeling," "Introduction," in *Hume's Enquiries* (Oxford: Clarendon Press, 1975; first published 1888), xxvi. Selby-Bigge concludes that the ethics of the *Enquiry* is virtually indistinguishable from Hutcheson's moral sense theory. See also Nicholas Capaldi, *Hume's Place in Moral Philosophy* (New York: Peter Lang, 1989). John Stewart argues that Hume has not revised his views of either sympathy or benevolence in the *Enquiry*. Rather, he says less about sympathy because he no longer aims to provide an account of the origin of the moral sentiments. See John B. Stewart, *The Moral and Political Philosophy of David Hume* (New York: Columbia University Press, 1963), especially pp. 328–39.

Second, Hume's notion of general benevolence is closer to what Hutcheson means by a public sense than to any of the forms of benevolence the latter describes. I will expand on these two points in turn.

Hume gives several examples of the communication of our passions or sentiments through sympathy (see EPM 5.26, 29, 38). Sometimes this happens as a kind of contagion; an example is our tendency to feel happy simply by being around a cheerful person (EPM 7.2). In the *Treatise,* sympathy was also referred to as a principle of the imagination that works analogously to custom: sympathy conveys what Hume calls the "liveliness" of the impression of self to an idea we have of another's emotion or sentiment, thereby transforming that idea into the same emotion that the other person feels. This earlier explanation of how sympathy works depended on Hume's associationist theory to which he makes only a brief appeal in the second *Enquiry.* Nevertheless, Hume suggests in the *Enquiry* that he still regards sympathy as a principle of the imagination, and that we typically first form an idea of another's emotion (see EPM 6.3, n.26; EPM 8.15). Our sympathetic response to others is more lively or intense when the situation is physically close to us, or is brought closer through, for example, skillful storytelling. As in the *Treatise,* sympathy is not itself any particular feeling, but explains why we respond sympathetically to a broad range of emotions: "no passion, when well represented, can be entirely indifferent to us; because there is none, of which every man has not, within him, at least the seeds and first principles." We can be swayed by others' opinions or sentiments, both good and bad. Hume specifically takes note of the "less laudable effects of this social sympathy" in producing "popular sedition, party zeal," and factions (EPM 5.30, 35). As noted above, the detailed account of sympathy in the *Treatise* relied on the principles of association. First, I infer that someone is experiencing some emotion or other by her behavior or from her situation, and because she resembles me, some of the liveliness of the conception I have of myself is transferred to the idea of the person's emotion so that I come to feel that very emotion. Second, in morally evaluating a person's character, we sympathize with the effects of it on the agent or her associates, that is, with their responses, which will include a range of feelings and attitudes such as love, gratitude, hatred, or contempt, and it is from my sympathy with their pleasures or pains that I in turn experience moral approbation or blame toward the person's character. Since Hume gives a different account of moral evaluation and the standard of virtue in the second *Enquiry* (see the next section), we have reason to think he saw as problematic the associationist account of sympathy and moral evaluation. In the *Enquiry*, he no longer appeals to association to explain sympathy, and at one place writes

It is needless to push our researches so far as to ask, why we have humanity or a fellow-feeling with others. It is sufficient, that this is experienced to be a principle in human nature. We must stop somewhere in our examination of causes; and there are, in every science, some general principles, beyond which we cannot hope to find any principle more general.... It is not probable, that these principles can be resolved into principles more simple and universal, whatever attempts may have been made to that purpose. (EPM 5.17, n.19)

It is a brute fact of our nature that we take an interest in others and are responsive to them, and that we can be influenced by their opinions and feelings.

Hume argues that it is obvious that sympathy exerts as strong a force in our lives as does self-interest. Sympathy is not merely a real or imagined self-interest, but makes it impossible for us to be completely indifferent to the concerns of others. We need only to think of our reactions to drama or poetry where we enter into the passions of fictional characters. The news from distant states, especially when it centers on tragedy or is presented to us vividly, engages our compassion for complete strangers. The same principle explains the genuine feelings we have for historical figures. Most of us naturally see ourselves as sociable creatures, taking pleasure from friendships and company, and losing out on enjoyment if we are condemned to solitude. Perhaps most telling are those occasions when self-interest and morality diverge, and yet we still feel approval for, or recognize as praiseworthy, the virtues of those who oppose us (EPM 5.17). It thus seems a weak and implausible "subterfuge" to claim that our approbation of the distant virtuous character depends on our imagining ourselves as the beneficiaries of her virtue. It is far more plausible and consistent with our experience to concede that we just do admire useful or agreeable traits of character, and blame harmful and disagreeable traits.

So what are we to make of the *Enquiry's* linking of sympathy with the sentiments of humanity and benevolence? I think we can get clearer on this by comparing Hume's view with that of Hutcheson, since some scholars claim that Hume moves closer to the latter's view. Hutcheson recognizes four distinct internal senses: that of imagination (or the aesthetic sense); the public sense, which is most like Hume's principle of sympathy; the moral sense; and the sense of honor. The public sense explains our tendency to be pleased by the happiness of others and pained by their misery. There is nothing inherently moral about this tendency, and Hutcheson notes that it often operates in people without their giving any thought to virtue or vice. The moral sense is an independent internal sense that responds to kind or unkind affection. Hutcheson also distinguishes between particular benevolence and what he calls general calm benevolence. We act from particular benevolence in response to a situation calling for compassion, friendship, gratitude, or one of the other benevolent motives. General benevolence, in contrast, is a general calm desire for the good of particular persons or societies. Hutcheson recognizes yet a third kind of benevolence, universal calm benevolence, which is directed toward the species in general. Particular benevolence (including calm particular benevolence) neither necessarily arises from nor presupposes universal benevolence; in fact, we often find that people have particular benevolent affections but ("through want of reflection") possess neither universal nor general benevolence. All three forms of benevolence, particular, general, and universal, count as virtues for Hutcheson, with universal benevolence being the most esteemed.[7]

In the *Enquiry*, Hume distinguishes between two kinds of benevolence, general and particular. We act from particular benevolence, as we saw earlier, when we are kind, grateful, compassionate, charitable, and the like, toward particular other persons. Particular benevolence motivates us to act on behalf of another, or take an attitude of concern toward someone, and is always virtuous. In contrast, when Hume talks in the *Enquiry* about *general* benevolence or

---

[7] See Francis Hutcheson, *An Essay on the Nature and Conduct of the Passions and Affections, with Illustrations on the Moral Sense,* ed. Aaron Garrett (Indianapolis: Liberty Fund, 2002), Sect. II.

sympathy, he clearly means something like Hutcheson's public sense. That is, sympathy makes us tend to feel glad about others' happiness or pained by their misery, and it is not any active desire, even a calm or general one, to promote others' well-being or express an attitude such as gratitude that would strengthen our relationship to them. General benevolence commonly operates in those cases where "we have no friendship or connexion or esteem for the person, but feel only a general sympathy with him or a compassion for his pains, and a congratulation with his pleasures" (EPM App. 2, n.60). General benevolence or sympathy is our sensitivity and responsiveness to the emotions or interests of others, rather than a motive to action. As Hume puts it, our sympathetic responsiveness need be nothing more than "a cool preference of what is useful and serviceable to mankind, above what is pernicious and dangerous" (EPM 9.4). There may be nothing particularly moral about sympathy, as when emotions are communicated as if by contagion. Yet, as we shall see below, we can cultivate a more delicate sympathy or sense of humanity, which is itself a virtue. Moreover, and in contrast to Hutcheson's view, Hume thinks that without sympathy or general benevolence to render us sensitive to the happiness or misery of others, we would neither perceive moral distinctions such as virtue and vice, nor respond to them with moral approbation or disapprobation (EPM 5.39).

Nevertheless, one wishes that Hume had been clearer about the exact nature of the relationship between sympathy and humanity on the one hand, and the moral sentiments on the other. In at least one place he suggests that our sympathetic concern for the happiness and misery of society, as these are affected by virtuous or vicious character traits, *is the same as* the moral sentiment: our sympathetic preference for the useful above the harmful is a distinction "the same in all its parts, with the *moral distinction*, whose foundation has been so often, and so much in vain, enquired after." The suggestion is that since utility is a source of merit, then our sympathetic preference for a useful character trait is the same as our moral approbation of it. Hume concludes from this line of reasoning "that these sentiments are originally the same" (EPM 6.5). Yet this conclusion introduces some ambiguity. The text suggests two possible readings, although these are not incompatible with one another.

On the one hand, Hume could mean that the origin of our natural preference for the useful character trait and our moral approbation of the trait is the same. Both have their origin in our capacity for sympathy. This interpretation is consistent with Hume's aim of showing that the moral sentiments are not the deliverances of an innate moral sense (as they are for Hutcheson). Rather, the moral sentiments are reflection-informed responses that correct the influence of interest and imaginative propensities such as favoring what is close over what is remote. On the other hand, Hume might mean that originally, in some earlier stage of the moral development of human society, a natural sympathetic preference for what one perceived as useful or harmful constituted moral approbation or blame. Hume suggests something like this in Section 9 when he writes "a rude, untaught savage regulates chiefly his love and hatred by the ideas of private utility and injury, and has but faint conceptions of a general rule or system of behaviour.... But we, accustomed to society, and to more enlarged reflections, consider, that this man [our enemy] is serving his own country and community.... And by these suppositions and views, we correct, in some measure, our ruder and narrower passions" (EPM 9, n.57). That is, as human society develops and expands, we learn to sympathize with more general preferences, rather than with private or partial ones.

Notice that on either reading, sympathy is the source of the moral sentiments, but those sentiments must be corrected or cultivated. And in either case, we may safely say that sympathy is the source or foundation of the moral sentiments. At one point Hume claims that sympathy always has "*some* authority" over our moral sentiments. Without sympathy, we would be indifferent to moral distinctions such as virtue and vice. For example, someone of "cold insensibility...unaffected with the images of human happiness or misery...must be equally indifferent to the images of vice and virtue." Similarly, an absolutely malicious creature "must be worse than indifferent to the images of vice and virtue," and his sentiments must be "directly opposite to those, which prevail in the human species." Hence, our sympathetic concern for the happiness and misery of society, as these are affected by useful or harmful character traits, is "a principle, which accounts, in great part, for the origin of morality" (EPM 5.39–40, 17).

IV. SYMPATHY, SENTIMENT, AND JUDGMENT

In both the *Treatise* and the *Enquiry*, Hume draws attention to the natural partiality of sympathy and to the means by which we correct it. Just as particular benevolence makes us care more about particular other persons, sympathy tends naturally to follow our particular affections and so itself exhibits partiality. We naturally sympathize easily with the people to whom we have special ties such as those of family, friendship, or nationality. Our sympathy tends to be less engaged when we are considering cases distant from us in time or place. So a question arises about how the moral sentiments can be grounded in sympathy if sympathy varies. In cases where partiality or nearness influence sympathy, we judge that two characters are the same, even if we *feel* more strongly about the one closest to us. That judgment "corrects the inequalities of our internal emotions" (EPM 5.41). We make a similar correction when our sentiments are aroused by the actual consequences of someone's action instead of the character trait that motivated it. For example, suppose someone who is well-off performs generous actions simply to have people think well of her, rather than out of a concern for others' well-being. Hume notes that we must separate "the character from the fortune, by an easy and necessary effort of thought," and assess the character rather than the results (EPM 5.41, n.24). The person in our example is unlikely to act generously when such a response is needed, or to be appropriately sensitive to what others most need. Erratic, ill-timed, or inappropriate instances of giving are not the actions of a generous character (although they may suggest the person is trying to cultivate generosity).

In both texts Hume's explanation focuses on how we establish a "standard of virtue." The standard of virtue is the standard to which our sentiments should conform if they are to be accepted as appropriate moral responses of praise or blame. But the account of how we establish the standard of virtue differs in the two texts. In the *Treatise* we *extend* our sympathy to take up the point of view of those who are affected by an agent's character. Hume asserts that the responses of those in the agent's sphere are more constant than our own variable responses, and so they comprise the standard of virtue by which we calibrate our approbation and disapprobation

(T 3.3.1.18, 30). One problem with this strategy is those in the agent's sphere might themselves respond to her character with a natural partiality or a pernicious bias, and Hume offers no explanation of how we might distinguish between appropriate and inappropriate responses.[8]

In the *Enquiry*, Hume does not appeal to sympathy with someone's circle of associates as the means for establishing the standard of virtue. While the *Treatise* mentions the importance of conversation, the *Enquiry* places the emphasis more squarely on language and shared conversation about what is useful or harmful. It is through conversation with one another that we form "a general standard of vice and virtue, founded chiefly on general usefulness" (EPM 5.42, n.25). Hume here distinguishes between the language of self-love and the language of morality. For example, "when a man denominates another his *enemy*, his *rival*," he uses the language of self-love, and expresses how things look to him from the perspective of his private interest. In conversing with others, we become "familiarized" to the more general preferences and interests of the community. We "invent a peculiar set of terms, in order to express those universal sentiments of censure or approbation, which arise from humanity." With moral terminology in place, "VIRTUE and VICE become then known: Morals are recognized: Certain general ideas are framed of human conduct and behaviour" (EPM 9.6, 8). We learn to affix praise or blame to actions and characters in conformity to these shared moral sentiments. And we use the language of virtue and vice, of approbation and blame, with the expectation that others will agree with our assessments. Shared reflection on general preferences leads to a shared moral discourse, grounded in our common humanity, and renders us "intelligible to each other" (EPM 5.42).

We can now consider the relation between moral sentiment, or "taste," and reason. Hume stresses the positive contribution of each faculty, and he suggests that the person in whom the two faculties are working together properly will possess the virtues of good evaluation. To be sure, it is this internal "feeling, which nature has made universal in the whole species," rather than truth-discovering

---

[8] I develop more fully the argument that Hume sets out a different and better set of criteria for the standard of virtue, that is, for good moral judgment or evaluation, in "Hume on the Standard of Virtue," *Journal of Ethics* 6 (2002): 43–62.

reason, that "renders morality an active principle" (EPM 1.9). But as we have just seen, our moral sentiments do not reflect merely idiosyncratic or individual preferences. Our conversations about general preferences will invoke reflection on past experience to establish which stable traits of character tend over time to promote the happiness of the agent or others. Similarly, the "due medium" of any character trait is determined by considerations of utility and by reflecting on the consequences of having too much or too little of the quality (EPM 6.2). The "bounds of duty" with respect to the actions and practices that exhibit particular traits are also determined with reference to what is most useful for the interests of society. For example, we need to ascertain which instances of giving really do some good, and which extinguish the independence of the recipient, and thus are done from weakness rather than from virtue. The "boundaries of moral good and evil" are thus adjustable as we learn more about how to promote the interests of society, or as social circumstances shift (EPM 2.17–18).

In Section 1 Hume specifically appeals to the elements of good reasoning: "in order to pave the way for such a sentiment, and give a proper discernment of its object, it is often necessary, we find, that much reasoning should precede, that nice distinctions be made, just conclusions drawn, distant comparisons formed, complicated relations examined, and general facts fixed and ascertained." While some forms of "taste" remain unsusceptible to the evidence of reason, our moral taste "demands the assistance of our intellectual faculties" if it is to have a proper influence on the mind (EPM 1.9). Hume repeats the point in the first Appendix, insisting that an "accurate *reason* or *judgment*" must inform our sentiment-based responses (EPM, App. 1.2).

While it is clear that some people will be better moral evaluators than others, Hume suggests that the cultivation of good reasoning is often a collective endeavor that takes place through active debate and discourse. Sometimes we need good reasoning to make sense of complex moral situations: to gather and sort through the relevant facts, to make the right sort of distinctions, to compare the current case to past situations, and so on. In other cases it is difficult to figure out just which motives, actions, or social policies and practices really will tend to the best interests of society. It is especially difficult to make assessments concerning utility in the case of justice. Hume appeals to the importance of the "debates of civilians; the reflections of politicians; the precedents of history and public records" to guide our assessments of the tendencies of particular laws or policies (EPM App. 1.2).[9] Yet since there is no antecedent fact of the matter about such things as property rights or contracts, lawmakers and judges must often exercise "taste and imagination" where no precedent or positive law exists to guide them (EPM App. 3.10). Thus while appropriate moral sentiments must be informed by reason and reflection, so also are taste and imagination sometimes needed to supplement reason.

Hume thus makes the case for the virtues of good evaluation: "a warm concern for the interest of our species"; a "delicate feeling of all moral distinctions"; an "accurate reason or judgment"; and the "enlarged reflections" acquired through moral conversation. In general, debate and conversation increase our awareness of and sensitivity to the complexities of moral situations: "the more we habituate ourselves to an accurate scrutiny of morals, the more delicate feeling do we acquire of the most minute distinctions between vice and virtue" (EPM 5.39, App. 1.2, 5.14). With a sufficient number of good judges, our sense of morality displays "the force of many sympathies." By "surveying ourselves" and keeping "in review" our own character and conduct, a concern for our own reputation as well as for the welfare of others becomes "the surest guardian of every virtue" (EPM 9.10–11).

V. THE SCOPE OF MERIT

The second part of Section 6 and the fourth Appendix of the *Enquiry* contain arguments that Hume had presented in two of the final sections of the *Treatise*. These arguments are meant to establish, first, that sympathy is the source of our admiration of whatever it is about a person that contributes to her own interests or those of others. So our admiration of natural talents, wealth, bodily endowments, and beauty (and our disdain for the opposite qualities) has the same

[9] Civilians were those who commented on the laws of societies. Two civilians with whose work Hume was familiar are Hugo Grotius, author of *On the Law of War and Peace* (1625), and Samuel Pufendorf, author of *On the Law of Nature and of Nations* (1672).

source in sympathy as does our moral admiration of virtue. Second, Hume argues that all of the mental qualities, including talents and self-regarding qualities, and not merely the social qualities usually styled virtues, are on the same footing insofar as they contribute to assessments of an individual's "personal merit." In the *Enquiry*, Hume pointedly directs these arguments against dogmatic theological moralists. But we should also notice that Hume's argument differs markedly from that of moral sense theorists such as Hutcheson and Shaftesbury. Sympathy makes it possible to find pleasing, and hence to ascribe merit to, a broad range of qualities in addition to benevolence. Our moral sentiments, Hume suggests, do not derive from an innate moral sense, but are forms of the natural sympathetic responses that we cultivate and correct in conversation with one another.

Throughout the *Enquiry*, Hume has focused on "personal merit" rather than more narrowly on "virtue." He has considered all the qualities of mind in which someone might take pride on reviewing her character and conduct. In addition to the social virtues or qualities of the "heart," such as benevolence, Hume includes as virtues self-regarding qualities, such as industriousness, and qualities of the "head" or talents, such as wit or perseverance. We also praise involuntary qualities, those qualities that people may not be able to achieve through their own efforts. Some involuntary qualities we might typically think of as gifts of fortune, including, for example, wit or eloquence. But Hume also thinks that some qualities we regard as typical virtues may be involuntary. For example, we might disapprove of the fearful or impatient person despite his efforts to cultivate courage or patience. Some virtues, such as magnanimity, require that one occupy a certain social station, something that often lies beyond the control of most people. The qualities of courage, patience, and magnanimity are useful or agreeable, so we admire them and deplore their opposites. Hume observes that the ancient moralists paid little regard to the distinction between voluntary and involuntary, and included all the laudable qualities of mind among the virtues. Our use of language in modern times shows that we do the same (EPM, App. 4.2, 11–20).

Remarking on the broad range of qualities that can contribute to a person's merit, Hume writes that he has represented "virtue in all her genuine and most engaging charms" so that the "dismal dress falls off, with which many divines, and some philosophers have covered her." First, he recognizes self-regarding qualities as important components of merit and demerit. In contrast to the habits of self-denial (the "monkish virtues") advocated by these divines, Hume has championed the self-regarding qualities that help individuals advance in the world and live well (EPM 9.15, 3). Indeed, he has all along emphasized that cultivating both the self-regarding and the social virtues enhances a person's reputation. Benevolence is "more essentially requisite," for example, in those with "ordinary talents" and who lack wealth or influence (EPM 2.3). And as we saw earlier, Hume argues in Section 9 that looking at the four different categories of virtue from the perspective of our long-term interest shows that the "agreeable sentiment, a pleasing consciousness, a good reputation" that come with the cultivation of virtue establish our "interested *obligation* to it" (EPM 9.21, 14).

In addition, Hume notes that our languages mark no precise boundary between *talents* and virtues. This is because our internal sentiments of praise or blame, pride or shame, make little or no distinction between the different kinds of qualities that contribute to or detract from personal merit. Attention to language also helps Hume to make his case against a theological morality. "Divines" in the guise of philosophers pay little regard to "the phenomena of nature, or to the unbiassed sentiments of the mind, hence reasoning, and even language, have been warped from their natural course." The theological moralists want to designate as virtues only those qualities that people can acquire voluntarily, but they make the error of "treating all morals, as on a like footing with civil laws, guarded by the sanctions of reward and punishment." Hume argues that "speculative philosophers" (in contrast to "moralists" who see their task as that of exhorting us to virtue) should see the ancient philosophers as having an advantage over at least those moderns who want to narrow the scope of morality and thereby exclude the sentiments of praise and blame that we experience in daily life (EPM, App. 4.21).

But does Hume's broadening of the scope of merit turn out to be a problem for his moral theory? How can the account of a sympathy-based moral sentiment provide the means of clearly distinguishing our estimation of "mental endowments" from our estimation of physical endowments and external advantages such as wealth? Sympathy is the common source of our various forms of disapproval, and

Hume writes that "a blemish, a fault, a vice, a crime; these expressions seem to denote different degrees of censure and disapprobation; which are, however, all of them, at the bottom, pretty nearly of the same kind or species" (EPM, App. 4.22). Sympathy also grounds our admiration of whatever we find pleasing about a person, whether a mental or a physical quality, and whether the quality is voluntarily acquired or a matter of fortune. We esteem the physically beautiful, wealthy, and powerful, as well as the virtuous. Yet Hume claims that we can separate such expressions of esteem when directed toward someone because of his or her wealth or social standing, from the sentiments of esteem we direct toward someone's character. For example, he writes that someone who values virtue over wealth "may, indeed, externally pay a superior deference to the great lord above the vassal; because riches are the most convenient, being the most fixed and determinate, source of distinction: But his internal sentiments are more regulated by the personal characters of men, than by the accidental and capricious favours of fortune" (EPM 6.34). But are our estimations of character so easily separated from our admiration of the other valuable qualities or advantages people possess? Hume's inclusion as meritorious the immediately agreeable qualities of genteelness, decency, cleanliness, and good manners – qualities most likely to be found in those among the higher social ranks – suggests that someone's social standing does inform our conception of the person's character as well as our ethical attitudes toward him. In the *Treatise* and in some of his essays, Hume spends more time discussing how someone's social standing affects our perceptions of the person's character. Indeed, in the *Treatise* the more detailed discussion of sympathy is put to use to explain how we acquire skills of social discrimination and how we tend to ascribe qualities to one another on the basis of social standing. That is, the generalizations we form on the basis of social categories inform our recognition and ascription of character traits. It may thus not be possible to locate purely ethical forms of praise and blame that are independent from our everyday discourse of respect or contempt.

VI. THE VARIABILITY OF MERIT

In discussing the scope of merit, Hume notes several times that the hesitation about including talents as meritorious qualities indicates at most a verbal dispute, and he advises that "it is of greater consequence to attend to things than to verbal appellations" (EPM, App. 4.22). This suggests that if we rely on our corrected responses of praise or admiration to useful or agreeable qualities as recommendations of merit, then we will reach broad agreement on which agreeable qualities belong in the "catalogue" of virtues and which disagreeable ones belong in the "catalogue" of vices (EPM 1.10). In one sense this is true. Hume identifies a universal feature of morality that transcends cultures or historical ages, namely, the sentiment of praise directed toward useful and agreeable qualities, and of blame toward qualities with the opposite tendencies. But Hume's answer about which qualities we find useful or agreeable, and their opposites, is more complicated. One of the most interesting aspects of the *Enquiry*, not present in the *Treatise*, is the attention Hume gives to cultural and historical variability in the qualities, actions, and practices that we find praiseworthy or blameworthy. This issue of historical and cultural variability is the focal point of "A Dialogue," the short work appended to the *Enquiry*. It is also a theme in several of Hume's essays.

We should first notice that Hume is attentive, as he was in the *Treatise*, to variation *within* a particular society. This kind of variation typically corresponds to the different social roles people have: for example, to a person's "station" (what we think of as socioeconomic class), "sex" (akin to our notion of gender), age, or profession. The variation in question may relate to the *degree* of a virtue a person is expected to have, or to a difference with respect to *which* virtues someone should have. Modesty, for example, is an important virtue for everyone, but at the time Hume was writing it was one especially important for women and young men. The expectation would be that women and young men show a greater degree of modesty than other people. There are also qualities or virtues that we expect to find in some individuals rather than others. For example, Hume identifies chastity as important for women, courage for soldiers, and discretion for politicians. We esteem the person who has the talents and qualities "which suit his station and profession" more "than he whom fortune has misplaced in the part which she has assigned him." Although as Hume notes, "he is more excellent, who can suit his temper to any circumstances" (EPM 6.20, 9).

We may sometimes regard historical changes in customs and laws as another kind of intracultural variation. Tyrannicide, for example, was "highly extolled" in ancient times, because it was almost the only means available for dealing with oppressive regimes. We, however, have learned from "history and experience" that this method produces tyrants who are more cruel (EPM 2.19). In Section 6, Hume argues that the ancients valued memory, physical strength, and courage more than do the moderns because of the circumstances of their way of life: a focus on oratory, rather than writing, made memory important, while in a martial or heroic society strength and courage were of greater value than many other qualities (EPM 6.19, 26). In contrast, the conventions of justice and the resulting stability of modern times enable industry and the arts to flourish. Such stability also allows us to form "enlarged reflections" about the general preferences of society, and these stand in contrast to the private or "narrower" ideas of utility held by those in martial or less complex societies (EPM 9.1, n.57). By learning how to make our moral sentiments more general we can apply praise and blame more uniformly across the boundaries of family, tribe, or nation. Hume suggests that we can here regard ourselves as the inheritors of a common past from which we have learned and can learn more.

The differences in values between cultures, and the implications of intercultural differences for the nature of morality (is it relative or universal), form the main topic of "A Dialogue." The dialogue takes place between Palamedes and an unnamed narrator, and begins with Palamedes describing a country called Fourli in which the values of the inhabitants are "diametrically opposite" to those of the eighteenth-century British. This country attaches positive value to practices such as homosexuality, incest, suicide, and parricide, and to actions that we would describe as treachery, perjury, and infidelity. The narrator, hardly believing Palamedes, asserts that "such barbarous and savage manners" are incompatible with "a civilized, intelligent people," and perhaps even with human nature (D 2, 12). Palamedes then reveals that he has been talking about ancient Greece, apparently the favorite culture of the narrator, and one of which Palamedes himself is highly critical. The narrator in turn describes a culture in which adultery, betrayal, dueling, and torture are praised rather than blamed. He is speaking, as Palamedes guesses, of eighteenth-century France.

This dialogue raises several issues about moral relativism. With respect to ancient Greece, the issue of relativism is in part about a "relativism of distance"[10] – about, that is, an older way of life with which we can have no actual encounter, and that is not (at least not in its entirety) a viable option for us. We can be critical of past moralities and ways of living, but our criticism cannot reform *their* values. According to the narrator, we need to try to understand the customs and manners of different ages, and to judge past ages by their own standards rather than by our own. Contemporary comparisons raise different and more general questions. How deep do the differences between societies run? What explains these differences? What explains any commonality that might exist between the different societies of the world, past or present? The two characters in the dialogue consider answers to these questions. Palamedes speculates that there may be no commonality, and urges that "fashion, vogue, custom, and law" are "the chief foundation of all moral determinations." The narrator takes a contrary view, arguing at length, that we must trace matters higher in order to examine "the first principles, which each nation establishes, of blame or censure." Even if customs and manners differ, such qualities as knowledge, friendship, courage, and honor are always valued. And, consistently with the arguments in the *Enquiry*, these qualities are said to be valued precisely because they are useful or agreeable, either to the person possessing them or to others. So all differences in morals "may be reduced to this one general foundation, and may be accounted for by the different views, which people take of these circumstances" (D 25–6, 37).

According to the narrator, the same moral sentiments of praise for what is useful or agreeable, and blame for the contrary comprise universally the foundation of morals. This argument admits, however, of two important qualifications. The first concerns the significance of the fact that the different circumstances (customs and laws, for example) of different societies may mean that the conception of character traits, and an understanding of how they are manifested in

---

[10] I take the term "relativism of distance" from Bernard Williams, *Ethics and the Limits of Philosophy* (Cambridge, MA: Harvard University Press, 1984), 162.

virtuous behavior, will vary. The second concerns the difficulty for both societies and individuals to reconcile or achieve all the good ends of life.

In the language of recent social theory, social institutions, including familial, economic, political, and religious institutions, are ways of organizing human activities which generate practices that sustain these activities and their related ways of life. Hume appeals to custom to explain the same sort of phenomena. The ancient custom of infanticide may be explained by scarcity and an unwillingness to raise a child in poverty, while some of the ancient marriages that we would deem incestuous simply reflect the boundaries set on intimate relations by the Greeks, in contrast to those we ourselves set. Thus, the caring parent of ancient Greece acts quite differently from the caring parent of modern times, and the notion of a faithful spouse differs between ancient and modern times. Nonetheless, parental care and spousal fidelity are valued in both cultures (D 29–30).[11]

Since customs and manners vary between societies, they also produce different views about which qualities are useful or agreeable, and consequently have moral merit (EPM 6.20). In several of his essays, as well as in "A Dialogue," Hume argues that the form of a society's government structures to a great extent the opportunities available to its members, and exerts an influence on the qualities that are valued.[12] In a monarchy, politeness and the arts are at the fore, whereas a republic tends to foster industry and scientific advance. Politeness corresponds to the stricter social hierarchy typical of monarchies, whereas republics promote relatively generous civil liberties. Through the narrator, Hume takes note of several "peculiar circumstances" (is a nation at war or enjoying peace? is it politically united or divided? has it an abundance of material resources or does it face scarcity? are its people educated or ignorant?), each of which can vary the sense and utility of some actions and qualities. He also observes that how women are treated, whether they have an active and essential role in business and "mutual discourse," or are excluded "from all social commerce," is "the most

---

[11] Hume gives a more negative assessment of the ancient practice of infanticide in his essay "Of the Populousness of Ancient Nations"; see E-PA 398–400.

[12] Hume argues the case at some length in an early essay "Of the Rise and Progress of the Arts and Sciences," and it is also a theme in "Of Refinement in the Arts."

material" difference occurring in the domestic sphere and produces "the greatest variation in our moral sentiments" (D 38, 43).[13]

This brings us to the second consideration about the relativity of virtue and morals. As we have just noted, one of the natural effects of different customs is a preference for certain virtues over others. Although we may identify a number of good ends and advantages in life that cultivating a virtuous character helps one to achieve, Hume argues that circumstances may render one quality or, more typically, one set of qualities more valuable than another. Eighteenth-century French society, with its strong norms of politeness, stresses the agreeable qualities over the useful, whereas the British esteem more a man who is useful to himself and his society. Chance also plays a role in what opportunities are available to people, since we have no choice about the society into which we are born. Even in a well-ordered and pluralistic society, individuals cannot achieve every advantage in life. In choosing some ends, we invariably sacrifice others. Despite these variations with respect to virtue and vice both within and between cultures, the narrator of "A Dialogue" maintains that the customs and manners that produce them "vary not the original ideas of merit . . . in any very essential point" (D 51). It is the moral sentiments that favor the useful and agreeable that are the chief foundation of all moral determinations, and not the variable customs and manners that embody more particular views about which qualities, actions, and practices are useful or agreeable.

VII. LANGUAGE AND MORAL SENTIMENT

We have seen that in the second *Enquiry* Hume makes several important claims about the relation between language and moral sentiment. Moral language, particularly the terms we use to praise or blame character traits, is "moulded upon" our sentiments of praise of useful and agreeable qualities, and blame of harmful and disagreeable ones (EPM 9.8). The language of morals is thus distinct from that of private interest. In turn, we employ the moral terminology

---

[13] Hume pursues the theme of the treatment of women in the essays as well as in the *Treatise*. See the important discussions in *Treatise* 3.1.12, "Of chastity," and in his essays "Of the Rise and Progress of the Arts and Sciences" and "Of Polygamy and Divorces."

of common life, and especially the terms we use to name character traits or mental qualities, to guide philosophical investigation into the general principles and foundation of morality. An examination of one set of moral terms, those connected with benevolence, establishes the fact that human nature includes other-regarding motives, as well as self-interested ones. Finally, moral language is something in which we must *acquire* a competence. We find that our conversations with one another help us to improve in our discernment of virtue and vice.

Nevertheless, what Hume has to say about moral language in connection with the issues of cultural and historical variability threatens his claim that a common moral discourse renders us mutually intelligible to one another. At the beginning of "A Dialogue," Palamedes says that during his visit to Fourli he had to "submit to double pains; first to learn the meaning of the terms in their language, and then to know the import of those terms, and the praise or blame attached to them" (D 2). His claim highlights how both the description of a character trait and the value attaching to it can vary throughout history and across cultures.

Hume extends his discussion of this point in his 1757 essay, "Of the Standard of Taste." In this essay Hume claims, as he does in the *Enquiry*, that all cultures share the fundamentals of moral discourse, including terms of praise and blame, as well as the more particular terms that refer to the character traits and actions to which praise and blame are directed. So, for example, all cultures have terms, such as *shameful, honorable, admirable,* or *odious,* expressing praise or blame at a general level. We also find universally such terms as *virtue* and *vice,* terms that refer to praiseworthy or blameworthy character traits or actions. And all cultures appear to recognize and evaluate similar character traits, and use the same names (*prudence, honesty,* or *cowardice,* for example) for them. Moreover, a term such as *prudence* both refers to a trait of character that we can describe further *and* indicates some evaluative stance on our part (for example, admiration in the case of prudence). But Hume's attitude in this essay is really more skeptical than this account suggests. He argues that the "very nature of language," that is, the fact that our moral terms are translatable from one tongue to another, accounts for what is only a "seeming harmony." When we examine what various cultures mean by a particular trait term, we find that the description of the trait differs between cultures. Even the general terms *virtue* and *vice* admit of differences about which traits comprise admirable or blameable characters. Homer's description of Ulysses's prudence, for example, includes more "cunning and fraud" than does the description of that same character's prudence by the seventeenth-century writer Fénelon. What Homer and his fellow ancients admired, we may find reprehensible, although both ancients and moderns employ the same terms. If the meanings of our terms vary, then our use of a common moral discourse may not be evidence that we have a *shared* discourse. We may be *unintelligible* to one another unless we submit to the pains of understanding the cultural point of view of others (E-ST 3, 228).

Hume offers a bit more help with the issue of mutual intelligibility in "Of the Standard of Taste." Although what he says concerns aesthetic taste (or what he terms "criticism"), we may apply a similar point to morals. With respect to the "true standard of taste and beauty," the disagreement at issue is not about what is beautiful, but rather about who is a competent critic of beauty. A "true judge" is one who possesses the virtues relevant for judging well. Hume concedes that we may disagree about who has these virtues, yet says he really needs to prove only that all taste "is not upon an equal footing," and that some "will be acknowledged by universal sentiment to have a preference above others" (E-ST 23, 25; 241, 242). This is an interesting move, since, if we apply it to the case of morality, we can dismiss the need for a criterion (other than utility or agreeableness) for assessing the actions, attitudes, and practices of different cultures. We can instead maintain that it is the acquisition and exercise of the virtues of good judgment that yield apt evaluations of different moralities.

Of particular importance for evaluating the moralities of different cultures is the use of *"good sense"* to check the influence of prejudice on our moral sentiments (E-ST 22, 240). We must place ourselves in that point of view from which we can appreciate *as theirs* the "peculiar views and prejudices" of historically or culturally different communities (E-ST 21, 239). While we should not let the manners of our own culture pervert our sentiments, we may nevertheless be guided by what we take to be a modern improvement in moral values, namely, the cultivation of the sense of humanity and decency.[14] We may be "justly jealous" of a moral standard that values humane treatment and moral inclusion, and so in certain cases, whatever allowance we make for different ways of life, we will not let our sentiments be perverted by inhumanity (E-ST 31, 33; 246, 247).

Of course, disagreement about the descriptive content or valuation of trait terms can also occur *within* a society. As Hume was well aware, there may be within a society extreme factions that refuse to subscribe to the goal of mutual intelligibility. Members of a society may differ about the meaning of *patriotism* or *compassion*, for example. For the most part, though, these are issues to be worked out along the lines Hume has suggested, through a process of civil conversation and debate. In this respect, Hume's later moral philosophy, in the *Enquiry* and *Essays*, shows a maturity lacking in the earlier moral philosophy of the *Treatise*. The emphasis on the need to converse and even debate with others about what we find useful and agreeable, and on the virtues of good judgment, including good sense and humanity, suggests that Hume had developed a deep appreciation of the complexities of our moral sentiments and the influences on them. Hume recognized that the development of a universally shared morality will require great, and continuous, effort, but he is optimistic about the possibility of making this kind of moral progress.[15]

SUGGESTIONS FOR FURTHER READING

In addition to the works cited in the notes to this essay, for further reading the following are recommended.

General Background

Stewart, M. A. "Two Species of Philosophy: The Historical Significance of the First *Enquiry*." In *Reading Hume on Human Understanding*, edited by P. Millican. Oxford: Clarendon Press, 2002. 67–95.

---

[14] Hume pursues the theme of humanity as a modern concept in several essays; see, e.g., "Of the Populousness of Ancient Nations," "Of Refinement in the Arts," and "Of Polygamy and Divorces."

[15] I presented versions of this essay at the Southern California Philosophy Conference at UC Irvine in 2004, where Mark Collier commented, and at the Third International Reid Symposium at the University of Aberdeen in 2004.

On Virtue, Moral Evaluation, and Deliberation

Baier, Annette C. *"Enquiry concerning the Principles of Morals:* Incomparably the Best?" In *A Companion to Hume*, edited by E. S. Radcliffe. Oxford: Blackwell Publishing, 2008.

Falk, W. D. "Hume on Practical Reason." *Philosophical Studies* 27 (1975): 1–18.

On Sympathy

Abramson, Kate. "Sympathy and the Project of Hume's Second *Inquiry.*" *Archiv für Geschichte der Philosophie* 83 (2001): 45–80.

Debes, Remy. "Humanity, Sympathy and the Puzzle of Hume's Second *Enquiry.*" *British Journal for the History of Philosophy* 15 (2007): 27–57.

Vitz, Rico. "Sympathy and Benevolence in Hume's Moral Psychology." *Journal of the History of Philosophy* 42 (2004): 261–75.

On the Sensible Knave

Baier, Annette C. "Artificial Virtues and the Equally Sensible Non-Knaves: A Response to Gauthier." *Hume Studies* 18 (Nov. 1992): 429–40.

Gauthier, David. "Artificial Virtues and the Sensible Knave." *Hume Studies* 18 (Nov. 1992): 401–28.

On "A Dialogue"

Mazza, Emilio. "Cannibals in *A dialogue* (in Search of a Standard for Morals)." In *Instruction and Amusement: Le ragioni dell'Illuminismo britannico*, edited by E. Mazza and E. Ronchetti. Milan: Il Poligrafo (2005). 45–66.

11 The Structure of Hume's Political Theory

David Hume believed that most of the views about society and politics prevalent in his day had roots in one or another of "two species of false religion," *superstition* and *enthusiasm*. Both were developments of conflicting theological doctrines that appealed to two different types of personalities. Both had come to be associated with opposing political interests. Both sprang from ignorance. And, while the two species had been universally present in society and in individuals in varying degrees throughout history, the peculiarity of modern post-Reformation Europe was the violent oscillation between them, as evidenced by the many wars of religion. Their more extreme adherents were also, not least, responsible for the plight of modern Britain, both north and south. One of the tasks of the philosophical historian, Hume believed, was to explain the preponderance at particular times of one or the other of these persuasions. The task he set for his political theory was to explain why both were philosophically misconceived, empirically untenable, and, in their extreme forms, politically dangerous.

I. THE POLITICS OF RELIGION

One part of humanity, Hume notes, has a tendency to "weakness, fear, [and] melancholy, together with ignorance." In this state the imagination conjures up forces operating under the surface, and the mind is prone to grasp methods of influencing these forces by "ceremonies, observances, mortifications, sacrifices, presents, or [by] any practice, however absurd or frivolous which either folly or knavery recommends to a blind and terrified credulity." This condition and these practices Hume calls *superstition*. In religion, priests, church

341

establishments, and rituals are used to mediate between the individual and these forces. In society and in politics, the superstitious person is disposed to accept established forms and powers as inherent in the nature of things and to see society as a hierarchical structure with a monarch as the unitary source of authority and sovereignty as a divine right (E-SE 2, 74).

In contrast, another part of humanity has a tendency to "hope, pride, presumption, [and] a warm imagination, together with ignorance." In this state, which Hume calls *enthusiasm*, individuals take flights of fancy from the real world, presume direct rapport with higher powers, and incline toward ungovernable self-assertion. In religion, priests, church establishments, and rituals are rejected. In society and politics, enthusiasts assert the rights of the individual. They often incline to forceful remodeling of authority and generally see self-government as the only proper government, at least in principle. Enthusiasts favor contractualist accounts of such authority as they will accept and insist on the protection of individual civil liberties (E-SE 3, 74).[1]

Hume's political theory is more than an outright rejection of such received ideas as those associated with superstition and enthusiasm. He meant his political writings to be also political *acts*, shaping the opinions or beliefs that in turn shaped politics and society. To achieve this end, he sought to provide a theory of the nature of social and political phenomena different from those that served to reinforce superstition and enthusiasm. On the one hand, he proceeds by analyzing those beliefs that in recent history had tended to modify the ideal types of superstition and enthusiasm; on the other hand, he argues that such analysis in itself forms a set of opinions or beliefs with direct and beneficial political consequences. Speaking in the idiom of the time, he showed how his principles led him to take one or the other side in current debates. Often, of course, his topical conclusions obscured the theoretical premises, not only for his contemporaries but for subsequent generations of interpreters as well. The main problem in explaining Hume's political thought has always been how to provide a clear understanding of the close

---

[1] For examples of Hume's analysis of the origins of prominent modern forms of enthusiasm, namely, Congregationalism and Quakerism, see HE 57.27–31, 62.71–9; 5:441–3, 6:142–6.

coherence between the general and the particular and the theoretical and the historical. His theory of the nature of social and political phenomena is mainly to be found in the third book of the *Treatise* and in the second *Enquiry*, while the particulars of the historically contingent situation of modern Britain and Europe are analyzed in many of his *Essays* and in the *History of England*. In order to understand either, we have to grasp the sense in which basic social and political institutions are, according to Hume, *artificial*. This can best be achieved by looking at the *philosophical* ideas underpinning superstition and enthusiasm. Elsewhere this might have been called his metaphysics of politics; Hume's aim was to unmask the politics of religious metaphysics.

II. MORALS – FOUND OR CONSTRUCTED

Hume was keenly aware of the continuing influence of ideas derived from Aristotle and mediated by scholastic tradition. From this perspective, social forms (such as property and contract) and political roles (such as magistracy) have their foundation in essences, in inherent structures found in nature itself. On such a theory, specific actions are only property-holding, contracting, or governing insofar as they are an attempt to actualize the inherent meaning or the essence signified by these words. Moral, social, and political relations between people are not constructed by the individuals involved; such relations are established with reference to something over and above the persons concerned, namely, an objective structure of reality and meaning on which individuals try to draw. Hume saw these ideas as the philosophical equivalent of the religious hocus-pocus of superstition (transubstantiation, for example). Like most such ideas, this philosophy supported the need for authoritative interpreters of the meanings supposedly inherent in, or essential to, life in society. It was, in other words, the philosophy behind Catholicism, High Church Anglicanism, old-fashioned Toryism, absolutism, and divine-right monarchism.

The reactions in post-Reformation Europe to these directions in religion and politics were, as Hume realized more clearly than most, immensely complex and often contradictory. It was possible, however, to discern some of the philosophical ideas that were basic to much Reformation thought, and that were eventually spelled out with great clarity by natural law philosophers such as Hugo Grotius, Thomas Hobbes, Samuel Pufendorf, and John Locke. This Protestant natural jurisprudence was an intellectual phenomenon so pervasive that thinkers who were very far from being natural law theorists also adopted parts of its conceptual apparatus. It was also clearly part of the context in which Hume developed his views. With the partial exception of Grotius, these writers held that there were no moral or political meanings inherent in the structure of things. All meaning, or value, is willed or constructed and imposed on a natural world that *in itself* is amoral and apolitical. The basic act of will is that of God who, in choosing the particular human nature He did, delegated to humans the task of creating moral and political forms that would make possible the culture of humanity. According to most Protestant natural law thinkers, human reason could, unaided by revelation, derive from the *character* of human nature and the human position in the world a certain guidance in morals and politics, and this is what they called the law of nature. Generally speaking, the basic law of nature held that, since people were sociable and, indeed, had to be sociable in order to exist at all, various measures had to be taken. These measures were contained in derivative laws of nature that specified the creation of moral and political institutions ranging from marriage and property to civil government and the law of nations. A few thinkers, notably Grotius and Hobbes, tried to formulate a theory that weakened the role of natural law as a guide for the human will. On this view, social and political forms are settlements negotiated between individuals with often conflicting claims and intentions, or *rights*. Natural law in this scheme is simply the lessons learned from such settlements, not the prescription for how to make them in the first place.[2]

The division between a natural law direction and a natural rights direction in Protestant natural law theory was of fundamental

---

[2] In addition, the law of nature was, of course, considered a positive law of God as revealed in His Word, but in this guise it could only be considered a law for those who received the Word, namely, Christian believers. Concerning the relationship between natural law and natural rights in Grotius and Hobbes, see Knud Haakonssen, *Natural Law and Moral Philosophy: From Grotius to the Scottish Enlightenment* (Cambridge: Cambridge University Press, 1996), Chap. 1; and Richard Tuck, *Natural Rights Theories* (Cambridge: Cambridge University Press, 1979), esp. Chaps. 3 and 6; and *Hobbes* (New York: Oxford University Press, 1989).

importance for the further development of political thought, as we shall see. For the moment, however, the significant point is that both forms of natural law theory apparently subscribed to the view that the institutions of moral and political life are contractually constructed by individuals.

These ideas of personal autonomy, of individual rights, of the absence of mediating factors between God and man, and of the consequent construction of morals and politics according to our own lights – ideas identified since with "constructivists" – these parts of the philosophical argument could be taken to the extremes of enthusiasm in religion and fanatical factionalism in politics. This had happened repeatedly in many parts of Europe, in Hume's opinion, but never with more devastating effects than in seventeenth-century Britain, marked as it was by religious strife and civil warfare. Even in his own time the political effects of the enthusiastic cast of mind remained a danger to be guarded against; as Hume grew older, he sometimes feared that the battle against it might yet be lost.[3]

III. HUME ON JUSTICE

The theory of social artifice presented in the third book of the *Treatise* is an attempt to formulate a position mediating the two philosophical traditions briefly outlined in the preceding section. Hume, of course, has no time for scholastic essences, and his naturalism precludes any role for the divine voluntarism of much Protestant natural law. Hume's individuals can expect neither inherent structures nor transcendent guidance. Only Hobbes had isolated humanity metaphysically and religiously as completely as Hume, yet the two thinkers reach very different conclusions about the human condition. It is not only that Hume gives a good deal more credit to the generous side of human nature. He also gives an account of the social relations between individuals that, while sharing the individualistic naturalism of Hobbes, is profoundly un-Hobbesian.

---

[3] In a number of letters in the late 1760s and early 1770s, Hume expressed his fear and loathing for the London mobs rioting in support of the reelection to Parliament of the outlawed John Wilkes. Hume saw it as a degeneration of the demand for liberty to a senseless fanaticism that English freedom allowed to feed on itself, thus creating factionalism and "barbarism" of a sort that could endanger this very freedom. See HL 2:180–1, 191–2, 209–11, 212–13, 216, 261; NHL 196, 199.

The actions that spring from the *natural virtues* and vices (beneficence, clemency, moderation, and their opposites, for example) are, according to Hume, "entirely natural, and have no dependance on the artifice and contrivance of men" (T 3.3.1.1).[4] Each of these actions is a simple or self-contained act that establishes relations between particular agents and particular patients. An act of benevolence, or its opposite, is completed as one act or one occasion when that virtue, or vice, is being expressed, for example, by the giving of a gift or the denial of a service. Such an activity may stretch over time, but it is nevertheless in a significant sense one act. Acts of benevolence may, of course, prompt reactions, such as gratitude, but these reactions are clearly *other* acts. Acts that result from natural virtue and vice are coherent and self-contained because they have a point or a meaning when taken *in isolation* – even when seen as nothing more than relations between specific individuals, a point Hume emphasizes by noting that we value each performance of a natural virtue (T 3.3.1.11–12).

The natural virtues, "commonly denominated the *social* virtues, to mark their tendency to the good of society," provide the basis for family life and intimate circles of friendship, but social life at large requires something else entirely, namely, a set of *artificial virtues* (T 3.3.1.11; cf. 3.2.2.4–6). When I as agent abstain from taking the fruit of my neighbor's pear tree, pay my landlord his rent, or answer the government's military call-up, my actions cannot be understood *in isolation* as mere expressions of inherent features of my nature. These actions have reference to something else, to something beyond the other person or persons, the patient(s) affected by them. This patient may be unknown to the agent or may have been undeserving of the agent's behavior: the neighbor may never harvest his fruit, the landlord may be excessively rich and grasping, the government may be conducting an unjust war. In such cases an agent's behavior can only have meaning and only be evaluated through its relation to some additional factor beyond both the agent(s) and patient(s) involved. It has meaning only within a framework that is in an important sense objective and distinct from individuals and their

---

[4] For another discussion of the distinction between the natural and the artificial virtues, see in this volume the essay "Foundations of Morality in Hume's *Treatise*," Part III A.

qualities. The relations between people who hold property to the exclusion of others, who contract for exchange of goods or services, and who owe allegiance or support of some sort – these relations can be established only because the people involved have something other than each other's intentions to refer to, something that can shape their intentions. My giving money to another person does not constitute "paying rent" merely because we have, respectively, intentions of giving and receiving. The transaction is given its particular meaning because it involves a social practice or institution, in this case a special form of contract. In other words, individual actions of this sort are not self-contained and complete. We cannot see their point and evaluate them without invoking the social practice to which they relate or on which they rely. Individual actions can be approved of as instances of such institutionalized practices as holding private property, keeping promises and contracts, paying allegiance, and the like, *because* such practices already exist and are approved of. This peculiar circumstance is, as Hume explains, well illustrated by actions that seem absurd when taken in isolation, but that acquire meaning and can be evaluated once we assume their reference to a social practice of the sort mentioned. Consequently, when we see a poor person paying money to a rich one, we assume that a loan is being settled or goods paid for (T 3.2.1.9).

Hume's analysis of the nature of social actions is a thorough rejection of will theories, such as contract theories. That is, he rejects theories according to which such social actions as respecting property claims acquire meaning because they derive from acts of will of the participating individuals. Like thinkers in the Aristotelian and Thomistic tradition, Hume holds that acts of will can only establish social relations *outside intimate groups* if these acts are given meaning by something over and above themselves.[5] In contrast to

---

[5] The scholastic theory of contract derives from Aquinas's theory of promises, *Summa Theologica* 2.2.88. The late scholastics, especially in the Spanish schools, made a sophisticated combination of this doctrine and the Roman law on contracts. This combination had an enormous influence through the seventeenth and eighteenth centuries – on even the natural lawyers who helped undermine the philosophical basis for the doctrine – and we find it in civilian lawyers like Jean Domat and Robert Joseph Pothier, who influenced the French *Code Civil* (1804). See Domat, *Les loix civiles dans leur ordre naturel* (Paris, 1689), Book I; Pothier, *Traité des obligations* (1761–4). The modern alternative to the Aristotelian-Thomistic idea of contracts as the actualization of the inherent essence of contracting was commonly seen to

that tradition, however, Hume rejected the view that there are fixed and essential meanings for such social institutions as property and contract. Such institutions are no more than practices, a fact he signals by calling them and their associated virtues and vices – justice and injustice, for example – artificial (T 3.2.1.17–19). They are artificial because they are human creations. At the same time, Hume has deprived himself of the simple contractualist account of these institutions as expressions of will. On his account, property and contract must exist as social practices prior to any acts of will relating to them. Hume has thus saddled himself with a genetic problem, namely, how to account for the origins of the social practices that constitute basic social institutions.

The solution, Hume suggests in *Of the origin of justice and property* (T 3.2.2), involves luck, moderate foresight, and imitative behavior. We inevitably live in family units, and although this is largely a response to natural passions and natural virtues, as well as to "the numberless wants and necessities" with which nature has lumbered human beings, it provides some experience with relative divisions into *mine* and *thine* and with trust (T 3.2.2.2). It requires only modest luck and prudence to attempt to imitate this in relations with people outside the family group. The scarcity of goods and abilities, in relation to needs and desires, puts a premium on making a success of such attempts. It is therefore easy to see how it may become common practice to respect people possessing, transferring, and exchanging things that in one way or another are associated with them, and then coming to trust each other's word about future actions. The general pattern of such practices may be explained by the way the imagination works along empirically established associative lines (see T 3.2.3–5).

be the combination of nominalistic definitions and will theories in thinkers like Hobbes and Locke. See Hobbes, *Leviathan*, ed. Richard Tuck (Cambridge: Cambridge University Press, 1991), 94–5; Locke, *An Essay concerning Human Understanding*, ed. P. H. Nidditch (Oxford: Clarendon Press, 1975), 1.3, 2.28, 4.4; see also Locke, *Two Treatises of Government*, ed. P. Laslett (Cambridge: Cambridge University Press, 1960), 2.81. It must be stressed, however, that the scholastic form of teleology was widely replaced by the teleological scheme of natural religion, and the latter was not much more suited to support pure will theories of promising and contracting than its predecessor. Eighteenth-century theories of promise and contract – legal as well as political – are therefore mostly complicated and confused, a circumstance that makes Hume's theoretical clarification the more remarkable.

It is a question of how such practices gain sufficient strength to withstand the pressure of conflict, for instance, in situations of social expansion and scarcity. The two basic requirements are that each practice should come to be valued independently of its individual instantiations and should be seen as binding or obligatory on the individual. Rather than being just the sum total of what people do, social practices have to become independent rules specifying what is good and to be done.

Hume here offers a radical solution to what had proved to be one of the most intractable problems in moral philosophy, the relationship between *goodness* and *obligation*. At one extreme were those who thought that human nature had been so impaired by original sin that humankind had no insight into moral goodness and could be directed and governed only by being obliged to certain forms of behavior. The obliging wills might be those of a hierarchy of authorities, terminating in God, as in much Lutheran thought; or they might be those of each individual, reflecting directly the will of God, as in much Calvinist thought. Either way, we have a will theory of morals and politics of the sort Hume thought impossible, and we do not have an account that makes any necessary link between moral goodness and being obliged. In contrast to this line of thought were a wide variety of theories that all allowed that, even in its fallen state, humanity was left with some natural capacity for moral insight. In Hume's recent past, they ranged from Cambridge Platonism and the rationalism of Samuel Clarke to the moral sense theories of Shaftesbury and Hutcheson. The proponents of such theories all had the task of explaining whether and how insight into moral goodness had implications for moral obligation. They all thought it did, and they all had extreme difficulty in accounting for it.[6]

The problem was a serious theological one. If each person had a natural moral faculty that could bring moral understanding, and if such understanding imposed a moral obligation, then God's moral role in human life was severely curtailed. The morally good person would not need God, whose moral function would be reduced to that of policing the morally wayward. This was clearly unacceptable, for it would make morals ideally independent of God. Accordingly, in all

---

[6] See Stephen Darwall, *The British Moralists and the Internal 'Ought,' 1640–1740* (Cambridge: Cambridge University Press, 1995).

these theories we find some residual element of divine voluntarism. Generally speaking, a way out was sought in some variation on the following theme. Since the relationship in God's nature between moral insight and moral will is unbroken – whatever account of the relationship theologians may give – and since humans to some extent share in the moral insight, a pale reflection of this relationship may be established in human nature if men and women can partake in God's will and in some measure make it their own. The chief way of accounting for this without resort to revelation was teleological. The particular and confined moral good that each person and community is able to effect may be understood as a contribution to the overall good of the moral universe of all moral agents past, present, and future. This universal good is understood to be the intention of the divinity as shown in the purposefulness of creation. Consequently our particular will to do the particular good in our power is part of God's general will for the moral creation as a whole. If on occasion we lack that particular will, or if it is weak and undecided, the thought of the teleological arrangement, that is, of God's will, is able to supply the want. We are then acting out of a sense of obligation.

This type of teleology and the associated Christian utilitarianism, as it is now often called, was probably the most pervasive style of moral and political thought in the eighteenth century.[7] An early formulation by Richard Cumberland had some influence, but the most important version was undoubtedly Francis Hutcheson's.[8] This line of argument provided the basis for the empirical "science of morals" that characterized a great deal of Enlightenment social thought. Since so much depended on the teleological arrangement of the universe, an important task of the science of morals was to provide a map of the moral world showing how its various components ideally fitted together. The popular science of morals was thus a description of the proper working of the moral institutions

---

[7] See J. E. Crimmins, "John Brown and the Theological Tradition of Utilitarian Ethics," *History of Political Thought* 4 (1983): 523–50.

[8] See Haakonssen, "The Character and Obligation of Natural Law according to Richard Cumberland," in *English Philosophy in the Age of Locke*, ed. M. A. Stewart (Oxford: Clarendon Press, 1993), 29–47, and *Natural Law and Moral Philosophy*, 63–99. For further discussion of Hutcheson's theory, see in this volume, "Foundations of Morality in Hume's *Treatise*," Part I.

currently making up society – *proper* being defined in terms of making social life possible as a contribution to the general happiness of humankind.

Hume matched this agenda point for point. Once such forms of behavior as respect for the possessions of others and keeping of promises have become fairly common, it will be evident to all that they are socially useful by allowing things to be done collaboratively that otherwise could not be done. This social utility, or public good, is merely the outcome of individual actions, but it appears as though it were the result of a shared design. Consequently individuals are inclined to approve of the behavior that brings about the public good, for it appears as though such behavior were aimed at this outcome, and, contrariwise, to disapprove of behavior having contrary effects. In this way the basic rules of justice pertaining to property and contract come to be accepted as moral rules. In short, while the purposefulness of certain general patterns of behavior is only apparent, the perception of this apparent purposefulness, or teleology, in itself becomes an independent cause of such behavior in the future.

The problem is that not every *application* of the rules of justice produces good results for all the individuals concerned, or, in extreme cases, for anyone. Nonetheless, because of their general public utility, we still think that the rules should be kept, or that they are obligatory. While the popular moral philosophy sketched previously invoked what we may call the internalization of God's will in order to account for obligation, Hume suggests instead that we internalize a social "will." In a social group where just behavior is generally approved as good because it produces social utility, people who in a particular case lack any motive for justice – perhaps because neither they nor any other assignable person stand to gain anything from the action in question – will tend to have a motive supplied. Because everyone generally approves of just behavior *as if* it sprang from a separate laudable motive, people lacking such a motive will feel morally deficient as compared with their surroundings and will come to disapprove of or hate themselves on that account. In this they will be reinforced by the disapproval of their fellows. This self-loathing becomes the motive or the will by which people act justly as a matter of obligation.

We may also say that just behavior has become an artificial accretion on the natural person. We disapprove of deficiencies – a lack of a certain degree of benevolence, for example – in the natural moral qualities and see it as an obligation to reinstate benevolence to its "natural" place among our motives. In the same manner we have learned to see the failure to have a motive for justice as a deficiency. Since there is no motive to be reinstated in this case, we have to "invent" one, namely, the will to be full moral characters like other people in our society. A crucial concept in Hume's analysis of obligation is thus that of character. Part of our moral character is natural, part of it derives from social living. Deficiencies in the former evoke a natural, in the latter a socially induced, desire to repair our character. These desires are, respectively, our obligation to the natural and to the artificial virtues.[9] This causal account of the moral obligation to pursue the artificial virtues, typified by justice, is the crowning effort in Hume's subversion of the reigning paradigms of moral and political philosophy. It had a number of no less subversive repercussions.

IV. THE BASIS FOR AUTHORITY

The rules of justice form the basis of social life in extended groups. Yet the obligation to obey the rules of justice depends on nothing more than each person's perception of the general social *opinion* of these rules. Although the formation of such opinion is a strong and universal tendency in human life, it is clearly subject to severe disruption and fluctuation. People accordingly seek to protect the rules of justice by the institution of government (T 3.2.8.5). But then one must ask, what is the basis for the authority of government to administer justice or to do anything else? Or in Hume's language, what is the source of allegiance to government? In answering this question, he follows a pattern similar to that employed in his analysis of the rules of justice.

---

[9] See T 3.2.1.4–8, 3.2.2.23–8, 3.2.5.4–7, 10–13, 3.2.8.7, 3.3.3.2, and the whole of Sect. 3.3.1 (*Of the origin of the natural virtues and vices*). For further discussions of Hume's theory of obligation, see Haakonssen, *The Science of a Legislator: The Natural Jurisprudence of David Hume and Adam Smith* (Cambridge: Cambridge University Press, 1981), 30–5. See also in this volume "Hume's Moral Psychology" (Part V) and "Foundations of Morality in Hume's *Treatise*" (Part III). Both of these essays consider Hume's account of obligation and the role of *sympathy* in his moral theory. The latter also considers Hume's account of justice.

The traditional Tory notion that authority is inherent in the social world in the form of a divine right has to be rejected because it invokes forces about which humans can know nothing. The traditional Whig notion that authority derives from contractual arrangements is, Hume argues, empirically false and conceptually confused.[10] The essential feature of a contractual arrangement is that it involves *choosing* whether or not to enter into the arrangement: but a choice that is unknown to a chooser is not a choice. It seems impossible to identify any contract by virtue of which any group living under a particular government owes allegiance to that government. The generality of humankind knows nothing of such a contract, and even if there had been some contract in the past, it would not carry authority beyond the original contractors. Hume thus finds incoherent the common suggestion that there is a "tacit" contract, a contract about which a people does not know or think. Furthermore, individuals on the whole have no choice. We are generally born into societies that are already subject to government and find ourselves obliged to obey the laws of that government. People of a particularly enthusiastic cast may, of course, say that they always have the choice of dying rather than living with what they consider a tyrannical government. These are exactly the people Hume fears most of all because in their fanaticism they could destroy existing government, and their wildness of temper could never sustain a lasting government (see T 3.2.7–9).

---

[10] Hume explains the labels "Whig" and "Tory" in HE 68.12, 6:381, and accounts for the emergence of the Whig and Tory parties at the Revolution of 1688–9 in HE 71.56–72, 6:523–34. The basic party principles and their connection with the later division between court and country interests are laid out in E-PGB 6–12, 69–72, and E-CP. Pre-Revolution Tory ideas of divine right to rule owed a great deal to Robert Filmer's *Patriarcha* of 1680; see *Patriarcha and Other Writings*, ed. J. P. Sommerville (Cambridge: Cambridge University Press, 1991); among many post-Revolution restatements, Charles Leslie's voluminous output is representative, for example, *The Constitution, Laws, and Government of England Vindicated* (London, 1709) and *The Finishing Stroke* (London, 1711). The role of John Locke's *Second Treatise of Government* (1689; in *Two Treatises of Government*) for the formation of Whig principles continues to be a matter of dispute, as does the significance of radical contractarianism in general. Representative examples of the sort of Whiggism Hume has in mind are the anonymous *Vox Populi, Vox Dei: Being True Maxims of Government* (London, 1709); Daniel Defoe, *The Original Power of the Collective Body of the People of England, Examined and Asserted* (London, 1702); and Benjamin Hoadly, *The Original and Institution of Civil Government Discuss'd* (London, 1710), esp. Part 2.

The contract theory of allegiance to government is in any case muddled in exactly the same way as the contractual account of property. It tries to reduce allegiance to acts of will by individuals, but in doing so it *presupposes* that there is a government, that is, an authority with some claim to allegiance to which individuals pledge that allegiance. Individual acts of obedience, in the form of promises, for instance, can only be recognized as expressions of allegiance if the object of such behavior is the sort of person or group of persons to whom allegiance is due. Governmental authority must therefore rest on something existing prior to any such promise of allegiance. In the terms used in the account of property, we can see that the subjects of government must have an interest in government distinct from their interest in keeping their pledge of allegiance. The interest in question is, in general terms, an interest in external and internal protection and, especially, in the administration of justice. To the extent that such interest establishes obedience as a general pattern of behavior, allegiance becomes, like justice, another artificial accretion on the natural personality of those involved. Once this has happened, the absence of sentiments of allegiance is perceived as a personal deficiency. In this way, allegiance, like justice, becomes a matter of not only "the *natural* obligations of interest . . . but also the *moral* obligations of honour and conscience" (T 3.2.8.7).

Hume's idea of the obligation of allegiance has a certain similarity with a form of contract theory that had some currency in his time, but that he never mentions at all, namely, implied contract. In fact, in his rejection of tacit contract, he seems to suggest that he did not see any difference between these two theories. Those who did distinguish between tacit and implied contracts saw the former as a voluntary commitment signaled in a nonverbal way, but still as an identifiable behaviorial event. On the other hand, an implied contract does not arise from any particular event; there is no act of will. The commitment of an implied contract follows from, is implied by, what a person is or what position or office (spouse, child, doctor, neighbor, citizen, magistrate) he or she holds. This was a way of thinking about social relations that had Aristotelian, Stoic, and Christian origins, and that had been translated into the common teleologically based systems of morals outlined here. Hume, too, thought that duties arise from what a person is, but this could not be accounted for teleologically in terms of the overall aim of the system of moral beings, nor, because there is no act of will involved, was there any reason to invoke "contract" to account for these duties.

Hume's theory of allegiance also saddles him with a genetic problem: how to account for the first origins of government. In his earlier works he is content to give a brief and bland explanation to the effect that, since government is superimposed on social groups that already recognize the rules of justice, including the obligation to keep promises, it is possible to see the first institution of government as a matter of mutual promises. It is clear, however, that his concern is to discredit the idea that this has any implications for a continuing allegiance to government (T 3.2.8.3; E-OC 8, 470–1). After a lifetime of reflecting on the problem and, presumably, after discussing it with his friend Adam Smith, Hume altered his argument in the last essay he wrote, "Of the Origin of Government." In this essay he suggests that government has its origins in people's habit of submission to military leaders in time of war. Such leadership would naturally attract nonmartial functions, for example, the administration of justice and the collection of revenue, and gradually become commonplace between bouts of warfare (E-OG 6, 39–40).[11]

V. OPINION AND THE SCIENCE OF POLITICS

Irrespective of the historical account of the origins of government, Hume always maintained his position that contract and consent are not, and cannot be, the basis for continued allegiance to governmental authority. The basis for government is a combination of the two factors discussed in the *Treatise* and noted in the preceding section: a people's perception of the public interest in protection, especially through enforcement of the rules of justice, and their perception of their obligation to allegiance. In the *Essays* he provocatively formulates this view by saying that it is "on opinion only that government is founded." This "opinion is of two kinds, to wit, opinion of

---

[11] See Adam Smith, *Lectures on Jurisprudence*, ed. R. L. Meek, D. D. Raphael, and P. G. Stein (Oxford: Clarendon Press, 1978), Report of 1762–3, 5:114–19, 127–8, 134–8; Report of 1766: 15–18, 93–6. On Smith, see Haakonssen, *The Science of a Legislator*, 129–31, and Duncan Forbes, *Hume's Philosophical Politics* (Cambridge: Cambridge University Press, 1975), 76.

INTEREST, and opinion of RIGHT" (E-FP 1–2, 32–3). People are generally born into, and continue to live in, societies that are under some
form of government. The opinions of these subjects that their government can care for the public interest, and has the right to exercise
authority, are the foundation of this government. Consequently the
central task of the science of politics is to account for the formation
and transformation of these fundamental opinions.

Some of the causes of opinion are so universal that they can
be explained in completely general terms; they are operative in
practically all circumstances of human life. This applies to beliefs
concerning the interest and obligation on which pregovernmental
institutions rest – the rules of justice pertaining to property and
contract – and to the beliefs underlying government itself. A few
additional features of politics may be explained in similarly general
terms, but it soon becomes necessary to draw on more particular
factors, factors that are more historically specific. Although it is
possible to discuss in general terms the relationship between "liberty" and "slavery" in government, one cannot introduce concepts
like "parties" into one's account without drawing on the experience
of particular forms of government. This requires knowledge of specific events in individual countries. Consequently Hume's science
of politics ranges from a consideration of what some of his contemporaries would have called the "natural history" of the human
species, that is, from his examination of human understanding and
the principles of morals, through historically based general maxims, to the civic history of particular cultures and states. This entire
range of material is necessarily part of his *science* of politics because,
even in the explanation of the most specific event, there will be references to the universal principles of human nature underlying all
moral thought, and to the institutions to which those principles have
led. Only rarely will our explanations depend on the idiosyncratic
whims of individuals. And even in those rare cases, as, for example,
the extremes of enthusiastic madness, deviations from principle can
only be understood as such because we know the regularity that
is being broken. At the same time, the full range of explanations,
from the most general to the most specific, is part of a science of
politics because all explanations are concerned with the formation
of those opinions that support the institutions of society. The more

general part of politics explains that such institutions are the kind of things that must have a history, while the more specific parts reveal the history they have actually had. The general principles of politics teach us that political action must start from an understanding of the particular political conditions to which history has brought us. Hume's political theory is, in other words, an explanation of why political theorizing in abstraction from historical conditions is futile and often dangerous. Hume was acutely conscious of the fact that this was in itself a political opinion calculated to inform political conduct at a particular time and place. Indeed, this was undoubtedly part of the reason why he went to such lengths to popularize his theory by means of his *Essays* and the *History.* The formation of sound political opinions is the most basic political activity, and Hume's political theorizing was such an activity. There is often a sense of urgency in Hume's political writings, for he was always keenly aware that people's opinions are fickle. Under the influence of passions – of avarice, of factional or dynastic or confessional allegiances, of utopian dreams of perfection – our understanding of our situation and that of our society too often becomes clouded, particularly in situations of uncertainty and instability. When there is uncertainty about who has authority or about what those in authority may do, our habitual ways of thinking and behaving are broken. Under such circumstances opinions and actions are much more likely to be influenced by imagined situations than by actual conditions, and passionate flights of fancy tend to take over. Since opinions are formed by experience, we can only have empirically well-founded opinions about who is doing what in society if there is a certain regularity of behavior. The message of Hume's theory concerning the basic features of society is that such regularity cannot come from individual minds and wills alone; it depends on something outside the individual, namely, regular or rule-bound institutions that can guide our behavior and consequently our expectations of each other. If such institutions, once acquired, are lightly given up, we lose habit and regularity; we lose, that is, the most important means of orienting ourselves to others. Consequently we cannot know what we ourselves may do with success, and we will have lost our most elementary freedom. This is the rationale for the enormous emphasis Hume placed on institutional stability.

VI. THE DISTRIBUTION OF JUSTICE

Stability can be seen from two perspectives: the stability of what those in authority *do* and the stability of whom they *are*. These two topics are fundamental to Hume's political thought.

The conduct of government is only stable and predictable if it follows publicly known general rules – only if it is government in accordance with law. Government must therefore be concerned with issues that are suitable subjects of law. These are primarily forms of behavior that are in the public interest, but not necessarily in the interest of each individual concerned in the particular instance.

We are, therefore, to look upon all the vast apparatus of our government, as having ultimately no other object or purpose but the *distribution of justice*, or, in other words, the support of the twelve judges. Kings and parliaments, fleets and armies, officers of the court and revenue, ambassadors, ministers, and privy-counsellors, are all subordinate in their end to this part of administration. Even the clergy, as their duty leads them to inculcate morality, may justly be thought, so far as regards this world, to have no other useful object of their institution. (E-OG 1, 37–8, emphasis added)

Although at first sight an example of the hyperbole to which Hume occasionally resorts in the *Essays,* this passage makes clear what carries most weight. Hume has no doubt about the necessity of a governmental agenda in defense and foreign affairs as well as in economics and culture, but he gives priority to maintaining those two basic institutions of justice – property and contract – that make social life possible. Insofar as the populace has a clear opinion that this balance of priorities constitutes the public interest and that the government protects this interest as well as any possible government could, to that extent the government has a secure source of allegiance (E-FP 2, 33).

It follows from this that Hume must reject policies that significantly break the rules of justice. He disparages, for example, the suggestion that governments should treat individual citizens according to their natural merit. Such a policy would create the greatest uncertainty. Merit is so dependent on each particular situation that it is impossible to formulate general rules for it; consequently, no orderly allocation of goods could be based on it. The same criticism applies to all other schemes for the distribution of goods or status on the basis of alleged personal merits or virtues. Hume criticizes in particular the claims of those religious fanatics who say *"that dominion is founded on grace, and that saints alone inherit the earth,"* and points out that England had experienced such enthusiasm from the Puritans and from one of their political subsects, the Levellers, who claimed that there ought to be "an equal distribution of property" (EPM 3.23–5).

Regarding the distribution of property, Hume adds some further considerations of importance. Even if we assume that equality of property could somehow be achieved, its maintenance would be "extremely *pernicious* to human society. Render possessions ever so equal, men's different degrees of art, care, and industry will immediately break that equality." In order to keep people equal in their possessions, these "virtues" would have to be controlled. To do so would require a "most rigorous inquisition," would impoverish society, and would break down social subordination and order (EMP 3.24–6). These remarks make it clear that Hume's notion of justice is not purely formal and procedural. The rule that everyone should have the same quantity of external possessions is as universal in form as Hume's rules concerning the allocation of property. But he rejects such a rule because it would require tyrannical interference with individuals' natural qualities – with their virtues and with their personal freedom. The object of just laws is thus individual liberty, and, since the most obvious and most endangered expression of such liberty is the acquisition and use of property, justice is centrally concerned with property, and, it follows, with contracts.

This order of justification is noteworthy, for in the *Treatise* Hume has sometimes seemed to limit the object of the rules of justice to securing property per se. He there says that we have three "species of goods," the "internal satisfaction of our mind, the external advantages of our body, and the enjoyment of such possessions as we have acquir'd by our industry and good fortune." Of these, the first cannot be taken from us, and the second, while transferable, can be of no use to others. "The last only are both expos'd to the violence of others, and may be transferr'd without suffering any loss or alteration; while at the same time, there is not a sufficient quantity of them to supply every one's desires and necessities" (T 3.2.2.7). External goods are, accordingly, the *direct* objects of justice. What the passages from the second *Enquiry* make clear is that through the protection of property the two other species of goods are being *indirectly* protected as well (EPM 3 Part 2).

VII. THE ROLE OF RIGHTS

Hume scarcely used the traditional notions of *rights* in his moral and political philosophy. Writers on these subjects commonly used a scheme based on materials from Roman law and developed by natural lawyers from Hugo Grotius onwards.[12] On this scheme, certain features were inherent in each person qua human being, while others were acquired and added to the person through his or her activity in life. The former were natural or innate rights and correspond roughly to Hume's natural virtues; the latter were adventitious or acquired rights and correspond roughly to Hume's artificial virtues. Some of the natural rights were "imperfect," others were "perfect," as were all acquired rights. Kindness, benevolence, gratitude, and the like could be claimed as rights only imperfectly because the qualities of the claimant that would justify the claim were too uncertain and variable to be the subject of law, and the moral urgency of claims for them was too limited to warrant the use of legal force to secure them. But the perfect natural rights, life, liberty, personal judgment – or bodily, behaviorial, and mental integrity – and their adventitious or artificial extension of the person to property and contractual relations were sufficiently ascertainable to be regulated by law, and their protection by the force of law was deemed so important that it provided the main justification for the institution of government. The distinction between perfect and imperfect rights in respect of their certainty and enforceability sounds very much like Hume's distinction between artificial virtues such as justice and the natural virtues such as beneficence. Yet, as we saw at the end of the previous section, he recognized that in addition to property, certain natural qualities – the goods of mind and body – require the protection of law, and that they receive such protection when property is legally safeguarded. These natural qualities or goods are the areas of life that, in theories of natural law, are protected as perfect natural rights. In other words, in substance, Hume was in agreement with the popular natural law

---

[12] On rights in Protestant natural jurisprudence, see Haakonssen, *Natural Law and Moral Philosophy*, 15–62, 310–41, and "The Moral Conservatism of Natural Rights," *Natural Law and Civil Sovereignty: Moral Right and State Authority in Early Modern Political Thought*, ed. I. Hunter and D. Saunders (Basingstoke: Palgrave Macmillan, 2002), 27–42.

systems of morals, but he could not use the concept of rights to formulate his argument. When he does talk of rights, it is casually and in connection with property and contract, or it is in the context of authority – the right to govern.

Hume could not use the concept of rights because both of the rights traditions were unpalatable to him. On one view, rights were qualities of the person as a moral agent; they were the primary feature of all morals, and all moral institutions, such as rules of property or structures of authority, arose when individuals adapted their respective rights to each other. This view had been approximated by Grotius and had received a daring philosophical formulation by Hobbes, for whom the qualities, or rights, in question were nothing more mysterious than the various claims of individuals on their surrounding world and on each other. In many respects this view was close to Hume's way of thinking, but there were two good reasons why he could not accept it. First, this form of rights argument led directly to the contractarian will theories of social institutions that we have seen him reject. Only if he had found a way of seeing the ascription of rights to individuals as part of the process of socialization could he have reconciled rights with his moral theory.[13] A second reason for rejecting this form of rights argument was probably that it was too readily associated with politico-religious enthusiasm and was politically dangerous. Religiously based claims to a freedom of the spirit to govern oneself were only too easily couched in terms of rights.

On a second view, rights, far from being the primary moral feature of the person, were derivative from a natural law that ascribed duties and rights to individuals. This was by far the most pervasive view of the philosophical status of rights and was shared by thinkers who otherwise were extremely different, ranging from the neoscholastic Gottfried Wilhelm Leibniz and Christian Wolff, the Cambridge Platonists and their associate Nathaniel Culverwell,

---

[13] This was one of the most significant philosophical achievements of Adam Smith, who explained justice in terms of rights, rights in terms of injury, and injury in terms of the reactions of spectators who were conditioned by their circumstances. See Smith, *Lectures on Jurisprudence*, Report of 1762–3, 1.1, 9–25; Report of 1766: 5–11; Haakonssen, *The Science of a Legislator*, 99–104.

the quasi-Cartesian Richard Cumberland, to the eclectic volun-tarists Samuel Pufendorf and Christian Thomasius.[14] One leading characteristic of these theories was that rights, and especially per-fect rights, were dependent on duties; when one person has a right to something, others have a duty to abstain from it. This is similar to Hume's reasoning about the moral quality of the rules of justice. But if in these circumstances Hume had invoked a concept of rights, he would have been in great danger of being misunderstood. He had to avoid the traditional argument entirely because, as we have seen, the natural law involved was commonly considered part of a teleological and providentialist scheme of justification.

In sum, there are very good reasons embedded in Hume's theory of morals and politics for rejecting all the common theories of rights. But this did not lead him to reject the entire jurisprudential approach to politics. His basic ideal of stable governmental action is couched in the juridical terms of the rules of justice, and these rules cover the central areas of private jurisprudence in the systems of natural law. They cover, that is, the protection of natural and adventitious rights, especially real and personal rights such as property, succes-sion, contract, and delict.

This ideal of government, or "the rule of law," was, in the British political debate, associated with "free" governments, whether purely republican like those of the Italian city states and the United Provinces (Netherlands), or "mixed" like the British government. One of Hume's most provocative contributions to this debate was his partial divorce of the question of the nature and stability of government from that of the nature and stability of governmen-tal action. He showed, first, that absolute monarchies like France were under certain circumstances perfectly able to adopt the rule of law and serve the public interest; and, second, that "free" gov-ernments like the British one harbored forces that tended toward anarchy, and thereby tyranny and the undermining of the public interest.

---

[14] For an overview of the seventeenth-century thinkers, see Haakonssen, *Natural Law and Moral Philosophy*, 15–62, and of those in the eighteenth century, "German Natural Law," *Cambridge History of Eighteenth-Century Political Thought*, ed. M. Goldie and R. Wokler (Cambridge: Cambridge University Press, 2006), 251–90.

VIII. THE RIGHT TO GOVERN

Having seen what Hume meant by stability of governmental action, we are left with a second question about stability, the question of who governs. All governments, Hume says, are founded on two opinions, opinion of right and opinion of interest. We have discussed opinion of interest, or what Hume describes as the "sense of the general advantage which is reaped from government," in terms of the regular administration of justice as the ideal of what good government should do and what citizens should seek from their government. Opinion of right is concerned with who the people think should rule, and it is divided into two kinds: "right to POWER and right to PROPERTY" (E-FP 3, 33). A government generally held by the people to have a right to power and to serve the public interest will be stable, unless its constitution allows for some popular influence, as in a republican or mixed constitution. In these cases people's opinion of the right to property normally includes the idea that there should be *some* proportionality between property and political influence. Hume remarks that a "noted author [James Harrington] has made property the foundation of all government; and most of our political writers seem inclined to follow him in that particular" (E-FP 4, 33-4).[15] But Hume rejects Harrington's claim that the balance of political power is directly dependent on the balance of property. There is a certain tendency for power to gravitate toward the propertied, but this process is normally influenced by several other factors, such as reverence for settled constitutional forms – that is, it is influenced by the opinion of right to power. Otherwise the British government would have become republican, given the weight of the propertied gentry represented in the House of Commons. In constitutions where property can have influence, there is always a danger that this may conflict with beliefs about the right to power, and consequently there is a danger of instability. This is the framework for Hume's analysis of factionalism in "free" government in general

---

[15] Hume is referring to one of the central theses of James Harrington in such works as *Oceana* and *The Prerogative of Popular Government*. See Harrington, *The Political Works*, ed. J. G. A. Pocock (Cambridge: Cambridge University Press, 1977), 163–5, 181–2, 231ff., 404ff., 458ff. Hume discusses Harrington in E-BG 1, 47–8, and E-IPC 4–5, 50, 514–16, 522–3.

and in that of Britain in particular. The danger of instability is not great in governments that rest primarily on the opinion of right to power, such as absolute monarchies, but monarchies may be fraught with other dangers.

Hume's analysis of the opinion of a government's right to power is in accordance with his general views regarding the connections between habitual behavior, the creation of expectations, and the making of moral judgments.[16] He suggests that the factors that form such opinion may be divided into five categories, *long possession, present possession, conquest, succession,* and *positive laws* (T 3.2.10.4–15).

Long possession of power is the strongest and most common source of authority, as was dramatically demonstrated in Britain by the continuing influence of the Stuarts long after they had exhausted most other sources of authority, including that of present possession. *Present possession* of power will always influence people's opinion about to whom they owe allegiance, as is shown by the repeated changes of sovereignty in Britain during the seventeenth and early eighteenth centuries. *Conquest* is a particularly forceful demonstration of present possession and has been used efficiently throughout recorded history. In the eyes of some, the accession of William of Orange to the British throne was an example of conquest. By *succession,* Hume means a situation in which the son succeeds to the father's authority as if this authority were property even though such succession had not been long established. Finally, *positive laws* that regulate who should hold power will always have some impact on a people's opinion of rightful authority, and this would undoubtedly be the case in Britain following the Act of Settlement (1701), which secured the Hanoverian succession to the throne of England (after 1707, also that of Scotland). All these principles influence people's opinion of rightful authority, and if they all concur, the government has "the strongest title to sovereignty, and is justly regarded as sacred and inviolable." Often, of course, the principles do not point in the same direction, and there is no general principle that will effectively sort them out. In the end, all politics is "entirely subordinate to the interests of peace and liberty" (T 3.2.10.15). Whatever the

---

[16] This process is outlined in connection with the obligation to justice in Part III of this essay.

principles on which a government may try to rest its authority, if it too grossly invades these interests, the rationale for government has been removed. In that sense the people always have a "right" to resistance.

Irrespective of the principle or principles on which a government bases its claim to sovereignty, the invocation of history will soon play a role. In monarchies the importance of history is reflected in the weight laid on the hereditary principle. Elective monarchies tend to be unstable but often make up for it through the principle of succession. In republics and mixed governments, historical justification is sought in the ancient origins of the constitutional forms followed. These invocations of the past for the purposes of legitimation are often mere myths, of course, and Hume certainly rejected as pure fiction the various Whig ideas of an ancient English constitution.[17] He clearly took it as one of the hallmarks of modern civilization that such myths could be subject to criticism without endangering the stability of government. Much of his historical and political writing was meant to educate modern Britons in this regard. By giving a candid view of the past, Hume hoped to provide a realistic understanding of how the passage of time influences the present. "Time and custom give authority to all forms of government, and all successions of princes; and that power, which at first was founded only on injustice and violence, becomes in time legal and obligatory" (T 3.2.10.19). This was crucially important in Britain. Even if the accession of William of Orange could be seen as usurpation in 1688, the course of history had lent legitimacy to the whole of the succession set in train then. It was the latter that was important for the allegiance of British subjects in the middle of the eighteenth century. The task of nonpartisan, philosophical history in the service of the science of politics was to disregard factions and factional myths and explain the process by which the nation had arrived at its particular present: by this process the "interests of peace and liberty" had been shaped. It was necessary for the politically relevant part of the population to hold enlightened opinions about the government's rights on the basis of its present performance with regard to these interests. One of the most remarkable features of modern Europe was,

---

[17] For further discussion of this topic, see in this volume the essay "David Hume: 'The Historian,'" Part IV.

Hume suggested, that this enlightenment was taking place not only within the mixed constitution of Britain, but also in the continental monarchies, or at least in France, the most modern of these.

Traditionally monarchies had whenever necessary created suitable opinions of governmental authority through the tyrannical and arbitrary exercise of force. Among Britons this was still the entrenched caricature of French "slavery," a caricature that Hume thought it was important to dislodge. France was in the vanguard of an entirely new species of monarchy, the civilized monarchy.[18] This admittedly did not have the dynamism to generate the central elements of civilization in the first place; it imitated free societies like Britain. Once adopted, however, civilized modes of life were fairly secure in a monarchy, in some respects perhaps even more secure than under a mixed constitution.

Hume's analysis of the process of civilization is subtle and rich and beyond easy summary. The three main foci are the expression of the human spirit in arts and sciences, the protection of the person by means of law, and the acquisition and exchange of the goods of the external world (see T 3.2.2.7). In dealing with these three factors, Hume is showing the relationship between merely living and living well, to use the Aristotelian distinction. For a society to live at all, it needs, in addition to a government strong enough to protect it externally, a minimal system of justice and the wherewithal to feed itself. In a society where the government, for whatever reason, is restrained from doing much more than securing these things, a spirit of enterprise and individualism will tend to predominate. There will be a growth of knowledge arising from experiments in living and producing, and it is on this basis that a commercial society like the British emerges. By living at all, a free society comes to live well. Intriguingly, monarchies can also become civilized by wanting to live equally well: in realizing this wish, they may adopt some of the basic features of a free society. Monarchies are characterized by a crust of nobility, whose status is dependent on the good

---

[18] Hume's analysis of modern monarchy in general and of that of France in particular is scattered through the *Essays*. The most important passages on which the present discussion is based are E-LP 2, 10–11; E-PR 10–11, 21–4; E-CL; E-RP 5–15 and 25–40, 112–19 and 124–33; E-OC 45, 485–6. The issue is discussed in Forbes, *Hume's Philosophical Politics*, 152–60; and Nicholas Phillipson, *Hume* (London: Weidenfeld & Nicolson, 1989), 61–70.

will of the monarch rather than their own enterprise, and whose life is guided by codes of honor and ritualized show. Such a class will feed off the arts and crafts developed in a free society and then will often outstrip that society in the finer arts, as exemplified by the superiority of French literature. Cocooned as they are within such a class of culture, monarchs are little inclined to take much interest in the life of society at large, and no social group is sufficiently propertied to make it necessary for them to do so. As long as the civil order is maintained by the enforcement of law, society can be left alone, and this freedom, combined with the need for foreign goods, eventually leads to the growth of commerce. This was the model of the modern civilized monarchy emerging in France, which Hume admired and about which he tried to enlighten his countrymen. It was within the framework of this political analysis of civilization that Hume developed his political economy. However, this perspective may be turned around, and it has in fact been argued that Hume's fundamental concern was with commerce as a new form of sociability, and that his political theory was derived from this concern.[19]

Despite his admiration for France, Hume never forgot that such a society enjoyed a regular administration of justice only by default. There were no constitutional guarantees because there was no constitutional counterweight to the crown. For all its freedom and civilization, modern monarchy had no political liberty. Hume thought social life with political liberty highly precarious, and in his more pessimistic periods, when faced with libertarian excesses such as the Wilkes riots in London in the 1760s, he thought a civilized monarchy the safest long-term solution. What he feared in a free constitution was its tendency to breed factions and the tendency of factionalism to degenerate into fanaticism, disorder, and anarchy, out of which would grow tyranny. In other words, the very engine of civilized

---

[19] See Istvan Hont's imposing *Jealousy of Trade: International Competition and the Nation State in Historical Perspective* (Cambridge, MA: Harvard University Press, 2005), which provides a rich European, not least French, context for Hume; see esp. 5–37 and Chaps. 3 and 4. Also John Robertson in *The Case for the Enlightenment: Scotland and Naples 1680–1760* (Cambridge: Cambridge University Press, 2005) marginalizes Hume's political theory in favor of political economy derived from what is seen as neo-Epicurean elements in Hume's moral thought. In comparison, see the account of Hume's economic views in the essay "Hume's Principles of Political Economy" in this volume.

living, namely, freedom under law, found its most refined protection in a system of political liberty that inevitably harbored forces that could become destructive of that engine. This could happen when an ignorant people suffered from historical delusions, stoked by corrupt politicians, such as the need to be jealous of France and fearful of its ambitions for "universal monarchy." Such madness was leading the country to meet an imagined danger militarily at the cost of a mounting public debt, a policy that in Hume's eyes was being transformed into commercial empire building through arms, something he feared would lead to disaster. This was the situation in which contemporary Britain found itself, and the anatomy of factionalism was consequently a central concern in Hume's literary intervention in public life: his *Essays* and much of the *History*.

The new and difficult point Hume had to impress on his readers was that in a free constitution political differences could not be *about* the constitution; they had to be *within* the constitution. Factionalism as he knew it was inconsistent with this: "the influence of faction is directly contrary to that of laws" (E-PG 2, 55). The general danger in factionalism was that it would lead to fragmentation by pitting group interests against each other at the expense of the public interest. Even worse, it tended to transform the recurring question of who should discharge the offices of government into a question of the balance between the powers of the constitution itself. This was particularly dangerous in a mixed constitution such as the British, where the main factions naturally would form around two different principles of government, the monarchical and the republican. The extraordinary thing was that Britain, as Hume saw it, was in the process of breaking away from this division. But his contemporaries did not appreciate this and, by continuing the old factional rant, they endangered the precarious constitutional and political balance that was emerging. A readable analysis of factionalism was needed.

IX. ABOVE PARTIES

Factions, or parties – Hume often uses the two words interchangeably – fall into two broad categories, personal and real. Personal factions are held together by personal relations, normally extensive family ties. Although such relations can play a role in any party, they most easily dominate politics as a whole in small republics, such as those of Italy. Real factions are the ones that can help us understand larger states, and especially Britain. "*Real* factions may be divided into those from *interest*, from *principle*, and from *affection*.*" Factions based on *interest* typically arise when two different social groups, like the nobility and the common people, have, or think they have, opposing interests. Since interest is inevitably a driving force in all human endeavor, such factions are "the most reasonable, and the most excusable." In England it had often been thought that there was a fundamental opposition between the interests of "the *landed*" and those of the "*trading* part of the nation," and this belief was an important aspect of the division of the political nation into "*Court*" and "*Country*" factions. But the belief was simply not justified. If people are to avoid such false oppositions, they must be enlightened so that the pursuit of interest, which is constitutive of human behavior, is guided by the belief that the public interest is also the most important private one (E-PG 9–10, 59–60).

In contrast, political factions inspired by "*principle*, especially abstract speculative principle, are known only to modern times, and are, perhaps, the most extraordinary and unaccountable *phænomenon*, that has yet appeared in human affairs" (E-PG 11, 60). The key word here is "speculative." If division between factions is concerned only with differences of a speculative or theoretical sort, then there is no objective necessity for any division in political behavior. That is to say, there is nothing outside the minds of those involved over which to divide. If the factional principles concerned things like power or goods that only one or other party could have, then there would be a prima facie case for division. In matters speculative, however, each mind could hold its own, were it not for a natural tendency to convince other minds to conform to one's own and thus to one's group. The factor that gave this natural tendency such sway in the modern world was, in Hume's opinion, the Christian religion. In its origins, Christianity, in contrast to most other religions, was not an establishment faith. It could survive only by developing a strong priesthood to protect the sect against secular power. The priesthood therefore had a vested interest in continuing to govern their flock in separation from the state and from other sects. In order to do so, they had to invent speculative principles around which to rally their followers, and in this the priests sought reinforcement from speculative philosophy. When the universal church broke up, the opposing forces burst on modern Europe in the disastrous religious wars. "Such divisions, therefore, on the part of the people, may justly be esteemed factions of *principle*; but, on the part of the priests, who are the prime movers, they are really factions of *interest*" (E-PG 13, 62). The danger from the people is factions based on enthusiasm; from the priests, factions primed by superstition.

Hume feared factionalism based on the opposing principles of superstition and enthusiasm most of all because of its rabble-rousing potential. Couching their rhetoric in whatever was the political jargon of the day, leaders could take to the streets and the meeting-houses and appeal to the large section of the population that was outside the reach of proper education. The only way to deal with such factionalism was to enlighten the potential leaders of the factions. To this purpose Hume supported every move that could secure the inclusion of the clergy in the world of letters. Clergymen of taste and learning would tend to see issues of doctrinal theology as matters for discussion among the educated rather than as reasons for social divisions, and they would see their role vis-à-vis their congregations as a moralizing and civilizing one rather than as a sectarian one.

The British political system, however, also bred leaders of secular factions who based their causes on *principle*. In the wake of the constitutional settlement after the Revolution of 1688, members of the old Tory and Whig factions had been weaving a complicated (and shifting) patchwork, the main components of which were a government or court faction consisting largely of modern Whigs *and* a country opposition consisting of groups of Tories and old-fashioned Whigs who were only rarely able to act coherently as a group. Hume thought that this factionalism should be dealt with in two ways. At one level the principles invoked by the factions should be criticized. At another level this criticism should not take the usual form of political polemics but rather the detached form of polite literary debate. Politics had to be made polite and subject to civilized manners just like art and literature; it had to be written about according to literary standards – as in Hume's *Essays* and *History* – and not in the form of polemic or diatribe. The substantial criticism of factional principles Hume approached in a variety of ways. In the

Treatise, the second *Enquiry,* and some of the *Essays,* he tried to show the untenability of the basic philosophical principles behind the factions that we considered at the beginning of this essay, that is, the ideas of natural hierarchy and authority, on one side, and will theories of contract, on the other. In the *History* and some of the *Essays* he rejected as spurious the historical authority invoked for party principles.[20] And in several of the *Essays* he argued that the factions were politically blind to the realities of the contemporary situation and therefore potentially disastrous. This was not least the case with factions arising from affection, as distinct from those from interest and from principle.

Factions from *affection* "are founded on the different attachments of men towards particular families and persons, whom they desire to rule over them" (E-PG 15, 63). Such factions were powerful forces in history, and Hume analyzed at some length the attachment of Englishmen and Scotsmen to the Stuarts, and of the new breed of Britons to the Hanoverians, an issue that remained at the forefront of British politics until the defeat of the last Jacobite rising in 1745 (E-PS; E-PGB 10–12; HE 71.70–2, 6:530–4). Political opposition based on such principles was irrational since it could seldom serve the real interests of those involved. The voice of reason could only try to persuade people of this and, more generally, try to show that it mattered less who governed than how they governed. The best constitution was one of such stable procedures that even poor rulers might govern in the public interest. At least in his more optimistic moments before the pessimism of the 1760s and 1770s set in, Hume thought that the British constitution was approaching, or could approach, such a stable and positive form. The problem was that factional cant was blinding Britons to this possibility.

X. THE STABILITY OF GREAT BRITAIN

The loudest charge against the British political system as it operated after the Revolution of 1688, and especially against the long regime of Sir Robert Walpole, was that of "corruption," by which was meant the manipulation of the House of Commons by the Crown and its ministers. Rejecting the use of such charged language, Hume

---

[20] As David Wootton shows in his essay "David Hume: 'The Historian,'" Part II.

pointed out that it was in fact a system of mutual dependence and the very thing that, however precariously, enabled political liberty to be combined with stability in a mixed constitution. The Crown was economically infinitely weaker than the property represented in the Commons taken as a whole, a state of affairs constitutionally ratified in the Crown's dependence on Parliament for supply. In balance, the Crown had acquired a measure of control over parts of the lower house taken individually and in that way secured the stability of the policy pursued at any given time. This was possible because of the respect given to traditional constitutional forms and because the Crown was a great deal richer than any individual subject. Through distribution of offices in government and church, pensions and honors, procurement of secure parliamentary seats, and the like, the king and his ministers enrolled members of Parliament in support of court positions on decisive issues. The motives and indeed the characters of those involved might not stand the closest moral scrutiny, but that was not to be expected of people in power in any system. The point was that this system converted private – and not so private – vices into public interest.

The same could not, in Hume's eyes, be said about the other part of the charge of corruption, the undermining of the economy through public debt. The government increasingly financed its business, including successive large-scale wars, by means of public loans from the community, guaranteed by the public treasury. Trading in these bonds became a major part of the finance market. The stability of this whole system was assumed to depend on the ability of the government to honor the loans, and as the public debt grew and grew, it seemed that the only barrier to national bankruptcy was trust in the future, which meant trust in the stability of the government to secure a future. Like many more traditional thinkers, Hume believed that landed property was a stabilizing influence on government. Since real estate could not be removed from the country, the landed interest was the interest of the country. But, in a commercial society where land itself was increasingly a commodity and subject to the fluctuations of financial exchange, even land did not provide a terra firma for a government engaged in loan financing on a large scale. The whole financial system appeared increasingly to be a mental construct of the players involved, a kind of economic superstition, with decreasing reference to anything objective and extra-mental. It was left to Hume's only peer in such matters, Adam Smith, to show that in this regard financial systems operated on rules not much different from the rules of justice, as Hume had expounded them. The fact that such systems were useful and the result of choice distinguished them from those based on superstition.[21]

XI. OPENING THE EYES OF THE PUBLIC: TWO CENTURIES OF READING HUME

In the Preface to the first edition of his *Essays* (1741), Hume sets his new literary effort into the context of the polite essays of the time, referring to *The Spectator* of Addison and Steele and to *The Craftsman* in which Bolingbroke published some of his most important political writings (W 3:41–2). It is unclear, because unexamined, how much impact Hume's intervention had on the public debate in general or how far it compensated for the ineffectiveness of the *Treatise.* While Hume had clearly damned himself as an infidel who could not be appointed to a university chair in philosophy, he was probably of no great significance in the public discussion of morals and politics until he published his *Political Discourses* (1752) and, especially, the Stuart volume of his *History of England* (1754). In an age when the political battles of the present were habitually fought through the past, Hume judged correctly that history – English history – was the most effective medium for his political views. Yet effectiveness was bought at a price. The philosophically based attempt at impartiality and balance between Tory and Whig readings of the past served only to concentrate the public attention on the party-political issue, to the detriment of discussion of the underlying philosophical ideas. Despite private protestations and public pursuit of even finer balance in subsequent volumes of the *History,* the work effectively marked him out as a Tory apologist in his principles. The posthumous publication in 1702–4 of Clarendon's *History of the Rebellion* and a string of subsequent histories had so inured the British public to seeing their past and therefore their present in Tory-Whig terms that Hume's principles of impartiality had little chance of being perceived and, typically, it was primarily on the battleground of history

---

[21] Smith also rejected Hume's theory of trade-led economic development.

that he had to be countered, for example, in the monumental Whig history of Catharine Macaulay.[22]

Hume's *History* became the standard work of its kind for sixty or seventy years, until eventually overtaken by T. B. Macaulay's great work, which was explicitly designed as a Whig replacement. Thus, even in its demise, Hume's work served to maintain the narrow agenda of Tory versus Whig. Throughout the nineteenth and the first half of the twentieth century Hume was rarely thought of as a political theorist at all, except occasionally on the issue of the social contract.[23] Not until the 1960s and, especially, the 1970s did Hume figure as much more than a Tory historian who rejected the original contract.

It was Duncan Forbes's detailed scholarship and J. G. A. Pocock's grand vision of Anglo-American political culture that effectively drew attention to Hume as a complex social and political theorist.[24]

---

[22] Edward Hyde, First Earl of Clarendon, *The True Historical Narrative of the Rebellion and Civil Wars in England*, 3 vols. (London, 1702–4); Catharine Macaulay, *History of England from the Accession of James I to that of the Brunswick Line*, 8 vols. (London, 1763–83). The histories *post* Clarendon, which helped create the climate in which Hume's efforts at political-philosophical history have to be understood, include Laurence Echard, *History of England from Julius Caesar to 1689*, 3 vols. (London, 1707–18); White Kennett, *Complete History of England* (London, 1706) and *A Compassionate Enquiry into the Causes of the Civil War* (London, 1708); Viscount Bolingbroke (Henry St. John), *Remarks on the History of England* (London, [1743]); Paul de Rapin-Thoyras, *Histoire d'Angleterre*, 10 vols. (The Hague, 1723–7; English trans., London 1726–31); John Oldmixon, *Critical History of England*, 2 vols. (London, 1724–6) and *History of England during the Reigns of the Royal House of Stuart* (London, 1730); Daniel Neal, *The History of the Puritans*, 4 vols. (London, 1732–8); James Ralph, *The History of England during the Reigns of King William, Queen Anne, and King George I; With an Introductory Review of the Reigns of the Royal Brothers Charles and James* (London, 1744); William Guthrie, *History of England from the Invasion of Julius Caesar to 1688*, 4 vols. (London, 1744–51); Thomas Carte, *A General History of England*, 4 vols. (London, 1747–55).

[23] See, e.g., Ernest Barker's *Social Contract. Essays by Locke, Hume, and Rousseau* (Oxford: Clarendon Press, 1947).

[24] The most central works are Duncan Forbes, *Hume's Philosophical Politics*; "Sceptical Whiggism, Commerce, and Liberty," in *Essays on Adam Smith*, ed. A. S. Skinner and T. Wilson (Oxford: Clarendon Press, 1975), 179–201; and "Hume's Science of Politics," in *David Hume: Bicentenary Papers*, ed. G. P. Morice (Edinburgh: Edinburgh University Press, 1977), 39–50. J. G. A. Pocock, *The Machiavellian Moment. Florentine Political Thought and the Atlantic Republican Tradition* (Princeton: Princeton University Press, 1975) and "Hume and the American Revolution: The Dying Thoughts of a North Briton," in *McGill Hume Studies*, ed. D. F. Norton, N. Capaldi, and W. Robison (San Diego: Austin Hill Press, 1979),

Forbes set in train the search for connections between Hume's purely philosophical principles, especially in the *Treatise,* and his application of these to formulate a "sceptical" or "scientific" Whiggism that not only cut across the old Tory-Whig divide but also, and much more importantly for our understanding of Hume's immediate situation, sorted out the division between court and country factions that had come to dominate British politics since 1688. The question of the coherence between Hume's philosophical endeavor in the *Treatise* and *An Enquiry concerning the Principles of Morals* and his political principles has subsequently dominated studies of his political thought. In a particularly useful introduction to Hume's political philosophy, David Miller argued that there is a gap between Hume's general skepticism and his political conservatism and that this gap is filled by what he calls Hume's "ideology." This thesis was rejected by John B. Stewart, who argued that Hume's view of practical knowledge led him to the principles of liberalism. In a book that presents the most detailed account of Hume's idea of the artificiality of sociopolitical institutions, Frederick Whelan argued for the coherence of Hume's political thought, while Donald Livingston suggested that such coherence arose from Hume's narrative approach, not only in his histories and essays but also in the more narrowly philosophical writings.[25]

The picture painted by Duncan Forbes was simultaneously and independently given depth and nuance by Pocock's evocative image of an Atlantic political debate centrally concerned with the civic-humanist values of classical republicanism that had been revived in

---

325–43, now republished in Pocock, *Virtue, Commerce, and History* (Cambridge: Cambridge University Press, 1985), 125–41, a work that further deepens Pocock's interpretation. See also the Introduction to *Wealth and Virtue: The Shaping of Political Economy in the Scottish Enlightenment,* ed. I. Hont and M. Ignatieff (Cambridge: Cambridge University Press, 1983). The point made in the text is not meant to imply that there were no valuable contributions to scholarship on Hume's politics prior to these works, but only that none were particularly effective in creating, in the scholarly debate, a broader view of Hume's politics.

[25] David Miller, *Philosophy and Ideology in Hume's Political Philosophy* (Oxford: Clarendon Press, 1981); John B. Stewart, *Opinion and Reform in Hume's Political Philosophy* (Princeton: Princeton University Press, 1992); Frederick Whelan, *Order and Artifice in Hume's Political Philosophy* (Princeton: Princeton University Press, 1984); Donald W. Livingston, *Hume's Philosophy of Common Life* (Chicago: University of Chicago Press, 1984).

the Italian city-states of the Renaissance. The ideal of a polity consisting of citizens of property sufficient to keep them independent
and armed to protect their freedom was, it was suggested, the background against which we had to understand the post-1688 debates
about the corrupting influence of transient commercial wealth, as
opposed to permanent real estate; about civic or public virtue; about
the virtues of a citizen militia and the dangers of a standing army;
about the balance of the constitution between executive and citi-
zenry and, consequently, about the duration and independence of
Parliament.[26] When set against this general framework, Hume, it
became clear, had a political agenda of hitherto unsuspected rich-
ness. Part of this agenda was the writing of philosophical history,
and this has been extensively explored in a vast European context in
Pocock's most recent major work.[27]

The notion of an Atlantic Machiavellian moment of neoclassical
republicanism strengthened the attention to another public whose
eyes Hume might have opened. In the 1960s American scholars,
in their attempts to understand the meaning of America, rediscov-
ered republicanism and its associated civic ethics as an alternative to Lockean liberalism.[28] This was reinforced by the continuing
European, and especially British, discussion of republicanism. The
general proposition was this.[29] In their search for principles in the
light of which they could understand their problems and justify their
solutions, the North American colonists were particularly receptive
to the neorepublican and anticourt ideas of the country opposition
in the mother country. But among the problems they faced after
independence was the classical dogma that a republican form of

---

[26] Concerning Hume and the militia issue, see John Robertson, *The Scottish Enlightenment and the Militia Issue* (Edinburgh: John Donald, 1985), esp. Chap. 3.

[27] Pocock, *Barbarism and Religion*, Vol. 2: *Narratives of Civil Government* (Cambridge: Cambridge University Press, 1999), Chaps. 11–15.

[28] The literature on this topic is extensive and beyond brief summary. The pioneering
studies were Bernard Bailyn, *The Ideological Origins of the American Revolution*
(Cambridge, MA: Belknap Press of Harvard University Press, 1967); and Gordon S.
Wood, *The Creation of the American Republic 1776–1787* (Chapel Hill: University
of North Carolina Press, 1969).

[29] Again, Pocock's work was the most important in clearing the ground; see esp. *The
Machiavellian Moment*, Chap. 15, and *Virtue, Commerce, and History*, 160–8,
183–8, 263–76.

government could exist only in a small country. The solution to this problem, as outlined by James Madison in *Federalist* No. 10, was, it was suggested, directly inspired by Hume's speculative "Idea of a Perfect Commonwealth."[30]

While the explosion of scholarly interest in the Scottish Enlightenment has benefited Hume scholarship generally, his political (and moral) thought has been particularly well served by much new work on Adam Smith. The better we understand Smith's work, the better we may appreciate the sharpest reading Hume's politics has received. It was the publication of a new set of students' notes from Smith's lectures on jurisprudence, as part of the new collected edition of Smith's works, that began to open up the question of how Hume's theory of justice related to traditional theories of natural law.[31] Smith's theory was, it was suggested, in effect offering a Humean basis for a jurisprudential system that hitherto had rested on entirely different philosophical foundations.[32] The relationship between natural law and Hume's politics had already been put under debate by Duncan Forbes's pioneering sketches.[33] This and the new work on Smith inspired further work on natural law, and it soon became clear

---

[30] This problem was studied early in an article that has become a classic, Douglas Adair, " 'That Politics May Be Reduced to a Science': David Hume, James Madison and the Tenth *Federalist*," *Huntington Library Quarterly* 20 (1957): 343–60; republished in Adair, *Fame and the Founding Fathers: Essays by Douglas Adair*, ed. T. Colbourn (Indianapolis: Liberty Fund, 1998), 132–51. For a wide-ranging discussion of Hume in the context of eighteenth-century ideas of constitutionalism, see David Wootton, "Liberty, Metaphor and Mechanism: 'Checks and Balances' and the Origins of Modern Constitutionalism," in *Liberty and American Experience in the Eighteenth Century*, ed. D. Womersley (Indianapolis: Liberty Fund, 2006), 209–74.

[31] Adam Smith, *Lectures on Jurisprudence*, ed. R. L. Meek, D. D. Raphael, and P. G. Stein (Oxford: Clarendon Press, 1978), part of The Glasgow Edition of the Works of Adam Smith, 6 vols. (Oxford: Clarendon Press, 1976–83).

[32] See Haakonssen, *The Science of a Legislator;* and Donald Winch, *Adam Smith's Politics: An Essay in Historiographical Revision* (Cambridge: Cambridge University Press, 1978), which include important discussions of Hume.

[33] Forbes, *Hume's Philosophical Politics*, Chaps. 1–2, and "Natural Law and the Scottish Enlightenment," in *The Origins and Nature of the Scottish Enlightenment*, ed. R. H. Campbell and A. S. Skinner (Edinburgh: Edinburgh University Press, 1982), 186–204. See also Stephen Buckle, *Natural Law and the Theory of Property: Grotius to Hume* (Oxford: Clarendon Press, 1991); Russell Hardin, *David Hume, Moral and Political Theorist* (Oxford: Oxford University Press, 2007).

that civic humanist republicanism lived side by side with a similarly ancient and revived natural jurisprudence.[34] If Hume's interventions in the public political debates around him had to be understood against the background of civic humanism, his underlying political philosophy had, among other things, to be appreciated in its critical relationship to Protestant natural law. For a major branch of this current of thought, deriving in particular from Samuel Pufendorf, prepared the way for Hume's and Smith's decisive rejection of metaphysical forms of natural law.[35] At the same time, natural jurisprudence as a general genre dominated the Scottish moral philosophy courses, at least in Glasgow and Edinburgh, as well as the teaching of law.[36] It was in many ways the systematic framework for a common social ethics which all of Hume's readers would have accepted as a matter of course.

This debate about the major conceptual worlds to which Hume's politics had to be related was being further complicated by the work of Istvan Hont, who argued that Hume followed by Smith were the thinkers who fully understood the most fundamental change to occur in the early modern world. This was the emergence of a new form of social intercourse, namely, national and international commerce as the basis for political society. This "unsocial sociability" – which Hont also saw being prepared by Pufendorf – marginalized all traditional political discourse, and Hume's essays in political economy were the pioneering effort in this regard.[37] More recently this primacy of political economy in Hume's thought has been forcefully argued by John Robertson on a different, though largely compatible basis. Robertson sees Hume's political economy (and that of Smith)

---

[34] The relationship between republicanism and natural law is discussed by J. G. A. Pocock, "Cambridge Paradigms and Scotch Philosophers: A Study of the Relations between the Civic Humanist and the Civil Jurisprudential Interpretation of Eighteenth-Century Social Thought,"*Wealth and Virtue*, 235–52; and in Haakonssen, *Natural Law and Moral Philosophy*, esp. Chap. 2.

[35] See Haakonssen, "Protestant Natural Law Theory: A General Interpretation," in *New Essays on the History of Autonomy: A Collection Honoring J. B. Schneewind*, ed. N. Brender and L. Krasnoff (Cambridge: Cambridge University Press, 2004), 92–109.

[36] See the Introduction to *Thomas Reid, on Practical Ethics. Lectures and Papers on Natural Theology, Self-Government, Natural Jurisprudence and the Law of Nations*, ed. K. Haakonssen (Edinburgh: Edinburgh University Press, 2007).

[37] Hont, *Jealousy of Trade*, which includes his major papers stretching back to the 1980s.

as the implication and practical application of a moral philosophy derived from neo-Epicurean stock, especially from Pierre Bayle and Bernard Mandeville. This is part of a claim for a unitary Enlightenment characterized in this way and reaching its epitome in Hume.[38]

Interest in the connections between Hume's science of politics and Adam Smith's incomplete science of a legislator meant that Hume became part of the explorations of the fate of the latter. As a result, we can now see that in the generation following his death Hume was not read exclusively as a Tory historian but also as a thinker of mixed political principles and as a pioneer empirical historian of politics.[39]

SUGGESTIONS FOR FURTHER READING

For further reading on this topic, the following are especially recommended.

Forbes, Duncan. *Hume's Philosophical Politics.* Cambridge: Cambridge University Press, 1975.

Hardin, Russell. *David Hume, Moral and Political Theorist.* Oxford: Oxford University Press, 2007.

Hont, Istvan. *Jealousy of Trade: International Competition and the Nation State in Historical Perspective.* Cambridge, MA: Harvard University Press, 2005.

Livingston, Donald W. *Hume's Philosophy of Common Life.* Chicago: University of Chicago Press, 1984.

Miller, David. *Philosophy and Ideology in Hume's Political Philosophy.* Oxford: Clarendon Press, 1981.

Phillipson, Nicholas. *Hume.* London: Weidenfeld & Nicolson, 1989.

Pocock, J. G. A. *Barbarism and Religion.* Vol. 2: *Narratives of Civil Government.* Cambridge: Cambridge University Presss, 1999. Chaps. 11–15.

"Hume and the American Revolution: The Dying Thoughts of a North Briton." In Pocock, *Virtue, Commerce, and History.* Cambridge: Cambridge University Press, 1985. 125–42.

---

[38] Robertson, *The Case for the Enlightenment,* 289–324, 360–76.

[39] See esp. Stefan Collini, Donald Winch, and John Burrow, *That Noble Science of Politics: A Study in Nineteenth-Century Intellectual History* (Cambridge: Cambridge University Press, 1983), Chaps. 1–2; Biancamaria Fontana, *Rethinking the Politics of Commercial Society: The "Edinburgh Review" 1802–1832* (Cambridge: Cambridge University Press, 1985), esp. Chap. 3; and Mark Salber Phillips, *Society and Sentiment: Genres of Historical Writing in Britain, 1740–1820* (Princeton: Princeton University Press, 2000).

Robertson, John. *The Case for the Enlightenment: Scotland and Naples 1680–1760*. Cambridge: Cambridge University Press, 2005.

Stewart, John B. *Opinion and Reform in Hume's Political Philosophy*. Princeton: Princeton University Press, 1992.

Whelan, Frederick. *Order and Artifice in Hume's Political Philosophy*. Princeton: Princeton University Press, 1984.

12 Hume's Principles of Political Economy

David Hume's essays were "the cradle of economics," suggested John Hill Burton, in his important biography of Hume.[1] Although this may be a biographer's exaggeration, there can be no doubt that Hume's work provided an important contribution to political economy as a discipline, together with a significant critique of the "mercantile" system that was later attacked by his friend Adam Smith.

I. ECONOMICS: THE BACKGROUND

Mercantilism is difficult to define. As the historian P. J. Thomas put it: "Mercantilism has often been described as a definite and unified policy or doctrine, but that it has never been. In reality it was a shifting combination of tendencies which, although directed to a common aim – the increase of national power – seldom possessed a unified system of policy, or even a harmonious set of doctrines. It was a very complicated web of which the threads mingled inextricably."[2] In the seventeenth and eighteenth centuries the object of policy was the enhancement of the power of the nation state, a strategy that was to be attained in a number of ways, at least one of

---

[1] *Life and Correspondence of David Hume*, 2 vols. (Edinburgh, 1846), 1:354.

[2] P. J. Thomas, *Mercantilism and the East India Trade* (London: P. S. King & Son, 1926), 3. The classic authorities on the mercantile system include Gustav von Schmoller, *The Mercantile System and Its Historical Significance* (London, 1896); Edgar S. Furniss, *The Position of the Labourer in a System of Nationalism* (Boston: Houghton Mifflin, 1920); Jacob Viner, "English Theories of Foreign Trade before Adam Smith," *Journal of Political Economy* 38 (1930): 249–301, 404–57; P. W. Buck, *The Politics of Mercantilism* (New York: Henry Holt, 1942); Joseph A. Schumpeter, *History of Economic Analysis* (London: Routledge, 1954), 335–76; Eli Heckscher, *Mercantilism* (London: George Allen & Unwin, 1955).

which was economic. The power of this state was to be enhanced by the accumulation of treasure through trade, the maximization of employment, and the encouragement of population growth.

Hume, unlike Adam Smith, made no attempt to treat the "mercantile system" as a *system*. But despite the fact that he approached mercantilism as a policy, he did also treat it at the *theoretical* level. As will be seen below, Hume in his economic essays identifies, criticizes, and sometimes uses a number of the "threads" associated with mercantilism. Mercantilists supposed, for example, that foreign trade is more important than domestic, a point of view admirably summarized by the title of Thomas Munn's *England's Treasure by Forraign Trade. Or, The Ballance of our Forraign Trade is the Rule of our Treasure* (1630). Hume, too, thought foreign trade of great importance, but his reasoning is substantially different from that of the mercantilists. The rate of interest, mercantilists supposed, is dependent on the supply of money. Hume focused on this issue, but presented a broader account of the determinants of interest rates. Mercantilists supposed that state regulation of trade was both necessary and beneficial. This position is neatly caught in William Petty's *Britannia Languens* (1680): "Nothing can so effectually and certainly secure the peace of the Nation, as the Regulating of our Trade, since it will set all Mens heads and hands at work in all manner of Innocent and Profitable Imployments, and introduce a general satisfaction and Harmony."[3] Although fundamentally committed to free trade, Hume accepted a modified form of this mercantilist view – in some circumstances, he granted, the state would have to produce legislation to promote and regulate industry. Mercantilists held that low wages are an incentive to industry – the utility of poverty argument.[4] Hume saw that low wages could in some circumstances provide an incentive to an established industry, but also saw that relatively high wages would produce additional markets for goods.

---

[3] *Britannia Languens, or a Discourse of Trade: Shewing the Grounds and Reasons of the Increase and Decay of Land-Rents, National Wealth and Strength*, cited from *A Select Collection of Early English Tracts on Commerce*, ed. J. R. McCulloch (London, 1856), 501. McCulloch's work includes eight texts first published from 1621 to 1701.

[4] See Furniss, *Position of the Labourer*, esp. Chap. 4, and E. A. G. Johnson, "Unemployment and Consumption: The Mercantilist View," *Quarterly Journal of Economics* 46 (1932): 698–719.

It would be wrong, however, to suggest that the mercantilists among Hume's predecessors provide an adequate expression of the nature of economic theory at the time Hume was composing his essays. By the seventeenth century speculation on economic questions was beginning to follow a new and different methodology, even as mercantilists continued to argue the merits of closely regulated trade.[5] A striking example of this methodological revolution is provided by William Petty:

> The method I take ... is not very usual; for instead of using only comparative and superlative words, and intellectual arguments, I have taken the course (as a specimen of the political arithmetic I have long aimed at) to express myself in terms of number, weight, or measure; to use only arguments of sense, and to consider only such causes, as have visible foundations in nature; leaving those that depend upon the mutable minds, opinions, appetites, and passions of particular men, to the consideration of others.[6]

Another example of the new method is provided by Gregory King's posthumously published *Political Arithmetic*. The manuscript of this work may have had a profound influence on Charles Davenant's classic works *An Essay on the East India Trade* (1697) and *Discourses upon the Public Revenue and Trade* (1698). Pioneering work on population statistics was done by Petty's friend John Graunt, whose *Political Observations on the Bills of Mortality* appeared in 1662. Edmund Halley further advanced population studies in his *Degrees of Mortality of Mankind* (1693).

An additional remarkable example, but this time in a Cartesian mode, is provided by Sir Dudley North's *Discourses upon Trade* (1691). North, like Davenant, was an advocate of free trade. In the Preface to this work Roger North acknowledged the debt of Sir

---

[5] Writers who review this debate include Schumpeter, *History of Economic Analysis*, and E. A. G. Johnson, *Predecessors of Adam Smith: The Growth of British Economic Thought* (New York: Prentice Hall, 1937); William Letwin, *The Origins of Scientific Economics: English Economic Thought, 1660–1776* (London: Methuen, 1963); and Terence W. Hutchison, *Before Adam Smith: The Emergence of Political Economy, 1622–1776* (Cambridge: Basil Blackwell, 1988). My debts to these works, and especially to that of Hutchison, will be evident in what follows in this section. Douglas Vickers, *Studies in the Theory of Money, 1690–1776* (London: Peter Owen, 1959), remains the classic account of monetary theory in the period and is highly recommended.

[6] *Political Arithmetic* (London, 1690), quoted from Hutchison, *Before Adam Smith*, 37.

Dudley, his brother, to Descartes, whose "excellent" *Discourse on Method* is "so much approved and accepted in our Age." Of his brother's work, North remarks: "I find Trade here Treated at another rate, than usually hath been; I mean Philosophically: for the ordinary and vulgar conceits, being meer Husk and Rubbish, are waived; and he begins at the quick, from Principles indisputably true; and so proceeding with like care, comes to a Judgment of the nicest Disputes and Questions concerning Trade." To this he added: "And hence it is, that Knowledge in great measure is become Mechanical; which word I need not interpret farther, than by noting, it here means, built upon clear and evident Truths."[7]

It is tempting to see subsequent developments in economics as involving a combination of two different methodological approaches. In his *Principles of Political Oeconomy* (1767), Sir James Steuart explicitly adopted the techniques of both induction and deduction while making a formal approach to the construction of theory. But there were other, and earlier, examples – notably Henry Martin's *Considerations upon the East-India Trade* (1701). In his prefatory remarks to this work Martin notes that he "has endeavour'd after the manner of the *Political Arithmetick*, to express himself in Terms of Number, Weight, and Measure; and he hopes, he shall not be thought to speak with confidence, of any thing that is not as certain as the very Principles of *Geometry*."[8]

There were still further developments that could have attracted Hume's attention. Especially important were the works of those who placed emphasis on the economic consequences of the fundamental principles of human nature, and, more particularly, on the important role played by self-interest. The first and most obvious of these writers was Bernard Mandeville, author of *The Fable of the Bees* (1705–23), whose influence Hume acknowledges in his *A Treatise of Human Nature* (T Intro. 7). Less obvious is Pierre de Boisguilbert, whose *Detail de la France* (1695) places self-interest at center stage and gives prominence to issues that Hume was later to emphasize, namely, the interdependence of economic phenomena and the

---

[7] Cited from McCulloch, *Early English Tracts*, [514–15].
[8] On Steuart, see *Sir James Steuart, Principles of Political Oeconomy*, ed. A. Skinner (Edinburgh: Edinburgh University Press, 1966), lx–lxii. Martin's *Considerations* is reprinted in McCulloch, *Early English Tracts*, 541–629.

operation of the circular flow of money. Isaac Gervaise, less interventionist than Boisguilbert, attempted to put the case for the freedom of trade on scientific grounds, and successfully articulated the concept of the balance of trade, a concept later emphasised by Hume.[9] Jacob Vanderlint's contribution, *Money Answers All Things, or an Essay to make Money Plentiful . . . and increase our Foreign and Domestick Trade* (1734), advanced theses similar to those we will find Hume to have adumbrated and further anticipated the role of self-regulating mechanisms in international trade. Dugald Stewart was to compare Vanderlint with Hume "in point of good sense and liberality," while Marx was to charge that Hume followed Vanderlint's work "step by step."[10]

While Stewart identified a *parallel* between Hume and Vanderlint, *debts* are more difficult to establish. But Burton has drawn attention to Hume's knowledge of Sebastian Vauban, Marshall of France, whose *Dixme Royale* (1701) is remarkable for its empirical content and for the analysis of taxation – another important theme in Hume's essays. Burton has also reminded us of Hume's debt to Montesquieu.[11] Given that Hume read some of Josiah Tucker's work in manuscript and corresponded with him,[12] it is likely that he was familiar with the latter's *Essay on Trade* (1749), a work that also emphasized the need to place economic studies on a scientific basis. Hume also cites Jean-Francois Melon's *Essai Politique sur le Commerce* (1734), Dutot's *Reflections Politiques sur le Commerce et les Finances* (1738), and Joseph Paris-Duverney's commentary (1740) on the latter's work (E-Mo, 8n, 287–8).

Hume's knowledge of the work of Francis Hutcheson opens up intriguing possibilities even if it is likely that the shape that Hutcheson gave to the study of economics had a greater influence on his student Adam Smith than it did on Hume.[13] Like Hume (and later Smith), Hutcheson treated questions of political economy as integral

---

[9] Hutchison, *Before Adam Smith*, 126–9.

[10] *The New Palgrave: A Dictionary of Economics*, s.v. "Vanderlint, Jacob."

[11] *Life and Correspondence*, 1:92, 304–5.

[12] See HL 1:270–72; 2:180, 182, 205.

[13] W. R. Scott, *Francis Hutcheson* (Cambridge, 1900), 230–43; see also W. L. Taylor, *Francis Hutcheson and David Hume as Predecessors of Adam Smith* (Durham, NC: Duke University Press, 1965), 12–28; and *The New Palgrave: A Dictionary of Economics*, s.v. "Hutcheson, Francis."

with issues in ethics and jurisprudence.[14] We are thus reminded of another, distinctive, approach to the study of political economy, one that took its origins, in part, from the work of Grotius and Pufendorf, and that was further stimulated by philosophical considerations.[15] But the path Hume was to follow was largely his own. It differs from that of Hutcheson and from that of John Locke, another major philosopher of an earlier age who made a significant contribution to the development of scientific economics.[16]

II. FUNDAMENTAL PRINCIPLES OF HUME'S ECONOMICS

Psychology

In his valuable introduction to *David Hume: Writings on Economics*,[17] Eugene Rotwein reminds us that Hume's discussion of economic issues relies heavily on principles elaborated in his *Treatise of Human Nature*. Rotwein notes especially Hume's conviction that "all the sciences have a relation, greater or less, to human nature; and that however wide any of them may seem to run from it, they still return back by one passage or another. Even *Mathematics*, *Natural Philosophy*, and *Natural Religion* are in some measure dependent on the science of MAN; since they lie under the cognizance of men, and are judg'd of by their powers and faculties" (T Intro. 4).

Hume was also convinced that the science of man itself must be founded "on experience and observation." But, because this science cannot make experiments purposely, he concluded that we

must therefore glean up our experiments in this science from a cautious observation of human life, and take them as they appear in the common course of the world, by men's behaviour in company, in affairs, and in their

---

[14] Richard F. Teichgraeber III, *"Free Trade" and Moral Philosophy: Rethinking the Sources of Adam Smith's* Wealth of Nations (Durham, NC: Duke University Press, 1986).

[15] Schumpeter, *History of Economic Analysis*, Chap. 2.

[16] See, e.g., Locke's *Consequence of the Lowering of Interest* (London, 1691), and *Further Considerations concerning the Raising of the Value of Money* (1695).

[17] Eugene Rotwein, *David Hume: Writings on Economics* (Edinburgh: Nelson, 1955). Professor Rotwein has provided the most important commentary on Hume's economic writings thus far published. His edition incorporates correspondence between Hume; Charles de Secondat, Baron Montesquieu; James Oswald of Dunniker; Henry Home, Lord Kames; Anne-Robert-Jacques Turgot; and the Abbé Morellet, 1740–76.

pleasures. Where experiments of this kind are judiciously collected and compar'd, we may hope to establish on them a science, which will not be inferior in certainty, and will be much superior in utility to any other of human comprehension. (T Intro. 7, 10)

This approach to his subject gives Hume grounds for maintaining a point of view that was to prove profoundly influential in the eighteenth century, namely, that both human nature, and, to a lesser extent, human behavior, are uniform – that, as he was to put it in *An Enquiry concerning Human Understanding*, "there is a great uniformity among the actions of men, in all nations and ages, and that human nature remains still the same, in its principles and operations" (EHU 8.7).

Among the constant principles Hume identified as essential to human happiness are "action, pleasure, and indolence." In practice, he placed the most emphasis on the first of these. "There is," he said, "no craving or demand of the human mind more constant and insatiable than that for exercise and employment; and this desire seems the foundation of most of our passions and pursuits." He makes a direct application of this need for action to the sphere of economics: "In times when industry and the arts flourish, men are kept in perpetual occupation, and enjoy, as their reward, the occupation itself, as well as those pleasures which are the fruit of their labour" (E-RA 3, 269–70; E-In 11, 300; see also T 2.3.10.6).

Self-Interest and the Pursuit of Gain

In addition to isolating the importance of the love of action, Hume also calls attention to the desire for gain: "Avarice, or the desire of gain, is an universal passion, which operates at all times, in all places, and upon all persons" (E-RP 6, 113). This desire is linked to vanity and pride: "We found a vanity upon houses, gardens, equipages, as well as upon personal merit and accomplishments," but the most common of these sources of vanity is property (T 2.1.9.1, 2.1.10.1). Indeed, "riches are to be consider'd as the power of acquiring the property of what pleases," and the "very essence of riches consists in the power of procuring the pleasures and conveniencies of life. The very essence of this power consists in the probability of its exercise, and in its causing us to anticipate, by a *true* or *false* reasoning, the real existence of the pleasure" (T 2.1.10.3, 10).

Hume used this argument to throw important light on what Adam Smith was later to describe as man's drive to better his condition, and in so doing anticipated Smith's claim that this drive has generally a social reference inasmuch as it is rooted in the desire for approbation. As Hume put it: "There are few persons, that are satisfy'd with their own character, or genius, or fortune, who are not desirous of showing themselves to the world, and of acquiring the love and approbation of mankind" (T 2.2.1.9). This position he elaborated by arguing that the

> *satisfaction* we take in the riches of others, and the *esteem* we have for the possessors may be ascrib'd to three different causes. *First,* To the objects they possess; such as houses, gardens, equipages; which, being agreeable in themselves, necessarily produce a sentiment of pleasure in every one, that either considers or surveys them. *Secondly,* To the expectation of advantage from the rich and powerful by our sharing their possessions. *Thirdly,* To sympathy, which makes us partake of the satisfaction of every one, that approaches us. (T 2.2.5.2)

In his explanatory practice, Hume placed the most emphasis on the third of these causes, *sympathy,* saying that "the pleasure of a stranger, for whom we have no friendship, pleases us only by sympathy. To this principle, therefore, is owing the beauty, which we find in every thing that is useful.... Wherever an object has a tendency to produce pleasure in the possessor, or in other words, is the proper *cause* of pleasure, it is sure to please the spectator, by a delicate sympathy with the possessor" (T 3.3.1.8).[18]

Self-Interest and Constraint

Hume drew attention to a problem created by the active pursuit of gain, namely, the problem of maintaining social order. Our avidity to acquire "goods and possessions for ourselves and our nearest friends," he writes, "is insatiable, perpetual, universal, and directly

---

[18] Adam Smith was critical of Hume's contention that the "same principle produces, in many instances, our sentiments of morals, as well as those of beauty" (T 3.3.1.9). Smith's criticism is found in *The Theory of Moral Sentiments,* ed. D. D. Raphael and A. L. Macfie (Oxford: Oxford University Press, 1976), Part 4, 179–93; this work was first published in 1759. But Smith accepted, and indeed elaborated on, Hume's use of sympathy to explain economic phenomena.

destructive of society," and our natural benevolence to strangers is too weak a passion to "counter-ballance the love of gain." In fact, we find that our natural self-interest can be constrained only by itself, and redirected to constructive ends: "There is no passion, therefore, capable of controuling the interested affection, but the very affection itself, by an alteration of its direction." This redirection or "alteration" as Hume calls it, "must necessarily take place upon the least reflection; since 'tis evident, that the passion is much better satisfy'd by its restraint, than by its liberty, and that by preserving society, we make much greater advances in the acquiring possessions, than by running into the solitary and forlorn condition, which must follow upon violence and an universal licence" (T 3.2.2.12–13).

We see, then, the importance of society – and of the conventions of justice on which society is founded – as basic preconditions of the social order we find beneficial and prize. Justice itself originates, Hume writes, *"from the selfishness and confin'd generosity of man, along with the scanty provision nature has made for his wants"* (T 3.2.2.18). Having observed "that 'tis impossible to live in society without restraining themselves by certain rules," humans have (perhaps without conscious forethought) devised the needed rules. But, once the rules are in place, it happens that we "receive a pleasure from the view of such actions as tend to the peace of society, and an uneasiness from such as are contrary to it." This fact and "the public instructions of politicians, and the private education of parents, contribute to the giving us a sense of honour and duty in the strict regulation of our actions with regard to the properties of others" (T 3.2.6.11).[19] As the reference to politicians perhaps indicates, the final condition for social order, and one that is essential to the conduct of economic affairs, is some system of government. Given that we as individuals "are, in a great measure, govern'd by interest," it is obvious that we need to institutionalize some form of control over these individual interests. We need to "change our circumstances and situation, and render the observance of the laws of justice our nearest interest, and their violation our most remote." This we have done by establishing a relatively few persons as magistrates or

---

[19] For further discussion of these points, see in this volume the essays "The Foundations of Morality in Hume's *Treatise*" and "The Structure of Hume's Political Theory."

"governors and rulers." These are individuals who are meant to "have no interest, or but a remote one, in any act of injustice; and being satisfied with their present condition, and with their part in society, have an immediate interest in every execution of justice, which is so necessary to the upholding of society.... These persons, then, are not only induc'd to observe those rules in their own conduct, but also to constrain others to a like regularity, and enforce the dictates of equity thro' the whole society" (T 3.2.7.1, 6).

The Use of History

The student of Hume's writings on economics should be aware that the great bulk of his published work was historical, and of his conviction that "history is not only a valuable part of knowledge, but opens the door to many other parts, and affords materials to most of the sciences." It is an invention that "extends our experience to all past ages, and to the most distant nations" (E-SH 6, 566).[20] Looked at in this way, historical studies afford invaluable information with regard to the principles of human nature and to the fact that the expression of these principles would be profoundly affected by the socioeconomic environment that may happen to exist and by changes in habits, customs, and manners.

To the economist the most interesting parts of Hume's *History of England* may initially be the appendices and reports of miscellaneous transactions introduced throughout the work. These answered to Hume's desire to "take a general survey of the age, so far as regards manners, finances, arms, commerce, arts and sciences. The chief use of history is, that it affords materials for disquisitions of this nature; and it seems the duty of an historian to point out the proper inferences and conclusions" (HE 62.65, 6:140).

Hume applies this procedure to his account of the entire range of English history, from the time of Julius Caesar to the Revolution of 1688.[21] Quite apart from the intrinsic value of the material, Hume's

---

[20] Hume withdrew the essay "Of the Study of History" in 1760, but it does not follow that he thought the essay mistaken in all respects.

[21] For the titles of the several volumes of *The History of England*, and information about the order in which the volumes appeared, see Part I of the Bibliography to this volume.

accounts are informed by an attempt to understand specific policies in their institutional, economic, and political settings, with the importance of economic liberty emphasized throughout. Thus, for example, in his discussion of the ecclesiastical affairs under Henry VIII, Hume remarks that "Most of the arts and professions in a state are of such a nature, that, while they promote the interest of the society, they are also useful or agreeable to some individuals; and in that case, the constant rule of the magistrate, except, perhaps, on the first introduction of any art, is, to leave the profession to itself, and trust its encouragement to those who reap the benefit of it."[22] Unless the process is "disturbed by any injudicious tampering, the commodity is always sure to be at all times nearly proportioned to the demand" (HE 29.2, 3:135). The same emphasis is apparent in the treatment of the regulation of interest, wages, the prohibitions on the export of specie, and, above all, in the context of international trade: "It is evident, that these matters ought always to be left free, and be entrusted to the common course of business and commerce" (HE 26.40, 3:78).

At the same time it has to be recognized that the *History* was primarily concerned with the broader theme of the study of civilization and with the interconnections between the growth of commerce, the changing forms of government, and liberty. In short, Hume's concern was with the origins and nature of the present establishments in Europe, where the economic dimension was only one part of a wider whole. Hume's perception of the interplay between economic growth and liberty moved Adam Smith to remark:

Commerce and manufactures gradually introduced order and good government, and with them, the liberty and security of individuals, among the inhabitants of the country, who had before lived almost in a continual state of war with their neighbours, and of servile dependency upon their superiors. This, though it has been the least observed, is by far the most important of all their effects. Mr. Hume is the only writer who, so far as I know, has hitherto taken notice of it.[23]

---

[22] This is a preamble to Hume's argument in favor of an established church. Such an institution, he argues, curbs the "pernicious" and "interested diligence of the clergy."

[23] *An Inquiry into the Causes of the Wealth of Nations,* ed. R. H. Campbell, A. S. Skinner, and W. B. Todd (Oxford: Clarendon Press, 1976), 3.4.4 (1:412). This work was first published in 1776.

The relevance of these positions for the contemporary understanding of Hume's treatment of economic theory and policy will be readily apparent.[24]

III. THE ECONOMIC ESSAYS

It is usual to identify nine of Hume's essays, eight of which were first published in 1752, the ninth in 1758, as the economic essays.[25] These are *essays*, rather than a treatise or a work that addresses separate subjects from one point of view. Yet Hume believed economic questions to be amenable to scientific treatment largely as a result of his belief in the constant principles of human nature and the emphasis that he gave to self-interest. In a famous passage he asserted that "it is certain, that general principles, if just and sound, must always prevail in the general course of things, though they may fail in particular cases; and it is the chief business of philosophers to regard the general course of things" (E-Co 2, 254).

Hume also noted that there are areas of experience about which generalization is difficult: "*What depends upon a few persons is, in a great measure, to be ascribed to chance, or secret and unknown causes: What arises from a great number, may often be accounted for by determinate and known causes.*" From this principle he concludes that the "domestic and the gradual revolutions of a state must be a more proper subject of reasoning and observation than the foreign and violent." He also concludes that it is easier to "account for the rise and progress of commerce in any kingdom, than for that of learning; and a state, which should apply itself to the encouragement of the one, would be more assured of success, than one which should cultivate the other" (E-RP 2, 5, 6, 112–13).

It should also be observed that the separate essays show a unity of purpose.[26] All of them illustrate the fundamental propositions in

---

[24] Duncan Forbes suggests that the essay "Of Refinement in the Arts" is an abridged version of those aspects of the *History* briefly touched on here. *Hume, The History of Great Britain*, ed. Duncan Forbes (Harmondsworth: Penguin, 1970), 297.

[25] The nine essays are "Of Commerce," "Of Refinement in the Arts," "Of Money," "Of Interest," "Of the Balance of Trade," "Of the Jealousy of Trade," "Of Taxes," "Of Public Credit," and "Of the Populousness of Ancient Nations." Those published in 1752 were a part of the immediately successful *Political Discourses*. "Of the Jealousy of Trade" was published in 1758.

[26] This point has been made by Rotwein, *Hume: Writings on Economics*, cv.

Section II. It is this unity of purpose and method that enables us to identify three major themes: historical dynamics, or the process of historical change; the use of the historical method; and Hume's use of both of these perspectives in the treatment of international trade.

Historical Dynamics and the Exchange Economy

"As soon as men quit their savage state, where they live chiefly by hunting and fishing," Hume suggests in "Of Commerce," they become farmers or manufacturers, "though the arts of agriculture employ *at first* the most numerous part of the society." In an early anticipation of the theory that humanity has passed, by stages, from hunting and gathering to the commercial society of eighteenth-century Europe, Hume noted that where there is little stimulus to change, "people must apply themselves to agriculture." Because they cannot exchange any surplus for other commodities, humans in this situation have no temptation to "encrease their skill and industry." As a result, the "greater part of the land lies uncultivated. What is cultivated, yields not its utmost for want of skill and assiduity in the farmers" (E-Co 5, 10, 256, 260–1).

In contrast, Hume continued, "When a nation abounds in manufactures and mechanic arts, the proprietors of land, as well as the farmers, study agriculture as a science, and redouble their industry and attention. The superfluity, which arises from their labour, is not lost; but is exchanged with manufactures for those commodities, which men's luxury now makes them covet" (E-Co 11, 261). In short, Hume suggests that there is likely to be a gradual progression toward the interdependence of the two main sectors of activity. Playing an important supporting role are the merchants, "one of the most useful races of men, who serve as agents between those parts of the state, that are wholly unacquainted, and are ignorant of each other's necessities" (E-In 10, 300).

Hume's argument has it roots in his deployment of a favorite thesis of the eighteenth century, namely, that men have natural wants that gradually extend in a self-sustaining spiral: "Every thing in the world is purchased by labour; and our passions are the only causes of labour" (E-Co 11, 261). It was this thesis that Mandeville addressed with such amusing consequences in *The Fable of the Bees*, and that drew from Hume the comment that to "imagine, that the gratifying of any sense, or the indulging of any delicacy in meat, drink, or apparel, is of itself a vice, can never enter into a head, that is not disordered by the frenzies of enthusiasm (E-RA 1, 268).

But there is more to the thesis than a concentration on a gradual institutional change; it is also a part of Hume's argument that the emergence of what came to be known as the *stage of commerce* would induce an accelerating rate of change due to changes in habits and manners – notably by encouraging the desire for gain and by giving progressively increasing scope to man's active disposition.[27] The historical process of economic development had been stimulated by the discovery of gold, for example, and this had been a factor, Hume thought, in the rapid rate of economic growth during the reign of Charles I and during the period from the Restoration to the Revolution of 1688 (E-Mo 7, 286; HE 62.83, 6:148; 71.81, 6:537).

Hume went on to observe that "industry and arts and trade encrease the power of the sovereign as well as the happiness of the subjects" insofar as they "store up so much labour, and that of a kind to which the public may lay claim" through taxation. Here again the modern commercial state has an advantage, for "when the riches are dispersed among multitudes, the burthen feels light on every shoulder" (E-Co 9, 11, 17; 260, 262, 265). He warned against such arbitrary impositions as a poll tax, expressing a strong preference for taxes on consumption in order to minimize disincentives:

The best taxes are such as are levied upon consumptions, especially those of luxury; because such taxes are least felt by the people. They seem, in some measure, voluntary; since a man may chuse how far he will use the commodity which is taxed: They are paid gradually and insensibly: They naturally produce sobriety and frugality, if judiciously imposed: And being confounded with the natural price of the commodity, they are scarcely perceived by the consumers. Their only disadvantage is, that they are expensive in the levying. (E-Ta 5, 345)

Indeed, Hume even contended that taxation *could* prove an *encouragement* to industry: "Where taxes are moderate, are laid on gradually, and affect not the necessaries of life," he writes, they "often serve to excite the industry of a people, and render them more

---

[27] Rotwein, *Hume: Writings on Economics,* 19, suggests that the historical variability of moral standards is a theme of Hume's "A Dialogue," a work routinely published at the end of *An Enquiry concerning the Principles of Morals.* For Smith's views, see *The Theory of Moral Sentiments,* 5.2 (194–211).

opulent and laborious, than others, who enjoy the greatest advantages" (E-Ta 2, 343).[28]

The modern state has a further advantage in that it can borrow present resources through the sale of securities that "are with us become a kind of money," a development that encourages "a set of men, who are half merchants, half stock-holders" and who are willing to trade in securities for small profits. Consequently, more individuals, those "with large stocks and incomes, may naturally be supposed to continue in trade, where there are public debts; and this, it must be owned, is of some advantage to commerce, by diminishing its profits, promoting circulation, and encouraging industry" (E-PC 8–9, 353–4).[29]

The essays are also remarkable for the emphasis that Hume gave to the other, noneconomic advantages that accrue from the process of historical development: "The minds of men, being once roused from their lethargy, and put into a fermentation, turn themselves on all sides, and carry improvements into every art and science. Profound ignorance is totally banished, and men enjoy the privilege of rational creatures, to think as well as to act, to cultivate the pleasures of the mind as well as those of the body." He noted that the "more these refined arts advance, the more sociable men become"; they "flock into cities; love to receive and communicate knowledge" (E-RA 4–5, 271). He also emphasized sociological and political developments in a notable passage in the *History*. During the reign of Henry VII, he writes,

The common people, no longer maintained in vicious idleness by their superiors, were obliged to learn some calling or industry, and became useful both to themselves and to others. And it must be acknowledged, in spite of those who declaim so violently against refinement in the arts, or what

---

[28] See M. Arkin, "The Economic Writings of David Hume – A Reassessment," *South African Journal of Economics* 24 (1956): 204–20. Hume corresponded with Turgot on the subject of taxation; see especially Turgot to Hume, 7 September 1766 and 25 March 1767 (Rotwein, 206–7; 210–13), and Hume to Turgot, September 1766 (HL 2:93–4).

[29] Hume was for some years convinced that government borrowing served to reduce interest rates. From 1752 to 1764 "Of Public Credit" included a note reading: "On this head, I shall observe, without interrupting the thread of the argument, that the multiplicity of our public debts serves rather to sink the interest, and that the more the government borrows, the cheaper may they expect to borrow; contrary to first appearance, and contrary to common opinion. The profits of trade have an influence on interest" (E-PC Variants, 637).

they are pleased to call luxury, that ... an industrious tradesman is both a
better man and a better citizen than one of those idle retainers, who formerly
depended on the great families; so much is the life of a modern nobleman
more laudable than that of an ancient baron. (HE 26.37, 3:76–7)

    This theme is elaborated in "Of Refinement in the Arts." Where
"luxury nourishes commerce and industry," Hume writes, "the peasants, by a proper cultivation of the land, become rich and independent; while the tradesmen and merchants acquire a share of the property, and draw authority and consideration to that middling rank of
men, who are the best and firmest basis of public liberty." This
development brought about major constitutional changes, at least
in England, where the "lower house is the support of our popular
government; and all the world acknowledges, that it owed its chief
influence and consideration to the encrease of commerce, which
threw such a balance of property into the hands of the commons.
How inconsistent then is it to blame so violently a refinement in
the arts, and to represent it as the bane of liberty and public spirit!"
(E-RA 16–17, 277–8).

    This dynamic environment, buttressed by "equal laws," further
enhances the possibilities for economic growth.[30] But it is important
to note here that Hume also offered a sharp critique of egalitarianism:
however attractive and compelling the "ideas of *perfect* equality
may seem, they are really, at bottom, *impracticable*; and were they
not so, would be extremely *pernicious* to human society. Render
possessions ever so equal, men's different degrees of art, care, and
industry will immediately break that equality" (EPM 3.26).

The Historical or Institutional Method

Hume's interest in the historical process led him quite naturally to
develop a distinctive technique for dealing with purely economic
questions; in turn, this technique led him to give prominence to
institutional background and, in particular, to the role of customs

---

[30] In "Of Commerce," Hume says that, "Every person, if possible, ought to enjoy
the fruits of his labour, in full possession of all the necessaries, and many of the
conveniences of life." He went on to note that "in this circumstance consists
the great advantage of ENGLAND above any nation at present in the world or that
appears in the records of any story" (E-Co 17, 265). The link between commerce
and liberty is one of the themes developed in "Of Civil Liberty."

and manners. While this technique shapes all the essays, three in particular stand out in this regard: the essays on population, money, and interest.

In the long essay "Of the Populousness of Ancient Nations," a work that has scarcely received the attention it deserves, Hume addressed a proposition advanced by Robert Wallace in his *Dissertation on the Numbers of Mankind in Ancient and Modern Times* (1753). Wallace maintained that population levels had been higher in ancient than in modern days.[31] In response, Hume argued that "there is in all men, both male and female, a desire and power of generation, more active than is ever universally exerted." Consequently, in addressing the question at issue it is necessary to know the "situation of society" and to compare "both the *domestic* and *political* situation of these two periods, in order to judge of the facts by their moral causes" (E-PA 4, 3, 5; 381, 383).

In arguing that modern society was the more populous one, Hume pointed out that the use of slavery in ancient times had been "in general disadvantageous both to the happiness and populousness of mankind." He also pointed out that ancient times had been characterized by a relatively high incidence of military conflict and by political instability. But perhaps the most striking aspect of his argument is his claim that "Trade, manufactures, industry, were no where, in former ages, so flourishing as they are at present in EUROPE" (E-PA 34, 83; 396, 416). In short, Hume saw that population is ultimately limited not just by political factors, but also by the food supply, and this in turn is affected by the type of economic organization prevailing.

Hume granted "that agriculture is the species of industry chiefly requisite to the subsistence of multitudes; and it is possible, that this industry may flourish, even where manufactures and other arts are unknown and neglected" (E-PA 88, 419). But, he added,

The most natural way, surely, of encouraging husbandry, is, first, to excite other kinds of industry, and thereby afford the labourer a ready market for his commodities, and a return of such goods as may contribute to his pleasure

---

[31] Wallace's work was not published until after Hume's, but Hume had seen the manuscript, and apparently encouraged Wallace to publish it. See Rotwein, *Hume: Writings on Economics,* 184. Hume also cites Montesquieu, with whom he corresponded on the subject (E-PA 3, 379–80). For a summary of the theory of population in this period, see Schumpeter, *History of Economic Analysis,* 250–8.

and enjoyment. This method is infallible and universal; and, as it prevails more in modern government than in the ancient, it affords a presumption of the superior populousness of the former. (E-PA 89, 419–20)

It is clear, then, that Hume saw no simple relationship between population and the food supply. Much depends on the form of economic organization, on the degree to which sectors of activity are interdependent, and on the degree to which men are motivated by the desire for gain.

The same basic view informs "Of Money." There Hume rejects the conventional wisdom that money can be regarded as wealth, and goes on to state the famous relationship between changes in the money supply and the general price level: "If we consider any one kingdom by itself, it is evident, that the greater or less plenty of money is of no consequence; since the prices of commodities are always proportioned to the plenty of money."[32] Less familiar is the fact that Hume consistently contrasted the situation of a primitive economy with a more sophisticated version. In a primitive economy, "we must consider, that, in the first and more uncultivated ages of any state, ere fancy has confounded her wants with those of nature, men, content with the produce of their own fields, or with those rude improvements which they themselves can work upon them, have little occasion for exchange, at least for money, which, by agreement, is the common measure of exchange." In a more advanced state of society, "Great undertakers, and manufacturers, and merchants, arise in every commodity; and these can conveniently deal in nothing but in specie. And consequently, in this situation of society, the coin enters into many more contracts, and by that means is much more employed than in the former" (E-Mo 1,14–15; 281, 290–1).

The changed form of economic organization heralds a change in manners by giving greater scope to individual effort and must therefore massively increase the supply of commodities that are subject to exchange. Hume thus concluded that although prices in Europe had risen since the discoveries in the West Indies and elsewhere, these prices were in fact much lower than the increase in the money supply itself might suggest:

[32] Hume's initial statement of this relationship occurs in a letter of 10 April 1749, to Montesquieu (HL 1:136–8). For a summary of treatments of the quantity theory of money, see Schumpeter, *History of Economic Analysis*, 311–17.

And no other satisfactory reason can be given, why all prices have not risen to a much more exorbitant height, except that which is derived from a change of customs and manners. Besides that more commodities are produced by additional industry, the same commodities come more to market, after men depart from their ancient simplicity of manners. And though this encrease has not been equal to that of money, it has, however, been considerable, and has preserved the proportion between coin and commodities nearer the ancient standard. (E-Mo 17, 292–3)

The essay "Of Interest" discusses an instance of the fallacy of taking "a collateral effect . . . for a cause." A lowered rate of interest "is ascribed to the plenty of money; though it be really owing to a change in the manners and customs of the people" (E-Mo 22, 294). The contention is that high interest rates arise from three circumstances: "A great demand for borrowing; little riches to supply that demand, and great profits arising from commerce," while a low rate of interest will reflect the contrary circumstances (E-In 6, 297).

In a primitive economy, the essay goes on, there will be little evidence of frugality, but often a considerable demand for borrowing for the purpose of consumption. This state of habits or manners is consistent with high rates of interest. In the modern economy there will be high levels of demand for funds to be used for productive purposes, but also an enhanced supply of such funds because

Commerce encreases industry, by conveying it readily from one member of the state to another, and allowing none of it to perish or become useless. It encreases frugality, by giving occupation to men, and employing them in the arts of gain, which soon engage their affection, and remove all relish for pleasure and expence. It is an infallible consequence of all industrious professions, to beget frugality, and make the love of gain prevail over the love of pleasure. (E-In 12, 301)

In short, the increase of commerce "by a necessary consequence, raises a great number of lenders, and by that means produces lowness of interest." This result is accompanied by a further tendency to reduce the rate of profit: "when commerce has become extensive, and employs large stocks, there must arise rivalships among the merchants, which diminish the profits of trade." Hume thus concluded that the most important single factor was not simply the supply of money, but a change in manners and in the form of economic organization. Interest, he wrote, is "the barometer of the state, and its lowness is a sign almost infallible of the flourishing condition of a people" (E-In 13–14; 302–3).[33]

The technique just considered counsels caution in offering generalizations in economics. The way in which economic relationships develop will necessarily be affected by manners and by the prevailing institutional structures. It is therefore important to note Hume's awareness of a further fact, namely, that economic relationships will be affected by the condition of an economy even where the institutional structure is stable. He makes this point regularly, but aptly illustrated it in "Of Money": "It seems a maxim almost self-evident, that the prices of every thing depend on the proportion between commodities and money, and that any considerable alteration on either has the same effect, either of heightening or lowering the price. Encrease the commodities, they become cheaper; encrease the money, they rise in their value" (E-Mo 12, 290).

This statement seems clearly to mean that an increase in the money supply will generate a change in the price level in cases where resources are fully employed, while a similar change in the supply of money could be expected to result in an increase in the supply of commodities if there are unemployed resources. Hume's analysis of the process by virtue of which changes in the money supply affect the economy embraces both results and at the same time takes the argument a step further:

Here are a set of manufacturers or merchants, we shall suppose, who have received returns of gold and silver for goods which they sent to CADIZ. They are thereby enabled to employ more workmen than formerly, who never dream of demanding higher wages, but are glad of employment from such good paymasters. If workmen become scarce, the manufacturer gives higher wages, but at first requires an encrease of labour; and this is willingly submitted to by the artisan, who can now eat and drink better, to compensate his additional toil and fatigue. He carries his money to market, where he finds every thing at the same price as formerly, but returns with greater quantity and of better kinds, for the use of his family. The farmer and gardener, finding, that all their commodities are taken off, apply themselves with alacrity to the raising more; and at the same time can afford to take

---

[33] Rotwein, *Hume: Writings on Economics*, xiv–xvi; Schumpeter, *History of Economic Analysis*, 327–34; and Hutchison, *Before Adam Smith, passim,* provide additional information about eighteenth-century views of interest rates.

better and more cloths from their tradesmen, whose price is the same as formerly, and their industry only whetted by so much new gain. It is easy to trace the money in its progress through the whole commonwealth; where we shall find, that it must first quicken the diligence of every individual, before it encrease the price of labour. (E-Mo 7, 286–7)

This reasoning, Hume added, leads us to the conclusion that the domestic happiness of a country is entirely independent of the size of the supply of money. All that matters – what constitutes "good policy of the magistrate" – is that the supply of money continually increase. If the magistrate can achieve that goal, "he keeps alive a spirit of industry in the nation, and encreases the stock of labour, in which consists all real power and riches" (E-Mo 9, 288). But as we shall see, a rather different appreciation of this matter was to emerge in the course of Hume's discussion of international trade.

International Trade

The final major aspect of Hume's discussion of these issues concerns the problem of international trade; his discussion again proceeds at a number of levels. He first draws attention to the general benefits of foreign trade. In "Of Commerce," for example, he points out that if "we consult history, we shall find, that, in most nations, foreign trade has preceded any refinement in home manufactures, and given birth to domestic luxury" (E-Co 15, 263). In the same essay he makes the further point that, as Smith was later to put it, imitation leads domestic manufactures to emulate the improvements of foreign ones.[34] Hume repeats this claim in "Of the Jealousy of Trade," asking us there to compare "the situation of GREAT BRITAIN at present, with what it was two centuries ago. All the arts both of agriculture and manufactures were then extremely rude and imperfect. Every improvement, which we have since made, has arisen from our imitation of foreigners; and we ought so far to esteem it happy, that they had previously made advances in arts and ingenuity" (E-JT 2, 328).

This sentiment sets the tone of this particular essay, which explicitly criticizes what Hume took to be a characteristic feature of

---

[34] *Wealth of Nations,* 3.4.4 (I:414). See also HE 33.58, 3:328.

mercantilist policy, namely, an unfounded jealousy or suspicion of the commercial success of other nations. "Nothing is more usual, among states which have made some advances in commerce," he wrote,

> than to look on the progress of their neighbours with a suspicious eye, to consider all trading states as their rivals, and to suppose that it is impossible for any of them to flourish, but at their expence. In opposition to this narrow and malignant opinion, I will venture to assert, that the encrease of riches and commerce in any one nation, instead of hurting, commonly promotes the riches and commerce of all its neighbours; and that a state can scarcely carry its trade and industry very far, where all the surrounding states are buried in ignorance, sloth, and barbarism. (E-JT 1, 327–8)

In a passage that may well have struck a chord with the French economist J. B. Say, who first formulated his famous law while discussing exactly this topic, Hume continued:[35]

> The encrease of domestic industry lays the foundation of foreign commerce. Where a great number of commodities are raised and perfected for the home-market, there will always be found some which can be exported with advantage. But if our neighbours have no art or cultivation, they cannot take them; because they will have nothing to give in exchange. In this respect, states are in the same condition as individuals. A single man can scarcely be industrious, where all his fellow-citizens are idle. . . . Nor needs any state entertain apprehensions, that their neighbours will improve to such a degree in every art and manufacture, as to have no demand from them. Nature, by giving a diversity of geniuses, climates, and soils, to different nations, has secured their mutual intercourse and commerce, as long as they all remain industrious and civilized. (E-JT 3–4, 329)

He closed the essay with a passage that must have attracted the attention of Adam Smith:

> I shall therefore venture to acknowledge, that, not only as a man, but as a BRITISH subject, I pray for the flourishing commerce of GERMANY, SPAIN, ITALY, and even FRANCE itself. I am at least certain, that GREAT BRITAIN, and all those nations, would flourish more, did their sovereigns and ministers adopt such enlarged and benevolent sentiments towards each other. (E-JT 7, 331)

---

[35] Say's Law is that supply creates its own demand. On the origin of this law, see my "Say's Law: Origins and Content," *Economica* 34 (1967): 153–66.

The second aspect of Hume's analysis supports this attitude toward foreign commerce on grounds that are essentially technical. Building on the analysis found in "Of Money," Hume examined the case of two or more economies with no unemployed resources with a view to demonstrating the futility of the mercantilist preoccupation with a positive balance of trade. Against this mercantilist concern, Hume contended that a net inflow of gold would inevitably raise prices in the domestic economy, while the loss of gold from the foreign economies would reduce the general price level in them. The net result would be an increase in the competitiveness of the foreign economy and a decrease in the competitiveness of the domestic economy. In "Of the Balance of Trade" Hume had concluded that "money, in spite of the absurd jealousy of princes and states, has brought itself nearly to a level," just as "all water, wherever it communicates, remains always at a level" (E-BT 15, 11; 314, 312). In the same essay he goes on to conclude:

From these principles we may learn what judgment we ought to form of those numberless bars, obstructions, and imposts, which all nations of EUROPE, and none more than ENGLAND, have put upon trade; from an exorbitant desire of amassing money, which never will heap up beyond its level, while it circulates; or from an ill-grounded apprehension of losing their specie, which never will sink below it. Could any thing scatter our riches, it would be such impolitic contrivances. (E-BT 35, 324)

The third dimension to Hume's treatment of foreign trade is much more complex. It is based on the premise that countries have different characteristics and different rates of growth, thus opening up a different and distinctive policy position as compared to those so far considered.

The *presence* of an argument reflecting a judgment that economic conditions are likely to be diverse is not perhaps surprising in a writer such as Hume. As Richard Teichgraeber has pointed out, Hume's perspective was Euro-Centric, rather than Anglo-Centric.[36] While critical of Montesquieu's claim that manners and customs depend on physical factors, Hume was nonetheless conscious of the fact that different countries could have different physical endowments,

---

[36] Teichgraeber, *"Free Trade" and Moral Philosophy*, 106.

and was clearly aware that climate could have some influence on economic activity (E-Co 21, 267; see also E-NC).

It is worth recalling here that the use of the historical method involved the comparison of different economic types, while emphasis on the dynamic element draws attention to the importance of individual effort and to an accelerating rate of change as institutions and manners themselves change. On the one hand the reader is reminded of the importance of a "diversity of geniuses, climates and soils," while on the other hand emphasis is placed on the fact that the extent to which men make use of "art, care, and industry" may vary in one society over time, and between different societies at any given time. Other factors that will affect the rate of growth and cause variations in rates of growth in different communities include the form of government and the degree to which public policies such as trade regulations, taxes, and debt are deployed with intelligence.

Hume illustrated this new aspect of the problem by referring to the issue of regional imbalance (a concern he shared with Josiah Tucker), citing the case of London and Yorkshire (E-PC 11, 354–5). In his early essay "That Politics May Be Reduced to a Science," he made the interesting further claim that, "though free governments have been commonly the most happy for those who partake of their freedom; yet are they the most ruinous and oppressive to their provinces" (E-PR 9, 18–19).This regional dimension is as relevant to the rich country–poor country debate (can a poor country hope to catch and overtake a rich country?) as is the international dimension, although it was on the latter that Hume chose to place most emphasis.

Hume's treatment of the performance of the modern economy, especially in "Of Money" and "Of Interest," implies that an increase in productivity may give the developed economy an advantage in terms of the price of manufactures. He also recognized that an inflow of gold into a growing economy need not generate adverse price effects. As he observed in a letter to James Oswald: "I never meant to say that money, in all countries which communicate, must necessarily be on a level, but only on a level proportioned to their people, industry, and commodities." To this he added, "I agree with you, that the increase of money, if not too sudden, naturally increases people and industry" (HL 1:142–3). Looked at from this point of view, Hume might have agreed with Tucker's belief that "the poor country, according to my apprehension, can never overtake the rich, unless it be through the fault and mismanagement of the latter"[37]

In "Of Money" Hume had already noted that where "one nation has gotten the start of another in trade, it is very difficult for the latter to regain the ground it has lost; because of the superior industry and skill of the former, and the greater stocks, of which its merchants are possessed, and which enable them to trade on so much smaller profits" (E-Mo 3, 283). But he observed that the historical increase in the quantity of money that quickened diligence could also result in a general increase in the price level, an increase that would be disadvantageous in the context of international trade. The advantages enjoyed by a relatively advanced economy, he continued,

are compensated, in some measure, by the low price of labour in every nation which has not an extensive commerce, and does not much abound in gold and silver. Manufactures, therefore gradually shift their places, leaving those countries and provinces which they have already enriched, and flying to others, whither they are allured by the cheapness of provisions and labour; till they have enriched these also, and are again banished by the same causes. And, in general, we may observe, that the dearness of every thing, from plenty of money, is a disadvantage, which attends an established commerce, and sets bounds to it in every country, by enabling the poorer states to undersel[l] the richer in all foreign markets. (E-Mo 3, 283–4)

Hume clearly felt that these trends were beginning to manifest themselves in England. There, "some disadvantages in foreign trade by the high price of labour, which is in part the effect of the riches of their artisans, as well as of the plenty of money," were already felt (E-Co 19, 265). The position which he was striving to formulate was well put in a letter to Lord Kames in the course of a discussion of advantages enjoyed by rich countries:

The question is, whether these advantages can go on, increasing trade *in infinitum*, or whether they do not at last come to a *ne plus ultra*, and check themselves, by begetting disadvantages, which at first retard, and at last finally stop their progress.... It was never surely the intention of Providence, that any one nation should be a monopoliser of wealth: and the growth of all bodies, artificial as well as natural, is stopped by internal causes, derived

---

[37] Quoted from Rotwein, *Hume: Writings on Economics*, 205.

from their enormous size and greatness. Great empires, great cities, great commerce, all of them receive a check, not from accidental events, but necessary principles. (HL 1:271–2)

These sentiments expand on a point that had already been made in "Of Money," where Hume had said that there "seems to be a happy concurrence of causes in human affairs, which checks the growth of trade and riches, and hinders them from being confined entirely to one people" (E-Mo 3, 283).[38]

The possibilities that Hume outlined are not without their implications for economic policy. A relatively backward economy might, for example, find it in its interest to adopt a policy of protection for infant industries. More advanced economies confronting a general loss of markets might have to adopt a policy of protection to sustain the level of employment. Hume regarded the possibility of such a response with some equanimity, noting that "as foreign trade is not the most material circumstance, it is not to be put in competition with the happiness of so many millions" who might otherwise find themselves unemployed (E-Co 19, 265).

Thus, although there is in Hume's writings a marked presumption in favor of free trade, he also recognized that government intervention may be beneficial. But any policies so instituted must always be consistent with the prevailing circumstances. This perspective is itself entirely consistent with that which Hume adopted when dealing with questions of a more purely theoretical nature.

Hume's concern with policy serves to remind us of other aspects of his contribution to economic theory. As we saw when discussing *historical dynamics*, Hume's tone is thoroughly optimistic in the sense that he saw economic change as resulting from a series of

---

[38] The rich country–poor country issue was the subject of considerable debate. See, for example, James Oswald to Hume, 10 October 1749 (Rotwein, 190–6) where it is argued, among other things, that rich countries are likely to enjoy continuing advantages. Hume took issue with this position in a letter to Oswald dated 1 November 1750 (HL 1:142–4). The topic is also addressed in correspondence between Hume and Kames (HL 1:270–1) and Josiah Tucker and Kames (Rotwein, 202–4). On this debate see also Istvan Hont, "The 'rich country–poor country' debate in Scottish classical political economy," in *Wealth and Virtue: The Shaping of Political Economy in the Scottish Enlightenment*, ed. Istvan Hont and Michael Ignatieff (Cambridge: Cambridge University Press, 1983), 271–315.

institutional changes whose net result is to give increasing scope to humanity's active disposition and in particular to the pursuit of riches. This vision of the future is, however, qualified by the introduction of the classical thesis of growth and decay, a thesis that manifests itself in Hume's belief that mature economies will eventually and necessarily confront constraints to their further development.

A further qualification of Hume's optimism emerges from his discussion of what he believed to be a characteristic feature of the modern state, namely, public credit. In this modern institution Hume saw several dangers. First, "national debts cause a mighty confluence of people and riches to the capital, by the great sums, levied in the provinces to pay the interest." Second, public stocks "being a kind of paper-credit, have all the disadvantages attending that species of money."[39] Third, holders of this kind of stock "have no connexions with the state" and can "enjoy their revenue in any part of the globe"; they are a group liable to "sink into the lethargy of a stupid and pampered luxury, without spirit, ambition, or enjoyment." Fourth, this form of wealth conveys "no hereditary authority or credit to the possessor; and by this means, the several ranks of men, which form a kind of independent magistracy in a state, instituted by the hand of nature, are entirely lost; and every man in authority derives his influence from the commission alone of the sovereign" (E-PC 11–12, 23; 354–5, 357–8). Hume concluded that the modern state relying on public credit could be affected by those circumstances that would offset the political and constitutional advantages that had been emphasized in "Of Refinement in the Arts": "No expedient remains for preventing or suppressing insurrections, but mercenary armies: No expedient at all remains for resisting tyranny: Elections are swayed by bribery and corruption alone: And the middle power between king and people being totally removed, a grievous despotism must infallibly prevail" (E-PC 23, 358).

---

[39] See also "Of Money" (E-Mo 4, 284) and "Of the Balance of Trade" (E-BT 21–2, 317). These concerns reflect the doubts rased by John Law, *Money and Trade Considered* (Edinburgh, 1705), whose position was echoed in part by George Berkeley in his *Querist* (1735–37). It is interesting to note that both these writers were concerned with the problems of underdeveloped economies; see Hutchison, 184.

IV. CONCLUSION

The major Scottish figures who contributed to the development of political economy in the two decades following the publication of the *Political Discourses* were Sir James Steuart and Adam Smith. The two men could hardly have been more different. Steuart had been a committed Jacobite whereas Smith was a Whig. As economists, the former was, seemingly, an advocate of interventionism, whereas the latter is now regarded as a leading advocate of economic liberalism. Yet Steuart and Smith had two things in common: both were profoundly influenced by Hume's economic essays, and both enjoyed his close friendship.

From a biographical point of view, Steuart's known links with Hume are few indeed. We do know that Hume visited Steuart in his ancestral home of Coltness, in Lanarkshire, on a number of occasions, during at least one of which the two men discussed Hume's *History.* The *Principles* (1767) also figures in the one long letter from Steuart to Hume that has survived, a letter that is remarkable for its good humor and familiarity and that attests the "many proofs you have given me of your friendship." Hume had probably given some assistance in the vexed question of Steuart's pardon, but had also read the *Principles* in draft. In a letter dated 11 March 1766, Professor Rouet wrote to Baron Mure that "George Scott and David Hume have looked into our friend's manuscript and are exceedingly pleased with it" although Hume was later said to have been critical of its "form and style."[40]

It is not difficult to see why Hume might have approved at least of the structure of the *Principles.* The book parallels Hume's preoccupation with the social and political implications of economic growth and places a similar emphasis on the role of natural wants. In it too there are discussions, similar to those found in Hume, of the theory of population and of the nature of the exchange economy. Indeed, it could be claimed that Steuart carried Hume's argument further in the sense that he addressed the problems that could be faced by an economy in the process of transition from an advanced agrarian stage to a primitive stage of the exchange economy. Steuart also went further than Hume in addressing the issues presented by

---

[40] Skinner, *Sir James Steuart,* xlv–xlvi.

variations in rates of growth both regionally and internationally; an analysis that resulted in a generalized statement of the three stages of trade: infant, foreign, and inland.[41]

If Sir James Steuart offered a legitimate development of Hume's treatment of political economy, it is equally true that Adam Smith more fully comprehended the latter's views as to the appropriate shape and scope of this discipline. It is now a commonplace that Smith endeavored to link philosophy, history, and economics as part of a grand plan that was announced in the closing pages of the first edition of *The Theory of Moral Sentiments* and repeated in the advertisement to the sixth and last edition of that work. But when we take the *Treatise of Human Nature* in conjunction with the *Essays Moral Political and Literary*, it becomes apparent that the outlines of the model had already been established by Hume. He it was who saw the close relationship between the "Understanding *and* Passions," the subjects of the first two books of the *Treatise*, and "Morals, Politics, *and* Criticism," the remaining subjects he projected as part of a five-volume *Treatise of Human Nature* (T Adv.).

It is important to note that Adam Smith had a close knowledge of Hume's philosophy, so close that Dugald Stewart would conclude that the "Political Discourses of Mr Hume were evidently of greater use to Mr Smith than any other book that had appeared prior to his lectures."[42] It is equally noteworthy that Smith should have acknowledged Hume's historical analysis of the links between commerce and liberty. Smith would have agreed with the view that Hume "deserves to be remembered... for his more fundamental attempt to incorporate economics into a broader science of human experience."[43]

But Smith's formal economic analysis differs from that of Hume (and of Steuart) partly because it was finally developed after the appearance of some of the great systematic performances of the period. Notable among these is Richard Cantillon's *Essai sur la Nature du Commerce en General*, written in the 1730s but not

---

[41] See my "David Hume: Precursor of Sir James Steuart," in *Discussion Papers in Economics* (University of Glasgow), No. 9003; and "The Shaping of Political Economy in the Enlightenment," *Scottish Journal of Political Economy* 37 (1990): 145–65.

[42] Dugald Stewart, "Account of the Life and Writings of Adam Smith," in *Essays on Philosophical Subjects* (Oxford: Clarendon Press, 1980), 320–1.

[43] Rotwein, *Hume: Writings on Economics*, cxi.

published until 1755. Cantillon's teaching was disseminated, in part, by the Marquis de Mirabeau in the *Ami des Hommes* (1756) and probably had a profound influence on the Physiocrats.[44] The most notable of this group include Francois Quesnay, whose *Tableau Economique* (1757) provided a coherent account of a macroeconomic model, and Turgot, whose *Reflections on the Formation and Distribution of Riches* dates from 1766.[45]

Adam Smith was to object that the members of the Physiocratic School "all follow implicitly, and without any sensible variation, the doctrine of Mr. Quesnai."[46] Perhaps with this in mind, Hume in 1769 wrote to the Abbé Morellet:

> I hope that in your work you will thunder them [the Physiocrats], and crush them, and pound them, and reduce them to dust and ashes! They are, indeed, the set of men the most chimerical and most arrogant that now exist, since the annihilation of the Sorbonne. I ask your pardon for saying so, as I know you belong to that venerable body. I wonder what could engage our friend, M. Turgot, to herd among them; I mean, among the economists. (HL 2:205)

But the truth is that writers such as Quesnay and Turgot produced a model of a capital-using system in which a number of sectors of activity were featured. In addition, socioeconomic groups were presented as being fully interdependent. Adam Smith knew of this work, and it seems to have influenced the macroanalysis of Book 2 of the *Wealth of Nations*.[47] Hume's essays, mostly written by 1752, are innocent of a model of this kind – and so too was Steuart's *Principles*, the first two books of which were completed in the isolation of Tübingen early in 1759. Hume's economic essays do not compare with the great systematic treatises of his friends, different

---

[44] Richard Cantillon, *Essai sur la nature du commerce en general*, ed. Henry Higgs (London: Macmillan, 1931); Henry Higgs, *The Physiocrats; Six Lectures on the French Economistes of the 18th Century* (London: Macmillan, 1897); Ronald L. Meek, *The Economics of Physiocracy* (London: Allen and Unwin, 1962). For a brief discussion of the views of the Physiocrats, see *The New Palgrave: A Dictionary of Economics*, s.v. "Physiocracy."

[45] The latter work is included in *Turgot on Progress, Sociology and Economics*, ed. and trans. Ronald L. Meek (Cambridge: Cambridge University Press, 1973).

[46] *Wealth of Nations*, 4.9.38 (2:678–9).

[47] See my *A System of Social Science* (Oxford: Oxford University Press, 1979), Chap. 5.

as they were in character, or to the analytical contributions of the Physiocrats.

That being said, it must be noted that Hume made significant contributions in the fields of population and of money, especially to quantity theory and to the analysis of specie flow. There his work "remained substantially unchallenged" until the 1920s.[48] Hume also succeeded in establishing that there is a relationship between the production of commodities and the level of aggregate demand, a relationship more commonly associated with the work of J. B. Say. Certainly Hume's analysis of the sectoral division of labor, his treatment of the theory of population, and his consideration of international trade separately and severally prompt a conclusion that, in the words of Say, "may at first sight appear paradoxical; viz. that it is production which opens a demand for products."[49]

If Hume's essays do not constitute a single coherent treatise, they do, as this essay has endeavored to show, disclose evidence of systematic treatment. Perhaps the most important single feature of this treatment is to be found in the use of history and of the historical method: Hume consistently sought to link economic *relationships* with the environment and the state of manners. This position was to find later expression in the work of the German Historical School and of the American Institutionalists.[50] But it is important to note that Hume's historical technique is different from that later adopted by Adam Smith. In Smith's hands, the history of civil society is essential for our understanding of the exchange economy and of the social and political environment which it may produce. But in Smith history is the *preface* to political economy rather than integral to the treatment. In fact, it has been said that Smith did *not* use the *historical method* in dealing with economic questions:

One may say that, despite its pronounced emphasis on economic development, Smith's approach to its more general aspects is less basically genetic or evolutionary than Hume's.... With regard particularly to his treatment

---

[48] Schumpeter, *History of Economic Analysis,* 367; see also Vickers, *Theory of Money,* 217–39.

[49] Quoted from my "Say's Law: Origins and Content," *Economica,* New Series, 34, no. 134 (May 1967): 159.

[50] Leo Rogin, *The Meaning and Validity of Economic Theory: A Historical Approach* (New York: Harper & Brothers, 1956), 1–13.

of the theoretical issues of political economy, Smith clearly exhibits the tendency to abstract from historical influences which was so characteristic of Ricardo and the later classical economists.[51]

A further point of interest to the modern economist is Hume's systematic comparison of different economic stages and his concern with the process of transition between them. This procedure throws important light on the problems of economic and social development. So too does his concern with international trade between economies with different characteristics and different rates of growth. Hume's argument effectively introduced the "rich country–poor country" debate that was also addressed by, among others, Tucker, Wallace, and Steuart. Such a perspective means that *policy* recommendations must always be related to the circumstances that prevail. Joseph Schumpeter's description of the work done by another eighteenth-century economist, the Italian Ferdinando Galiani, thus applies, despite Hume's belief in the uniformity of human nature, equally to Hume:

One point about his thought must be emphasised...he was the one eighteenth-century economist who always insisted on the variability of man and of the relativity to time and place, of all policies; the one who was completely free from the paralysing belief, that crept over the intellectual life of Europe, in practical principles that claim universal validity; who saw that a policy that was rational in France at a given time might be quite irrational, at the same time in Naples.[52]

The analytical success of the *Wealth of Nations* in the first two decades of the nineteenth century had some unfortunate results.[53] The dominant classical orthodoxy made it possible to think of economics as quite separate from ethics and history, thus obscuring the true purposes of Smith and Hume. In referring to these problems, Hutchison was moved to remark, in a telling passage, that Smith was unwittingly led by an invisible hand to promote an end not part

[51] Rotwein, *Hume: Writings on Economics*, cix–cx; see also Hutchison, *Before Adam Smith*, 213–14.
[52] Schumpeter, *History of Economic Analysis*, 293–4.
[53] Richard F. Teichgraeber III, "'Less abused than I had reason to expect': The Reception of The Wealth of Nations in Britain, 1776–90," *Historical Journal* 30 (1987): 337–66.

of his intention, that "of establishing political economy as a separate autonomous discipline."[54]

The dominance of a version of Smith's economic system in the nineteenth century led to the belief that the history of the subject dated from 1776, thus obscuring, temporarily at least, the contributions of Smith's predecessors, English, French, Italian, and Scottish. The acceptance of Smith's account of the mercantile system also caused advocates of intervention, such as Steuart, to be regarded as mercantilists on this ground alone, and sometimes to cause commentators to view with mild embarrassment the occasional departures of the enlightened Hume, not from the *principle*, but from the *application*, of a policy of free trade.

SUGGESTIONS FOR FURTHER READING

In addition to the works cited in the notes to this essay, for further reading the following are recommended.

Hont, Istvan. *Jealousy of Trade: International Competition and the Nation State in Historical Perspective*. Cambridge, MA: Harvard University Press, 2005.

Rotwein, Eugene. "David Hume." In *The New Palgrave: A Dictionary of Economics*, edited by J. Eatwell, M. Milgate, and P. Newman. London: Macmillan, 1987.

Schabas, Margaret. "David Hume on Experimental Natural Philosophy, Money, and Fluids." *History of Political Economy* 33 (2001): 411–35.

Schabas, Margaret, and Carl Wennerlind, eds. *David Hume's Political Economy*. London: Routledge, 2007.

---

[54] Hutchison, *Before Adam Smith*, 355.

13 Hume on the Arts and "The Standard of Taste"
Texts and Contexts

Hume's observations on the arts are set in the framework of social life. That is why he considers both the making of, and response to, works of art as human actions subject to the analysis he has offered of other human actions. He never published his intended treatise on "criticism" (T Adv.), and no developed theories of beauty, art, or criticism are to be found in his works. But by bringing together his scattered remarks on these subjects, and by looking at his general aims and the context in which he wrote, we can identify his principal views on these topics.

I. CULTURAL CONTEXT

It is always important to establish the context and date of a writer's views; it is especially important when setting out Hume's ideas on what today we call aesthetics. His interests and references, in almost every respect except the crucial one of classical literature, were narrower than those of an informed modern reader. We need to know what he might, and what he could not, have experienced, and to recognize that his cultural environment differed essentially from ours: concepts of, and attitudes to, the various mediums of art in the 1740s were evolving rapidly, as were artistic practices and expectations. Excepting only the very rich, and their households, most Scots and the majority of the English had very limited access to what count as the arts today.

Most of Hume's observations were made within a thirty-year period beginning in the late 1720s, at the outset of social and intellectual revolutions that were to gain rapid momentum in the second half of the eighteenth century and to transform Europe, although

there were significant geographical variations. Aesthetics, understood primarily as reflection on the nature of the arts and of discussion about them, achieved its modern forms only after Hume's
death. Its development is inseparable from many intellectual, social,
political, and economic factors: the spread of wealth and increase
of leisure among the middle classes in many European countries;
greater ease of travel, and the beginning of public concerts and
public museums (in which works would be removed from their
original contexts); a decline in individual patronage, and a resulting freedom for artists to satisfy a growing luxury market, or to
survive by following their own preferences; the beginning of the
formal study of the arts, especially literature, by nonpractitioners
and nonowners in colleges and universities, thus augmenting an
informed audience; a greater availability of books and illustrations
as secondary sources of information about the arts; the increasing
influence of critics, through journals; and the institutionalization of
the arts and sciences and thus of professional distinctions between
them.

Hume's references to arts other than literature are infrequent and
fleeting. He almost never refers to music, or to sculpture, his asides
on painting are inconsequential, and architecture gains more than a
passing mention only in his letters from the mainland of Europe in
1748; what little theoretical or philosophical writing was available
to him on these arts receives almost no mention.[1] His critical views

[1] The musical scene in eighteenth-century Scotland is explored in David Johnson,
Music and Society in Lowland Scotland in the Eighteenth Century (Oxford: Oxford
University Press, 1972). See also Neal Zaslaw, ed., *The Classical Era: From the
1740s to the End of the 18th Century* (London: Macmillan, 1989); Enrico Fubini,
Music and Culture in Eighteenth-Century Europe (Chicago: University of Chicago
Press, 1994); Ruth Smith, *Handel's Oratorios and Eighteenth-Century Thought*
(Cambridge: Cambridge University Press, 1995); William Weber, *The Rise of Musi-
cal Classics in Eighteenth-Century England* (Oxford: Clarendon Press, 1992); Cyn-
thia Verba, *Music and the French Enlightenment* (Oxford: Clarendon Press, 1993);
Thomas Christensen, *Rameau and Musical Thought in the Enlightenment* (Cam-
bridge: Cambridge University Press, 1993); Donald Burrows and Rosemary Dunhill,
Music and Theatre in Handel's World (Oxford: Oxford University Press, 2002).

The contexts of painting and architecture in Britain are analyzed in John Sum-
merson, *Georgian London* (London: Pleiades Books, 1945); Iain Pears, *The Discovery
of Painting: The Growth of Interest in the Arts in England, 1680–1768* (New Haven,
CT: Yale University Press, 1988); Basil Skinner, *Scots in Italy in the 18th Century*
(Edinburgh: National Galleries of Scotland, 1966); James Holloway, *Patrons and
Painters: Art in Scotland 1650–1760* (Edinburgh: Scottish National Portrait Gallery,

seem to have been formed with mainly poetry and drama in mind, although it was commonplace in his day to compare and even identify poetry with painting, as Dryden had done in his preface to the translation of C. A. du Fresnoy's poem *De Arte Graphica* (The Art of Painting), entitled *A Parallel betwixt Painting and Poetry* (1695).[2] This work was widely quoted by contemporaries such as George Turnbull and Alexander Gerard,[3] and Hume may even allude to it (T 2.2.5.19). Hume accepted a standard view of his time that paintings could convey a narrative or act as an historical record or symbol, but he more often regarded them as essentially pieces of usefully decorative furniture – like James Norie's fashionable overmantle paintings in Edinburgh and the Lowlands. The painter Allan Ramsay was a close friend, and, of course, Hume visited Scottish Border and

1989); George Fairfull-Smith, *The Foulis Press and the Foulis Academy* (Glasgow: Glasgow Art Index, 2001).

For gardens, see A. A.Tait, *The Landscape Garden in Scotland 1735–1835* (Edinburgh: Edinburgh University Press, 1980). The French context for architecture, painting, and criticism is examined in Joseph Rykwert, *The First Moderns* (Cambridge, MA: MIT Press, 1980); Antoine Picon, *French Architects and Engineers in the Age of Enlightenment* (Cambridge: Cambridge University Press, 1992); Thomas E. Crow, *Painters and Public Life in 18th-Century Paris* (New Haven, CT: Yale University Press, 1985). See also Andrew Wilton and Ilaria Bignamini, eds., *Grand Tour: The Lure of Italy in the Eighteenth Century* (London: Tate Gallery Publishers, 1996); John Ingamells, ed., *A Dictionary of British and Irish Travellers in Italy 1701–1800* (New Haven, CT: Yale University Press, 1997); J. Paul Hunter, *Before Novels: The Cultural Contexts of Eighteenth-Century English Fiction* (New York: Norton, 1990); M. H. Abrams, "Art-as-Such: The Sociology of Modern Aesthetics," *American Academy of Arts and Sciences* 38 (1985); Rémy G. Saisselin, "The Transformation of Art into Culture: From Pascal to Diderot," and *Studies on Voltaire and the Eighteenth Century* 70 (1970); idem, "Painting, Writing and Primitive Purity," *Studies on Voltaire and the Eighteenth Century* 217 (1983): 257–96; Bernard Denvir, *The Eighteenth Century: Art, Design and Society 1689–1789* (London: Longman, 1983).

[2] John Dryden, *A Parallel betwixt Painting and Poetry*, in C. A. du Fresnoy, *De Arte Graphica: The Art of Painting* (London, 1695). On the list of books in the library organized by Professor Robert Steuart in 1724, called the Physiological Library, and to which Hume had access as a student, see Michael Barfoot, "Hume and the Culture of Science in the Early Eighteenth Century," in *Studies in the Philosophy of the Scottish Enlightenment*, ed. M. A. Stewart (Oxford: Clarendon Press, 1990), 151–90. For a study of comparisons between poetry and painting, see R. W. Lee, *Ut Pictura Poesis: The Humanistic Theory of Painting* (New York: W. W. Norton, 1967).

[3] George Turnbull, *A Treatise on Ancient Painting* (London, 1740); Alexander Gerard, *An Essay on Taste* (London, 1759); Henry Home, Lord Kames, *Elements of Criticism* (London, 1762).

Lowland houses, and possibly also the best houses in Rheims and La Flèche, when studying there in the 1730s (HL 1:5, 12). Nevertheless he had probably seen rather few paintings other than portraits until he accompanied General St. Clair to Vienna and northern Italy in 1748 (HL 1:64). We should remember that strict Calvinist churches displayed no paintings, and that the label "portrait" covered fanciful historical likenesses as well as "faces" of actual sitters. Until after the midcentury there were few collectors in Scotland: the Clerks of Penicuik and the second Marquis of Annandale certainly had notable collections, although the Duke of Argyll did not, and several prominent Scots known to Hume made the Grand Tour, as patrons or tutors. But even in England the market and audience for painting, together with critical debate, had not developed to the extent Hume witnessed in Paris in the 1760s. There were, of course, illustrated books and engravings, but some engravings were both reversed and consisted only of outlines of the main forms in a painting. In any case their small scale and content encouraged a literary approach. Unlike George Turnbull in his *Treatise on Ancient Painting* (1740) – for whom Ramsay commissioned engravings while they were both in Italy – Alexander Gerard in his *Essay on Taste* (1759), or even Lord Kames in his later *Elements of Criticism* (1762), Hume makes no reference to the influential ideas of Roger de Piles, Charles Alphonse du Fresnoy, or Andre Félibien; and of Jonathan Richardson, whose challenging writings first appear in 1715, there is not a word.[4] There is ample textual evidence, nevertheless, that Hume derived many of his ideas about "criticism" from French writers, and we now know that he owned, at some stage, many important French texts.[5]

---

[4] Roger de Piles, *Conversations sur la connoissance de la peinture et sur le jugement qu'on doit faire des tableaux* (n.p., 1677); Charles Alphonse du Fresnoy, *De Arte Graphica* (Paris, 1668); André Félibien, *L'Idée du peintre parfait* (Paris, 1707); Jonathan Richardson, *Two Discourses. I. An Essay on the whole Art of Criticism as it relates to Painting. II. An Argument in behalf of the Science of a Connoisseur* (London, 1719). De Piles, in the opening book and in a very brief essay, "Of Taste," with which he ends *The Art of Painting* (2nd ed., London, 1744), lists a number of ideas taken up by Dubos, and later by Hume. In Scotland, Kames, in particular, discussed architecture at some length; Smith wrote about music late in his life, but in the context of Hume's essay, the most interesting discussion of music is by John Gregory, *A Comparative View of the State and Faculties of Man* (London, 1765).

[5] For a detailed analysis of Hume's views on the arts and criticism see my *Hume's Sentiments: Their Ciceronian and French Context* (Edinburgh: Edinburgh University Press, 1982). I discuss the possible influence on Hume of Ephraim Chambers,

Hume displays no interest in music, but he was not without opportunity to learn about it. Although formally constituted only in 1728, the Edinburgh Musical Society had flourished since the 1690s, providing encouragement for several good amateur performers and composers; but unlike Kames, William Cullen, or Joseph Black he seems not to have been a member. There was a strong tradition of dance and folksong throughout much of Scotland, however, with which Hume would have been familiar. English opera arrived in Edinburgh in 1751, but we have proof only that Hume attended the opera in Turin in 1748 and in Paris in 1764, and reported that he had heard the castrato Angelo Maria Monticelli in Vienna, also in 1748, but possibly not in opera. There are no references to the concerts of the eight-year-old Mozart in Paris in 1764. In the first half of the century, there was little theoretical discussion of music outside France, and Hume refers to no one other than Abbé Jean-Baptiste Dubos, although he must have heard about the dispute between Jean Jacques Rousseau and Jean Philippe Rameau in the 1750s. He also came to know Dr. Charles Burney, the great historian of music, Count Algarotti, who wrote on opera, and Jean-Francois Marmontel, who wrote several opera libretti. By way of contrast, Alexander Gerard, John Gregory, and James Beattie, in Aberdeen, along with Kames and Adam Smith, all wrote something about music. Although Hume later seems to have owned other books that discussed music, by authors such as D'Alembert, William Duff, Daniel Webb, the Marquis de Chastellux, as well as libretti by Abato Pietro Metastasio, their ideas appear nowhere in his own writings.

Cyclopaedia: or an Universal Dictionary of Arts and Sciences (London: Ephraim Chambers, 1728) in "Hume and the Beginnings of Modern Aesthetics," in *The Science of Man in the Scottish Enlightenment,* ed. P. Jones (Edinburgh: Edinburgh University Press, 1989). Information about the Hume Library is taken from David Fate Norton and Mary J. Norton, *The David Hume Library* (Edinburgh Bibliographical Society, 1996). Earlier studies on Hume and his context include T. Brunius, *David Hume on Criticism* (Stockholm: University of Uppsala, 1951); W. J. Hipple, Jr., *The Beautiful, The Sublime, and the Picturesque in Eighteenth-Century British Aesthetic Theory* (Carbondale: Southern Illinois University Press, 1957). See also Rémy G. Saisselin, *The Enlightenment against the Baroque: Economics and Aesthetics in the Eighteenth Century* (Berkeley: University of California Press, 1992). See also my "Italian Operas and Their Audiences," in *The Enlightenment World,* ed. Martin Fitzpatrick et al. (London: Routledge, 2004).

It would be natural for architecture, rather than painting or music, to capture the attention of someone engrossed, as Hume was, in the debate between the Ancients and Moderns; Addison had himself demonstrated that fact, and countless authors before and after Hume liked to refer to the Divine Architect when comparing the works of God and man.[6] Hume owned at least three of the major volumes that essentially championed the moderns.[7] He furthermore comments on the debate in letters written during his Viennese mission, and in 1767 expresses pride in the architectural achievement of Robert Adam (HL 1:118–27; 2:173). He refers to, and thus presumably had seen, the beautifully illustrated translations of Andrea Palladio that were available from the 1720s; and he quotes a significant passage from Claude Perrault's influential commentary on the Roman writer Marcus Vitruvius Pollio (EPM App. 1.15; T 2.1.8.2).[8] Like Pascal, both Charles and Claude Perrault emphasized fashion as influencing architectural styles and details, and this point was

---

[6] See my "Hume on Context, Sentiment and Testimony in Religion," in *Religion and Hume's Legacy*, ed. D. Z. Phillips and Timothy Tessin (New York: St. Martin's Press, 1999), 251–77.

[7] Norton and Norton indicate that the following works were in the Hume Library, and they may well have been there before Hume wrote his essay of 1757: Charles Perrault, *Parallèles des anciens et des modernes* (Amsterdam, 1693; 1st ed., 1688); William Wotton, *Reflections upon Ancient and Modern Learning* (London, 1694); Jean-Baptiste Dubos, *Réflexions Critiques sur la poésie et sur la peinture* (Utrecht, 1732). Hume owned an edition of Bernard le Bovier de Fontenelle, *Oeuvres* (Paris, 1742) and was certainly familiar with its contents, such as *Digression sur les anciens et les modernes* (Paris, 1688), and *Dialogues des Morts* (Paris, 1683): and he also owned Dominick Bouhours, *Les Entretiens D'Ariste et D'Eugene* (Paris, 1671); Houdar de la Motte, *Réflexions sur la Critique* (The Hague, 1715); James Harris, *Three Treatises, Concerning Art, Music, Painting, Poetry, and Happiness* (London, 1744); and Roger de Piles, *Art of Painting* (London, 1744). The last work originates in de Piles's original translation of and commentary on Du Fresnoy, *De Arte Graphica* (Paris, 1668). See Thomas Puttfarken, *Roger de Piles' Theory of Art* (New Haven, CT: Yale University Press, 1985); Edgar Wind, *Hume and the Heroic Portrait* (Oxford: Clarendon Press, 1986); William Hogarth, *The Analysis of Beauty*, ed. R. Paulson (New Haven, CT: Yale University Press, 1997; first published 1753).

[8] On Robert Adam, see John Fleming, *Robert Adam and His Circle* (Cambridge, MA: Harvard University Press, 1962); Geoffrey Beard, *The Work of Robert Adam* (Edinburgh: John Bartholomew & Son, 1978); Joseph and Anne Rykwert, *The Brothers Adam* (London: Collins, 1985). Claude Perrault, *Les Dix Livres d'architecture de Vitruve* (Paris, 1673). Professor Steuart's class library list of 1724 cites a copy of Perrault's *Abrégé* of Vitruvius, along with works on the construction and geometry of fortifications.

adapted and broadened by both Allan Ramsay and Adam Smith in their discussions with Hume about taste. But what else had Hume read? There was little on architecture of a philosophical nature in either France or England before the 1760s. There were practical handbooks for patrons and builders, of course, and what were essentially pattern books, but there is no reason to think that they were of interest to Hume.[9] Vitruvius, Leon Battista Alberti, Palladio, Sebastiano Serlio, Vincenzo Scamozzi, and Giacome Barozzi da Vignola were all available in English, and Hume could readily have consulted the work of Fréart de Chambray as well as that of Perrault.[10] But if 1757, and the appearance of his essay on taste, is taken as the last date for influencing Hume's published philosophical thoughts on such matters, Marc-Antoine Laugier's (as then anonymous) *An Essay on Architecture* (1753, Eng. trans., 1755) was available, but Sir William Chambers's *A Treatise on Civil Architecture* (1759) is ruled out. There were also the articles on architectural matters in the early volumes of the famed *Encyclopédie ou Dictionnaire Raisonné des Sciences, des Arts et des Métiers* (Paris, 1751–80), and several works by Robert Morris, but Hume refers to these no more than to the others.[11] And yet, even if only indirectly, Hume absorbed ideas from some of these writers. For example, Vitruvius had insisted, and almost all his followers emphasized the point, that some form of

[9] Some key references are John Archer, *The Literature of British Domestic Architecture 1715–1842* (Cambridge, MA: MIT Press, 1985); Eileen Harris, *British Architectural Books and Writers, 1556–1785* (Cambridge: Cambridge University Press, 1990); Howard Colvin, *A Biographical Dictionary of British Architects 1600–1840*, 3rd ed. (New Haven, CT: Yale University Press, 1995).

[10] Marcus Vitruvius Pollio, *The Ten Books of Architecture* (1st English trans. of Perrault's *Abridgement*, 1692); Leon Battista Alberti, *De Re Aedificatoria* (Florence, 1485; 1st complete English trans., 1726); Andrea Palladio, *I Quattro libri dell'architettura* (Venice, 1570; 1st complete English trans., 1715); Sebastiano Serlio, *Architettura*, (Venice and Paris, 1537–47; 1st English trans., 1611); Vincenzo Scamozzi, *L'Idea della architettura universale* (Venice, 1615; 1st English trans., 1676); Giacome Barozzi da Vignola, *Regole delle cinque ordini d'architettura* (Rome, 1563; 1st English trans., 1655); Roland Fréart, Sieur de Chambray, *Parallèle de l'architecture antique et de la moderne* (Paris, 1650; 1st English trans., 1664).

[11] Marc-Antoine Laugier, *An Essay on Architecture* (London, 1755); William Chambers, *A Treatise on Civil Architecture* (London, 1759); Robert Morris, *Lectures on Architecture* (London, 1734, 1736). On the *Encyclopédie*, see Kevin Harrington, *Changing Ideas on Architecture in the* Encyclopédie, *1750–1776* (Ann Arbor, MI: UMI Research Press, 1985).

expert judgment is needed in both making and responding to works, albeit judgment not hide-bound by rules. London witnessed a huge building program throughout the eighteenth century, and the increased wealth of English patrons provided opportunities for designers such as Thomas Chippendale, who were quick to publicize their work. But Hume saw little of this until after he had written the *Treatise* and early *Essays,* and he died before more than a handful of elegant houses had appeared in Edinburgh's New Town.[12] Forty years earlier, in the *Treatise,* he had stated that buildings, furniture, and utensils are made to fulfill specific functions, and that their beauty derives largely from their success in this regard: "Most of the works of art are esteem'd beautiful, in proportion to their fitness for the use of man," and the beauty of "tables, chairs, scritoires, chimneys, coaches, sadles, ploughs," and indeed "every work of art" is "chiefly deriv'd from their utility" (T 3.3.1.8, 2.2.5.17).[13] Such views had, in fact, been canvased by Claude Perrault, explicitly referring to the role of the association of ideas. Moreover, Perrault also declared that theory was often neither uppermost, nor present, in the minds of craftsmen, and should not therefore be the object of a spectator's or critic's search: assumptions about theory have been generated by "men of letters," although "there is no great obstacle to believing that the things for which they can find no reason are, in fact, devoid of any reason material to the beauty of the thing."[14] Parallel to such views were passages in Cicero, quoted by numerous writers throughout the eighteenth century, to the effect that almost everybody is able to judge art without the need of any theory (*De Oratore,* 3.1.195). Several issues overlapped in such discussions. Throughout the evolving debate between the ancients and

---

[12] Hume's own more modest New Town house, situated on what is now called St. David Street, at the southwest corner of St. Andrew Square, was built for him in 1770–1. For further details, and speculation about the naming of St. David Street, see Ernest Campbell Mossner, *The Life of David Hume* (Edinburgh: Thomas Nelson & Sons, 1954), 562–6.

[13] "Art" meant "skill," and the phrase "work of art" was used well into the 1750s to mean any works involving skill; the term was not synonymous with "the fine arts," which denoted painting and the decorative arts.

[14] *Ordonnance des cinq espèces de colonnes selon la méthode des Anciens* (Paris, 1683); cited from the translation by Indra Kagis McEwen (Santa Monica, CA: Getty Center for the History of Art and Humanities, 1993), 58.

moderns, much ink was spilt on the widening gap between practitioners and commentators, between professionals and amateurs. Professionals caused things to happen, and initiated change; amateurs, by contrast, experienced and savored the effects of such changes, and became active only in their subsequent parasitic reflections. In addition, however, a transition was taking place between a view of the fine arts as pleasurable luxuries, useful to forestall boredom, and a view of them as the product of citizens whose primary moral task was to be publicly useful. J.-F. Blondel, a practicing architect with an unusually extensive interest in theory, rejected a favorite distinction of the amateurs between use and pleasure as a means of identifying the arts, and his colleague Denis Diderot claimed that *"speculation"* and *"pratique"* were both essential in the successful execution of any "art."[15] Since antiquity, it had been recognized that architecture differed from the other arts, and fitted comfortably into none of the existing categories of endeavor. It is a physical and social phenomenon, occupying, ordering, and enclosing spaces: experience of it involves all the senses. Alberti had seductively argued that the merit of a work of architecture is inseparable from its intended use or function, and might not be explicable in terms of rules. J.-G. Sulzer, who translated Hume and was a friend of Kant, argued for a rigorous contextualism in judging architecture, and agreed with Aristotle that in all the arts particular rules are discovered and understood before any formulation of general principles – where "rules" are understood to be "practical means to desired ends." He also held that a resolution between the demands of reason and taste was "part psychological and part political."[16]

Hume always proclaimed that literature was his principal passion, and he certainly knew, met, or corresponded with almost everyone of note in his day associated with the arts, in Britain and France. He was widely read in classical, English, French, and Italian authors and frequently alludes to them. But it must be emphasized again that for him literature was a general category that included history and philosophy. That explains why he assesses literature, of almost any

---

[15] Diderot's remarks occur in his entry for "Art" in *L'Encyclopédie ou Dictionnaire Raisonné des Sciences, des Arts et des Métiers* (Paris, 1751), 1.714.

[16] Sulzer's remarks occur in the entries for "Architecture," "Art," and "Esquisse" in *Supplément à L'Encyclopédie* (Amsterdam, 1776–7), 1.540, 588, 595; 2.872.

kind, as the coherent expression of thought. Moreover, the notion of *judgment*, which became associated with that of *critic*, involved three decisions about the appropriateness of expression: namely, to the speaker's state of mind, to the intended listener's own capacities, and to the particular context. Eighteenth-century British and French writers alike claimed Joseph Addison's eleven papers, "On the Pleasures of the Imagination," and a preceding paper on taste, for the *Spectator* of 1712, as significant sources of their theoretical ideas. Hume admired Addison's skill and success as a popular essayist and, of course, refers to these papers, but he did not think the explicit Lockean account of imagination used in them could explain the philosophical issues raised. Other insights Hume adopted from Jean de la Bruyère, Nicolas Boileau-Despreaux, or Bernard le Bovier de Fontenelle needed a more substantial grounding than could be provided by the passing reflections of Anthony Ashley Cooper, third Earl of Shaftesbury, or his avowed champion Francis Hutcheson.[17] Hume found many of the conclusions he wanted to adopt in a French work that for at least fifty years was the most influential work of its kind throughout Europe: but with the Abbé Jean-Baptiste Dubos, Hume's task was to provide a stronger and non-Cartesian philosophical underpinning for those conclusions, by reference to his own theory of human nature.

The Abbé Dubos was Secretary of the French Academy from 1723 until his death in 1742; he had been a friend of the Huguenot scholar Pierre Bayle, whose philosophical skepticism he found increasingly congenial and who greatly inspired Hume. At the beginning of the century Dubos had also helped to publicize *An Essay concerning Human Understanding* by his friend John Locke, in Pierre Coste's French translation. Like Fontenelle, whose work he admired, Dubos was a learned and cultured man, and his volumes abound in references to ancient and modern works, and in allusions to recent

---

[17] Jean de La Bruyère, *Les Caractères* (Paris, 1688); Nicolas Boileau-Despreaux, *Oeuvres diverses* (Paris, 1701); Bernard le Bovier de Fontenelle, *Oeuvres diverses* (La Haye, 1728); Anthony Ashley Cooper, third Earl of Shaftesbury, *Characteristicks of Men, Manners, Opinions, Times* (London, 1711); Francis Hutcheson, *An Inquiry into the Original of our Ideas of Beauty and Virtue, Treatise I, Concerning Beauty, Order, Harmony, Design* (London, 1725). For Claude Perrault, see his *Ordonnance des cinq espèces de colonnes selon la méthode des Anciens* (Paris, 1683); for J.-G. Sulzer, see *Supplément à l'Encyclopédie*.

scientific discoveries. Nowhere is this more apparent than in *Réflexions critiques sur la Poésie et sur la Peinture*, which appeared first in 1719, went through several editions, and was translated into English in 1748. Hume referred to it in his "Early Memoranda" (possibly of the early 1740s), and its impact is discernible both in the *Essays Moral and Political* of 1741–2, especially when the topic is art, and most dramatically in his "Of the Standard of Taste" of 1757.[18] (Adam Smith, in the 1780s, also adopted from Dubos a significant portion of his ideas about the arts.) Like many influential writers, Dubos was not himself very original: his skill lay in synthesizing many of the critical ideas "in the air" – even if they were mutually contradictory – and in the range of issues he identified as calling for analysis and reflection.

The *Réflexions*, among other things, is a contribution to the debate between the Ancients and Moderns, Hume's interest in which is everywhere apparent in his 1741 *Essays*.[19] Writers in England had imported this debate on the relative merits of ancient and modern learning and culture from France, and by the early 1700s several issues were being discussed. These included the nature of judgments of taste and the influence of history and society on such judgments; the limits of criticism and the role of rules in it; the nature of beauty and the respective roles of experts and the public in its determination; overall comparison between the Ancients and the Moderns, with particular dispute over the stature of Homer; and the nature of progress, particularly as revealed in modern institutions and practices, and in relation to Christianity. Hume expressed views on all these matters, and although his hero was in most things Cicero,

---

[18] See Ernest Campbell Mossner, "Hume's Early Memoranda, 1729–1740," *Journal of the History of Ideas* 9 (1948): 492–518, esp. 500; and especially M. A. Stewart, "The Dating of Hume's Manuscripts," in *The Scottish Enlightenment: Essays in Reinterpretation*, ed. P. Wood (Rochester, NY: University of Rochester Press, 2000), 267–314. For a full discussion of Hume's debts to Dubos, and the debate between the Ancients and Moderns, see my *Hume's Sentiments*.

[19] See P. O. Kristeller, "The Modern System of the Arts," in *Journal of the History of Ideas*, vols. 12 and 13 (1951, 1952); R. F. Jones, *Ancients and Moderns: The Battle of the Books* (St. Louis, 1936); H. Rigault, *Histoire de la querelle des anciens et des modernes* (Paris: L. Hachette, 1856); Charles Kerby-Miller, ed., *The Memoirs of the Extraordinary Life, Works, and Discoveries of Martinus Scriblerus* (New Haven, CT: Yale University Press, 1950); Joseph M. Levine, *Between the Ancients and the Moderns* (New Haven, CT: Yale University Press, 1999).

his admiration for recent political progress and material advance, together with his refusal to appeal to authority or to Christianity, aligned him with the moderns. Moreover, Hume's debt to Dubos goes some way to explain why almost all of his own remarks on the arts are set in the framework of our social life.

Hume's recorded artistic preferences, together with his critical observations on particular works, are entirely orthodox for the age, and are – like those of his friend Adam Smith – rather uninteresting. These references are securely anchored in classical and modern neoclassical literature. In 1741 he asserted that Virgil and Racine represent the peaks of ancient and modern literary achievement, and that France possibly surpasses ancient Greece in artistic merit. At the same date he objects to anything falling under the eighteenth-century notion of "Gothic," and to any excess ornament (E-SR 4, 193; E-CL 6, 91). In 1757 he objected to Homer because of the moral attitudes represented (E-ST 31, 246), and at about the same time he declares that Donne is guilty of the "most uncouth expression" and that Shakespeare, although a genius, is too often tasteless (HE App. 4, 5:151–2). On his journey to Paris in 1763 he carried with him the works of Virgil, Horace, Tasso, and Tacitus – his Homer was too large (HL I:401). Such flat verdicts, which appear in his *History of England* of the late 1750s, should be juxtaposed, however, with his patriotic and romantic enthusiasm for John Home's *Douglas* (1755) and, initially, for James Macpherson's putative translations of Gaelic poetry in the 1760s. But Hume's broad notion of literature must be underlined, since he never displayed as much interest in poetry and drama as in history and philosophy. Indeed, none of his allusions to works of art reveals special knowledge, interest, or insight, and many are derived second-hand, from *texts* about them. In 1739, at least, his proposed treatise on "criticism" would have been part of his overall account of the science of man, and would not have taken its departure from particular concern with one or more of the mediums of art, or of individual works: we have no evidence that he conceived of a project of this kind at any time in his life.

II. BEAUTY AND JUDGMENTS OF BEAUTY

In *A Treatise of Human Nature* Hume hardly mentions the arts, but he attempts to mark out the domain of reason and sentiment in

matters of beauty. Although his remarks on beauty are strictly subordinate to other, usually moral, concerns, they are relevant to his
later reflections on the arts because of his observations on judgment
in general, and disinterested evaluation in particular.

In outline his view is that beauty is an indefinable "power" in
objects that causes a pleasurable sentiment (T 2.1.8.2); beauty is
not itself a sentiment, nor even a property discernible by the five
senses, but rather a property whose presence is felt (by a sixth or
even seventh sense, as Dubos and Hutcheson, respectively, said) only
when objects with certain detectable properties causally interact,
under specifiable conditions, with minds having certain properties
(E-Sc 13–18, 164–6; EPM App. 1.15).[20] Discussion can focus on the
object in which a person takes delight, and by altering his perceptions
of it, can set off a new causal chain that results in a new sentiment.

Hume distinguishes beauty, perception of beauty, and judgments
of beauty, but he concentrates on the last, further distinguishing,
in line with Shaftesbury, between beauty of form, of interest, and
of species.[21] Hume gives two closely related examples of intrinsic
beauty, perception of which is barely, if at all, mediated by conceptual judgment. He says we might attend to the beauty of the "form"
of "some senseless inanimate piece of matter"; or we might find that
"some species of beauty, especially the natural kinds, on their first
appearance, command our affection and approbation" (T 2.2.5.16;
EPM 1.9).[22]

Two important principles operate in judgments of beauty: comparison and sympathy. The first functions in our classification of
objects: "We judge more of objects by comparison, than by their

---

[20] Dubos probably derived his notion of a sixth sense (Dubos 2.22) from Fontenelle,
  Entretiens sur la pluralité des mondes 3 (1688), but it was commonplace to cite
  Cicero (*De Oratore* 3.1.195) as the classical source of the idea. On Hutcheson, see
  Peter Kivy, *The Seventh Sense* (New York: B. Franklin, 1976).

[21] Shaftesbury, *Characteristics*, ed. J. M. Robertson, 2. vols. (Indianapolis: Library of
  Liberal Arts, 1964), 2:136–8.

[22] The references here to natural kinds are echoed later in Immanuel Kant, *The
  Critique of Judgement* (1790), trans. J. C. Meredith (Oxford: Clarendon Press, 1952),
  154–5. Kant maintained that "the empirical interest in the beautiful exists only in
  society," and that interest can combine with a judgment of taste only "after it has
  once been posited as a pure aesthetic judgment." Hume would probably reply that
  his own agreement with the former point was part of his attempt to avoid anything
  like the latter.

intrinsic worth and value." Sympathy operates whenever we think
of objects in association with people; thus our sympathy with the
owner of a house enables *us* to derive pleasure from the "convenience" of *his* house (T 3.3.2.4, 2.2.8.2, 2.2.5.16).

The justification of judgments of beauty depends on the species
and nature of the object to which it is attributed. Beauty of utility
is relative to species, whether the utility benefits the animal itself,
or the owner of an object; it also varies between cultures (T 2.1.8.2,
3.2.1.18, 3.3.5.3). Although it is detected by a sentiment, beauty
is as "real" as color and other allegedly secondary qualities; moreover, discussion of it can be objective, however difficult to achieve
this may be. Three factors are necessary to the objectivity of such
judgments: the conventions of language, the universal psychological
make-up of human beings, and the possibility of publicly shareable
viewpoints.

Everyone acknowledged that reference to utility required the exercise of judgment, and Hume emphasizes the importance of both
the kind of beauty in question and the kind of thing that is said
to be beautiful. Every community, Hume thinks, agrees on how to
describe what most concerns it. No special mystery surrounds the
conventions governing such discourse, although their historical and
psychological origins may be obscure; but within any social group
it is only deviation from the conventions that calls for explanation.
Thus, what counts as a beautiful plain depends on a particular community's notion of a plain, and in Hume's context – poor agricultural
land almost everywhere – a plain cannot be both "overgrown" and
"beautiful." If we limited our attention to some aspect of its form,
say, its color, or thought of it as something other than a "plain," we
might then be able to *think* of the new 'it' as beautiful, but not to *feel*
it to be so, because such beauty would be "merely of imagination"
(T 2.2.5.18, 3.3.1.20–3, 2.1.20.4).

For the required causal interaction to occur between object and
observer, for our judgments to be objective, and for social communication to take place at all, it is necessary to establish and agree on
appropriate viewpoints. The metaphorical notion of viewpoint here
covers the descriptions under which an object is considered, as well
as the observers' beliefs, attitudes, and interests.

It is central to Hume's position that "'tis impossible men cou'd
ever agree in their sentiments and judgments, unless they chose

some common point of view, from which they might survey their object, and which might cause it to appear the same to all of them." This general viewpoint is the ground of the "general inalterable standard, by which we may approve or disapprove of characters and manners. And tho' the *heart* does not always take part with those general notions, or regulate its love and hatred by them, yet are they sufficient for discourse, and serve all our purposes in company, in the pulpit, on the theatre, and in the schools" (T 3.3.1.30, 3.3.3.2). Such standards are revisable, because they serve the needs of the community, and those needs may change. Moreover, "*general rules* are often extended beyond the principle, whence they first arise; and this in all matters of taste and sentiment" (EPM 5.42, 4.7; T 2.2.5.12); only close attention to the context will enable us to distinguish between the origins of a principle and its present foundations – in other words, it has a history, and may have changed (E-OC 4, 469). It is contingent, of course, which standards are accepted within a particular context, since the judgment is made on grounds of utility; but it is necessary that there are some standards.

We can adopt the required "*general* points of view" only "in our thoughts," but they are necessary to all social life: "'twere impossible we cou'd ever make use of language, or communicate our sentiments to one another, did we not correct the momentary appearances of things, and overlook our present situation." Strictly speaking, the adoption of a "general" viewpoint enables us to correct our language rather than our sentiments; first, because "our passions do not readily follow the determination of our judgment," and change more slowly than the operations of the imagination; second, because our sentiments are not influenced immediately, but only mediately by judgments (T 3.3.1.15–18).

Such passages support the view that Hume is one of the first British writers to emphasize the central importance of *context* to our critical judgments. "The passion, in pronouncing its verdict, considers not the object simply, as it is in itself, but surveys it with all the circumstances, which attend it" (E-Sc 35, 172), while "in many orders of beauty, particularly those of the finer arts, it is requisite to employ much reasoning, in order to feel the proper sentiment" (EPM 1.9). We may have to learn what complexities need to be considered, but discussion can change how we think of something, and thereby set off a new causal sequence ending in new sentiments and verdicts.

III. EARLY ESSAYS

In the *Essays* of 1741–2 there are several discussions of the origins and social development of the arts, and Hume frequently echoes Dubos's conclusions, without necessarily agreeing with the implied route to them. Hume agrees with Dubos that the fine arts can develop only when groups or societies exist beyond the conditions of bare subsistence, and indeed only when production of the necessities of life exceeds demand, views that Adam Ferguson explicitly rejects. (J.-G. Sulzer is unique among Hume's contemporaries for recognizing that the choices of color, size, shape, decoration, or texture of containers or dwellings, among so-called early peoples, might be regarded as art or incipient art.)[23] Like Dubos, Hume claims that the arts and sciences arise only among peoples who have what he calls a "free government," and some measure of security; moreover, strong rival states stimulate invention while also curbing territorial expansion. Those arts that require patronage are likely to flourish best in a civilized monarchy, whereas sciences typically flourish in a republic, but in both domains there are cycles in which perfection is necessarily followed by decline. The notion of cycles referred less to skills, as such, than to the fact that both styles and content can fall out of favor through overfamiliarity or repetition, or when particular practices seem to be exhausted. Hume holds that nothing can be done to alter anyone's personal, inner constitution, although it exerts a crucial influence over individual taste. And reasoning has important roles to play because it can modify the ways we perceive and describe things. Dubos had echoed ancient writers in emphasizing how physical and physiological factors, such as aging, affect our critical judgments; by contrast, Hume emphasizes social or "moral" factors. He argues that happiness, consisting in a balance between action, pleasure, and indolence, is necessary to the physical well-being of individuals, as well as to the political health of society.

Dubos argued that works of art raise artificial, not natural, passions, and that everyone except fellow artists and scholars reads works of art for pleasure. The contrast between artists and scholars, on the one hand, and spectators, on the other, is important. Fellow-artists are interested in techniques and know-how, but as

[23] J. G. Sulzer, in his article on "Art" in *Supplément à l'Encyclopédie*, 1.588.

rival craftsmen and potential competitors for attention, they cannot, in that frame of mind, adopt a properly disinterested attitude. (Dubos may have been the first to use this notion in an exclusively aesthetic context.) Dubos insists that we can derive sustained pleasure from a work only if we understand it in some way, and the minimal requirement is for *ordre* – which might be translated as "discernible structure." The "public," and not the self-proclaimed professional critics, are the proper judges of art because, having no self-interest in the transaction, they can more easily answer the primary question of whether they have been moved or affected by a work – and that question is not the task of reason but of an internal sense called *sentiment*.[24] The task of reason is to identify the features of a work that cause us pleasure, and thereby justify the verdict of sentiment. These tasks of identification and justification typically belong to the critic. There are important distinctions, therefore, between an artist who makes, a spectator who responds, and a critic who explains. The "public," it should be added, turns out to be a privileged group that has learned through experience to exercise comparative taste; they are the "true amateurs," because the learned connoisseurs are in danger of losing touch with the very point of the arts, which is to please.

Dubos influenced Hume not only in his reflections on the physical, social, and political conditions of the arts, but also when he came to consider the conditions for the proper responses to them. This will become apparent in the next section. Before examining Hume's most important essay on matters of criticism, however, brief mention should be made of a short essay he published at the same time, under the title "Of Tragedy." There, Hume takes up the fashionable topic of why spectators should derive pleasure from representations of tragic events that in real life they would abhor. Most well-known

---

[24] It should be emphasized that the ambiguity in the French term *sentiment*, deplored by French and English writers alike, is precisely mirrored in Hume's term "sentiment," by which he sometimes means "emotion, passion," and sometimes "judgment, opinion"; indeed, for him, the term treacherously covers both feeling and thought. Adam Smith, in 1762, used the term to mean "moral observations"; see his *Lectures on Rhetoric and Belles Lettres*, ed. J. C. Bryce (Oxford: Clarendon Press, 1983), Lecture 11, 58. In the same year, Kames defined it: "Every thought suggested by a passion or emotion, is termed *a sentiment*"; *Elements of Criticism*, 2:149.

writers in France and Britain had something to say on the subject, including Addison, Dubos, and Lord Kames. Hume combines the views of Dubos and Fontenelle, and augments them.[25] He agrees with them that we never fail to know that we are in a theater, that almost any passion is better than none, and that almost any form of imitation or representation arrests our attention and pleases us. The clue, he thinks, lies in the mastery of language and presentation, which allows one of the conflicting passions to become dominant over the other. The intense horror we experience from the story is itself converted to something pleasing by the overwhelming pleasure from the beauty with which it is presented. The conversion can occur only when the story is fictional, or at least is narrated about the past. Since antiquity, of course, the skill with which a sculptor or painter represented horror, had been admired – as in the case of Laocoon. In the field of music, by the mid-eighteenth century, a staple criterion of merit consisted in the resolution achieved by a skillful composer in first setting himself, and then overcoming, difficulties – achievements detectable, of course, only by an informed listener. By 1759 it was becoming commonplace to complain that, in Voltaire's words from *Candide*, "music today is nothing but the technical skill of performing scores that are hard to play" (Chapter 25). In connection with tragedies, however, Hume does not mention the notion of sympathy, perhaps because it would diminish pleasure to the extent that it induced identification with the sufferers (E-Tr).

IV. "OF THE STANDARD OF TASTE"

In 1755 the Edinburgh Society for Encouraging Arts, Sciences, Manufactures, and Agriculture in Scotland had proposed, but failed, to award a medal for "the best essay on taste." Adam Smith, Lord Kames, William Robertson, Adam Ferguson, and Hume were members of the society, as was Allan Ramsay, who had just published his own "A Dialogue on Taste." The Society renewed its proposal in 1756 and awarded a gold medal to Alexander Gerard: he explored his ideas further in the Aberdeen Philosophical Society in 1758,

---

[25] Addison, *The Spectator*, no. 418; Dubos, *Réflexions critiques*, 1.1; 1.44; Henry Home, Lord Kames, *Essays on the Principles of Morality and Natural Religion* (Edinburgh, 1751), 1.1; Fontenelle, *Réflexions sur la poetique*, 36.

in the presence of Thomas Reid, John Gregory, and George Campbell, all of whom later wrote on aspects of the problem. Gerard's
expanded submission was published, at Hume's urging, in 1759 as
An Essay on Taste, together with "three dissertations on the same
subject," by Voltaire, d'Alembert, and Montesquieu; these last were,
in fact, unacknowledged translations from entries under "Goût" in
volume 7 of the *Encyclopédie.*[26]

In the same year Smith published *Theory of Moral Sentiments,*
which includes his discussion of taste, while Lord Kames published
his discussion in *Elements of Criticism* in 1762. Meanwhile, in 1757
Hume had published (in *Four Dissertations*) an essay of his own, "Of
the Standard of Taste," together with "Of Tragedy" and two other
essays; he told a correspondent that his essay on taste was a substitute for one on geometry that Lord Stanhope persuaded him to withdraw. Ramsay, like Hume, cites Shaftesbury as a point of departure
when discussing whether there could be a standard of taste, and offers
a sociological explanation of changes in fashion, placing great weight
on habit and social status. Hume's own essay is condensed and adopts
many of Abbé Dubos's conclusions, albeit now implicitly supported
by his own philosophical system. Indeed, Hume seeks to find in
human nature, as well as in social practices, a resolution for the problem Ramsay located only in social practices. Gerard's much longer
book takes its departure from a Humean position and discusses many
of the same issues: the need for attention and comparison in order to
establish the ends and merit of a work; the need for good sense, reasoning, and models; the parallels between taste and virtue; the need
to ground our conclusions in experience. Likewise, Kames's even
longer book clearly addresses Hume's views, and includes unusually
detailed discussions of architecture, gardens, and music.

Reason, Sentiment, and Judgment

In "Of the Standard of Taste" Hume, in effect, extends his reflections from *An Enquiry concerning the Principles of Morals* on the

---

[26] Allan Ramsay, "Dialogue on Taste," *The Investigator* 322 (1755); H. Lewis Ulman,
ed., *The Minutes of the Aberdeen Philosophical Society 1758–1773* (Aberdeen:
Aberdeen University Press, 1990). James Adam wrote to Kames from Rome about
the matter in 1761 and drafted his own essay on "architectural theory" the following year: the essay is reprinted in Fleming (see note 8 above).

respective roles of reason and sentiment in the realm of values. Some so-called judgments of taste are, he believes, palpably foolish and indefensible: "the taste of all individuals is not upon an equal footing," and we should not give unrestricted license to the claim that it is "fruitless to dispute concerning tastes." He recognizes that those who introduce sentiment into the analysis must nevertheless avoid claiming that everyone is equally right in matters of sentiment. Indeed, if rational discourse is even to be possible, there must be some "standard," "rule," or criterion by which disputes can be resolved. Consequently, Hume hopes to show that criticism is a factually based, rational, social activity, capable of being integrated into the rest of intelligible human discourse, and he attempts to establish that sentiment can be a criterion. Of course, if there are "rules," whether of composition or criticism, they must not be thought of as "fixed by reasonings *a priori*, or . . . be esteemed abstract conclusions of the understanding" (E-ST 25, 7, 6, 9; 242, 230, 229, 231).

Hume holds that to discern the subtle or the defining properties of something, a purely passive attitude is not enough. The observer must self-consciously attend to the object in question and, moreover, be in a proper state of mind when doing so; a merely causal reaction will be replaced by an appropriate causal interaction, to which the observer significantly contributes. Following Dubos, Hume states that three traits are needed: "A perfect serenity of mind, a recollection of thought, a due attention to the object" (E-ST 10, 232). In art the problem is complex: "In order to judge aright of a composition of genius, there are so many views to be taken in, so many circumstances to be compared, and such a knowledge of human nature requisite, that no man, who is not possessed of the soundest judgment, will ever make a tolerable critic in such performances" (E-DT 4, 6). There are three main "causes" of failure to respond properly to works of art, and each one is derived verbatim from Dubos: a person may lack delicacy, may lack good sense, or may suffer from prejudice. These are all transliterated seventeenth-century French technical terms, essentially Cartesian and cognitive in force, familiar to all of Hume's learned contemporaries (E-ST 14, 20–1, 234, 239–40). Hume holds that delicacy of feeling enables one to "be sensibly touched with every part of" a work (E-DT 2, 4): such discriminating perception clearly requires judgment of some kind. Cartesians had defined good sense as true judgment of sensible things, its role being to guard against false judgment, or prejudice. Hume accepts the point: "reason, if not an essential part of taste, [not, that is, the defining element] is at least requisite to the operations" of it. "To form a true judgment" a critic "must place himself in the same situation" as the audience for whom the work was conceived, and to whom it was originally addressed. In other words, an approximation to the original context is a first condition of discerning what was achieved. Good sense attends to four features of the context: the ends for which a work has been calculated, the effectiveness of the means to those ends, the mutual relations of the parts and of the parts to the whole, and the intelligibility of the whole. For example, "the object of eloquence is to persuade, of history to instruct, of poetry to please by means of the passions and the imagination. These ends we must carry constantly in our view, when we peruse any performance." In addition, "every kind of composition, even the most poetical, is nothing but a chain of propositions and reasonings," so that intelligibility is central (E-ST 21, 22, 239, 240). Hume's friend Adam Ferguson, in *An Essay on the History of Civil Society* (1767), agreed that a knowledge of context is indeed essential for understanding human achievements, but insisted that we too often ascribe design, intention, and theory where none existed (in Part 3, Section II, for example). The "antitheory" view of many practicing artists was accepted by several philosophers in both France and Britain throughout the eighteenth century, and several critics of Hume's *History* who disapproved of his political interpretations also objected to his implausible attribution of rational thought and planning to his chosen subjects.

Practice, Comparison, Interpretation

To overcome failures caused by prejudice or the lack of delicacy and good sense, two steps are necessary (again from Dubos): practice and comparison. *Practice* is necessary to overcome superficial first impressions, since any "very individual performance" should be "more than once perused by us, and be surveyed in different lights with attention and deliberation." Only in this way can we determine "the relation of the parts" and their respective merits. Likewise, *comparison* is essential "between the several species and degrees of excellence," because someone "who has had no opportunity of comparing the different kinds of beauty, is indeed totally unqualified to pronounce an opinion with regard to any object presented to him. By comparison alone we fix the epithets of praise or blame, and learn how to assign the due degree of each." A prejudiced critic fails to place "himself in that point of view, which the performance supposes," and "obstinately maintains his natural position." Hume insists that "every work of art, in order to produce its due effect on the mind, must be surveyed in a certain point of view, and cannot be fully relished by persons, whose situation, real or imaginary, is not conformable to that which is required by the performance" (E-ST 18–21, 237–9). We see here Hume's view that a work of art is an intentional act, calling for self-conscious mental action on the part of the spectator.

Although he rarely uses the term, Hume is clearly concerned with the nature and conditions of "interpretation" which leads to an understanding of a work (see EPM 9.4); practice is needed in order to achieve discrimination, and comparison in order to place a work in its proper categories. A passage in Section 3 of *Philosophical Essays concerning Human Understanding* of 1748 (later retitled as *An Enquiry concerning Human Understanding*) is here significant. There Hume argues that the principles of human agency are themselves represented in, or at least leave traces in, what we do; and they underlie the spectator's acts of interpretation. That is why he says, in 1757, "the same address and dexterity, which practice gives to the execution of any work, is also acquired by the same means, in the judging of it" (E-ST 18, 237). For Hume, our capacity to understand the world depends on our capacity to understand the causes in operation. In *An Enquiry concerning Human Understanding* he asks causal questions about each of the issues he raises later in "Of the Standard of Taste": the artist and the conditions of creation, the art product which results, and the audience and the conditions of response. Moreover, like Dubos, Hume's interest centers on broadly representational works of art, and he asks causal questions about the things or events represented, in order to determine the consistency and intelligibility of the work's content. His internal questions about the consistency of the work itself presuppose answers to the external matter of the proper viewpoint, and the relations between the work and other things – such as society at large, or morality. He declares that

As man is a reasonable being... he seldom acts or speaks or thinks without a purpose and intention.... In all compositions of genius, therefore, it is requisite, that the writer have some plan or object... there must appear some aim or intention, in his first setting out, if not in the composition of the whole work. A production without a design would resemble more the ravings of a madman, than the sober efforts of genius and learning. (EHU 3.4–5)

In "narrative compositions," it is a rule that "admits of no exception," that the narrated events "must be connected together by some bond or tye," must "form a kind of *Unity*, which may bring them under one plan or view, and which may be the object or end of the writer in his first undertaking." Above all, it is necessary that such works "have a sufficient unity to make them be comprehended" (EHU 3.6–17).[27]

The Mind's Contribution

In the *Treatise* Hume argued that consistency of ideas ensures their "easy transition," together with "the emotions or impressions, attending the ideas"; the natural requirement for such easy transitions lies behind demands for consistency of treatment and tone in literature, and for balanced figures in painting and statuary (T 2.2.8.18–20, 2.2.5.19; EPM 6.6). "The designs, and projects, and views of men are principles as necessary in their operation as heat and cold, moist and dry" (T 3.1.2.9); they are, in brief, the conditions of human agency, and a knowledge of them is a precondition for understanding what a man does.

We require art to be intelligible precisely because it is a human activity; "*durable*" pleasure, indeed, is dependent on understanding in the relevant ways (T 2.2.4.5, 2.3.10.6). Our affections are aroused,

---

[27] The first five editions (1748–60) of EHU included an additional paragraph in which Hume said that it "is incumbent on every Writer, to form some Plan or Design, before he enter on any Discourse or Narration, and to comprehend his Subject in some general Aspect or united View, which may be the constant Object of his Attention." See the Clarendon edition of EHU, 237.

or at least sustained, only if the actions of our fellows display what might be called a certain *transparency*.

Even if, as he maintained in the second *Enquiry*, the "final sentence depends on some internal sense or feeling, which nature has made universal in the whole species," a "judgment on any work of art" involves more than a mere report of such a feeling (EPM 1.9; E-ST 23, 241). Judgment involves identifying the causes of the pleasurable sentiment and, although they are detectable only from certain viewpoints, these causes are to be found among the properties of the work itself. Like Sancho's kinsmen, in Cervantes's *Don Quixote* (2.13), who were vindicated by the discovery of the leather thong (Hume gets the story slightly wrong), a critic who identifies the causes of his sentiment will have "justified the verdict" (E-ST 16, 235); he will have established its appropriateness by establishing its repeatable causal conditions. Dubos had claimed, in 1719, that the role of reason was to justify the judgment that sentiment had already made (*justifier le jugement que le sentiment a porté*), by determining the "causes" of our pleasure; critics, indeed, can tell us the cause of an effect one has already felt (*la cause d'un effet qu'on sentait déjà*) only if, on Hume's view, the antecedent is identifiable, and the relation repeatable.[28] "Reason," therefore, that is, inductive, experimental reasoning, is "requisite to the operations" of taste (E-ST 22, 240) because the proper sentiment depends on the proper discernment, which in turn involves thinking of the work in particular, determinate, ways. "Critics can reason and dispute more plausibly than cooks" (E-Sc 11, 163) because cooks are concerned solely with the physical causes of sensations and require minimal mental contribution from the customer, and their dishes are not bearers of meaning; concepts still operate, of course, and children are not alone in rejecting unfamiliar dishes they fail initially to classify as soup. By contrast, critics require sound judgment in order to discern the consistency and meaning of an intentional human performance, and in order to understand it. Of course, many ancient and modern writers insisted, in Shaftesbury's words, that "we may judge well of poetry without being poets or possessing the least of a poetic vein."[29] It must be stressed, nevertheless, that a genuine man

---

[28] Dubos, *Réflexions critiques*, 2.22, 32.
[29] Shaftesbury, "A Letter Concerning Enthusiasm" (1708), in *Characteristics*, 1.30.

of taste must experience a pleasurable sentiment when he attends to
a work in specified ways, because that is the sentiment – his signal –
whose cause and justification he wishes to locate in the work itself.
In brief, the "proper sentiment" is a complex response to a work,
involving causal interaction between it and a spectator who attends
to it in specifiable ways; a critic's task includes the determination
of the spectator's viewpoint, and he justifies his verdicts by bringing others to perceive and think of the work in the way he has. It
could even be suggested that by replacing a purely causal account
of response by one essentially involving interaction, Hume reveals a
new context in which Newtonian thinking, by the midcentury, had
displaced the earlier Cartesian model.

Pretenders and Bad Critics

When discussing the causes of failure to feel the proper sentiment,
Hume raises two important questions, although he directly answers
only one of them. First, he asks how we should "silence the bad
critic" who insists on his sentiment in the face of counterevidence
to his causal claims (E-ST 16, 236). Hume's answer is that we must
appeal to parallel cases whose relevance the bad critic acknowledges.
Hume's view is that in the absence of established models and general principles, time will ultimately vindicate any critical judgment;
someone with unusual powers of discrimination may fail to convince his peers, but we should all hope that truth triumphs in the
end. He would admit, however, that even if an established critic
can convince his audience about a new case, we are left in ignorance as individuals or as unestablished critics, because self-doubt
will typically accompany our failure to convince others. This point
leads to the second issue: in the context of art criticism, how can
pretenders be detected? In contrast to the bad critic, who insists on
his own sentiment, the pretender says what others do say or are
willing to say, but either experiences no pleasure, or derives it from
properties other than those he claims to be the cause of the pleasure. Hume's question about pretenders – unjustified claimants – is
a legacy of the search for a criterion of knowledge, and of debates
about genuine faith in religion. The question forces us to clarify the
role of the calm passions in his theory. If, as is possible, a pretender's
judgments eventually gain acceptance, they do so in spite of the

fact that he does not have the same sentiments as his listeners. But what matters to them, as to each one of us, is not what the pretender personally feels, although they happen to be deceived about that, but finding the viewpoints from which properties of the work can be discerned. Supporting this idea is an ancient insight, much trumpeted in the eighteenth century, that we all begin by learning what to say from others, and no one can begin by being a pretender: pretence is parasitic on knowledge, and knowledge in principle is public. Hume has already emphasized that it is by comparison that we learn how to assign "the epithets of praise or blame" (E-ST 20, 238). Even a pretender must first learn the same conventions as his peers, in order to be able to communicate at all. In brief, no human being can proclaim special authority for a self-absorbed report of his or her thoughts about the world, without first having learned from others how to formulate and express thoughts of such a kind: in this respect, judgments about art differ not at all from anything else.

In the *Treatise* Hume observed that "in changing the point of view, tho' the object may remain the same, its proportion to ourselves entirely alters" (T 2.2.10.3); and later he noted that "a very small variation of the object, even where the same qualities are preserved, will destroy a sentiment" (EPM 5 n.17). So disagreements in judgments may have their source in variations between the observers, or in the objects observed, or in the viewpoints adopted. But Hume never doubts the possibility of reaching agreement on descriptions of states of affairs, although it is an empirical fact whether a particular community possesses adequate conventions to achieve them.

What sort of person is a pretender? If inner sentiments play no role in discussions of public objects, a pretender must be someone who wants to be admired for his judgments on those things, even though he knows he lacks the normal pleasurable sentiments derived from attending to them. There are many possible motives for wanting to deceive others about our internal states. Hume believes that men want to agree primarily because they are social beings; the bond of social sympathy is so strong that we can rarely hold out against the general opinion of others (T 3.3.2.2, 2.1.11.2; DP 2.10, W 4:152). Moreover, as members of a community we begin by being told what to say, and only subsequently discover any internal accompaniments to our utterances. No one thrust into a new culture and society, as Shaftesbury and others recognized, would know what judgments it was appropriate to make, and at first would not even know how to describe the matters in hand. Of course, as Hume often states, education can lead to purely mechanical reactions that, in this case, might mean judgments made in the absence of the inner sentiments that are their ground (EPM 5.3, 3.23). But a man can become a pretender only when he discovers that his internal life differs from those of his peers, and by then he may well have established alternative associations that act as cues. Hume's pretender in criticism, indeed, has much in common with a color-blind man. Both, for the most part, can get by with their learned responses; both, in his view, suffer from a defect in their mental constitution, as a result of which they are lacking in certain basically natural reactions (E-Ep 6, 140); neither, once we know their handicap, is to be relied on as our guide.

In the concluding pages of the essay Hume continues to echo Dubos. Psychological facts about individuals, and social facts about communities, explain residual variations within otherwise agreed judgments. Thus, Ovid, Horace, and Tacitus are all worthy of esteem, although at different times of his life a man may prefer one above another. Such preferences are "innocent," because "it is almost impossible not to feel a predilection for that which suits our particular turn and disposition." It often requires "some effort" to judge the works of other ages and cultures, but adverse verdicts should be restricted to those which confound the boundaries of vice and virtue (E-ST 30, 31, 33; 244, 244–7; see also EPM 5.15). Hume implied a moral distinction between a bad critic and a pretender, because in the worst cases, a pretender, setting out to deceive, may secure approval of what is really reprehensible.

V. CONCLUSION

For Hume, the notions of mistake, error, falsity are associated with a critic's failure to convince a suitable peer group, over a suitable period of time, about the alleged facts; the possibility of mistakes entails the possibility of correction, and a bad critic is one who persists in his mistakes. It is a question of fact who the arbiters of taste are at any particular time, and how they gain recognition, although Hume believes that most of us "are apt to receive a man for whatever he has a mind to put himself off for" (E-IM 2, 553). On this view he could claim that most critics are self-proclaiming. Few people are properly qualified to be critics, however, because it is rare to find the combination of "strong sense" and "delicate sentiment, improved by practice, perfected by comparison, and cleared of all prejudice" (E-ST 23, 241).

Some modern commentators have alleged that Hume's account is entirely circular: the standard of taste is established by, or recognized in, the true critics; and the true critics are recognized by adherence to the standard of taste.[30] But this is not Hume's position. He holds that when learning social practices, and the conventions that govern them, we learn at the same time who currently counts as the experts, and what are accepted as the best examples. But if this is true when a practice is already established, it does not explain how the first experts in a given field gain recognition, or how established judgments are modified or, exceptionally, overturned. Hume cannot appeal solely to the passing of time since, by itself, that does nothing to establish either correctness or appropriateness; and it is useless as a criterion in the present. He admits that eighteenth-century responses to Homer and the Greek tragedians differ from those of their own time, but he also holds that, once prejudices are removed, audiences can perceive the lasting and true beauties of the works. Yet once the properties of a work are truly discerned, the endorsement of later times does little more than clarify which works should function as models at different stages in a tradition. Hume does not raise the question of whether long admired works either are or must be understood differently at different times; nor whether some works admit of significantly varying interpretations; although, in his *History*, he does observe of political matters that "it seems unreasonable to judge of the measures, embraced during one period, by the maxims, which prevail in another" (HE 52.66, 5:240). Since, at least in 1741, he canvassed a cyclical view of the progress of the arts, it is surprising that he did not directly analyze the factors in changing tastes. If every individual is constrained in his judgments by the traditions he has inherited, he is unlikely to witness the vindication of any large-scale reassessments he may attempt. And since Hume also holds that whatever pleases cannot be a fault (E-ST 9, 232), it may be asked whether someone might not derive greater pleasure

---

[30] Peter Kivy, "Hume's Standard of Taste: Breaking the Circle," *British Journal of Aesthetics* 7 (1967): 57–66.

from a work that, in the view of experts, he has misunderstood or misperceived.

At the end of "Of the Standard of Taste," having conceded that the expression of merely personal likes and dislikes admits of no worthwhile discussion, Hume asserts that the overall merit of a work stands or falls on an estimate of its moral stance, if there is one. Three kinds of observation can be made by a critic, therefore: "I like the work," "The work is good of its kind," "The work is morally praiseworthy." Reference to the standard of taste covers the conditions for establishing what something is, the models against which it is to be measured, and the true moral standards. Hume is quite clear that, even if pleasure is the occasion of sustained attention to a work, the critic's task is to concentrate on the work, not on himself. In the *Treatise* he stated that "our approbation is imply'd in the immediate pleasure" (T 3.1.2.3), and in this sense a man himself needs no justification for the pleasures he experiences. But as a social being he wishes to communicate that pleasure, and to seek reassurance that he does not deviate markedly from his peers. This he can do only by getting agreement from others over the causes of shareable pleasures. Hume himself, for example, admits distress at being unable to change his sentiments to accord with those of men he respects; he hopes that the long-term verdict of posterity will vindicate him (HL 2:133). In another letter he remarked that we often conceal our dislike of something because of our inability to give reasons for our verdict (HL 1:30). To express our dislike is often to publicize our deviation from the accepted evaluation, and, as such, our judgment calls for explanation. We can retreat, of course, in the direction of our psychological idiosyncrasies, but to do so is to withdraw our original verdict from public discussion. But if instead we advance toward a viewpoint available to others, we then advance toward objective verdicts.

Hume nowhere discusses questions about the *meaning* of works of art, even though he was entirely familiar with long-running battles over the interpretation of biblical and other historical texts. This is partly because he believes that, in the general context of communication, any distortion of the "natural meaning" of terms is socially irresponsible. It is surprising, however, that he did not discuss the implications of the fact that no traditions can be relied on uncritically, since they can change within a lifetime, and we frequently project our present concerns onto the past – as Anthony Collins and other freethinkers forcefully insisted.[31] It should also be noted that, compared with the absolute necessities of life, art is one of life's "superfluities"; this aside, the habit of conversing together, and of contributing to each other's pleasures, increases the level of both knowledge and humanity (E-RA 7, 272).

The overall view can be outlined as follows. Someone becomes conscious of pleasure in a certain object. He needs only a vague awareness of its properties to be able to concentrate more fully, and to render his first "obscure and confused" sentiment "clear and distinct" (E-ST 18, 237; T 2.3.9.12). But it is not, strictly, the original sentiment that becomes clear. Attention requires the fullest perceptual and intellectual effort, and the spectator naturally seeks a state of equilibrium and consistency. D'Alembert, for example, underlines the importance of sustained interest, and this notion clearly fits Hume's scheme.[32] For, if a spectator can make some sense of what he perceives, he will experience new sentiments; these will displace his earlier ones, and may loosely be described as enhancing them. To determine the focus of his pleasures he must appeal to publicly discernible things, using the conventions of his community, and these conventions secure all the objectivity we need for our judgments and verdicts. Moreover, as a social being, a spectator wishes to reassure himself that his responses resemble those of his neighbors, and to share with them what he enjoys.

VI. FINALE

This essay began with the claim that Hume's observations on art are set in the framework of social life, and that this is why he considers both the making of, and the response to, works of art as human actions subject to the analysis he has offered of other human actions. In the broadest sense, works of art are pleasurable means of communication between human beings, and so the preconditions

---

[31] Anthony Collins, *An Essay Concerning the Use of Reason in Propositions* (London, 1707); *A Discourse of Free-Thinking* (London, 1713); *A Philosophical Inquiry* (London, 1715); *A Collection of Tracts written by Mr . . .* (London, 1717).

[32] Jean le R. d'Alembert, "De la liberté de la musique," in *Mélanges de literature, d'histoire, et de philosophie* (Amsterdam, 1759), 4.404.

of effective communication apply to art as much as to other means. Certain works please us because of the particular properties they possess; one of our tasks is to identify these causes in order to enable others to share in our enjoyment. We cannot comprehend a work of art merely by being in its presence, however. Two properties that belong to human actions, and that are goals of our comprehension, are meaning and value; neither is discernible by the five ordinary senses alone. The mind must be actively involved. Just as inference beyond the present data is necessary for all factual reasoning, so interpretation is necessary to establish the meaning of what another person has done. Hume's commitment to classical learning, and in particular to the views of Cicero, explains his interest in the practice and theory of rhetoric. From that domain he derived the view that one can, and should, ask a set of questions of any text, in order to grasp its meaning: who wrote it? for whom? about what? how? when? where? why? He did not sufficiently consider, however, how complex or difficult some of these questions can be.

No one in the first part of the eighteenth century envisaged the multiple interpretations of works of art that, today, are commonplace. Hume's emphasis is primarily on the context in which works are encountered. The great danger, as Dubos saw, is that the critic becomes a parasite: a disengaged nonpractitioner who passes judgment and exercises authority over the lives of both makers and spectators, and who transforms the critical role from that of a dispensable intermediary to that of an indispensable oracle. At that stage criticism has assumed autonomy as a practice in its own right, but one that fundamentally depends on the agency of others. Indeed, from the seventeenth century onwards – and probably earlier – artists in many fields deplored a growing tendency in their audiences to substitute talk for close scrutiny and, in the absence of any practical knowledge themselves, to impute theories to artists when none had been entertained.[33]

Hume's views on taste were discussed, sometimes at considerable length, by his immediate contemporaries, such as Lord Kames,

---

[33] Almost a century after Perrault, Hume's acquaintance Dr. Charles Burney forcefully made the same point; see Jones, "Italian Operas and Their Audiences," 326. Charles Burney, *A General History of Music from the Earliest Ages to the Present Period* (London, 1776–9).

Adam Smith, Edmund Burke, Alexander Gerard, Thomas Reid, George Campbell, and Hugh Blair. Hume's close friend Adam Smith accepted most of his views on the arts, and those of Dubos, but underlined the implication of Hume's emphasis on context by stressing that our overriding concern is with the meaning of works.[34] Immanuel Kant undoubtedly conceived the first part of his *Critique of Judgment* as a response to Hume, whose essay on taste Sulzer translated for him. On the continent of Europe a few writers during the nineteenth century, in Russia, Hungary, Italy, and Greece, for example, became interested in Hume's views, often through the mediation not only of Kant, but also the works of Hugh Blair, Kames, and articles in encyclopedias.[35] After a gap of almost 200 years, several Western philosophers have turned to Hume's essay; their work is best described as "inspired by Hume," rather than as thought plausibly ascribable to Hume himself.[36] Hume's own experience of the arts increased dramatically from the 1760s, but we have no evidence that he later revised any of his earlier thoughts about the arts or taste. Although he regarded philosophy as anchored in and referrable back to daily life, we regrettably do not know how he expected his views on taste, in particular, to be absorbed into either creative or critical practice.

The precise nature of the context in which Hume was writing, and its profound differences from our own, are usually ignored by modern commentators on Hume, who see no need to anchor their

---

[34] For an analysis of Smith's views, see my "The Aesthetics of Adam Smith," in *Adam Smith Reviewed*, ed. P. Jones and A. S. Skinner (Edinburgh: Edinburgh University Press, 1992), 56–78.

[35] See *The Reception of David Hume in Europe*, ed. P. Jones (London: Thoemmes Continuum, 2005); Peter Jones, "Why Bother with Hume and Kames on Criticism and the Arts?" in *Instruction and Amusement*, ed. E. Mazza and E. Ronchetti (Padova: Il Poligrafo, 2005), 27–44.

[36] Some anachronism may be inevitable in the interpretation of past texts and contexts; see Peter Jones, *Philosophy and the Novel* (Oxford: Clarendon Press, 1975). Most twentieth- and twenty-first-century philosophers reflect their view of philosophy itself by "using" texts from the past for their own purposes in their own contexts. For variations in this approach: Mary Mothersill, *Beauty Restored* (Oxford: Clarendon Press, 1984); George Dickie, *The Century of Taste* (Oxford: Oxford University Press, 1996); Paul Guyer, "The Standard of Taste and the 'Most Ardent Desire of Society,'" in *Pursuits of Reason; Essays in Honor of Stanley Cavell*, ed. T. Cohen, P. Guyer, and H. Putnam (Lubbock: Texas Tech University Press, 1993), 37–66.

own reflections in practical knowledge of one or more of the arts. Moreover, it is often claimed that philosophy must not be conflated with the history of ideas, and that the essential logic of an argument, whatever the contingencies of its expression, is context-independent. However much his own practice varied, Hume himself is unlikely to have sympathized with such a view. Those who find Kantian aesthetics largely convincing ask whether an empiricist aesthetics, along Humean lines, is even possible, within some specified context. The roles of imagination and the emotions, in both creation and response, which Hume did not explore in detail, still require satisfactory analysis; the issues of interpretation and meaning occupy many modern theorists of language and criticism, as do the complex social contexts in which works of art are made, recognized, and assessed, and that accelerate changes in the central concepts themselves. Every reader, however, should ask what, in their optimistic moments, Hume and his colleagues hoped might or could happen as a result of publishing their views in the way they did.

SUGGESTIONS FOR FURTHER READING

Of the works cited in the notes to this essay, the following are especially recommended.

Dickie, George. *The Century of Taste: The Philosophical Odyssey of Taste in the Eighteenth Century.* Oxford: Oxford University Press, 1996.

Guyer, Paul. "The Standard of Taste and the 'Most Ardent Desire of Society.'" In *Pursuits of Reason: Essays in Honor of Stanley Cavell*, edited by T. Cohen, P. Guyer, and H. Putnam. Lubbox: Texas Tech University Press, 1993. 37–66.

14 David Hume: "The Historian"

The first volume of Hume's *History of England*, dealing with the early Stuarts, appeared in 1754. The final volumes, covering the period from the invasion of Julius Caesar to 1485, appeared in 1762, although Hume was occupied with revisions of the whole work until his death.[1] In writing history, Hume was partly creating, partly responding to, a new market. In 1757 he thought history "the most popular kind of writing of any" (HL 1:244). In 1770 he wrote, "I believe this is the historical Age and this [Scotland] the historical Nation" (HL 2:230). He knew of no fewer than eight histories that were currently being written. The year before, in England, he had declared, "History, I think, is the Favourite Reading" (HL 2:196). Hume and his friend William Robertson were in large part responsible for this new popularity of history, much of it written by Scotsmen for English readers.[2] Hume himself had received unprecedented payments for his *History* (for which he sold the copyright on each volume, rather than collecting royalties): he made at least £3,200 on the whole, at a time when a friend of his could consider himself well

---

[1] My title comes from the entry for our David Hume in the British Library catalog, which, to the puzzlement of generations of philosophers, distinguishes him from others of the same name by identifying him as "the historian."

[2] Robertson's *History of Scotland* appeared in 1759. For a recent discussion of Robertson, see M. Fearnley-Sander, "Philosophical History and the Scottish Reformation," *Historical Journal* 33 (1990): 323–38. Hume and Robertson had a low opinion of their chief English competitor, Tobias Smollett, whose *History of England* appeared in 1757 (HL 1:302). When Gibbon published the *Decline and Fall*, Hume expressed surprise that an Englishman could have been capable of such a work. He expected Gibbon to understand that it was the highest of compliments to say that the book had been well received by "all the Men of Letters in this Place [Edinburgh]" (HL 2:309–12).

447

to do on £80 per annum (HL1:193, 255, 266, 314). Although in practice his *History* seems to have sold less well during his lifetime than the various volumes of his *Essays,* Hume was consistently of the opinion that this was his bookseller's fault. The market for history books was potentially far larger (HL 2:106, 229, 233, 242).

I. THE HISTORICAL AGE

Hume was the beneficiary of an immense expansion in the reading public that took place in the mid-eighteenth century.[3] Much of that public was middle class and female, and perhaps its favorite reading was the new genre that seems to have been invented especially for it, the novel: Richardson's *Pamela* appeared in 1740, *Clarissa* in 1748.[4] As early as 1741, however, Hume had felt that the history book could supplant the novel. "There is nothing which I would recommend more earnestly to my female readers than the study of history," he wrote, "as an occupation, of all others, the best suited both to their sex and education, much more instructive than their ordinary books of amusement, and more entertaining than those serious compositions, which are usually to be found in their closets." Only a woman who was acquainted with the history of her own country, and with those of Greece and Rome, could engage in conversation that "can afford any entertainment to men of sense and reflection." Moreover, history provided the best way of becoming "acquainted with human affairs, without diminishing in the least from the most delicate sentiments of virtue." The same could not be said for the actual "practice of the world," or for poetry, since poets "often become advocates for vice." Philosophy, for its part, could rarely move the passions; it is historians who are "the true friends of virtue" (E-SH 1, 5, 7, 563, 566–7).

It was as a friend of virtue, one writing in competition with novelists, that Hume deliberately sought to move his audience to tears by his account of the execution of Charles I (HL 1:210, 222, also

---

[3] Jerome Christensen, *Practicing Enlightenment: Hume and the Formation of a Literary Career* (Madison: University of Wisconsin Press, 1987).

[4] We do not know what Hume thought of Richardson. In 1773 he thought Laurence Sterne's *Tristram Shandy* the "best Book that has been writ by any Englishman these thirty years" (HL 2:269).

344; MOL 11).[5] He was certainly successful: indeed, we have letters from female admirers testifying to how his history had moved
their passions. One of them told him that she had never had such a
good opinion of herself as when reading his history: evidently Hume
had inspired virtuous sentiments in her, and thereby made her feel
virtuous and admirable (HL 2:347, 366–7).[6]

Hume thus early saw a central role for history in contemporary
culture. He had himself long thought of writing history, and he was
evidently spurred on by the conviction that "there is no post of
honour in the English Parnassus more vacant than that of History."
Previous historians – even Paul de Rapin-Thoyras, the most widely
admired of them – had lacked "style, judgement, impartiality, care"
(HL 1:170).[7] Only a contemporary historian could hope to meet the
first test. In 1741 Hume was able to write: "The first polite prose
we have, was writ by a man [Swift] who is still alive" (E-CL 8, 91).
Since there were no contemporary British historians of note, Hume
had to look abroad for his models. Horace Walpole thought Hume's
style was influenced by Voltaire, but Voltaire's *Siècle de Louis XIV*
did not appear until 1751.[8] The models Hume himself refers to were
more distant in time. He tells us he was writing "after the manner
of the Ancients," at least in that he was writing a concise narrative
(HL 1:170). The *Annals of Imperial Rome* (c. A.D. 117) by Gaius
Cornelius Tacitus were soon to be his model for working backwards
rather than forwards in time (HL 1:378), and it is probably from
Tacitus that he took his habit of explaining what different types of
people thought about events at particular moments of crisis: Hume

[5] J. C. Hilson, "Hume: the Historian as Man of Feeling," in *Augustan Worlds*, ed.
J. C. Hilson, M. M. B. Jones, and J. R. Watson (Leicester: Leicester University Press,
1978), 205–22.

[6] Hume's *History of England* was translated into French by Octavie Guichard,
Madame Belot, and published in Amsterdam in 1763. The leading Whig reply to
his *History* was Catherine Macaulay's eight-volume *History of England from the
Accession of James I to that of the Brunswick Line* (1763–83); see NHL, 80–2.
Hume and Macaulay are compared in Natalie Zemon Davis, "History's Two Bod-
ies," *American Historical Review* 93 (1988): 1–30.

[7] The first volume of Rapin's *Histoire d'Angleterre* appeared in 1724, followed by an
English translation in 1725.

[8] "In this Countrey, they call me his Pupil, and think that my History is an Imitation
of his Siecle de Louis XIV. This Opinion flatters very much my Vanity; but the
Truth is, that my History was plan'd, & in a great measure compos'd, before the
Appearance of that agreeable Work" (HL 1:226).

thus took over a version of the fictitious speeches beloved of ancient historians.

In 1758 Hume apologized to Walpole for not having provided footnote references to his sources in the volumes on the Stuarts: it was a defect he was to remedy when he revised them (HL 1:316, 379). His apology provides us with the best guide to his more recent models: "I was seduc'd by the example of all the best historians even among the moderns, such as Matchiavel, Fra paolo, Davila, Bentivoglio; without considering that that practice [of providing references] was more modern than their time, and having been once introduc'd, ought to be follow'd by every writer" (HL 1:284).[9] (Machiavelli, the oldest, was born in 1469; Bentivoglio, the youngest, died in 1644.) Fra Paolo Sarpi (1552–1623) in particular was singled out for praise in the *History:* his account of the Council of Trent was an admirable example of historical writing, so effective that the Roman Catholic church would, Hume thought, never dare call another general council while there was a prospect of such a historian being alive to write about it (HE 39 n.F, 4:388–9). Sarpi had thus single-handedly changed the course of history: Hume could hope no more of his own undertaking.[10]

Niccolò Machiavelli, Sarpi, Enrico Davila (author of the *Historia delle guerre civili di Francia* [1630]), and Guido Bentivoglio (author of *Della guerra di Fiandra* [1632–9]) have more in common than that they are all sixteenth-century Italians, and all influenced by Tacitus. They had all taken an active part in political life, and had written about events within the memory of their contemporaries. For them, history was a practical account of how power politics functioned, and

---

[9] The striking peculiarity amongst this list of "the moderns" is the omission of Francesco Guicciardini, Machiavelli's contemporary, and his superior as a historian. But Hume was familiar with Guicciardini's work, and mentions him on three separate occasions in *An Enquiry concerning the Principles of Morals,* and once in the *Treatise.*

[10] On Sarpi, see my *Paolo Sarpi: Between Renaissance and Enlightenment* (Cambridge: Cambridge University Press, 1983). Those, such as Richard H. Popkin, who think that one of Hume's major achievements was to break with providentialist and prophetic history, attribute to Hume a transformation that Hume himself would probably have attributed to late Renaissance Italy. See "Hume: Philosophical versus Prophetic Historian," in *David Hume, Many-Sided Genius,* ed. K. R. Merrill and R. Shahan (Norman: University of Oklahoma Press, 1976), 83–95. The standard work on the subject is E. Cochrane, *Historians and Historiography in the Italian Renaissance* (Chicago: University of Chicago Press, 1981).

an indispensable education for those who planned to participate in political life. Their natural audience was composed of the members of the political elite – all, of course, men. In order to make himself like such men, Hume had set out in 1748 to acquire a knowledge of courts and camps by entering the service of General St. Clair (HL 1:109; see also NHL 23). But Hume's *History*, as it was finally written, places little emphasis on court intrigues and military prowess. It sees events, above all, from the point of view of the intelligent spectator, not the participant, just as its readers are expected to be spectators: Addison's *Spectator* had provided the model for some of Hume's moral and political essays, and had done much to educate the new polite public that Hume sought to address. If Hume had a model among historians, it is likely, once again, to have been Sarpi: for if the audience to which Sarpi directed his *History of the Inquisition* was one of Venetian politicians, the intended audience of the *History of the Council of Trent* (1619) was much wider. He made the notion that a general council expressed the will of God incredible to an educated public who did not participate in church politics but wished merely to decide what to believe about the church.

Hume's *History* sought to address a new audience: an audience neither of politicians nor of antiquarians, but of those who aspired to participate in polite conversation. This gave history a new role: that of retelling a story already told. We take it for granted that there will be more than one history dealing with a particular subject, but to those living in the eighteenth century there was something novel about this idea. As Hume set to work on the *History*, Charles Rollin had recently published his *Histoire Romaine* (1738–41): this was the first attempt to retell the history of ancient Rome for a modern audience.[11] Until then it had always been assumed that those who wanted to learn about Roman history would do so through a direct reading of the great historians of ancient Rome, Gaius Sallustius Crispus (Sallust: c. 86–35 B.C.), Titus Livius (Livy: c. 59 B.C.–A.D. 17), and Tacitus (c. A.D. 56–120). This assumption was also held about English history. In the same letter to Walpole, Hume defended himself against a view that he felt Walpole "rather insinuated than advanc'd; as if it were superfluous to rewrite the English history, or publish on that subject any thing which has ever before in any shape

---

[11] An English translation began to appear in 1739.

appeard in print." Hume insisted, first, that there was too much material for anyone but a professional to come to grips with it all: "The original books, which instruct us in the reign of Q. Elizabeth alone, would require six months reading at the rate of ten hours a day" (HL 1:285). The historian thus, in part, provided a précis, and it was partly as a précis of English history that Hume's volumes had such astounding success: seven complete editions during his lifetime, and 175 in the century after his death.[12] Why, though, beyond the fact that Hume was more concise, read Hume on the Civil War rather than the great historian and statesman Edward Hyde, Earl of Clarendon (1609–74)? It was Clarendon, not Hume, who embodied the traditional ideal of the historian: an intelligent participant in the events he himself described. Hume's response was that most people who read the original sources "wou'd attain but a very confus'd idea of the transactions of that period." The problem was not merely the abundance of material, but the difficulty of making sense of it: "To allege therefore the number of historical monuments against composing a history seems not much better founded, than if one shoud give it as a reason for not building a house, that he lay near a quarry" (HL 1:285). Thus the accounts of contemporaries were no longer to be regarded as self-sufficient narratives, but to be treated as mere sources, a quarry for the modern historian. It was wrong to think that history, once written, need never be rewritten. At the heart of Hume's undertaking was, therefore, a novel, and largely unstated, conception of progress in historical knowledge.

Hume turned to the writing of history partly in deliberate pursuit of literary fame, though, despite what he says in his autobiography, this can scarcely have been his overriding motive, for his *Essays* had already won him renown. Just as important was his desire to explore, through the writing of a historical narrative, philosophical, political, and moral questions that lay at the heart of his previous enquiries.[13]

---

[12] David Berman, "David Hume on the 1641 Rebellion in Ireland," *Studies: An Irish Quarterly Review* 65 (1976): 101–12, 110; *David Hume: Philosophical Historian*, ed. D. F. Norton and R. H. Popkin (Indianapolis: Bobbs-Merrill, 1965), 109, 413–17.

[13] The point is well made in David Fate Norton, "History and Philosophy in Hume's Thought," in *David Hume, Philosophical Historian*, xxxii–l, which is particularly helpful on the links between Hume's skepticism and historical study.

II. HISTORICAL CRITICISM

What did Hume have to tell his readers that was new? Before we look at the substantive content of the *History*, we need to understand in what sense Hume was a "philosophical" historian.[14] One Hume scholar has rashly claimed that there was no philosophy of history in the eighteenth century.[15] In fact, there was a well-established literature on historical methodology, one that dealt with philosophical problems central to Hume's own interests. The founding text for this literature was *La logique, ou l'art de penser*, commonly known as *The Port-Royal Logic*, written by two Jansenist theologians, Antoine Arnauld and Pierre Nicole, and first published in 1662.[16] In that work Arnauld (for he seems to have been primarily responsible for the chapters of interest to us) had invented modern probability theory by arguing that a number of different activities – games of chance, the authentication of legal documents, belief in

[14] "Philosophical history" is sometimes identified with "conjectural history," a term invented by Dugald Stewart (1753–1828), and one that he took to be identical with Hume's term "natural history" as used in *The Natural History of Religion*. Since this work lies outside the scope of the present chapter, I have not discussed conjectural history here. See, for example, H. H. Hopfl, "From Savage to Scotsman: Conjectural History in the Scottish Enlightenment," *Journal of British Studies* 17 (1978): 19–40. I also do not discuss here the view that Hume's insistence in the *Treatise* on the uniformity of human nature meant that his outlook was fundamentally ahistorical: see, e.g., L. Pompa, *Human Nature and Historical Knowledge: Hume, Hegel, and Vico* (Cambridge: Cambridge University Press, 1990). Pompa is remarkable for failing to grasp that Hume's concept of historical knowledge is intended to be a response to sceptical arguments (28–9, 33), and for failing to consider Hume's actual practice as a historian.

[15] Donald W. Livingston, *Hume's Philosophy of Common Life* (Chicago: University of Chicago Press, 1984), 211. It may be admitted that there was little philosophy of history in English: characteristically indifferent to philosophical questions is [P. Whalley], *An Essay on the Manner of Writing History* (London, 1746). A good guide to the way in which historical writing was conceived when Hume was writing the *History* are lectures 17–20 of Adam Smith's *Lectures on Rhetoric and Belles Lettres* (1762–3), ed. J. C. Bryce (Oxford: Clarendon Press, 1983). Smith, who was a close friend of Hume's, was aware that modern history was different from ancient history because it was preoccupied with proving matters of fact, but disapproved of this because it interrupted the narrative (102). He also continued to think that the best historians were generally those who wrote about events of which they had personal experience (93–4).

[16] On the significance of this work for Hume's philosophy of history, see my "Hume's 'Of Miracles': Probability and Irreligion," in *Studies in the Philosophy of the Scottish Enlightenment*, ed. M. A. Stewart (Oxford: Clarendon Press, 1990), 191–229.

miracles – were philosophically related because they all involved judgments of probability. Courts had established rules to determine which documents could be admitted in a trial because they wanted to minimize the chance of fraud, misrepresentation, and error. Historians, when they reported that Augustine had witnessed a miracle, were agreeing to give credence to Augustine's testimony despite the inherent improbability of the events described: Augustine's good character and intelligence eliminated the possibility of fraud, misrepresentation, or error.

Arnauld thus sought to formulate the rules that should govern the criticism of sources by applying probability theory. Crucially, he separated judgment of the actual likelihood of an event in itself (he agreed miracles were improbable in themselves) from judgment of the quality of the testimony (good testimony could make an improbable event likely). From this analysis there derived a series of works that sought to formulate the rules that should be employed in assessing historical testimony, and that insisted that several independent witnesses should be given credence if they contradicted one isolated individual, and that direct participants and eyewitnesses were to be believed when they contradicted those who relied on second-hand information.[17] An immediate consequence of this was a downgrading of the reliability of oral tradition: a point made with particular force by Protestants such as John Locke, since it undermined the Catholic claim that theological truths are based in traditional knowledge.[18]

The new (largely French) literature on historical source criticism threw up a number of key problems, all of which Hume sought to address. First of all, how could we claim to have first-hand knowledge of the existence of Julius Caesar when the sources we relied on were in fact copies of copies? *De bello Gallico* was only in appearance a primary source: such a work was in fact a secondary authority, since the reader had to trust in the fidelity of generations of printers, and,

---

[17] C. Borghero, *La certezza e la storia* (Milan: Franco Angeli, 1983), gives an excellent account of late-seventeenth- and early-eighteenth-century philosophies of history.

[18] Daniel Woolf, "The 'Common Voice': History, Folklore and Oral Tradition in Early Modern England," *Past and Present* 120 (1988): 26–52; and my "Hume's 'Of Miracles,'" 198, 222–3.

before them, of scribes. For ancient history there were, on this view, virtually no primary sources at all. In the *Treatise* Hume insisted that this skeptical argument was specious: scribes and printers were generally to be trusted (T 1.3.13.6). The most important theorist in this field (and one who was almost certainly known to Hume) was Nicolas Fréret, whose *Réflexions sur l'étude des anciennes histoires et sur le degré de certitude de leurs preuves* (1729) was a response to the skeptical arguments of J. Lévesque de Pouilly's *A Dissertation upon the Uncertainty of the History of the first four ages of Rome.*[19] Fréret argued that we could trust historians like Livy when they reported events that we could no longer confirm by appealing to independent sources, for they had access to sources now lost to us.[20] There was nothing inherently impossible about knowledge of the past.

To make this claim, Fréret had to justify a critical reading of Livy. Livy freely reported natural prodigies and even miracles. Fréret argued that we could be skeptical of the first and incredulous with regard to the second but still trust Livy's accounts of military and political conflicts. In "Of Miracles," Hume set out to justify a systematic skepticism with regard to all reports of miraculous events through a novel application of probability theory. Originally intended for publication in the *Treatise,* this essay would have balanced his defense of the reliability of our sources for the knowledge of ancient history, paralleling Fréret's treatment of the subject. His argument (which was eventually published in the *Enquiry concerning Human Understanding*) proceeded by imagining a miracle for which there was apparently unimpeachable testimony. Yet one would have to balance this testimony against the inherent unlikelihood of an event contrary to the constant course of nature. Thus "external" and "internal" evidence would seem almost perfectly balanced. Take into account, though, the fact that those who advocated a belief in miracles were self-interested witnesses who were trying to win adherents to their own cause, and at once it becomes clear

---

[19] Ian Ross tells me that it was probably Adam Smith who arranged for de Pouilly's essay, which first appeared in French in 1729, to be published in English, in *The Philological Miscellany*, vol. 1 (1761).

[20] See my "Hume's 'Of Miracles,'" 200–3.

that their testimony must not be taken at face value. The "internal" evidence must always outweigh the "external," and one could only properly believe in a miracle if the testimony in favor of it were so strong that it would take a miracle for it to be false – that is, only if the alternative to belief in a miracle was belief in a greater miracle.

In his long and brilliant essay "Of the Populousness of Ancient Nations" (first published in 1752), Hume presented a tour de force in the criticism of sources. Regularly one found apparently reliable ancient sources reporting cities with enormous populations and battles involving armies of extraordinary size: it was easy to conclude that the ancient world was far more populous than the modern. Hume set out to show that these claims were inherently implausible: slaves had few opportunities to breed and raise children; massacres and destructive wars were common; the small physical space that cities occupied was irreconcilable with the claims made for their populations; and high interest rates were infallible evidence of primitive economies, economies consequently incapable of supporting dense populations. Thus by drawing together different types of evidence from an immense range of sources, Hume showed that ancient claims with regard to population sizes were completely unreliable; round numbers, like reports of miracles, represented a special category of evidence to be treated with extreme skepticism. Hume's detailed and technical argument was not of merely antiquarian importance: it provided decisive evidence for the claim that modern civilization was superior to ancient. Hume emerged victorious from a debate with Robert Wallace, one of the last major battles in the long-running war between those who saw history as a record of decline from ancient glory, and those who saw it in terms of (at least temporary) progress toward modern sophistication.[21]

In *The History of England*, source criticism also had a central role to play, for factual claims about the past were crucial to contemporary debates between Whigs and Tories, and between Protestants and Catholics. One of Hume's central purposes was to expose party

---

[21] See in this volume the essay "Hume on the Arts and 'The Standard of Taste,'" Part I, and, for the seventeenth-century origins of the controversy, R. F. Jones, *Ancients and Moderns*, 2nd ed. (Berkeley: University of California Press, 1965).

myths: parties, like religions, depended on historical claims that could be subjected to impartial criticism. Detailed historical enquiry into such claims could lead one to conclusions that no reasonable person would question and could in the process provide evidence that decisively undermined the rhetoric of political extremists. Hume identified three episodes that played a crucial role in contemporary historical mythologies, and it was no little part of his purpose in the *History* to show how historians could separate fact from myth with regard to episodes such as these:

There are indeed three events in our history, which may be regarded as touchstones of partymen. An English Whig, who asserts the reality of the popish plot, an Irish Catholic, who denies the massacre in 1641, and a Scotch Jacobite, who maintains the innocence of queen Mary, must [in the light of Hume's *History*] be considered as men beyond the reach of argument or reason, and must be left to their prejudices. (HE 39 n.M; 4:395)[22]

Hume's position on these questions inevitably involved him in controversy, even with those, such as Robertson, whose judgment he usually respected. In his view, one side was obviously right, the other wrong. This was not the case with an equally vexed question, that of the authorship of the *Eikon Basilike*. This work, supposedly by Charles I and published immediately after his execution, was undoubtedly the most successful piece of political propaganda in English history. It portrayed the king as pious, honest, and concerned with the welfare of his subjects. Its popular success played a major part in preparing the way for the Restoration. But did it really provide an insight into the king's secret thoughts, or was it, as many claimed, the hypocritical concoction of a royalist chaplain,

---

[22] Hume's choice of three events in particular is presumably governed by his desire to have one each from English, Irish, and Scottish history. The reality of the Popish Plot – a supposed plot to assassinate the king and impose Catholicism on England by force – was firmly asserted by Shaftesbury in 1678, and it was the campaign to hunt down the plotters that brought the Whig party into existence. Numerous Protestants were murdered in a Catholic Irish uprising in 1641: this provided the justification for Cromwell's savage campaign against the Irish. Queen Mary of Scotland, the mother of James I of England, was complicit in the murder of her husband, Darnley: this was held to justify her expulsion from the throne, a precedent for the expulsion of James II in 1688, the legitimacy of which was denied by Jacobites.

Dr. Gauden? Hume, who wanted to defend Charles's good character, had an interest in finding the book to be by Charles himself,
but he did not in any way understate the difficulty of reaching a
decision:

> The proofs brought to evince, that this work is or is not the king's, are
> so convincing, that, if an impartial reader peruse anyone side apart, he will
> think it impossible, that arguments could be produced, sufficient to counter-
> balance so strong an evidence: And when he compares both sides, he will be
> some time at a loss to fix any determination. Should an absolute suspense
> of judgment be found difficult or disagreeable in so interesting a question,
> I must confess, that I much incline to give the preference to the arguments
> of the royalists. The testimonies, which prove that performance to be the
> king's, are more numerous, certain, and direct, than those on the other side
> [though Hume added a footnote admitting this might be an overstatement].
> This is the case, even if we consider the external evidence: But when we
> weigh the internal, derived from the style and composition, there is no
> manner of comparison. These meditations . . . are so unlike the bombast,
> perplexed, rhetorical, and corrupt style of Dr. Gauden, to whom they are
> ascribed, that no human testimony seems sufficient to convince us, that he
> was the author. (HE 59.144, 5:547–8)

Here Hume had found a real case that appeared at first sight to
correspond to the hypothetical case he had discussed in "Of Miracles," one where two bodies of evidence are in perfect balance. As
in that case, Hume goes on to insist on the superiority of internal
over external evidence: in the one case, the inherent improbability
of an event contrary to the laws of nature; in the other, the inherent
improbability of Dr. Gauden's prose being transformed. Such evidence could be so strong that no testimony could serve to contradict
it: the case against Dr. Gauden's authorship was precisely as strong
as the case against miracles.

Hume had argued that unskilled individuals, even if they could
spare the time and energy to study the monuments of the past, would
not necessarily know what to make of them. Conflicting claims
regarding the casket letters, supposedly written by Mary Queen of
Scots (in Hume's view her authorship could be demonstrated), or the
authorship of *Eikon Basilike*, could only breed confusion unless one
had an adequate training in historical method and understood the
philosophical principles involved in the assessment of testimony.

III. HISTORICAL ARCHITECTURE

When we speak nowadays of the philosophy of history we sometimes mean to refer to the detailed philosophical analysis of the nature of historical evidence, and sometimes to large-scale theories that claim to identify a pattern or a meaning in the course of history. Hume was familiar with both sorts of philosophy of history. He would not have thought it unreasonable to regard his history as a test of the large-scale theories of James Harrington (1611–77), Charles-Louis de Secondat, baron de Montesquieu (1689–1755), and Anne-Robert-Jacques Turgot, baron de l'Aulne (1727–81), who would have been in his eyes the most important exponents of the second sort of philosophy of history.

Harrington was an important figure for the analysis of English politics for four reasons: first, he had in *Oceana* (1656) given an account of an ideal commonwealth, laying down principles according to which a free state ought to be established, and providing a standard by which the eighteenth-century English constitution could be measured. Second, Harrington believed that, by grounding his ideal state in the principle of self-interest, he had constructed a new science of politics, although he acknowledged that in this respect he was indebted to Machiavelli and to Thomas Hobbes. Third, he had provided an account of English history according to which the mid-seventeenth-century political crisis was the inevitable outcome of a long period of social change. Fourth, his followers after the Restoration had mounted a sustained attack on two contemporary developments that they believed had shifted the balance of power in favor of the monarchy: the development of a professional or "standing" army, and the growth of royal revenue and royal bureaucracy to the point that the king could significantly influence the political process by the offer of places and pensions, by bribery and corruption.

Hume engaged with all four aspects of the Harringtonian and neo-Harringtonian position.[23] In the "Idea of a Perfect Commonwealth," he largely approved of Harrington's ideal model of a republic, while offering some improvements. Second, in "That Politics may be reduced to a Science" and in "The Independency of

---

[23] James Moore, "Hume's Political Science and the Classical Republican Tradition," *Canadian Journal of Political Science* 10 (1977): 809–39.

Parliament," he accepted the Harringtonian position that political institutions created a framework within which people pursued their interests; and that it was therefore possible to predict how they would behave. Such predictions must be based on the assumption that people would act selfishly: although in fact not everyone was selfish, enough people were to undermine any institution that relied on men acting selflessly. The key to politics was thus the study of institutions, not men; good institutions would cause men to act as if they themselves were good. Third, in "Of the Protestant Succession," he by and large accepted the Harringtonian account of the social changes that had made an increase in the power of the Commons inevitable in the mid-seventeenth century. In "The Independency of Parliament," however, he sought to show that Harrington was wrong to conclude from this that the monarchy was bound to be abolished. Finally, in "Whether the British Government inclines more to Absolute Monarchy, or to a Republic," he accepted the neo-Harringtonian account of the rising power of the Crown.

Hume is never uncritical in his attitude to Harrington, but he is always a friendly, never a hostile, critic (see, for example, "Of the First Principles of Government"). Harrington had constructed the first determinist account of history: he had argued that the distribution of landed property determined the distribution of military strength, and that this in turn must predetermine the outcome of political conflict. All one had to do was to extend his definition of property to include commercial wealth to have a species of economic determinism. If one then argued that commercial activity had civilizing consequences, one would have a new economic explanation for the progress of liberty. Adam Smith believed one could find this argument in Hume's *History*. He wrote in *The Wealth of Nations:*

commerce and manufactures gradually introduced order and good government, and with them, the liberty and security of individuals, among the inhabitants of the country, who had before lived almost in a continual state of war with their neighbours, and of servile dependency upon their superiors. This, though it has been the least observed, is by far the most important of all their effects. Mr. Hume is the only writer who, so far as I know, has hitherto taken notice of it.[24]

---

[24] *An Inquiry into the Causes of the Wealth of Nations,* ed. R. H. Campbell, A. S. Skinner, and W. B. Todd (Oxford: Clarendon Press, 1976), 3.4.4 (1:412); C. N. Stockton, "Economics and the Mechanism of Historical Progress in Hume's *History,*" in

Hume would certainly have agreed with Smith that the subject had hitherto been ignored. In 1741 he had written:

Trade was never esteemed an affair of state till the last century; and there scarcely is any ancient writer on politics, who has made mention of it. Even the ITALIANS have kept a profound silence with regard to it, though it has now engaged the chief attention, as well of ministers of state, as of speculative reasoners. The great opulence, grandeur, and military atchievements of the two maritime powers [England and Holland] seem first to have instructed mankind in the importance of an extensive commerce. (E-CL 2, 88–9)

Thus, writing a century after Harrington, Hume was bound to give much more importance to commerce than Harrington had done. A major purpose of a history of England must be to trace the role of commercial expansion in the country's rise to opulence and grandeur. What was not to be expected was that Hume, instead of treating political liberty as a cause of commercial expansion, as he often had done in the *Essays* (see E-CL 10, 92–3; E-RA 6, 113; E-Co 17–19, 265–6), would reverse the order of causation and insist that commerce, in England at least, had caused the appearance and expansion of liberty. It was in the towns that political liberty had first existed; it was the development of the money economy that made serfdom an anachronism that the lords saw no need to preserve; and the rise of personal freedom "paved the way for the increase of political or civil liberty" (HE 23.42, 2:524). Hume did not offer a "four stages theory of history" that explained historical change in terms of the development of the means of production: this was to come later, in Smith and his associates.[25] But he certainly had provided a new type of economic explanation of history, which we may term a commercialized Harringtonianism.

Hume, like Harrington, saw in the rise of the gentry the profound cause of the shift in the balance of power that undermined the monarchy in the early seventeenth century. If the Harringtonian character of his analysis is not always obvious, it is because Hume saw in the rise of the gentry the explanation, not of the Civil War, but of the constitutional revolution that preceded the Civil War itself. Social change (combined with the fact that Parliament provided an

Hume: A Re-evaluation, ed. D. W. Livingston and J. T. King (New York: Fordham University Press, 1976), 296–320.

[25] See Andrew Skinner's essay in this volume, and R. L. Meek, "Smith, Turgot and the 'Four Stages' Theory," *History of Political Economy* 3–4 (1971–2): 9–27.

institutional context within which that change could find political expression) might explain the events of 1640–1; only religious enthusiasm could explain Parliament's inability to come to terms with the king. Harrington saw the execution of the king as the natural outcome of the political process he had traced; Hume saw the mixed constitution of the early eighteenth century as its natural outcome. For the aberration of the Cromwellian regime, other explanations were necessary. Harrington had failed to take account of the fact that "though men be much governed by interest; yet even interest itself, and all human affairs, are entirely governed by *opinion*" (E-BG 5, 51).

It is much harder to be sure about Montesquieu's influence on Hume than it is about Harrington's, for the simple reason that Hume's thinking seems to parallel Montesquieu's before as well as after the publication of *The Spirit of the Laws* (1748). On one key issue he certainly disagreed with Montesquieu: "Of National Characters" (1748) reads as a refutation of Montesquieu's account of the role of climate in shaping political and cultural life. It is not impossible that this is exactly what it is, for Hume may have known something of the arguments of *The Spirit of the Laws* prior to their publication.[26]

In other respects Hume's thinking is so close to Montesquieu's that reading Montesquieu can help in the interpretation of Hume's *History.*[27] Montesquieu and Hume both work with a threefold typology of regimes: despotisms, civilized monarchies, and constitutions based on liberty, such as the English. England is for both of them the most singular example of liberty the world has seen. Both use the word "liberty" in several distinct senses, but both are primarily concerned with one that commentators sometimes call "private" or "civil" liberty, and for which representative government served as merely a means.[28] Montesquieu defined "political liberty" as "that

---

[26] P. E. Chamley, "The Conflict between Montesquieu and Hume," in *Essays on Adam Smith,* ed. A. S. Skinner and T. Wilson (Oxford: Clarendon Press, 1975), 274–305.

[27] Montesquieu, Charles-Louis de Secondat, baron de, *The Spirit of the Laws,* trans. and ed. A. M. Cohler and others (Cambridge: Cambridge University Press, 1989), esp. 18, 22, 156–66, 197, 325–33, 388, 456, 608.

[28] David Miller, *Philosophy and Ideology in Hume's Political Thought* (Oxford: Clarendon Press, 1981), 148–9; Duncan Forbes, *Hume's Philosophical Politics* (Cambridge: Cambridge University Press, 1975), 125–92.

tranquillity of spirit which comes from the opinion that each one has of his security, and in order for him to have this liberty the government must be such that one citizen cannot fear another citizen."[29] Hume, in a posthumously published essay, stressed (surely following Montesquieu on the division of powers) the need for citizens to have no cause to fear, not only each other, but also their government:

The government, which, in common appellation, receives the appellation of free, is that which admits of a partition of power among several members, whose united authority is no less, or is commonly greater than that of any monarch; but who, in the usual course of administration, must act by general and equal laws, that are previously known to all the members and to all their subjects. In this sense, it must be owned, that liberty is the perfection of civil society. (E-OG 7, 40-1)

Thus both see the key to English liberty as lying in the establishment of a division of powers between legislative and executive, but both regard other constitutional developments as indispensable: the jury system, habeas corpus, an independent judiciary, and the freedom of the press are pillars of liberty. Both believe that the competing interests of legislative and executive must necessarily create conflicting parties in support of these different interests, and that these parties will inevitably rewrite history to justify their policies.[30] Finally, both believe that the essential pattern of the evolution of English history since the Norman Conquest has been one of feudal anarchy, which gave way to despotism, which itself gave way to the liberty of a mixed constitution. Both agree that there never has been a civilized monarchy in England, partly because such an institution depends on a strong nobility, while the English nobility was fatally weakened before the emergence of a strong monarchy.

Finally, Montesquieu's *The Spirit of the Laws* forcefully reminds us of a central problem that faced Hume as he wrote the *History*. The

[29] Montesquieu, *The Spirit of the Laws*, 157. Montesquieu writes, "I have had new ideas; new words have had to be found or new meanings given to old ones." Hume, "I wish, that People do not take a Disgust at Liberty; a word, that has been so much profand by these polluted Mouths [the supporters of Wilkes], that men of Sense are sick at the very mention of it. I hope a new term will be invented to express so valuable and good a thing" (NHL, 196).

[30] Hume thought (letter to Montesquieu) that Montesquieu somewhat underestimated the dangers of constitutional conflict (HL 1:138).

classical models for historical writing were all almost entirely narrative in form. Montesquieu, however, showed that one could analyze
a constitution and a culture at a moment in time, presenting it as an
ideal type. Indeed, one needed to do this if one was to grasp the logic
of events. Hume therefore committed himself to extended digressions explaining the character of the constitution at different times,
and surveying events (for example, developments in the arts and sciences) that did not fit comfortably within a narrative framework.
Nevertheless, these digressions seemed to him at odds with the narrative form proper to historical writing, and in later editions of the
History he moved parts of them into notes (HL 1:294).[31] Moreover,
although Hume clearly felt that constitutional institutions and practices were crucial to the explanation of political events, he resisted
following Montesquieu so far as trying to establish a close relationship between developments in a nation's culture and those in its
political life: Hume never claimed to identify a single spirit running
through all aspects of the life of an epoch.

Turgot, unlike Harrington and Montesquieu, had little influence
on Hume, but his views provide a helpful contrast to Hume's own. It
is not possible to determine when Hume first read Turgot's "On Universal History" (1751), which argues that all history is the history of
progress. In 1768, full of pessimism over the demands for "liberty"
made by Wilkes, Hume pointed to events in England as a refutation
of Turgot's views: "I know you are one of those, who entertain the
agreeable and laudable, if not too sanguine hope, that human Society is capable of perpetual Progress towards Perfection.... Pray, do
not the late Events in this Country appear a little contrary to your
System?" Hume was convinced that dangerous policies – above all
the growth of the national debt – could endanger civilization. He
was not even persuaded by Turgot's view that "since the Discovery
of Printing we need no longer Dread the usual Returns of Barbarism
and Ignorance" (HL 2:180). On the contrary, reading the first volume
of Edward Gibbon's *Decline and Fall of the Roman Empire* (1776)

---

[31] He was obviously happier with another type of digression: the discussion of an
individual's character. This was necessary, both to evoke the readers' sympathies
and passions, and to make it possible for them to make moral judgments. In Hume's
view it is character rather than individual actions that ought to be judged when
assessing the moral value of a person.

made him remark on the "marks of Decline" in England, where "the Prevalence of Superstition...prognosticates the Fall of Philosophy and Decay of Taste" (HL 2:310). He foresaw "a new and a sudden Inroad of Ignorance, Superstition and Barbarism" (NHL 199). Turgot's confidence that progress was guaranteed by providence must indeed have seemed to Hume to be itself a sophisticated superstition. He was much happier with Voltaire's *Candide, ou l'optimisme* (1759): "It is full of Sprightliness & Impiety, & is indeed a Satyre upon Providence, under Pretext of criticizing the Leibnitian System" (NHL 53). History itself, in Hume's view, provided no grounds for any faith in providence, even in the secularized form of a belief in the inevitability of progress.

IV. WHIGS AND TORIES

We come now to the central, and most difficult, question in the assessment of Hume as a historian: that of the politics of the *History*.[32] Scholars have adopted a number of views on this question, and Hume's own explicit descriptions of the political significance of the *History* in his letters are open to more than one interpretation. For some, the *History* presents a conservative view of politics: it reflects the growing conservatism of Hume's views after the Jacobite uprising of 1745 and was revised further in a conservative direction after Hume responded with hostility to the "Wilkes and Liberty" campaigns. It is thus essentially a "Tory" history.[33] According to another view, the whole point of the *History* is its impartiality: Hume presents the views of the different parties involved in English politics and admits that all have a certain justification.[34] However, on this view Hume held that past practice was almost the only basis for establishing whether a government was legitimate. Hume's declared support for the Revolution of 1688 in the *Treatise*, and the

---

[32] For Hume's own summary account of party politics in England, and his explanation of terms such as "Court" and "Country," "Whig" and "Tory," see E-PGB.

[33] Giuseppe Giarrizzo, *David Hume Politico e Storico* (Turin: Einaudi, 1962), and "Ancora su Hume storico," *Revista storica italiana* 83 (1971): 429–49.

[34] Duncan Forbes, "Politics and History in David Hume," *Historical Journal* 6 (1963): 280–95; *Hume's Philosophical Politics*; and his introduction to Hume's *History*, a reprint of the first edition of the early Stuart volume (Harmondsworth: Penguin, 1970).

History involved him, it is argued, in no little inconsistency. A third view is that Hume wrote to defend the existing constitution, and that he approved those men and measures that brought it about, even though they could only be seen to have been admirable with the advantage of hindsight and had no proper idea of what they were doing at the time.[35] Hume certainly describes in the *Treatise* the psychological process that causes one to make retrospective judgments in the light of the outcome of events (T 3.2.10.19), but a history written from such a point of view would fail in what was for Hume its essential purpose, that of distinguishing virtue from vice: to do this the historian would have to give up the advantage of hindsight. A fourth view holds that Hume thought that the contemporary absolutist monarchies of Europe were superior to the mixed monarchy of England, that he not only hoped to see absolutism established in England in his own day, but regretted the failure of the Stuarts to establish it in the seventeenth century.[36] Beyond Hume's insistence that civilized absolutist governments are legitimate where they are already established, this view seems to me to have little evidence to support it. I must admit to a certain sympathy with a fifth view, namely, that the *History* is informed throughout by Hume's love of liberty, although it would be quite wrong to equate liberty, as Hume understood the term, with democracy.[37]

There is no doubt that the first volume of the *History* was well received in France partly because it gave the Stuart monarchy a sympathetic treatment. During the reaction to the French Revolution, Hume's hostility to the execution of Charles I made him seem the first counter-revolutionary historian, a precursor of Burke.[38] Louis XVI's own response to the news of his death sentence was to set about

---

[35] Livingston, *Hume's Philosophy of Common Life*, 257–8.
[36] Nicholas Phillipson, *Hume* (New York: St. Martin's Press, 1989).
[37] J. V. Price, "Hume's Concept of Liberty and *The History of England*," *Studies in Romanticism* 5 (1966): 139–57. *Liberty in Hume's* History of England, ed. N. Capaldi and D. W. Livingston (Dordrecht: Kluwer, 1990), collects a number of essays that defend this view. David Miller, *Philosophy and Ideology*, provides a balanced assessment. An important contribution to this debate is John B. Stewart, *Opinion and Reform in Hume's Political Philosophy* (Princeton: Princeton University Press, 1992).
[38] Laurence L. Bongie, *David Hume: Prophet of the Counter-Revolution* (Oxford: Oxford University Press, 1965).

rereading Hume's account of Charles's execution.[39] Even before the French Revolution, the anti-Wilkes reaction had increased Hume's popularity in England. He wrote in 1768:

Licentiousness, or rather the frenzy of liberty, has taken possession of us, and is throwing everything into confusion. How happy do I esteem it, that in all my writings I have always kept at a proper distance from that tempting extreme, and have maintained a due regard to magistracy and established government, suitably to the character of an historian and a philosopher! I find on that account my authority growing daily; and indeed have now no reason to complain of the public. (HL 2:191–2)

Such readings, however, ignore important aspects of Hume's argument, aspects that survived his many revisions of his work, all of which, he said, favored the Tories. He described the 1770 revisions as follows:

I am running over again the last Edition of my History in order to correct it still farther. I either soften or expunge many villainous seditious Whig Strokes, which had crept into it. I wish that my Indignation at the present Madness, encourag'd by Lyes, Calumnies, Imposture, and every infamous Art usual among popular Leaders, may not throw me into the opposite Extreme. I am, however, sensible that the first Editions were too full of those foolish English Prejudices, which all Nations and all Ages disavow. (HL 2:216)

It would be wrong, however, to overestimate Hume's conservatism, even toward the end of his life. Not only was he, as he put it, "an American in my Principles" (HL 2:303), unconditionally supporting American independence from an early date, but he was also happy to say bluntly that the French monarchy would have to be overthrown so that the French people could escape the burden of the government debt (HL 2:242). Indeed, it gave Hume great pleasure to think people would have trouble categorizing him: "Whether am I Whig or Tory? Protestant or Papist? Scotch or English? I hope you do not all agree on this head; & that there [are] disputes among you about my principles" (HL 1:196). Clearly he would delight in the continuing disputes over how to categorize him.

---

[39] Livingston, *Hume's Philosophy of Common Life*, 317.

To make sense of Hume's *History*, we must take more seriously than commentators usually do the fact that his is a narrative history describing changing social and political circumstances. Hume's emphasis on change was, indeed, one of the most original aspects of his history. Tory historians before 1688, such as Robert Brady, the first volume of whose *Complete History of England* appeared in 1685, and Jacobite historians, such as Thomas Carte, author of *A General History of England* (1747–55), had insisted that the ancient constitution of England was that of divine-right monarchy: the revolutions of 1642 and 1688 were scarcely forgivable from this point of view, and the mid-eighteenth-century constitution an outrage. Whig historians before 1714 had argued the opposite case: the ancient constitution of England was one that guaranteed the liberties of the subject. On this view, which was supported by James Tyrrell in his *General History of England* (1696–1704) and later by Rapin, Parliament, including the House of Commons, was an institution of Saxon origin, and one with an unbroken history. The Stuarts had sought to undermine this ancient constitution; the Revolution of 1688 had restored it. In Hume's day, elements of this view were adopted by Tory opponents of the court, such as Henry Saint-John, viscount Bolingbroke.[40] This country opposition attacked the court for corruption, and attacked the Whig government, particularly Walpole in the period immediately before his fall, for extending executive power. The reply of the court Whigs to this assault was a novel one. Lord Hervey, for example, argued that there had been no ancient constitution.[41] The constitution of England had been constantly in flux. There had been no secure liberty before 1688. The present administration should be judged not by its fidelity to a mythical set of constitutional principles, but by its ability to preserve effective and beneficent government.

Placed in this context, there is no doubt that Hume, for all his claims to impartiality, effectively ended up supporting the argument

---

[40] Bolingbroke was the author of "A Dissertation upon Parties" (1733–4) and of *Letters on the Study and Use of History*, 2 vols. (London, 1752). For a selection of Bolingbroke's works, see *Historical Writings*, ed. I. Krammick (Chicago: University of Chicago Press, 1972).

[41] John, Baron Hervey, *Ancient and Modern Liberty Stated and Compared* (London, 1734). Hume did not share the court Whigs' favorable assessment of Walpole (E-CR 574–6).

of the court Whigs. The first volume he wrote was the volume on the early Stuarts. Although in writing that volume he came increasingly to suspect that traditional Whig history was deficient, and although he defended at length the character and motives of Charles I, he still tended to the Whig view that the Stuarts were innovating to the detriment of Parliament. Once he had worked on the Tudor period, he became convinced that Tudor rule had been despotic and revised his account of Stuart aspirations accordingly.[42] Hume's revisions of his *History* may have been hostile to Whig prejudices, but they brought him closer to the court Whig position.

In Hume's view, the barbarism of the Middle Ages and the despotism of the Tudors were not surprising: they were precisely what one would expect to find in a primitive society. A vast gulf separated us from the world of our ancestors. In place of traditional Tory and Whig arguments, which stressed constitutional continuity and paid little attention to social change, Hume stressed the distance at which we stood from both the social and the political life of our ancestors: he attacked, alongside the Whig myth of the ancient constitution, the myth of the Roast Beef of Old England. A poor diet and a despotic government were intimately related. In correspondence he explained his view bluntly:

My Notion is, that the uncultivated Nations are not only inferior to civiliz'd in Government, civil, military, and eclesiastical; but also in Morals; and that their whole manner of Life is disagreeable and uneligible to the last Degree. I hope it will give no Offence (and whether it do or not, I must say it) if I declare my Opinion, that the English, till near the beginning of the last Century, are very much to be regarded as an uncultivated Nation; and that even *When good Queen Elizabeth sat on the Throne*, there was very little good Roast Beef in it, and no Liberty at all. The Castle of the Earl of Northumberland, and no doubt that of the Earl of Warwick, the *King Maker* and others, was no better than a Dungeon: No Chimney to let out the Smoak; no Glass Windows to keep out the Air; a glimmering Candle here and there, which coud scarce keep their Ragamuffins of Servants and Retainers from breaking their Shins or running foul of each other: No Diet but salt Beef and Mutton

---

[42] The full extent of Rapin's deficiency was obviously not apparent in 1753: HL 1:170; contrast HL 1:258. For the comparison between the Tudors and the Stuarts, HL 1:264, 461. For later revisions: HL 1:379; HL 2:216, 260–1; NHL 69–71. For Hume's views in 1758, E-CP 493–501. For an analysis, see E. C. Mossner, "Was Hume a Tory Historian?" *Journal of the History of Ideas* 2 (1941): 225–36.

for nine Months of the Year, without Vegetables of any kind: Few Fires and these very poor ones.... When Queen Catherine of Arragon had a Fancy to eat a Sallad, she coud not find one in all England, she was obligd to send a Messenger to the Low Countries for that Purpose: And I suppose when her Tyrant of a Husband [Henry VIII] thought she was with Child, and that the Life of his royal Issue depended upon it, he woud indulge her in that Caprice. (NHL 198)

Hume himself came from what had long been, by his description, "the rudest, perhaps, of all European Nations; the most necessitous, the most turbulent, and the most unsettled" (HL 2:310). The extraordinary rapidity of social change in the Scotland of his day made him, along with the rest of the enlightened Scots, acutely sensitive to the social evolution that had taken place in the past; the continuing backwardness of the Highlands must have provided them with a vivid picture of medieval life in France or England.

Nevertheless, Hume was prepared to find even in the Middle Ages the stirrings of modern liberty. Although he insisted on placing the Magna Carta, the great charter of liberties of 1215, in a feudal and baronial context, he was also prepared to see in it statements of principle that would have met with the approval of a Locke or a Sidney:

It must be confessed, that the former articles of the Great Charter contain such mitigations and explanations of the feudal law as are reasonable and equitable; and that the latter involve all the chief outlines of a legal government, and provide for the equal distribution of justice, and free enjoyment of property; the great objects for which political society was at first founded by men, which the people have a perpetual and unalienable right to recal, and which no time, nor precedent, nor statute, nor positive institution, ought to deter them from keeping ever uppermost in their thoughts and attention. (HE 11.56, 1:445)

This is hardly the language of the thirteenth century, and it comes perilously close to approving views that Hume had attacked in his essay "Of the Original Contract."[43] When he describes the execution of Algernon Sidney (d. 1683), who had been convicted because he had defended, in a private manuscript, views such as these, Hume,

---

[43] On which, see in this volume the essay "The Structure of Hume's Political Theory."

far from attacking contractarianism, cautiously defends it: Sidney "had maintained principles, favourable indeed to liberty, but such as the best and most dutiful subjects in all ages have been known to embrace; the original contract, the source of power from a consent of the people, the lawfulness of resisting tyrants, the preference of liberty to the government of a single person" (HE 69.48, 6:436). Though he had indeed been involved in a conspiracy against Charles II, his conviction was contrary to law, his sentence iniquitous.

Such passages, taken in isolation, would appear to justify a court Whig reading of Hume: although liberty had not been long established, the principles of liberty had always been admirable. Hume himself insisted: "My views of *things* are more conformable to Whig principles; my representations of *persons* to Tory prejudices. Nothing can so much prove that men commonly regard more persons than things, as to find that I am commonly numbered among the Tories" (HL 1:237). Duncan Forbes, whose study of *Hume's Philosophical Politics* is the most influential account of Hume's historical thought, prefers to emphasize Hume's own claims to impartiality, and dismisses this particular remark as superficial: Hume had no commitment to Whig principles.[44] But Hume's claims to impartiality are also misleading unless one notes that Hume claims to support Whigs and Tories *alternately:* in other words, he is always partial, even if he is not always on the same side (HL 1:179, 369). The key to the volume on the early Stuarts lies, in fact, in the following description: "I am not surely unfavorable to the Parliament. Till they push'd their Advantages so far as to excite a civil War, so dangerous & unnecessary, I esteem their Conduct laudable; & to this Extremity nothing carry'd them but their furious Zeal for Presbytery: A low Bigotry, with which they sully'd a noble Cause" (HL 1:222). Indeed, Hume's *History* is Parliamentary, not Royalist, in its account of the period from 1604 to 1641, and Parliamentary again in its account of the period from 1681 to 1688.

There is nothing arbitrary about this changing of sides: in Hume's view, it was a characteristic of English history that the "disinterested" (that is to say, the impartial) "fluctuated between the factions; and gave the superiority sometimes to the court, sometimes to the opposition" (HE 66.43, 6:307–8). The history was written from

---

[44] Forbes, *Hume's Philosophical Politics,* 292.

the point of view of such disinterested individuals, whose concern was with the public good. Such people, Hume believed, supported Parliament until the end of 1641, until the Grand Remonstrance made war inevitable. They ought to have admired John Pym and John Hampden, Parliament's leading spokesmen, and approved the Petition of Right of 1628 and the constitutional revolution of 1640 and 1641, which had established the principles of the mixed constitution. They should have continued to support Parliament despite the execution in 1641 of Thomas Wentworth, Earl of Strafford, the king's chief minister, an event that foreshadowed the trial of Charles himself. But thereafter it was Parliament, not the king, that endangered stability (despite, for example, the king's attempt to arrest the leaders of the Commons, including Pym and Hampden, in 1642). The king had accepted that his was a limited monarchy, and there was nothing in his character to suggest that he could not be trusted. Only their "low Bigotry" drove men on to resistance, while those who were not bigots rallied to the royalist side.

The true heroes of Hume's account were thus the men who had known when to change sides, Clarendon and Lucius Carey, viscount Falkland, who had joined the king in 1642.[45] He willingly echoes Clarendon's praise of Falkland, attributing to him the authorship of the king's reply to the Parliament, *His Majesties Answer to the Nineteen Propositions* (June 1642), in which for the first time the principles of the modern English constitution were described and defended. Falkland, who died in battle in 1643, was the epitome of Hume's conception of virtue:

devoted to the pursuits of learning, and to the society of all the polite and elegant, [he] had enjoyed himself in every pleasure, which a fine genius, a generous disposition, and an opulent fortune could afford. Called into public life, he stood foremost in all attacks on the high prerogatives of the crown; and displayed that masculine eloquence, and undaunted love of liberty, which, from his intimate acquaintance with the sublime spirits of antiquity, he had greedily imbibed. When civil convulsions proceeded to extremities, and it became requisite for him to chuse his side; he tempered

---

[45] It is worth noting, however, that Hume regarded Bulstrode Whitelocke as a more impartial historian than Clarendon (HE 64, 6:215). Since Whitelocke supported Parliament while Clarendon supported the King, this judgment scarcely accords with a view of Hume as a Tory.

the ardour of his zeal, and embraced the defence of those limited powers, which remained to monarchy, and which he deemed necessary for the support of the English constitution. Still anxious, however, for his country, he seems to have dreaded the too prosperous success of his own party as much as of the enemy; and, among his intimate friends, often after a deep silence, and frequent sighs, he would, with a sad accent, re-iterate the word, *Peace*. (HE 56.59, 5:416–17)

Once we see Hume changing sides, we can recognize that, whether he writes in favor of king or Parliament, he always gives his support to the mixed constitution. For those who favored such a constitution the key question at the end of 1641 was, he believed, "Can the king be trusted?" Hence the importance of Hume's account of Charles's character, and the strategic significance of his claim that the arguments of the royalists in 1642 were strongest when discussing not principle, but the past behavior of the king. Similarly, between the Exclusion Crisis and 1688, the key question is the behavior of James II. Hume refuses to take sides between the Whigs who trumped up the charges against Tories during the Popish Plot (1678), and the Tories who led the witch hunt against Whigs after the Rye House plot (1683).[46] But from 1682 James's behavior toward Scotland was unambiguous. He sought to execute men guilty only of having conversed with others who were suspected of having been rebels. Two women were tied to stakes and slowly drowned by a rising tide because they refused to take an oath of loyalty. James himself was believed to have participated in the torturing of suspects. If Clarendon represents the reasonable men and women who converted to Royalism before the outbreak of the Civil War, Archibald Campbell, ninth earl of Argyll, represents the loyal subjects who were forced to turn against James. Tried for his life because of his loyalty to Protestantism and the constitution, he was driven into exile late in 1682: from this moment, conspiracy against James was justified.

There was, of course, an important difference between 1642 and 1682: after the Restoration, Charles II and James II had no excuse for failing to recognize that England was now a limited monarchy.

---

[46] The Rye House Plot was a plot by leading Whigs, including Algernon Sidney, to assassinate Charles II and his brother James.

As Hume had argued in the *Treatise,* in any limited monarchy there must be a right of rebellion in defense of the constitution, for otherwise there will be no effective limits on royal power. If Hume had good reason to defend rebellion in 1688, even on his own conservative principles, one is bound to ask, On what grounds could he justify Parliamentary innovation in 1641? Perhaps, in the words of the *Treatise,* "nothing is more essential to public interest, than the preservation of public liberty" (T 3.2.10.16), but what right can the public claim to construct public liberty where there has been none before? Even if they know that liberty will benefit society, how can they be confident that the attempt to establish it will not fatally undermine authority, and that innovation will not cause more harm than good?

In attempting to answer this question, the first thing to note is that England under the Tudors did not have what Hume termed a "civilized monarchy" (E-RP 28, 125). It suffered under a species of despotism. Thus, under Henry VIII the English "were so thoroughly subdued that, like eastern slaves, they were inclined to admire those acts of violence and tyranny, which were exercised over themselves, and at their own expence." Under Elizabeth, the government of England bore "some resemblance to that of Turkey at present: The sovereign possessed every power, except that of imposing taxes" (HE 33.47, App. 3.10; 3:323, 4:360). This limitation, as in Turkey, could only have pernicious consequences while the monarch sought to exercise absolute power (E-Ta 11, 347–8). In England it meant that the Crown had recourse to forced loans, or rather arbitrary confiscations, and to the sale of monopolies and privileges. Over time, the first practice would have destroyed all security of property, while the second would have destroyed all trade, reducing English society to the poverty of Turkish. An absolute government in which the monarch could levy taxes would have been preferable, for then the monarchy would have had an interest in the wealth of its subjects. Tudor despotism was thus dangerous to civil liberty and economic prosperity: it was in the public interest that such despotism should give way, either to civilized absolutism or to a mixed constitution.

In his Appendix to the reign of Elizabeth, Hume says that one should generally limit one's questions about constitutions to questions about the facts: to finding what has in practice been established.

If any other rule than established practice be followed, factions and dissentions must multiply without end: And though many constitutions, and none more than the British, have been improved even by violent innovations, the praise, bestowed on those patriots, to whom the nation has been indebted for its privileges, ought to be given with some reserve, and surely without the least rancour against those who adhered to the ancient [that is, established] constitution. (HE App 3.1, 4:355; see also 23.24–5, 2:513–15)

When Hume first wrote the *History*, he thought that in the early seventeenth century both Royalists and Parliamentarians had sought to undermine the existing constitution. In time he came more and more to believe that many of the rights claimed by the Stuarts were established in previous practice; nevertheless, they could not be cleared of the charge of trying to innovate by making the king master of taxation. Since Parliament refused to finance the government adequately, such innovation might be justifiable, but, alas, the result would have been not a civilized absolutism, but an almost unparalleled concentration of power.

Hume thought that most supposedly absolute governments were in fact limited. As he put it in "Of the Origin of Government," "The sultan is master of the life and fortune of any individual; but will not be permitted to impose new taxes on his subjects: a French monarch can impose taxes at pleasure; but would find it dangerous to attempt the lives and fortunes of individuals" (E-OG 7, 40). Charles I, however, was able both to tax and to imprison at will. In many countries, Hume says, religion acts as a restraint on power, and indeed in his account of the "eleven years'" tyranny (1629–40), Hume says that the Church of England was the only effective restraint on royal authority (HE 53.1, 5:250). The comment was deliberately ironical, for this was the church of Laud, a church that preached unrestricted divine-right monarchy.

In France, as Montesquieu had stressed, the power of the nobility provided a practical restraint on the king's will; in England, by contrast, the nobility had declined in the fifteenth century, creating a power vacuum that the monarchy had sought to fill. In France, the Parlements provided a guarantee of due process in law; in England, the Star Chamber could circumvent the normal processes of law, even common law judges served at the royal pleasure, and juries were easy to intimidate (HE App. 3.3–8, 4:356–60). In France, the church was in large measure independent of the Crown; in England, it was entirely under royal control. Such comparisons, implicit rather than explicit in Hume's *History*, could alone justify the innovations to which the Long Parliament resorted in its first sessions. Hume was thus able to conclude his account of the Tudors:

On the whole, the English have no reason, from the example of their ancestors, to be in love with the picture of absolute monarchy; or to prefer the unlimited authority of the prince and his unbounded prerogatives, to that noble liberty, that sweet equality, and that happy security, by which they are at present distinguished above all nations in the universe. (HE App. 3.32, 4:370)

The key to English liberty, equality, and security did not lie, however, as we might think, in representative government. Representative government was not on its own a guarantee of freedom, for elections provided scope for the Crown to bring its influence to bear, and the small number of members of Parliament made it possible for it to make full use of its powers of patronage. Hume would, in principle, have preferred more decisions to be taken, either by the electorate as a whole, or by much larger representative bodies. Liberty derived, in fact, from the constant effort to restrict royal authority within the mixed constitution. It was this that had given birth to institutions that were, in Hume's eyes, unprecedented advances toward civil liberty. First among these was habeas corpus, unique to England, of which he wrote: "as it has not place in any other form of government, this consideration alone may induce us to prefer our present constitution to all others" (HE 67.59, 6:367). Second was the liberty of the press, also unique to England, of which he was prepared to claim (until the disadvantages of too much liberty became apparent to him during the Wilkes and Liberty crisis): "this liberty is attended with so few inconveniencies, that it may be claimed as the common right of mankind, and ought to be indulged them almost in every government" (E-LP 6.13n, 604 [published 1741–68]).[47]

Hume's support for Parliament under the early Stuarts thus rests, not on any principled commitment to representative government, but on the conviction that only the gentry, represented in Parliament and given a political voice by it, were in a position to control what showed every sign of becoming a tyrannical power.

[47] The only exception Hume recognized was ecclesiastical government, which he took to be incompatible with freedom of discussion.

Fortunately the spread of learning had ensured that many of the gentry entertained noble ambitions: "A familiar acquaintance with the precious remains of antiquity excited in every generous breast a passion for a limited constitution, and begat an emulation of those manly virtues, which the Greek and Roman authors, by such animating examples, as well as pathetic expressions, recommend to us" (HE 45.35, 5:18–19). The House of Commons was the only potential restraint on royal power, and Hampden and his associates were right to rally to its defense. The success of the Parliamentary cause, however, owed more to bigotry than to good judgment and noble sentiment: "And though it was justly apprehended, that such precedents [as the imprisonment of Hampden], if patiently submitted to, would end in a total disuse of parliaments, and in the establishment of arbitrary authority; Charles dreaded no opposition from the people, who are not commonly much affected with consequences, and require some striking motive, to engage them in a resistance of established government." It was an irony that without religious bigotry (which was to provide the "striking motive"), liberty might never have been established in England in 1640, and that, without the invasion of William of Orange in 1688, it might never have been secured. Recognition of such ironies was, Hume believed, one of the pleasures of historical study (HE 53.1, 5:249–50; 23.31, 2:518–19).

Hume thus writes in favor of the mixed constitution to which both moderate Parliamentarians and Royalists aspired in 1641, and that was finally established in 1688. Toward the end of the *History,* he tells us that the English have established "the most entire system of liberty, that ever was known amongst mankind" (HE 71.70, 6:531), and, in one of the volumes written last, he claims that the main utility of history lies in instructing us to cherish the present constitution (HE 23.45, 2:525). Earlier he had written of "*that singular* and happy *Government which we enjoy at present.*" In 1772, in a fit of "Spleen and Indignation," he struck out the words "and happy," but his considered opinion was that they should be restored, for "the English Government is certainly happy, though probably not calculated for Duration, by reason of its excessive Liberty" (HE 49.34, 5:114; HL 2:260–1). Thus, the English had established more liberty than had ever existed at any other time or in any other place; too much liberty, perhaps, for the stability of their political system, but not too much for the philosopher or the historian as he sought to go about his business. Hume, in impartially weighing the merits of Whig and Tory principles, was taking full advantage of that liberty of the press that was unique to England. The conclusion to the History might well have been the same as the epigraph to the *Treatise*, a famous sentence from Tacitus: "Rara temporum felicitas, ubi sentire, quæ velis; & quæ sentias, dicere licet" (The rare good fortune of a time when you may think what you like and say what you think; *Histories* 1.1). Hume may have been increasingly unsure how much liberty was compatible with stability; he never doubted that it was "the perfection of civil society."

SUGGESTIONS FOR FURTHER READING

In addition to the works cited in the notes to this essay, the editors recommend the following.[48]

Hume, David. *David Hume: A History of England*. A variorum edition, edited by F. van Holthoon. Charlottesville, VA: InteLex Corporation, 2000. A digital text of Hume's *History of England*.

Articles

Cohen, Alix. "In Defence of Hume's Historical Method." *British Journal for the History of Philosophy* 13 (2005): 489–502.

Evnine, Simon. "Hume, Conjectural History, and the Uniformity of Human Nature." *Journal of the History of Philosophy* 31 (1993): 589–606.

Perinetti, Dario. "Philosophical Reflection on History." In *The Cambridge History of Eighteenth-Century Philosophy*, edited by K. Haakonssen. 2 vols. New York: Cambridge University Press, 2006. 2:1107–40.

Phillips, Mark Salber, and Dale R. Smith. "Canonization and Critique: Hume's Reputation as a Historian." In *The Reception of David Hume in Europe*, edited by P. Jones. London: Thoemmes Continuum, 2005. 299–313.

Slater, Graeme. "Hume's Revisions of the *History of England*." *Studies in Bibliography* 45 (1992): 130–57.

Spencer, Mark G. "Hume and Madison on Faction." *William and Mary Quarterly* 59 (2002): 869–96.

Stewart, M. A. "Hume's Historical View of Miracles." In *Hume and Hume's Connexions*, edited by M. A. Stewart. Edinburgh: Edinburgh University Press, 1994. 171–200.

---

[48] For their assistance in compiling this list, the Editors gratefully acknowledge Dario Perinetti and Mark Spencer.

Van Holthoon, F. L. "Hume and the 1763 Edition of His *History of England*: His Frame of Mind as a Revisionist." *Hume Studies* 23 (1997): 133–52.

Wood, Paul. "The Natural History of Man in the Scottish Enlightenment." *History of Science* 28 (1990): 89–123.

Books

Fieser, James, ed. *Early Responses to Hume's* History of England. In *Early Responses to Hume*, 2nd ed. 10 vols. Bristol: Thoemmes Continuum, 2005. Vols. 7–8.

Foster, Stephen Paul. *Melancholy Duty: The Hume-Gibbon Attack on Christianity*. Dordrecht: Kluwer Academic, 1997.

Herdt, Jennifer A. *Religion and Faction in Hume's Moral Philosophy*. Cambridge: Cambridge University Press, 1997.

Phillips, Mark Salber. *Society and Sentiment: Genres of Historical Writing in Britain 1740–1820*. Princeton, NJ: Princeton University Press, 2000.

Spencer, Mark G., ed. *Hume's Reception in Early America*. 2 vols. Bristol: Thoemmes, 2002. 2:1–182.

15 Hume on Religion

Hume's critique of religion and religious belief is, as a whole, subtle, profound, and damaging to religion in ways that have no philosophical antecedents and few successors. Some of the damage and a little of the subtlety will, I trust, become evident in Part II of this essay, where Hume's seminal discussions of the design argument for the existence of God, miracles, morality, and natural belief are examined. Before this, however, certain preliminaries need attention. First, there is the difficulty caused by the old-fashioned or unfamiliar terminology used by Hume and his commentators in describing and assessing what he has to say. Second, although the scale of Hume's writing on religion is reasonably obvious (it exceeds his output concerning any other subject except history), the fact that it is dispersed over a number of publications and partly embedded (sometimes none too clearly) in several more, as well as having to be drawn from essays, letters, and minor writings, needs to be understood before any informed discussion is possible. Third, there is the problem of seeing what he wrote not as ad hoc criticisms turned out piecemeal, but as a comprehensive critical strategy. Finally, a problem of interpretation results from Hume's "abundant prudence" in covering his real opinions with ambiguous irony and even, on occasions, with denials of his own apparent conclusions.

I shall attempt some clarification of these four preliminary issues in Part I of this essay, beginning with the terminology, a matter that infects and informs all else that can be said.

I. TEXT AND CONTEXT

Terminology

A basic classification of religious information according to its source
in reason or in historically particular disclosures has long been established in the contrast between *natural theology* or *natural religion,*
on the one hand, and *revelation* or *revealed religion,* on the other.
Natural religion (the phrase usually does duty in the eighteenth century for the now more common term *natural theology*) is the system
of conclusions about God's (or the gods') existence and nature supposedly attainable from evidence and by reasoning accessible to any
intelligent person irrespective of any special information conveyed
in the Bible, Koran, or other revelatory source. For example, the conclusion that a designing agent, not chance, is needed to explain the
order of the cosmos is part of natural not revealed religion. *Revelation* or *revealed religion,* on the other hand, is the body of alleged
truths about the divine that can be obtained only from particular historical and supposedly inspired sources such as the Bible or Koran.
For example, the claims that an individual human person can expect
resurrection after death, or that God once sent his son into the world,
are parts of a revelation. A distinction is sometimes made between
particular revelation and *general revelation. Particular revelation*
is revelation as just described. *General revelation* is the supposed
general experience of the presence of God in the religious life of each
believer.

Within natural religion, two types of argument in various versions are, and always have been, conspicuous. These are called by
Hume (and some others who use the pre-Kantian terminology) *the
argument a posteriori* and *the argument a priori. The argument a
posteriori* is the phrase by means of which Hume usually refers to
versions of what we would normally call the design argument, that
is, the argument that God exists because his creative intelligence can
be observed in the order or purposiveness to be found in the natural
world (DNR 2.5, 9.1; 143, 188, for example). *The argument a priori* in
Hume's usage refers to his paraphrase of the particular cosmological
argument to be found in Samuel Clarke's Boyle Lectures for 1704,
later published as *A Discourse concerning the Being and Attributes
of God.* The argument in Hume's words begins "Whatever exists

must have a cause or reason of its existence," and concludes with the claim "We must, therefore, have recourse to a necessarily existent Being, who carries the REASON of his existence in himself; and who cannot be supposed not to exist without an express contradiction" (DNR 9.3, 188–9).

Both the positive rejection of revelation as a source of religious knowledge and one of the possible conclusions attainable from the arguments and evidence of natural religion can be referred to as *deism*. The term *deism* was widely used in the eighteenth century, but with vague meaning, to indicate a view of religion that held that our reliable knowledge of God is based on reason alone (that is to say, on natural religion and not on revelation). The term is not much used by Hume except to reject its application to himself.[1] It is also a term used to indicate belief (arrived at from reasoning alone) in a god who set the universe in motion or caused the universe to exist and then left it alone. Another way of expressing this limited view is to say that deism is the claim to rationally substantiated belief in a god lacking *providence. Providence*, while sometimes used as a synonym for God, is more particularly used to refer to that aspect of God's (or the gods') nature that consists in exerting control, guidance, or forethought in the moral affairs of human beings or the physical processes of the world. Hume uses *providence* in just this sense in Section 11 of the *Enquiry concerning Human Understanding*, where he argues that there is no evidence for God's providence.

When the God (either on the evidence of revelation, or natural religion, or in some other way) is held to be a single and eternal God who created all things (possibly ex nihilo) and continues to sustain and work within his creation (that is, to exercise providence), the belief is usually called *theism*. Thus the common root of the Judaic, Christian, and Islamic religions is theism.

Two corruptions of religion were of great concern to Hume and other eighteenth-century writers. These corruptions were *superstition*, usually associated with idolatry and with the Church of Rome, and *enthusiasm*, usually associated with the newly converted and with extreme Protestant sects. *Superstition* is the state in which "unknown evils are dreaded from unknown agents." Its source is

---

[1] See my "Hume's Attenuated Deism," *Archiv für Geschichte der Philosophie* 65 (1983): 160–73.

"weakness, fear, melancholy, together with ignorance," and it manifests itself in "ceremonies, observances, mortifications, sacrifices, presents" directed toward the unknown agent. *Enthusiasm* is religion corrupted by emotional fanaticism or religious mania: "raptures, transports, and surprising flights of fancy" that are "attributed to the immediate inspiration of that Divine Being, who is the object of devotion" (E-SE 2–3, 73–4).[2]

An attitude to religion often associated in the late seventeenth and eighteenth centuries with enthusiasm, but also having a pedigree that includes Tertullian, Pascal, and possibly St. Paul, was sometimes referred to by Hume's near contemporaries as "implicit belief" or "blind belief" or "the submission of reason to faith." In the nineteenth century this attitude was developed into the position known since about 1870 as *fideism.* This is the view, argued by some Christian apologists to be reinforced by Hume's skepticism, that religious belief is justified by faith alone, quite apart from reasons or evidence, because *all* knowledge rests on premises accepted by faith.

Finally there are two confusing terms that both contain the word *natural,* but that are used in different senses: the eighteenth-century term *natural history* and the twentieth-century term *natural belief. Natural history* (as in Hume's *Natural History of Religion*) indicates an account of something as a natural phenomenon. In the title of Hume's work, the account is of the causes and conditions that "naturally" produce religion (as, for example, the presence of air and water "naturally" produces rust on iron) without reference to any reasons that can be produced in favor of or against the religion in question. *Natural belief* on the other hand is not a phrase to be found in Hume's own writings. It is a phrase introduced by Norman Kemp Smith,[3] and much used since, to indicate basic or indispensable beliefs.

---

[2] For more on Hume's distinction between superstition and enthusiasm and true religion, see his unpublished Preface to what has become Vol. 6 of his *History of England,* quoted in full in Ernest Campbell Mossner, *Life of David Hume* (Edinburgh: Thomas Nelson, 1954), 306–7. For a discussion of the political dimensions of the distinction, see in this volume the essay "The Structure of Hume's Political Theory."

[3] Norman Kemp Smith, *The Philosophy of David Hume* (London: Macmillan, 1941), particularly 104–37, 442–63. See also note 25 below.

484   J. C. A. GASKIN

The Works

Hume's two main works directly on religion are the *Natural History of Religion* (1757) and the *Dialogues concerning Natural Religion* (1779, but first written in the 1750s). The former deals with religion's natural origins in human nature and society – its causes. The latter examines the supposed rational grounds for belief in God or gods – its reasons. Parts of the latter examination had already been given a preliminary run in Section 11 of the *Enquiry concerning Human Understanding* (1748) in which there also appeared the chapter "Of Miracles," Hume's celebrated onslaught on the credentials of the Christian revelation. But the *Enquiry* as a whole also develops an epistemological attack on metaphysics and "philosophical religion" whose final outcome is not unlike the conclusions of twentieth-century logical positivism (EHU 12.24–34). Less obviously, the second *Enquiry*, the *Enquiry concerning the Principles of Morals* (1751), is also concerned with religion. In it Hume gives an account of a morality in which what is added by religion to the secular core all too often amounts to spurious virtues and imaginary crimes that result in cruel, bigoted, and anti-utilitarian interferences in human affairs. Some of these interferences are chronicled in his *History of England* (published between 1754 and 1762).

Among Hume's fifty or so individual essays, there are numerous reflections on religion. These range from the lengthy footnote on the hypocrisy of the clergy, which is attached to "Of National Characters," to the damaging account of the two concepts developed in "Of Superstition and Enthusiasm." This account would seem to leave little of true religion once the two corruptions of religion have been understood. But by far the most important essays are the two that ought to have appeared in 1757 along with the *Natural History of Religion*. These are "Of Suicide" (which argues that suicide is neither immoral nor irreligious) and "Of the Immortality of the Soul" (which argues that there is good evidence for man's mortality). Both essays were withdrawn by Hume before publication after threats against him or his publisher. An authorized and somewhat inaccurate printing appeared in 1777, the year after Hume's death. Hume's authorized text is preserved in the National Library of Scotland.

Finally, letters and short documents apart, there is the *Treatise of Human Nature* (1739–40). The *Treatise*, Hume's first work, is, to our eyes, not overtly concerned with religion. Part of the reason for this is that Hume excised some of its "nobler parts" before publication, including some version of "Of Miracles" (which could have been located in Book 1, Part 3, between sections 13 and 14),[4] and possibly some version of "Of the Immortality of the Soul" (which could have formed the concluding pages to the section of Book 1 entitled *Of the immateriality of the soul*). But a more important reason that the *Treatise* as published does not seem to us much concerned with religion is that our sensitivities regarding what would constitute an attack on religion are much weaker than those of Hume's contemporaries. The nature of their sensitivities is illuminated by the pamphlet *A Letter from a Gentleman*. The text is drawn from a letter by Hume and was rushed into print on his behalf in 1745 when he was a candidate for the Chair of Moral Philosophy at Edinburgh University. In this brief work Hume is defended against six "charges," four of which are that the *Treatise* subverts religion (L 7–8, 15–18, 21–35). To us the most obvious charge is that some of his arguments about causation (particularly the section in Book 1 entitled *Why a cause is always necessary*) constitute a significant criticism of the a priori argument for God's existence.

The Structure of Hume's Critique

Suppose we put the fundamental question thus: Why does anyone believe in God or gods, or cleave to the teachings of such theistic religions as Christianity or Islam? The answer may be given (nonexclusively) in terms of either reasons or causes, and it is under this division that Hume's examination of religion begins to look like a comprehensive critique rather than a collection of challenging but discrete sections.

In traditional (and particularly eighteenth-century) religious apologetic, the reasons for belief in God usually took the form of appeals to arguments and revelation. The appeal to revelation was neither to the general revelation associated with dedicated religious practice nor to individual claims to have direct information about

---

[4] The suggestion is endorsed in David Wootton's article "Hume's 'Of Miracles'," in *Studies in the Philosophy of the Scottish Enlightenment*, ed. M. A. Stewart (Oxford, 1990), 199. Wootton is mainly concerned with the background influences on Hume.

the Divine, but specifically to the particular revelation of Christianity as set out in the New Testament. This, it was supposed, carried with it certain guarantees of its own authenticity. These guarantees were that the revelation fulfilled prophecy and was attended with miracles. Miracles could be brought about only by God (and not any god, but only by the one true God). Therefore a rational man had *grounds* for accepting the Christian revelation as genuine. It is, of course, precisely these grounds that Hume set out to undermine in Section 10 of the first *Enquiry*, where incidentally, he treats fulfilled prophecy as a species of miracle (EHU 10.41).

The appeal to arguments to support belief in God was most commonly an appeal to those types of argument that Hume calls the argument a priori (cosmological arguments) and the argument a posteriori (design arguments). These were the traditional core of natural religion. The former is dismantled by Hume in the *Treatise,* the first *Enquiry,* and again in Part 9 of the *Dialogues.* The latter is subjected to a uniquely thorough and hostile examination in Section 11 of the first *Enquiry* and again throughout the *Dialogues.*

But if, as Hume contends, the arguments of natural religion do not establish the existence of any deity that could be an object of religious belief, and if revelation is not authenticated in any way that could convince a rational man, then it might seem that the only answer that can be given to the question "Why does anyone believe in God or gods?" is that the belief has natural *causes.* An investigation of these is Hume's subject in the *Natural History of Religion.* At the heart of his analysis is the contention that the origin of belief in gods is to be found in fear of the unknown causes of the sometimes malevolent, sometimes benevolent, and frequently capricious events that govern human life (NHR 2.4–5, 3.1–6, 8.1–2, 13.1–6, 14.7–8).

That, I think, is the main structure of Hume's critique of religion, but its details extend vastly further: to a "mitigated scepticism" (carefully developed in the first *Enquiry*) that would put religious metaphysics beyond our understanding; to a sharpened theological dilemma (EHU 8) between God's omniscience and man's moral answerability; to a separation of morality and religion (implied in the *Treatise* and emphasized by the second *Enquiry*) with comments on particular issues such as suicide; to a philosophical account of personal identity and of the soul (T 1.4.5–6), which invites the rejection of immortality contained in "Of the Immortality of the Soul"; to an exposé in the *History of England* of the misery produced by religious fanaticism and superstition; and on to letters that contain all manner of detailed comments and criticisms (note, for example, his remarks on the psychology of worship and the inappropriateness of prayer in NHL 13).

Hume's Stance and the Problem of Interpretation

The problem with the interpretation of Hume is that, although his arguments and the facts he adduces are regularly highly critical of religion and damaging to any belief in the divine, his affirmations (and sometimes the conclusions that he seems to draw) do not always look like the real outcome of his criticisms. Thus, for example, the *Natural History of Religion* reads like a reduction of religion to its causes in human nature, but in his brief "Introduction" to the work Hume remarks: "The whole frame of nature bespeaks an intelligent author; and no rational enquirer can, after serious reflection, suspend his belief a moment with regard to the primary principles of genuine Theism and Religion" (NHR Intro. 1).

Similar affirmations appear at least five times in the main text. Seventeen years earlier, in a footnote to the Appendix to the *Treatise*, Hume had unequivocally countermanded whatever damage to belief in God the *Treatise* might have been supposed guilty of: "The order of the universe proves an omnipotent mind; that is, a mind whose will is *constantly attended* with the obedience of every creature and being. Nothing more is requisite to give a foundation to all the articles of religion" (T 1.3.14.12, n.30).[5] And yet the argument to God's existence from the order of the universe, described in the first *Enquiry* as the "chief or sole argument for a divine existence" (EHU 11.11), is there, and again and most celebratedly in the *Dialogues*, subjected to devastating criticism. Most paradoxically of all, this criticism is itself followed by an affirmation from the skeptic Philo that "A purpose, an intention, or design strikes everywhere the most careless, the most stupid thinker" (DNR 12.2, 214). Another instance of Hume's arguments apparently being at odds with his conclusion

---

[5] This note was added by means of the Appendix published in 1740, at the end of the third and final volume of the *Treatise*.

is in his onslaught on miracles. There his attack on the credentials of revelation concludes with a recommendation to faith: "Our most holy religion is founded on *Faith*, not on reason" (EHU 10.40). Somewhat similarly, his aphoristic demolition of the grounds for believing in immortality in "Of the Immortality of the Soul" begins and ends with a recommendation to "the gospel alone, that has brought life and immortality to light" (E-IS 1, 43, 590, 598).

It is not possible within present constraints of space to discuss these issues in full. They are complex and have, moreover, already been examined at depth in recent Humean exegeses.[6] But an outline interpretation will be useful. In the first place neither Hume nor any other writer in eighteenth-century Britain (or elsewhere in Europe for that matter) was free to express atheistical or antireligious views without the threat of or actual prosecution or social penalties of a very nasty sort. Hence we would expect Hume to cover his apparently skeptical views with protestations of orthodoxy with which he could defend himself when need arose. In this he is in company with most other eighteenth-century expressions of religious skepticism or atheism.[7] His isolated direction to faith as the foundation of "our most holy religion" is thus almost certainly a defensive irony following on his attack on miracles, or a rueful acknowledgment of the ultimate irrationality of religious belief, not a sincere fideistic defense of what religious belief "really" is. It would also be possible to construe some of his blander affirmations of belief in God as the designer in this way, particularly the fulsome and then highly qualified concession by the skeptic Philo in *Dialogues*, Part 12.

But having acknowledged the prudential irony, there remains an impression, from the careful complexity of his arguments, from his skepticism about metaphysical arguments, and from letters and anecdotal evidence, that Hume really was unwilling to deny the existence of God and all lesser supernatural agents in the unequivocal sense now conveyed by the notion of atheism. It is as if he was too consistent a skeptic to pronounce positively on any "remote and

[6] For a full development of the interpretation that follows, see my *Hume's Philosophy of Religion*, 2nd ed. (London: Macmillan, 1988). For further works in the same area and other recent exegesis of the *Dialogues*, see note 8 below.
[7] The matter is documented by David Berman in his *A History of Atheism in Britain* (London: Croom Helm, 1988).

abstruse subjects" (EHU 1.12), atheism included; and, moreover, it is as if the closer he looked at the defects of the design argument, the more something of it remained unrefuted, so that, at the end of the *Dialogues*, in a paragraph very probably added to the initial version of the manuscript in 1757, he can write, surely without hint of irony:

> If the whole of natural theology, as some people seem to maintain, resolves itself into one simple, though somewhat ambiguous, at least undefined proposition, *that the cause or causes of order in the universe probably bear some remote analogy to human intelligence*: If this proposition be not capable of extension, variation, or more particular explication: If it afford no inference that affects human life, or can be the source of any action or forbearance: And if the analogy, imperfect as it is, can be carried no farther than to the human intelligence; and cannot be transferred, with any appearance of probability, to the other qualities of the mind: If this really be the case, what can the most inquisitive, contemplative, and religious man do more than give a plain, philosophical assent to the proposition, as often as it occurs; and believe that the arguments, on which it is established, exceed the objections which lie against it? (DNR 12.33, 227)[8]

So I would suggest for working purposes that one should take as prudential irony Hume's affirmations where they are blandly at variance with any straightforward reading of what precedes or follows them. But one should also acknowledge that his regard for the limitations of human understanding, and his caution concerning "so extraordinary and magnificent a question" as the being and nature of God (DNR 12.33, 227), make him genuinely unable to advocate straightforward atheism of the sort later associated with D'Holbach or Russell. Thus his skepticism about all theological and other claims based on "abstruse metaphysics" does not at the end permit him to reject in toto "obvious" claims based on the order apparent in the universe. But these "obvious" claims amount to very little as far as any real religion is concerned. They imply no duties and no action or forbearance from action. They involve no

---

[8] Smith supposes this paragraph was added in 1776, but M. A. Stewart shows that the paper, watermarks, and spelling on the page on which the paragraph was written all support a 1757 date. See M. A. Stewart, "The Dating of Hume's Manuscripts," in *The Scottish Enlightenment: Essays in Reinterpretation*, ed. P. B. Wood (Rochester, NY: University of Rochester Press, 2000), 267–314, esp. 288–305, 307–8, and Figure 14. I am indebted to Prof. Stewart for correspondence bearing on this question.

devotion. I have elsewhere suggested that such an emasculated concession to the proposition "there is a god" should be called "attenuated deism."[9] This is deism in which such evidence and reasons as
remain uncontroverted add up to no more than a dim possibility that
some nonprovidential god exists, a possibility too ill-understood to
be affirmed or denied by a "wise man."

But whether the designation "attenuated deism" is appropriate
or not, it is Hume's actual arguments that contribute to the philosophy of religion, together with the excitement of the challenges
that he brings to bear on questions concerning religion and the existence of God or gods. These arguments and challenges for the most
part stand or fall on their own philosophical merits without need to
refer to Hume's own hard-to-identify stance. In what follows, and for
present purposes, I shall therefore take Hume to be identified with
any interesting position set out in his own works.[10]

II. ARGUMENT AND OUTCOME

The Core of Natural Religion

In the first *Enquiry* Hume refers to the design argument as "the
chief or sole argument for a divine existence" (EHU 11.11). He is
here not making a judgment but reporting a fact. There are strong

---

[9] See my *Hume's Philosophy of Religion*, 219–23.

[10] The only case where this may need special justification is the *Dialogues*, where the
three speakers are in evident conflict and it is not always clear who has the better of
the argument. Given that Hume's model is Cicero, and the balanced presentation
exemplified by *De Natura Deorum*, and not Plato, with (generally) his pro-Socratic
yes-men, it is still possible to say that (a) Demea speaks very little for Hume and
in good part for both the high rationalism of Samuel Clarke and, somewhat per-
versely, for such "blind belief" as Hume admits into the discussion; (b) Cleanthes
speaks somewhat more for Hume, especially when he opposes Demea, but mostly
for the moderate rationalists and users of the a posteriori arguments whose best
known representative is Joseph Butler; (c) Philo is closest to Hume's mouthpiece
but inclined to overstate his position so that retreat is occasionally possible. There
is a considerable literature on the interpretation of the *Dialogues*. See in particular
Kemp Smith's "Introduction," *Dialogues*, ed. N. K. Smith (London: Thomas Nelson, 1935); James Noxon, "Hume's Agnosticism," *Philosophical Review* 73 (1964):
248–61; my *Hume's Philosophy of Religion*, Chap. 12; Nelson Pike, "Hume on
the Argument from Design," *Dialogues concerning Natural Religion*, ed. N. Pike
(Indianapolis: Bobbs-Merrill, 1970).

hints of the argument in the Bible.[11] It played a significant part in Greek philosophical monotheism.[12] In its teleological version it appears as the Fifth Way of Aquinas. In eighteenth-century literature its soundness is virtually taken for granted, and the same applies for much nineteenth-century literature. It has even enjoyed some rehabilitation in the twentieth century.[13]

Apart from numerous short references, Hume attempts three statements of the argument:[14]

1. The religious philosophers... paint, in the most magnificent colours, the order, beauty, and wise arrangement of the universe; and then ask, if such a glorious display of intelligence could proceed from the fortuitous concourse of atoms, or if chance could produce what the greatest genius can never sufficiently admire. (EHU 11.10)

2. The curious adapting of means to ends, throughout all nature, resembles exactly, though it much exceeds, the productions of human contrivance; of human design, thought, wisdom, and intelligence. Since therefore the effects resemble each other, we are led to infer, by all the rules of analogy, that the causes also resemble, and that the Author of nature is somewhat similar to the mind of man; though possessed of much larger faculties, proportioned to the grandeur of the work, which he has executed. (DNR 2.5, 143)

3. Consider, anatomize the eye: Survey its structure and contrivance; and tell me, from your own feeling, if the idea of a contriver does not immediately flow in upon you with a force like that of sensation. (DNR 3.7, 154)

In effect (although I do not think it can be shown that Hume intended anything so systematic) these three statements show the design argument in distinct versions. In (1), the argument is presented as what I have elsewhere suggested should be called the nomological argument,[15] namely, as the appeal to the inexplicability

---

[11] Note, e.g., Psalm 19; 2 Maccabees 7:28; Romans 1:20.

[12] See, e.g., Xenophon: *Memorabilia*, 1.4, 6–7; Plato: *Timaeus*, 47; Cicero: *De Natura Deorum*, 2.34–5.

[13] Note particularly the remarkably modern sounding *The Fitness of the Environment* by L. J. Henderson (New York: Macmillan, 1913), and, among more recent books, Alvin Plantinga, *God and Other Minds* (Ithaca, NY: Cornell University Press, 1967), and R. G. Swinburne, *The Existence of God* (Oxford: Clarendon Press, 1979), Chap. 8.

[14] It is difficult even now to identify any definitive statement of the design argument and we know Hume encountered the same problem. See HL 1:155.

[15] See *An Encyclopaedia of Philosophy*, ed. G. H. R. Parkinson (London: Routledge, 1988), 339–42.

of natural *order* if this is not accounted for as the outcome of intelligent design. In (2), Hume makes a very careful attempt to represent the form of what is usually called the teleological argument: the appeal to the significance of the *purposes* supposedly evident in natural phenomena. In (3), Cleanthes, the advocate of the argument in the *Dialogues*, is not so much presenting a new version of the argument as suggesting that its conclusion is something verging on the perceptually obvious. We cannot see the structures of nature, or become *aware* of the all pervading regularities we express as laws of nature, without "feeling" their source as intelligent. The question then becomes whether this "feeling" is justifiably related to what elicits it (like our feeling of fear about atomic radiation) or unjustifiably related (like some people's feeling of fear about darkness per se).

In the *Dialogues* and the first *Enquiry*, Section 11, Hume subjects these arguments to an intricate and cumulatively devastating series of objections, the majority of which apply to both the nomological and the teleological arguments. His main objections are as follows:

a. If we suppose God (or gods) to be the cause of order in the world, then since all that we can infer about God (or gods) is inferred from the world, we can *only* attribute to God (or the gods) whatever degree of power, intelligence, foresight, and so forth is sufficient to produce what we actually find in the world (EHU 11.12–23). In particular, Hume argues, when applied to divine providence, that it is impossible to *infer* from the world infinite or even very great benevolence in its designer (DNR 10–11). As Philo in the *Dialogues* puts it, "The whole presents nothing but the idea of a blind nature, impregnated by a great vivifying principle, and pouring forth from her lap, without discernment or parental care, her maimed and abortive children" (DNR 11.13, 211). Hume is also at pains to point out in the *Dialogues* and first *Enquiry* that we may torture our brains (to adapt Hume's phrase from EHU 11.17) into *reconciling* the suffering of living things with the presupposition that God is perfectly benevolent, but what we cannot do is justify that presupposition by *inference* from the given suffering.

b. If valid, the inference from design could equally well establish a number of conclusions incompatible with monotheism: for example, that the universe, like most human contrivance, is the product of cooperating designers; that it is a discarded experiment in universe making or the product of a second-rate god; that it is the creation of a deistic god, that is, one who has set it all going and then let it run on at its own devices; and so on (DNR 5, 166–9).

c. Hume argues extensively in his general philosophy that the concept of cause applies only to *kinds* of object. That is to say we have warrant for calling A the cause of B only if objects of *kind* A have constantly occurred prior to, and contiguously with, objects of *kind* B. When this has happened, we both have evidence that, and believe that, As cause Bs. Given this analysis of causation, it makes no sense to talk about a unique object such as "the universe as a whole" being causally produced by a unique and otherwise unknown entity "outside" (in the sense of not being one among) the repeating causal sequences of the universe itself. Evidently we cannot have experience of an event or events prior to, contiguous with, and constantly conjoined with the beginning of the universe (EHU 11.30; DNR 2.24–8, 149ff.).

d. The analogy, Hume contends, between artifacts – objects known to proceed from design – and natural objects is too weak and remote to suggest similar causes. (This objection is developed almost throughout the *Dialogues*.)

e. The relation between order and design is experience based: "order, arrangement, or the adjustment of final causes" is not a priori proof of design, it is indicative of design "only so far as it has been experienced to proceed from that principle" (DNR 2.14, 146).

f. The design argument takes it as obvious that the order in nature (or more generally the material world per se) *requires* an explanation: that it cannot itself be accepted as the ultimate brute fact. But, Hume argues, if this is so, and the explanation of natural order has to be sought in something other than itself – namely, in the activity of an intelligent agent taken to be what theistic religions call "God" – then what is it about this explanation which legitimately blocks the quest for further explanation? "But if we stop [at the agent explanation]... why go so far? Why not stop at the material world?" (DNR 4, 161).[16] Hume's question is absolutely crucial.

---

[16] For a critical discussion of this and some of Hume's other objections to the design argument, see R. G. Swinburne, "The Argument from Design," *Philosophy* 43 (1968): 199–212. See also L. Dupre, "The Argument from Design Today," *Journal*

It challenges the most fundamental of all Jewish, Christian, and Islamic assumptions: that there is something about God that makes it more reasonable to stop all "why?" and "where from?" questions with that entity than with the most fundamental realities of the material world itself.

Each of the above requires, and is given by Hume and the secondary literature which follows his agenda, detailed philosophical discussion that cannot be attempted here. But at least one other important and highly original counter to the design argument related to (f) above is suggested by Hume. We can all agree that the inference to a designer depends on the assumptions that (1) the order in nature *needs* explanation and that (2) no explanation is possible other than by reference to some designing intelligence. In Part 8 of the *Dialogues* both these assumptions are questioned.

The first had been classically challenged by a tenet of the Epicurean (or Greek Atomist) system that attracted much ancient ridicule and criticism. This was Epicurus's contention that the world just happened by the unguided collision and grouping of numberless primary particles taking place over an infinite time in infinite space. Thus Balbus, one of Cicero's characters in his dialogues in *De Natura Deorum* (2.37), derides the Epicureans:

Should it not astound me that anyone . . . can persuade himself . . . That a world of the utmost splendour and beauty is created by an accidental combination of those [primary particles]? I do not see how the person who supposes that this can happen cannot also believe that if countless instances of the twenty-one letters were thrown into a container, then shaken out onto the ground, it were possible they might form a readable version of the *Annals* of Ennuis. I'm not sure that luck could manage this to the extent of a single line!

The fundamental claim against the Epicureans is that order, beauty, and the arrangement of the universe *need* explanation, and random collisions of infinite numbers of primary particles do not provide a probable one. The same claim is elicited by the seventeenth-century revival of Epicurean atomism.

of *Religion* 54 (1974): 1–12; Gary Doore, "The Argument from Design: Some Better Reasons for Agreeing with Hume," *Religious Studies* 16 (1980): 145–61; and my *Hume's Philosophy of Religion*, Chaps. 2–3.

In 1682, at Oxford, a translation into English verse of Lucretius's "six books of Epicurean philosophy" appeared, to be followed by paraphrases by Dryden and others. An angry reaction to the popularity of such an irreligious work followed, and in 1712 there appeared an answer on an epic scale: *The Creation* by Sir Richard Blackmore. At several points Blackmore confronts the Epicurean account of the origin of the *ordered* universe in precisely the manner in which it had been confronted by Balbus in Cicero's dialogue sixteen hundred years earlier:

> Could Atomes, which with undirected flight
> Roam'd thro' the Void, and rang'd the Realms of Night;
> Of Reason destitute, without Intent,
> Depriv'd of Choice, and mindless of Event,
> In Order march, and to their Posts advance
> Led by no Guide, but undesigning Chance?

The challenge is again clear: the order manifested by the universe *needs* explanation. But does it? Hume is inclined to answer – see (f) above – that it does not; or rather, if we think it does, then having traced its origin to a divine orderer, the order in *that* ought just as much to require explanation as the order in matter:

To say, that the different ideas, which compose the reason of the supreme Being, fall into order, of themselves, and by their own nature, is really to talk without any precise meaning. If it has a meaning, I would fain know, why it is not as good sense to say, that the parts of the material world fall into order, of themselves, and by their own nature? Can the one opinion be intelligible, while the other is not so? (DNR 4, 162)

Hume adds that we have indeed "experience of ideas, which fall into order, of themselves, and without any *known* cause" (presumably our own ideas), but "we have a much larger experience of matter, which does the same." A reply to Hume is that the reduction of two sorts of autonomous order, material and mental, to one, mental order, effects a desirable elimination of a superfluous explanatory entity.[17] The problem for the theist, however, is to show, against

---

[17] This and related matters were investigated in the Swinburne-Olding exchange in the early 1970s. See A. Olding, "The Argument from Design – A Reply to R. G. Swinburne," *Religious Studies* 7 (1971): 361–73; R. G. Swinburne, "The Argument from Design – A Defence," *Religious Studies* 8 (1972): 193–205; A. Olding, "Design – A Further Reply to R. G. Swinburne," *Religious Studies* 9 (1973): 229–32.

496   J. C. A. GASKIN

the ever rising tide of scientific evidence, that mental order, and not material order, has explanatory primacy: that material order is explainable in terms of mental order and not vice versa, and that mental order and material order are genuinely different categories.

But there is a further reason to think that the order manifested in the universe is *not* in need of special explanation. The point is that Cicero's Balbus, and Blackstone, and others who have walked in their footsteps have assumed that in some sense a chaotic universe is more probable, at least would be less in need of explanation, than the orderly cosmos we find. But this assumption is in need of justification. Why? Because the assumption implies that we can compare the ordered cosmos that actually exists with a chaos that does not exist, and find the existent cosmos less probable than the nonexistent chaos. But the crucial point is that we cannot make such a comparison. We have absolutely *no* grounds for supposing that what actually exists has any probability at all by comparison with anything else, since in this special instance *there is nothing else.* Similarly we have absolutely no grounds for holding that order in nature is more (or less) in need of explanation than chaos would have been. Order is what we have, and there is nothing else by contrast with which that order is in any sense probable or improbable.

Even if at best Hume himself can do no more than shed doubt on the need to explain natural order, or on the usefulness of doing so, the second assumption required for inference to a designer remains, namely, that there is no explanation of natural order if we do not attribute it to a designing intelligence. However, we (but not Hume) might be able to argue, in the light of the big bang theory favored by modern cosmology, that the initial event out of which all subsequent sequences of events emerged could (at least we have no reasons to think that it could not) have set absolutely any sort of universe developing. But having set going this universe, those first developments were continuous with what we subsequently read as the laws of nature. The initial event having set things going in *one* way (that is, the way it actually did), that *one* way is what we see as natural order, and indeed no existent things can develop in any other way given the initial event. There is even a hint of this type of thinking in the *Dialogues* (although it is arrived at in a somewhat different way): "Instead of admiring the order of natural beings, we should clearly see, that it was absolutely impossible for them, in the smallest article, ever to admit of any other disposition" (DNR 6, 175). But in the pages of the *Dialogues* that follow this remark, Hume develops without aid from our big bang theory an extensive reply to the traditional Stoic and Christian assumption that order *could not* have emerged from chaos without intelligent design.

Hume's "new hypothesis of cosmogony" (DNR 8, 183) is a form of the Epicurean theory revised by the assumption that the number of primary particles of matter is very large but not, as Epicurus supposed, infinite. Suppose, says Hume, in a passage of remarkable insight, "matter were thrown into any position, by a blind, unguided force" and that this force was not exhausted at the moment of the first throw, but remained active in every part of matter so that movement continued (DNR 8, 184). Is what we actually find – namely, stable structures composed of disorderly primary particles – not a possible outcome of such a finite amount of matter undergoing transpositions over a very long period of time? In particular, certain structures and sequences, once struck on, will be of a character that enables them to endure.

In effect Hume is suggesting that given an initial blind force (a big bang?) subsequent random movements of a large but finite amount of matter *could* produce the stable entities and sequences we now observe in the universe. Laws of nature and inorganic structures, just as much as natural species, *could* be arrived at by a process akin to that of natural selection: "It is in vain, therefore, to insist upon the uses of the parts in animals or vegetables, and their curious adjustment to each other. I would fain know how an animal could subsist, unless its parts were so adjusted?" (DNR 8, 185).

Even if the best reading of the available evidence would now seem to show that the most fundamental laws of nature have not evolved, but have operated uniformly from the remotest accessible past, Hume's "new hypothesis" (DNR 8, 183) remains astonishingly impressive as an attempt to provide an alternative to the "religious hypothesis" (EHU 11.18). It is, moreover, an attempt that, when fleshed out by Darwin's observations, vastly devalues the teleological argument even if the nomological argument partially escapes.

What then is Hume's achievement in this area? At the very least he put a massive and permanent question mark against a crucial piece of religious apologetic previously taken as unquestionable. In the process he brilliantly anticipated later ideas and established the grounds on which all subsequent philosophical discussions have taken place.

The Credentials of Revelation

Two-and-one-half centuries after its publication, "Of Miracles," Section 10 in the first *Enquiry,* is still spawning book-length responses together with an unabated stream of discussion articles.[18] Indeed, "Of Miracles" is manifestly one of those rare philosophical pieces whose very inconsistencies and ambiguities are more fruitful than the cautious balance of a thousand lesser works. Its main structure is simple.

In Part 2 a number of case histories and what have been called a posteriori arguments are reproduced (for the most part they are not original to Hume) to show that "there never was a miraculous event established on so full an evidence" that the falsehood of the evidence would be "a real prodigy" (EHU 10.14). In effect Part 2 is concerned with the criteria for good evidence, with the significance of incompatible religious claims based on rival miracles,[19] and with the general conclusion Hume draws from his arguments – that "a miracle can never be proved, so as to be the foundation of a system of religion" (EHU 10.36). Given the contemporary background of controversy concerning miracles, and the use of miracles to validate a particular revelation of Christianity, I have suggested that this guarded conclusion should be unpacked as "The Resurrection can never be proved in such a way that it can function as a good reason to accept the Christian revelation."[20]

---

[18] The first book-length reply was William Adams, *An Essay on Mr. Hume's Essay on Miracles* (London, 1752). George Campbell's critique, *A Dissertation on Miracles* (Edinburgh, 1762), elicited from Hume one of his rare philosophical replies: see HL 1:348–51. An interesting recent discussion of the general philosophical problems concerning reported prodigies can be found in C. A. J. Coady, *Testimony: A Philosophical Study* (Oxford: Clarendon Press, 1992). See also the works by Earman, Fogelin, and Johnson cited below in note 21.

[19] See my "Contrary Miracles Concluded," *Hume Studies* 10 (Suppl. 1985): 1–14.

[20] The controversy is most readably documented by Sir Leslie Stephen in his *History of English Thought in the Eighteenth Century,* Chap. 4, Sect. 4 (originally published in 1876). The area has been more thoroughly and more recently reviewed by R. M. Burns in *The Great Debate on Miracles* (Lewisburg, PA: Bucknell University Press, 1981). For the interpretation of "Of Miracles" as a comment on the evidential significance of the Resurrection, see my "David Hume and the Eighteenth Century Interest in Miracles," *Hermathena* 99 (1964): 80–92.

In Part 1 an a priori argument (so called by commentators on Hume) is produced to act as a "check" on superstition. The argument purports to show that no "wise man" (that is one whose belief is proportioned to the evidence) could believe reports of miracles. A paraphrase of Hume's argument is as follows:

1. A weaker evidence can never destroy a stronger.
2. A wise man proportions his belief to the evidence.
3. Some things happen invariably in our experience, for example, that men die. In matters of fact these invariable experiences constitute certainties and are called, or form the basis of, laws of nature – "a firm and unalterable [unalterable because *past*] experience has established these laws." (EHU 10.12)
4. Other things happen less than invariably in our experience, for example, that one will survive a heart attack. In matters of fact these variable experiences constitute probabilities which admit of degrees ranging from strong (almost always happens) to weak (very seldom happens).
5. The veracity of human testimony is, from experience, normally a strong probability and as such amounts to a proof that what is reported took place. But sometimes the veracity of human testimony is a weak probability (as is always the case, according to Hume's arguments in Part 2, with reports of miracles). *Therefore*, from 3 and 4, when testimony is given that is contrary to our invariable experience, a probability, whether weak or strong, is opposing a certainty, and (from 1 and 2) the wise man will believe the certainty.
6. But a miracle is *"a transgression of a law of nature* [see 3] *by a particular volition of the Deity."* Therefore, "There must ... be a uniform experience against every miraculous event, otherwise the event would not merit that appellation. And as a uniform experience amounts to a proof, there is here a direct and full *proof*, from the nature of the fact, against the existence of any miracle." (EHU 10.12 and n.23)

The above argument has provoked some fundamental questions, including the following, which can only be stated here: (1) What is meant by a law of nature, and how can one distinguish between an event that falsifies a law (shows that it is an inaccurate description of the way things are in the natural world) and an event that results from a suspension of the law or an intrusion into the natural world by a supernatural agent such as a god or other invisible spirit? (2) Can Hume, on the basis of what he says elsewhere in the *Treatise* and first *Enquiry*, formulate any concept of natural causation strong enough to give content to the notion of its violation? (3) Is Hume's definition of a miracle (which is entirely reportive) in need of supplementation, particularly by the qualification "of religious significance," so that mere inexplicable freaks of nature do not get counted as miracles? (4) Is Hume correct in implying (EHU 10.11–13) that in order for something to be called a miracle it must not happen more than once? And if, as biblical reports would seem to suggest, he is not correct, at what stage will repeated "miracles" become clusters of "para-normal" phenomena in need of explanation *within* the natural world? (5) Can Hume, or anyone arguing on his behalf, or on behalf of those who need such a concept in their definition of what a miracle is, give adequate content to the notion of a physically impossible event?

But there is a further and crucial question. Hume's a priori argument is addressed to *reports* of events, not to our own eye-witnessing of them, and his argument depends on our reluctance – whether rational or irrational remains to be established – to accept as veridical reports that are contrary to "our uniform experience." So, (6) with what justification can we use the exceptional nature of an event as grounds for rejecting testimony that the alleged event took place? It is this final question that is crucial in assessing and understanding Hume's a priori argument since, it must again be emphasized, the argument is addressed to *reports* of events, not to our own eye-witnessing of them.

The position I would defend with regard to question (6) is this: Hume's argument is an accurate formal representation of the norm of rationality we all in fact apply, or try to apply, in our search for historical truth. Furthermore, when applied to the reports to which Hume has to apply it in order to damage the credentials of the Christian revelation – namely, to the biblical reports of miracles in general and to the Resurrection in particular – the norm is successful in showing that these reports would be rejected for the reasons he gives, if they occurred in historical contexts in which religious faith was not involved.

Consider a nonbiblical example. Toward the end of his dialogue *Agricola,* the august Roman historian Tacitus describes a decisive battle with the aboriginal tribes north of Perth in Scotland at "Mount Grampius." The location of the battle has never been identified, but supporting archaeological traces of Agricola's campaign have been discovered, and there is nothing improbable about a battle, in the circumstances Tacitus describes, that would invite the application of Hume's argument. *Hence* we accept the testimony. Now, at the end of the same historian's account of Germany, when he surveys the land to the east, he concludes: "What comes after them is the stuff of fables: Hellusii and Oxiones with the faces and features of men, but the bodies and limbs of animals. Concerning such unverifiables I will express no opinion." Since the judicious Tacitus merely itemizes fables and then suspends judgment, we are not faced with a report to assess, however far-fetched. But suppose he had written:

In the borderlands of the world to the east of the Dnieper there are human-like creatures who (A) have a single eye in the middle of their skulls, and (B) do not move as other creatures do, but when they desire to traverse a distance they merely wish it so, whereupon they disappear in the place they were in and reappear in the place where they wish to be. These creatures are called cyclopoids.

What would be the result of applying Hume's norm of historical rationality to this supposed report? Item (A) has some trace of corroboration in the *Odyssey* but lacks any zoological or archaeological support, and never has occurred in our experience. Hence, despite Tacitus' reputation, we are unlikely to accept as true the report I am supposing him to have given. It is too *improbable.* Item (B) is of a different order. Like the reconstitution of a dead body into a living man, such wish-locomotion would be violation of a whole cluster of what we are justified in taking as laws of nature, and as such there is a "direct and full *proof,* from the nature of the [alleged] fact" against its existence. Cyclopoids (B) just do not exist. The report is at variance with the norm of historical rationality formalized in Hume's argument because the report concerns *the impossible* as that concept would normally be understood and is commonly applied.

Now, it is largely agreed that despite his obvious *inclination* to regard miracles as impossible, Hume did not put forward the official version of his a priori argument in order to *prove* that miracles are

impossible. What he set out to show was that it would never be reasonable to believe on the basis of reported evidence that a miracle
had taken place. But once it is granted that he, and you and I, never
have ourselves experienced a miracle in the sense of something that
is clearly at variance with what we call laws of nature, the effective *practical* difference between "never reasonable to believe" and
"impossible" becomes negligible. In terms of what we have rational
warrant to believe, there is no difference between rejecting ancient
testimony to cyclopoid (B) – or the Resurrection – on the grounds that
it conflicts with all our experience as codified in the laws of nature,
and saying that cyclopoid (B) – or the Resurrection – is "impossible"
as that word is commonly employed. It is this, I suggest, that gives
Hume's a priori argument, his "check to all kinds of superstitious
delusion" (EHU 10.2), its peculiarly sharp ambiguity in which one
feels, and is, taken to a more radical conclusion than one believes to
be warranted.[21]

The "Preposterous Distribution... of Praise and Blame"

The attention justly given to the *Treatise* as, among other achievements, Hume's main contribution to analytic moral philosophy has
tended to eclipse his other account of social and personal morality in
the second *Enquiry.*[22] This account, supplemented by the final part

---

[21] As already indicated, the literature is very extensive. Among modern discussions of
the logic and the interpretation of Hume's argument the following provide some of
the basic discussion: Antony Flew, *Hume's Philosophy of Belief,* 2nd ed. (London,
1961), Chap. 8; and *David Hume, Philosopher of Moral Science* (Oxford: Oxford
University Press, 1986), Chap. 5; my *Hume's Philosophy of Religion,* Chap. 8. The
above paraphrase of Hume's a priori argument is drawn from this latter work,
152 f. A useful collection of highly relevant articles (including Hume's essay) is
provided in *Miracles,* ed. R. G. Swinburne (New York: Macmillan, 1989). Useful
additions to the literature include Dorothy Coleman, "Hume, Miracles, and Lotter-
ies," *Hume Studies* 14 (1988): 328–46; J. Houston, *Reported Miracles: A Critique
of Hume* (Cambridge: Cambridge University Press, 1994); John Earman, *Hume's
Abject Failure: The Argument against Miracles* (New York: Oxford University
Press, 2000); Robert J. Fogelin, *A Defense of Hume on Miracles* (Princeton, NJ:
Princeton University Press, 2003). See also notes 18–20 above, and 33 below.

[22] For example, in *Hume's Moral Theory* (London: Routledge & Kegan Paul, 1980), J.
L. Mackie mentions the second *Enquiry* in his first sentence and then continues
an otherwise admirable book as if only the *Treatise* existed. Similar treatment of
the two works is evident in Jonathan Harrison's *Hume's Theory of Justice* (Oxford:

of the *Dialogues* and the essay "Of Suicide," has two things to say about religion that to many people are as unacceptable at the beginning of the twenty-first century as they were when Hume first published his ideas in the middle of the eighteenth. The first is that the precepts of morality and our practical obligations to observe them are independent of religious beliefs and religious sanctions. The second is that when religion does intrude into morality, it serves only to distort natural morality by the introduction of "frivolous species of merit" and the creation of artificial crimes. This distortion results in "a preposterous distribution . . . of praise and blame" and in gratuitous human suffering (DNR 12.16, 222).

1. The independence of morality. It is a matter of fact everywhere observable, Hume contends in the second *Enquiry*, that normal human beings are not absolutely indifferent to the weal and woe of others physically or imaginatively near to them. This responsiveness to other people is, according to Hume, ultimately traceable to the operation of "sympathy," the natural trait by means of which we actually share in or are directly moved by, the feelings of others. (In the *Treatise*, Hume had attempted to trace the origins of sympathy back to more fundamental features of human nature than he is concerned with in the second *Enquiry*. In the later work he explicitly takes the operation of sympathy as an experienced fact about human beings that, in an account of social morality, need not be provided with any deeper explanation. See EPM 5.17, n.19, App. 2.5, n.60.) Now, continues Hume, since human beings have to a certain extent a common nature, what is misery to one, is misery to most; and what produces happiness in one, produces happiness in most. Thus it is that certain devices and doings attract our *general* condemnation because they commonly produce misery, while others attract our *general* approval because they commonly promote happiness. This generality of approval for whatever promotes happiness in human society is, according to Hume, the ultimate source

Clarendon Press, 1981). Both Mackie and Harrison typify the standard and disproportionate emphasis on the *Treatise* as the only worthwhile source for Hume's contribution to ethics. A study that gives some attention to *An Enquiry concerning the Principles of Morals* is Nicholas Capaldi, *Hume's Place in Moral Philosophy* (New York: Lang, 1989). For further discussions of Hume's ethics, see the essays in this volume by Terence Penelhum, David Fate Norton, and Jacqueline Taylor.

of moral discriminations. On this showing moral rules (and the particular laws of a state) will, in the absence of distorting prejudices or misinformation, express the general policies that have been found to promote the objectives of minimizing misery and maximizing happiness. The sources of moral rules are thus located in the good of society and its members, and not in man's relation to God or to some other nonworldly or "spiritual" entity. The point was well made by the Emperor Julian in 361 A.D. when he rejected the Judeo-Christian claim to have had a special moral revelation in the Ten Commandments: "Except for the commandment 'Thou shalt not worship other gods' and 'Remember the sabbath day,' what nation is there... which does NOT think it ought to keep the other commandments?"[23] Hume would have agreed. The *other* commandments commend themselves to us quite apart from religion because they are perceived to codify some of the conduct generally needed to ensure the happiness of any society, and this perception is true, as a matter of common human experience, not as a result of surprising information conveyed by a God on Mount Sinai.

But even if it is conceded that moral rules have, or need have, no source beyond our open-minded and "natural" (I return to this word below) approval of what is generally useful in promoting happiness, surely our commitment to observing them depends on religion? Do we not to this day, and not infrequently, come across utterances by politicians, religious believers, and laymen blaming the increase of crime and the drop in standards of behavior on *lack* of religious belief and teaching? And if religious teaching (as Hume and the Emperor Julian would have it) is not a necessary precondition for "discovering" that, for example, stealing and murder have to be prohibited, then it must at least be the case that religion is a necessary condition for our enforcement of these commandments on ourselves as individuals when we are disinclined to obey them. In short, religion is the source of moral *obligation.*

Hume would disagree: "the *moral obligation* holds proportion with the *usefulness*" (EPM 4.3). Yes, but that is to assert a proportion between obligation and usefulness, not to give an account of the source of the obligation. We may agree that the more something

---

[23] The Emperor Julian, *Against the Galilaeans,* 152D (Spanheim-Neumann pagination).

contributes happiness to individuals or to society, the more we ought to do it. But the nature of "ought" is not thereby explained.

Hume's explanation, his highly distinctive secular analysis of obligation, is for the most part located in the conclusion to the second *Enquiry* (EPM 9.14–15). What he there produces is an account of what he calls "our interested *obligation*" to virtue. It is "interested" because it is a combination of all the factors that press on us, as mentally normal people in our normal social relations with ourselves and others. These factors include our self-interest in doing to others what we would wish others to do to us, our natural interchange of sympathy, our desire to be well thought of by our neighbors, our wish to live at ease with ourselves when "inward peace of mind, consciousness of integrity, a satisfactory review of our own conduct" is part of what is required to be a happy person (EPM 9.23). But if these are some of the factors that interest us in what is called morality, how do they add up to an *obligation?* Because, apart from being understandable and capable of analysis into separate influences, they constitute something naturally *felt,* and feelings, unlike thoughts or facts in Hume's estimation, constitute direct sources of action. Feelings, or, in Hume's preferred term, "passions," are the mainsprings of action.

Now, clearly a lot more deserves to be said and will no doubt be said about Hume's account of social morality, but for present purposes the point is that however debatable the outcome, what Hume offers is a serious account of morality that makes no reference whatsoever to God, or to religious belief or teaching. But Hume goes further than a separation of religion and morality. He also holds that the input of religion into morality is positively mischievous in the sense that religion invents crimes (such as suicide or the use of contraceptives) that are not natural crimes, that is, are not activities that normally produce misery; and it invents virtues (such as self-mortification or doctrinal orthodoxy) that are not natural virtues, that is, are not activities that normally promote happiness in oneself or others.

2. The religious distortion of morality. The key to the point Hume is making is to be found in my insistent use above of such phrases as "in the absence of distorting prejudices," our "natural approval," as "normal people." The point is that Hume is attempting to characterize morality as it is or would be when it operates between

normal people in *natural* conditions: "normal" in the sense (a) that
the person or persons concerned are not pathologically defective
(from whatever cause) in their emotional responses, feelings, or levels of intelligence, and "natural" in the sense (b) that the conditions
do *not* include special influences that overcome normal feelings.
Item (a) will make a special case of, for example, the criminally
insane, or those whose conduct is explainable in terms of their real
lack of the feelings that commonly operate between persons (for
example, the person whose hurting of children really does not feel
to him or her as a harm because that was the way he or she was
treated). In such cases those who follow the direction of Hume's
thought would conclude that special treatment, not *moral* disapproval, is called for: *moral* disapproval being reserved for the voluntary actions of people who are normal in the sense just given.
Item (b), vastly more serious because capable of vastly more general
operation than (a), attempts to single out as "unnatural" conduct
that overrides the natural system of morality (based on happiness) in
the interests of nonmoral "superstitions." The superstitions Hume
was thinking about as overriding natural morality were religious,
those in which the commitment to the religion overcame all sense
of natural good, for example, in the burning of witches and heretics
and the righteous infliction of pain on others for their (nonnatural)
good, or for the good of the religion per se. But the twentieth century
could add political superstitions – National Socialist and Marxist –
in which all feelings of natural good have given way (and have *really*
given way in the feelings of the many concerned) to the nonnatural
good that consists of loyalty to the party or state irrespective of the
happiness resulting, or the misery caused to actual men and women.

Hume's substantial account of secular, this-worldly, utilitarian
morality in the second *Enquiry* is certainly polished literature, but it
is also, as I hope to have shown, revolutionary thought of ever widening application. The revolution is still going on, and the thought is
still contentious.[24] If it were not, it is difficult to see why so often
religion and morality are still popularly linked, or how, for example,
a major religion can still stigmatize as sinful the natural (Hume's
sense) good inherent in effective family planning.

---

[24] For further discussion, see David Fate Norton, "Hume, Atheism, and the Autonomy of Morals," in *Hume's Philosophy of Religion*, ed. M. Hester (Winston-Salem,
NC: Wake Forest University Press, 1986), particularly 120–33.

Natural Belief

If, as Hume maintains, the evidence of natural religion is at best highly problematic and ambiguous, if the evidence of revelation is such as would not be accepted if it came from a nonreligious source, if we can both understand the natural causes of religion and deplore its unnatural effects on conduct, and if, as seems to be Hume's argued position at the beginning and end of both the first *Enquiry* and the *Dialogues*, all speculations about "the powers and operations of one universal spirit" are beyond our understanding (DNR 1, 135), why is it that religious belief persists, even among well-informed people?

One possible answer is that which seems to be implied by a full reading of Hume on religion: that belief in the divine retains just enough wisps of rational support for our propensity to see the world as intelligible, in conjunction with the still-operating causes of religion, to sustain religion despite philosophical criticism. Another answer, not strictly an answer at all, is characterized by the gesture of astonishment with which Hume ends his essay on miracles in the first *Enquiry:* the gesture that has led some apologists into the false view that Hume is advocating fideism as a defensible account of how we do and why we should retain religious belief. But a third, and potentially very fruitful answer, is sometimes given on Hume's behalf: that belief in the divine is a natural belief.

The concept of a natural belief was assembled by a number of twentieth-century commentators on Hume from the characteristics of those few and very general beliefs that Hume identifies as ultimately resistant to all skeptical argument – belief in the continuous existence of an external world independent of our perception of that world, belief that the regularities of the past will continue into the future, that our senses are normally reliable, are examples.[25] The characteristics of these natural beliefs are the following:

a. That they are arrived at prior to any process of reasoning, and cannot for long be dislodged by any process of skeptical reasoning because:

b. They are indispensable as presuppositions of knowledge and conduct for any sentient being who lives in a coherent

---

[25] The concept was first developed by N. K. Smith in his article "The Naturalism of Hume," *Mind* 14 (1905): 149–73, 335–47. This material reappears as Chaps. 4–6 of his *Philosophy of David Hume.*

relation to the given appearances of things. In practical terms no one can act in the world unless he or she has these beliefs. Hence:

c. These beliefs are universal – not merely the cherished or dominant or unquestioned assumptions of a particular culture or of a learned or unlearned population, but such as all human beings always and everywhere have.

Set out thus, it is all but obvious that belief in the divine does not have the characteristics of a natural belief.[26] Even if it could be shown that for most, or at least for many people, religious belief is attained and retained according to (a), it is an incontrovertible matter of fact that religious belief is not universal in the manner of (c). It is also evident that individuals can and do act perfectly adequately in the world without religious belief, and that religious belief is not an epistemic requirement for any coherent relation to the given appearances of things, that is, (b) does not hold either.

There is, moreover, no clear evidence that Hume ever seriously entertained the thought that belief in the divine might be an instinct of nature impervious to skepticism in the way that our belief in an external world is. The nearest we get to such a thought is Cleanthes' restatement of the design argument in which there is an appeal: "tell me, from your own feeling, if the idea of a contriver does not immediately flow in upon you with a force like that of sensation" followed by a reference to the universal and "irresistible" influence of the argument (the design argument) for theism (see DNR 3, 154,

---

[26] The thesis that belief in the divine is a natural belief was first argued at length by R. J. Butler in "Natural Belief and the Enigma of Hume," *Archiv für Geschichte der Philosophie* 42 (1960): 73–100. It is discussed, and rejected, in my *Hume's Philosophy of Religion*, Chaps. 6–7, and is subject to additional refinements in Terence Penelhum's important *Themes in Hume: The Self, the Will, Religion* (Oxford: Clarendon Press, 2000), Chap. 10. With the advantage of a century of discussion behind us it may be felt that the term "natural belief," which is not found in Hume's own writings, was unfortunate. There is a lack of clarity about how it relates to terms which he did use, such as "original principles," "original instinct," "primary impression of nature," or "natural propensity." Some account of these terms in relation to natural belief is given by Miriam McCormick in "Hume on Natural Belief and Original Principles," *Hume Studies* 19 (1993): 103–16. But the philosophically important point remains: that whatever we decide to call these beliefs – Hume's device for rejecting the sustained application of skepticism to beliefs in the absence of which human beings could not, for example, learn from experience or anticipate the future – belief in God is not one of them.

quoted as (3) in Section II above). The force of Cleanthes' point seems to be that our natural propensity to see and expect order in nature is so close to seeing an *orderer* that our natural belief in the former brings with it the latter. But even if Cleanthes, contrary to the majority view among commentators, can be taken to be speaking for Hume, his view is defective in this matter. In the first place, as Philo points out near the end of Part 4 of the *Dialogues* and again in Part 7, the activity of an ordering agent is not the only possible explanation of order; and second, even if the *feeling* that "a contriver" is responsible for the ordered universe is difficult to keep at bay with skeptical argument, it is not "irresistible" because it is resisted, and it is not universal because at least some people do not succumb to the influence of the argument for theism. That something is widely felt, influential, and difficult to dislodge by argument, is not of itself sufficient to give it the exceptionally privileged status of a natural belief. But this still leaves Hume with the difficulty – which he partly faces in the *Natural History of Religion* – of explaining the persistence of religious belief once the arguments and evidence for it are shown to be all but negligible.

Hume did not and perhaps could not have anticipated the nineteenth-century explanation for this persistence developed by Schopenhauer, Feuerbach, and above all by Freud. Namely, that we are so constituted that emotionally and psychologically (but not rationally and epistemically) we *need* some sort of religious belief. Nor could Hume have expected (1) that his skeptical philosophy of religion would lead to a redeployment of fideism or (2) that his "natural belief" counter to extreme skepticism would suggest the development of other and new defenses of Christianity. How did this come about?

In the first place, Hume's undermining of the traditional rational grounds for belief in God was so thorough that once his position had been absorbed into the mainstreams of European thought (via, among others, D'Holbach, Kant, and Shelley) a fundamental reappraisal of the nature of religion commenced. Thus first Schleiermacher (1768–1834) and later Kierkegaard (1813–55) sought to make religion rely less on evidence and reason, and more on feeling, subjective experience, and faith. Such a fideistic reliance largely evades Hume's rationalistic critique, but it does so at the risk of making religious belief arbitrary, while at the same time both inviting Hume-type accounts of its "natural history" and leaving intact his criticism of its moral and social effects.

Theological fideism has a philosophical counterpart in what Terence Penelhum has called "The Parity Argument."[27] The argument can be used by someone who agrees, as Hume does, with the skeptical tradition "that at least some of the fundamental philosophical commitments of secular common sense are without rational foundation" but who nevertheless yields to our natural tendency to believe them: "The Parity Argument suggests to such a person that he is inconsistent if he refuses to yield also to the demands of religious belief merely because he considers that it, too, does not have a rational foundation."[28]

The core objection to this argument is that the inconsistency claimed is not an inconsistency unless it can be shown that the pressure to yield to religious belief is *equal in all respects* to the pressure to yield to natural beliefs. But set against the criteria (a), (b), and (c) above, we have already seen that the metarational demands to believe in the divine are in many respects *not* equal to the demands to believe in, for example, an external world. An additional objection to the Parity Argument is that if it justifies belief in the divine, it also justifies *any* cherished personal or group belief for which there is no rational foundation, for example, that there are witches with diabolical and supernatural powers. It will be noted that Hume's account of "natural beliefs" cannot be used to justify such cherished irrationalities because the criteria for a natural belief are enormously tougher than the irrationality criterion appealed to in the Parity Argument.

Despite the failure to identify belief in the divine as a genuine natural belief, modern philosophical theology is marked with attempts to employ some notion of natural belief for apologetic purposes. Thus, for example, John Hick asserts an analogy between "the religious person's claim to be conscious of God and any man's claim to be conscious of the physical world as an environment, existing independently of himself."[29] The same thought turns up in the

---

[27] See Terence Penelhum's important work *God and Skepticism* (Dordrecht: Reidel, 1983), particularly Chaps. 2, 5, and 6.

[28] Penelhum, *God and Skepticism,* 139.

[29] John Hick, *Arguments for the Existence of God* (London, 1970), 110.

writings of John Macquarrie: "It is not inappropriate to compare the conviction of the independent reality of God to the conviction of the independent reality of the world or of other selves,"[30] and again, more recently, in the writings of Hans Kung: "The history of modern epistemology from Descartes, Hume, and Kant to Popper and Lorenz – it seems to me – made clear that the fact of any reality at all independent of our consciousness can be accepted only as an act of trust," *hence* a like act of trust is appropriate to belief in God.[31] A similar move, but differently presented, is evident in the American school of "Basic Belief Apologists," associated with Alvin Plantinga.[32]

These moves derive from Hume's "natural belief" counter to excessive skepticism, but the derivation is less acceptable than Hume's original counter for the two reasons already identified in connection with the Parity Argument, namely, the derivation admits *any* belief that one may choose to assert baselessly, and it fails to differentiate between an optional belief like belief in God (optional since plainly some of us do not have it) and a nonoptional belief like belief in an external world:

To whatever length any one may push his speculative principles of scepticism, he must act, I own, and live, and converse like other men; and for this conduct he is not obliged to give any other reason than the absolute necessity he lies under of so doing (DNR 1, 134).

No such absolute necessity attaches to any particular belief in the divine.

I said above that there are three possible ways in which Hume could have responded to the puzzle about the resistance of religious belief to skeptical reasoning. He does not take the way of natural belief. He works at the way of causal explanations for religion coupled with a vestigial rationality. The third way, characterized by

---

[30] John Macquarrie, *God-Talk* (London, 1967), 244.
[31] Hans Kung, *Eternal Life?*, trans. E. Quinn (London: Collins, 1984), 275. See also Kung's *Does God Exist? An Answer for Today*, trans. E. Quinn (Garden City, NY: Doubleday, 1980), 568–83. I am indebted to Philip Barnes for these references.
[32] See particularly Alvin Plantinga, "Rationality and Religious Belief," in *Contemporary Philosophy of Religion*, ed. S. Kahn and D. Shatz (New York: Oxford University Press, 1982); and *Faith and Rationality: Reason and Belief in God*, ed. A. Plantinga and N. Wolterstorff (Notre Dame, IN: Notre Dame University Press, 1983).

the gesture of astonishment with which Hume ends his essay "Of Miracles," is perhaps a very realistic perception of the fundamental irrationality of human beings concerning those specially cherished beliefs called religious: "So that, upon the whole, we may conclude, that the CHRISTIAN religion not only was at first attended with miracles, but even at this day cannot be believed by any reasonable person without one" (EHU 10.41). This is not, as some would have it, to clear the way for fideistic Christianity – a conception alien both to Hume's mitigated skepticism and to his worldly morality. It is simply to note the "continued miracle" by which religious faith survives in the secular world against all the intellectual odds.

SUGGESTIONS FOR FUTURE READING

In addition to the works cited in the notes to this essay, for further reading the following are recommended.

Bernard, Christopher. "Hume and the Madness of Religion." In *Hume and Hume's Connexions*, edited by M. A. Stewart and J. P. Wright. Edinburgh: Edinburgh University Press, 1994. 224–38.

Fogelin, Robert J. "What Hume Actually Said about Miracles." *Hume Studies* 16 (1990): 81–6.

Garrett, Don. "Hume on Testimony concerning Miracles." In *Reading Hume on Human Understanding*, edited by P. Millican. Oxford: Clarendon Press, 2002. 303–34.

Gaskin, J. C. A. "Religion: The Useless Hypothesis." In *Reading Hume on Human Understanding*, edited by P. Millican. Oxford: Clarendon Press, 2002. 349–69.

Herdt, Jennifer. *Religion and Faction in Hume's Moral Philosophy*. Cambridge: Cambridge University Press, 1997.

Johnson, David. *Hume, Holism, and Miracles*. Ithaca, NY: Cornell University Press, 1999.

O'Connor, David. *Routledge Philosophy Guidebook to Hume on Religion*. London: Routledge, 2001.

Owen, David. "Hume versus Price on Miracles and Prior Probabilities: Testimony and the Bayesian Calculation." In *Reading Hume on Human Understanding*, edited by P. Millican. Oxford: Clarendon Press, 2002. 335–48.

Phillips, D. Z., and T. Tessip, eds. *Religion and Hume's Legacy*. New York: St. Martin's Press, 1999.

Reich, Lou. *Hume's Religious Naturalism*. Lanham, MD: University Press of America, 1998.

Stewart, M. A. "Hume's Historical View of Miracles." In *Hume and Hume's Connexions*, edited by M. A. Stewart and J. P. Wright. Edinburgh: Edinburgh University Press, 1994. 171–200.

Yandell, Keith. *Hume's 'Inexplicable Mystery': His Views on Religion*. Philadelphia: Temple University Press, 1990.

APPENDIX: HUME'S AUTOBIOGRAPHIES

I. A KIND OF HISTORY OF MY LIFE

In the spring of 1734, Hume accepted a position with a Bristol merchant. His philosophical endeavors were not going well, and so he determined to put these "aside for some time, in order the more effectually to resume them." As he traveled to Bristol, he wrote to an unnamed physician, probably either John Arbuthnot or George Cheyne,[1] to ask advice about how to get on with his philosophical work. Whether Hume actually sent such a letter is not known, but the surviving manuscript furnishes us with a valuable account of the first years of his adult life. The text printed here is based on the original manuscript deposited in the National Library of Scotland, and is published with the permission of the Royal Society of Edinburgh. The title is taken from the first paragraph of the letter.

Sir

[1]   Not being acquainted with this hand-writing, you will probably look to the bottom to find the Subscription, & not finding any, will certainly wonder at this strange method of addressing to you. I must here in the beginning beg you to excuse it, & to perswade you to read what follows with some Attention, [and] must tell you, that this gives you an Opportunity to do a very good-natur'd Action, which I believe is the most powerful

---

[1] For a helpful discussion of this letter, see John P. Wright, "Dr. George Cheyne, Chevalier Ramsay, and Hume's Letter to a Physician," *Hume Studies* 29 (2003), 125–41.

515

Argument I can use. I need not tell you, that I am your
Countryman, a Scotchman; for without any such tye, I dare rely
upon your Humanity, even to a perfect Stranger, such as I am. The
Favour I beg of you is your Advice, & the reason why I address
myself in particular to you need not be told. As one must be a
skilful Physician, a man of Letters, of Wit, of Good Sense, & of
great Humanity, to give me a satisfying Answer, I wish Fame had
pointed out to me more Persons, in whom these Qualities are
united, in order to have kept me some time in Suspense. This I say
in the Sincerity of my Heart, & without any Intention of making a
Complement: For tho' it may seem necessary, that in the beginning
of so unusual a Letter, I shou'd say some fine things, to bespeak
your good Opinion, & remove any prejudices you may conceive at
it, yet such an Endeavor to be witty, wou'd but ill suit with the
present Condition of my Mind; which, I must confess, is not
without Anxiety concerning the Judgement you will form of me.
Trusting however to your Candor & Generosity, I shall, without
further Preface, proceed to open up to you the present Condition of
my Health, & to do that the more effectually shall give you a kind
of History of my Life, after which you will easily learn, why I keep
my Name a Secret.

[2]   You must know then that from my earliest Infancy, I found
alwise a strong Inclination to Books & Letters. As our College
Education in Scotland, extending little further than the Languages,
ends commonly when we are about 14 or 15 Years of Age, I was
after that left to my own Choice in my Reading, & found it encline
me almost equally to Books of Reasoning & Philosophy, & to
Poetry & the polite Authors. Every one, who is acquainted either
with the Philosophers or Critics, knows that there is nothing yet
establisht in either of these two Sciences, & that they contain little
more than endless Disputes, even in the most fundamental
Articles. Upon Examination of these, I found a certain Boldness of
Temper, growing in me, which was not enclin'd to submit to any
Authority in these Subjects, but led me to seek out some new
Medium, by which Truth might be establisht. After much Study, &
Reflection on this, at last, when I was about 18 Years of Age, there
seem'd to be open'd up to me a new Scene of Thought, which
transported me beyond Measure, & made me, with an Ardor

natural to young men, throw up every other Pleasure or Business to apply entirely to it. The Law which was the Business I design'd to follow, appear'd nauseous to me, & I cou'd think of no other way of pushing my Fortune in the World, but that of a Scholar & Philosopher. I was infinitely happy in this Course of Life for some Months; till at last, about the beginning of Septr 1729, all my Ardor seem'd in a moment to be extinguisht, & I cou'd no longer raise my Mind to that pitch, which formerly gave me such excessive Pleasure. I felt no Uneasyness or Want of Spirits, when I laid aside my Book; & therefore never imagind there was any bodily Distemper in the Case, but that my Coldness proceeded from a Laziness of Temper, which must be overcome by redoubling my Application. In this Condition I remain'd for nine Months, very uneasy to myself, as you may well imagine, but without growing any worse, which was a Miracle.

[3]   There was another particular, which contributed more than any thing, to waste my Spirits & bring on me this Distemper, which was, that having read many Books of Morality, such as Cicero, Seneca & Plutarch, & being smit with their beautiful Representations of Virtue & Philosophy, I undertook the Improvement of my Temper & Will, along with my Reason & Understanding. I was continually fortifying myself with Reflections against Death, & Poverty, & Shame, & Pain, & all the other Calamities of Life. These no doubt are exceeding useful, when join'd with an active Life; because the Occasion being presented along with the Reflection, works it into the Soul, & makes it take a deep Impression, but in Solitude they serve to little other Purpose, than to waste the Spirits, the Force of the Mind meeting with no Resistance, but wasting itself in the Air, like our Arm when it misses its Aim. This however I did not learn but by Experience, & till I had already ruin'd my Health, tho' I was not sensible of it.

[4]   Some Scurvy Spots broke out on my Fingers, the first Winter I fell ill, about which I consulted a very knowing Physician, who gave me some Medicines, that remov'd these Symptoms, & at the same time gave me a Warning against the Vapors, which, tho I was laboring under at that time, I fancy'd myself so far remov'd from, & indeed from any other Disease, except a slight Scurvy, that I despis'd his Warning. At last about Aprile 1730, when I was

19 Years of Age, a Symptom, which I had notic'd a little from the beginning, encreas'd considerably, so that tho' it was no Uneasyness, the Novelty of it made me ask Advice. It was what they call a Ptyalism or Watryness in the mouth. Upon my mentioning it to my Physician, he laught at me, & told me I was now a Brother, for that I had fairly got the Disease of the Learned. Of this he found great Difficulty to perswade me, finding in myself nothing of that lowness of Spirit, which those, who labor under that Distemper so much complain of. However upon his Advice, I went under a Course of Bitters, & Anti-hysteric Pills. Drunk an English Pint of Claret Wine every Day, & rode 8 or 10 Scotch Miles. This I continu'd for about 7 Months after.

[5]   Tho I was sorry to find myself engag'd with so tedious a Distemper yet the Knowledge of it, set me very much at ease, by satisfying me that my former Coldness, proceeded not from any Defect of Temper or Genius, but from a Disease, to which anyone may be subject. I now began to take some Indulgence to myself; studied moderately, & only when I found my Spirits at their highest Pitch, leaving off before I was weary, & trifling away the rest of my Time in the best manner I could. In this way, I liv'd with Satisfaction enough; and on my return to Town next Winter found my Spirits very much recruited, so that, tho they sunk under me in the higher Flights of Genius, yet I was able to make considerable Progress in my former Designs. I was very regular in my Diet & way of Life from the beginning, & all that Winter, made it a constant Rule to ride twice or thrice a week, & walk every day. For these Reasons, I expected when I return'd to the Countrey, & cou'd renew my Exercise with less Interruption, that I wou'd perfectly recover. But in this I was much mistaken. For next Summer, about May 1731 there grew upon [me] a very ravenous Appetite, & as quick a Digestion, which I at first took for a good Symptom, & was very much surpriz'd to find it bring back a Palpitation of Heart, which I had felt very little of before. This Appetite, however, had an Effect very unusual, which was to nourish me extremely; so that in 6 weeks time I past from the one extreme to the other, & being before tall, lean, & rawbon'd became on a sudden, the most sturdy, robust, healthful-like Fellow you have seen, with a ruddy Complexion & a chearful Countenance. In excuse for my Riding,

& care of my Health, I alwise said, that I was afraid of a
Consumption; which was readily believ'd from my Looks; but now
every Body congratulate me upon my thorow Recovery. This
unnatural Appetite wore off by degrees, but left me as a Legacy, the
same Palpitation of the heart in a small degree, & a good deal of
Wind in my Stomach, which comes away easily, & without any bad
Gout, as is ordinary. However, these Symptoms are little or no
Uneasyness to me. I eat well; I sleep well. Have no lowness of
Spirits; at least never more than what one of the best Health may
feel, from too full a meal, from sitting too near a Fire, & even that
degree I feel very seldom, & never almost in the Morning or
Forenoon. Those who live in the same Family with me, & see me at
all times, cannot observe the least Alteration in my Humor, &
rather think me a better Companion than I was before, as choosing
to pass more of my time with them. This gave me such Hopes, that
I scarce ever mist a days riding, except in the Winter-time; & last
Summer undertook a very laborious task, which was to travel 8
Miles every Morning & as many in the Forenoon, to & from a
mineral Well of some Reputation. I renew'd the Bitters &
Antihysteric Pills twice, along with Anti-scorbutic Juices last
Spring, but without any considerable Effect, except abating the
Symptoms for a little time.

[6]   Thus I have given you a full account of the Condition of my
Body, & without staying to ask Pardon, as I ought to do, for so
tedious a Story, shall explain to you how my Mind stood all this
time, which on every Occasion, especially in this Distemper, have
a very near Connexion together. Having now Time & Leizure to
cool my inflam'd Imaginations, I began to consider seriously, how I
shou'd proceed in my Philosophical Enquiries. I found that the
moral Philosophy transmitted to us by Antiquity, labor'd under the
same Inconvenience that has been found in their natural
Philosophy, of being entirely Hypothetical, & depending more upon
Invention than Experience. Every one consulted his Fancy in
erecting Schemes of Virtue & of Happiness, without regarding
human Nature, upon which every moral Conclusion must depend.
This therefore I resolved to make my principal Study, & the Source
from which I wou'd derive every Truth in Criticism as well as
Morality. I believe 'tis a certain Fact that most of the Philosophers

who have gone before us, have been overthrown by the Greatness of their Genius, & that little more is requir'd to make a man succeed in this Study than to throw off all Prejudices either for his own Opinions or for th[ose] of others. At least this is all I have to depend on for the Truth of my Reasonings, which I have multiply'd to such a degree, that within these three Years, I find I have scribled many a Quire of Paper, in which there is nothing contain'd but my own Inventions. This with the Reading most of the celebrated Books in Latin, French & English, & acquiring the Italian, you may think a sufficient Business for one in perfect Health; & so it wou'd, had it been done to any Purpose: But my Disease was a cruel Incumbrance on me. I found that I was not able to follow out any Train of Thought, by one continued Stretch of View, but by repeated Interruptions, & by refreshing my Eye from Time to Time upon other Objects. Yet with this Inconvenience I have collected the rude Materials for many Volume; but in reducing these to Words, when one must bring the Idea he comprehended in gross, nearer to him so as to contemplate its minutest Parts, & keep it steddily in his Eye, so as to copy these Parts in Order, this I found impracticable for me, nor were my Spirits equal to so severe an Employment. Here lay my greatest Calamity. I had no Hopes of delivering my Opinions with such Elegance & Neatness, as to draw to me the Attention of the World, & I wou'd rather live & dye in Obscurity than produce them maim'd & imperfect.

[7]   Such a miserable Disappointment I scarce ever remember to have heard of. The small Distance betwixt me & perfect Health makes me the more uneasy in my present Situation. Tis a Weakness rather than a Lowness of Spirits which troubles me, & there seems to be as great a Difference betwixt my Distemper & common Vapors, as betwixt Vapors & Madness.

[8]   I have notic'd in the Writings of the French Mysticks, & in those of our Fanatics here, that, when they give a History of the Situation of their Souls, they mention a Coldness & Desertion of the Spirit, which frequently returns, & some of them, at the beginning, have been tormented with it many Years. As this kind of Devotion depends entirely on the Force of Passion, & consequently of the Animal Spirits, I have often thought that their Case & mine were pretty parralel, & that their rapturous Admirations might

discompose the Fabric of the Nerves & Brain, as much as profound Reflections, & that warmth or Enthusiasm which is inseperable from them.

[9]   However this may be, I have not come out of the Cloud so well as they commonly tell us they have done, or rather began to despair of ever recovering. To keep myself from being Melancholy on so dismal a Prospect, my only Security was in peevish Reflections on the Vanity of the World & of all humane Glory; which, however just Sentiments they may be esteem'd, I have found can never be sincere, except in those who are possest of them. Being sensible that all my Philosophy wou'd never make me contented in my present Situation, I began to rouze up myself; & being encourag'd by Instances of Recovery from worse degrees of this Distemper, as well as by the Assurances of my Physicians, I began to think of something more effectual, than I had hitherto try'd. I found, that as there are two things very bad for this Distemper, Study & Idleness, so there are two things very good, Business & Diversion; & that my whole Time was spent betwixt the bad, with little or no Share of the Good. For this reason I resolved to seek out a more active Life, & tho' I cou'd not quit my Pretensions in Learning, but with my last Breath, to lay them aside for some time, in order the more effectually to resume them.

[10]   Upon Examination I found my Choice confin'd to two kinds of Life; that of a travelling Governor & that of a Merchant. The first, besides that it is in some respects an idle Life, was, I found, unfit for me; & that because from a sedentary & retir'd way of living, from a bashful Temper, & from a narrow Fortune, I had been little accustom'd to general Companies, & had not Confidence & Knowledge enough of the World to push my Fortune or be serviceable in that way. I therefore fixt my Choice upon a Merchant; & having got Recommendation to a considerable Trader in Bristol, I am just now hastening thither, with a Resolution to forget myself, & every thing that is past, to engage myself, as far as is possible, in that Course of Life, & to toss about the World, from the one Pole to the other, till I leave this Distemper behind me.

[11]   As I am come to London in my way to Bristol, I have resolved, if possible, to get your Advice, tho' I shou'd take this absurd Method of procuring it. All the Physicians, I have consulted,

tho' very able, cou'd never enter into my Distemper; because not being Persons of great Learning beyond their own Profession, they were unacquainted with these Motions of the Mind. Your Fame pointed you out as the properest Person to resolve my Doubts, & I was determin'd to have some bodies Opinion, which I cou'd rest upon in all the Varieties of Fears & Hopes, incident to so lingering a Distemper. I hope I have been particular enough in describing the Symptoms to allow you to form a Judgement; or rather perhaps have been too particular. But you know 'tis a Symptom of this Distemper to delight in complaining & talking of itself.

[12]   The Questions I wou'd humbly propose to you are: Whether among all these Scholars, you have been acquainted with, you have ever known any affected in this manner? Whether I can ever hope for a Recovery? Whether I must long wait for it? Whether my Recovery will ever be perfect, & my Spirits regain their former Spring & Vigor, so as to endure the Fatigue of deep & abstruse thinking? Whether I have taken a right way to recover? I believe all proper Medicines have been us'd, & therefore I need mention nothing of them.

II. MY OWN LIFE

By April 1776, Hume was convinced that the bowel disorder that had afflicted him for some months would soon lead to his death. Just prior to setting out for Bath, there to seek a cure from the waters, he prepared his will and the brief autobiography that follows. The title, My Own Life, *is Hume's own; the text printed here is that of the first edition of this work,* The Life of David Hume, Esq. Written by Himself, *London, 1777.*

[1]   It is difficult for a man to speak long of himself without vanity; therefore, I shall be short. It may be thought an instance of vanity that I pretend at all to write my life; but this Narrative shall contain little more than the History of my Writings; as, indeed, almost all my life has been spent in literary pursuits and occupations. The first success of most of my writings was not such as to be an object of vanity.

[2]   I was born the 26th of April 1711, old style, at Edinburgh. I was of a good family, both by father and mother: my father's family is a branch of the Earl of Home's, or Hume's; and my ancestors had been proprietors of the estate, which my brother possesses, for several generations. My mother was daughter of Sir David Falconer, President of the College of Justice: the title of Lord Halkerton came by succession to her brother.

[3]   My family, however, was not rich, and being myself a younger brother, my patrimony, according to the mode of my country, was of course very slender. My father, who passed for a man of parts, died when I was an infant, leaving me, with an elder brother and a sister, under the care of our mother, a woman of singular merit, who, though young and handsome, devoted herself entirely to the rearing and educating of her children. I passed through the ordinary course of education with success, and was seized very early with a passion for literature, which has been the ruling passion of my life, and the great source of my enjoyments. My studious disposition, my sobriety, and my industry, gave my family a notion that the law was a proper profession for me; but I found an unsurmountable aversion to every thing but the pursuits of philosophy and general learning; and while they fancied I was poring upon Voet and Vinnius, Cicero and Virgil were the authors which I was secretly devouring.

[4]   My very slender fortune, however, being unsuitable to this plan of life, and my health being a little broken by my ardent application, I was tempted, or rather forced, to make a very feeble trial for entering into a more active scene of life. In 1734, I went to Bristol, with some recommendations to eminent merchants, but in a few months found that scene totally unsuitable to me. I went over to France, with a view of prosecuting my studies in a country retreat; and I there laid that plan of life, which I have steadily and successfully pursued. I resolved to make a very rigid frugality supply my deficiency of fortune, to maintain unimpaired my independency, and to regard every object as contemptible, except the improvement of my talents in literature.

[5]   During my retreat in France, first at Reims, but chiefly at La Fleche, in Anjou, I composed my *Treatise of Human Nature*. After passing three years very agreeably in that country, I came over to

London in 1737. In the end of 1738, I published my Treatise, and immediately went down to my mother and my brother, who lived at his country-house, and was employing himself very judiciously and successfully in the improvement of his fortune.

[6]   Never literary attempt was more unfortunate than my Treatise of Human Nature. It fell *dead-born from the press*, without reaching such distinction, as even to excite a murmur among the zealots. But being naturally of a cheerful and sanguine temper, I very soon recovered the blow, and prosecuted with great ardour my studies in the country. In 1742, I printed at Edinburgh the first part of my Essays: the work was favourably received, and soon made me entirely forget my former disappointment. I continued with my mother and brother in the country, and in that time recovered the knowledge of the Greek language, which I had too much neglected in my early youth.

[7]   In 1745, I received a letter from the Marquis of Annandale, inviting me to come and live with him in England; I found also, that the friends and family of that young nobleman were desirous of putting him under my care and direction, for the state of his mind and health required it. – I lived with him a twelvemonth. My appointments during that time made a considerable accession to my small fortune. I then received an invitation from General St. Clair to attend him as a secretary to his expedition, which was at first meant against Canada, but ended in an incursion on the coast of France. Next year, to wit, 1747, I received an invitation from the General to attend him in the same station in his military embassy to the courts of Vienna and Turin. I then wore the uniform of an officer, and was introduced at these courts as aid-de-camp to the general, along with Sir Harry Erskine and Captain Grant, now General Grant. These two years were almost the only interruptions which my studies have received during the course of my life: I passed them agreeably, and in good company; and my appointments, with my frugality, had made me reach a fortune, which I called independent, though most of my friends were inclined to smile when I said so; in short, I was now master of near a thousand pounds.

[8]   I had always entertained a notion, that my want of success in publishing the Treatise of Human Nature, had proceeded more

from the manner than the matter, and that I had been guilty of a very usual indiscretion, in going to the press too early. I, therefore, cast the first part of that work anew in the Enquiry concerning Human Understanding, which was published while I was at Turin. But this piece was at first little more successful than the Treatise of Human Nature. On my return from Italy, I had the mortification to find all England in a ferment, on account of Dr. Middleton's Free Enquiry, while my performance was entirely overlooked and neglected. A new edition, which had been published at London of my Essays, moral and political, met not with a much better reception.

[9]   Such is the force of natural temper, that these disappointments made little or no impression on me. I went down in 1749, and lived two years with my brother at his country-house, for my mother was now dead. I there composed the second part of my Essays, which I called Political Discourses, and also my Enquiry concerning the Principles of Morals, which is another part of my treatise that I cast anew. Meanwhile, my bookseller, A. Millar, informed me, that my former publications (all but the unfortunate Treatise) were beginning to be the subject of conversation; that the sale of them was gradually increasing, and that new editions were demanded. Answers by Reverends, and Right Reverends, came out two or three in a year; and I found, by Dr. Warburton's railing, that the books were beginning to be esteemed in good company. However, I had fixed a resolution, which I inflexibly maintained, never to reply to any body; and not being very irascible in my temper, I have easily kept myself clear of all literary squabbles. These symptoms of a rising reputation gave me encouragement, as I was ever more disposed to see the favourable than unfavourable side of things; a turn of mind which it is more happy to possess, than to be born to an estate of ten thousand a year.

[10]   In 1751, I removed from the country to the town, the true scene for a man of letters. In 1752, were published at Edinburgh, where I then lived, my Political Discourses, the only work of mine that was successful on the first publication. It was well received abroad and at home. In the same year was published at London, my Enquiry concerning the Principles of Morals; which, in my own opinion (who ought not to judge on that subject), is of all my

writings, historical, philosophical, or literary, incomparably the best. It came unnoticed and unobserved into the world.

[11]   In 1752, the Faculty of Advocates chose me their Librarian, an office from which I received little or no emolument, but which gave me the command of a large library. I then formed the plan of writing the History of England; but being frightened with the notion of continuing a narrative through a period of 1700 years, I commenced with the accession of the House of Stuart, an epoch when, I thought, the misrepresentations of faction began chiefly to take place. I was, I own, sanguine in my expectations of the success of this work. I thought that I was the only historian, that had at once neglected present power, interest, and authority, and the cry of popular prejudices; and as the subject was suited to every capacity, I expected proportional applause. But miserable was my disappointment: I was assailed by one cry of reproach, disapprobation, and even detestation; English, Scotch, and Irish, Whig and Tory, churchman and sectary, freethinker and religionist, patriot and courtier, united in their rage against the man, who had presumed to shed a generous tear for the fate of Charles I. and the Earl of Strafford; and after the first ebullitions of their fury were over, what was still more mortifying, the book seemed to sink into oblivion. Mr. Millar told me, that in a twelvemonth he sold only forty-five copies of it. I scarcely, indeed, heard of one man in the three kingdoms, considerable for rank or letters, that could endure the book. I must only except the primate of England, Dr. Herring, and the primate of Ireland, Dr. Stone, which seem two odd exceptions. These dignified prelates separately sent me messages not to be discouraged.

[12]   I was, however, I confess, discouraged; and had not the war been at that time breaking out between France and England, I had certainly retired to some provincial town of the former kingdom, have changed my name, and never more have returned to my native country. But as this scheme was not now practicable, and the subsequent volume was considerably advanced, I resolved to pick up courage and to persevere.

[13]   In this interval, I published at London my Natural History of Religion, along with some other small pieces: its public entry was rather obscure, except only that Dr. Hurd wrote a pamphlet against

it, with all the illiberal petulance, arrogance, and scurrility, which
distinguish the Warburtonian school. This pamphlet gave me some
consolation for the otherwise indifferent reception of my
performance.

[14]   In 1756, two years after the fall of the first volume, was
published the second volume of my History, containing the period
from the death of Charles I. till the Revolution. This performance
happened to give less displeasure to the Whigs, and was better
received. It not only rose itself, but helped to buoy up its
unfortunate brother.

[15]   But though I had been taught by experience, that the Whig
party were in possession of bestowing all places, both in the state
and in literature, I was so little inclined to yield to their senseless
clamour, that in above a hundred alterations, which farther study,
reading, or reflection engaged me to make in the reigns of the two
first Stuarts, I have made all of them invariably to the Tory side. It
is ridiculous to consider the English constitution before that period
as a regular plan of liberty.

[16]   In 1759, I published my History of the House of Tudor. The
clamour against this performance was almost equal to that against
the History of the two first Stuarts. The reign of Elizabeth was
particularly obnoxious. But I was now callous against the
impressions of public folly, and continued very peaceably and
contentedly in my retreat at Edinburgh, to finish, in two volumes,
the more early part of the English History, which I gave to the
public in 1761, with tolerable, and but tolerable success.

[17]   But, notwithstanding this variety of winds and seasons, to
which my writings had been exposed, they had still been making
such advances, that the copy-money given me by the booksellers,
much exceeded any thing formerly known in England; I was
become not only independent, but opulent. I retired to my native
country of Scotland, determined never more to set my foot out of
it, and retaining the satisfaction of never having preferred a request
to one great man, or even making advances of friendship to any of
them. As I was now turned of fifty, I thought of passing all the rest
of my life in this philosophical manner, when I received, in 1763,
an invitation from the Earl of Hertford, with whom I was not in the
least acquainted, to attend him on his embassy to Paris, with a near

prospect of being appointed secretary to the embassy, and, in the meanwhile, of performing the functions of that office. This offer, however inviting, I at first declined, both because I was reluctant to begin connexions with the great, and because I was afraid that the civilities and gay company of Paris, would prove disagreeable to a person of my age and humour: but on his lordship's repeating the invitation, I accepted of it. I have every reason, both of pleasure and interest, to think myself happy in my connexions with that nobleman, as well as afterwards with his brother, General Conway.

[18]   Those who have not seen the strange effects of modes, will never imagine the reception I met with at Paris, from men and women of all ranks and stations. The more I [recoiled] from their excessive civilities, the more I was loaded with them. There is, however, a real satisfaction in living at Paris, from the great number of sensible, knowing, and polite company with which that city abounds above all places in the universe. I thought once of settling there for life.

[19]   I was appointed secretary to the embassy; and, in summer 1765, Lord Hertford left me, being appointed Lord Lieutenant of Ireland. I was *chargé d'affaires* till the arrival of the Duke of Richmond, towards the end of the year. In the beginning of 1766, I left Paris, and next summer went to Edinburgh, with the same view as formerly, of burying myself in a philosophical retreat. I returned to that place, not richer, but with much more money, and a much larger income, by means of Lord Hertford's friendship, than I left it; and I was desirous of trying what superfluity could produce, as I had formerly made an experiment of a competency. But, in 1767, I received from Mr. Conway an invitation to be Under-secretary; and this invitation, both the character of the person, and my connexions with Lord Hertford, prevented me from declining. I returned to Edinburgh in 1769, very opulent (for I possessed a revenue of 1000 l. a year), healthy, and though somewhat stricken in years, with the prospect of enjoying long my ease, and of seeing the increase of my reputation.

[20]   In spring 1775, I was struck with a disorder in my bowels, which at first gave me no alarm, but has since, as I apprehend it, become mortal and incurable. I now reckon upon a speedy dissolution. I have suffered very little pain from my disorder; and

what is more strange, have, notwithstanding the great decline of my person, never suffered a moment's abatement of my spirits; insomuch, that were I to name the period of my life, which I should most choose to pass over again, I might be tempted to point to this later period. I possess the same ardour as ever in study, and the same gaiety in company. I consider, besides, that a man of sixty-five, by dying, cuts off only a few years of infirmities; and though I see many symptoms of my literary reputation's breaking out at last with additional lustre, I knew that I could have but few years to enjoy it. It is difficult to be more detached from life than I am at present.

[21]   To conclude historically with my own character. I am, or rather was (for that is the style I must now use in speaking of myself, which emboldens me the more to speak my sentiments); I was, I say, a man of mild dispositions, of command of temper, of an open, social, and cheerful humour, capable of attachment, but little susceptible of enmity, and of great moderation in all my passions. Even my love of literary fame, my ruling passion, never soured my temper, notwithstanding my frequent disappointments. My company was not unacceptable to the young and careless, as well as to the studious and literary; and as I took a particular pleasure in the company of modest women, I had no reason to be displeased with the reception I met with from them. In a word, though most men any wise eminent, have found reason to complain of calumny, I never was touched, or even attacked by her baleful tooth: and though I wantonly exposed myself to the rage of both civil and religious factions, they seemed to be disarmed in my behalf of their wonted fury. My friends never had occasion to vindicate anyone circumstance of my character and conduct: not but that the zealots, we may well suppose, would have been glad to invent and propagate any story to my disadvantage, but they could never find any which they thought would wear the face of probability. I cannot say there is no vanity in making this funeral oration of myself, but I hope it is not a misplaced one; and this is a matter of fact which is easily cleared and ascertained.

April 18, 1776.

SELECTED BIBLIOGRAPHY

Part I of this Bibliography provides readers with a chronological list, by date of first publication, of Hume's principal philosophical, historical, and literary works, and recommends currently available editions of these works. Part II recommends several helpful and generally reliable (but incomplete) printed and online bibliographies of work on Hume and three biographies. Part III recommends seventeen anthologies of articles on a wide range of Hume's thought. Part IV recommends approximately fifty monographs on Hume or some aspect of his thought. Those who are able to look at the bibliographies listed in Part II will realize that there are now thousands of articles and books devoted to Hume's work, and that no complete bibliography is available.

For a list of the editions and abbreviations used in this volume, see above, "Method of Citation."

I. HUME'S WRITINGS

We present here, in the approximate chronological order of original publication, the principal works of Hume. We also provide cross-references to the "Method of Citation" at the beginning of this volume, because this indicates which currently available editions we have recommended by using them in this volume.

At the end of this list we discuss some of the currently available electronic editions of selected works.

A Treatise of Human Nature: Being an Attempt to introduce the experimental Method of Reasoning into Moral Subjects. 3 vols. London, 1739–40. The critical edition of this text published by Oxford University Press is used in this volume. For details, see T, "Method of Citation."

An Abstract of a Book lately Published; Entituled, A Treatise of Human Nature, &c. *Wherein the Chief Argument of that Book is farther Illustrated and Explained.* London, 1740. Prior to the rediscovery of this work

531

by J. M. Keynes and P. Sraffa in the 1930s it was supposed that this missing work had been written by Adam Smith, even though those who had seen the work attributed it to Hume until about 1825. Scholars are now widely agreed that Hume was its author. The critical edition of this text published by Oxford University Press is used in this volume. For details, see A, "Method of Citation."

Essays, Moral and Political. 2 vols. Edinburgh, 1741–2. For additional details, see below, *Essays, Moral, Political, and Literary* in *Essays and Treatises on Several Subjects.*

A Letter from a Gentleman to His Friend in Edinburgh: Containing Some Observations on A Specimen of the Principles concerning Religion and Morality, said to be maintain'd in a Book lately publish'd, intituled, A Treatise of Human Nature, &c. Edinburgh, 1745. The critical edition of this text published by Oxford University Press is used in this volume. For details regarding facsimile and critical editions of this work, see L, "Method of Citation."

An Enquiry concerning Human Understanding, first published as *Philosophical Essays concerning Human Understanding.* London, 1748. The critical edition of this text published by Oxford University Press is used in this volume. For details, see EHU, "Method of Citation."

An Enquiry concerning the Principles of Morals. London, 1751. The critical edition of this text published by Oxford University Press is used in this volume. For details, see EPM, "Method of Citation."

Political Discourses. Edinburgh, 1752. The essays in this work were eventually included in *Essays and Treatises on Several Subjects,* a collection first published 1753–6. For details, see E, "Method of Citation."

Essays and Treatises on Several Subjects. Beginning in 1753, the first *Enquiry* (EHU), second *Enquiry* (EPM), and essays (including materials included in the *Political Discourses* of 1752 and, beginning in 1758, the *Four Dissertations* of 1757) were brought together and published under this title. Hume saw through the press editions that were were published in 1753–6, 1758, 1760, 1764, 1767, 1768, 1770, 1772, and prepared the text of the first posthumous edition, that of 1777.

Four Dissertations. London, 1757. The four items included in this volume ("The Natural History of Religion," "Of the Passions," "Of Tragedy," and "Of the Standard of Taste") were from 1758 included in *Essays and Treatises on Several Subjects.* The critical texts of *A Dissertation on the Passions* and *The Natural History of Religion,* published by Oxford University Press, are used in this volume. For details, see DP and NHR, "Method of Citation."

The History of England, from the Invasion of Julius Caesar to The Revolution in 1688. The work now published under this title was first published in six volumes over an eight-year period, 1754–62. Hume first published (1754, 1757) two volumes on the period 1603–88, then two more (1759) about the period 1485–1603, and, finally, two volumes (1762) about the period from c. 50 B.C. to A.D. 1485. For details about the edition used in this volume, see HE, "Method of Citation." For information about some of the more than 175 posthumous editions of this work, see *David Hume: Philosophical Historian.* Edited by D. F. Norton and R. H. Popkin. Indianapolis: Bobbs-Merrill, 1965. Appendix A.

The Life of David Hume, Esq. Written by Himself. London, 1777. Published in the Appendix to this volume. For details, see MOL, "Method of Citation."

Dialogues concerning Natural Religion. London, 1779. First edited and published by Hume's nephew, David Hume the Younger. For details of the edition used in this volume, see DNR, "Method of Citation."

The Letters of David Hume. Edited by J. Y. T. Greig. 2 vols. Oxford: Clarendon Press, 1932.

New Letters of David Hume. Edited by R. Klibansky and E. C. Mossner. Oxford: Clarendon Press, 1954.

Many additional letters of Hume have been published since 1954, in many journals and books. A few of the hundreds of letters to Hume are published in *Letters of Eminent Persons Addressed to David Hume,* ed. J. H. Burton (Edinburgh, 1849). A catalog of several hundred such letters is included in *Calendar of Hume Mss. in the Possession of the Royal Society of Edinburgh,* ed. J. Y. T. Greig and H. Beynon (Edinburgh: Royal Society of Edinburgh, 1932).

Computer-Readable Collections

As this volume goes to press the most comprehensive collection of Hume's texts available in electronic form is that in the Past Masters Series of the InteLex Corporation. This collection contains the works, including the three volumes of Hume's letters, mentioned above. Unfortunately, with one exception, the *texts* available from this source are assembled from a hotchpotch of inauthentic and casually prepared editions, some of which modernize spelling and punctuation, and only one of which derives from authentic editions prepared for the press by Hume himself. The one exception is *The History of England.* The InteLex text of this work is based on the edition published in 1778, an edition that Hume revised before his death in 1776, but did not see through the press.

Fortunately, Oxford University Press plans to make available online the critical editions published as part of the *Clarendon Edition of the Works of*

David Hume (General editors: T. L. Beauchamp, D. F. Norton, and M. A. Stewart). These are: *A Treatise of Human Nature, An Abstract* of the *Treatise, A Letter from a Gentleman, An Enquiry concerning Human Understanding, An Enquiry concerning the Principles of Morals, A Dissertation on the Passions,* and *The Natural History of Religion.* In addition, the text of the 1777 edition of *An Enquiry concerning Human Understanding,* another text that Hume revised before his death in 1776 but did not see through the press, is available at www.etext.leeds.ac.uk/hume/.

PART II. SELECTED BIBLIOGRAPHIES AND BIOGRAPHIES

A. Bibliographies

Fieser, James. For an online list of many of the responses to Hume's works, 1739–1900, go to http://www.utm.edu/staff/jfieser/humebib/.

Hall, Roland. *Fifty Years of Hume Scholarship: A Bibliographical Guide.* Edinburgh: Edinburgh University Press, 1978. This bibliography includes the principal writing on Hume for the years 1900–24 and a comprehensive list of Hume literature, 1925–76.

Hall, Roland, William E. Morris, and James Fieser. "The Hume Literature for 1976." *Hume Studies* 2 (1977): 94–102, and subsequent years. *Hume Studies* has published annual bibliographies of work on Hume for the years 1976–2003. These bibliographies have been prepared by Roland Hall (1977–85), William E. Morris (1986–2003), and, from 2004, James Fieser.

Jessop, T. E. *A Bibliography of David Hume and of Scottish Philosophy from Francis Hutcheson to Lord Balfour.* London: Brown and Son, 1938. Facsimile edition, New York: Garland, 1983.

B. Biographies

Burton, John Hill. *Life and Correspondence of David Hume.* Edinburgh, 1846.

Greig, J. Y. T. *David Hume.* Oxford: Oxford University Press, 1932.

Mossner, Ernest Campbell. *The Life of David Hume,* 2nd ed. Oxford: Clarendon Press, 1980.

PART III. SELECTED ANTHOLOGIES ON HUME

Capaldi, Nicholas, and Donald W. Livingston, eds. *Liberty in Hume's History of England.* Dordrecht: Kluwer, 1990.

Chappell, V. C., ed. *Hume: A Collection of Critical Essays.* New York: Doubleday, 1966.

Cohon, Rachel, ed. *Hume: Moral and Political Philosophy*. Aldershot, England: Dartmouth, 2001.

Frasca-Spada, Maria, and P. J. E. Kail, eds. *Impressions of Hume*. Oxford: Oxford University Press, 2005.

Jacobson, Anne Jaap, ed. *Feminist interpretations of David Hume*. University Park: Pennsylvania State University Press, 2000.

Jones, Peter, ed. *The Reception of David Hume in Europe*. Bristol: Thoemmes-Continuum, 2005.

Livingston, Donald W., and James T. King, eds. *Hume: A Re-evaluation*. New York: Fordham University Press, 1976.

Mazza, Emilio, and Emanuele Ronchetti. *New Essays on David Hume*. Milan: FrancoAngeli, 2007.

Millican, Peter, ed. *Reading Hume on Human Understanding: Essays on the First Enquiry*. Oxford: Clarendon Press, 2002.

Morice, G. P., ed. *David Hume Bicentenary Papers*. Edinburgh: University of Edinburgh Press, 1977.

Norton, David Fate, Nicholas Capaldi, and Wade L. Robison, eds. *McGill Hume Studies*. San Diego: Austin Hill Press, 1976.

Owen, David W. D., ed. *Hume: General Philosophy*. Aldershot, England: Dartmouth, 2000.

Read, Rupert, and Kenneth A. Richman, eds. *The New Hume Debate*. London: Routledge, 2000.

Schabas, Margaret, and Carl Wennerlind, eds. *David Hume's Political Economy*. London: Routledge, 2007.

Stewart, M. A., ed. *Studies in the Philosophy of the Scottish Enlightenment*. Oxford Studies in the History of Philosophy, vol. 1. Oxford: Clarendon Press, 1990.

Stewart, M. A., and John P. Wright, eds. *Hume and Hume's Connexions*. Edinburgh: Edinburgh University Press, 1994.

Traiger, Saul, ed. *The Blackwell Guide to Hume's Treatise*. Oxford: Blackwell, 2006.

PART IV. SELECTED MONOGRAPHS

A. Eighteenth- and Nineteenth-Century Works

Beattie, James. *An Essay on the Nature and Immutability of Truth; In Opposition to Sophistry and Scepticism*. Edinburgh, 1770.

Brown, Thomas. *Inquiry into the Relation of Cause and Effect*. 3rd ed. Edinburgh, 1818. Originally published as *Observations on the Nature and Tendency of the Doctrine of Mr. Hume concerning the Relation of Cause and Effect*. Edinburgh, 1805.

Campbell, George. *A Dissertation on Miracles: Containing an Examination of the Principles Advanced by David Hume, Esq; in an Essay on Miracles.* Edinburgh, 1762.

Fieser, James, ed. *Early Responses to Hume.* 2nd ed. 10 vols. Bristol: Thoemmes-Continuum, 2004.

Green, T. H. "General Introduction" and "Introduction to the Moral Part of the *Treatise.*" In *A Treatise of Human Nature,* edited by T. H. Green and T. H. Grose. 2 vols. London, 1874. 1:1–299, 2:1–71.

Home, Henry, Lord Kames. *Essays on the Principles of Morality and Natural Religion.* Edinburgh, 1751.

Leland, John. *A View of the Principal Deistical Writers of the Last and Present Century.* 3rd ed. 3 vols. London, 1755–7.

Paley, William. *View of the Evidences of Christianity.* London, 1794.

Priestley, Joseph. *Letters to a Philosophical Unbeliever.* Bath, 1780.

Reid, Thomas. *An Inquiry into the Human Mind, on the Principles of Common Sense.* Edinburgh, 1764.

Shepherd, Lady Mary. *Essay upon the Relation of Cause and Effect, Controverting the Doctrine of Mr. Hume.* London, 1824.

Warburton, William, and Richard Hurd. *Remarks on Mr. David Hume's Essay on the Natural History of Religion.* London, 1757.

Whately, Richard. *Historic Doubts Relative to Napoleon Buonaparte.* London, 1819.

B. Twentieth- and Twenty-First-Century Works

Árdal, Páll S. *Passion and Value in Hume's* Treatise. 2nd ed. Edinburgh: Edinburgh University Press, 1989.

Baier, Annette C. *A Progress of Sentiments: Reflections on Hume's* Treatise. Cambridge, MA: Harvard University Press, 1991.

Baxter, Donald L. M. *Hume's Difficulty: Time and Identity in the* Treatise. New York: Routledge, 2008.

Bongie, Laurence L. *David Hume: Prophet of the Counter-Revolution.* Oxford: Clarendon Press, 1965.

Box, M. A. *The Suasive Art of David Hume.* Princeton: Princeton University Press, 1990.

Bricke, John. *Mind and Morality.* Oxford: Clarendon Press, 1996.

Buckle, Stephen. *Hume's Enlightenment Tract: The Unity and Purpose of An Enquiry concerning Human Understanding.* Oxford: Clarendon Press, 2001.

Costelloe, Timothy M. *Aesthetics and Morals in the Philosophy of David Hume.* New York: Routledge, 2007.

Flew, Antony. *Hume's Philosophy of Belief: A Study of His First Inquiry.* London: Routledge & Kegan Paul, 1961.

Fogelin, Robert J. *A Defense of Hume on Miracles.* Princeton: Princeton University Press, 2003.

Forbes, Duncan. *Hume's Philosophical Politics.* Cambridge: Cambridge University Press, 1975.

Garrett, Don. *Cognition and Commitment in Hume's Philosophy.* New York: Oxford University Press, 1997.

Haakonssen, Knud. *Natural Law and Moral Philosophy: From Grotius to the Scottish Enlightenment.* Cambridge: Cambridge University Press, 1996.

Hendel, Charles W. *Studies in the Philosophy of David Hume.* Princeton: Princeton University Press, 1925; 2nd ed., Indianapolis: Bobbs-Merrill, 1963.

Herdt, Jennifer A. *Religion and Faction in Hume's Moral Philosophy.* Cambridge: Cambridge University Press, 1997.

Jones, Peter. *Hume's Sentiments: Their Ciceronian and French Context.* Edinburgh: Edinburgh University Press, 1982.

Kail, P. J. E. *Projection and Realism in Hume's Philosophy.* New York: Oxford University Press, 2007.

Laird, John. *Hume's Philosophy of Human Nature.* London: Methuen, 1932.

Livingston, Donald W. *Hume's Philosophy of Common Life.* Chicago: University of Chicago Press, 1984.

Loeb, Louis E. *Stability and Justification in Hume's Treatise.* New York: Oxford University Press, 2002.

Mackie, John L. *Hume's Moral Theory.* London: Routledge & Kegan Paul, 1980.

MacNabb, D. G. C. *David Hume: His Theory of Knowledge and Morality.* 2nd ed. Hamden, CT: Archon Books, 1966.

Mall, R. A. *Experience and Reason: The Phenomenology of Husserl and Its Relation to Hume's Philosophy.* The Hague: Martinus Nijhoff, 1973.

Mercer, P. *Sympathy and Ethics: A Study of the Relationship between Sympathy and Morality, with Special Reference to Hume's Treatise.* Oxford: Clarendon Press, 1972.

Miller, David. *Philosophy and Ideology in Hume's Political Thought.* Oxford: Clarendon Press, 1981.

Norton, David Fate. *David Hume: Common-Sense Moralist, Sceptical Metaphysician.* Rev. ed. Princeton: Princeton University Press, 1984.

Orr, James. *David Hume and His Influence on Philosophy and Theology.* New York: Scribner's, 1903.

Owen, David, *Hume's Reason.* Oxford: Oxford University Press, 1999.

Passmore, John. *Hume's Intentions.* 2nd ed. New York: Basic Books, 1968.

Penelhum, Terence. *David Hume: An Introduction to His Philosophical System.* West Lafayette, IN: Purdue University Press, 1992.

Price, H. H. *Hume's Theory of the External World.* Oxford: Clarendon Press, 1940.

Rivers, Isabel, *Reason, Grace, and Sentiment: A Study of the Language of Religion and Ethics in England,* 1660–1780. 2 vols. Cambridge: Cambridge University Press, 1991, 2000.

Russell, Paul. *Freedom and Moral Sentiment: Hume's Way of Naturalizing Responsibility.* New York: Oxford University Press, 1995.

The Riddle of Hume's Treatise: Skepticism, Naturalism, and Irreligion. New York: Oxford University Press, 2008.

Siebert, Donald T. *The Moral Animus of David Hume.* Newark: University of Delaware Press, 1990.

Smith, Norman Kemp, *The Philosophy of David Hume: A Critical Study of Its Origins and Central Doctrines.* London: Macmillan, 1941.

Spencer, Mark G. *David Hume and Eighteenth-Century America.* Rochester, NY: University of Rochester Press, 2005.

Stewart, John B. *Opinion and Reform in Hume's Political Philosophy.* Princeton, NJ: Princeton University Press, 1992.

Strawson, Galen. *The Secret Connexion: Causation, Realism, and David Hume.* Oxford: Clarendon Press, 1989.

Stroud, Barry. *Hume.* London: Routledge & Kegan Paul, 1977.

Waxman, Wayne. *Hume's Theory of Consciousness.* Cambridge: Cambridge University Press, 1994.

Whelan, Frederick G. *Order and Artifice in Hume's Political Philosophy.* Princeton, NJ: Princeton University Press, 1985.

Wright, John P. *The Sceptical Realism of David Hume.* Manchester: Manchester University Press, 1983.

Zabeeh, Farhang. *Hume: Precursor of Modern Empiricism.* 2nd ed. The Hague: Martinus Nijhoff, 1973.

INDEX

fallibilism, 210, 225, 235
fancy, *see* imagination
Fearnley-Sander, M., 447n2
Federalist, The, Hume's influence on, 377
Feiser, James, 311n2
Félibien, André, 417
Fénelon, François de Salignac de la Mothe-, 338
Feuerbach, Ludwig, 509
fictions, 47, 51–2, 59n19, 142, 189, 191, 212–13, 232
fideism, 483, 507, 509–10
Filmer, Robert, 353n10
Fleming, John, 419n8, 432n26
Flew, Antony, 27n41, 105n1, 112n13, 216, 502n21
Fodor, Jerry A., 43n4, 68n29
Fogelin, Robert J., 37, 105n1, 111n8, 112nn13, 14, 498n18, 502n21
Fontana, Biancamaria, 379n39
Fontenelle, Bernard le Bovier de, 419n7, 423, 426n20, 431
Forbes, Duncan, 355n11, 374–5, 392n24, 462n28, 465n34, 471
Four Dissertations, 432
France, 366–8, 418, 424, 466, 475, 523, 524
Franklin, James, 111n8, 113n17
Frasca-Spada, Marina, 110n7
Frede, Michael, 112n15, 113n16, 114n19, 234n25
free trade, 382–3, 406, 413
freedom and necessity, 18n23, 21–2, 149n4, 251–5
and liberty of indifference, 253–4
and liberty of spontaneity, 252–3
Fréret, Nicolas, 455
Freud, Sigmund, 267, 509
Fubini, Enrico, 415n1
functionalism, 62–3
Furniss, Edgar S., 381n2, 382n4

Galiani, Fernando, 412
Galileo, 41, 241
Garrett, Don, 86n20, 94n33, 149n4, 171–4, 196n22
Gaskin, J. C. A., 38, 149n5, 204n26
Gassendi, Pierre, 113n17
Gauden, John, 458

general rules, 53, 100, 300–2, 428
generosity, *see* benevolence
geometry, 36, 119n26, 121–7, 142, 216, 432
standard of equality for, 122–3
See also mathematics
Gerard, Alexander, 416, 417, 418, 431–2, 445
Gervaise, Isaac, 385
Gettier problem, 54n12
Giarrizzo, Giuseppe, 465n33
Gibbon, Edward, 447n2, 464
God, gods, 149, 160–1, 163–4, 179, 344–5, 349–51, 480–2, 484–90, 492–4, 504–5, 508n26, 509, 511
Goldie, M., 362n14
Goldman, Alvin, 54n13
good, 19–20, 77–8, 246–9, 274, 282, 291
government, 335, 389–90
ecclesiastical, 476n47
right of, 352–6, 363–8, 465–6
and security, 354, 355–6, 460, 463
stability of, 357–9, 372, 396, 476–7
Grant, James, 524
Graunt, John, 383
Great Britain, *see* Britain
Greece, ancient, 333–4, 425, 448
Green, T. H., 134n53
Gregory, John, 417n4
Grene, Marjorie, 162n19
Grotius, Hugo, 2n1, 328n9, 344, 360–1, 386
Grünbaum, Adolf, 111n10, 129n44
Guicciardini, Francesco, 450n9
Guichard, Octavie, 449n6
Guthrie, William, 374n22
Guyer, Paul, 445n36

Haakonssen, Knud, 38, 229n21, 271n3
habeas corpus, 463, 476
habit, 34–5, 133, 152n7, 153–5, 160, 165–6, 173, 211
Hacking, Ian, 225n18
Halkerton, Lord, 523
Halley, Edmund, 383
Hampden, John, 472, 477
Hanoverians, 364, 371
happiness, 283, 319, 322–4, 387, 429, 503–5
Hardin, Russell, 377n33

CPSIA information can be obtained at www.ICGtesting.com
Printed in the USA
LVOW061015100713

342103LV00003B/253/P